Perspectives of Reality

असतो मा सद्गमय।
तमसो मा ज्योर्तिगमय।
मृत्योर्मामृतं गमय।।

(यजुर्वेद ब्रह. उपनिष्द् १/२/२७)

From the unreal lead me to the real
From darkness lead me to light
From death lead me to immortality

Bṛhadāraṇyaka Upanisad 1:3:28

Perspectives of Reality

An Introduction to the Philosophy of Hinduism

With a Foreword by John Koller

Jeaneane Fowler

sussex
ACADEMIC
PRESS

BRIGHTON • PORTLAND

2 4 6 8 10 9 7 5 3 1

First published 2002 in Great Britain by
SUSSEX ACADEMIC PRESS
PO Box 2950
Brighton BN2 5SP

and in the United States of America by
SUSSEX ACADEMIC PRESS
5824 N.E. Hassalo St.
Portland, Oregon 97213-3644

British Library Cataloguing in Publication Data
A CIP catalogue record for this book is available from the British Library.

Library of Congress Cataloging-in-Publication Data
Fowler, Jeaneane.
Perspectives of reality : an introduction to the philosophy of Hinduism / Jeaneane Fowler.
p. cm.
Includes bibliographical references and index.
ISBN 1–898723–93–1 (alk. paper) — ISBN 1–898723–94–X (pbk. : alk. paper)
1. Philosophy, Hindu. 2. Vedanta. I. Title.
B131 .F66 2002
181'.4—dc21 2002021716

Cover illustration: The Sanskrit "Aum" design is used by permission of Himalayan Academy Publications, *Sacred Aums* CD.

Typeset & designed by G&G Editorial, Brighton
Printed by TJ International, Padstow, Cornwall
This book is printed on acid-free paper.

Contents

Foreword by John M. Koller

Today it is clear that our very survival depends on cooperation among people whose lives are guided by diverse values and ideas. But this cooperation is impossible unless we understand the basic ideas and values that shape the cultures and guide the societies of the peoples with whom we must cooperate. These ideas and values are rooted in the philosophical and religious traditions that underlie every society's institutions and practices. In India, home of one-fifth of the world's people, it is Hinduism that has been the major source of the ideas and values that guide the life choices and social practices of most of the people. If we are to understand India, the world's largest democracy, a major nuclear power and home of the world's greatest spiritual traditions, we must understand Hinduism.

In this carefully researched and clearly written introduction to Hinduism's philosophical traditions Dr Fowler provides a foundation for insight into today's India by helping us understand how Hinduism has answered the fundamental questions about existence and human life: Who am I? What is real? How do we know? What is the right thing to do? What is the ultimate goal of life? For three thousand years Indian thinkers have been exploring these questions and examining various answers to them in their efforts to find ways of life that satisfy the deepest needs of a person. Building on the visions of the great thinkers of the Vedas and Upanisads dating from 1500–500 BCE that provide the foundations for Hinduism's profound spirituality, India produced six enduring philosophical traditions in its efforts to answer the fundamental questions of human life. *Perspectives of Reality: An Introduction to the Philosophy of Hinduism* is a splendid guide to understanding these traditions, known as *darśanas* (visions) into reality.

Beginning with the foundational visions of the Vedas, Dr Fowler examines each tradition's vision of reality in a systematic way that focuses on how it understands the self, the highest reality, causality, knowledge, and liberation. Because the six major Hindu philosophical traditions – Mimamsa, Samkhya, Yoga, Nyaya, Vaisesika, and Vedanta – complement each other in important ways as well as compete with each other in some ways, this systematic comparison of the fundamental topics of each tradition enables us to see the beautiful tapestry of the Hindu way of life that these traditions have created. This book offers the reader who wishes to understand the philosophical basis of Hinduism a clear and comprehensive introduction. It also provides a solid foundation for the reader who wishes to go on to advanced and detailed studies of any of the Hindu philosophical traditions.

Because *Perspectives of Reality* focuses exclusively on Hinduism, the reader who wants to understand India's other spiritual and philosophical traditions – Buddhism, Jainism, and Islam – may wish to also consult John M. Koller, *The Indian Way* (London: Collier Macmillan, 1982). Readers interested in an even broader approach that includes Indian and Chinese thought may wish to consult John M. Koller, *Asian Philosophies* (Upper Saddle River, New Jersey: Prentice-Hall, 2002).

John M. Koller
Great Neck, New York
June 2002

Preface and Acknowledgements

A few years ago I wrote *Hinduism: Beliefs and Practices* as an introduction for students who knew nothing at all about Hinduism. That book was designed to generate enthusiasm for, and motivate further inquiry into, this fascinating religion. It was designed to open the minds of students to a culture and religion that is so remarkably broad in its dimensions and yet so deep in its underlying philosophies. The present text examines the breadth of those philosophies, those that emerged from the various orthodox schools of Hindu philosophical belief, as well as the "depths" of their thought that have informed so much of Hinduism. It is the beliefs of the six orthodox philosophical schools of Hinduism that form a highly important core of ideas, rather like the hub of a wheel is essential for the balance and function of the wheel itself. For, in many ways, these schools attempted to provide balance and function for Hinduism itself, often pragmatically so, in terms of providing justification for trends like devotionalism in Hinduism, but also necessarily so, in terms of the need to confront challenges like Buddhism. Thus, the many strands of Hinduism are not so much like spokes of a wheel added to its philosophical hub. The philosophical schools are more like the hub extracted from tradition, and attached to the wheel. No student of Hinduism can get far without encountering the theories of these schools.

Like *Hinduism: Beliefs and Practices*, this book is written as an *introduction* to the philosophy of Hinduism. It therefore assumes no prior knowledge of the philosophical schools or their beliefs, though it does assume some knowledge of Hinduism in general. The book is written in response to student need of a clear, focused analysis of the major concepts that emerge from the philosophical strands. Each of the six orthodox philosophical schools of Hinduism will be dealt with in the pages that follow. But it is also part of the purpose of the book to present some of the background of Hindu religious tradition that will provide a basis for understanding the schools and, in fact, that served as the foundation for the schools themselves. This will be the scriptural tradition, *Veda*, or Knowledge.

Whoever we are, and wherever we are, there are often times when we raise fundamental questions about our purpose, our destiny, our best direction in life. Times of birth, death, great happiness, sorrow, loss and grief often make us more reflective beings. But no one individual has the answers to life; none has the complete picture, though there are many contributions to it. The Hindu philosophical schools also try to answer the deeper questions about life, about what can be real in a world where everything is subject to change, decay and death. They ask critical questions about our means of knowledge, and ask what it is that we can *really* know. They inquire into the nature of the self, searching for the self that is real and permanent, the self that transcends the finitude and transience of time. They reflect on the interrelatedness of phenomena – like the mighty oak that stems from the small acorn – and the relation between causes and their effects that can bring this about. They search for *freedom*, often for the happiness and bliss that can only exist when the self is liberated from its suffering in the world. And they search for God, some to find him unnecessary, some to find him distant, some to find him close. But, like human beings themselves, no one school can paint the complete picture – although each school believes it has the definitive answers. The fundamental questions about life are, therefore, answered differently by each school. But the quests of each are virtually the same – a search for the real in the world of the unreal, a search for light in the darkness of the world, and a search for immortality in the face of death.

I am indebted to a number of people who have assisted me in a variety of ways throughout the preparation of the text. In particular, I need to convey my gratitude to the Library and Learning Resources Centre at the Caerleon Campus of the University of Wales College, Newport. As always, Lesley May, Deputy Head of Library and Learning Resources, has given every possible support. I owe special thanks also to Library Assistant Nigel Twomey, who has procured so many texts for me from inter-library lending services. Without the continued help of these two excellent colleagues, I could not have completed the work. I am also very grateful to my colleague Margaret Swabey in Reprographics at UWCN for her speed and efficiency in reproducing the text at its various stages. A number of postgraduate students assisted with the proof reading of the chapters while absorbing the content for their MA in Philosophy and Religious Studies at UWCN. To these students – Judith Anderson, John Derosaire, Kate Healey, Helen Hobbs, David Meredith, Alexis Niziol, Jill Peterson, Joe Richardson, Rob Ward and Alf Williams – I owe my thanks, not least for the blend of humour and hard work with which they analysed the contents. This is not the first text that I have prepared for Sussex Academic Press, and I am very happy to continue my association with such a superb and efficient Press. As the publisher, Anthony Grahame has given me the space to proceed with care, and without pressure. As editor, he has given me sound advice on the text. It was a complex book to prepare, and every effort has been made on my part to remove any errors. For any that remain I take full responsibility. Where printed errors occurred in quoted material – particularly in some of the older texts – I have quietly corrected them, though not in any way that offends the original sense.

I am very grateful, also, to John Koller for his kindness in writing the *Foreword* to this book. His own books have been an inspiration to my students of Eastern religions for many years. In particular his work *The Indian Way* is a masterful introduction to the broader canvas of Indian and Islamic religions, not least because as an author he possesses the remarkable ability to approach these cultures with a deep sensitivity that penetrates to the heart of their respective philosophies. He is a wonderfu writer.

Finally, a very good colleague and friend of mine, Glyndwr Harris, died recently.

Both my husband and myself were students of his long ago at UWCN. He was a deeply personal and religious man, but with a mind that radiated out to embrace the ideas and philosophical concepts of other cultures. He had always been ahead of his time, and was an inspiring tutor. It is a privilege for me to pay tribute to him here, for he set both my husband and myself on our own academic careers, and he left a lasting legacy to Philosophy and Religious Studies at UWCN, where we both now teach. It is to Glyn that I dedicate this book.

The more insights we can get, the more aspects of the Divine we can perceive,
the more we see of divinities beyond the different aspects of the universe,
the more elements we can assemble to build up some conception of
the origin of things, of the destiny and purpose of life, the nearer
we are to understanding something of what divinity is.

A. Daniélou, *The Myths and Gods of India*

Then there were neither death nor immortality,
Nor was there then the torch of night and day.
The One breathed windlessly and self-sustaining.
There was that One then, and there was no other.
. . .
But, after all, who knows, and who can say
Whence it all came, and how creation happened?
The gods themselves are later than creation,
So who knows truly whence it has arisen?

Whence all creation had its origin,
He, whether he fashioned it or whether he did not,
He, who surveys it all from highest heaven,
He knows – or maybe even he does not know.

A. L. Basham, *The Wonder that was India*

In our mind we can conjure up an ideal, a passion, etc., and identify with it to such an extent as to forget that we are individuals above and beyond passions and ideas. We can dream while wide awake . . . and identify with our dreams to such a degree that we lose our identity.
This happens to the majority of people; in fact, they are not persons but teachers, politicians, tradesmen, fathers, mothers, children etc.; they are everything and anything but entities aware of their true and profound reality.

Raphael, *The Pathway of Non-Duality*

We not only do not know what we ourselves really are, but do not also know
what the world about us is.

S. Dasgupta, *A History of Indian Philosophy*

Here, within our own Self, we gain an infallible guide to the absolute Being
which we are seeking.

P. Deussen, *The System of the Vedanta*

We may be nearer to a mental representation of divinity when we consider
an immense number of different gods than when we try to stress their
unity; for the number one is in a way the number farthest
removed from infinity.

A. Daniélou, *The Myths and Gods of India*

There is no need for taking active steps to achieve peace (liberation) in the Self.
All souls are eternally at rest, unborn, and completely withdrawn by nature,
homogeneous and non-different from one another. That is, the Self,
as a metaphysical principle, is unborn, homogeneous and pure,
and hence there is no need to *produce* the state of blessed
abstraction or liberation. Action can have no effect on
that which is eternally of the same nature.

Śaṃkara, *Gauḍapādakārikābhāṣya* 90
trans. Alston, *Śaṃkara on the Soul*

We can either become congealed on one particular level, or we can broaden out
and learn to master other sectors of this enormous keyboard,
to explore the different dimensions of reality,
or at least open ourselves to them.

G. Feuerstein, *The Yoga-Sūtra of Patañjali*

Introduction

The nature of philosophy

Hindu philosophical inquiry is set against a backdrop of the vastness of an infinite cosmos and infinite time. The parameters of philosophical inquiry in Hinduism extend to a search for Truth in this chasm of space and time, and are often directed beyond both. Such an inquiry is one into the nature of reality. However, the human dimension is never lost on the vast canvas of Hindu cosmic and extra-cosmic reality. For the whole purpose of the search for reality is to emerge with answers to fundamental questions about existence – What is the real nature of the self? What is the fate of the self at death? How can the self be free of suffering? What can we really know? Can we really know anything in a world that is impermanent and transient? How do cause and effect operate to bring about the interrelatedness of the universe in which we live? Is there a First Cause, and is this God? What is the nature of God? How can a permanent and infinite God be involved in an impermanent and finite world? These are the kinds of questions with which Hindu philosophical schools have been involved, and which they felt would be answered through the *quest for reality*.

Philosophy is a love of wisdom, a love of knowledge that results in a search for ultimate truths about the way things are. Even in the ordinary realm of living experience, each human being is bound to ask questions about his or her life. These questions may not be *ultimate*, yet they are likely to relate to the problematic areas of the existential life-condition in which each human being is placed. Often, also, they relate to issues that take the individual to deeper reflections that lie beyond the mere acceptance of the day-to-day world. The essential nature of such philosophical questions is put succinctly by Chatterjee and Datta: "Desire for knowledge springs . . . from the rational nature of man. Philosophy is an attempt to satisfy this very reasonable desire. It is not, therefore, a mere luxury, but a necessity."[1] Philosophical inquiry is, thus, a natural part of life, of what it is to be human. While the academic philosopher engages more ardently in such inquiry, perhaps dedicating many years to the task of discovering the truth about things, none of us can do without some form of rational inquiry into the lives we live. Such an inquiry need not be intellectual *per se*, but can be viewed as an essential ingredient to approaching life:

There are no people who could be impervious to the demands of this world for an expla-

> nation of its apparent chaos and contradictions. Only an all-embracing explanation of life, consistent with experience, would satisfy the requirements of reason, man's highest instrument for the regulation of life. For this reason, philosophy cannot be a mere exercise of the intellect or a pursuit for sheer aesthetic interest or curiosity. It must have a spiritual raison d'être and must satisfy man's spiritual need. It must deal with problems which force themselves on our thought and press for a solution, viz., what man is, why he is conditioned as he is, what his goal is and how he is to attain it.[2]

These words suggest that our philosophical moments in life are also the more spiritual ones, the times when we are inclined to think more deeply and reflectively about life and the way we live it. But any search for a deeper rationale to life, or for a more ultimate kind of reality, suggests that there is a common ignorance that pervades our normal view of things – the ordinary levels of reality. The individual may be aware of this dichotomy in the search for happiness and the search for greater quality of life. But Hindu philosophy takes this basic human desire to its limits, searching for answers to the restrictions on the human self and human life – answers that will free the human soul for all time, and that will overcome all ignorance. The search for Reality, for Truth, becomes synonymous with the quest for liberation from all suffering, especially from the concomitant endless cycles of reincarnation.

What this book will explore, then, are the answers posited to fundamental questions about life by the various orthodox philosophical schools of Hinduism. There are six major such schools, though one, Vedānta, will be divided into three. I shall therefore examine *eight* separate schools of philosophy. Each school supplies a "view", a *darśana*, of "reality" that differs from the next, though there is some common ground between them all. As far as possible I shall structure the analysis of each school under the same, or similar, headings. The topics that will be generic to the treatment of each school are likely, then, to be:

- *General background* to provide a context for each school of philosophy, mainly in terms of its historical background.
- *Main proponents and commentators.*
- *General features.* For some schools it may be necessary to introduce some general information pertinent to the overall philosophy of the school, though in most cases this will be subsumed under the heading of:
- *Reality*, which will detail the view of the world according to the particular school.
- *Categories of reality* accepted by each school differ. For some schools it will be necessary to detail these under a separate heading. In other cases, especially when they have been adopted from, and therefore explored in, another school, separate treatment will be unnecessary.
- *Epistemology*, the theory of knowledge, will be an important topic common to all the schools.
- *Pramāṇas*, the means of valid knowledge, while critical to the epistemology of each school, are usually important enough to be treated under a separate heading.
- *Error* in knowledge will also sometimes need a separate section, though this is an area that sometimes will be subsumed in general epistemology, particularly in the context of the means of valid knowledge, the *Pramāṇas*.

Four topics will consistently be dealt with separately in the material for each school. These are:

- *The self*
- *Causality*
- *The concept of God*
- *Liberation.*

The structure outlined above will facilitate a thematic perusal of the book by undergraduate students in particular. Any student studying the Hindu concepts of the self, the divine, or liberation, for example – key issues of Hindu religion generally – will find appropriate relevant material in each chapter under clear and separate headings. The undergraduate reader will also find much that is relevant to the study of devotional Hinduism, *bhakti*, in the final two chapters of Viśiṣṭādvaita and Dvaita. But the book is also designed for postgraduate students with some previous knowledge of Hinduism. Here, the more complex issues of epistemology, reality and causality will also be relevant. One purpose of this Introduction to Hindu Philosophy is to identify the major philosophical contributions of each of the schools without the usual complicated analysis of ideas across the schools. To some extent the approach adopted here is problematic, since so much of the tradition and literary output of each school was spent in criticizing those of the others. Fierce philosophical debate and refutation of the theories of others was what these schools were about in their search for Truth. But the complexities of such cross-analysis are offputting for students, and are unnecessary in a strict *introduction* to Hindu philosophy. My aim is to make Hindu philosophy more accessible to students. Having said this, such philosophy abounds with Sanskrit terms, some of which are essential for the student who will want to journey further. I have limited the use of such terms to essential words. Those that are used will be defined when first used: thereafter, the reader is advised to consult the *Glossary* at the end of the book. Then, too, the proponents of each of the schools are numerous, and each introduces nuances of philosophical thought that, in some cases, subdivide the major schools considerably. I intend to deal only with the major proponents of each of the schools.

The traditions of the Hindu schools of philosophy stretch back over two millennia, having their origins in ancient oral and, eventually, literary traditions. The language of these traditions is, by today's standards, somewhat sexist. To modernize such language and refer to *humanity* instead of *man* would be very misleading in the context of much Hindu thought, for its literature is traditionally sexist and deals most definitely with man and not woman. Here is one textual aspect that I shall need to retain in most places. Eastern philosophy also lends itself to traditional translations of words that do not appear in English dictionaries. It is traditional to write of the *un*manifest aspect of reality or God, rather than the non-manifest, and words like *beginningless* and *evolutes* might seem at first glance to be non-grammatical inventions of the writer, but are standard in this field of study, and are intentional. A number of other words of this kind will occur from time to time in the text.

While the different schools form the main focus of this book, chapter 1 is devoted to an analysis of different types of religious belief. These types underpin the views of the respective schools, and it is important to understand their precise character from the outset. The eight schools that are dealt with in this book are *orthodox* schools, so called because they base their views on orthodox traditions of Hinduism – some stringently so, and some only cursorily. However, chapter 2 will look at the literary basis of the schools, examining the knowledge, the *Veda*, on which subsequent orthodox philosophy was built. Then each of the schools, the *darśanas*, is dealt with in turn. Chapter 3 is concerned with Pūrva Mīmāṃsā, a school that is best dealt with first because of its more pertinent connection to the ritual knowledge of the *Veda*, in the previous chapter. The two atomistic schools of Vaiśeṣika and Nyāya follow in chapters 4 and 5 respectively. Chapter 6 examines the school of Sāṃkhya and chapter 7 the related school of Yoga. The school of Vedānta is divided into three: Advaita in chapter 8, Viśiṣṭādvaita in chapter 9 and Dvaita in chapter 10. In order to avoid confusion between the use of the school of Vedānta and the literary tradition that marks the end of the *Veda* as *Vedānta*, I shall italicize the latter throughout.

The *darśanas*

The six orthodox systems of Indian and Hindu philosophy were attempts to uphold the ancient tradition of the *Veda* – that part of Hindu scripture called *śruti* "heard" because it was revealed to the ancient sages – in the face of trends away from orthodoxy. Each was a view, a *darśana*, of that tradition. Yet even these orthodox schools pursued philosophical inquiry sufficiently independently to diverge occasionally from the *Veda*. Sāṃkhya is a case in point, for this school denies all sense of an Absolute divinity – despite so much contrary evidence in the *Upaniṣads*, the more philosophical writings at the end of the *Veda*. The *darśanas* were not, then, complementary analyses of reality, of the self, God and liberation, for they differ radically on a number of issues, and a good deal of the material in each was aimed at refuting the views of the others. Indeed, each school had to understand fully the views of the other schools before it could articulate its own with any credence. Philosophical analysis and debate, and logical and systematic presentation of belief, were essential to each of the schools: it was not an issue of faith that motivated them; it was a spirit of rational inquiry, of philosophical expertise. The schools that will be featured in this book represent the major orthodox ones, but there were other attempts to defend the *Veda* against the unorthodox schools of those such as the Materialists (the Cārvākas), the Jains, and the Buddhists. The teachings of each of the schools was handed down in a chain from generation to generation, preserving the particular philosophical traditions of each over a long period of time – in most cases more than a millennium.

The major orthodox schools as we know them today are best traced through their literary development. The compilation of *sūtras* was the first step on the path to organized schools and organized philosophy in each case. The *sūtras* were aphoristic compositions that sought to systematize the original inspired visions of the seers: they were "threads", that threaded together the oral teachings of a school or a number of schools, which had been handed down for centuries. At the same time the schools wanted to condense the material into short aphorisms. Bādarāyaṇa began this process with his *Brahmasūtra*, which was a systematization of the teachings in the *Upaniṣads*. But short aphoristic statements, *sūtras*, are understandable only to the higher echelons of the initiated, and even for devoted disciples there was a need for them to be explained. The next literary stage, then, and the next stage of development and consolidation of the schools, was the writing of commentaries, *bhāṣyas*, on the *sūtras*. In this way each of the systems grew and evolved, elaborating and refining its teachings with newer, deeper commentaries on *sūtras* and commentaries on commentaries. At each step of this literary path, discussion, *vārttika*, was essential for development. This all led to an intricacy and complexity of literature pertinent to the various strands of each school, exacerbated by the stringent analysis and criticism of opposing schools of thought – both orthodox and unorthodox. Indeed, the final stage of development of each school might be said to be the rational defence of its position against all rival schools.

The dating of the schools has always been a complex issue and one that will always defy solution. For each school, dating varies widely for a number of reasons. To begin with, founders of the individual schools are often shrouded in mystery; little is known about them that might assist in any dating. Even the *sūtras* they are said to have written are, in some cases, the work of composite authors. Then, too, each school liked to claim ancient status, which in some part was legitimate in view of the early oral traditions that informed it. What can safely be said is that the beginnings of the philosophical systems occur from about 400 BCE to about 500 CE and some of the commentaries stem from this early date of about 400 BCE. It is likely that the schools emerged in a more structured form in about the second century BCE. Sāṃkhya is probably the oldest of the schools for it does not suggest knowledge of any of the others and appears to be pre-Buddhist. Mīmāṃsā is also old, if its date is judged by its terminology. Vaiśeṣika might be said to be earlier than its sister school Nyāya in view of its less developed epistemology. These two last schools are normally treated together since their theories coalesce and complement each other. Nyāya is concerned with the nature of knowledge, logical thought and reasoning, while Vaiśeṣika is concerned with the atomic composition of reality. While the major proponents of the schools of Vedānta – Śaṃkara (eighth century), Rāmānuja (eleventh century) and Madhva (twelfth–thirteenth century) – are easily datable, the origins of their respective philosophies date well back. Each proponent interprets the *Veda* in his own way, and all used Bādarāyaṇa's *Brahmasūtra* as the basis for their schools of Vedānta – Advaita, Viśiṣṭādvaita, and Dvaita, respectively. While there are many proponents of Vedānta philosophy, in this book these three major ones will be the focus of separate chapters.

Reality

Reality and Truth are synonymous in Hindu philosophy and may or may not be equated with Absolute divinity. Reality or Truth is termed *sat*, a word that can also mean "existence" and "being", that is to say existence and being as opposed to non-existence and non-being that are unreal.[3] Where a concept of God is accepted, then the ultimate and definitive essence of divinity often becomes the ultimate Reality and Truth, in relation to which other kinds of reality are but lower levels. This is rather like the differences in reality we experience in states of waking, dreaming and deepest sleep. The search for ultimate

Reality – whether or not this is equated with God – is a logical projection of the human mind. It is an attempt to get to the bottom of things, an attempt to find what it is that is behind the universe as we perceive it.

In the human search for a Reality that is ultimate and that underpins the universe there is a search also for a Reality that is beyond the limitations of our normal conceptions of reality. This is not to say that our ordinary conceptions of how things are, are necessarily denied, it is just that there is some conception of a Reality that is not bound by any constraints and flaws. In the human context, such constraints are the nature of suffering, perpetual reincarnation and bondage to the laws of cause and effect, *karma*. So if the human being can reach out, or inward, to ultimate Reality, then the self can experience the same kind of unbound freedom, and the loss of all limitations that lesser levels of reality bring: the experience is one of liberation. The search for ultimate Reality, then, is a search for the liberation of the soul, the very essence of the self.

How far Reality that is ultimate is connected with the reality – or non-reality – of the world in which we exist, varies from one philosophical school to another. One school, Advaita Vedānta, is idealist in its approach to reality. That is to say, it regards our normal perceptions of reality as only apparent ones, projections of the ideas in our minds that create an apparent world of reality that, all the time, hides the ultimate Reality that is the essence of all things. This is a difficult view of reality, for it raises the question of what causes us to view the world in the way we do. And if the answer is our own ignorance, then what causes that ignorance? Advaita posits illusion or *māyā* as the cause. *Māyā* is a principle that makes a unified Reality appear diverse, that veils ultimate Reality, and that *is* the ignorance that makes us think, act and perceive the way we do. The only way Truth can be experienced is by transcending the apparent reality of the world – removing the veil, like polishing the dust from a mirror. This will involve a path of increasing knowledge, a loss of attachment to the world, and a loss of the egoism that separates the self from its true Reality as identical with divinity.

But most of the schools accept the reality of the world in some form or other. Most are pluralists and realists. That is, they accept the plurality and separate identity of all the different things that we see in the world. There is no unity of the essence of things that undermines our natural perceptions of them. This is a common sense view of the world, and accords well with the views of the *Veda*, which do not render much support for the world as an illusion. Yet there is a good deal in the *Veda* to suggest that there is a unity to reality, and that the dualities that we perceive are a result of our propensities for differentiating between this and that in order to make sense of the world. A certain interconnectedness of reality is posited in so much *Vedic* tradition and in the cause–effect processes of life itself. The unity of reality is posited by Advaita Vedānta, and Viśiṣṭadvaita, but is denied by the pluralistic and realistic schools of Mīmāṃsā, Nyāya and Vaiśeṣika.

A dualist perspective of reality is held by two schools, Sāṃkhya and Dvaita, though the way that dualism is expressed in both these schools is very different. Sāṃkhya divides reality into two, pure spirits and matter, but while all matter, which represents everything in the universe, is unified as one, the spirits are multiple, representing the individual souls of each human being. There is no hint of divinity in this school, unlike that of Dvaita, where its dualism serves to separate every aspect of worldly reality from the divine.

Whatever the perspective of reality, there is always present the idea that the ordinary self is not experiencing the deeper level of Reality, the Truth of existence, because of over-involvement in the phenomenal world. Self-centred egoism is usually the block that prevents the liberation of the self to Truth. In the more theistic schools like Viśiṣṭādvaita and Dvaita, egoism is not so much wrong as misdirected. Surrendering one's whole being to the divine in loving-devotion, concomitant with pursuit of knowledge of God, brings about a gradual shift in the perspective of reality from a self-centred to a God-centred viewpoint. In all schools, Reality is experienced through changes in the self. All the schools have a substance view of reality that makes it permanent and unchanging at its deepest level. When, through knowledge, the soul permeates this level, it realizes its natural state as a permanent, eternal substance, ever free, ever real.

Where the reality and plurality of the world are maintained, there is a quest to establish the fundamental constituents of reality – the stuff of which the world is composed. These are sometimes called *tattvas*, literally "reals" or "truths". Most of the schools posit a number of such "reals" as composing the universe, or are prepared to take on board those put forward by another school. These "reals" are *categories* of reality, and the Sanskrit term for these is *padārthas*. It will be the schools accepting pluralistic realism that will be most concerned with such categories, and each of these will accept different ones.

Whoever we are, we cannot fail to perceive the transient and finite nature of the world in which we live. Moments pass and are irretrievable except through memory. We seem to be the same person through our childhood and maturity, and yet, like all life, we are perpetually subject to change. We know that, one day, the finitude of our present life will be presented to us in the form of death. We can be happy, but we can also be sad. We can experience great joy, but we can also grieve. We can laugh heartily and fully, but we can cry desperately and forlornly. We are humans, and human life is bound in vicissitudes as much as great things, in evil as much as good, in suffering as much as pleasure, and the suffering and vicissitudes of some are greater than others. One question this book seeks to answer is how the different perspectives of reality in each school offer solutions to this. And how does God fit into this kind of picture of reality? If God is *God*, in what way is he involved in this impermanent and transient world where humans suffer? And if he is God, and Reality at its ultimate, what is his role in the reality of the world? In short, how can a permanent, Absolute divinity be involved in an impermanent, finite world of change? It is a question I shall return to in the treatment of each school.

Epistemology: the theory of knowledge

In any search for the deepest levels of reality and truth, it is knowledge that provides the means. In Hindu thought, to experience knowledge that is ultimate is to discover the answers to life, to perfect life, and to transcend it in liberation. Thus there was a search for perfect knowledge. There are different kinds of knowledge. Much of our knowledge, for example, is knowledge *about*, knowledge *that* something is the case. This kind of knowledge is essential to our daily living and well-being, to our abilities to progress and evolve in life, and to the living of our lives competently. At this level of knowledge we make use of *percep-*

tion through our senses, aided with our abilities to classify and make appropriate comparisons of the data we receive from our senses. Memory is the servant of all such sense perceptions, and the mind is the medium for synthesizing all the sense stimuli we receive. And yet there is a difference between knowledge that is *immediate*, knowledge acquired *directly* through the senses, and something recalled through memory. The perception I have now of the view from my study window, for example, is much more reliable and exact than my memory of the same view yesterday. This suggests that immediate and direct knowledge through the senses has greater *validity* than knowledge gained from memory, which might be said to have much less, or even no, validity at all.

Some of our knowledge is not direct and immediate, however, but *indirect* and *mediate*. Inferred knowledge is of this type. I know, for example that if the roads and fields and flowers, and all that I can see are wet, then it must have rained – especially since my experience tells me that *every* time I perceive such wet things, it has rained. *Inference*, then is another important means of our general knowledge about life. Then, again, so much of our knowledge is acquired from other people. Here we have to differentiate between what is a reliable source – perhaps a particular person, or book, or newspaper – and what is unreliable. This is knowledge gained from the *testimony* of others.

Perception, inference and testimony are the generally accepted means of valid knowledge in Hindu philosophy, though some schools will add other means, as will be seen. Valid knowledge is termed *pramā*, and the means or causes of valid knowledge are called *pramāṇas*.[4] Each of the schools sets out its views on the valid means of knowledge, and this will be an area that will need to be examined carefully in each of the chapters related to the schools. Sometimes, of course, our perceptions deceive us, and the knowledge we have proves to be erroneous. *Error* in knowledge is also something that occupied the thoughts of the different schools.

The relationship between knowledge and the self is critical to Hindu philosophy. If I cannot know *anything*, can there be an "I", a self? On the one hand it could be said that cognition, knowledge, is essential for awareness of the self: when I am in deepest sleep, for example, or when I am under anaesthetic, no knowledge at all takes place until I wake up. So where is the self in this state of absence of cognition? On the other hand, the continued involvement of the self in its knowledge of the material world is the major factor in its continued bondage in the interminable cycle of reincarnation. This suggests that the self must be ever present, despite times when it knows nothing. It might also suggest that cessation of knowledge is the key to liberation, for without knowledge there can be no bondage to worldly sense stimuli. As will be seen, some of the Hindu schools accept this idea, equating the state of liberation with a total loss of knowledge similar to that in deep sleep. But if this is the case, of what value is the liberated state? Is it not better for the soul to retain some knowledge, or a degree of consciousness that can appreciate its freedom? It is particularly the theistic schools like Viṣiśtādvaita and Dvaita, that will see the importance of knowledge that recognizes the divine in the liberated state. Advaita Vedānta, on the other hand, as well as some strands of other schools, accept a pure state of consciousness, a pure *sat*, Truth or Reality, as the ultimate state of liberation.

The link, then, between knowledge, ultimate Reality and liberation is a critical one. Clearly the kind of knowledge that impedes the evolution of the self – and that is the kind of knowledge that feeds the desires and aversions encountered in the material world – traps each individual in ignorance. It is removal of that ignorance that brings experience of a level of reality that is more ultimate: knowledge is usually the means for this though, ultimately, it itself may be transcended.

The self

Central to Hindu philosophical inquiry is the nature of the self. All the orthodox schools of philosophy accept the cycle of reincarnation of each self through millions of existences. However, they accept that there must be a final end to the process of rebirth, a point at which the individual is forever free. It is the egoistic and self-assertive involvement of the self in the world that causes reincarnation, for each action of the self is a cause, a cause that, at some time in the present life, or in future existences, will come to fruition. It is the self's involvement in the world that builds up a network of causes that will create a future for it. Understanding the nature of the self, why it exists, its purpose, its destiny, and why it suffers, is critical in pointing the way forward to release from reincarnation. Hindu philosophy generally accepts a substance view of the self. That is to say, the self is an eternal substance that can exist in a state of freedom, providing it finds the means to realize this ultimate goal. This is the function of Hindu orthodox philosophy: it is also the function of much Hindu scripture – especially the *Upaniṣads*. We are what we make of ourselves, and all levels of reality are open to experience, providing we have the means. This centrality of the self in its perspective of reality is put rather well by Sharma:

> The self is the immediate starting point of all experience. It is so borne in upon us as to easily usurp the place of honor. The existence of things outside of us in time and space and even the reputed existence of a Deity are, after all, secondary, being reached only through acts of private consciousness and may, for aught we know, be illusory or at any rate, not so irrefragably real as the self. From an opposite point of view, matter which can be moved and measured and is therefore tangible, could be set up as a sterner reality than either God or the souls, who seem to shrink into shadowy abstractions by its side.[5]

It is precisely because the self is the centre of all experience of reality, and because matter is the reality that it understands, that it cannot release itself from its own egocentric involvement with the world.

But how can we assume that the self is something more than the body, the senses and the mind? Why is the self not merely identifiable with ordinary consciousness and mind functions? Hinduism's answers to such questions are various. But it is eager to establish the eternal nature of a self that transcends the body, mind and senses. The existence of the self is often inferred in the process of knowledge: I can say "I" know, where "*I*" am the subject and the knowledge is a characteristic I have. I don't say I *am* the knowledge that I have. It seems, too, that I can know my own mind, and while it is so often difficult to control the mind processes entirely, to a certain extent we can all direct our minds in directions we desire. All this might suggest that the nature of the self is pure consciousness, a consciousness that can obtain independently of processes of knowledge that present objects for that consciousness. Some Hindu philosophers took this stance, but others preferred to see consciousness as a quality of the self, something that could come and go, as when we lose consciousness in deep sleep when no impressions are conveyed by the mind. The analogies of the waking, dreaming and deep sleep states, were often used by the proponents of the schools to analyse this difficult aspect of consciousness. For others, the self consists of a pure consciousness that is devoid of objects, dualities and differentiation.

A substance view of the self is of a permanent *ātman*. The *ātman* is often referred to as the soul, the part of the self that is permanent, unlike the transient bodily self and the psychological self. This stands in sharp contrast to Buddhist process views of the self in which the self never is, but is always in a process of becoming: it is never permanent, and there can never be a permanent soul. Differentiating between the eternal soul, the *Self*, as opposed to the egoistic personality *self*, will be important throughout this book. While the word "soul" has too many western connotations, and can sometimes be misleading, there are occasions when it is the more apt term. Generally, however, I shall refer to the eternal self as the Self or, to use the Sanskrit term, *ātman*. This should differentiate it from the ordinary self, the *jīvātman*. But in the early parts of the *Veda*, the *ātman* referred to the concrete, psychological self. It was only later, at the end of the *Veda*, the *Vedānta*, that the conception of it changed to one of a more subtle and transcendental nature. Either way, however, it was deemed eternal.

The transcendental shift in the conception of the self was what linked its essence, its essential and permanent component, with the divine and with ultimate Reality. It became identified with God either partially, or totally, and/or equated with a level of Reality that transcended the ordinary finite one of the world of matter. Concomitant with this more transcendent view of the self was a turning inward to conceive of the depth of the self as the true Self, the soul, and consonant with Reality, while the ordinary self was that which was outward focused on the material world. Realization of the Self was, then, often God realization, though certainly not for every orthodox school. The link between the *ātman* and the divine was sometimes pressed to the non-dual level of identity, as in Advaita Vedānta, but in most cases the *ātman* remained in dualistic relationship to the divine, and this was essential to the retention of overt theism.

One critical question that will need to be taken up in the treatment of the different philosophical views, is the extent to which individual ego is to be lost for experience of a more ultimate Reality and, in most cases, divinity. Ego, *ahaṃkāra*, is the epitome of the personality self, the *jīvātman*. It is the ego that is responsible for self-assertiveness, when it is involved in reactions to the sense stimuli of the environment. In response to such stimuli, the egoistic self differentiates between this and that, desiring one thing and not another, thus pursuing some things and avoiding others. Since it is because of this kind of interaction with the world that the law of *karma* ensures appropriate effects for each individual according to that interaction, then it presupposes that interaction with the world is inimical to the evolutionary journey of the self, and its realization of liberation. Thus it is self-centredness that has to be transcended. But does this mean a loss of the ego, the "I"? The schools answer this difficult question differently. For some, the retention of personal identity is essential to the dualistic relationship between human and divine. For the most part, the emphasis shifts from a self-interested to a disinterested viewpoint, but in some cases, the ego is lost entirely.

Causality

We all know that causes are related to effects. If I do *x*, then I expect *y* to follow, and by this means life is ordered sufficiently for individual and collective progression. But while we accept such cause–effect processes, where does the process start? Is there a first, uncaused cause that starts the ball rolling? After all, if there is no first cause, then this suggests that causes can come into being without being caused to do so. And if this is the case are such uncaused causes real causes, or are they effects without causes? It is questions like these with which the proponents of the different philosophical schools of Hinduism were occupied. Processes of cause and effect are critical to reality, to epistemology, and to the means of liberation.

Most schools view the world as an effect, or a multiplicity of interrelated effects. But to understand the reality of the effect that is the world, it is essential to know the nature of the causes or cause by which it came about. And how can there be valid means of knowledge if we do not know the nature of the causes of the objects in existence, or the way those objects themselves can be causes? Even more critical to the Hindu mind was the cause of bondage of the soul, and the suffering involved in perpetual transmigration. If the causes of such bondage and suffering could be identified, and the relationship between cause and effect overcome, then liberation would be the end effect and the termination of all effects.

All the schools accept the law of cause and effect, the law of *karma*, which operates to bring positive effects to good actions and negative ones to bad or evil ones. This is a "reap what you sow" principle, and if there are effects to be reaped, then an individual has to remain in a transmigrating existence until all the effects of previous causes have been exhausted. Overcoming this is the key to liberation. The body serves the purpose of associating a self with a material medium, as a means for working out fruitive *karma*. It is a temporary union of an eternal soul with an impermanent, material substance.

There are three main theories of causality in the Hindu orthodox schools. One is *satkāryavāda*, the view that effects *exist* latently in their causes. Milk, for example, may be the cause of curds, the effect. But the curd is simply a *transformation* of the cause into the effect; nothing new has come into being, for there has been no material change in the effect. So this view accepts that effects exist in their causes *before* they become manifest, that effects are always related to causes, and that cause and effect are unified. The opposite view is that of *asatkāryavāda*. Here, effects do not pre-exist in their causes, so the causes must be antecedent to the effects, and the effects do not exist until they actually become manifest. And when this happens, these effects are something *new*, they are not just transformations of causes, but new existences in themselves. It is a theory that rejects remote causes and looks only to immediately antecedent causes. When the effect comes into being – as the oak tree that comes from the acorn – the cause ceases to exist, leaving the reality of the new effect.

The third theory of causality is *satkāraṇavāda*, which sees effects as no different at all from causes. Thus, causes alone are real, and there are no effects. Nothing new can come into being, and all effects are illusory. However complex effects may appear, they are only apparent and not real. All reality is unified into one cause, denying all differentiation between cause and effect, and between all dualities like light and dark, good and evil, male and female, this and that, and so on.

What these three major theories of causality aim to do, is to understand the relationship between causes and effects in order to get to grips with what is needed to transcend the causative processes. Such a process is necessary in order to reach out, or in, to ultimate Reality, to divinity – where the latter is accepted – and to experience the true nature of the soul.

While causality is of the essence of all existence, facilitating the phenomena of the universe, the universe itself is subject to similar processes of cause and effect in its cycles of creation and dissolution. What causes this process to occur will form part of the inquiry into the nature of causality in the remit of each school. Only one school, Pūrva Mīmāṃsā, rejects the cyclical nature of the universe, as will be seen. In some cases, it is God who is the ultimate cause of creation. This might be as the *material* cause, in which case, something of the nature of the divine emanates forth to compose the world. Pantheistic and panentheistic types of belief incorporate God as a material cause. A particular problem here will be how to avoid linking the divine nature with the changeability, contingency, finitude, evil and suffering in the world. In other cases, God is the *efficient* cause of creation, he that causes the cyclical processes of creation and dissolution of the universe, but who does not form the universe from part of his own being. Either, both, or neither of these theories are to be found in the different schools of thought.

The concept of God

For the most part, the concept of deity in the various schools is radically different, ranging from overt atheism to devotional theism. The school of Pūrva Mīmāṃsā rejects a concept of God outright, and Sāṃkhya also has no concept of deity. In the former school the autonomous law of cause and effect, and the concomitant potency that permits each cause to ripen to an appropriate effect, are all that are needed for humanity to create its own world. However, the *Veda*, here, is centripetal to the best possible functioning of human beings in their self-determining capacities. In the latter, Sāṃkhya, reality is dual – matter and spirits. Matter needs only its own self-energizing principle for its materialization, initiated by the proximity of spirits. And the spirits are independent of each other, thoroughly plural, and in no need of a deity to unify them, or the matter in which they become entrapped. For Vaiśeṣika and Nyāya, God is he that directs the process of cause and effect, the efficient cause of the different combinations of atoms to form the differentiated phenomena of the world. In the school of Yoga, too, God fulfils the same kind of role in the causation processes, but acts also as a focus for meditation and *yogic* practice – only to be abandoned when liberation is realized.

These rather low-profiled views of the divine seem to fall short of the highly developed concepts of divinity that are articulated in the *Upaniṣads*, the great texts of the *Veda* on which the schools themselves claim their orthodoxy. And, indeed, without a developed concept of deity, it is difficult to see just why some of these schools could have been granted orthodox status. Clearly, they all have developed epistemologies and theories of reality, and they all accept the ultimate cessation of reincarnating life at the attainment or realization of *mokṣa*, liberation. But it is left to the Vedānta school, in its non-dual, qualified non-dualistic and dualistic aspects, to provide the most philosophical and profound concepts of deity. It is in the broad spectrum of Vedānta philosophy that both the indescribable Absolute and the cosmic describable and transcendent God of the *Upaniṣads* become the whole focus of the entire philosophy of the respective schools. These are orthodox *darśanas* in the truer sense, in that they complement and interpret the philosophical strands of the *Veda* more closely.

Ontology[6] is the nature of *being*, the fundamental Reality that underpins the universe, the only existent that simply *is*. It is a substance view of all reality, suggesting that there is an ultimate Reality, a fundamental, uncaused substratum that is *sat*, pure being. It is along these lines that Vedānta takes its philosophies. For Advaita Vedānta this *sat* is a unifying essence with which all is equated. Knowledge is the key to its discovery in the depths of the self: the removal of ignorance brings experience of this absolute ultimate Reality that is the self. But in other Vedānta schools the identity with the absolutely ultimate divine can never be complete. For Viṣiśṭādvaita this is because divinity is something forever beyond the self – not completely, but like the soul is ever superior to the body: they are at one, and yet different. In the school of Dvaita, this separation will be far more distinct, and will be manifest in outright dualism between God and all aspects of the world, and the self.

Earlier I stated that the different schools should not be seen as complementary to one another. Nowhere is this better exemplified than in the wide differences in the concept of deity. While at one end of the scale we find a conception of a totally transcendent Absolute, on the other, there may be no God at all. Then, too, while a totally transcendent Absolute is essential to the school of Advaita Vedānta, for other Vedānta schools the dualistic separation of human and divine permits a depth of theistic devotion that is so integral to, and essential for, religious practice. But the more theistic the philosophy, the greater the problems of the involvement of God in the world. Where God is either the material or efficient cause of the world, it is expected that questions like the relation between an omnipotent and good God, with a world in which evil and suffering exist, are bound to emerge. Here, again, is the problem of how a permanent divine entity can be involved with an impermanent, contingent and finite world. These are important issues to be taken up in the chapters that follow.

Liberation

While the concept of God is sufficiently underplayed in some of the schools as to caste doubt on the legitimacy of their orthodoxy, the one doctrine that qualifies all of them for the rank of orthodoxy is the belief in liberation, *mokṣa*. The need for liberation from suffering – especially in its form of endless reincarnation – underpins Indian philosophy.

Liberation is the lynchpin of orthodox Hindu philosophical inquiry. The means to it were supplied by knowledge, or by *bhakti*, the devotional and theistic focus on the divine. The former path of knowledge is normally the harder path, and even *bhakti* itself is usually informed by an emphasis on knowledge. Either way, disinterested non-attachment to the fruits of one's own actions – to the effects of the causes one makes – would be essential to rid the self of the *karma* that accrues to it and causes rebirth. But Hinduism does not have exclusive and definitive means to *mokṣa*, and the schools will reflect this diversity. Yet there are some common denominators that inform them all in the quest for liberation. Knowledge of reality is essential, that is to say, knowing by what means something can be said to be true, and knowing what is real *ultimately*. Knowledge of how cause and effect operate to keep the self bound, also underpins the quest for liberation. Then, too, there is a common quest to know the nature of any ultimate cause and, most importantly, the quest for the nature of the real self. While the proponents of the various schools may seem at times to be preoccupied with the minutiae of epistemology, logic, meanings of words, ritual practices and the like – so that one wonders sometimes whether such intricacies have lost sight of the ultimate questions – it should be remembered that ultimate Truths cannot be answered simply and conveyed without logic and rational argument. Careful and meticulous statement of argumentation was essential to arm a proponent against those of other schools, as well as to give credence to one's own.

1

Types of belief

Hinduism is a remarkable religion in that it has accommodated a broad spectrum of ideas and beliefs throughout its very long tradition. It is also something of a unique religion in that persistent accommodation of ideas has meant that it tolerates very diverse perspectives of what it is to be "Hindu". Such perspectives allow for simple worship of stones or trees, for example, alongside metaphysical introspection of the nature of the divine and the transcendence of the senses until unity with the cosmos and the Absolute of divinity is experienced. Hinduism, then, is characterized by many, and not just one, type of belief. The western world is used to the word *monotheism* to describe the religions of Judaism, Christianity and – if people are sufficiently aware of the nature of the religion – Islam. But Hinduism cannot be so neatly confined to any one particular belief type, not only during its historical past but, also, in its present expression. As an umbrella term, "Hinduism" incorporates within it types of belief ranging from atheism to polytheism, some of these types of belief co-existing in the same period of time or even in the same location in space, others being characteristic of certain periods of historical tradition. It will help, then, to examine in detail some of these types of belief that will be pertinent to the study of reality in Hindu religion and philosophy.

Theism

The term *theism* comes from the Greek *theos* "god", which merely has *-ism* added to it to make it a *type* of belief. It is a word that can incorporate a number of meanings, however, its basic meaning is belief in a deity or deities as opposed to its opposite of *a*-theism, which has no such belief at all. It is a term originally used in western philosophy of religion, and in order to arrive at a working definition, it will be useful to examine its meaning in relation to western thought. Its past usage in western philosophy is in relation to the Christian view of the divine as one God expressed as a Trinity, and we sometimes find the word theism being used to refer specifically to monotheistic Christianity, as opposed to other religions that are polytheistic or pantheistic. Those who study world religions might find this definition rather narrow and outdated, almost suggestive that theism cannot obtain in religions outside Christianity. At one time the word would have been alien to other religions, but is now commonly used beyond western philosophy in the context of any religion.

Another more restrictive sense of the word theism is also found in western philosophy to depict belief in a God who has *revealed* himself to his people, a God who thus has some kind of *personal* involvement with humanity. Theists would often wish to be differentiated from *deists*, those who have a belief in a God as Creator, but not in one that is subsequently involved in creation in any way. This is rather like a watchmaker who makes a watch, winds it up, and then leaves it to work on its own. Deists do not accept that God reveals himself to humanity in any way at all, so theism is a term sometimes used to express the opposite view. Theism incorporates the notion of a God as Creator and also Sustainer of the universe in a very real way, a God who reveals himself to humanity in many ways and with whom human beings have a personal relationship. This *personal* relationship is an important characteristic of all theism, but is particularly important to Judeo-Christian theism.

These are rather specific "western" views of theism and result in the term being used in confined senses. Peter Bertocci, for example, limits his definition of theism to belief in "one self-existent God, who alone is worthy of worship".[1] His definition is expanded to include the concept of a revealed God who intervenes in the world and a God on whom everything in existence is dependent but, essentially, it confines theism to belief in *one*, male, God.

But even for western contexts, definitions of theism can be fairly diverse because of different concepts of deity. These range from very transcendent perspectives of the divine as a self-existing being that surpasses all possible understanding and human knowledge, to more describable aspects of divinity to which humanity can more readily relate. Bertocci deals with his topic of theism mainly through the old theistic "proofs" for the existence of God, and this is a useful approach for western analysis of theism, since theists often accept one or more of the "proofs" as the basis of their religious philosophy. Thus, ontological[2] theists believe that God is a perfect being, so great that nothing greater than him can be envisaged. Cosmological[3] theists accept God as the self-existent, infinite and unchanging being who is the cause of the finite and changing world, and who creates the interconnected order between causes and their effects within the universe. Many people have come to accept this theory because there must be some cause, they say, which makes everything happen the way it does, otherwise we would live in chaos. Teleological[4] theists have a similar view that there is a purposeful *design* to the world, one that serves the purpose of pointing ultimately to God.

Despite the diversity of theistic belief, however, it is always essentially *dualistic* in its perspective of the divine. That is to say, God and the world and God and human beings are dualistically related to each other. Such dualism is essential to theism because without it, God could not be worshipped, prayed to and experienced, and he could not have discourse with humanity, intervene in history, send his prophets, save his people, and so on: he could not be a God of revelation, a revealed God. And this duality between God and human means that God is describably different from humans; he is depicted as omnipotent, omniscient, omnipresent, eternal, perfect, ultimate goodness, and so on.

These are characteristics of the divine that are important to western theism. So because of dualism, predicated statements can be made about God; we can say God is x, God is y, God is z. But making statements about God can lead to philosophical difficulties – and theism leaves itself wide open to problems. Consider, for example, the implications of a question posed by Quinn and Taliafero: "Can God make a stone so heavy that even God cannot lift it?[5] Whichever way one answers, the power, the omnipotence of God – so important to theism – is challenged.

Whether one accepts ontological, cosmological or teleological theistic views of God and the world, it would have to be claimed that God would need to be assigned some kind of rational will, and some kind of self awareness. Otherwise, how could he be perfect and create connected order or purposeful design in the world? Theists, therefore, often give God *Personhood*, though recognizing at the same time the essential *otherness* of God. If theism accepts God's involvement with the world, with creation and with humanity, then it is difficult to make him impersonal. And if God is not impersonal and is always dualistically related to humanity and the world, then theism as a belief system means that we can ask questions – albeit limited ones – about God: "What is God?" "What sort of a Person is God?" "What is the nature of God"? Strictly speaking, however, philosophical theism retains a belief in the transcendence of the divine which makes ultimate questions about divinity difficult, yet it accepts the immanence of the divine which is more readily able to be experienced.

Western theism is usually very careful to differentiate between Creator and created and is antagonistic to any theory or belief type that might seek to conjoin the two too closely. For this reason creation is *ex nihilo*, "out of nothing". In the creation narrative of Genesis 1, God creates by command, "Let there be". Nothing *emanates* from God to cause creation. Quite the opposite is the case for much Hindu theistic belief which, while retaining the dual distinction between Source and creation, is more content to see the universe as an emanated manifestation of an ultimately indescribable Source. The relationship between human and divine and between the world and the divine is therefore much closer in Hindu theistic belief because something of the divine resides in each entity in the cosmos.

All belief types have their particularly problematic areas, but theism perhaps lays itself open to some insurmountable problems, mainly because God is given attributes. Some of the major difficulties are set out below:

1 One of the greatest problems remains the question of theodicy, and I say "remains" because I do not consider that it is one solved by western theistic systems unless the omnipotence of the theistic God is jeopardized. Theodicy is the problem of evil and the relation of God to it. How can a morally good, omnipotent and perfect God permit evil? If he is all-powerful, why doesn't he do something about it? If he is not all-powerful, and cannot, then is he really God? Theists usually find one way out of this is to accept – and much western theism does – that individuals have freedom of choice; they are free to choose good or evil. But then there are pointless or gratuitous evils, evils that seem to have no possible cosmological, teleological or ontological purpose at all. Why does the theistic God permit these? Why did he

allow the Holocaust? But *because* he is theistically viewed, it allows me to pose these difficult questions and to search for reasons why a perfect, omnipotent God can seem to be otherwise.

2 Theism often accepts some kind of moral norm by which good/evil, right/wrong are judged. And if the theistic God is sustaining his creation, then we have to assume that within it are universal moral "norms" for humanity to follow. Some western Christians see "conscience" as supplying awareness of such moral norms, while Hindus might refer to the old *Vedic* concept of *ṛta*, or to *dharma*. The theist suggests that something is right if the omnipotent divine will says it is. But this raises the question: Is something right because it is the divine will or does God will it because it is right? If the former, then God *could* will something evil, but it is right because God wills it: if he can't or doesn't will evil then he is not omnipotent. But if God only wills what is right, then what is right exists independently of God, and God is not needed for moral behaviour. In this case his omnipotence is again in question. Many western theists fall back on the epistemic distance between God and humanity to solve this question, which means that we cannot know the reason why God allows certain evils, even pointless ones. The best answer to such a problem in the West is to place limitations on the power of God – he sees, but cannot avoid, because he has given total freedom to his created beings. Generally, Hinduism has less of a problem with theodicy: the law of cause and effect places the blame for evil – and the fruits of it – squarely on the shoulders of each individual being: we reap what we sow.

3 In making predicative statements about God, theism runs the danger of limiting the divine. Negative theology sometimes overcomes this. That is to say, saying what God is *not* as opposed to what God is – non-predicative as opposed to predicative statements – serves to retain the inscrutable nature of the divine. Hinduism sometimes uses the expression *neti neti* "not this, not this" to refer to the indescribable Absolute.

4 The dual nature of divine and human and the predicative statements about the divine are usually of a transcendent but immanent being in western theism. But in its wider sense theism can incorporate non-transcendent and overly anthropomorphic views of the deity – to an extent that they jeopardize the essential transcendence of divinity, and restrict the divine nature.

5 Theism is a culture-bound belief type in that it is built up within, and conforms to, a particular religion. Hindu theism, then, would differ from Christian, Jewish, or Islamic theism. Christian theism, for example, accepts a Trinity of God, an incarnation of God, and a spirit of God – something that would be rejected by both Islam and Judaism. Hindu theism can also accept the descent of the divine into human form, but can maintain, at the same time, more transcendent expressions of theism that accept the ultimate Absolute as indescribable. But all expressions of theism in Hinduism are equally culture bound.

6 It is theistic statements that tend to be antagonistic to scientific fact. Less theistic, more metaphysical assertions about religion, which go beyond theism, have less tangibility, are less language-bound in character. Theism makes many statements

about the divine, and the more statements that are made, the more problematic are many of the claims encompassed in them.

7 When theism, as in western religions, seeks to separate the divine from the temporal, the result is to rid creation of any sense of sacredness or holiness. It strips Nature of any status in creation. Wainwright comments:

> Christian theism maintains that nothing contingent is inherently holy. Places (Sinai, Jerusalem) persons (prophets, priests, divinely anointed kings) artifacts (the ark), and so on, aren't intrinsically holy; any holiness they possess is extrinsic – conferred upon them by God from without. Nature is no longer regarded as divine and therefore becomes an appropriate object for manipulation and detached observation.[6]

This distinct duality between temporal and divine is problematic for Christianity for a number of reasons. It exists in order to maintain a clear separation in the nature of the Creator and creation, and this maintains in turn, the transcendence and power of the divine. But the corollary of this is that western humanity has tended to place the same distance between itself – believed to be made in the image of God – and the rest of creation. So western religious theism has been partly blamed for conditioning human beings to accept their superiority over Nature, and the harnessing and control of Nature as inferior. It is an attitude that is not helping the ecology of the planet, endangered species and the holistic development and evolution of individuals one with another. In theory, Hinduism has a totally different viewpoint in that, since there is a more intimate link with an ultimate divine Source, then all, including Nature, is divine; all is sacred.

These, then, are some of the fundamental problematic areas of theism, and the more the concept is expanded, the more numerous the problems become. Theistic belief is a characteristic of most religions in some form, and is the most readily adaptable and fluid of the types of religious belief. It is theism that is often channelled into anthropomorphic expression – an important dimension of much religious belief. The word *anthropomorphism* is of Greek origin and has two basic meanings; first, the giving of human form, attributes and character to the divine; and, second, the giving of human personality to what is impersonal and irrational, for example animals. Theism readily lends itself to anthropomorphism because of belief in a personal deity or deities, and a revealed God can only be known in terms understandable to the human being. Strict western philosophical theism has a tendency to avoid anthropomorphism, but it abounds in established religion and popular thought, and has become a widespread characteristic of theistic belief and practice in many religions. The height of anthropomorphic expression in theism is found in the human forms of the divine – the incarnation of God in Christianity, and the *avatāras* of Viṣṇu in Hinduism. The extent to which Christocentricity predominates over theocentricity in Christianity, and of Kṛṣṇaism, for example, over the ultimate Absolute of Brahman in Hinduism, suggest how powerful anthropomorphic theism is in most religious expression.

Theism is, thus, a varied phenomenon, and is really a generic term for a multiplicity of theisms – each with its own distinctive character. It is "a complex web of assertions about God's reality, character, and relations with the universe", writes Evans.[7] Indeed, theism allows for a greater multiplicity of expressions, greater diversity, than other belief types. Now that theism is a term used in the context of all religions, it needs to be broadened from its western definition in order to be comprehensively applicable elsewhere – in this context, to Hinduism. Taking into account the western origin and perspectives of theism, and yet the wider application of the term to the broader expression of religion, theism can be said to be: *belief in a deity or deities (God, Goddess, Gods and/or Goddesses) with whom human beings have a dual and personal relationship.* The meaning of theism can be further qualified by prefixes – *mono-*, *poly-*, *pan-*, *panen-*. Importantly, all these qualified theisms retain the dualism of the relationship between the individual and the divine.

Monotheism

Monotheism as a belief system is not quite so simple as the term suggests. The word is, again, Greek in origin, *mono* "one", "single", *theos* "god" and *-ism*. In western philosophy, the terms monotheism and theism are almost interchangeable.[8] Just as western theism accepts God as the perfect, immutable, omniscient, omnipotent Creator, so monotheism is often defined in the same way. And this really is the problem of defining monotheism, because definitions are so thoroughly western. It could be claimed, on one hand, that monotheism is the doctrine or belief that *there is only one God.* In the West, this is likely to be interpreted that the Christian God is the *only* God, and none other exists. On the other hand, in the East, this same definition might be interpreted as the existence of only one God, but that that God is worshipped differently, and by different names, by different people and in different cultures. This is a definition that monotheism is *belief in, or worship of, one God.* It is a more fluid one and is better suited to an analysis of eastern ideas. Because monotheism is essentially theistic belief, it infers the same dualistic relationship with, and *personal* belief in, the deity. I propose, then, a working definition of monotheism as: *belief in one divine being (male, female or other) with whom the individual has a dual and personal relationship.*

However, monotheism is a varied phenomenon, and it would be wise to observe the comment of Ludwig that: "Monotheism is like a river with many springs and many tributaries."[9] Ludwig also suggests – and it is a very valid point – that there will often be significant differences between the theoretical monotheism of a particular faith, and that faith in practice.[10] Thus an Eastern Orthodox or a Roman Catholic church may contain more images than a Hindu temple, and the former could appear visually polytheistic like the latter. Similarly in Hinduism, the religion portrayed in the sacred literature is vastly different from the religion of the villages and towns. This should warn us about definitions that are too narrow and too scripturally and philosophically confined.

Monotheism is a dualistic principle, one that separates the divine from the world and from humanity. As was seen in the case of theism, the monotheism of Judaism, Christianity and Islam considers the nature of the divine to be separate from creation in order to maintain divine transcendence and omnipotence. In Hindu monotheistic expression this separation is often far less pronounced in relation to the divine and the individual,[11] though the degree to which the world is separate from the divine is more variable. The point of the dualism of monotheism is that, as theism in general, devotion to, worship of, prayer to, praise to, adoration of, supplication to, a deity are each possible, but are intensified because of the focus on one single deity. Utter devotion to many deities is difficult for any human being, but monotheism supplies the kind of focus that makes a more fervent devotion possible, and the intensity of the personal relationship between divine and human is given its fullest expression. Very often, to allow for a more personal approach to the divine, a particular *aspect* or *attribute* of the divine may be the focus of the worshipper. The incarnation of the divine in Christianity is a good example, or the "descents" of Viṣṇu in Hinduism as Kṛṣṇa or Rāma. Aspects of the divine, such as a symbol of the reproductive energy of Śiva for Hindu Śaivites, may be the focus of attention.

Those who relate to a deity monotheistically would find it difficult to bestow the same kind of devotion on another deity. This point raises some important issues. Can the definition of monotheism support worship of one particular deity to the exclusion of all others, one particular deity as a chosen one amongst others, or one particular deity while accepting that there *are no* others? Judaism and Islam certainly accept the last of these suggestions, and are critical of Christianity for dividing divinity into a Trinity. Since, however, monotheism accepts the worship of different aspects or attributes of one divinity, Christianity defends itself with the claim that the Trinity is three aspects of one being, albeit that Christians tend to focus primarily on the incarnated aspect. Likewise, it could be claimed that where Hinduism accepts an ultimate Absolute, Brahman, which subsumes in it all other deities as aspects of itself, then monotheism must obtain in Hinduism too. This is so even if a particular individual devotes himself or herself to one of these deities to the exclusion of all others, or to one chosen deity amongst many. Some may wish to suggest the term *henotheism* for worship of one deity as supreme while recognizing the existence of other deities, and *monolatry* as worshipping one supreme deity while accepting others as inferior. But, either way, the focus on, and devotion to, *one* personal deity is a *mono* theism – and I do not think that there is a need to qualify the term further. In recognizing one specific deity as the focus of devotion, the worshipper is assigning to that deity the omnipotence and supremacy that any other expression of divinity does not appear to possess to the same extent.

In point of fact, many so-called monotheistic religions incorporate polytheistic ideas and aspects: attributes of a deity sometimes fall into this category, depending on the degree of personhood associated with an attribute. Where evil is separated from the perfection of the divine being and assigned to another dualistic force, for example in some Christian theology, and in late Zoroastrianism, then we have really moved away from a strictly *mono* theism.[12] Many monotheistic faiths have a host of supporting divine beings – angels, saints, spirits and so on, and where incarnations obtain there is often focus on the incarnation in a way that can only be described as dividing the incarnated form from its divine source.

There are both positive and negative aspects and outcomes of monotheism. On the one hand it is natural for human beings, in the context of religion, to focus on one divine being alone. This fulfils the particular innate needs of a human being and helps that person to make sense of the world as we know it. On the other hand, western monotheism is currently criticized for its monarchical and patriarchal natures, both of which can give the impression of a dictatorial deity, the patriarchal head of his people and the dictatorial chairman of the board. These are notions of deity that can oppress and suppress the human psyche – especially the feminine one – and can be exclusivist to all other approaches to the divine.

In approaching Hinduism I feel there is a need to define monotheism more loosely. Many Hindus regard themselves as monotheists because, ultimately, all deities are one – the Absolute, Brahman. The unity of the divine in Hinduism is, for most aspects of the religion, fundamental. It is a unity that may sometimes become blurred at the village and urban level where local deities are the main focus of worship, but the unity nevertheless obtains. There is often a difference between the theoretical conceptualization of religion and its expression in practice. Then, too, given the number of manifestations of Brahman, the Absolute of Hinduism, it is natural that many will have one chosen deity who will be the focus of devotion, even though other deities might be worshipped for other functional reasons. I would claim that this is monotheistic practice, defining monotheism as above: *belief in one divine being (male, female or other) with whom the individual has a dual and personal relationship.*

Polytheism

"Polytheism" stems from the Greek *poli* "many" and *theos* "god" with the addition of *-ism*. And, again, it contains the inference of dualistic, personal relationships with divinity, in this case, with more than one, or many deities. Polytheism, then is: *belief in more than one deity, or a plurality of deities, with whom there is a dual (and sometimes personal) relationship.* Importantly, a plurality of deities makes divinity accessible, supplying human beings with the means to make sense of, and provide meaning to, their environment and the cosmos. Thus, a local deity may have more significance for daily existence than an omnipotent supreme God, and elements of the cosmos can be explained and brought within the scope of human understanding if they are associated with divine entities. There is so much variation in polytheism that, as one author comments: "The historical variety is not easily reducible to a common denominator."[13] Indeed, conclusions about polytheism in one culture are often immediately contradicted by those in another.

Polytheism is usually regarded as an inferior belief system to monotheism, and many consider it to be a primitive stage in the development of religion, the more sophisticated cultures inevitably becoming monotheistic. This, however, is hardly true because there have been very civilized cultures that have been polytheistic – even, as Werblowsky has noted, in *advanced* cultures like India, the Near East, Greece and Rome.[14] On the other hand, some suggest that monotheism was the earlier form of religion and this degenerated into polytheism, perhaps to return, later, to monotheism again. Either way, polytheism is seen as inferior to monotheism. But Hinduism does not, in fact, conform to either of these views. Primitive Hinduism certainly bears witness to overt polytheism in its early Indus Valley civilization (a highly advanced and sophisticated culture), as well as in the early *Vedic* period. But subsequent periods characterized by both monotheism in the strictest sense of the term, and metaphysical monism, have been replaced by a plurality of deities, albeit ultimately unified in Brahman. It seems likely that polytheistic belief is something that belongs to the archetypal psyche of humankind – which is probably why it appears so often in disguise in monotheistic systems. All individuals collectively simply cannot envisage the same deity, even in the same religious culture; and it is from this fact that plurality in divine form and conception stems. It is probable, too, that polytheism relates better to cultures dependent on fertility, where it makes sense to people to see the microcosmic environment as dominated by male and female forces. Conversely, cultures stemming from tribal religions, where patriarchal, dominant, male leadership of the tribe was essential, may orientate towards a monotheistic religion that is devoted to a male deity.

Polytheism as a belief system seems not to be taken very seriously as an appropriate or legitimate approach to the divine. Indeed Werblowsky comments that "polytheism is treated as an important phenomenon or stage in the history of religions but hardly ever philosophically or theologically, as a live option".[15] Alain Daniélou, on the other hand, posits some of the advantages of a polytheistic belief. He takes the concept of God away from the One to the Many, suggesting that the more perceptions and perspectives we can have of what is understood to mean "God", the nearer we get to some perception of what divinity is. Just as we need different views of a sculpture to appreciate it as a whole, he says, so we need multiple views of deity in order to come close to a more valid concept of deity – albeit never a complete one. He writes:

> The more insights we can get, the more aspects of the Divine we can perceive, the more we see of divinities beyond the different aspects of the universe, the more elements we can assemble to build up some conception of the origin of things, of the destiny and purpose of life, the nearer we are to understanding something of what divinity is.[16]

Daniélou presents an attractive and perfectly valid suggestion of the advantages of polytheism over monotheism, for if the divine is absolute then it must contain all perspectives. Human beings cannot possibly glimpse *all* dimensions of the divine but, collectively, their varied perceptions can contribute to the immensity of a concept which, after all is said and done, must remain transcendently inscrutable. Daniélou takes the point a stage further when he suggests that the pluralistic approach of polytheism is a superior one to that of either monotheism or, he implies, monism: "we may be nearer to a mental representation of divinity when we consider an immense number of different gods than when we try to stress their unity; for the number one is in a way the number farthest removed from infinity".[17] This multiple view of deity, in a way, suits Hinduism well, for there is always present the multiplicity of diversity, within the unity of the Absolute, Brahman. If, for example, all existence comes forth from one Ground of all Being – as some Hinduism suggests – then there is no end to the possible manifestations which divinity can take. The fact that many monotheistic religions incorporate polytheistic trends might also suggest that, because humanity is plural and multiple, no two conceptions of divinity can be expected to be the same: each individual needs, and has, a different view of the divine. And there are those who prefer a plural conception of deity. Hinduism allows for multiple conceptions of divinity in the concept of perpetual reincarnation – *saṃsāra* – which enables each individual soul to "journey" and evolve over countless lives. Naturally, then, a person's concept of the divine will depend on his or her particular stage of evolution on this long path through time. And where the divine is in, or is, all things, and all emanates from the divine, then it can be approached through the simplest of ways, for it is both the simple and the profound itself. We should certainly not, then, approach any evidence of polytheism in Hinduism with the closed minds of western monotheistic superiority.

Werblowsky asserts that no deity can be omnipotent in a polytheistic system of belief, for this is only possible in monotheism.[18] But in the context of Hindu underlying monotheism and *surface* polytheism, this is hardly the case. A Vaiṣṇavite will see Viṣṇu as the supreme, omnipotent deity, and worship him as such. A Śaivite, on the other hand, will see the deity Śiva in the same way. But both the Vaiṣṇavite *and* the Śaivite will recognize the perspective of the other. It could be claimed that each relates monotheistically to his or her respective, and omnipotent, deity but, nonetheless, accepts a plurality of deities. Given the uniting factor of the impersonal Absolute of Brahman, omnipotence can be given, for example, to Viṣṇu, Śiva or the Mother Goddess. It might be argued here that this is a case of neither monotheism nor polytheism, but henotheism, a belief type that gives superiority to one deity but recognizes, at the same time, the existence of others. But I doubt whether this nuance of meaning is particularly applicable to Hinduism in view of its recognition that there are numerous valid paths to the divine. As Werblowsky points out, henotheism is often considered to be an intermediate stage between polytheism and monotheism,[19] and this, I believe is erroneous. We live in an age of religious pluralism, where the deities of other cultures are no longer considered "pagan" or "heathen", but are given validity in view of the depth of conceptualization of divinity. It might be said, then, that where a western person has a belief in a particular, omnipotent deity, but can accept that a Hindu or Muslim or Sikh, for example, has a different, but valid deity, then this is suggestive of a henotheistic perception of deity. Certainly, the Hindu would accept the western view of deity as valid, if we turned the proposition around. My point here is (and I think Daniélou would agree), that henotheism in this sense might be said to be an evolutionary stage ahead of monotheism, if that monotheism is over-exclusive. Henotheism, in fact, is perhaps a stage of religious belief to which many thoughtful westerners may be moving, a stage perhaps to be eclipsed by the perception of one ultimate divinity manifest in many forms within different cultures.

Pantheism

The word *pantheism* stems from the Greek *pan* "all, entirely, altogether", and *theos* "god", with the addition of *-ism.* The word thus indicates a meaning that all, everything, is God or, put the other way round, God is all things, the totality of the cosmos. Despite the Greek origins of its components the word was not in currency until the early eighteenth century, when it had a somewhat derogatory association with atheism. The term *pantheist* was first used by John Toland (1670–1772) to depict his own personal religious standpoint. It is the theory that God and the universe are identical; God is everything, and everything is God. Therefore, if we take divinity in this belief type to its furthest point, the equating of it with the universe necessitates the loss of any personality for God on the one hand and, on the other, an utter denial of the transcendence of God over the universe. It is easy to see, then, why this type of belief stands in contrast to the traditional western theism that holds the opposite view. There is also a further nineteenth-century meaning of the word *pantheism* to suggest worship of *all* gods, as, for example, that which obtained in ancient Rome, but this meaning is a somewhat confined one, and no longer in use.

Western theism has always maintained that God and Nature are entirely separate; pantheism makes them identical and makes God identical with the whole universe. There is, then, one universal being and each individual is a part of that being like the multiple radii that make up a circle. This last point is important because pantheism is not totally divorced from theism in terms of the relationship between the individual and God. Both accept the dualistic and personal relationship of the individual with the divine. This can obtain in pantheism because the divine is *everything*, not just one thing. Indeed, the fact that pantheists can so frequently refer to "God" reiterates this personal and dual relationship. Critics of pantheism suggest that God becomes impersonal – at the ultimate level, a point against which it is difficult to argue. But, while there are some forms of pantheism that retain the total non-theistic, impersonal conception of the divine, maintaining that there cannot be a personal relationship with a God who is the totality of the universe, in others, aspects of a personal God are still retained. Indeed, a God who is all things is also all feelings, emotions and fears, and can therefore be the object of intense personal devotion. Yet this draws God into the world in a way that compromises his transcendence: and this is anathema to the strict western theist. Western theism deliberately avoids pantheism in order to retain the supremacy of God *over* the universe and to retain the omnipotence of God. Yet pantheism, while asserting omnipresence of the divine, does not really jeopardize omnipotence and need not jeopardize omniscience, for if God is all then he must know all, and *only* God *is* all.

While pantheism is an attractive belief system in that it could be the means for many people to experience God in the beauty of the natural world, we have to remember that the natural world contains its adverse sides as well as its attractive ones. And the most obvious adverse side of Nature is its finitude, its expression in death, and its utter contingency – the uncertainty of future events. God, we usually think, can be none of these things, for God is *necessary existence*, he is self existing. But if we are to claim that God *is* everything, then he or it must also be the contingency of the world, he is finite as much as infinite, temporal as much as eternal, form as much as formless. We should have to think of God as two sides of a coin, both sides being necessary to the existence and definition of God and, in this case, finitude, and so on, become part of the nature of God, but not the whole nature. While we know that perpetual change is a characteristic of the world, if that world is equated with God – even partially – then this suggests that God, too, must be subject to change. And if there are no "ifs" about life, no contingencies at all, and God is pulling the strings of human life and the strings of the natural order, then life becomes totally determined: contingency must cease to exist if God determines all, and the universe is then reduced to a machine-like automaton. While this might solve the relationship between contingency and the self-existence of God, there are few who would wish to deny the freedom of the human being. So pantheism, if it wishes to retain the free will of humanity, has to accept that the effects of that free will alter the divine as the totality of existence.

The complexities of the problem give rise to considerable discussion and result in equally considerable diversity as to definitions of pantheism.

Another side to the problem of pantheism concerns the absolute nature of God. There is a sense in which God, as Absolute Reality, needs to contain the change and finitude of the world otherwise his absolute nature is forfeited – something would exist beyond God. Reality, then, must include the necessity of God *and* the contingency of the world. But if God is also the contingency of the world, then, as has been noted, there are aspects of God that must be changeable alongside his immutability. The question is how we interpret the word absolute: not to include negative aspects like finitude means that they are beyond God, and yet to include them lends partial finitude to the divine. It seems to me that the word "absolute" is compromised less by the latter proposition than the former. Pantheism really has to accept that God is not only cause, but also effect, but that the cause and effect processes are held in the absolute nature of God. Pantheism is thus involved with dualities – Creator and created, absolute and relative, necessary and contingent, infinite and finite, and so on. In this sense it is very different from monism as a belief system, although there are those who give the two systems a certain degree of synonymy.

Hinduism has less of a problem with the concept of pantheism especially where it incorporates emanationist theories of existence. For much Hindu thought, the immutable Absolute, Brahman, exists as the inner *ātman* of all things, so all is eventually subsumed in the divine, even if finitude overlays the existence of *ātman* in the world. This finite and transient element of the cosmos is sometimes referred to as *māyā* "illusion", or the result of divine *līlāvibhūti* "cosmic sport" or "play". Where the Absolute as Brahman is posited as the Source of all manifest existence it is the motivator of what is called *prakṛti* – all the evolutes of existence and their whole cause and effect process.[20] The divine in much Hinduism is the centripetal point of all existence, just like the radii of a circle relate to, and cannot obtain without, the one point at the centre. Where such an Absolute is accepted in Hinduism, like the centre of the circle, it becomes the point at which dualities meet, thus good and evil and so on are cancelled out in the totality of the divine. In this sense pantheism can sometimes suggest that the dualities – and therefore the contingencies of life – are ultimately unreal, or at best a lesser reality.

An important corollary of pantheism is the widening of forms of religious experience because the divine is everywhere, not in an immanent sense as in theism, but in a much more tangible and dynamic way. Nature, especially, affords a medium for experience of the divine, something illustrated well by the words of the poet Wordsworth:

> . . . with bliss ineffable
> I felt the sentiment of Being spread
> O'er all that moves, and all that seemeth still;
> O'er all that, lost beyond the reach of thought
> And human knowledge, to the human eye
> Invisible, yet liveth to the heart;
> O'er all that leaps, and runs, and shouts, and sings,
> Or beats the gladsome air; o'er all that glides
> Beneath the wave, yea, in the wave itself,
> And mighty depth of waters. Extract from *The Prelude*[21]

. . . and I have felt
A presence that disturbs me with joy
Of elevated thoughts; a sense sublime
Of something far more deeply interfused,
Whose dwelling is the light of setting suns,
And the round ocean, and the living air,
And the blue sky, and in the mind of man:
A motion and a spirit, that impels
All thinking things, all objects of all thought,
And rolls through all things. *Lines composed a few miles above Tintern Abbey*[22]

Some of the most beautiful poetry and prose has been the result of pantheistic experience of the divine, especially as a result of the ability to transcend normal conditions of life to experience the divine in Nature. Strict western theism cannot accept such perceptions, but the concept fits comfortably into Hindu ideas of God. There is a sense of unity of the cosmos which is, at times, mystically experienced; in short, the pantheist is often such because he or she *feels* the presence of the divine in all things, and *feels* the cosmic unity of all that equates with the divine. Pantheists, then, believe that God is *in* Nature, not above it.

The diversity of pantheism as a type of belief is considerable. This is because there are nuances of meaning between God being everything or *in* everything and, also, because the solution to the relationship between the necessity of God and the finitude of the world provides a number of variables. God may be seen as the natural order of the universe itself, the cosmos, or perhaps an aspect of the natural order. Similarly, God may be seen as an essence that pervades the cosmos: the *ātman* equated with Brahman in Hinduism can be seen in this way.[23] Fundamental to pantheism, however, is the fact that God is not seen as a being separate from the cosmos itself. One frequent explanation of pantheism is to see the world as the "body" of the divine and God as the soul of the world. This is a perfectly rational explanation of pantheism providing the body is not entirely discarded through inferiority to the soul. But certainly in western thought, the old Plato–Cartesian dualism of body and soul/mind suggests the total superiority of the latter over the former; some forms of Hinduism will do so, too. Where such is the case, then the divine (as the soul) is greater than the world (as the body) and would be indicative of panentheism rather than pantheism. Modern western pantheism is expressed best by the views of Charles Hartshorne[24] who views God and the world as one unit, just as composite parts of anything serve to make up a whole. The composite parts may act independently of God but each action and each moment in time has an effect on the whole. So God would be a totality that is changed by the contingency of the world. It is a view that finds contingency in the divine credible, but that retains individualism and individual personalities in existence. It is the acceptance of contingency that is particularly rejected by theists. But Hartshorne does well to point out that individualism is not alien to pantheism – a point which, quite erroneously, critics of pantheism believe pantheism can never have.[25]

While pantheism can be variously defined, a working definition is needed that will not do violence to the broad remit of the concept, but which is sufficiently adaptable to Hindu perspectives. The many forms of pantheism are dependent on the degree of identity between the divine and the world, and Hinduism – having for the most part a concept of *ātman* which is partly or wholly identical to the divine Absolute, Brahman – presses this identity far beyond that of western pantheism. I shall therefore define the term simply as: *the belief that the divine is the totality of all things, though each thing is dualistically related to the divine.* It is the latter part of this definition that serves to distinguish pantheism from monism.

Panentheism

Panentheism is a term that is derived from the Greek *pan* "all", *en* "in", *theos* "God", with the addition of *-ism*. Again, it is a recent term, being coined by the German philosopher K. F. Krause (1781–1832). It accepts, according to Hartshorne, "a plurality of active agents within the reality of the supreme agent".[26] Individuals exist as distinctly free individuals, but they are ultimately subsumed in the divine. They can thus choose to do good or evil. Indeed, all such dualities of existence are accepted as part of a pluralistic world, but the pluralism of the world is united in the divine. Each entity of existence is thus dualistically related to the divine, but panentheism accepts the superiority of the divine to the cosmos: the term can thus be defined as: *God is in all things, and all things are in God, but God is greater than all things.* Western panentheistic views accept God as Creator of a finite world and as present in all things within that creation. It is a presence, I suggest, that is stronger than immanence, being far more of an indwelling, far more of an *essence* of the divine in all things. At the same time there is a transcendence of the divine so dear to theism, and this transcendence does not in any way jeopardize the dual and personal relationship that is possible between the divine and the human. God is thus both the Source and what emanates from the Source. God is also eternal, but is also infused into the temporal, is Absolute, but is part of the finitude of the relative.

Panentheism solves a number of the problems that pantheism poses. To begin with it can permit the retention of intensely theistic personal devotion, enhanced somewhat by a refusal to separate the divine from the world through remote transcendence, and yet the ultimate omniscience and omnipotence of the transcendent divinity are maintained alongside an indwelling omnipresence in the whole cosmos. Divine status is given to all things in the cosmos, in the same way as pantheism, but alongside that divine status is the space for freedom of choice and this, therefore, solves to some extent the problem of evil in existence. In the case of Hinduism, the transcendent divinity is, as in pantheism, that point at which the dualities such as good and evil cease to exist. Like pantheism, panentheism widens the experience of the divine through the multiple manifestations of it in existence, particularly through Nature itself, avoiding the outcome of manipulation and subjugation of Nature as separate and inferior from God and humankind. There is a sense, too, in both panentheism and pantheism, of an evolutionary goal for each individual to realize the dimension of divinity within his or her self. In Hinduism this is given the added perspective of reincarnation, by which the individual has countless lives to realize the point of liberation. Panentheism does not entirely solve the problem of linking the divine with contingency of the world in western thought, but emanationist ideas of Hinduism do not lend to the term the same difficulties.

Dualism

Dualism means essentially "of two parts" and refers in religious and philosophical thought to two, independent and juxtaposed principles like God and the world, temporality and eternity, infinitude and finitude, mind and matter, body and mind, body and soul, idealism and materialism, and good and evil. Dualism is a problematic principle in that it can sometimes limit and minimize the omnipotence of God. This is particularly so in the case of good and evil. To accept that there is a separation of good and evil into distinct entities (and western theological thought mostly refers to this particular dualism) is helpful in that it absolves God from evil. But it is problematic in that it limits the omnipotence of God because he has no control over a whole dimension of the universe. And if such a dualism is coexistent, that is to say, it were not created by God, then creation could not have emerged as the result of divine volition. Indeed, creation could only be half good! The dualism of good and evil has been a constant thorn in the side of all western theistic belief.

Hinduism generally accepts the unity of the cosmos, though there are philosophical schools of thought, as will be seen, that will deny this and posit both duality and plurality. But where unity is accepted, it is equated with ultimate Reality so that all the dualities of life like good and evil, time and eternity, light and darkness, you and I, are only apparent. It is the dualities on the microcosmic level of the world in which we live – dualities that are built up by our egoistic perceptions and choices – that blur the real unity of all things in the cosmos. In reality, for many aspects of Hinduism, everything is unified by the essence of the divine that infuses all. And since all dualities are united in the essence of the divine, good and evil do not exist apart from the egoistic perception of them. Thus there is essentially a unity to all existence and a unity with the divine. Sometimes this unity between the world and the divine is taken to the point of total identity – God and human beings are one – but more usually a dualistic separation of the divine and the world/humankind is maintained within this context of unity. Providing dualism between the individual and the divine is accepted, theism in any form – monotheism, polytheism, pan(en)theism – can obtain. All theism necessarily maintains a dual perspective of the relationship between individual and divine. The converse, however, is not true: not all dualism between the human and divine is theistic.[27]

Pluralism

In philosophical terms pluralism is a theory or type of belief that accepts more than one ultimate principle in existence. It has been neatly defined as: "Any metaphysical theory which is committed to the ultimate existence of two or more kinds of things":[28] this includes dualism. Pluralism, then, accepts that there is more than one element that constitutes reality as we know it and this stands in stark contrast to monism that posits one fundamental Reality in the universe. Pluralism can be viewed at two levels, and defined in both:

- *as a metaphysical or philosophical term to suggest the lack of total unity between human and divine and the world and the divine.*

- *as a term designating that an independent reality is evident to all things in the perceived world. That is to say, whatever we see is given its own independent identity and reality and there is nothing connecting one thing and another to suggest any unity of them.*

Monism

The word *monism* comes from the Greek *monos* "single" with the addition of *-ism*. It was a term first used by a German philosopher, Christian Wolff (1679–1754). As a philosophical and metaphysical term it refers to the acceptance of one single, ultimate, principle as the basis of the cosmos, the unity and oneness of all reality, and stands in contrast to pluralism and to any kind of dualism. And if it is opposed to dualism then it is opposed to any differentiation between divine and human, or divine and the world. Differentiation, indeed, is not encompassed within the term. Thus, there can be no differentiation or duality between good and evil, matter and mind, and so on: all is one.

In western philosophy monism has generally been used to depict the concept of one God in contrast to the dual proposition of a God of goodness in opposition to a God of evil. But it is also used to indicate the holistic nature of the mind and body as inseparable and non-dual. That is to say, there is no division between soul and body or between the spiritual self and the material self.

The close association between mysticism and monism has been noted by McDermott,[29] and it is an association that is certainly evidenced in the Hindu tradition. He suggests that this connection between mysticism and monism is likely to be because of the "unitive quality of the mystical experience itself".[30] Indeed, the transcending of the dualities of life, and the non-differentiation between this and that, are indicative of enlightenment (*nirvāṇa* or *mokṣa*) in much eastern religion. However, while experience of the unity, the monism, of the cosmos is perhaps the height of much mystical experience, true monism must really include unity with the divine at the same time, otherwise, a dualism is maintained. So in fact, I prefer to see unity – and this means identity – with the cosmos as pantheism if that unity excludes complete identity with the divine. For true monism to exist there should be absolutely no separation between the divine and humanity, the divine and the individual, the divine and the world but, instead, *total* identity. In such monism, then, the I–Thou relationship between the individual and the divine cannot exist; there can be no theism, and there can be no term "God". And, like the experience of unity itself, the Absolute of monism is inexplicable.

Monism is one type of belief that, rather than being adapted from western to suit eastern philosophical discussion, has a model *par excellence* in that put forward by the eighth-century Indian philosopher Śaṃkara, who is associated with the school of thought of Advaita Vedānta. Since this is one of the systems of reality that are to be examined I do not propose to discuss it here, but suffice it to say that – at least when monism is discussed – the emphasis originates from eastern rather than western philosophical thought.

It is the question of reality that is important to many monistic systems for there is a certain necessity to deny the transient and changeable reality of the world for a deeper, valid, and unitive Reality behind it. It is the experience of this that is the high point of mystical experience. And it is the issue of Reality – what is real in a world characterized by finitude and surface knowledge – that is the quest of the schools of philosophical thought that are to be examined. Reality, these schools claim, is founded in the kind of knowledge that is valid, so the theory of knowledge, *epistemology*, is one important aspect of the remit in examining the schools of philosophical thought. The monistic strand will emphasize the more intuitive type of knowledge that is knowledge of the deepest aspect of the self, an aspect that is equated totally and monistically with the divine.

One factor dominates monistic thought and that is the inscrutable nature of the One Ultimate Principle, the Absolute that is the fundamental Reality permeating the universe. Hindus call it Brahman or Puruṣa, many stressing that it is *neti neti* "not this, not this"; it is beyond all the apparent particularities and dualities of existence. Greek philosophers called it the One. Later Hindu *Vedic* hymns referred simply to *Tat* "That", or *Tat Ekam* "That One", the indefinable Absolute as the Source of all the gods which, though a monotheistic expression in the *Vedas*, became the monistic essence of all the cosmos in the *Vedānta*. However, monistic belief has to deal with the complex question of manifest existence, and may deny its reality entirely or assign it to a lower level of reality. The Absolute may be manifest in some way in the world as God the Creator, like some western monistic thought, or as Īśvara "Lord" in Hindu thought, as part of this lesser reality. Ultimate Reality, however, remains empty of the particularities of all manifest existence, and it is knowledge – of the deep intuitive kind – that reveals it, and that transcends all distinctions of the world and, sometimes, even itself.

The problem of monism as a belief type is, in fact, the degree of reality given to particulars of existence, the degree of reality given to the plurality of the world that we know from the experience of our – albeit egoistic and subjective – selves. Total denial of the world, as well as the egoistic self, as illusionary, really denies an *aspect* of the unified cosmos, since if abstract or concrete illusions create effects in chains of causality then these, too, should be part of ultimate Reality. Some monists, then, will not jeopardize the reality of the manifest world.[31]

Like the other concepts that have been examined monism is something of an umbrella term that will be expressed differently by different people. It is thus aptly stated that: "There is agreement only on the oneness of ultimate reality but no agreed definition of what that unity is, whether it is 'being itself', or idea, soul, substance or material reality."[32] As a working definition, however, I shall define monism as: *the belief that Reality is one single principle, which is to say that all things are ultimately at one with, and identical to, another. In terms of the divine, the same unity and identity of all things with it obtains.*

Non-dualism

In spite of the fairly consistent equating of non-dualism with monism there is a sense in which the former can be considered a far stronger term than the latter. Monism, as the etymology of the word suggests, is based on the concept of *One*. But if we consider this term *One*, then it would have to be conceded that it is one as opposed to two, or one as opposed to many. In other words, it is one part of a duality, albeit itself indivisible. If this is the case then non-dualism should be beyond even one. The point is clarified somewhat by the standpoint of philosophical Taoism where the Tao is not reducible to the One as some suggest[33] but is beyond the One. The *Tao Te Ching* of Lao-tzu makes this clear:

> The Tao begot one.
> One begot two.
> Two begot three
> And three begot the ten thousand things.[34]

The One here is the cosmic energy of *ch'i*, the Tao being the incomprehensible unmanifest Source of it.[35] The Tao of classical Taoism, then, expresses the inexpressible beyond monism and might be said to be pure non-dualism. This is something that the Sanskrit term for non-dualism, *advaita*, might incorporate, and we shall explore it in the context of the Vedānta school of thought. Suffice it to say that the simple equating of monism with non-dualism – perhaps resulting from its usage in western philosophy – is not necessarily accurate in analysis of eastern thought. While it would be true to say that all monism should, strictly speaking, be non-dual, non-dualism can stand as a principle independently of monism. Perhaps this is what the *Advayatāraka Upaniṣad* (3:3) means by the "non-dual Immensity". Alain Daniélou makes the point that:

> A SUPREME CAUSE has to be beyond number, otherwise Number would be the First Cause. But the number one, although it has peculiar properties, is a number like two, or three, or ten, or a million. If "God" is one, he is not beyond number any more than if he is two or three or ten or a million. But although a million is not any nearer to infinity than one or two or ten, it seems to be so from the limited point of view of our perceptions.[36]

Daniélou's reasoning is valid, and it indicates that there is a need to be specific in the use of the term non-dual when analysing aspects of ultimate Reality in Hinduism.

In conclusion a number of points need to be raised. First, many of the terms I have selected for discussion have their basis in western philosophical thought and, as such, are sometimes difficult to apply directly to eastern concepts. It is for this reason that encyclopedic or dictionary definitions of the terms are sometimes unhelpful in the clarification of meanings. Then, too, each term is something of an umbrella term, and can encompass a variety of different beliefs in the context of a single name. The definitions I have proposed for each belief type are designed to suit the eastern context of Hinduism, though I have tried as far as possible to maintain the parameters of western original meanings. Additionally, the terms are not mutually exclusive: theism can be further qualified as monotheism, pantheism, for example, and there is no reason why beliefs such as pantheism or panentheism cannot also be monotheistic. They are useful terms, but they are also flexible ones, and it is necessary to bear in mind that they are, after all, alien to the Indian language.

2
Veda

Indian philosophy and metaphysics is essentially a search for Truth, for Reality that is ultimate, for the true nature of the self, and for the kind of knowledge that makes the experience of Truth and ultimate Reality possible. While it might be claimed that science offers the same kinds of goals to the West, science, unlike philosophy, is less intimately involved with individual and collective life. Everyone has a philosophy of life, whoever he or she is, and wherever he or she live. It may be a very simple philosophy of life, or it may be highly developed and evolved. Indian philosophy has the more evolved quest of exploring some of the fundamental questions involved in human existence – What is the purpose of life? Who am I, and what is my *real* self? What is real in a world of change? Why do human beings suffer? Why does evil exist? What kinds of things can we *really* know? From what or whom did the universe arise? And so on. While we may not have elaborate answers to such questions, they are the kinds of questions that many people ask themselves at various points in their lives. Philosophy, then, is intimately connected with life. While western science pushes the boundaries of its inquiry further into the cosmos, Hindu philosophical inquiry has usually been characterized by a search for Reality, Truth and knowledge that transcends both space and time. For space and time impose on life the transience, impermanence and changeability that challenge the reality of the world in which we live.

Schools of Indian philosophy

While this book is concerned with the six orthodox schools of Hindu philosophy it is important to realize that these six systems provide only some viewpoints of how the philosophical questions, such as those noted above, are able to be answered. And even here, there is a considerable variety of beliefs. Although the six systems represent the core of Hindu philosophy, there are also other attempts to present answers to the fundamental questions of life in the wider Hindu and Indian context. A summary might be helpful at this point.

Orthodox (āstika)

• *Mīmāṃsā*	*inspired by ritualistic Vedic texts*
• *Vedānta*	*inspired by speculative Vedic texts*
• *Sāṃkhya*	*accepts Vedic authority*
• *Yoga*	*accepts Vedic authority*
• *Nyāya*	*accepts Vedic authority*
• *Vaiśeṣika*	*accepts Vedic authority*

Heterodox (nāstika)

• *Cārvāka*	*materialist and atheist; rejects Vedic authority*
• *Buddhism*	*rejects Vedic authority*
• *Jainism*	*rejects Vedic authority*

As can be easily seen from the above summary, the acceptance of *Vedic* authority is the central issue in the legitimization of the orthodox systems. But even where it is rejected by the heterodox schools, it is so deeply entrenched in the Indian mind, that common concepts (such as belief in *karma* and *saṃsāra*) underpin much thought outside orthodoxy. Before embarking on an examination of the philosophical views of the six orthodox schools of Indian philosophy, therefore, it will be necessary to explore, in some detail, what is meant by "*Vedic* authority".

Veda: wisdom

The word *Veda* means "knowledge" or "wisdom" and refers to a broad spectrum of Hindu religious literature, generally referred to as *śruti*, "heard" or "revealed" sacred truths. While this literature is really one composite "wisdom" it is usually divided very clearly into two distinct groups of writings, roughly *Vedas* and *Upaniṣads*. This is because the former are concerned primarily with ritual, and the latter, with more philosophical and metaphysically speculative material. And since the *Upaniṣads* are relatively later than the *Vedas*, occurring at the end of them, the term *Vedānta* "end of the *Veda*" distinguishes this more philosophical material from the earlier ritualistic literature. Because the *Vedas* are ritualistic they are concerned with correct ritual action, *karman*; they are thus the *karmakāṇḍa* "ritual action portion" of the *śruti* literature. The *Vedānta*, on the other hand, is concerned with knowledge, *jñāna*. This is knowledge of the deep and intuitive type and is the medium for revealed wisdom. The *Vedānta* is, thus, the *jñānakāṇḍa*, the "knowledge portion" of *śruti* literature, in which wisdom is synonymous with knowledge. Here, I propose to deal with the *Vedas* primarily, before examining the *Upaniṣads*, the *Vedānta*, but it is important to bear in mind that the knowledge that both impart belongs to the same *śruti* tradition. The transition between the two is not abrupt for other *śruti* literature overlaps and integrates with both: the transitional literature is also relevant material in an exploration of "*Vedic* authority".

Śruti literature was experientially received by the ancient seers or *ṛṣis* and was, and is still, accepted as revealed from the divine, like the breath of the divine breathed out on, and inhaled in by, humanity. There is, thus, a direct perception of wisdom, though it was wisdom certainly not available to all, but only to those of heightened consciousness. Later Hindu sacred scripture is differentiated from this kind of revealed scripture by the designation *smṛti*. This latter is interpretative material – material that develops the earlier *śruti* but does not "receive" it in the same way. *Śruti* literature was considered so sacred that it was eventually committed to written form very reluctantly, and reflects, therefore, a long period of oral transmission during which it was meticulously handed down to each generation of priests. Dasgupta suggested that the term *śruti* in fact refers to the memorized material that was "heard" by *Brahmin* priests from their preceptors.[1] This is perhaps a more practical interpretation of the term *śruti*, but does not depict so well the nature of the scripture as revealed ultimate Truth and wisdom – perspectives held by some of the philosophical systems and maintained in much subsequent Hindu thought and practice. While the more popular *smṛti* scriptures dictate the religious genre of present and much past Hindu practice, it is *śruti* tradition on which it is based.

Dating in Indian history and philosophy is nearly always problematic, for it was, and is, not important to the Indian mind. I do not propose to deal with it except briefly, but I wish to point out that there is considerable variance. *Vedic* literature, however, is certainly very ancient, the *Vedas* and earlier *Upaniṣads* easily predating the Buddha, and the oral transmission of the material perhaps stretching back to at least the middle of the second millennium BCE or even the third.[2] It is small wonder that Hindus themselves regard the *Veda* as timeless. The earliest of the hymns of the main *Vedic* text, the *Ṛg Veda*, are certainly very old and we are therefore thinking in terms of a long spell of transmission lasting from at least 1200 BCE down to about 500 BCE.

So far *śruti* literature has been divided into *Vedas* and *Upaniṣads*, but other literature is also included, and the *Vedas* themselves are divided into four. Dealing with the latter first, the four *Vedas* are the *Ṛg*, which is the "Royal" knowledge and is the most important of the four (indeed, much of the material that comprises the other three *Vedas* is taken from the *Ṛg*); the *Sāma Veda*, which is knowledge of chants, the sacred melodies to which the hymns of the *Ṛg Veda* were set; the *Yajur Veda*, which deals with sacrificial ritual; and the *Atharva Veda* which contains magical formulas, incantations and spells. The material of each of the *Vedas* is also given the term *Saṃhitā*. All subsequent *śruti* literature is based on these four *Vedas*, so each has its commentary or *Brāhmaṇa* that deals with the rites and ceremonies of the respective *Saṃhitā*. Each, too, has its *Āraṇyakas* or forest writings, as well as specific *Upaniṣads*. The *Saṃhitās* and the *Brāhmaṇas* form the *karmakāṇḍa* (ritual portion) and the *Āraṇyakas* and the *Upaniṣads* the *jñānakāṇḍa* (knowledge portion). I shall deal with much of this literature below, but suffice it to say here that, despite the immense variety of ideas in *śruti* literature, and a loose arrangement of the material, it is felt, as a whole, to be connected and composite. The *Saṃhitās* in their written form are in a very old Sanskrit, and are sometimes difficult to understand. Since the chief concern was with ritual, the hymns contained in the *Saṃhitās* were not systematically, but selectively, committed to written form; many hymns were probably omitted as not wholly relevant to ritualistic purpose. In the *Ṛg Veda* the hymns are arranged in relation to the deities who are worshipped, such as Indra or Agni; the whole of the ninth *maṇḍala*, for example, is devoted to Soma, at once a deity and a powerful consumable liquid that heightened consciousness.

Much of the material of the *Ṛg Veda* is repeated in the other three *Vedas* and so it is generally regarded as the most important and the earliest of the four. It has just over one thousand hymns or *mantras* divided into ten books or *maṇḍalas*, all addressed to deities. The hymns are variously dated, some being very old, perhaps earlier than the Aryan migration to northern India, others being composed many centuries later. They are, therefore, the result of many authors. Apart from their religious and cultural value, the hymns reflect the many stages in the growth of Aryan society. Coming from the plains of Central Asia east of the Caspian Sea, the Aryans were one group of many Indo-Europeans who filtered out from this area from about 2000 BCE. They settled in northern India, bringing with them their specific religion and their orally transmitted *Vedas*. To those hymns they brought with them were added others as the centuries passed, and so we are left with a remarkable insight into Aryan or *Vedic* culture.

Vedic religion

Vedic or Aryan religion is often depicted as nature worship, the Aryans having brought with them the nature religion of their forebears. But to describe *Vedic* religion as simply nature worship is a little misleading and tends to suggest a level of primitivism that is an over simplification. Since there is so much symbolism in *Vedic* thought we should be wary of treating *Vedic* religion at its surface level. It was not so much nature itself that was worshipped, as the impersonal *powers*, the *forces*, or *essences*, that underpinned the *Vedic* universe of earth, atmosphere and heaven. Generally, then, *Vedic* deities symbolized aspects of earth, sky or heaven, and allowed Aryan man and woman to make sense of the world around and beyond them. This profound connection with the less tangible aspects of the universe often tends to make *Vedic* deities somewhat elusive in character rather than overtly anthropomorphic. A somewhat shifting nature of deity is evident in *Vedic* religion as a result, and, if at one time pivotal to human existence, the deities came to be secondary to the whole complex process of ritual celebration. Then, too, the forces that the *Vedic* gods symbolized were sometimes very similar: Agni as Fire, for example could be similar to Sūrya as the Sun, or Indra as Lightning. Thus the characters of *Vedic* deities were often blurred and only rarely distinctive. Close to nature they may have been, but they are normally characterized by too much symbolic intangibility to be completely personalized and wholly anthropomorphized.

Nevertheless, the gods, at least in the early stages of Aryan religion as we know it from the *Vedas*, were certainly propitiated for what, to the Aryan mind, were the essentials of existence – wealth, particularly in cattle, longevity, success in battle, and progeny. Hiriyanna points out that this kind of communion with the divine gave way to virtual demand and compelling of the gods through the medium of sacrificial ritual.[3] Yet at the popular level it is likely that the simpler folk continued to propitiate the gods for their basic needs in life, and to overcome their fears of evil forces. The *Atharva Veda*, especially, bears witness to such popular religious thought and practice, with its spells and incantations for everything from a reluctant lover to gambling success. But, certainly, the power of the priests as the conductors of sacrifice rose to a level that appeared to usurp the role of the deities, a suggestion that the school of Pūrva Mīmāṃsā endorses. But perhaps, as Hiriyanna elsewhere suggests, the transference of power was not from god to priest but from god to *Veda*.[4] This great reverence for *Vedic* authority, and belief in the power of the sacrificial ritual of the *Vedic* religion, is the key to understanding the religion of the Aryans in the earlier centuries of their settlement in India.

The whole complex *Vedic* ritual was called *yajña*, sacrificial ritual that assumed increasing importance to the point that it was felt to regulate and maintain all aspects of creation. Without it the sun would not rise and the patterns and rhythms of the natural world would no longer obtain. The tiniest mistake in any aspect of the ritual – an incorrect tone in the chants, a mispronounced word, a careless action, a misplaced item, the wrong amount of a material – it was believed, could have the most disastrous effects on the Aryan environment – indeed, on the cosmos itself. It is easy to see how the priests, who were solely responsible for the meticulous conducting of ritual – some of which was elaborate enough to continue for many months – rose to considerable power and prestige. It is also easy to see that, providing the sacrifices were carried out perfectly, then the gods became almost superfluous: *Vedic* ritual itself would bring about the necessary effects. It suggested to the Aryan mind that there was some kind of potent magical force that transformed the sacrifice into the desired effects; this will be an important issue that will need to be taken up in the later discussion of the philosophical systems.

The sacrificial ritual was considered to be correct action, *karman* or *kriyā*. Dasgupta pointed out that the effects of such *karman* could be directed to both positive results and negative ones (such as causing harm to an enemy).[5] Could this be, then, the origin of the later doctrine of *karma*, the law of cause and effect by which a good action is rewarded by a good result and the converse action by adverse results? It would seem distinctly possible that this is so, for the efficacy of the cause–result process in *yajña* becomes a fixed principle that would need only the extension to those actions outside religious ritual to make it a more universal law. And the fact that sacrifice was an action that was an established *duty* is also a link with later ideas of religious duty – in all kinds of prescribed and non-prescribed forms – as a means to good fruitive *karma*. The goal of life for the *Vedic* Indian was, indeed, both correct ritual worship and a righteous existence, presupposing the established doctrines of *karma* and *dharma* that are characteristic of later thought.

Śruti literature is mainly priestly (*Brahmin*)[6] focused, that is to say, it pertains almost entirely to priestly study, transmission, practice, knowledge and expertise. The priests belonged to different family groups and were responsible for specific aspects of ritual; each group of priests was concerned with a specific *Saṃhitā* as opposed to another. Then, too, the associated *Brāhmaṇas* and *Āraṇyakas* and subsequent *Upaniṣads* were also associated with specific *Brahmin* groups. In this way, the many priestly schools developed, being associated with specific scriptures and the production of additional texts. Each school would be responsible for transmitting its traditions orally.[7] There was certainly scope for considerable interpretation of the *Saṃhitās* in the commentaries of the *Brāhmaṇas*, and the complexities of ritual, therefore, led, also, to complexities of scripture. The control of the priests in every area of the complex ritual made Aryan religion wholly elitist, and it should be borne in mind that it is exactly this elitist tradition that has been handed down to us now in written form. For the religious practice of many others in Indian life – the ordinary village folk, for example – we can know relatively little. But I would not wish to leave the reader with the impression that *Vedic* religion is so ritualistic that it has little spirituality or feeling. The *Saṃhitās* are poetic hymns that speak of the beauty of the dawn, personified in the beautiful goddess Uṣas, the wonder of the setting sun, the marvel of the cow that produces milk. Because deities were assigned to the three parts of the universe – heaven, sky or intermediate region, and earth – the writers of the hymns, the *mantras*, had plenty of scope with storm, wind, rain, lightning, stars, sun, moon, and so on, in order to express their ideas. The view of life and death was a linear one, not cyclical. One life was all that was allotted to human beings who, if they had lived it well, could hope for reward in a physical heaven, a realm of light where they would experience physical pleasures in the company of the gods. But for those who had not the moral fibre, a realm of darkness and punishment awaited them. A similar, linear, perspective of the universe is evident, at least in the sense that it has a beginning, a distinct creation, even if less is evident about the end. There is no belief in transmigration of souls or of cyclical evolving and involving of the universe in the *Ṛg Veda* but the connection between action and its appropriate good or bad result is established quite clearly.

The Aryan view of the world was a common sense one of a plurality of things and of beings, the reality of which was never questioned. Yet, given the fact that ritualistic practice was believed to have its effects on the immediate and cosmic environment, a certain interconnectedness of all things has to be presupposed. The divine and human worlds were believed to coalesce to some extent but one was not thought to be more real than the other. So there is nothing in the *Ṛg Veda* to suggest that the world is unreal, as in some later philosophical thought. Despite the transience and changeability obvious in the nature of the self, it remained real, though the personality, the *jīvātman,* was believed to be separate from the soul, the *ātman*, the latter being that part of the self that continued eternally. In no way, however, was the *ātman* linked with the divine; it was, rather, considered to be the vital breath (*asu*) of a being that separated from the body at death and was associated with the thought and emotions of a person (*manas*). It is not until the *Brāhmaṇas* and *Āraṇyakas* that the word *ātman* can be found to hint at a more unifying world Self.[8]

Polytheism of the *Vedas*

The initial picture one has of the religion of the *Vedas* is that it is polytheistic, and in the earlier hymns this certainly seems to be so if we take the meaning of the term to be belief in more than one divine being. Some, however, have been critical of this description of early *Vedic* religion as simplistic. Dasgupta suggested that the religion reflected in the earliest hymns is not actually sufficiently developed to be called polytheism: "The gods here do not preserve their proper places as in a polytheistic faith, but each one of them shrinks into insignificance or shines as supreme according as it is the object of adoration or not."[9] It is true that deities wax and wane in *Vedic* literature as a whole, and the exploratory nature of early *Vedic* religion necessitates the extolling of one deity as opposed to another for specific reasons. The more this-worldly deity Indra, for example, supplies very different needs than a more cosmic and omnipotent and omniscient deity like Varuṇa. But I do not see why this kind of changeable nature of *Vedic* deities cannot be depicted, at least on the surface, as polytheistic. Hindu religion at most of its stages rarely fits the neat classifications of western thought or the linear thinking that polytheism as an inferior system must precede monotheism. It was inevitable that one deity had to be supreme in a specific ritualistic context and that other deities had to take a back seat until an appropriate time: this need not compromise the term polytheism.

Later *Vedic* hymns more clearly express a search for one ultimate Source of the gods, a Supreme Being that is the generator of all things. This was variously conceived of as Sun, Desire, Time, Water, Air, and so on. Coupled with this was the tendency, noted above, for the *Vedic* deities to become more closely identified with each other, fusing their respective characters and their respective roles – an extremely important development that prefigured much that was to emerge in *Upaniṣadic* thought. And just as the earlier period had a distinct kind of polytheism, so the move to a more monotheistic conception of the divine also has its own special features. It could be argued that it was the very lack of a well-defined polytheistic pantheon of deities in the earlier stage that paved the way for the kind of fusion of divine status that made the search for one ultimate Source viable. Hiriyanna points this out when he says:

> The conception of a unitary godhead which becomes explicit now may be said to lie implicit already in the thought of the earlier period. For, owing to the incomplete individualization of deities and the innate connection or mutual resemblance of one natural phenomenon with another (e.g. the Sun, Fire and Dawn), there is in Vedic mythology what may be described as overlapping of divinities. One god is very much like another.[10]

The polytheism of the early *Veda*, then, is not simply a primitive polytheism. It was not the kind of polytheism to set up the rigid distinctions of polytheistic pantheons, and its more fluid perception of divinity never develops into anything more concrete. It is not a primitive polytheism that becomes a developed polytheism, it is simply a different polytheism and remains so.

Monotheism of the *Vedas*

If there is a move to monotheism in the *Vedas* it is a move at times to a metaphysical monotheism, that is to say to belief in a more intangible and transcendent Reality from which all proceeds but which is elusive: it is a One behind the many. And no particular deity is associated with this One as supreme, it is more a fusion of them all:

> They call him Indra, Mitra, Varuṇa, Agni and he is the heavenly noble-winged Garutmān. To what is One, sages give many a title: they call it Agni, Yama, Mātariśvan.[11]

Some of the deities lend themselves well to an all-pervasiveness. Such is Sūrya, the Sun and Agni, Fire. For if the sun gives its light and warmth it does so pervasively and not selectively. And to the *Vedic* mind Agni, Fire, was One, not many. Basham aptly points out: "Agni, in fact, was here, there and everywhere. Was there only one Agni, or were there many Agnis? How could Agni be one and many at the same time?"[12] Unity of divinity, then, is prefigured in the *Ṛg Veda*:

> Kindled in many a spot, still One is Agni;
> Sūrya is One though high o'er all he shines.
> Illuminating this All, still One is Uṣas.
> That which is One has into All developed.[13]

This more speculative thought did not counteract the ritualism of the *Vedic* period, but was accommodated alongside it, and the polytheism underpinning *yajña* still obtained. But the search for a Source of the deities was moving in a direction of a search for the Source that caused all to *emanate* from it. This is to say, there is present the idea of a unifying link between Source and the world – divine or other – that would develop into panentheistic and monistic ideas. *Vedic* religion witnesses a thread of thought that searches not for the causes behind the natural phenomena of the universe, but for a First Cause that is the ultimate Source. At times, *Vedic* thought suggests a personal ultimate Source and at others an impersonal one. The move towards focus on One as opposed to many deities is a move to a more monotheistic religious outlook. But just as the polytheism of the *Vedas* is somewhat different to other polytheistic systems, the monotheism of the *Vedic* period is equally so, for there is no effort to make one of the deities supreme, and no evolution of a deity to ultimate status. Instead, totally new concepts are searched for, and this may be one reason why the status of *Vedic* gods – even a god like Indra – diminished at a later date.

So early *Vedic* polytheism and monotheism differ in some ways from the usual definitions of the terms: it could be claimed that the particular monotheism of pre-*Upaniṣadic* times developed the way it did because of the fluid nature of divinity that enabled one deity to become identified with another by an underlying similarity of *essence*. Nevertheless, the search for an ultimate Source saw the emergence of conceptually new deities as supreme. But, even here, they are the unifying principle *behind* all other deities and the Source of the universe. And so we find a range of supreme deities. Prajāpati "Lord of Creatures" is one, depicted as laying his seed in the waters of chaos in which he becomes a golden egg or embryo called Hiraṇyagarbha, from whom emanates the whole universe. The term *prajāpati* was originally a description of many gods but, in the attempt to find the Source and essence beyond the deities themselves, "lord of creatures" came to be personified as that Source from which all sprang. It is in the *Brāhmaṇas* particularly that Prajāpati is panentheistically featured. As a supreme Source who creates himself and projects himself into the world, he must ultimately transcend it even though he constitutes it. Such intimacy between Creator and created is reflected in his name as "Lord" or "Father" of all creatures, and in the *Brāhmaṇas* all gods are said to be subsumed in him.[14] He is a good example of *Vedic* monotheism (and panentheism) in which a god emerges quite separately from the other *Vedic* deities.

Hiraṇyagarbha "Golden Germ", who initially emanates from Prajāpati, becomes the Self of the world, the essence from which everything in existence derives its being. In later times he will become the creator divinity Brahmā. The *Ṛg Veda* says of Hiraṇyagarbha:

> In the beginning rose Hiraṇyagarbha, born Only Lord of all created beings. He fixed and holdeth up this earth and heaven. What God shall we adore with our oblation?
> Giver of vital breath, of power and vigour, he whose commandments all the Gods acknowledge: The Lord of death, whose shade is life immortal. What God shall we adore with our oblation?
> Who by his grandeur hath become Sole Ruler of all the moving world that breathes and slumbers; He who is Lord of men and Lord of cattle. What God shall we adore with our oblation?
> His, through his might, are these snow-covered mountains, and men call sea and Rasā his possession: His arms are these, his are these heavenly regions. What God shall we adore with our oblation?[15]

This magnificent hymn reflects the transcendent nature of the Source and Creator from which all emerges; he is the "God of gods, and none beside him", the hymn later says.[16] Another Source, Brahmaṇaspati is said to have blown out the created universe like a blacksmith and he, too, is equated with Brahmā. Another posited Source of all was Viśvakarman "Maker of Everything", "Creator of All", a kind of divine architect. Again, this term was one once given to other gods and then projected as a divine entity itself. Like Prajāpati, Viśvakarman does not emanate from any prior cause and represents an uncreated Source of all, generating all things. Again we have a move to one ultimate Source in a monotheistic sense, but a panentheistic emanation of that Source within the universe.

An interesting early attempt to find the Source behind the deities is reflected in the collective and unifying term Viśvadevas, "All gods". This attempt was more than a statement that all the gods were one; it was tantamount to suggesting that the monistic identity of all the gods was an essence that underpinned and informed them all, like a thread that unites many beads. Similarly, *Prāṇa*, "Vital Breath", was thought to be the essence that united all life, and this, too, became an ultimate principle for a while. Yet there were also more tangible sources suggested for the ultimate foundation behind all. These have been noted earlier – Air, Water, the Sun, Fire, Heat, Desire, Time – and were posited as the mediums by which the world came into being. But two hymns in particular have become the creation accounts best transmitted beyond the Indian world. One is the *Puruṣasūkta*, and the other the creation hymn 10:129, both from the *Ṛg Veda*. They are very different from each other, the former presenting a more tangible Source, the latter a highly metaphysical one, as the basic Reality behind the universe.

According to the *Puruṣasūkta* the universe emerged from a being that existed before all. And by the self-sacrifice of this being, *Puruṣa*, all things in the universe came to be:

> A thousand heads hath Puruṣa, a thousand eyes, a thousand feet. On every side pervading earth he fills a space ten fingers wide.
> This Puruṣa is all that yet hath been and all that is to be; The Lord of Immortality which waxes greater still by food.
> So mighty is his greatness; yea, greater than this is Puruṣa. All creatures are one-fourth of him, three-fourths eternal life in heaven.
> With three-fourths Puruṣa went up: one-fourth of him again was here. Thence he strode out to every side over what eats not and what eats.[17]

Later in the hymn it is related how the sacrifice of Puruṣa formed the four classes of Indian society – the *Brahmin*, the priest from his mouth; the *Kṣatriya* or *Rājanya*, the warrior, prince or king, administrators and officials from his arms; the *Vaiśya*, the merchant and farmer from his thighs; the *Śūdra*, the servant and worker from his feet. The moon is said to come from his mind, the sun from his eye, and all parts of the universe emanate from the various components of this huge sacrificial being. Yet it is clear from the verses above that only one quarter of Puruṣa becomes the universe, the rest remains transcendent over and beyond it. This is clear panentheism, a divine being who is the Source of all, who is in all, but who transcends all. It is a panentheistic monotheism that characterizes much of the more speculative hymns of the *Vedas*.

Thus, as Radhakrishnan pointed out clearly: "The world form is not a complete expression or manifestation of the divine Reality. It is only a fragment of the divine that is manifested in the cosmic process. The World-soul is a partial expression of the Supreme Lord."[18]

The height of metaphysical speculation occurs in one magnificent hymn of the *Ṛg Veda* in a poem that we might well term *The One*. Basham described the hymn as "one of the oldest surviving records of philosophical doubt in the history of the world",[19] and it is his translation that is included here:

Then even nothingness was not, nor existence.
There was no air then, nor the heavens beyond it.
What covered it? Where was it? In whose keeping?
Was there then cosmic water, in depths unfathomed?

Then there were neither death nor immortality,
Nor was there then the torch of night and day.
The One breathed windlessly and self-sustaining.
There was that One then, and there was no other.

At first there was only darkness wrapped in darkness.
All this was only unillumined water.
That One which came to be, enclosed in nothing.
Arose at last, born of the power of heat.

In the beginning desire descended on it –
That was the primal seed, born of the mind.
The sages who have searched their hearts with wisdom
Know that which is is kin to that which is not.

And they have stretched their cord across the void,
And know what was above, and what below.
Seminal powers made fertile mighty forces.
Below was strength and over it was impulse.

But, after all, who knows, and who can say
Whence it all came, and how creation happened?
The gods themselves are later than creation,
So who knows truly whence it has arisen?

Whence all creation had its origin,
He, whether he fashioned it or whether he did not,
He, who surveys it all from highest heaven,
He knows – or maybe even he does not know.[20]

Here is an unnamed and abstract Reality behind the phenomenal universe, an indescribable Source that can only be termed "That" or "That One", *Tat Ekam*. The One that breathes windlessly or breathlessly and self-sustaining obviously exists here before all other manifestations in the cosmos. So the manifest cosmos does not equate with it, for "That" is a limitless, indescribable, absolute principle that can exist independently of existence – otherwise it cannot be the Source of it. I doubt, then, whether this can be termed a "superpersonal monism"[21] or, even stronger, "the quintessence of monistic thought".[22] It is more expressive of a panentheistic, totally transcendent entity that can become manifest by its own power. It exists in itself, unmanifest, but with the potential for all manifestations of the cosmos.

But the fact that it precedes creation as neither this nor that, yet not *nothing*, places "The One" transcendent to the manifest universe. The hymn brings out well the differentiated opposites of our normal existence that cease to obtain in the darkness wrapped in darkness – the point where opposites merge to the state of no-thing but, clearly, not *nothing*. This, however, is probably the closest the *Vedas* come to overt, true monism; the hymn certainly expresses the fundamental principle of manifest existence emanating from an Unmanifest Source, and therefore all existence is a unity. It is heat, *tapas*, that is the latent power in the Unmanifest and that is depicted as the initial medium for creation to take place. But unity with that Unmanifest Source is partial and panentheistic, for the Source, although constituting what it creates, as the creative Cause also transcends what it creates.

This is really the height of the philosophical speculation of the *Vedas*, the placing of a First Cause at a point of utter mystery and indescribability, beyond both being and non-being. As to any other evidence for monism in the *Vedas*, I think it is doubtful. The deities may, indeed, have taken on one another's identities, or have been merged into One, but this only suggests a unity of divinity, and for true monism to occur the total identity of all things in the cosmos with the divine, both individually and collectively, would be expected. But the human individual is not equated with divinity in the *Vedas* even if he or she is accepted as being an emanation of divinity. A certain distance always remains between individual and ultimate. In contrast to this, Sharma writes of "no development from polytheism through monotheism to monism, but only of monism from the first Mantra portion to the last Upaniṣadic portion".[23] He gives many examples of what he considers to be monism in the *Vedas* but the examples are, in the main, of the unity of the deities rather than an *identity* of all things one with another and one with the divine. Certainly the deities can be considered as one, and I have yet to discuss the unifying principle of *ṛta*, but these examples point more to monotheism than monism. I believe it wise to differentiate clearly between a pantheistic emanation of the divine in all things, and a monistic identity of all things with each other and the divine, the latter being a more explicit monism. Generally, the *Vedas* indicate that the dualistic nature of self and divine is maintained.[24]

One very important concept in the *Vedas* that was a unifying principle in the three worlds of heaven, atmosphere and earth was *ṛta*. It was the right and orderly course of all things, a cosmic norm to which gods and humans were expected to conform, and which regulated all things. It was not an aspect of divinity since it was an impersonal law, and the gods themselves were subject to it, even if they were responsible for the preservation of aspects of the universe that came under its control. The deity Varuṇa was its overseer but was neither identified with it nor created it. *Vedic* ritualism was believed to conform to *ṛta* in that it was "right" and "orderly". There is a certain fundamental reality and truth to this all-pervading *ṛta* and an inviolability that is similar to the later law of *karma*. It also came to denote the course of moral order in the daily existence of Aryan man and woman and, as such, was the precursor of *dharma*. *Ṛta* thus pervaded all existence, regulating the rhythms of life and nature both microcosmically and macrocosmically. It was deeper and more fundamental than the gods themselves, an abstract unifying principle which, while not the precursor of the Brahman of the *Upaniṣads*, was at least sufficiently speculative and metaphysical to suggest identity in its all-pervasiveness.

Another mysterious force that operated in existence was the power and efficacy behind the multitude of sacrificial actions. What was it that ensured a certain result from a particular ritualistic cause? One of the reasons why the *Vedas* were accepted as being testimony of ultimate Truth was that the ritual they prescribed actually produced the appropriate effects. Two factors are important here: one is the unquestionable belief in *Vedic* testimony, and the other, the belief in the power or force operative between action and its result. These were issues taken up by some of the philosophical systems, in concepts like *apūrva* and *adṛṣṭa* – the unseen potency that is produced in causal actions, and that brings appropriate results.

The more metaphysical and speculative ideas that have been explored here are particularly characteristic of later *Vedic* thought. To the four *Vedas* are added the *Brāhmaṇas* and the *Āraṇyakas*. The *Brāhmaṇas* are written in prose, unlike the poetic hymns of the *Vedas* and, while they comment on and elucidate the sacrificial ritual of the *Vedas*, they also occasionally provide some philosophical thought. The *Upaniṣads* are appended to them, but are very different in nature. It is in the *Brāhmaṇas* that we see the elaboration of ritual ceremony to the extent that it usurps the power of the gods and changes their role from forces propitiated to intermediaries of the sacrifice. The word *brāhmaṇa* means "prayer", here, in the sense of correct ritual action that produces effects, and it is the whole dimension of *yajña* that occupies this particular literature. In the words of Dasgupta: "These works are full of dogmatic assertions, fanciful symbolism and speculations of an unbounded imagination in the field of sacrificial details."[25]

The *Āraṇyakas* are much more mystical and philosophical in nature. They are the forest treatises, so-called because they were "cognized" by the *vānaprasthas*, those who left society for the forest life. In the forest existence, ritual was less practically viable, and more mystically important, so the forest dwellers interpreted and found meaning for the sacrificial ritual in a more philosophical and metaphysical way. As such, the *Āraṇyakas* are more similar to the *Upaniṣads* than to the *Vedas* and *Brāhmaṇas* and include some of the older *Upaniṣads* as their concluding material. In the forests, where elaborate ritual could not be undertaken, the more active ritual was symbolically interpreted and led to a development away from ritual to knowledge – the hallmark of *Upaniṣadic* thought. The overlap between

Brāhmaṇa, *Āraṇyaka* and *Upaniṣad* is certainly evident, for they were originally parts of one composite literary tradition, and should not, therefore, be regarded as segregated material.

How, then, do we view pre-*Upaniṣadic* thought? There is certainly evidence of polytheism in its earliest phases, but not a polytheism that has a rigid pantheon of deities with clear identities and anthropomorphized characters. *Vedic* polytheism is far more intangible and fluid, and the fact that the deities can so easily be identified one with another, and that we can witness a certain overlapping of their functions, suggests a more intricate polytheism than systems such as ancient Canaan or ancient Greece. And is *Vedic* polytheism a primitive polytheism or is it subtle polytheism? If the former, we should expect a neat evolution to a more developed polytheism with a systematized pantheon of deities. But this we do not find. I favour a more subtle type of polytheism and a distinctly patriarchal one, in which the female is conspicuously underemphasized. It is a polytheism that develops comfortably into a search for an ultimate, abstract Reality that transcends all the phenomena of the universe.

I do not think, in fact, that Hinduism fits so neatly into established types of belief in this early period. And any desire to see a neat westernized idea of progression from polytheism to monotheism – with the idea that the latter is a more evolved position than the former – is unlikely to be applicable. It is true that the *Vedic* hymns display from time to time the tendency to raise one deity to supremacy to the apparent neglect of others. But this is not to be viewed as an "improvement" on a primitive polytheism, but more of an expediency of religious practice. Modern Hinduism adopts the same idea when it is expedient to pay homage to Santoṣī Mā if one desires a new washing machine, rather than to the remoter and more cosmic Dūrga who is not interested in such mundanities. And neither of these deities would suffice if one wished to open a new business, when Gaṇeśa would be far more appropriate. This same kind of expedient selection is likely to have obtained in *Vedic* ritual. It was Max Müller who coined the term *henotheism* as a stage between polytheism and monotheism, a stage when one deity is raised to supremacy with others accepted, but on the periphery. The definition, as most now accept, is an over-simplification. If Hinduism proceeds to monotheism it is a monotheism of a type that searches for something way beyond the anthropomorphized monotheism of a theistic deity, and this seems fairly clear from the trends evident in the *Vedas* and, particularly, the *Āraṇyakas*. The thread that seems the clearest in *śruti* literature is the move to more and more philosophical and speculative views of deity, and I do not think it is bound by the same conceptualizations as western theistic monotheistic views of deity. Nevertheless, there is clearly discernible a desire to find a Source behind all deities – not to deny that deities exist, but to find the Reality beyond them from which they emerge. And once the deities merge into this Reality then we have a One, as the Source of all. But there is no suggestion that the ritualism that is involved with all the other deities should disappear as a result. We do not find all *Vedic* deities disappearing totally from the scene, even if, in some of the hymns of the *Vedas*, deities become subsumed in one another. The picture is too fluid to categorize: different deities caught the fancy of Aryan people at different times and probably for different reasons. Without a clear pantheon of deities, such fluidity of selection was possible. So the *Vedas* reflect both polytheism and monotheism and a rather fluid blending of the two from time to time.

Vedānta

The latest of the *śruti* literature comes at the end of the *Vedas* and is called just that, *Vedānta* (*Veda* and *anta* "end"). The particularly philosophical and mystical nature and content of the literature which comprises the *Vedānta*, the *Upaniṣads*, tend to separate it from the rest of *śruti* literature. The search for an ultimate Reality and essence that underpins all existence is the specific quest of *Upaniṣadic* thought, and we see in it the ways in which the sages wrestled with the search. Some of the most ancient *Upaniṣads* represent the oldest attempt of humankind to provide a philosophical explanation of the universe, of ultimate Reality, of the nature of the self and the purpose of humankind. The *Bṛhadāraṇyaka Upaniṣad* expresses this quest in the beautiful words: "From the unreal lead me to the real, from darkness lead me to light, from death lead me to immortality."[26] *Vedānta* also means "end of the *Vedas*" in the sense of fulfilment of the *Vedas*, that is to say, the *Upaniṣads* brought out what was considered the real meaning behind *Vedic* ritual through the pursuit of true knowledge. Since the *Upaniṣads* are the sole literature pertaining to the *Vedānta* the two terms are synonymous. The importance of *Upaniṣadic* thought in the development of Hinduism is enormous, for it contains most of the developed concepts that we associate with Hinduism today – belief in the Absolute of Brahman, *karma*, *saṃsāra*, *mokṣa*, *dharma*, *ātman* in relation to Brahman, are just some of the most fundamental.

Despite the radically different nature of the *Upaniṣads* in relation to the *Vedas* it has to be remembered that the material of both form the *Veda* or "knowledge" which is *śruti* literature. So the *Upaniṣads* develop the ideas of the *Vedas* beyond their ritual formalism and should not be seen as isolated from them. But it is the more philosophical aspects of the *Vedas* that are more particularly emphasized in the *Vedānta*: the efficacy of *Vedic* ritual is not rejected, it is just that there is a search for the Reality that informs it. The fact that the *Upaniṣads* were attached to the *Brāhmaṇas* shows that they were regarded not only as ancient as them but, also, as being in their own way explicative of *Vedic* ritual. The nature of the monotheistic trends of the *Vedas*, I believe, sets the stage for this unique development of a totally transcendent Absolute. But, while the philosophical search in the *Vedas* for a Reality behind the deities and existence is extended in the *Upaniṣads*, there is also evident a new and profound interest in the nature of the true self. Yet even this inquiry is prefigured to a certain extent in the panentheism of *Vedic* hymns such as the *Puruṣasūkta*, in which the self, as all in life, is an emanation of the divine sacrificial being Puruṣa.[27] The synthesis of these two aspects – Reality and the soul – is the particular genius of the *Vedānta*. And in the nature of the inquiry into Reality and soul, and the fusion of the two, the more introspective and meditative approaches to the *Vedas* were adopted.

The *Upaniṣads*

The *Upaniṣads* reflect a long period of compilation preceded by oral tradition. Dating is precarious: in fact, as Olivelle aptly comments, "in reality, any dating of these documents that attempts a precision closer than a few centuries is as stable as a house of cards".[28] The earliest of them are likely to be the *Chāndogya* and the *Bṛhadāraṇyaka* dated to the seventh or sixth centuries BCE,[29] while the latest date to about a thousand years later. The older *Upaniṣads* probably date to before the time of the Buddha and are among the thirteen of the few hundred that are generally considered to be the most important.

The usual translation of the word *upaniṣad* is "sitting close to", presumably a *guru*, in order to hear the wisdom of one who had cognized the truths of the universe. The pupils, or *chelas*, sat around the *guru* listening to his teachings and engaging in dialogue with him. The *Upaniṣadic* literature contains a considerable amount of such dialogue between disciple and *guru* and the translation "sitting close to" is therefore an apt one. However, the word *upaniṣad* is a compound one, and the roots that compose it can have a variety of meanings. Dandekar, for example, suggests a meaning "placing side by side" or "equivalence, correlation", and this would reflect the *Upaniṣadic* theme of equating all things in life as of one fundamental essence.[30] Attractive, too, is the interpretation put forward by Alain Daniélou of a meaning "near approach" to the Absolute, Brahman. This, indeed, would reflect the main trend of *Upaniṣadic* thought.[31] Then, again, the *Upaniṣads* are essentially *esoteric* teachings, secretive teachings that are only for the initiated, and some disciples had to wait patiently for many years before they were deemed worthy by their teachers to receive them. Deussen, therefore, saw the word *upaniṣad* as denoting the idea of "secret", or "secret teaching", *rahasya*.[32] The proponent of Advaita Vedānta, Śaṃkara, took the basic meaning from the root *sad*, "to loosen, reach" or "destroy" suggesting the idea of loosening or destroying the ego and ignorance, which prevent knowledge of Brahman and Reality. All these meanings reflect the particular theses of their commentators, but, collectively, they highlight well the nature of the speculative ideas of the *Upaniṣads*, in meanings that are characterized by a certain overlap of thought.

The early *Upaniṣads* were, as stated, one strand of the composite *śruti* literature, but their very nature made them more suitable for the meditative recluse than the worshipping householder or, even for the individual who simply took up an abode in the forest. The knowledge imparted in them was probably added to over time, the original teaching being quite brief but profound, and this was then overlaid by the related discourse that took place. And one *Upaniṣad* may contain a number of such formulas, which may or may not be contradictory one with another. The composition of the *Upaniṣads*, therefore, is very varied, containing old ideas alongside new ones, the ideas of one teacher alongside those of another, and expositions on the teachings of many *gurus*, so that they end up bafflingly heterogeneous. They were written in poetic form or rhythmic prose but are, as Dasgupta said, "collations or compilations of floating monologues, dialogues or anecdotes".[33] Like the *mantras* of the four *Vedas* they were considered to be timeless and authorless, so the name of each of the early *Upaniṣads* is not derived from a compiler or author, but is the title of an old *Vedic* school or branch (*śakhā*). Each of these schools would have been associated with one or more of the *Upaniṣads*. However, some of the *Upaniṣads* feature sages of great repute such as Uddālāka Āruṇī and Yājñavalkya, and it is likely that these were the original teachers of the ideas associated with them. Most of these teachers would have been of the *Brahmin* class, but *Kṣatriyas* also seem to have contributed to the philosophical teaching, occasionally to the extent that they are depicted as instructing *Brahmins*. Tradition, however, retains anonymity of *śruti* literature as essential to the belief in its timeless nature, yet suggests an overall priestly transmission and development.

From the wide dating and varied composition, then, the content of the *Upaniṣads* is, itself, philosophically varied, and does not reflect homogeneous ideas. Many different solutions are offered to the metaphysical questions raised about the nature of the self, ultimate Reality and knowledge and the nature of the divine, and some texts may be more interested in one of these aspects than others. The material is sufficiently varied even in one *Upaniṣad* to contain contradictory ideas in this exploration, but they are similar in that they deal with religious experience and spirituality in all its variety. And, ultimately, the *Upaniṣads* were based on *Vedic* texts, so that any part of the considerable *Vedic* material could be taken up for discourse, philosophical analysis and discussion. As will be seen, the prominent message of the *Upaniṣads* is a monistic one, but this is by no means the only one in the melting pot of philosophical ideas that informed them.

The *Upaniṣads* deal with a quest for Truth that can only be known intuitively and not empirically. They are not, claimed Dasgupta, "reasoned statements, but utterances of truths intuitively perceived or felt as unquestionably real and indubitable, and carrying great force, vigour, and persuasiveness with them".[34] They represent a journey of the soul rather than the mind, and a quest to find the nature of the soul and the means to its liberation from a world of change, finitude and transience. The journey is not to be undertaken by the ordinary person, who is necessarily bound to the world. Rather, it is a journey for the initiated, who already display the capabilities of heightened consciousness and intuitive understanding. It is a spiritual journey. It would be to such individuals that the *gurus* would expound their teachings. This emphasis on intuitive knowledge and understanding in the *Upaniṣads* classifies them as *jñānakāṇḍa*, the "knowledge portion" of the *Vedic* material as a whole, as opposed to the ritual action portion, the *karmakāṇḍa* of the four *Vedas* and *Brāhmaṇas*. Each supplies a different route to the ultimate goal: the former, *jñānamārga*, is the path of knowledge; the latter *karmamārga*, is the path of works, actions.

Like all *śruti* literature the *Upaniṣads* are considered to be *sanātana*, timeless, and that is why they can only be known intuitively and not in the context of the empirical and finite world. Cognized or "seen" by ancient sages with the heightened consciousness necessary to receive direct revelation, they represent the kind of knowledge that needs comparable levels of consciousness in order to understand them. This is why a *guru* was so fundamental to the imparting of such wisdom, and why only the chosen few were initiated and taught. Some *gurus* required many years of austerities from would-be initiates before initiation. Indeed, Deussen's interpretation of the word *upaniṣad* as "secret", noted above, reflects well the secrecy attached to the knowledge, and its deeply esoteric nature. We should not expect *Upaniṣadic* thought, then, to be consistently clearly articulated, for the *Upaniṣads* often dealt with their material symbolically and were meant as formulas around which a good deal of oral discourse was necessary.

Dealing with the spiritual search for Reality, the *Upaniṣads*, generally, are idealist rather than realist. That is to say they deal with the knowledge experienced in the soul, and to some extent the mind, rather than with knowledge acquired by the senses. There is a thread that is common to most of the principal *Upaniṣads*, and that is, the acceptance of the world as a changeable reality at the root of which is a changeless Reality that is the fundamental basis of all. But this is not to say that realism barely features in the *Upaniṣads*. Olivelle points out the "diversity of goals that their authors pursue, chief among which are food, prosperity, power, fame, and a happy afterlife. There are rites to secure greatness, to win a woman's love, to harm the lover of one's wife, to ensure pregnancy, to guard against pregnancy, to assure a safe childbirth – the list can go on".[35] So the *Upaniṣads* have their mundane themes as much as their celebrated flights of metaphysical thought.

Nevertheless, it is the search for a unified Absolute Reality that is the main theme of the *Upaniṣads*, a search resulting in the articulation of knowledge that is both ultimate and infinite. Reality emerges in the *Vedānta* as single and as that which informs the apparent plurality of all things: it is this thread of thought that pervades its literature. There are some passages which, like the *Vedas*, suggest that the ultimate Reality behind the universe is elemental – Air, Water, Fire, Ether – other early ideas suggest *prāṇa*, "Vital Breath", *manas* "Mind", or the Sun. But what emerges as the main thread of thought in the *Upaniṣads* is the unified nature of Reality that underpins all and remains changeless in all the transience and finitude of existence. It is a Reality that is beyond the senses, a Reality unknowable by ordinary means and yet, since it informs all life and is its fundamental essence, it is intimately bound in all things. Nothing can exist outside it and all things take their *raison d'être* from this ultimate Source. So all the souls of existence are unified in one Reality and the whole of the physical universe. This is monism, the belief that Reality is one single principle in which all things are at one with, and identical to, another, and are identical to the ultimate Reality that is their Source.

An *underlying* Reality that is ultimate and changeless suggests that the phenomenal world that we observe, and which is subject to change, is comparatively unreal – either having no reality at all or, having only a lesser reality. The *Upaniṣads* can support both these concepts. They can, at times also support a more pantheistic view of reality, that is to say, the identification of the whole of the cosmos with ultimate Reality in a way that removes the latter as a Source that transcends the cosmos by preceding it. There are also theistic threads in the *Upaniṣads*, particularly in the later principal ones, but the main current that unites them is monism. Yet, broadly, these types of belief are united by an *emanationist* view of reality. That is to say, the world is considered, in some way, to have *come forth* from the ultimate Source and to have that ultimate Source as its fundamental essence. The link between each entity in the universe and its Source is therefore a profound one, but can be viewed very differently. The *Upaniṣads* and the philosophical schools seek to answer this particular problem among the many metaphysical questions they raise.

Brahman

The ultimate Reality, the Source from which all emanates, the unchanging Absolute, is termed *Brahman*. The word was originally associated with "prayer" or "devotional utterance" in the *Vedas*, and the related word *Brāhmaṇas* denotes the commentaries that pertain to the sacred prayers and devotions of the priests. The word *Brahman* is a kind of philosophical shift in emphasis of the word, an internalizing of it, a reflection of the *power* behind the efficacy of prayer and sacrificial devotion. Although it is a difficult word to pin down, many suggest a derivation from the root *bṛh* "to burst forth", or "to grow, increase",[36] reflecting, perhaps, the emanation of Brahman into the universe as the *Ground of all Being*, and the unlimited nature of Brahman. Some suggest a meaning "to be strong".[37] But whatever Brahman was or was not, It was mainly felt to be beyond the conceptions of human imagination. It was a Reality that was indescribable, though experienceable in the deepest part of the self: something in the depths of the ancient *Upaniṣadic* sages *knew* that it was the highest expression of Reality. Radhakrishnan expressed this superbly:

> The word suggests a fundamental kinship between the aspiring spirit of man and the spirit of the universe which it seeks to attain. The wish to know the Real implies that we know it to some extent. If we do not know anything about it, we cannot even say that it is and that we wish to know it. If we know the Real, it is because the Real knows itself in us. The desire for God, the feeling that we are in a state of exile, implies the reality of God in us, though we cannot tell what it is. All spiritual progress is the growth of half-knowledge into clear illumination. Religious experience is the evidence for the Divine. In our inspired moments we have the feeling that there is a greater reality within us, though we cannot tell what it is.[38]

These words epitomize well the fundamental link between the deepest self and the Ground of all Being that is Brahman. As the Ground of all Being, Brahman's manifestation or emanation in the universe lends to it a degree of reality. But it is a reality that the *Upaniṣads* generally consider to be hidden by either a lower reality, or by total illusion. These are aspects that require examination below. As the Cause and Source of the universe, Brahman is both the active generator of all things and yet is also the passive and unmoved Absolute. Pervading all, Brahman is yet unaffected by all and though the Source of space and time, and of cause and effect, Brahman is beyond them. Being beyond the limitations of human conception, Brahman is a neuter principle, an "It" rather than a he or she. The term "God" is therefore often inapplicable to Brahman. Brahman also transcends the dualities and differentiation of existence. It is not this as opposed to that, light as opposed to dark, good as opposed to evil, and so on. Brahman is *neti neti* "not this, not this".

Brahman is thus an abstract principle beyond human comprehension. It is *Tat*, simply "That", Absolute, and unknowable in the ordinary sense of the word. And yet it is the Source of all because everything emanates from it, is sustained by it, and returns to it. Brahman, therefore, is both Unmanifest and devoid of qualities (*nirguṇa*) and yet manifest in the universe and therefore with qualities (*saguṇa*). *Upaniṣadic* thought is inclined to focus on both these aspects at times. The Unmanifest and manifest aspects of Brahman are not different, but simply two aspects of reality, two sides of the same coin – unity in diversity. But the degree to which the world is considered as real will vary, as will be seen, for any linking of the essence of divinity with a world of change and finitude is problematic. This would suggest that Brahman is changeable in its manifest form, and what is subject to change is impermanent and not Absolute. And if the changing world is considered to be illusionary, then that illusionary nature must *also* emanate from Brahman. Conversely, if all form, or *rūpa*, is the manifestation of Brahman it must also be real, and because each form has an intrinsic reality given to it through *nāma*, "name", common sense will suggest it is real. These questions of the degree of manifestation of Brahman in the world, alongside the degree of reality ascribed to the world, are two important issues that are dealt with in the philosophical schools.

Related to these difficult questions is also the degree to which Brahman, as the Unmanifest Source of the manifestation of cause–effect processes in the universe, is also bound in those causes and effects. How can effects like you and I, and all other effects in the universe, emanate from the ultimate Cause of Brahman without Brahman, too, being effect as well as cause, and subject to the same changes that bring about effects? Are the changes that occur in the manifestations of Brahman, that is to say in each *rūpa* in existence, only apparent and not real changes, like clay that can become a pot, a jar, a plate and so on? Or are changes from cause to effect *real* changes in every way, so that the effect is something new? These are issues on which the *Upaniṣads* touch, but which the schools of philosophical thought take up more earnestly.

The two aspects of Brahman – *nirguṇa* and *saguṇa* – give rise to two different views of Brahman, *acosmic* and *cosmic* respectively; both feature in the *Vedānta*. The acosmic Brahman remains the indescribable and impersonal Absolute to which no qualities can be given, but the cosmic Brahman is a more personalized aspect of Brahman, manifested in the forms of deities like Śiva and Viṣṇu, and referred to as Īśvara "Lord". The impersonal is sometimes referred to as higher Brahman, and the personal form lower Brahman. The distinction between the two is often blurred in the *Upaniṣads*. The acosmic view of Brahman is of an Absolute in which all dualities cease to exist, and that is one reason why no attributes or qualities can be assigned to It. Any differentiation between this and that fails to understand the nature of ultimate Reality that is *neti neti*, "not this, not this". So Reality is non-differentiated, that is to say, when we differentiate between this and that we obscure the real which is not one or the other. The unity of the acosmic Brahman is therefore essential Reality and ultimate knowledge. It is *That* from which all springs and so is the ultimate subject in which all knowledge is subsumed as object so that the two are one. Sharma writes, "the Absolute is the Existence of all existences, the Truth of all truths, the Reality of all realities".[39] This indicates clearly the *ultimacy* of the Absolute, without which, nothing in existence can obtain.

The cosmic Brahman is that aspect of Brahman that is more involved in the manifestation of the universe, that which allows the universe to come forth, that sustains it and that draws it back into itself. It is the cosmic Brahman that may more easily be given the term "God" and the personal pronoun "he" or "him". The cosmic Brahman is like the clay that gives rise to many articles, the ultimate essence from which all is produced and can be reduced. It is the ultimate essence, like the clay, that is the *real* nature of the effect or form. Thus, the manifest world is rather like the *body* of Brahman, the essential reality that underpins it being the *soul*, Brahman. This view allows a degree of reality to the phenomenal world, a degree of differentiation and plurality, because the physical world itself is differentiated from Brahman, allowing for a certain duality in an overall unity.

The distinction between the cosmic and acosmic Brahman in the *Upaniṣads* is not always clear, for they are really two aspects of a single Reality – an undifferentiated unity that becomes the differentiations of the world. The creative power that brings this about is more readily depicted as God, as *Īśvara*, that which is the all-knowing and all-pervading subject, which has the world as its created object, and in whom all knowledge is held. Thus we have an impersonal Absolute that is without qualities (*nirguṇa*), without form (*nirākāra*) and indescribable, and a personal Brahman with qualities (*saguṇa*), with form (*sākāra*) as

Īśvara. Both can be united as one, and for some, Īśvara is the means of focus on the impersonal Brahman beyond the personal.

Since there is a more personalized Brahman in the *Upaniṣads* then there is space for theistic devotion, devotion to a personal God as the controller and sustainer of the universe. The *Kaṭha*, *Īśā*, *Śvetāśvatara*, and *Muṇḍaka Upaniṣads* are all infused with theistic thought. It is these later principal *Upaniṣads* that tend to incorporate concepts of a personal, omnipotent and omniscient God. The Hindu deity Śiva, for example, features in such a way in the *Śvetāśvatara Upaniṣad* and Viṣṇu in the *Kaṭha*, but not exclusively theistically, for the impersonal acosmic conception of Brahman is still evident. But, where theism is overt, there is a clear understanding that devotion to God is *the* means to liberation, and the understanding of this can only represent a completely dualistic relationship between individual and divine. Indeed, in the *Śvetāśvatara Upaniṣad* there is evident the idea that human beings are providentially controlled by the divine and a certain conception of the grace of God being available to the devout worshipper is evident. This is far removed from an impersonal, acosmic view of divinity. Such theism, however, is not a major current in *Upaniṣadic* thought and it is to the major trend of monism that this chapter will be directed.

Ātman

Some of the questions that were raised above concerning the relation of the changeless Brahman to the cause–effect process in the universe as the manifestation of Brahman, are answered by the key *Upaniṣadic* concept of *ātman*. *Ātman*, initially, is the word for "self". It is likely to be derived from the root *an* "to breathe" and, by extension therefore, suggestive of the breath of life that animates human beings.[40] But apart from being the general animated self, the *ātman* is also the soul, what Radhakrishnan depicted as "what remains when everything that is not the self is eliminated".[41] Since breath is the essential element of life – the *essence* of life without which human beings cannot exist – there came about in *Upaniṣadic* thought the concept of *ātman* as the *essence* of the self, the fundamental and *real* part of the self that underpinned the personality. Thus a transfer from *breath* to *essence* took place in the usage of the word. And the *ātman* in this sense of the true essence of the individual was believed to be separate in some way from the personality self, the *jīvātman*. It is the latter that is egoistically bound to the dualities of existence – this as opposed to that, happiness as opposed to sorrow, wealth as opposed to poverty, and so on. The *ātman* is the *still* part of the self, the deepest part of the self that transcends the phenomenal world, and is the eternal soul of each person. Concomitant with this conception of the *ātman* as the fundamental real essence of the self was the comparative unreality of the transient world in which we live, an unreality that, much later, was sometimes pressed as far as sheer illusion.

Thus the *ātman*, while interpreted differently in the various philosophical schools, came to be thought of as the permanent aspect of the self. To realize this ultimate Self, to experience the reality of it, became the goal. And this experience would transform the egoistic self into one devoid of the usual conceptions of "I" and "mine", for the *ātman* is pure and unconnected with the transient processes of life. It was the *ātman* that became conceived of as the substratum of all real knowledge about the world and, as the ultimate real aspect of the self, needed no validation for its existence.

Brahman-ātman

The particular brilliancy of the *Upaniṣads* is the synthesis of Brahman and *ātman*. It is a fairly logical conception in that, if Brahman is the unchanging and permanent but indescribable Absolute Reality that underpins all existence, and the *ātman* is the fundamental, real and permanent part of the self, then they are conjoined by their particular reality and permanence. Since all in the universe was believed to have emanated from Brahman, then at least the fundamental *essence* of all things must be equated either wholly or partially with Brahman. Once *ātman* had shifted its meaning to "essence" then not only human beings, but also all things in existence, animate and inanimate, were believed to contain this same essence that is Brahman. And, since all things have the same Source, the *same* essence that is Brahman informs all things, so at the deepest levels of life there is a fundamental and permanent Reality that runs through all things – *ātman*, which is Brahman. This, indeed, is the monism so typical of *Upaniṣadic* thought, by which all is one and each entity in the universe is identical to Brahman.

It is this equation of *ātman* = Brahman which is the brilliant star of *Upaniṣadic* thought, and which really provided the answer to so many of the philosophical questions that a search for Reality and Truth had engendered. The sages had at last emerged from the unreal to the real, from darkness to light and from death to immortality. Two different concepts had become synthesized in a unique way that would provide a basis for much philosophical thought in the centuries to follow, and provided, with some modifications, the core of much Hindu religious belief. The microcosmic world of humankind had become intimately equated with the whole of the macrocosm because of the presence of the *ātman* in all things. The inner self became projected out into cosmic identity and unity with all things as the permanent substratum of Reality equated with its divine Source. Each human being is thus identical to another, identical to the cosmos and identical to Brahman.

The characteristic philosophy of the *Vedānta*, then, is monism – the idea that everything in the cosmos is one. Differentiation between this and that, and the recognition of dualities in the universe, occur only because of ignorance (*avidyā*). But not only is everything in the cosmos one, each entity in it *is* Brahman – not a *part* of Brahman as in pantheistic or panentheistic belief, but totally identical with Brahman. And just as Brahman is indescribable and beyond human conception so the *ātman* is also beyond any empirical analysis; it, too, is indescribable and can only be experienced by the kind of deep, intuitive knowledge that penetrates to the hidden Reality in the depths of the self.

Of the many parts of the *Upaniṣads* that express this identity of *ātman* and Brahman it is the expression *Tat tvam asi*, "That you are", of the *Chāndogya Upaniṣad* that epitomizes this identity. Indeed, Halbfass refers to this specific text as "one of the most seminal texts in the history of Indian thought".[42] The story behind these words is that of Śvetaketu, a young boy who, at the age of twelve, embarked on his period of study with a *guru*. When he returned twelve years later at the age of twenty-four, somewhat conceited and arrogant with the amount of knowledge he had acquired, his father Uddālāka Āruṇī asked him whether he had requested from his *guru* that instruction "by which the unhearable becomes heard, the unperceivable becomes perceived, the unknowable becomes known?"[43] Of course, it is to the *ātman* and its identity with Brahman that Uddālāka is referring. But Śvetaketu does not know, and cannot see how such a question could be answered. His father explains that just as there is one substance like clay, from which all things made of clay come, so there is one Being from which the world of not-being is derived. But the example of clay is an easy one and Uddālāka directs his son to more subtle ideas. He asks his son what he can see when he cuts the fruit from a banyan tree in half. When it reveals the tiny seeds, his father asks him to cut one of the seeds in two and again say what he can see. This time Śvetaketu has to admit that he can see nothing, yet he knows that something within the seed must cause it to grow to the mighty banyan tree. Uddālāka is directing his son to the idea of the *essence* of things which, while hidden, we know to be present, and from there to the subtle essence of Brahman as the *ātman* in all things. He tells his son:

> My dear, that subtle essence which you do not perceive, verily, my dear, from that very essence this great nyagrodha tree exists. Believe me, my dear.
> That which is the subtle essence, this whole world has for its self. That is true. That is the self. That art thou Śvetaketu.[44]

Like air in a jar that is the same as the air outside it, the *ātman* in the self is identical to the cosmos and its Source, the Ground of all Being that is Brahman.

The empirical self

The self that we know in life is not the *ātman*. The self that we know is the egoistic personality that operates in the world from the self-consciousness of individual psyche. Our view of the world is based on our likes and dislikes, our positive and negative responses to our environment, our aims, drives, genetic make-up and interaction with others and the world at large. The sum total of our personality to date is termed the *jīvātman* "that which breathes", from the root *jīv* "to breathe".[45] It is the biological, psychological and social self that enjoys, suffers, acts, thinks, breathes, makes choices between this and that, and is subject to the experiences mediated by the five senses – all in contrast to the pure *ātman* that is the still, non-active, subtle and real Self. It is the *jīvātman* that is subject to reincarnation, a concept accepted by most Indian thought. Reincarnation, or *saṃsāra*, occurs because the *jīvātman* accumulates both positive and negative *karma* as a result of its actions in mind, speech and body. The whole notion of cause and effect is an important one in Indian philosophical thought and it will be necessary to return to it continually. The law of cause and effect known as *karma* suggests that a person has to be reincarnated in order to reap the results – negative and positive – of the accumulation of all his or her actions in life. And since physical and mental actions are taking place in every waking moment of life, the effects that have to bear fruit necessitate countless lifetimes. So at death it is only the body that ceases to exist, while the subtle accumulated *karma* of one's existence in the present and past lives continues into the next. Each *jīvātman*, then, creates for itself its specific personality in the next existence and the sorrows and joys that are the fruits of its actions in past existence(s).

Each individual then is, as Sharma puts it, "a mixture of the real and the unreal, a knot of the existent and the non-existent, a coupling of the true and the false".[46] And it is mainly to the false and unreal world that the *jīvātman* leans, and not to the subtle, eternal, real Self within. The only way that the *ātman* in life can be experienced is by transcending the "other" self, the *jīvātman*, and by transcending the dualities of life to experience the unity behind it. The inimical inhibitors of this are desire and aversion – our negative and positive responses to the multitude of stimuli in life – and the egoistic self that they create. The self is a bit like an onion with layers or sheaths covering the *ātman*. At the outer level is the gross body (*annamaya*), and as we peel off that layer we come to the vital breath that is the life force (*prāṇamaya ātman*). Then there is the will (*manomaya ātman*), beneath which is the consciousness (*vijñānamaya ātman*) and, finally, the deepest self that is the *ātman* of pure bliss (*ānandamaya ātman*). It is here, at this deepest level, that subject–object differentiation in life, the dualities of life, desire, aversion, ego, *jīvātman* and sense perceptions are all dissolved. All is passively still, like a rippleless lake.

It is the ego (*ahaṃkāra*) that causes the *ātman* to be obscured, like layers of dust on a mirror. And what creates ego are the responses we make to all the stimuli in life, desiring one thing and rejecting another, whether that be physical objects or mental thoughts. It is this egoistic response to stimuli that creates the kind of personal *karma* that must bear fruit in the future – hence the necessity for reincarnation. So if the ego can be lost, all that is left is the pure self, *ātman*, and for this to happen, the individual has to be less involved with the dualities of the phenomenal world, and overcome desire (*kāma*). The problem is that the *jīvātman* does not usually *want* to stop desiring this and that – the world is so attractive. And because the personality self is so keen on being involved in the world, detachment from it is something that has to be cultivated, but only in those who are prepared to undergo the rigorous pursuit of it. Through detachment (*vairāgya*) the slow process of eradication of desire and ego takes place. Being involved in the phenomenal world is rooting oneself in *avidyā* "ignorance", for the only knowledge that is ultimately real is that rooted in the *ātman* which is Brahman. This is the kind of knowledge by which a person experiences the unity of his or her self with all other animate and inanimate things in the universe. *Avidyā*, on the other hand, makes one believe that all the dualities of life are important, feeding the ego with desires and aversions, and engendering a false sense of separateness from all other beings and things. Through *avidyā* it is believed that the world is all there is to reality; it deludes us into belief that there is no need to search for the Real. And so, the *Upaniṣads* teach, humankind suffers and is subject to *saṃsāra*.

Liberation

To lose the egoistic perceptions of the world, the dualities which that perception engenders, and the desires that create the ego, are the goals of *Upaniṣadic* thought. It is a *liberation* from all that restricts, binds, and holds humans in ignorance. The term for such liberation is *mokṣa*. The early *Vedic* idea of liberation was that, at the end of one existence, the soul of the good would be recompensed in heaven and the soul of the evil punished in a dark abode, a somewhat undeveloped hell. The later *Upaniṣadic* idea of reincarnation is sometimes combined with this concept, so that an individual is believed to go on experiencing the results of *karmic* action accumulated in life in the context of some heavenly or hellish abode, only then to be reborn in order to reap the fruits of other positive and negative *karma*.

Liberation or *mokṣa* is not something that can be "reached" or "acquired". Since the *ātman* is already there as the fundamental essence of the self it is merely there to be experienced. But a certain amount of knowledge is necessary to reveal it, not, as we have seen, empirical knowledge, but deep, intuitive knowledge that is, like the *ātman* itself, indescribable. But it is *mokṣa* that brings the realization of *ultimate* knowledge, the unity with the cosmos that makes all sense of "I" disappear. The diversity of the world vanishes in the ultimate knowledge of the unity of all things, the identity of the *ātman* with Brahman is realized. A synonym of *mokṣa* is *mukti* and it is the term used more readily in some texts like the *Bhagavadgītā*. The term *mukta* is also used of one who has realized the *ātman*, has become liberated and enlightened, but who is still contained by the physical body, still living. Such a person is egoless, does not act from the level of the "I", perceives the unity of all things, and does not differentiate between this and that to feed any egoistic desire. The *jīvanmukta*, then, is one liberated while alive, one freed from personality, freed from fruitive *karma*, freed from *saṃsāra*. The ignorance, *avidyā*, that characterized all the past lives is removed, and its opposite *vidyā*, "wisdom", is experienced. But liberation does not mean that a *jīvanmukta* has to be divorced from the world. It simply means operating in the world in an egoless way. As the point at the centre of a circle is equidistant from all points on the circumference, so the *jīvanmukta* is equally poised between all dualities of life, observing all, actively engaged in all, but not from the level of desire of one thing more than another, or preference for this as opposed to that. There is no "person", or personality, or individuality for this to take place. After death, the enlightened one becomes *videhamukti*, that is to say liberated after losing the body, and truly becomes Brahman.

It would be wrong, however, to assume that the only perspective of *mokṣa* in the *Upaniṣads* is that of monistic identity with Brahman for there are times when the more dual and theistic perspectives of *mokṣa* are to be found. Here, there is a more intimate and personal relationship with the divine at *mokṣa*. The degree of identity with the divine will vary, but the overall impression is one that supports the belief *ātman* = Brahman, stemming from the acosmic view of the indescribable Absolute. Identity with Brahman permits a state of *mokṣa* that is depicted as *sat* "Truth" or "Being" (as opposed to the non-being of the changeable and finite world), *cit* "pure Consciousness", and *ānanda* "Bliss". It is not extinction, but the degree to which self-identity is lost will depend on the particular conception of the Absolute Brahman. To say that this cannot be personal in the *Upaniṣads* would be misleading, and a *Upaniṣad* like the *Kaṭha* even suggests that it is by the *grace* of the supreme Self that the *ātman* can be realized.[47] Where a personal Brahman is accepted then monism is lost for a panentheistic view of the relationship of the world, and the individuals in it, to the divine. This is evident in, for example, the *Śvetāśvatara Upaniṣad*.

Perspectives of reality in the *Upaniṣads*

The fundamental quest of the *Upaniṣads* is for what is real in a world of change, transience and finitude. There is no doubt that Brahman as the Ground of all Being is ultimate Reality, but does this, then, negate the world itself as having any reality? I have touched on this idea above in that, if Brahman *is* the Ground of all Being, then what emanates forth from it – namely the universe – should have a degree of reality itself, like its Source. The concept of *ātman* answers the question to some extent in that it is the subtle *essence* of all in existence, and this might lend to the unified essence of the universe a reality that is not necessarily as evident in the grosser aspects of all existence. But this is in danger of suggesting that the world is a partial emanation (as the subtle essence) of Brahman, while there is a whole aspect of the universe (the gross and physical) that is unconnected with Brahman. The *Upaniṣads*, however, would support this line of reasoning, so we have to suggest either that all physical phenomena *are* real, or, that they are illusionary, or, that they are a lesser reality. The last two propositions tend to compromise monistic identity of all things.

The real question here is how far the individual self, the *jīvātman*, is real? Is it a lesser reality than the *ātman*, is it an illusion, or is it, as an emanation of Brahman, *ultimately* real? To give the phenomenal world an *ultimate* reality in the same sense as Brahman and *ātman* is ultimate, rather makes the detachment of the self from the world, and the aim of an egoless self, a nonsense. It is necessary, then, to claim for the world, and each self in it, a *different* reality from that of Brahman-*ātman*, a reality that has its Source in Brahman, but is an empirical reality as opposed to an *ultimate* Reality. But while this maintains the concept that the world and selves can have no reality apart from Brahman, it really denies monistic identity on the physical level, even though it may accept it on the subtle level. And if the reality of the world and selves are accepted then the plurality of it would have to be considered as real also, a kind of external diversity (the phenomenal world) united in a subtle oneness (*ātman*). The alternative is to accept the world and individual selves as an illusion, but, even then, it would have to be claimed that Brahman as the Ground of all Being is the Source, also, of such illusion. The *Upaniṣads* support all these ideas, and they are ones integral to the schools of philosophy that seek to establish the nature of reality and what it is that we can really *know*.

One answer to the problems posed by the reality or unreality of the world might lie in the *nirguṇa* and *saguṇa* aspects of Brahman, the former being the unchanging, indescribable Reality, and the latter being the cause–effect process of the manifested Absolute. The world itself, then, becomes a blend of what is unmanifest (the *ātman*) and what is manifest (the phenomenal world), a mixture of Being (Brahman) and non-being (the manifested world of Brahman that is subject to change). Individual egos, in this case, would reflect this same blend and could be said to be real, though the *ātman* would be "super real". Thus, Radhakrishnan neatly stated that "the ego is a changing formation on the background of the Eternal Being",[48] which rather suggests a degree of reality for the changing, finite self as much as the changing finite world. So the incessant change and perpetual motion of the universe is the nature of matter that emanates from the Ground of all Being. But this view of the many things in the world as real (pluralism) coupled with the idea that matter is real (realism) tends not to be prominent in the *Upaniṣads*. Unity not pluralism in the cosmos is the main message, and the contradiction that this poses in the face of the common sense view of the diversity of the world is not articulated to a sound conclusion in the *Vedānta*. It was, however, taken up by the different philosophical schools of thought. The sages of the *Upaniṣads* were generally content to accept the world as real because it was an emanation of the divine, but its diversity was underpinned by a more ultimate kind of reality. It is a perspective tinged with dualism.

The main current of thought, however, is a rejection of the pluralism of the world as unreal, though not in the sense of almost total unreality given to it by Śaṃkara in the much later school of Advaita Vedānta. It is the monism of Reality that makes the *apparent* diversity and plurality of the world unreal. And the more we are involved with this diversity and pluralism, the further we are away from the Reality of *ātman*, and the more we are rooted in *avidyā* – which brings me to the idea of the world as illusion, *māyā*, the veil that obscures reality. *Māyā* is also *delusion*, and this depicts rather well the deluded involvement of egoistic selves with the apparent diversity and plurality of the phenomenal world as what is real, when the *real* is deep within the self. It is ideas such as these that logically *must* deny reality to the world at large in comparison to the reality of Brahman. The two can co-exist as *levels* of reality, but it makes no sense to equate them. Again, this tinges the concept with dualism. The analogy of clay as a basic substance from which pots, plates, jugs, pipes, ornaments emerge suggests that, at least outwardly, we can claim that the pot is different from the plate. But forms and names are but the end products of the base substance, and those who have the knowledge of the base substance have an added perception of reality. Pots and plates can have no reality without the clay from which they are made, just so, the world has no reality apart from Brahman as its Source. It is the perspective of the real and unreal that is important here.

Māyā is close in meaning to *avidyā* and, indeed, the latter may have been the term used by the earlier *Upaniṣads* as an equivalent.[49] While the idea of *avidyā* is met frequently, the concept of *māyā*, though evident in the *Upaniṣads*, is not always clearly articulated. There is a sense in which *māyā* is conceived of as the divine power and art that causes all things in the universe, but it is also used in the sense of *līlā*, divine sport or play – almost a deliberate veil placed over the world by the divine. The *Bhagavadgītā* articulates this very clearly.[50] This concept gives us some insight into the two aspects of Brahman, the Unmanifest *nirguṇa* Absolute on the one hand, and the manifest aspect that is dynamic and active – something inherent in the word *līlā*. As such the Unmanifest Brahman is the passive, pure subject while the world is *prakṛti*, the active object. Subject and object, passive and active, Brahman and *prakṛti* are intimately bound, but it is the *nirguṇa* aspect of Brahman that is the substratum of all. There is no problem in accepting the world as real providing it is seen as the unified manifestation of Brahman and is lived in from the perspective of the *ātman*. But if the egoistic self becomes pre-eminent then *māyā* will conceal ultimate Reality and there will be ignorance of what is real.

It is *avidyā* and *māyā* that cause individuals to differentiate between this and that, usually between what they desire and what they dislike, for human beings are rarely neutral to their environment. All life presents to us the choices between dualities and we tend to make sense of the world by comparing one aspect of a dual relationship, such as happiness or goodness, with its opposite, sadness and evil. But since Brahman is the non-differentiated Reality that is *neti neti*, "not this, not this", and is equated with the *ātman*, then the real self, once realized, is also characterized by a non-differentiating view of the world. The distinctions between subject and object, between one person and another, between the dualities of life, vanish, and all is seen as the manifestation of Brahman in the universe. The *essence* that is Brahman is experienced in all things as the unifying and equating factor. All matter, all *prakṛti*, is characterized by dualities for in all existence we have opposites. But all opposites – all diversities – unite in Brahman and cease to be real, again, just like the centre point of a circle is equidistant to all points on its circumference; the centre is not any of them, though no point can exist without relation to it.

The opposite of ignorance, *avidyā*, is knowledge, *vidyā,* and it is that knowledge by which all other things are known which is the pursuit of the *Upaniṣadic* sages and which was to be found in the *ātman*. And the presence of the *ātman* in all suggests that Brahman can be known, not in the ordinary sense, but only through a higher and more intuitive knowledge. It is a "higher" knowledge (*parāvidyā*) in comparison to the "lower" knowledge that is knowledge we have about the world around us, or even knowledge of the *Vedas*. Higher knowledge is knowledge of the "clayness" that informs clay, as opposed to the effects that are produced from clay, it is knowledge of the *essence* of things and of Brahman as that essence. It is true intuitive wisdom and knowledge, *jñāna*. Acosmically, it is perfect knowledge that is beyond sense perception and any subject–object differentiation, cosmically it is the more articulated knowledge of the deeper aspects of life. Either way, it is wisdom, and the *Upaniṣads* present it as eternal wisdom that is self-valid, that runs through all manifest existence, informing all. It is not, then, personal wisdom, but the wisdom that belongs to the universe.

The means to ultimate Reality

From what has been said it is easy to see that knowledge, *jñāna*, is the key to liberation. And unlike the *Vedas* which are the *karmakāṇḍa* or ritual action portion of *śruti* literature, it is the *Upaniṣads* that are the *jñānakāṇḍa* or knowledge portion. The *chelas* who attached themselves to *gurus* for the purpose of acquiring knowledge were searching for a spiritual path of intuitive knowledge rather than knowledge of anything in the material world. But it was a difficult path, to be undertaken only by the most dedicated of pupils. Given the esoteric and secretive nature of the material in the *Upaniṣads*, there must have been very few who proceeded to the end. Those who were attracted to the path sat at the feet of their *gurus* to hear the Truth and, through a process of critical analysis and discussion, proceeded to a second stage of intellectual knowledge and conviction of what had been heard. But it is the *practical* realization of wisdom, the third stage, which is the goal, that is to say, the inner, meditative and experiential cognition of the *ātman* that is all important. These three stages represent a period of faith, of understanding and of Brahman-realization respectively.

Considering the intuitive nature of the knowledge that has to be acquired, it is meditation or *yoga* that provides the means. When the mind is pulled away from its attractions to the sense stimuli of the environment then it can become calm and still and receptive to the inner experience of direct knowledge that is independent of the senses. *Yoga* provides the techniques by which the mind and intellect can be stilled and made more receptive to the deeper kind of knowledge that is ultimate. Renunciation (*nyāsa*) was particularly important and was (and still is) epitomized in the fourth stage of life, *saṃnyāsa*. This stage stood in contrast to the path of ritual action of the earlier *Vedas* but did not necessarily mean a total world denial and cessation of activity. Chatterjee and Datta, among others, point out that the discipline of *yoga* and the principle of renunciation often encouraged the acquisition of positive traits that were in many ways world-affirming, for example the development of compassion and generosity.[51] Yet, though inferior to renunciation, the practice of austerities, *tapas*, was an important means of developing the spiritual at the expense of the physical. It should be remembered that it is non-attachment of the ego to the stimuli of the world that is the aim; this is denial of the self and not necessarily the denial of the world *per se*. It is detachment of the self as opposed to attachment of the self. Yet it is easier to control the self when it is withdrawn from the world than when it is bombarded by the sense stimuli of daily existence. But the insistence on the observation of the four *āśramas*, the four stages of life of student, householder, recluse and *saṃnyāsin*, suggests a general well-balanced view of both worldly and spiritual pursuits.

The Hindu *darśanas*

It is obvious from what has been said so far that there was an abundance of material in the *Veda* as a whole that was open to wide interpretation and analysis. The search for the answers to the fundamental questions about life, the nature of the self, causality, valid knowledge and ultimate Reality did not end, but continued in the various traditions and commentaries, and an enormous amount of philosophical inquiry was amassed. It was partly a need to systematize this material on the one hand, and the need to justify certain traditions on the other, that paved the way for the development of the six orthodox schools of philosophical thought in Hinduism. Much early material relating to this development is lost, but that which has survived has been incorporated in their respective *Sūtras*, the "threads" – an apt name for the philosophical tenets of each of the different philosophical traditions. Such *Sūtras* and their related commentaries attempted to put forward particular philosophical perspectives with a rationale and carefully formulated argumentation for the propositions contained in them. But, at the same time, they set out reasons why the argumentation of other traditions was erroneous. This seems to suggest that the development of the six schools of philosophical thought was contemporaneous, but, in fact, it was not.

The development of the six philosophical schools stands against a background of *Vedic* tradition that, to some extent, had been challenged by the atheism and rejection of the *Veda* by the heterodox school of Buddhism. This is not to say that the ritualism of the *Vedas* was broadly rejected – in point of fact it increased – but the philosophical justification of it was felt to be exigent for some traditions. *Dharma* and *karma* had become very important concepts by the time the schools of philosophy were systematized: *dharma* pertained to everything that was right in the universe, in society, in the life of an individual and in societal interchange; and *karma* to the just rewards or adversities for those who conformed to, or deviated from, *dharma* respectively. The correct performance of ritual was still believed to accrue good *karma* and an appropriate *dharma* that led one to life in heaven or a good rebirth. Thus we find a profound belief in the principles of cause and effect to be operative in the Hindu psyche. All life was believed to be governed by this cause–effect law of *karma*, which operated impersonally in the universe and which was mainly irrevocable. The principle raises an important question. If everything that happens to an individual does so as a result of past actions of that individual, of what use or relevance is a divine being in a world that operates purely on such an irrevocable cause–result process? If my actions *now* determine what will happen to me in the future, either in this life or some future, distant life, then – assuming all others in life are subject to the same law of cause and effect – is there any need to posit an outside Source that underpins the process? Is a deity necessary? This is a question that will be answered by the schools of philosophical thought.

The Hindu systems of philosophy should also be seen against a rising devotion to a personal deity. This is evidenced in both Śaivism, the worship of Śiva as the supreme God, and also in Vaiṣṇavism with the worship of Viṣṇu. The concept of a personal supreme deity was one that emerged in the later principal *Upaniṣads* and was to take hold of the Hindu mind in a very profound way. The concept of *bhakti* or "loving-devotion" was an ecstatic outpouring of devotional love to the divine that transcended the personal ego – a process of utter surrender to God. An intense theism is thus also to be seen as the background to the rise of the orthodox systems of philosophy.

Just as the whole of the *Veda* was informed by a long period of oral tradition, so the different schools of Hindu philosophy began with oral teachings passed down through the generations of a variety of associated schools until the teachings were eventually crystallized and systematized in *Sūtras* of one main school. Each school of thought, then, had its own *Sūtras* text associated with a particular compiler, but had, preceding it, a long history. And because of this long oral tradition, only the main features of the teachings were committed to writing, for it was accepted that disciples of the various schools would have been conversant with much of the material – a bit like teaching points without the teacher's "asides" and explanations. The *Sūtras* consist, then, of aphorisms, brief statements that epitomize the main tenets of the school. Radhakrishnan summarized the prescribed rules for them: "They are intended to be as short as possible, free from doubt, able to bring out the essential meaning and put an end to many doubts; and they must not contain anything superfluous or erroneous. They try to avoid all unnecessary repetition and employ great economy of words."[52] As Radhakrishnan pointed out, the *Sūtras* are concise summaries of the ideas of many thinkers over many years, so that their precise origins are difficult to ascertain.[53] One important work is the *Brahmasūtras* of *Badārāyaṇa*, dated to the last few centuries BCE or somewhere in the first half of the first century CE. It outlined the fundamental teachings of the early *Upaniṣads* and was particularly important to the school of Vedānta. Yet the aphoristic nature of this, as other *Sūtras*, itself gave rise to further very divergent, interpretative material and necessitated, like all *Sūtras*, efficient commentaries. What emerged were commentaries on commentaries on commentaries, so that the literature of any one school became very complex and still has its interpreters to the present day. There were also *kārikās*, which were treatises written independently and which attempted to put forward the main points of a philosophical system. On these, too, and on other extraneous literature, commentaries were compiled.

But from all the attempts to systematize the *Veda* and present a coherent perspective of Reality, six philosophical schools emerged, providing six different views. Theos Bernard neatly points out that: "According to Indian tradition there is only one Ultimate Reality, but there are six fundamental interpretations of that Reality."[54] It is a point that may seem initially surprising for, after all, Reality should be Truth, and Truth should not be open to a variety of meanings. But Indian philosophy, being an attempt to grasp Reality and Truth that are *ultimate*, spends time and effort in the debate of it. So while this book will attempt to isolate the different philosophical perspectives of Reality held by the different schools, it is important to understand the *darśanas* as interlinking dialogues about the best possible methods of ascertaining what it is that can be real.

The six schools of philosophy are also called the six *systems* of philosophy or the six *Brahmanical* systems (because they are based on the priestly, *Vedic* traditions), or the six "insights" or "views", called *darśanas*, or *ṣaddarśana* "six views". This last term comes from the Sanskrit root *dṛś* "to see", and is the equivalent of the word "philosophy". The six *darśanas* are Mīmāṃsā, Vaiśeṣika, Nyāya, Sāṃkhya, Yoga, and Vedānta, and each presents its "view" or "vision of the Truth", its *darśana*. Each school is concerned with the perception of Truth, the vision and view of what is real, and each sets out the means by which we can come to know what is real, in terms of both ordinary and spiritual perception.

Exactly when the systems were first in currency is impossible to determine, but it is certain that they did not appear directly following the *Vedic* period. However, Dasgupta suggested the earliest beginnings as 600 BCE.[55] Because the oral traditions predate the literary ones it is difficult to place the chronology between the systems exactly. Some may have had their origins before the advent of the Buddha, others later, it is impossible to say. But because of their acceptance and origin in the priestly traditions of the *Veda* they are commonly referred to as the *āstika* systems, the "it is", orthodox systems, as opposed to the *nāstika*, "it is not", heterodox systems that totally reject *Vedic* authority.

The style of the material of the systems is very similar, most being characterized by the aphoristic style noted above, and all, therefore, are difficult to understand without a commentary. Each *darśana* believed that it was interpreting the doctrines of the *Veda* in the correct way, and was anxious to endorse its view by showing the erroneous logic of other schools. Given the lack of systematic philosophy in the *Upaniṣads* it was easy for each school to advance or suppress ideas there in order to put forward its own particular perspective. Moreover, the task of refuting the theories of other schools often caused the development of some aspect or other in quite a new way. Each school had to defend its position logically against the assertions of the others but in a way that did no violence to the past traditions of its own school. There were, however, significant changes that took place in the thought of each school over the centuries, but these were regarded as modifications rather than radical deviations. The resulting traditions, therefore, came into being through the most intricate of methods, rather like travelling to a far point through all the lanes and footpaths of the distance between, so that there is no direct route that we can highlight.

Thus, to present either a history of them or a neat dissection of ideas is not only difficult, but impossible.

The six systems have much in common, despite different views of reality. To begin with they each take on board the need of humankind to transcend the transience and suffering of life. They are concerned to find the purpose and meaning of human life and to direct the steps of their disciples to its ultimate goal. Their perspectives of reality will differ: some will be positivist and empirical, accepting a common sense realism and pluralism about the world we perceive. Others will deny the reality of the world in some way, pressing for a transcending of the phenomenal world to a higher and intuited Reality. But they are all united in saying that the purpose of life is to aim for ultimate Truth and knowledge and that the world that we ordinarily observe obscures these. Reaching out for ultimate Truth allows the self to be experienced in its true light and the liberated state to be realized. All the schools agree that this will necessitate a changed world-view, but that personal morality underpins all attempts to know the Self. The degree to which each school recommends withdrawal or involvement in the world will, however, differ considerably.

Hindu philosophy has what Chatterjee and Datta describe as an "unflinching devotion to the search for truth"[56] – a devotion that lies at the heart of each of the systems. The real, as will be seen, was something differently depicted by each of the schools, but they were united in agreeing that there was something ultimately real that underpinned a world of change. The search for true knowledge was critical to their thinking, for only knowledge of the true nature of life and matter could enable liberation of the self. So the search for liberation as the ultimate goal of all life is a common goal, too, even if it is differently conceived of. All six systems accept the law of *karma*, the law of cause and effect and its implications for the morality of human beings, and the whole nature of causality was one with which they wrestled. There was also a common belief in reincarnation amongst the systems, so that the evolution of the soul through countless lives to the point of liberation was the goal of all of them. The fourfold system of class was also accepted, as, too, with some modifications, the four life stages of student, householder, recluse and mendicant.

Common to all of the schools was the issue of ignorance as opposed to knowledge, the former being the reason why the human being was held to the cycle of reincarnation and its concomitant sufferings in countless lives. The presentation of the nature of, and means to, knowledge of Reality as the way to overcome this was the *raison d'être* of the schools. The realization of this knowledge, moreover, served to link the microcosmic world of the human being with the macrocosm at large. This kind of cosmic view is essential to most Indian thought and to the perspectives of reality that it proposes.

Most of the schools begin their basic investigation into the nature and means of *valid knowledge*, what are called *pramāṇas*. Such valid knowledge may be quite realist and logical, but it also serves to investigate the kinds of knowledge that are less obvious, but that can be regarded as reliable. The number of *pramāṇas* which the systems accept varies from one school to another, but each is keen to defend the premises on which acceptance of their own is based, at the same time putting forward the reasons why they reject those of other schools. Some *pramāṇas* are common to all schools. One *pramāṇa* that will be taken up in the discussion of the schools that follows is that of *testimony* as a valid and separate means of knowledge. And since the whole of the *Veda* is the basis for the speculations of the systems, the testimony of it as valid knowledge will be an important issue for each *darśana.*

The philosophical systems of Hinduism are a complex phenomenon, but no student of Hinduism can really come to grips with the religion in all its diversity without examining this philosophical core that has informed so much of Hinduism today. While few of the schools have survived to modern times, their influence has been considerable in developing particular aspects of the Hindu religion. Mīmāṃsā, for example, has influenced the Indian legal system considerably, while the school of Vedānta thrives today in many tributaries in all parts of the globe.

3
Pūrva Mīmāṃsā

Background to the school

While the school of Pūrva Mīmāṃsā no longer exists, its legacy to India is considerable. For it is the *darśana* of Pūrva Mīmāṃsā that has provided the interpretation of Hindu scriptures in their present contexts of Hindu life, and the school was important enough to influence the Hindu legal system even today. Thus, the ritual and ceremonial life of the Hindu, as well as moral conduct, are rooted in this particular school and, to quote Bernard, "Mīmāṃsā breathes life into the very super-structure of Indian culture."[1] Even under British rule the laws governing such legal aspects as property, inheritance and adoption were formulated by the old Mīmāṃsā regulations. Keith describes the school as "an investigation of texts in order to evolve an orderly system for their interpretation as a harmonious whole",[2] and while this refers to *religious* texts, the system was so prestigious that skill in Mīmāṃsā was almost essential for skill in civil law texts. Civil law itself thus remained heavily influenced by the Mīmāṃsā analysis of religious injunctions. It is Mīmāṃsā that has laid down just how *Vedic* duties are to be performed, with much explanatory rationale for them.

Like the Vedānta schools that developed from it, Pūrva Mīmāṃsā is deeply rooted in the *Vedic śruti* tradition and is thus highly orthodox. But whereas Vedānta is concerned with *Upaniṣadic* thought – as its name suggests – Mīmāṃsā is based on the earlier *Vedas* and *Brāhmaṇas*, and was concerned to establish rules pertaining to their interpretation, and explanations for their inconsistencies. Such characteristics owe much to the kinds of pressures placed on orthodox Hinduism by the non-orthodox system of Buddhism with its rejection of basic tenets of Hinduism, particularly its *śruti* tradition, as well as by rising devotional belief and practice associated with *bhakti*. Given its ritualistic nature, Mīmāṃsa has the least philosophical speculation, but it has enough to class it as a *darśana*. Although it confines its philosophy to ritual practice as opposed to the more metaphysical speculations about God and the universe, its epistemology, or theory of knowledge, is better developed.

The name Mīmāṃsā means "investigation", coming from a Sanskrit root *man* "to investigate, think, consider, examine", and it is the texts of the *Veda* that are the object of such investigation, especially those related to ritual practice. The term can also mean "reflection", or "revered thought",[3] and this is reminiscent of its reverence of *Vedic* truths, as much as its aim of reflection on them. But it is especially the *discussion* and *authentication* of particular points of practices as opposed to others that characterize the Mīmāṃsā school. It was an approach necessitated by the discrepancies between *Vedic Saṃhitās* and the commentaries on them – their associated *Brāhmaṇas*. The term Mīmāṃsā covers both the early or *pūrva* school as well as the latter or *uttara* school that is known as Vedānta. They are so called because the Pūrva Mīmāṃsā bases its inquiry on the earlier *śruti* texts of the *Vedas* and the *Brāhmaṇas*, while the Uttara Mīmāṃsā bases its inquiry on the *Upaniṣads* of the *Vedānta*. Pūrva Mīmāṃsā is therefore concerned with ritual action, *karman*, and Uttara Mīmāṃsā with knowledge, *jñāna*, exploring the *karmakāṇḍa* and *jñānakāṇḍa*, ritual and knowledge portions of the *śruti* texts respectively. It has become common practice to refer to the school of Pūrva Mīmāṃsā as simply Mīmāṃsā, and the school of Uttara Mīmāṃsā as Vedānta, and this practice will be adopted in the pages that follow. The Pūrva Mīmāṃsā school is also sometimes called the Dharma Mīmāṃsā because of its inquiry into *Vedic* truth as *dharma* and as ultimately right. It is also known as Karma Mīmāṃsā because of its emphasis on ritual action.

The origins of this school are obscure. Clooney places its origins in the formation of *Vedic* texts and rituals dating as far back as 1000 BCE, and to the succeeding centuries when doubtful material in the texts needed investigation.[4] But certainly by the early centuries BCE the validity of sacrificial ritual had come into question both from the challenge of Buddhism and from that of wandering *śramaṇas*, the more ascetic and philosophically rather than ritually minded of the priestly class.[5] To counteract this challenge, many different groups grew up dedicated to demonstrating the valid nature of the *Vedic* texts, and to formulating rules for their interpretation. Mīmāṃsā has its origins here. Such different groups came to be regarded as specific schools, and there must have been a number of these, but it is only the materials of one of these early schools that have come down to us, the school associated with Jaimini. Two major schools emerged in later years, one led by Kumārila Bhaṭṭa and the other by Prabhākara, both probably dated to the seventh century CE. Kumārila and Prabhākara had many views in common, but they also disagreed on fundamental points, enough to divide Pūrva Mīmāṃsā into two quite distinct schools. Together, however, they constitute the major pillars of this particular *darśana*, Mīmāṃsā.[6] Strictly speaking, however, Mīmāṃsā refers to a whole body of doctrines.

The primary aim of Mīmāṃsā was concerned with the validity of the *Veda*: first, to establish the validity of the injunctions of the *Veda* as the source of right action or *dharma* and, second, to establish the validity of the *Veda* as eternal with no human or divine author. This was mainly done by verifying the fundamental reality of meaning – the idea behind the words of the *Veda* – and by refuting any arguments against the claim that the *Veda* was infallible. An important perspective emerging from such approaches was establishing the self-validity of all knowledge. At the same time it was important to set out philosophical justification for the words contained in the *Veda* and to formulate principles by which they could be interpreted. Such was its diligence in this last aspect that the school accumulated over a thousand rules for interpretation.

Main proponents and commentators

While not the founder of Mīmāṃsā, Jaimini's *Mīmāṃsāsūtras* provides the foundation of our knowledge of the school or, rather, the main surviving strand. The major commentary, *bhāṣya*, on Jaimini's *Sūtras* was written by Śabara, after whom, and on whose work, there were many commentators: Kumārila Bhaṭṭa and Prabhākara are the most important. Jaimini made a compilation of the traditional teachings, basing his work on the earlier *Veda*. Here he parted company from his teacher Bādarāyaṇa who, as one who played a comparable role for the Uttara Mīmāṃsā, the Vedānta school, was more concerned with *Upaniṣadic* thought. We know little about Jaimini, not even when he lived – anything from 400 BCE to 200 CE is possible. However, it seems likely that he was motivated to defend the *Veda* against Buddhist opponents, and that might suppose a date some centuries after the Buddha's' demise. To search for an exact date is to act in vain, and speculation results in very wide possibilities.

As noted earlier, a *sūtra* is literally a "thread", the thread that weaves through things to hold them together. The *Sūtras* of all the schools, then, have the purpose of weaving together the tenets of their particular traditions. Each composite text of *sūtras* consists of short statements, aphorisms; Jaimini's work has 2,700 of these. These *sūtras*, which presuppose a lengthy previous tradition, are divided into twelve chapters (*adhyāyas*), most of which are further divided into four parts (*pādas*), each with further subdivisions. Nine hundred topics (*adhikaraṇas*) are discussed in these twelve chapters. Everything is laid out very logically, and in the first chapter Jaimini tells us that his purpose is to inquire into the nature of *dharma*, its cause, what is valid knowledge, and the validity of the knowledge in the *Veda*. The remaining sections are concerned with *dharmic* actions – *Vedic* injunctions; the differences between ritual actions, and the relative predominance or subservience of them; the motive behind ritual actions; their sequence; those who are entitled to perform them; the relations between actions; and so on. In short, *karman*, ritual action, is the entire focus of Jaimini's *Sūtras*. While this compilation of *sūtras*, or aphorisms, is the primary text of the school, there is also an abundance of other material. Jaimini's work, in common with other *Sūtras*, is barely intelligible without a commentary and the major commentary (though not the earliest one) on the *Mīmāṃsāsūtras* of Jaimini, is known as the *Śabarabhāṣya*, and was composed by Śabara. It is he who introduced a more concentrated philosophical character to Mīmāṃsā – something lacking in the approach of Jaimini. Again, it is difficult to date the work: a date somewhere in the first century BCE is suggested by some,[7] though others suggest the second or third century CE,[8] or even later.[9] Nothing is known of Śabara's life that might assist in dating him. Both Jaimini's *Sūtras* and the detailed *Bhāṣya* of Śabara aim to validate *Vedic* injunctions for ritualistic practices. Such practices were the only means of *dharma*.

The second most important school – at least in the sense that its teachings are known to us – was founded by Kumārila Bhaṭṭa sometime during the seventh century CE. He was probably an older contemporary of the Vedānta philosopher Śaṃkara. Some consider – and tradition accepts it – that Kumārila was the teacher of the main proponent of the other school, Prabhākara, but this is by no means certain. Indeed, the Prabhākara school may be, as Hiriyanna puts it, "nearer in spirit" to original Mīmāṃsā than the Bhaṭṭa school, and therefore earlier.[10] Kumārila wrote his own commentary on Jaimini's *Mīmāṃsāsūtras* as well as on the *Bhāṣya* of Śabara. His school, usually called the Bhaṭṭa school of Mīmāṃsā, is generally regarded as the more important of these two later schools, Prabhāraka presenting more difficult and controversial points.[11] Bhatt comments that "Kumārila appeared at the right moment as the savior of the Vedic religion and it is in this capacity that he will ever be remembered".[12] The "right moment" was at a time when Buddhism itself had produced outstanding thinkers and was challenging the very roots of *Vedic* ritual and thought. Kumārila had an unusually excellent knowledge of Buddhism itself, and was well placed to refute its ideologies. His outstanding works were the *Ślokavārtika*, *Tantravārtika* and *Ṭupṭīka*, which are commentaries on Śabara's *Bhāṣya*.

Prabhākara also wrote a commentary (called the *Bṛhatī*) on the *Bhāṣya* of Śabara but, while he takes no notice of anything that Kumārila has written about it, Kumārila, on the other hand, seems to take on board some of the ideas of Prabhākara.[13] This, together with his particular style of writing, might suggest that Prabhākara preceded Kumārila.[14] With the schools of Kumārila and Prabhākara – the two greatest exponents of Mīmāṃsā – any innovative philosophy in the Mīmāṃsā *darśana* ceases. But their time, as Bhatt puts it, "was an age of the most vigorous intellectual activity and philosophical fertility, in which Mīmāṃsā thought touched the loftiest heights in critical and speculative philosophy".[15]

General features of the school

In general, the doctrines of Mīmāṃsā seem to owe some debt to the Nyāya and Vaiśeṣika schools, accepting some of their doctrines while rejecting others. However, Mīmāṃsā is a system of philosophy that is atheistic and stands alone amongst the *darśanas* in rejecting any cycles of creation, evolution and dissolution of the world. Because it accepts that the *Veda* is eternal, having itself no author, but being *self-valid*, there cannot be a dissolution of the world when the *Veda* does not exist until the world's recreation. But to believe in the self-validity of the *Veda* means that Mīmāṃsā has to set about proving the self-validity of all knowledge and the eternal nature of words and their meanings. It also must set out to prove that *dharma* can only result from the stipulations of the *Veda*. The school is concerned mainly with ritualistic practice rather than with the hymns of the *Vedas*, and it is with the *Brāhmaṇas*, which deal so much with the elaborations and explanations of ritual, that Mīmāṃsā is mainly occupied.

It is the injunctions, or *vidhi*, of the *Veda* that form the basis of *dharma*, along with prohibitions (*niṣedha*). Hymns, names that define, and passages that explain, support these injunctions and prohibitions. And all are believed to be eternal Truths that are beyond empirical evidence for, because the *Veda* is eternal and authorless, no human error or experience can be incorporated in it. Indeed, Mīmāṃsā believed that the *Veda* contained knowledge that reached beyond normal sense experience: it is thus *supersensuous*. Hence it is self-valid, for its eternal knowledge transcends human reason and experience and any divine creation and preservation. Thus, the injunctions of the *Veda* are to be taken literally and to be accepted as what is right, *dharma*. This is not to say that the *Veda* cannot deal with ordinary experience, because it does. In such a case, the material could be interpreted more liberally than the ritual injunctions. Any actual contradictions in the *Veda*, Mīmāṃsā believed, were only apparent and merely needed correct interpretation. The practical outcome of this eternal and self-valid nature of the *Veda* was that certain actions were believed to be unconditionally obligatory as eternally right, and failure to observe them would result in sin. Obligatory *karmas* (summarized below), along with abstinence from prohibited actions, are the means to liberation. Other actions were optional.

- *Nityakarmas* actions that must be performed daily.
- *Naimittikarmas* actions that must be performed at auspicious times.
- *Kāmyakarmas* actions that are optional.
- *Pratiṣiddhakarmas* actions that are prohibited.

Dharma

Jaimini began his *Sūtras* with an inquiry as to the nature of *dharma*, which he defined as *Vedic* injunction. He followed his definition with statements concerning the *means* by which knowledge of it is obtained. These means consisted of conforming to the obligatory injunctions and prohibitions of the *Veda*. Ritualistic duty was essential because the *Veda* was believed to be the only eternal truth. It was also a means to ensure positive results through its practice. In short, ritualistic duty is *dharmic* and promotes *dharma*, so *dharma* is correct ritual action and, more particularly, the concomitant results of it. Clooney notes the *active* and *purposeful* nature of this elusive concept of *dharma* in Jaimini's *Sūtras*. He notes that all things, texts, words, actions, have their own particular *dharma* in the context of *Vedic* ritual.[16] *Dharma*, he writes, "indicates the functional description of a sacrificial element. To know the *dharma* of some element is to know what the element does, what is done to it, what it is related to, when it appears in the sacrifice and when it leaves it".[17] *Dharma* is also the interrelation of ritual elements and their necessary effects.

Dharma, however, is to be known only from the *Veda* and is extraneous to sense perception. While we can perceive the nature and characteristics of something, its *dharma* cannot be known. The *Veda* alone attests to *dharma*. Gaṇgānātha Jhā defines it succinctly thus in his commentary on the opening aphorisms of Jaimini's work:

> Dharma can be defined as that desirable thing which is mentioned or laid down by Vedic injunctions; that is to say, that which the Vedic injunction lays down as leading to a desirable end is Dharma; and from this it also follows that the Vedic Injunction is the sole means of knowing Dharma.[18]

Everything that is right or wrong can only be known from the yardstick of *Vedic* injunctions. *Dharma* was not only obedience to the *Veda* in correct ritual practice, but was synonymous with the term "religion". Even today, Hinduism lacks a distinct word for religion but will depict it as *dharma*. Coming from the root *dhar*, "to preserve", *dharma* is duty, or what is right; it is, therefore, the preservation of norms of daily, societal, class and universal existence in the widest sense, and the duty of preserving and obeying *Vedic* injunctions in the Mīmāṃsā sense. Thus, *Vedic dharma* is, as Halbfass notes, "completely different from a universal ethical code. It has as its center the Vedic ritual prescriptions or injunctions (*vidhi*, *codanā*), rules which apply to those who are within the Aryan order of 'castes' (*varṇa*)[19] and 'stages of life' (*āśrama*) and which are by definition trans-empirical and not susceptible to rationalization and universalization".[20] The religious and spiritual person, then, is the one who can obey the commands of the *Vedas* in terms of correct ritual practices. And the outcome, *dharma*, is what leads to the appropriate happiness or suffering in accordance with the extent the injunctions have been obeyed and the sacrificial ritual maintained. *Dharma*, then, encompasses its own means as ritual action, and its appropriate positive outcomes.

The opposite of *dharma* is *adharma*. Both are forces, and not qualities of the self, yet it is the self that reaps either. *Adharma*, for Mīmāṃsā, would result from neglect of obligatory *Vedic* injunctions and prohibitions. Such neglect would inevitably cause the suffering that is concomitant with *adharma*. To Kumārila the very fact of obeying *Vedic* rules was itself moral action that would reap its appropriate rewards or, for disobedience, its appropriate punishments. And such rewards, or the avoiding of punishments, would have been the motivating factors for moral behaviour and thorough conformity to *Vedic* prescription. Prabhākara, on the other hand, was keen to state that, although the operation of *dharma* could bring happiness or sadness, heaven or hell, good should be done, and *Vedic* commands obeyed, for the sake of good or duty itself, not for the sake of rewards. The Prabhākara school is thus less goal-orientated and incorporates greater disinterestedness of motive in observation of *Vedic* command. It is closer to the true nature of the *karmamārga* path here in its aim of action without ego-involvement.

The emphasis on *dharma* is all the more important when it is remembered that Mīmāṃsā does not have any concept of a God who transcends and controls the universe. *Dharma* becomes the all-important means that connects an action to its appropriate pleasant or unpleasant result, and therefore serves to explain the changes that we perceive in all life. And, unlike the other orthodox schools, the concept of *mokṣa* was not given credence in early Mīmāṃsā thought; *dharma* was conceived of as the ultimate end of life, as much as being the proximate goal of life. The idea of *mokṣa* – that is to say the kind of liberation of the self that might obliterate ego and self identity as we understand them, and that brings partial or complete identity with divinity – was alien to early Mīmāṃsā thought. For *dharma* could bring one to the delights of heaven as reward for the correct and dutiful observation of *Vedic* injunctions, and this was the goal of earlier thought. The more philosophical concept of *mokṣa* was not taken on board by the school until later.

The Mīmāṃsā school accepts that there are several means of knowledge (*pramāṇas*), but though they are valid in themselves they are inadequate means of establishing knowledge of *dharma*; only the *Veda* can do this because it deals with Truths that are eternal and beyond ordinary means of establishing valid knowledge. *Dharma* can *only* be realized through obedience to *Vedic* injunctions.

Reality: the Mīmāṃsā view of the world

Mīmāṃsā philosophy is pluralist, realist and materialist. Being pluralist it accepts that there is a plurality of separate phenomena that compose the world, and this includes individual selves. There is no sense at all of a unity to existence and, being mainly atheist, there is no divine God or Absolute to act as a unifying agent. Variety, then, is accepted in the universe, so each individual is different from the next, as are their souls that survive the body at death. There is variety, too, in the countless particles that are believed to make up material existence. Mīmāṃsā, then, has a realistic view of the world, assigning reality to the independent objects that we perceive. Kumārila said: "The idea that Cognitions have a real basis in the external world must be true, - because it is an idea that is never sublated, - just as the idea of Dreams being false is never sublated."[21] Such realism is essential to its theory of knowledge. Since one of its means of valid knowledge is the perception of real objects, and the knower, in order to know, must perceive these objects, realism is essential for the interrelation of subject and object and the knowledge or cognition that occurs in relation to the two. Such realism also accepts that the objects of knowledge – the phenomena of the world – exist independently of the knower. So if things exist independently of a knower, they exist *really*, and when the knower, who is also real, perceives them, he or she does so *really*: this is the simplest form of validity of knowledge common to realist philosophy. It is also a thoroughly *materialist* view of reality. Nevertheless, the Mīmāṃsā school is not *empiricist*, that is to say, it cannot be regarded as accepting that there is a means of testing, beyond doubt, the validity of all knowledge. Primarily, it is because the *Veda* is supersensuous that such non-empiricism must obtain. The idea of *dharma* is also non-empirical as, also that of *apūrva*, a concept to which I shall return below.

Yet, as Keith pointed out: "There is nothing to show that the question of the reality of the world had ever occurred to the framers of the *Mīmāṃsā Sūtra*".[22] It was not until the time of Śabara that articulated perspectives of reality were necessary in the face of the more widespread Buddhist denial of anything permanent in, or out of, existence. Kumārila, especially, was keen to refute the Buddhist idealist view of the non-reality of all objects. The Buddhist view is that waking experiences are as unreal as dreams because both are characterized by the same kind of cognitions. But Kumārila argued that dream cognitions are shown to be false by waking experience. However, there is nothing that eventually contradicts most of our experiences when we are awake. And one of the criteria for valid knowledge in Mīmāṃsā is that it should not be contradicted by any subsequent knowledge. If, then, nothing contradicts the fact that we all find the world real, and accord to all things an external and independent reality from ourselves, then pluralistic realism must obtain.[23]

Padārthas: categories of reality

All the philosophical schools seek to discover the basic *categories* that make up reality. It is the school of Vaiśeṣika that has the most highly developed atomic division of categories, and the Mīmāṃsā divisions owe much to this school. Kumārila accepted five such categories, and Prabhākara eight, though Prabhākara does not deal with them systematically. Categories common to them both are:

- substance *dravya*
- quality *guṇa*

- action/motion *karma*
- generality *sāmānya*

PRABHĀKARA ALONE ACCEPTS:

- inherence *paratantratā*
- potency/power *śakti*
- similarity *sādṛśya*
- number *saṃkhya*

AND KUMĀRILA ALONE ACCEPTS:

- non-existence *abhāva*

Potency, similarity and number are not independent categories according to Kumārila. Rather, he considers the three of them to be qualities. He keeps close to the Nyāya-Vaiśeṣika acceptance of non-existence as a separate category. But both reject the Nyāya-Vaiśeṣika category of particularity.

Like many of the schools, Mīmāṃsā accepts that there are basic *substances* called *dravyas* that underpin all existence. These *dravyas* are permanent and eternal and, just like clay is the basic substance from which clay things are made, so *dravyas* are the basic elemental substances from which all things emerge. While the end products of such *dravyas* are subject to change and impermanence, the *dravyas* themselves are permanent, so the same identity (of clay, for example) exists in different forms (in pots, saucers, ornaments etc.). The different *dravyas*, however, are not themselves unified, and so the Mīmāṃsā school retains its pluralistic outlook. But just as a child makes different things with plasticene, but the plasticene is always the basic substance, so the *dravyas* are expressed in the variety and change of the universe and yet are always the same – the same identity in different things.

A substance is that which is characterized by qualities. Prabhākara accepted nine substances – earth, water, air, fire, ether, *ātman*, mind, time and space. Kumārila added two more – darkness and sound. Earth, fire, water and air have the qualities of colour and touch, and are associated with the senses of sight and touch, so these substances are capable of being perceived via the senses. The other substances are imperceptible and, therefore, can only be inferred. Kumārila adds darkness as a substance because of its qualities of blueness and motion.

Prabhākara accepted seventeen *qualities* – colour, taste, smell, touch, number (which is also a separate category for Prabhākara, but only a quality for Kumārila), dimensioń, individuality (for eternal qualities only, but Kumārila accepted individuality for non-eternal qualities also), duality, conjunction, disjunction, priority and posteriority (both to do with space and time), pleasure, pain, desire, aversion, effort. Kumārila added gravity, fluidity, viscidity, cognition, impression (velocity, elasticity and mental impression), manifestation, tone, and potency.

As far as *action* or *motion* is concerned, Kumārila believed it to be perceptible. However, Prabhākara believed motion itself is imperceptible, and that it can only be inferred. This is because motion cannot belong to what moves. Things come together (conjunction) and apart (disjunction), but movement cannot itself belong to objects.

Generality is perceptible, real and eternal. We can perceive generality, like the "tree-ness" of trees, or the "cow-ness" of cows. Moreover, the class "cows" does not cease to exist when an individual cow does. For Prabhākara such class generality *inheres* in the individual thing, and *inherence* is a separate category. But Kumārila denied that this was possible. Substance, quality and action are all accepted as generalities by Kumārila, but Prabhākara only accepts the generality of substance – a substance-ness. Prabhākara added *similarity* as a category because we seem to prove its existence in our experience in life. It is also not a substance, quality or action, though it exists in them.

Kumārila's category of *non-existence* was essential for his theories of the relation between cause and effect. This can be seen in the four kinds of non-existence that he posited:

- negation — like the non-existence of curd in milk
- destruction — like the non-existence of milk in curd
- mutual — like the non-existence of a horse in a cow or a cow in a horse
- absolute — like the non-existence of the horns on a hare.

In perceiving the ground without an expected jar on it we come to *know* that a jar is not there. Its non-existence *there* is a separate reality for Kumārila. This was not, to Kumārila, a case of inference: we do not *infer* the jar isn't there, we cognize the negation of it. In short, when we know we are not perceiving something, the knowledge is real.

The combining of elemental particles and qualities is regulated by the totally autonomous law of *karma*, cause and effect. There is no outside agent like a divine being who combines the basic components of the universe together in a specific way, either to cause the universe or to dissolve it. And by particles, the Mīmāṃsakas did not mean *invisible* particles, but visible ones like the tiny specks we see in rays of sunshine. These particles, according to Kumārila, were of the distinct and independent elements of earth, fire, water and air.[24]

Epistemology

Mīmāṃsā claims that *all* knowledge, all cognition, is valid. It is the synonymy between knowledge and cognition that serves to make this so. At any point in time when we claim we *know* something, we consider knowledge to have taken place, and to be correct, to be valid – even if, at a later point, we may find that we are wrong. So cognitions occur, even if they are later proved incorrect. And when we know something, we generally act on that information, so it is often the testing of that knowledge in practice that ascertains whether it is correct or not. Thus, all knowledge when it occurs is valid, but it may become invalid later when it is proved wrong in some way. Self-validity of knowledge is called *svataḥprāmāṇya*. But valid knowledge for the Mīmāṃsaka is essentially *apprehension* (*anubhūti*). That is to say, one must *apprehend* knowledge in an *immediate* sense, through the senses. Memory, therefore, is discounted as valid knowledge, because it would be knowledge based on the impressions left by a previous, and not immediate, knowledge. When memory or remembrance is used we don't apprehend things directly and have to rely on *indirect* means and impressions. This does not deny the value of remembered knowledge, it simply denies its self-validity and its validity as a means of true knowledge. To a certain extent, this is problematic, for it suggests – as a Buddhist might claim – that what you know, once the moment has passed, is no longer valid because you have to recall it from memory!

To the Mīmāṃsāka, then, valid knowledge must also be *new* knowledge, since old knowledge is merely reliant on memory. There needs, then, to be an element of novelty in the knowledge we acquire in order for it to be valid, and we should not have apprehended the object before. Kumārila insisted that it would have to be presupposed that the sense organs that apprehend knowledge are intact or, where other means of apprehension of knowledge are used, that they are valid means. Knowledge arises when we come into contact with the objects of the world, and it *has* to occur. If it is wrong, then there is some fault in the means and conditions by which we gained that knowledge, or there may be contradiction with some other knowledge. But at the time of cognition it is believed to be valid. Here, then, is a very realistic view of knowledge, which maintains a pluralistic view of the world in that different cognitions are all regarded as true.

Thus the conditions that produce knowledge provide, at the same time, the validity of knowledge, so that the validity of knowledge is not dependent on anything extraneous to its immediate apprehension; it is intrinsic to apprehension. We automatically know that something is true, and believe so, when we say we know it. So valid knowledge presupposes the interrelation of a subject and an object and is indirectly inferred from that interrelation. It cannot exist independently outside that interrelation. Knowledge of validity and validity of knowledge are simultaneous. In some ways it would be difficult to argue that knowledge is not intrinsically valid, because to do so, it would have to be claimed that it has to be verified by another, second knowledge. But that, too, would not have intrinsic validity and would need a third knowledge, and so on *ad infinitum* – a position of infinite regress. This would suggest that *no* knowledge at all could be valid. In other words, we cannot validate knowledge unless it is self-valid. The premise of the self-validity of all knowledge will be essential to the Mīmāṃsā school in relation to proving the validity of the *Veda*. Thus, Dasgupta aptly stated that this self-validity of knowledge "forms the cornerstone on which the whole structure of the Mīmāṃsā philosophy is based".[25]

From what has been said it would have to be claimed that knowledge is imperceptible and supersensuous (bearing in mind that Mīmāṃsā rejects memory as valid). Śabara's view of knowledge was succinct. Knowledge is momentary and cannot know itself. The object of knowledge must be beyond it. In the process of knowledge the form of an object is cognized first, and this is followed by knowledge of the knowledge, so to speak. Such knowledge has to be presumed. Kumārila and Prabhākara differed in their views of the process by which valid cognitions occur and, thus, how they can be known. Kumārila believed firmly that knowledge cannot be perceived and that it is an aspect of the self. It is also a process and an action, and can be *inferred* in the process and act of apprehending an object. Sharma puts this neatly when he says: "It is the act of the self by which it knows an object and it is inferred by the fact that an object has become 'known' by the self. The cognitive act is inferred from the cognizedness of the object."[26] Knowledge is inferred from the act of knowing and is the proof of that act having taken place. It is proof of interaction between the self and the object of perception. In this case, a change has taken place in the knower, the subject, in that knowledge is inferred, and the object is *made manifest* in the process of cognition, the object being the result in the process of knowledge. The change that has come about makes the process of knowledge an action, a movement, an active process. There is an interrelation between subject and object in the process of that knowledge, something that affects the subject *and* the object that is known, because the object is illuminated. The object is not necessarily changed by that interrelation with the subject, but the fact that it is apprehended suggests to the Mīmāṃsaka that it *is* affected.

Kumārila saw the activity of knowledge as a *four-way* process involving the knower (*jñātā*), the object of knowledge (*jñeya*), an instrument of knowledge (*jñānakaraṇa*), and the resultant knowledge of the object, the cognition (*jñātatā*). The activity of knowledge is sometimes likened to the cooking of rice – the cook as the agent, the rice as the object, the heat as the instrument, and the soft rice as the result. This example makes it easier to see that there is a manifestation in the object, the result, that is as intrinsic to the process of knowledge as the self that cognizes it. The cognition, according to Kumārila, is inferred from the particular interaction of subject and object, and the interaction and relationship of subject and object are also inferred by the presence of the cognition. But the cognition, the knowledge, is not, according to Kumārila, self-luminous, because if it were, then it would itself be an object and would need another cognition to perceive it, and that another, and so on. So knowledge – cognition – is imperceptible and inferred, and is self-valid.

Prabhākara, on the other hand, posited a *tripartite* process of knowledge (*tripuṭīpratyakṣavāda*) involving the knower (*jñātā*), the knowledge (*jñāna*) and the object of knowledge (*jñeya*). Knowledge, he believed, was self-luminous, self-manifesting, but transient. When knowledge occurs, at the same time it reveals the self as the knower and the object as the known. While all cognitions incorporate these three aspects, they operate simultaneously, but neither the self as knower, nor the object, can be known *without* cognition; both are dependent on cognition, on knowledge, for their own revelation. So, in every incident in which knowledge occurs there is awareness of the self as the knower, the object as what is known, and the knowledge that is known to the self. For Prabhākara, cognition is *directly* known and not inferred, because it reveals the self as subject, the object, *and itself*. When we are in deep, dreamless sleep, and no kind of sense apprehensions can occur, then there is no self because there is no knowledge to illuminate it. Cognition, as far as Prabhākara is concerned, is never an object; only an object can be an object, and knowledge, he claimed, cannot be the object of the self. Knowledge cannot be the object of direct apprehension, but it can be known because an object, the known, is apprehended directly by the self.

So the nature of knowledge is self-valid: while it usually has a cause – whatever it is that causes us to know – it needs no other extraneous power beyond the conditions that bring it about, to occur. Taber put this pragmatically when he wrote: "*Svataḥprāmāṇya* says, in effect, that if a cognition appears in every way true, then it is. Falsehood cannot conceal itself forever; a cognition that is really false will eventually be revealed as such."[27]

Error

If we accept that all knowledge is valid, then we would have to ask how it is that some of our knowledge is wrong, and how we are to describe this. Mīmāṃsakas claim that errors arise because of the subject or object, *not* because of the cognition. Gaṇgānātha Jhā wrote:

> Nor again can there be any cause for the appearance of any such cognition as is not valid, *as cognition*; because what is regarded as the cause or origin of invalid cognitions is the presence of discrepancies in the cognitive agency; but upon examination we find that these discrepancies are totally devoid of creative energy, and as such, cannot produce anything; all that they can do is to put obstacles in the way of the cognition of things as they are; and thus the wrongness would pertain to the *thing cognised*, and not to the *cognition*.[28]

So all cognitions are still valid; if there is error, it lies in the object perceived or in some invalidity in the subject or object. Invalidity of the knowledge we have is usually inferred through some kind of later, contradictory knowledge or through some defect in the instrument of knowledge. An example of the former would be a rope mistaken as a snake, which subsequently is recognized as a rope, while defectiveness in the instrument is often likened to someone with jaundice who perceives things as yellow. Here, the instrument of the eye leads to error in knowledge. But in both cases it could not be said that knowledge did not occur. Mīmāṃsakas claim that that knowledge is valid – it is the object and subject that cause the confusion. So the self-validity of knowledge remains.

Later knowledge can only effect a change in knowledge because the initial conditions of knowledge have been defective in some way. When this happens, we *infer* that the first knowledge is incorrect. Of course, what is corrected by later, valid knowledge becomes invalid because it is remembered, and memory, according to Mīmāṃsā, is invalid knowledge. But in character with its realist and pluralist philosophy, Mīmāṃsā finds all belief normal and disbelief abnormal. And when we think of the instances in just one day when we accept the validity of our perceptions as opposed to doubting them, it would be common sense to accept this. It could be claimed that we don't wait to verify something in order to act, we simply act. Or, we might retort and say that we *do* verify things by recourse to our memories, albeit imperceptibly. But this process really only serves to *support* the cognition and is not a condition of the cognition taking place: the cognition has happened, and anything else is merely associated with its result. In other words, cognition has to be valid and can only be invalidated by something extraneous to itself.

Two classic examples of error of perception are that of a shell which appears to the observer as silver, and that noted above, the rope that is seen as a snake. In the former case, the cognition – that it is silver – is valid, even though subsequent knowledge proves that cognition to be wrong. We can test the validity of the claim that it is silver, but we cannot reveal validity itself, or produce it. Validity can only arise in the cognition that produces knowledge – whether that knowledge is right or wrong. According to Kumārila, in the shell and silver, or rope and snake, examples, what has occurred is the relating of two quite separate things. Both shell and silver would be valid cognitions, but they are erroneously combined. What is cognized is misapprehended, and there is partial misrepresentation (*anyathākhyāti*), a wrong synthesis of two real things. What has taken place is a partial straying from reality, and a positive view of error – one of commission.

Prabhākara, on the other hand, saw such error as non-apprehension, not misapprehension – a more radical straying from reality, and a negative view of error, one of omission. He claimed that the shell/silver cognition is really two cognitions incorrectly associated, and what actually takes place is the perception of the shell combined with the memory of the silver. The first perception of the shell is valid – a cognition has occurred. It is the second, memorized recollection of silver that is invalid, and the conjoining of the two results in erroneous knowledge. In fact, what is actually cognized when someone thinks a shell is a piece of silver is the *memory* of the silver, the shell doesn't enter into it. And so we have a case of non-apprehension, because it is the memorized silver that is envisaged, and the shell not at all. The common qualities of silver and shell are perceived, but the *differences* are not apprehended: memory is at fault here, and what was originally apprehended correctly, the silver, is not apprehended correctly when the shell is seen.

Sometimes the proximity of things produces error in knowledge, as when one object reflects the colour of another because of proximity. In this case, the apprehension of both objects supplies valid knowledge, but we fail to separate the distinctive characteristics of each. Prabhākara considered that the test of erroneous knowledge lay in its outcome in activity. If the knowledge acquired worked when actively applied, then it was obviously valid, if not, then it was simply abandoned. But when originally cognized it would have to be regarded as valid even if it were wrong.

The Prabhākara theory of error is known as *akhyāti* or non-apprehension, that is to say, the error arises through the non-apprehension of the unrelated nature between the two aspects of knowledge – shell and silver, or rope and snake. It is not a case of misrepresentation, for Prabhākara believed that if all knowledge is valid it cannot, therefore, misrepresent its object. But the omission of the distinction between two confused objects, the absence of discrimination, results in error. Sometimes cognitions are doubtful, as when we are not certain that we are looking at a man or a post. But, even here, what we really have are two distinct cognitions of memory – what a man looks like, and what a post looks like. But when looking at the post that may be a man, we combine the two. Valid knowledge lies in the immediate apprehension of the post/man, but not in the erroneous or doubtful interpretation of it.

Pramāṇas

All the *darśanas* put forward what they consider to be valid means of knowledge, and these are known as *pramāṇas*. Broadly, Mīmāṃsā accepts the following:

Pratyakṣa	Perception
Anumāna	Inference
Śabda	Testimony
Upamāna	Comparison or Analogy

Arthāpaṭṭi	Presumption, Postulation, Implication
Abhāva or *Anupalabdhi*	Non-apprehension

Not all proponents of the Mīmāṃsā schools accepted all these *pramāṇas*. Jaimini accepted only perception, inference and testimony, for example, and Kumārila rejected *upamāna*, which was peculiar only to the Prabhākara school. Prabhākara does not accept the *pramāṇa* of non-apprehension. However, all discounted recollection or memory as a *pramāṇa*.

Perception (pratyakṣa)

Mīmāṃsā accepts that ordinary perception is one means of knowledge, and this conforms to the pluralistic realism of the school. According to Śabara, valid perception is the knowledge arising from contact of the sense organs with an object, and this really claims the *svataḥprāmāṇya*, "intrinsic" or "self-validity", of all perceptual knowledge, though accepting that any knowledge may be contradicted by later knowledge. Perception is *immediate* knowledge, that is to say, the senses are the means by which we come to know something through direct apprehension. Other means of knowledge are mediate. In immediate perception, for example, we see something via the sense organ of the eyes, the eyes relay the picture to the mind, and the self – which Mīmāṃsā, like most Hindu philosophy, posits as separate from the mind – receives the image from the mind and acquires the specific knowledge.

Perception is in two stages, *indeterminate* (*nirvikalpaka*) and *determinate* (*savikalpaka*), both of which must be valid cognitions because Mīmāṃsā accepts all knowledge as valid. Indeterminate knowledge refers to that stage of simple awareness of things before we actually know what they are, before we have time to define the perception more clearly. Sometimes, we never proceed to a clearer defining of the object because to move to a more determinate knowledge is just not needed. I may, for example, have a number of things on my desk of which I am vaguely aware, but they are not essential in terms of what I am doing at the moment, so they remain in the background and not really determined in my mind as to *what* they are. It is only when I want a *particular* item that I actually have to shift the indeterminate knowledge that I have to a *determinate* level.[29] Tiny babies, too, exist in the indeterminate stage of knowledge until their perceptions are capable of being mentally articulated at the determinate level. According to Kumārila, indeterminate perception is of the individual nature of an object *and* its class character; but neither has any impact on consciousness. Prabhākara also accepted that individuality and class are *implicitly* perceived at the indeterminate stage, but without the comparison with other phenomena that occurs at the determinate stage.

At the determinate level, comparisons that allow for similarity and dissimilarity bring the object from indeterminate to determinate perception. What must be noted here are the valid knowledge of the *perception* and the invalid knowledge supplied by the *memory* of comparative objects: it is the perception of the object, and not its relation to other things in the memory, that permits valid cognition. Determinate knowledge, then, is that stage of perception when the object is truly known, and we can categorize it according to such things as class, quality, substance and action. Relating and comparing it to other things, from which it differs or is similar, brings about determinate knowledge. An element of memory, and therefore invalid cognition, is involved at this stage. But what are recalled from the memory at this time are the associations the object has with past experience, with other items of the same class, and so on. Mīmāṃsakas claim that all the necessary information for the cognition is there at the indeterminate stage of the process; nothing new is added at the determinate stage. What we see at the indeterminate stage is the object in its *pure* form, devoid of any classifications and particulars that we have yet to bring to mind, to determine, but by relating these at the determinate stage to other things, the self cognizes the object.

The mind (*manas*) is considered atomic and is regarded as a sense in all the processes of perception: just as the eye enables us to see, so the mind enables us to think. But knowledge is not a product of the mind for Mīmāṃsakas, it is an experience of the self; the mind is only the instrument by which knowledge is acquired by the self. While it has no qualities like colour, smell and taste, it acts as the medium of the self's experience of such things as pain or pleasure. But the mind remains an atomic substance, just like the other senses of the body. Gaṅgānātha Jhā described the function of the mind as follows:

> This *manas*, alone by itself, brings about such effects as cognitions, pleasure, pain, desire, aversion, effort, and so forth; it brings about remembrance when aided by impressions left by past cognitions. Thus then we have arrived at the conclusion that the *manas*, or *mind*, is an organ whereby the Soul obtains such cognitions as those of pleasure and pain &c. The mind however by, (*sic*) itself, is found to be devoid of any such qualities as colour, smell &c.; and as such it cannot lead the soul to experience or cognise these qualities; hence for this it stands in need of such other organs as may be characterised by these qualities.[30]

Thus the other sense organs serve the mind, the mediator of perception to the self. Most of our perceptions are sense-based; they are direct apprehensions that produce knowledge in the self of substances, classes or qualities. But it is the *self* that is the knower, not the mind. The mind cannot "know", because to know something "I" have to know that I know. "I" am the cognizer in the perception, not my mind. Yet it is the knowledge, the *jñāna*, that is the connecting and self-valid element between the knower and what is known. For Prabhākara these three aspects of knower, the object of knowledge, and the cognition that is knowledge, are simultaneous. But for Kumārila, as was seen above, it is a four-way process.

Inference (anumāna)

Śabara's definition of *anumāna* was simple – knowledge from the perception of one object that is known to be related to another that is not perceived at the time. Inferential knowledge occurs when two particular things are *always* associated with each other in a way that when we see one of these, we infer that the other must exist. Smoke and fire are the classic examples. There is a definite element of universality about this: if *every* time smoke arises, it has been known to occur because of fire, then we can assume that we can *know* that where there is smoke there is also fire. But, importantly for Mīmāṃsā, it is the *percep-*

tion of the smoke that gives rise to the knowledge, the latter part of the knowledge being the memorized aspect that there is no smoke without fire. It is the *perception* of the smoke that provides the valid cognition. Inference occurs where certain causes *always* produce certain effects, and in which certain things *always* coexist. The important factor here is not the perception but experience, for it is through experience of so many cases of, for example, smoke being the effect of fire, that we can infer a general principle, a *universal concomitance*, from it. As Radhakrishnan stated: "When a permanent relation of coexistence, identity or causal nexus is fixed up in the mind, one term of it reminds us of the other."[31] Yet memory here is a secondary process; it is the initial perception of, for example, the smoke, that is primary. And smoke carries with it, from experience, fire, as its cause.

Such inference is a means of valid knowledge that has been very finely and logically argued by the Nyāya school, and will be dealt with in more detail in that context. Indeed, most of the schools accept the fundamental logic of Nyāya in its analysis of inference. The key to valid inferential knowledge in Mīmāṃsā follows the Nyāya logic of the *universal concomitance* between two things. This is called *vyāpti* – the universal and major premise that inference asserts. It is the invariable concomitance of the two terms – in the example here, smoke and fire – that must obtain in order for the knowledge to be valid.

Memory, of course, is an invalid means of knowledge for the Mīmāṃsaka, but Kumārila argued that in the case of inference, knowledge from memory is not invalid, but it does not have the status of a *pramāṇa*. We also have to bear in mind the fact that, for knowledge to be valid it also has to have an element of novelty for Mīmāṃsā, and it could be claimed that universals such as *smoke is always an effect of fire* contain no novelty at all. But then, the smoke is rarely in the same place when it is perceived, so this is what adds the element of novelty.

Testimony (śabda)

The *śabda pramāṇa* is critical to all Mīmāṃsā philosophy, providing the rationale for the school. Testimony is verbal authority. Sharma says: "It is the knowledge of supra-sensible objects which is produced by the comprehension of the meanings of words".[32] And it is the *Veda* that is the source of knowledge through testimony *par excellence*, for its injunctions and prohibitions are the sole means of *dharma*. They are believed to be valid truths because they have been proved to work in practice, particularly because they are timeless and authorless. However, in the setting out of *śabda* as a *pramāṇa*, Mīmāṃsakas are keen to show exactly *why* the sacred text of the *Veda* is eternal and consists of valid knowledge. This knowledge is supersensuous, for it attests to the particular effects of action and is the *only* means by which *dharma* can be known. Other means of knowledge fail to apprehend what is supersensuous.

The *Veda* was considered to be *impersonal* testimony, that is to say, not the result of any human or divine source. But Mīmāṃsakas also accepted personal testimony, providing it originated from a reliable person. This personal testimony was, however, considered inferior to that of the impersonal testimony of the *Veda* itself. Kumārila, especially, accepted such personal and impersonal testimony as valid, though he differentiated between superhuman *Vedic* testimony and human testimony. But Prabhākara considered reliable personal testimony to belong to the *pramāṇa* of inference. Person A says such and such, A is a reliable person, so what A says must be right. But *Vedic* testimony is a *pramāṇa* in its own right – timeless and authorless. The testimony of the *Veda* was a source of information about existence, as well as direction in the form of injunctions of what ought to be done, and prohibitions about what ought not to be done. This kind of impersonal testimony was believed to be *intrinsically* valid. Thus, Prabhākara believed personal testimony to be valid only by inference, that is to say, it could be inferred because of the trustworthy nature of the person as its source, but might, at some later date, turn out to be wrong. In fact, only human sources can be proved to be unreliable, whereas an *impersonal* source such as the *Veda* cannot be subject to human error, neither can its knowledge be obtainable outside itself. And all the other *pramāṇas* are useless means of verifying *Vedic* knowledge, for it validates itself, and can never be demonstrated later as wrong.

Jaimini, in particular, made *śabda* the pre-eminent *pramāṇa*. One task of Jaimini was to establish the relative validity of the whole gamut of *Vedic* texts. But while injunctions were deemed to be *dharmic*, much other material was less pragmatic at first glance. One critical aspect that absorbed Jaimini's attention was the particular relevance of any part of the *Veda* that did not have any direct bearing on actions that should or should not be performed – in other words, injunctions. Was such superfluous material in the *Veda* to be regarded as useless and of no relevance to *dharma*? *Dharma* is action or non-action in a particular context: descriptive passages that might, for example, describe the god Vāyu as the swiftest of the gods, seemingly have no bearing at all on *dharma*. Similarly, absurd statements (like prohibiting the kindling of a fire in the sky), and the mention of clearly non-eternal things, might be rejected as not being of the eternal nature of *dharma*. But to Jaimini such statements were *supportive* and *auxiliary* to specific injunctions, in their special contexts. They illustrated a particular injunction and made it more meaningful. In short, Jaimini depicted *Vedic* injunctions as the best possible means of *dharma*-consciousness, and other, explanatory material, names, *mantras*, and *smṛtis*, as supplementary, supportive and valid means of such knowledge.

Even *smṛti* literature was accepted as supportive to the *Veda* as illustrative of it, and originating from it – particularly since its compilers were *Vedic* sages. *Vedic* authority, however, remained pre-eminent for Jaimini, though of comparable importance to the *smṛtis* as far as Kumārila was concerned. So apart from the important and central *Vedic Saṃhitas* and *Brāhmaṇas*, Kumārila cited the *Itihāsas*, the *Purāṇas*, and the *Manusmṛti* in particular, as authoritative *smṛti* literature, but only parts – those based on the *Veda* – were accepted as valid testimony. Prabhākara, while accepting such *smṛti* tradition as valid, did so only where no contradiction between it and *Vedic* authority was evident. Kumārila was more inclined to accept *smṛti* contradictions of *Vedic* authority as alternatives.

So Jaimini argued that those passages that might be regarded as superfluous to *dharma* are actually *syntactically* connected with injunctions.[33] The syntax of a *Vedic* sentence carries its own special eternality of meaning to which all parts are related. *Śabda* was the "Word" of the *Veda*, and Jaimini claimed that every word has within it an inherent power of meaning, and this meaning is, itself, eternal. The eternal meaning inherent in a word obtains irrespective of how the word is pronounced, or when it is not being articulated; the meaning in a word is not limited to the sound of it. And even if a word is spoken by many people, the meaning is still one single inherent and eternal meaning. Modifications of words are new words with new meanings and, whether spoken quietly or loudly, the meaning of a word is not at all altered. The absolute and eternal relation between a word and its meaning is termed *autpattika*. So a word and its meaning are not the product of human convention. Jaimini said: "the relation of the word with its meaning is inborn (and eternal); consequently injunction (which is a form of word) is the means of knowing dharma; and it is unfailing in regard to objects not perceived (by other means of knowledge)".[34] But while accepting the power in individual words, to Jaimini the grammatical connected sentence is a complete and unique unit of meaning, and it is that meaning that is intrinsic to the sentence. This is exactly what a *Vedic* injunction *is*. Take away any of the words, and that unity of meaning – the injunction – fails to have any power, efficacy and essence.

Meaning of words, then, is the key to the understanding of this *pramāṇa*, and when combined in particular sentences the relations between the meanings of the words can only be known in this way and not by something apart from them. They must, therefore, be valid. If I say, for example, "The trees are about to turn green", each word has inherent within it a particular meaning, and when the words are combined in a sentence, how can anything but the inherent meaning of that sentence be valid? Nothing else can point to the inherent meaning of this particular combination of words. We understand sentences because of the validity of their meanings. Problematic, however, is the fact that, while meanings of words may have their own validity – and this is carried into their particular sentence combination – the trees, as a matter of fact, may not be about to turn green at all. Eternality of meaning does not necessarily suggest that the external fact is also valid. In other words we can understand what words mean, but we don't have to believe what they indicate. But the words of the *Veda* and their associative meanings were not believed to have been composed by any human or divine author; they existed for all time and had within them the kind of power to create the appropriate effects if their validity were accepted and acted upon. And the efficacy of the effects as a result of *Vedic* sacrificial ritual served to endorse the validity of the testimony of the *Veda*. Clooney points out that, as far as Jaimini was concerned, words do not, in fact, have any hidden, esoteric or sacred meaning. Whether a word is used in everyday use, or in the *Vedic* context, no differentiation needs to be applied. But it is only the *Veda* that is the source of *dharma* that transcends ordinary existence. Clooney puts this succinctly when he writes: "The Vedic arranges the ordinary in a particular way for an extraordinary reason."[35]

Kumārila saw the meanings of the *Vedic* texts as inherent in the atomistic combinations of the meanings of *words* – the whole sentence was a combination of different, individual word-meanings. Unlike Prabhākara, he believed that *each* word possessed its own meaning, independent of its use in sentences. Prabhākara, however, stressed the particular relationships and arrangements of the words and, especially, the *letters* that composed them, as the important factors in testimony, each letter or syllable having the potency to combine with those associated with it and provide meaning. The letters here, then, are the key to valid cognition. But it is only when individual letters and words are combined syntactically as sentences that true knowledge is acquired. Thus, the sentence as a whole is necessary for an injunction with power.

But whether the individual words or the combinations of words are the key, the

Veda was believed to be the source of verbal cognition. This verbal cognition is knowledge through the words themselves or the combination of them, which cannot be gained by any other means, and would not be apprehensible to the senses. Ultimately, the *letters* of the words and their particular combinations are important as means of verbal cognition, the mind gaining an impression of each sound, which enables the next one to be interpreted, and so on. The power of a word comes from the power of the individual letters that composes it. This is important, because it illustrated that perception and inference could not possibly be valid means of ascertaining the meaning of the words.

The syllables that the letters form,[36] then, are the sounds that form a word, and are believed to be eternal, present everywhere, and unchanging, even though we as humans are inclined to articulate them differently. The letters that are written to correspond with these sounds are symbols of those eternal sounds. When arranged in a specific order, the syllables produce a unity that results in a word, and that word and its meaning are both eternal for Mīmāṃsakas, for they believed that language is intrinsically natural to existence and not the specific creation of human beings. The letter and sound *ba* exist as one, even though *ba* is used in a multiplicity of combinations, in different places and at different times, by a multiplicity of persons. But it is still one *varṇa*, one sound, *ba*, that transcends all the uses of it. *Ba*, then, exists independently of either its spoken sound (its *dhvani*) or its written form (its *rūpa*). It is the particular *order* of the syllables that make up the words in the *Veda* that is so important to the Mīmāṃsaka and it is this order that is regarded as timeless, unlike the order of sounds that constitutes ordinary speech that is transient. The order of the words in the *Veda* is not, unlike everyday language or other scriptural material, the work of one or more human beings. Tradition has never known an author for the *Veda*, and so its testimony and particular combination of sounds – as authorless – are said to be eternal. For Prabhākara, who was a pragmatist, only those parts of the *Veda* that led to *action*, such as the injunctions set down for active response and obedience, were considered as true *śabdapramāṇa*.

So it was accepted that every word had a particular denotive meaning and that that meaning was inseparable from the particular combination of syllables that made up the word. Since Mīmāṃsakas deny that the relationship between a word and its meaning is a matter of convention, the Sanskrit word for something cannot be exchanged by another word. The word and what it denotes, therefore, are a unit, and what a word denotes exists even if a person does not understand the meaning. Just because someone doesn't understand a meaning doesn't mean to say that it isn't *there* all the same. Two and two are still four, even if I don't know that they are, and the word sun denotes the sun irrespective of my knowledge of it. The word and its denotive meaning also exist in unmanifest form even when not being used. Being an aggregate of different eternal sounds, or *varṇas*, a word is indicative of a particular transient thing on one level, but also of an eternal and universally, unchanging meaning on another level. But if the *Veda* can be verbally cognized in the sense that every word that is spoken is acted on, and the sound and its denotive meaning are perfectly matched and obeyed, then *dharma* is the result. It was Prabhākara, especially, who stressed the importance of *activity* as a result of knowledge. Mīmāṃsakas believed that it was essential to put into practice the injunctions of the *Veda*. For the powerful effect of the words of the *Veda* applied in the sacrificial ritual, combined to bring about *dharma*.

Such was the impact of the Mīmāṃsā theories of word and sentence meaning that the school is also called Vākyaśāstra, "The Science of Sentences". The three facets to word meaning in sentences which the school postulated – *ākāṇkṣā* (mutual expectancy), *yogyatā* (consistency) and *saṃnidhi* (contiguity) – came to be accepted widely in Hindu literary analysis.

Analogy (upamāna)

Analogy as a means of cognition is based on the similar relationship of things. Simply, this is recognizing something from the past, B, as *similar* to an object presently perceived, A. Importantly, it is the *object that is remembered* that forms the cognition, not the object that is perceived. In other words something new – the element of novelty that must be present for valid knowledge – is perceived in the *remembered* object, and that is that it is like the *perceived* object. At first glance this *pramāṇa* appears to be based on memory, and memory, as we have seen, is an invalid means of knowledge. But this is discounted because, although the object B was seen in the past, it is its *similarity* to object A that is the cognition, and this similarity was not perceived in the past. The fact that similarity is the means of cognition means that perception is not. It is also not a case of inference, because the aspect of universal concomitance of the inference *pramāṇa* is missing; it would be impossible to claim that all cases of seeing object A create the same similarities in knowledge provided by the remembered B. And there is no causal link between A and B in the same way that there is, for example, with smoke and fire. The cognition occurs also because object A, the perceived object, is unknown, and is compared to the remembered object B; the example usually cited is that of a wild cow perceived for the first time which is compared with the ordinary cow known to the perceiver through memory. The reverse idea, the similarity of the wild cow to the cow, is not admissible here (because this would be a simple case of perception and determinate knowledge). Essentially, it is the *similarity* that is the valid knowledge, and this stands on its own as an independent *pramāṇa*. It is only Prabhākara that accepts this means of knowledge as a distinct *pramāṇa*. Kumārila regards the similarities of the two objects – perceived and remembered – as *qualities* pertinent to both.

Presumption/Implication (arthāpaṭṭi)

The *pramāṇa* of presumption or implication postulates an explanation not based on direct perception that can be the only possible one to make sense of something. It is the kind of postulation or implied knowledge we have when we want to account for something that goes against experience. In other words, what we see directly cannot be explained without a further assumption. The doubt that is characteristic of the implication prevents it from being a case of inference. For inference, there must be universal concomitance, and there is nothing for us to reconcile in this case, for there are no inconsistencies in the case of inferential knowledge. Two examples of *arthāpaṭṭi* or implication are usually given. If a man is getting fat, but does not eat in the day, there is the implication that he is eating at night. The implication that he is eating at night resolves the difficulty between the two irreconcilable facts that he is getting fatter but doesn't eat during the day, even though we do not directly perceive his nightly binges. We cannot *infer* that he is eating at night since there is no universal concomitance between getting fat and eating at night. Similarly, when we call on someone and that person is not at home, if we know that person is alive, then by implication he or she must be out. Thus implication reconciles the two facts person A is alive, and A is not at home. We use this kind of inferential knowledge a good deal when we have to imply the meaning of words from their contexts.

Prabhākara believed that *doubt* is an important factor in this *pramāṇa*, for this clearly separates implication from inference, in which there can never be doubt. So when I see a man getting fatter, or find my friend not at home, doubt is raised in my mind until I posit the presumption that reconciles the two facts, and the doubt whether the fat man *is* getting fatter, or whether my friend *is* alive, is removed. Kumārila, however, claimed that there is no element of doubt in implicated cognition, that is, whether the fat man is actually getting fatter, or, whether my friend is alive. It is therefore the *irreconcilability* of the two factors that was important to the Bhāṭṭa, the irreconcilability between two facts that are themselves known to be true. Again, the element of novelty in the cognition is evident in the postulating of a reconciling factor as a new truth.

Non-apprehension (anupalabdhi or abhāva)

The Bhāṭṭa school alone considers non-apprehension to be a *pramāṇa* in its own right. Non-apprehension is the absence of valid cognition when all the other *pramāṇas* have not ascertained valid knowledge. It thus recognizes the negative. When something is not there we normally know this through perception, or through inference; we either see something is not there or infer that it is not. Prabhākara turns non-existence of something into a positive perception, in that if I see there is no jar on the ground, what I am *actually* perceiving is the ground without the jar. But Kumārila maintained that we can sometimes know that we did not perceive something in the past, say earlier in the day. We cannot say that this is memory because it wasn't in the memory earlier, neither was it not perceived in the past since we were not looking for it then. Thus, if I think that I haven't seen object A today, that must be a valid cognition. And since it is not to be ascertained by perception, or inference (for there is no universality or cause–effect link), nor are the other *pramāṇas* of analogy and implication relevant, this non-apprehension must be a separate *pramāṇa*.

The self

The *Upaniṣadic* sages were concerned with the nature of the self, as much as with ultimate Reality, for it was the link between the two that somehow seemed capable of answering the purpose behind existence. While Mīmāṃsā was more concerned with the ritual portion, and not the knowledge portion, of the *Veda*, it still inherited something of the spirit of inquiry into the nature of the self that was such a marked feature of the *Vedānta*. And yet, without a concept of God, and a need to establish the relationship between the self and the divine, a more pragmatic picture of the self was inevitable.

The early Mīmāṃsā view of the *ātman* was as the egoistic self that acts in life and enjoys life. The idea of the ego, *ahaṃkāra*, being obliterated in a state of liberation was alien to early Mīmāṃsā. Action was essential to life and for reaping the appropriate rewards or punishments. *Dharma* would have been nullified without real human activity, and *Vedic* injunctions to no avail.[37] Even Kumārila and Prabhākara – though the latter less overtly – had to concede that the all-pervasive, essentially inactive *ātman* must be able to act when embodied – otherwise there could be no action leading to *karmic* effects. Action has to accrue to the *ātman*. Unlike Kumārila, however, Prabhākara saw ego as superimposed on the *ātman* in order for activity to come about.

The self is a real and permanent substance with which merit, demerit, pleasure, pain, and memory are associated. There is a plurality of selves, and one cannot know others, though it can infer that others exist because of the presence of a plurality of other physical bodies. Each self has to be permanent: if it were not, then a task could not be resumed by an individual after a long period of time. Indeed, the self is posited as eternal. This is important for Mīmāṃsā for, otherwise, the heaven spoken of in the *Veda* would be untrue. All the sacrificial ritual to make heaven possible would, then, also be invalidated. It was essential, therefore, for the eternal nature of the self to be proved, and for there to be a plurality of selves or souls that are able to reap their individual rewards in heaven, as a result of obeying *Vedic* injunctions. Some entity must, therefore, survive the body at death. It is an entity that pervades the life of each human being, despite the changes that take place in the body, life, character and nature of each one. "The sea remains, despite the movements of its waves; the serpent uncoils, without change of essence."[38] In early Mīmāṃsā, when the ultimate goal was heaven and not *mokṣa*, the soul returned to human existence after reaping its appropriate rewards in heaven or hell. Thus its existences were continued for all eternity. Later, when the concept of *mokṣa* was taken on board, the soul only continued to be associated with a body – whether on earth or in heaven or hell – until it had no merits or demerits to reap. These are two quite different perspectives of the ultimate fate of the self.

Given the general philosophical trend to refer only to the male self, and the exclusion of women from access to the *Veda*, it is worth noting that Jaimini took what Keith referred to as a "generous view of the position of woman".[39] She could certainly perform sacrifices when unmarried, and join her husband in their performance, if married. But, clearly, there were many practices that the husband/male alone could carry out. Śabara, in his *Bhāṣya*, stated that all those "desiring heaven" (*svargakāmaḥ*) could perform sacrifices, and that meant male *and* female.[40] For Śabara, it is the *smṛti* texts that seek to exclude woman from sacrificial ritual because she is herself "property" of father and husband, and has no property of her own. But Śabara is clear, "if the woman desires the results that are spoken of as following from a sacrifice, she should reject the authority of the *Smṛti*, acquire property and also perform the sacrifice".[41] However, a wife is only permitted to do that which is prescribed for her. Thus, "on account of inequality, the wife does not stand on the same footing as the husband (in the matter of the performance of details)".[42] However, *Śūdras* were definitely to be excluded from sacrificial performance: they were not considered to have the necessary knowledge to be of the "desiring heaven" disposition. Not being able to access the *Veda*, they could know nothing of the sacrificial ritual that was the means to heaven. The later trend was to exclude women in this way too.

The everyday self that we experience seems to have some awareness of itself as separate and different from the body, an awareness of itself as that which organizes the sense data it receives via the mind, and which recalls appropriate memory for the purpose of functioning in the world. Jaimini separated this self from mind and senses, but Śabara did not, for he saw the self as identical with consciousness, the subject of all objective knowledge, and a subject that knows itself and that cannot be known by others. For Kumārila the true Self as a substance is of the nature of *pure* consciousness. He said that it is necessary "to regard the Soul as being of the nature of Consciousness, eternal, omnipresent, capable of ensouling several bodies".[43] The soul "is itself *conscious*, as otherwise, it would not be the experiencer; it is *omnipresent*, otherwise, it could not occupy one body after another, which it does even without any locomotion".[44] However, for Prabhākara, it is the *substratum* of consciousness, and is therefore not consciousness itself. Here, the self is the knower underpinning what is known, the agent behind all activity leading to knowledge, and the experiencer of the results of knowledge. At the same time the self was believed to be infinite, omnipresent and ubiquitous. Kumārila believed *ordinary* consciousness to be a changing process in the self, an action or mode by which the self comes to know something. This cannot be the essence of the self. The self to Kumārila was basically the same substance but subject to transient changes, consciousness, modes and diversity – all underpinned by its basic substance of selfness. It is the substance aspect of the self that is the *free* self, the self without ordinary consciousness and sense perception – the *pure*, conscious self. It is the modal self, the changing and diverse self, which is subject to *karma* and reincarnation, and that is the knower of all knowledge.

While it might seem sensible to suggest that consciousness is intimately connected with self-identity, Kumārila argued that ordinary consciousness, in fact, has more to do with the *object* of knowledge than the subjective self. He argued that we cannot *know* consciousness, we can only indirectly infer it from the act of knowing something. And it is not even ordinary consciousness that reveals the self, but a higher level of consciousness, an "I" consciousness. This "I" perceives itself independently of the consciousness that takes place when knowledge of an object is acquired. The self is thus both the subject and object of itself. I can say, for example "I know myself". In ordinary cases of knowledge we do not always have a perception of the "self" as a knower in every cognition. I can observe something and say "That is a cat", but I don't always have a conception of my self knowing that at the same time. *Self*-consciousness, according to Kumārila is something quite distinct from ordinary consciousness of knowledge of an object. So when Kumārila equates the self with consciousness, he does so with this higher consciousness that is "I" awareness, independent of other ordinary cognitions. Knowledge, then, does not reveal the self. Knowledge is that which occurs when we look at something and locate it as familiar or unfamiliar and realize that we then have knowledge of it. That realization comes from *inference*. "If it appears to be familiar or previously known (*jñāta*), then from this character of familiarity or knownness (*jñātatā*) which the object presents to us, we *infer* that we had a knowledge of that object. Knowledge is thus known indirectly by inference on the ground of the familiarity or knownness observed in the object".[45] Knowledge comes about because there is an activity in the agent, the self, which interacts with the object, and the activity of cognition results. For Kumārila, then, knowledge is an action and a process, and resultant knowledge is inferred from the process, but the self is not always known in the action and process of cognition. Prabhākara's view of the self is somewhat different. He sees the self as the subject of every cognition. He discounted entirely the Bhāṭṭa idea of the true Self as pure consciousness. According to the Prabhākara theory, every time I know something, I am revealed as the subject; the self is thus known through cognition. Indeed, if I were not the subject of my own knowledge of an object there would be nothing to differentiate between my knowledge and somebody else's. As noted above in the context of epistemology, Prābhākaras believed that whenever something is known, three things are revealed at *exactly the same time* – the knower, the object that is known and the knowledge. And it is the *knowledge* that reveals both the subject as the self and the object: the knowledge also reveals itself. So unlike Kumārila, knowledge does not have to be inferred by the self, it is actually *known* by the self.

Far from accepting that the self is self-conscious, Prabhākara believed that the self was an unconscious substance, like that in deep sleep, and that it occasionally had the quality of consciousness – as when it is in the act of cognizing. All the things that the self experiences through consciousness are the results of past *karma*. All self-consciousness, then, is consciousness of knowledge. Since consciousness is only a quality of the substance of the self, the self is really unchanging, rather like a screen onto which is projected the images of perception. The screen, like the self, never changes, but the images, like the consciousness that occurs when we come to know something, are diverse and transient. So it is knowledge that imposes on the unconscious all the experiences that we have – perceptions, feelings, pain, happiness, activity, motion, qualities – all serving to create consciousness of an "I" that is the subject. However, the permanent, unconscious self is inferred from the fact that we can remember and recall past cognitions, so there must be some fundamental substantial self that can contain such memory unconsciously until it is recalled. This makes the self unchanging and also all-pervading because there is no knowledge that it cannot reflect, except that of another self. As pure substance, devoid of cognition, it is separate from the mind and the body and therefore from all the senses. The self is the *subject*, the *agent* of knowledge, the "I", in that it pervades each cognition presented by the mind. And each cognition then becomes a quality of the self. But the self can also exist without qualities – that is to say, cognitions – as it does in deepest sleep, or as it does when liberated.

It is the mind that acts as the mediator between the eternal self and the world with which it interacts when embodied. It is what facilitates consciousness, what gives the soul contact with, and knowledge of, the world in which it exists. All the enjoyment and suffering, the pleasure, pain, desire, aversion and effort of the self are mediated through the mind. The mind cannot exist without the body, but the self can, and that is to say that the self can be free of the sense impressions that cause it to react to the world and, hence, to reap *karmic* results. The realist and pluralist conception of the self by the Mīmāṃsakas allows for all individual experiences by different people. It is these experiences that produce the quality of consciousness in the self. And that consciousness is changeable and occurs only according to the nature of the sense stimuli that promote it.

The liberated Self is free from such changeable consciousness; it is free from the body, sense perception and from thought, and exists only in itself. It is the self that is not free from sense perceptions and consciousness that is subject to *saṃsāra* and this *karmic* self directs the body for each individual, *my* self directing the body differently from the next person and the next, and so on. Some selves direct their bodies and minds in a way that is *dharmic*, others as *adharmic*, and the operation of *karma* creates for each person his or her particular type of existence in the next life. This is a self, then, that is changeable and subject to modifications, and even though this self may ultimately transcend ordinary consciousness, it is always real and remains the self despite all the changes.

Causality

The realism and pluralism of the Mīmāṃsā school accepts the changeable and transient nature of all existence. All things are self-evolving and therefore change is essential to their nature. The changes that take place in human beings are those that result from all the past *karmas* coming to fruition. And such change is eternal, for there is no beginning of the universe or dissolution of it – no cycles of existence – which would prevent the constant processes of change. Kumārila stressed the theory of identity in difference, *bhedābheda*, in the changing nature of reality. That is to say things do change, but there is nevertheless a causal, single identity throughout the changes in each entity. Thus, a great oak tree emerges from a vastly different acorn, but all the causal changes that produce the oak tree are just examples of the diversity of causal change in *one* identity, and that identity prevents the acorn from turning into a sycamore tree. Thus, identity underlies difference, for most Mīmāṃsā, and the processes of change in anything create differences but not radically new things: the causal principle that permits change from one state to another does so without altering basic identity. Kumārila thus accepted what is called *satkāryavāda*, the belief that results inhere in their causes. So all objects of clay inhere in their causal clay, all articles of gold in their causal gold. Again, whatever changes take place, are only differences beneath which is identity.

The *Veda* is for the Mīmāṃsaka the clear and definite example of how cause and effect operate for the benefit of human beings. For, by obeying the injunctions of the *Veda* and carrying out the sacrificial ritual, it was proved that certain effects were assured. Thus if the *Vedic* injunctions could be followed by an individual, then the causes made would reap the respective rewards of heaven or, for later Mīmāṃsā, *mokṣa*. But the results transcend the individual, too. Clooney remarks that for Jaimini: "The human person may approach the sacrifice as he wishes, according to his desire for certain results. But once he has undertaken a certain sacrifice, the action is no longer governed by his viewpoint and desires. He himself is now part of a larger event not totally dependent on him."[46] However, while the *Veda* set out certain obligatory norms, it by no means regulated every aspect of life. Hiriyanna writes: "A lamp we hold in our hand when walking in darkness, shows the character of the ground we have to traverse; but it leaves the choice of the path we pursue to ourselves."[47] Similarly, as Hiriyanna points out, the *Veda* attests to a knowledge that cannot be found elsewhere, and it will illustrate how certain causes lead to certain effects, but it is not so prescriptive that it dictates every moment of how life ought to be lived. It is a compass not an ordnance map.

Karma

Mīmāṃsā accepts the law of *karma* like all other schools. It is a law of cause and effect that ensures appropriate effects for all actions, whether physical, mental or oral. For this school, *karma* is entirely autonomous, and operates independently of any divine force; it is also seen as that which regulates the basic structure of the universe. The *karma* of each individual provides the necessary changes that occur in his or her life and is the cause of all bondage and suffering. The obligatory (*nitya*) injunctions of the *Veda* should always be obeyed, and nothing but good can ensue from such actions. And as far as the optional injunctions (*kāmya*) that can be obeyed or neglected are concerned, the advantage of obeying them was the merit of a future life in heaven. Prohibited (*pratiṣiddha*) actions should never be undertaken, for it is these, especially, that result in negative *karma*.

Without such adherence to the *Veda* the soul becomes too involved with the physical body, with the senses and the mind. Additionally, all the past actions of a person bind him or her to the world, thus promoting such involvement. The self is the subject and experiencer of all the phenomena within the entire world as objects. Thus, the self becomes the subjective agent in the world, prone to activity resulting from the sense perceptions it receives. It is the self that stops being the subjective agent in the world, the self that is free from the shades of thought that detract it from its pure nature, that became the ideal.

Mīmāṃsā accepted a power, force or essence that was intrinsic to the nature of a thing, and that informed all the changes that characterized it. It is a power called *śakti* that provides the hidden energy by which the acorn becomes the shoot, the sapling, and eventually the oak tree. This *śakti* is an imperceptible potency that is one link between cause and effect. It is what makes fire burn, and is that which, generally, comes to fruition unless it is destroyed in its causal state. It is, say Chatterjee and Datta, "the power of burning in fire, the power of expressing meaning and inducing activity in a word, the power of illumination in light".[48] For Prabhākara it was a category in its own right, but this was rejected by the Bhaṭṭa school, in view of its more obvious nature of a quality existing in phenomena.

Apūrva

The real unperceived potency between cause and effect – even if the effect is not evident until a future existence – is called *apūrva*,[49] usually translated as "transcendental results". Radhakrishnan and Moore define this term in the following words:

> Acts are enjoined with a view to their fruits. Between an act and its result there is a necessary connection. An act performed today may achieve its result at some later date, and in the meantime the result is in the form of an unseen force or *apūrva*, which may be regarded either as the imperceptible antecedent of the fruit or of the after-state of the act itself. The deferred fruition of acts is possible only through the force of *apūrva*.[50]

Satkāryavāda, the theory that results inhere in their causes, is clearly portrayed by these words. In every cause there is an invisible and subtle potency. In the *Mīmāṃsāsūtras* Jaimini points out that if there were no such thing as *apūrva* the sacrificial ritual of the *Veda* would be useless. He said, "as the act of the *sacrifice* itself is perishable, so that if the sacrifice were to perish without bringing into existence something else, then the cause, having ceased to exist, the result (in the shape of heaven) could never come about".[51] If sacrificial ritual is not to result simply in a heap of ashes, then latent effects must inhere in their causes with an unseen potency that causes them to come to fruition in a particular way at some future point. So actions – of thought body or speech – produce their *apūrva* that in time will come to appropriate fruition for their agents. And in the individual this latent power for producing a result is embedded in the self, ready to produce its effect at the right time. This, indeed, is how the law of *karma* operates: though the latter is a more extensive and explicit law of cause–effect relationships, the principle of *apūrva* is a clearly related one, and in its origin was the precursor of the law of *karma*.[52] But, essentially, the words of the *Veda* themselves contain this same subtle, unseen potency of *apūrva*. The important issue here is that an action – whether it is a sacrificial one related to *Vedic* ritual, or an individual action of a human being – is transient; once done it disappears. The latent, but potent, effect of that action then remains, irrespective of the fact that the action itself no longer exists. That effect is literally "held" in suspension until the appropriate time for it to be manifest. Thus, "Apūrva", wrote Radhakrishnan, "is the metaphysical link between work and its result".[53] What remains unanswered, however, is what exactly it is that causes the *apūrva* to manifest itself in a given effect at a given time.

In the light of such necessary cause–effect potencies, Raju refers to Mīmāṃsā as a system of "ethical activism", and points out that it is such activism that controls the world processes. He writes:

> The world processes conform to the moral and the immoral, prescribed and prohibited activities of man by producing corresponding results. The freedom of man to do the prescribed or prohibited action is accepted; but once the act is done, the causal relation between that act and the result is fixed, and there is no freedom here. The act guides the processes of the world, which has its own laws. The Mīmāṃsā is activism so far as it asserts that the processes of the world are guided by ethical action: the controller of the world is ethical action.[54]

This leads him to the justified claim that it is *karma* that controls the causal processes, in place of God:

> All that man wants is that the forms of his environment must be conducive to his happiness; and he can bring about the required forms through action. Therefore, instead of accepting a hypothetical entity like God, about whose existence we can never be sure, it is better to accept that *karma* (action) itself as prescribed by the Vedas controls the world processes. *Karma* can control the world process, because it produces results according to its own good and evil nature. Thus *Karma* is made to occupy the place of God in the Mīmāṃsā.[55]

In no other school does *karma* play such a powerful role. Ultimately, it is humanity itself that directs its own destiny here *and* the destiny of the universe. For it directs its own *karmic* rewards and punishments. Raju is right to say that *karma* replaces God, but it is also right to say that it is humanity, the cause and reaper of *karma*, that really operates the world – albeit often blindly – in this system. This is reflected in Raju's definition of the spiritual world of Mīmāṃsā as "a sort of self-contained democracy of the *ātmans*",[56] each individual being solely responsible for the outcomes of his or her own actions, and for the universe in which he or she lives. The storing up of good *apūrva* was essential for the reaping of good rewards, and this could only come about from the right kind of activities: this justifies Raju's use of the term "ethical activism" entirely. The presence of the additional concept of *apūrva*, however, transcends the cause–effect process of *karma* and shifts causality to a more extraordinary level. *Apūrva* is a potential that arises as something new in a particular action. It is a new potential for an extraordinary result that comes about through correct performance of *Vedic* ritual. As such, it is closely interrelated with *dharma* though is not synonymous with it. It is also more potent than *karma* with which it is also, therefore, not synonymous. In the words of Halbfass, "the *apūrva*, the special result of the special ritual, is by definition stronger than any general retributive causality".[57]

Jaimini separated actions, or causes, into "primary" and "subsidiary". Primary causes are related to equally primary, and independent, *apūrvas* and results. Subsidiary actions or causes only serve to complement the primary ones, and so have no independent *apūrvas*. Thus, knowledge of what constitutes primary actions is essential for *dharma*, and this is something that Jaimini deals with in detail in the second section of his *Mīmāṃsāsūtras*. The relation between the causal activity of obeying a *Vedic* injunction and the expectant result was crucial to the argument for the validity of the *Veda*. Both Śabara and Prabhākara believed that subsidiary actions could have no *apūrva* of their own, but Kumārila accepted an *apūrva* for every injunction, whether primary or secondary. All primary and subsidiary actions are linked to the particular form, syntax and type of *Vedic* injunction. Thus, *apūrva* is specific to the actions that stem from the specific word order of *Vedic* hymns. The differentiation of such actions is also dealt with in detail in the second section of Jaimini's *Sūtras*. Knowledge of such differentiation is regarded as essential, both for the performance of the right kind of primary action, and for the manner of the performance itself; appropriate results could occur only through such knowledge.

Thus, causality in the Mīmāṃsā school is human designed. As far as the universe is concerned, it is subject to the same processes of cause–effect, and is affected by the very actions of humanity. It is human merits and demerits that account for the external nature of the universe and the production and destruction of all things in it. Impressions experienced in dreams are also the result of the operation of *apūrva* in accordance with the good or evil past *karmic* actions of individuals. These two forces of *apūrva* and *karma*, then, account for the way the world is and for all its processes of change. Nothing else needs to be posited to bring about such processes, and Kumārila, in particular, goes to great lengths to prove why there cannot be a creation–dissolution cycle of the universe, or any God that creates or supervises it.[58]

The concept of God

Because of the emphasis on the eternal nature of the *Veda* and its authorless status, Mīmāṃsā has to deny the existence of God, otherwise there would be something that was superior to the *Veda*, or even might be said to have composed it. And if God were inferior to the *Veda*, then the status of the divine would be compromised. Then, too, the role of a

God is usually connected in some way with both the creation and dissolution of the universe – a concept, also, that would only serve to limit the *Veda* in time and space, and inhibit its nature as eternal. Mīmāṃsakas, therefore, as has been stated above, are unique in rejecting any cyclical beginning or end of the universe. The impersonal systems of *karma*, *dharma* and *apūrva* operate in the universe without the necessity of any divine intervention. This, claims Hiriyanna, "is indeed a strange tenet to be held by a school claiming to be orthodox *par excellence*".[59] And it must be remembered that, while based heavily on the *karmakāṇḍa* portion of the *Veda*, Mīmāṃsā should also have accepted to some extent the *Vedānta* teachings of the *Veda*, and these are steeped in belief in an Absolute. But in dispensing with a concept of God, problems of theodicy do not arise: human beings are themselves responsible for their own *dharma* through the *karmic* results of the actions reaped in the past. Mīmāṃsā begins, then, with a fundamental atheism.

However, the *Veda* certainly accepts the existence of many deities, even if in the *Vedas* and *Brāhmaṇas* there is little postulation of any supreme Source. It is along these lines that Mīmāṃsā takes its belief in God, and Jaimini certainly does not bother to postulate any kind of supreme deity who interferes in the lives of human beings in any way at all. It was very late in the development of the school that Mīmāṃsakas found the lack of a divine being unsatisfactory, and a gradual shift in philosophy to include the principle of the divine was seen. Radhakrishnan suggested that Kumārila equated Brahman with the *Veda* itself. This is true in the sense that Kumārila nullifies God in the process, but there seems no evidence to suggest that he made God the general cause of things and the *Veda* as the "revelation of the mind of God".[60] Elsewhere, indeed, this same author referred to the argument of Kumārila against the existence and necessity of God in Kumārila's *Ślokavārtika*.[61] Indeed, the *Ślokavārtika* gives a very measured and logical explanation as to why God is rejected. It has to be admitted that this is mainly in the context of arguments against a creator God,[62] and it is possible that, while many Mīmāṃsakas deny the existence of God *as creator*, they may not necessarily deny God *in principle*. However, Mīmāṃsakas are really intent on proving that the *Veda* exists for all time and is authorless, and any discussion about God would have to serve this end. They are not interested in the existence of God *per se*. In the absence of a well-formulated belief in a transcendent Absolute it must be claimed that Jaimini, Śabara, Kumārila and Prabhākara supported an atheistic stance. Thus, there can be no problem of theodicy here, for humankind's response – or lack of it – to *Vedic* authority, is the only means by which appropriate happiness, pain and sorrow, are reaped. It made no sense to the Mīmāṃsakas to posit a creator god of a world that was so evidently full of sin and sorrow. It is evident, however, that followers of both major schools came to accept a theistic stance from about the fourteenth century[63] in the very latest stages of Mīmāṃsā. During its period of decline, both the concept of God and a belief in cyclical creation and dissolution of the universe were taken on board. These were concepts that would have been anathema to the earlier great thinkers of the school.

So despite a *saṃsāric* cycle for individuals on the microcosmic level, Mīmāṃsā rejects a similar cycle of evolution and involution, creation and dissolution on the macrocosmic level of the universe itself. This stands in sharp contrast to the beliefs of the other *darśanas*. The world for the Mīmāṃsaka is eternal and self-existent, though it is subject to the change and flux of causation – the beginning, decay and death of things on the microcosmic level. The many gods of the *Veda* are accepted against this realism and permanence of the universe. And since the universe is self-existent and there is no need for any supreme deity, one wonders why a profusion of deities in an overtly polytheistic belief system was supported by Mīmāṃsā. But it is sacrificial ritual that is all important to the Mīmāṃsaka and, while the hymns of the *Vedas* are addressed to many deities, it was the ritual rather than the gods that came to the fore, and the deities "gradually recede and fade into mere grammatical datives".[64] The god becomes simply one in whose name a particular ritual is conducted, but nothing more: the important thing is to comply with *Vedic* injunctions not to propitiate the gods. And it is the *Veda* itself that will provide the appropriate *dharma*, not the gods whose names appear in so many hymns.

Chatterjee and Datta are inclined to suggest that this rather inferior role of the deities calls into question the nature of the polytheism of the system.[65] For the deities are so undermined that they can hardly comprise a type of belief at all, and their very existence is questionable. In the Mīmāṃsā school, these deities are totally removed from any anthropomorphic theism that might be suggested in the *Vedic* hymns and cease to have any function beyond a titular role in ritual: any reality given to them is superfluous in function.

Deities, then, are subsidiaries in ritual, rather than principal aspects that pertain to ritual action. They are focuses for, and incentives to, the performance of ritual sacrifices, are not propitiated, and are not, in a sense, real. So they have almost no function. It is not they who apportion reward and punishment to humankind – this is fulfilled by *apūrva*. And it is *apūrva*, too, that ensures the appropriate effects that accrue to the varieties of sacrificial ritual. In effect, there is nothing for a god to create, sustain or supervise: the sacrificial rites and relative obedience or disobedience to *Vedic* injunctions are sufficient to reap the appropriate effects. Neither is God necessary in the directing of individual lives: the individual does this for him or her self through the operation of the law of *karma*.

Liberation

Early Mīmāṃsā was not interested in liberation as much as right action. And there is no doubt that in the early Mīmāṃsā school heaven (*svarga*) was the ultimate goal, the point at which the human being was absolved from *Vedic* ritual for a time, and enjoyed its rewards. Liberation (*apavarga*) of the self from the endless reincarnating lives became the goal much later, and a life of happiness and bliss in heaven were the best rewards one could have in the earlier stages. There was certainly no concept of *mokṣa* in the sense of a loss of self, egoistic identity. In fact, it was only the first three of the four basic aims of Hinduism – *artha* "wealth", *kāma* "pleasure", *dharma* "what is right" – that were accepted by the early Mīmāṃsakas. *Mokṣa*, as the fourth of the aims, was only accepted later. Heaven was not permanent. It was a reward, a result, which, when exhausted, brought another life.[66] Neither was heaven a physical place. Rather, it was conceived of as a state of happiness. But time in that state was limited, because it was a *karmic* effect. And like all such effects, once experienced and enjoyed, it came to an end, and new causes – reaping new effects – had to be made.

The self that reached this heaven was conceived of as being an *ātman* without bodily form, a soul, although Jaimini believed that the liberated Self was omnipotent, omniscient, and possessed a different kind of body, with full senses. For Śabara, as Jaimini, heaven was clearly the goal acquired by those who performed *Vedic* ritual. He said: "Thus we find that it has been well said that the 'Sacrifice' is the *subordinate*, and 'Heaven' the *principal*, factor."[67] Heaven was the ultimate reward for whoever was obedient to the *Veda*. And, also clearly, it is the *desire* for heaven that promotes the need to follow ritual practices to the letter. The *only* way in which one could reach this heaven was by sacrificial ritual, the path of action, *karman*, and not knowledge.

It was the later major school of the Bhāṭṭas that was mainly responsible for shifting the emphasis from *dharma* to *mokṣa* and, with this change, there is a concomitant emphasis on release from *saṃsāra* as the ultimate goal, and not on life in heaven. Jaimini and Śabara do not deal with *mokṣa*. It is Kumārila and Prabhākara that do. Here, *svarga* or heaven was accepted alongside *mokṣa*, but the latter gradually became the more important goal. In this case, *dharma* became less important in view of the need to lose any fruitive *karma*, be it positive or negative, for liberation to occur. There was sufficient speculation about the state of *mokṣa* to result in considerably divergent views. But *mokṣa*, like *svarga*, still emphasized obedience to *Vedic* injunctions as the *means* to the end, it is just that the emphasis on *mokṣa* stressed the loss of the egoistic self through disinterested obedience to the *Veda*. Kumārila said:

> For those who have understood the real nature of the Soul, all their past *Karma* having become exhausted through experience, and there being no further Karmic residum (*sic*) left to wipe off, there comes no further body; as it is only for the experiencing of the reactions of past *Karma* that the Soul is burdened with the Body; therefore the seeker for Liberation should not do any such act as has been forbidden or even what has been enjoined for certain purposes; (as both these would bring about Karmic reaction which would have to be expiated by experience); but he should continue to perform the compulsory acts, as the omission of these would involve sin, which have (*sic*) to be expiated by painful experience through a physical Body.[68]

Beyond consciousness, the liberated Self remained a substance in its own intrinsic nature, though there were some of the Bhāṭṭa school who accepted the liberated soul as experiencing a state of bliss. This is not surprising given the acceptance of a state of pure consciousness at liberation. And with the emphasis on *mokṣa* there occurred perhaps a lessening of that on ritual, but this was certainly a late development.[69] Whereas the senses and consciousness would have to be posited for a happy existence in heaven, they would have to be annihilated for the realization of *mokṣa* or, at best, consciousness if retained, would be so pure that it senses nothing. Realistically, without a body, the self has no possibility of sense experience. So for Prabhākara, especially, the liberated soul is imperceptible: it just *is*, and continues, unlike *svarga*, for eternity.

For the liberated self there is neither *dharma* nor *adharma*, reward nor punishment – only absolute negation of the self. Liberation was the point at which the physical body was lost and all knowledge ceased. Kumārila, especially, believed that the liberated Self existed in pure consciousness, with absence of knowledge. Prabhākara, however, accepted a total lack of consciousness at *mokṣa*. Either way, there is nothing to be experienced by a soul devoid of all knowledge – not even the bliss that characterized the liberated state in some of the other *darśanas*. *Mokṣa*, here, is a thoroughly negative state.

In conclusion it needs to be said that it is this acceptance of *mokṣa* that really helps to classify Mīmāṃsā as a *darśana*, bringing it more in line with the other schools, even if its acceptance is late. It is the acceptance of *mokṣa* by later Mīmāṃsakas, too, that really paved the way for the development of the school of Advaita Vedānta, for this particular shift in emphasis necessitated a certain acceptance of knowledge, *jñāna*, alongside ritual, *karman*. For the Vedānta school the shift would be fully to an emphasis on knowledge. Kumārila is thus the link between the Pūrva and Uttara Mīmāṃsā, taking the concepts of the school a stage beyond Jaimini: it was sufficient to open a new door for Advaita Vedānta. In a way it is the adoption of the theory of *mokṣa* that lifts Mīmāṃsā to the level of a philosophy. In fact Raju, for one, considers that Mīmāṃsā lost its essential nature in this move. He writes:

> If all philosophy is *mokṣa-śāstra* or science of salvation, then the Mīmāṃsā is not philosophy, because it was not originally meant to be a *mokśa-śāstra*, but a *dharma-śāstra* or science of duty or right action. It was a philosophy of *karma* or action. Later Mīmāṃsā writers accepted the concept of *mokṣa* and made the Mīmāṃsā subservient to the Vedānta, thereby making it an incomplete and imperfect Vedānta and so an incomplete and imperfect philosophy. The Mīmāṃsā preaches *karma*; but the fashion of treating *karma* (action) as subservient to *bhakti* (devotion) and *jñāna* (knowledge, gnosis) has grown. Thus by interpreting the Mīmāṃsā as what it was not intended to be, it was represented as incomplete, imperfect and so unimportant; and thus the very spirit behind the philosophy was lost sight of. [70]

This is a pertinent point, and it would be true to say that Mīmāṃsā is taken less seriously than the other *darśanas*. But, had it not shifted its position to a *mokṣaśāstra*, its fate may have been worse. At least it represents one of the six orthodox schools of Hindu philosophy – and that would not have been possible without the significant adoption of a concept of *mokṣa*. A different, yet related, criticism of the school comes from Halbfass. He points out the difficulties posed by a school adopting approaches to religion that are long outmoded: "What the Mīmāṃsā does amounts to a retrospective reconstruction of the Veda as an idealized fountainhead of the unity and identity of the Āryan tradition. Although the Mīmāṃsaka advocates the Vedic rituals as the center of dharma, he is no longer at home in the world in which these rituals were originally developed and enacted. The historical conditions have changed; his world is different from the old magico-ritualistic universe of the Veda."[71] In particular, and as Halbfass points out, it is the massive animal sacrifice of the *Veda* that would be a "serious concern" to any who would wish to accept Vedic ritualism as thoroughly authentic and religiously necessary. For such sacrificial ritual was antagonistic to those who would wish to uphold any belief in the doctrine of *ahiṃsā*, "nonviolence". As he notes, the "tension and conflict between Vedic ritualism and *ahiṃsā* remains a characteristic phenomenon of later religious thought in India".[72] This is likely to be another reason why the school did not continue its traditions to the present day. As a contrast, and a conclusion, I cite the opinion of Dwivedi on the impact of Mīmāṃsā in the Hindu philosophy:

Massive and unique contribution of Mīmāṃsā to the philosophy of language, hermeneutics, exegesis and semiology, to the philosophy of religion, epistemology and above all to the philosophy of pragmatic active life affirming continuity of cultural tradition remains important for the intellectual pursuits in the world of knowledge and culture. Its influence on other branches of learning in India is formidable. No system of thought can be properly understood without a reference to Mīmāṃsā.[73]

4
Vaiśeṣika

Background to the school

The Vaiśeṣika school is noted for its attempt to explain the whole universe in logical and realistic terms through a mainly atomistic theory. Along with its associative school of Nyāya, it "offers one of the most vigorous efforts at the construction of a substantialist, realist ontology that the world has ever seen".[1] "Particularity" or "difference" – *viśeṣa* – is said to characterize the primary atoms that combine to create our diverse world, and this results in characteristics that distinguish one phenomenon from another. This makes its view of the world distinctly pluralistic with none of the underpinning unity that characterizes so many other strands of Hindu thought. The emphasis on *viśeṣa*, "particularity", as one aspect of valid knowledge, is possibly reflected in the name of the school.[2] And it is this aspect of particularity, along with its developed atomic theory of reality, which are the major contributions of the school, and which are its distinguishable features in, and contributions to, the allied (*samānatantra*) school of Nyāya. The complementary beliefs of the two schools are considerable, but there are sufficient differences in emphasis – indeed, also in belief – to warrant their separate discussion. Vaiśeṣika is believed to have supplied the metaphysics and cosmology, and Nyāya the epistemology. The result is what has been termed a "well-rounded synthesis",[3] and the view that: "A combination of the two was a logical necessity."[4] But there is a long history of Vaiśeṣika thought before the amalgamation of the two schools, which took place in about the fifth century[5] or later – even if, as Karl Potter states, the two schools "considered themselves as mutually supportive" from their early development.[6]

While Vaiśeṣika is an orthodox *darśana*, Hiriyanna is of the opinion that it was not originally so.[7] This is likely to have been the case, especially considering the pluralistic metaphysics of the school on the one hand, and the somewhat appended, low-profiled view of God on the other. Like most of the schools, a considerable period of debate and disputation, along with lost writings, prefigures our present knowledge of the origins of the school.[8] Its precise dating, therefore, remains problematic, and ranges from suggestions of 400 BCE[9] or even the sixth century BCE,[10] to as late as 200–400 CE.[11] But since the earliest extant *Sūtras* of the school seems to have no concern with Buddhism, or even with Nyāya material, there are some grounds for considering the date of this extant *Vaiśeṣikasūtras* as stemming from the first few centuries before the common era.[12] The school as we know it came about through a variety of traditions. Its teachings were handed down orally in the form of the usual aphorisms – *sūtras*. These short, cursory sayings were eventually committed to one, composite, written form, along with later explanatory additions. Since the system "had its beginnings at some indeterminate time B.C.",[13] the literary development of the school is as complicated as its dating. It was not until the fifth or sixth century CE that a more systematic formulation of the ideas of the school occurred.

Like its partnered *darśana*, Vaiśeṣika has the liberation of the self as its fundamental aim, a liberation that can be realized through a correct perspective of knowledge in terms of the real nature of the world. Without this knowledge, the self is bound to the constant chain of reincarnation because of ignorance. Realization of the atomic nature of the phenomenal world – and that includes the mind – will assist in the cessation of the desires and aversions by which each individual self relates to the world, and becomes bound to it. But the self, when liberated, retains its particularity, and there is no thought of the unity of the self with other selves, or with an Absolute divinity.

Main proponents and commentators

The main proponent of the school, referred to as the founder, was Kaṇāda, and it was he who is said to have compiled the foundational *Sūtras* of the school, the *Vaiśeṣikasūtras*. He was from the Kāśyapa family, and is sometimes referred to by that name, but the little that is known of him is more legendary than factual. While there may have been earlier major proponents of the school, Kaṇāda's *Sūtras* is the earliest that we know of. His name, Kaṇāda, is a compound of *kaṇa* "atom", "particle" or "grain", and *ad* "to eat", thus earning him the title "atom-eater",[14] though his real name was his family name. Legend has it that he used to meditate all day and, like an owl, eat only at night, so the school is sometimes called the *Aulūka* system from the word *ulūka* "owl". Nevertheless, as Potter comments: "It is pretty clear that we are dealing here with a mythical personage."[15] Be that as it may, I shall refer to the legendary Kaṇāda as author of the *Vaiśeṣikasūtras* throughout, in line with the traditions of the school. While there were a number of commentaries written on Kaṇāda's original *Sūtras*, the earliest extant one is that of Praśastapāda's *Padārthadharmasaṃgraha*. He was responsible for a more systematic presentation of the beliefs of the school in about the fifth or sixth century CE. His commentary, or *bhāṣya*, on Kaṇāda's *Vaiśeṣikasūtras* is more concerned with an elucidation of the major content than a systematic and chronological explanation of the aphorisms, and is a more refreshing rearrangement of the material, developing it considerably. His work has remained the seminal and authoritative work on the Vaiśeṣika school. While some later commentaries on Praśastapāda's *bhāṣya* were written, his work always remained definitive, and marked the end of the long, developmental period of the school. Here, in the context of this chapter, therefore, I shall be concentrating mainly on the older Vaiśeṣika of the so-called Kanāda, and Praśastapāda. Kaṇāda's *Vaiśeṣikasūtras* consist of ten parts or "books" each containing two sections. The whole work contains three hundred and seventy *sūtras*.

Its main purpose was to demonstrate how knowledge of the true nature of the self, and of the nature of reality as a whole, could provide the means to *mokṣa*.

Reality: the Vaiśeṣika view of the world

The Vaiśeṣka concept of reality is realist, pluralist and atomistic and it attempts to examine reality in a systematic and common-sense way. It is a "nature philosophy" as one writer puts it.[16] All the phenomena that we see in the world are given reality as objects – a reality that obtains irrespective of our subjective experience of them. Realism is fundamentally important to the school because it "invests every object with a self-hood; each object is significant by itself",[17] each object has its own individuality. And this is true of individual selves as much as all other things in existence. Indeed, such is the realism of all primal matter, that eternal souls stand alongside the eternal primary building blocks of all things, and are not projected to any greater significance. *Karmic* selves – of the kind that we understand to be the varied personalities that make up existence – are as different from each other as the non-*karmic* souls that are their basic substances. Diversity is at the fundamental level of all existence, and therefore characterizes the whole universe as we know it. And yet Vaiśeṣika is not materialistic, for it accepts the non-material nature of souls, of God, and the operation of the law of cause and effect in *karma* as well as the unseen potency existing between a cause and its related effect. Whereas some religious inquiry searches for an ultimate cause of existence, the Vaiśeṣika inquiry is different. Halbfass makes this clear when he writes: "The old mythical question: What *was* all this in the beginning? is translated into the question: What *is* it, in the ultimate analysis? In other words, what are the ultimate ingredients of the cycles, those constituents or elements of the world that are not affected by the recurrent cosmic processes?"[18] Vaiśeṣika sets out to answer this question about the basic stuff of the universe.

But while Vaiśeṣika's pluralistic realism accepts the plurality of, and therefore differentiation between, all objects, it nevertheless posits a certain relation between them, because they stem from fundamental, elemental atoms. Vaiśeṣika, writes Halbfass, "tries to understand the world in terms of a combination, aggregation, and separation, but also substitution and replacement of definite, actual, distinct entities".[19] Every item that we experience externally in the world is given reality as a particular combination of atomic parts, a combination of different conditions, though the liberated soul, and therefore the eternal soul, is not atomic. Each individual is real, is able to experience the results of his or her own actions, remains the same individual through all those experiences, and is different from the next individual, and from all others. All individual selves, as all things in existence, are located in time and space, both of which allow them to come into being, exist, and pass away.

Physical matter is derived from four primary types of elemental substances – earth, water, fire and air – called *mahābhūtas*, from which certain products are produced and also certain qualities. An additional substance, ether or *ākāṣa*, is the particular medium that facilitates the quality of sound. Thus we have:

Substances	**Earth**	**Water**	**Fire or Light**	**Air**	**Ākāśa**
Products	solids	liquids	luminosity	gases	etheric substance
Qualities	smell* taste colour touch	liquidity taste* colour touch viscidity	colour* touch	touch*	sound*
Kinds	bodies sense-organs objects of perception				
Special qualities	taste liquidity	luminosity	temperature		

* is the distinctive quality, the *viśeṣaguṇa*.

The four elemental, basic substances have indivisible atoms that combine in all sorts of ways to produce the world that we know. And everything that we know in the world is denoted by some name that serves to differentiate its particular combination from that of the next thing, and from everything else. These individual combinations of atoms, labelled by various names, are all real, even though their combination is temporary and finite: it is the reality of the basic, elemental atoms that lends to each individual object its own specific reality. The particular contribution of Vaiśeṣika lies in its classification of such objects of knowledge according to its atomistic view of the world. The four atomic element-types in the table above, form the basic material of the universe. To these are added another atomic substance of mind, and then four non-atomic substances of ether, space, time and selves – a total of nine primary substances. Inhering in these substances are both qualities and activities or motions. These three categories – *substance*, *quality* and *activity* – will be examined extensively below.

Vaiśeṣika assumed that things can be broken down to their basic atoms. These always remain separate, distinct and uncreated. Clearly, we would never be able to *perceive* such atoms, but they could be *inferred* from the fact that we know things are composed of parts, and those parts can be broken down again and again. Atoms are necessarily imperceptible; if they were not, and were perceptible, then they could not be permanent, because everything we see is subject to impermanence through decay. And since a different number of atoms are needed to make up a mountain than to make up a small mustard seed, there must be a limit to the division and subdivision of parts. If there were not, there would be no difference in their respective sizes – the mustard seed would have an indefinite number of atoms as its parts and would, logically, be as big as the mountain. The only way it can remain small is if its divisibility into parts ceases at the level of basic atoms. The mustard seed, then, will require less division and subdivision to reach its elemental state than the mountain. When each entity is broken down it reaches its primary state of an atom, a *paramāṇu*. Thus, to quote Frauwallner, "the whole world-occurrence is a play of the imperishable atoms which conglomerate and again separate but themselves remain permanent".[20] The question could be raised how impermanent aggregates of atoms can have any degree of reality. After all, a jar is only real in so far as it remains a jar. If I smash it into little bits, then this demonstrates all too well that its reality is somewhat limited. But Vaiśeṣika accepted the reality of a thing, and its newness, *separately* from the parts that composed it. A buttercup, then, is something that inheres in the aggregate of all the parts that combine together to make it, but is something *more than* these parts, with a different and separate reality from the parts. The reality of the whole stems not only from the reality of the basic atomic components it contains, but also from a universality of its whole to other "wholes" of its kind – buttercup-ness in general. Moreover, each primary atom has its own *particularity*, its own distinctive and real nature informed by both qualitative and quantitative characteristics. This will always lend to the aggregates that make up any phenomenon a degree of distinctive reality – albeit an impermanent one.

Heat is normally suggested by Vaiśeṣika as the medium by which atoms combine and separate. The process of combination is begun when two similar atoms combine to form what is called a *dvyaṇuka*, a dyad, or binary molecule. Such molecules are beyond knowledge through our senses. Three such binary molecules or dyads make a triad, a *tryaṇuka*, and this is, according to Vaiśeṣika, the first finite, perceptible entity – the tiny motes that we see in sunbeams. It is from triads that the whole of the universe is formed. These binary molecules then also combine together in groups of two or more. And so the combinations continue. The greater the number of combinations, the greater the mass that is produced. Importantly, when two similar atoms combine to form the binary dyad, there is a *relation* between the dyad and the primary atoms, but the resulting dyad is different and new, even though its relation to the original is one of *inherence* (*samavāya*). And the same is true of any further combinations.

Given the basic substances from which all things are composed, there is a certain inter-relatedness of all things, even though each combination of atomic molecules is a new effect of its causal atoms. So while it is possible to differentiate and distinguish between, and to compare and contrast, the various composites that make up reality, individualizing all things, there is a certain relational inherence of everything in basic, primary substances. Radhakrishnan commented on this interrelation of all things by saying: "The changing world of experience consists of a plurality of existent things standing in a complicated network of relations of all kinds with one another. The Vaiṣeśika has for its aim the representation of the universe as a systematic whole, a harmony of varying members".[21] However, Vaiśeṣika did not overplay the interconnection of all substances to the point that an underlying and harmonious reality could exist naturally. The theism of later Vaiśeṣika ensured that a divine being was responsible for the appropriate combination of atoms in order to effectuate causation according to past actions. This is something that will also need to be examined below.

All that exists, then, are substances with attributes or qualities added to them, which are at one and the same time, particularized and individualized, but are also interconnected and related to all other substances, "a mass of sense data which melt into one another", said Radhakrishnan.[22] The reality of existence is an interrelated, atomic and composite structure resulting from basic independent and eternal atoms. The idea of basic elements of earth, water, air and fire (or light) is one that has been popular in many systems of belief both within and without Hinduism. These basic elements are conceived of as eternal, their specific combinations accounting for the diversity of all life. But when combined together to form any entity in manifest existence, that coming together is non-eternal, a temporary combining of the basic atoms. The relatedness of things is very evident in the universality of certain classes of things, their generic nature or *sāmānya*, as well as by the inseparable connection or *samavāya* that exists between certain things. But, also, things have their own particularity, their *viśeṣa*. Universality (or generality), and particularity, are intimately linked; indeed, it is only the qualities of each that vary sufficiently to differentiate between them.

Epistemology

Following Nyāya, Vaiśeṣika came to regard knowledge, intellect, consciousness and perception as identical. Knowledge is a quality of the self, conveyed adventitiously by the mind. Thus, knowledge is sometimes absent in sleep, and can only exist through its dependence on the substrate of the self. So any knowledge that occurs does so through the agency of the self and must be knowledge of an object. There can be no "pure" consciousness, "pure" knowledge, that is the nature of a real self, for knowledge itself can never be a pure substance.

Pramāṇas

Perception

Whereas Nyāya accepts four *pramāṇas*, Vaiśeṣika accepts only two, perception and inference. Perception is accepted in the same sense as Nyāya of direct perception through the medium of the senses, and intuitively, without the senses. In particular, *yogic* extra-sensory intuition, extraordinary (*alaukika*) perception, is accepted as a valid means of knowledge. Perception is divided into indeterminate and determinate. The former is vague intuition, an apprehension of something without qualifications, attributes and class, whereas the latter moves to a point where these are distinguishable and known. Praśastapāda accepted memory as a type of valid knowledge. Nevertheless, because memory is triggered by perception or by cases of inference, it is subservient to these means. So memory is not, itself, a direct means of knowledge: it is merely supportive.

Inference

The only other means of valid knowledge that is accepted is inference. Comparison and verbal testimony are both included in this category. Inferential knowledge is knowledge gained through association or contact of one thing with another, as, for example, with the association of cause and effect, like fire and smoke. In this case there is an inseparable connection between two entities, and the smoke inheres in the fire. While later views of inference came in line with those of Nyāya, Kaṇāda, who seems to have been unaware of the Nyāya analysis here, gave more specific examples of inference – cause from effect; effect from cause; inferring one thing from another to which it is inseparably connected, or is opposed to, or inheres in. Praśastapāda's views are in line with Nyāya. He was more precise than Kaṇāda and divided inference into two kinds. The first is perceived resemblance between the knowledge of one member of a class when applied to another, new, perception of something of the same class. The second is a more general application of a principle: hard work by the peasants produces a good harvest, so one might infer that hard work by the priests through sacrificial ceremony, might also lead to a good reward.[23] Non-apprehension is considered to be inferential knowledge by Praśastapāda. Just as a cause *x* can be inferred from an effect *y*, so the non-existence of a cause can be inferred from the non-existence of an effect.

The two additional *pramāṇas* accepted by Nyāya are *upamāna* and *śabda*, comparison and verbal testimony, respectively. But Vaiśeṣika rejects testimony as a separate means of knowledge. The verbal testimony of the *Veda*, according to Vaiśeṣika, is not eternal and is not absolutely authoritative. However, the validity of it can be inferred from the reliability of its seers and, as such, it has a degree of reality that is exceptional and that contains accurate knowledge of reality from those whose consciousness could directly and intuitively perceive it. Later Vaiśeṣikas assigned the authorship of the *Veda* to God. All such verbal knowledge, Vaiśeṣika claimed, can only be inferred from the universal acceptance of the meanings, the denotations of words. Things, according to Kanāda are given names by convention, not by any eternal, timeless precedence.

Error

Invalid knowledge was regarded as doubt, misconception, indefinite cognition and dreams. Doubt occurs when what is seen resembles something that was seen in the past (like a piece of shell that resembles silver), or what was perceived in one form in the past appears differently in the present. Doubt is mainly caused by ignorance in some way or other. Inaccurate knowledge occurs through the imperfections of the senses, and through the imperfection of the impressions of the memory. In this last case, the shell is more readily accepted as silver. According to Praśastapāda, too, error occurs through defective sense perception when an aspect of something once perceived causes the mind to relay incorrect information to the self. *Karma* is the root of all such error.

Padārthas: categories of reality

The origins of the concept of "categories", *padārthas*, are obscure, but it is a concept integral to both Vaiśeṣika and Nyāya philosophy. However, it is the special contribution of the Vaiśeṣika *darśana* that is notable here. It is this school that meticulously analysed those objects or categories of knowledge that can be cognized – the *padārthas*, or objects denoted by words – and these may be physical or otherwise. Whereas Nyāya recognizes sixteen *padārthas*, Vaiśeṣika accepts only seven (though Praśastapāda accepted only six). In other words, there are only seven categories of real entities in the whole of the universe of which we can have consciousness and, therefore, that we can name. They are:

Perceptible objects of experience

1	Substance	*dravya*
2	Quality	*guṇa*
3	Activity	*karma*

Intellectually inferable and imperceptible

4	Universality	*sāmānya*
5	Particularity	*viśeṣa*
6	Inherence	*samavāya*
7	Non-existence	*abhāva* (not accepted by Praśastapāda)

These categories are of the nature of the following:

1 Substance (*dravya*)

Elemental
Air (*marut* or *vāyu*)
Fire (*tejas*)
Water (*ap* or *jala*)
Earth (*kṣiti* or *prithivī*)

Non-elemental
Ether (*ākāśa*)
Time (*kāla*)
Space (*dik*)
Soul (*ātman*)
Mind (*manas*)

2 Quality (*guṇa*)

Kanāda listed seventeen, but added "etc." at the end of the list, thus inviting more. Those accepted by Kanāda are indicated by an asterisk.

Universal
Tendency (*saṃskāra*)
Heaviness (*gurutva*)
Distance (*paratva*)*
Proximity (*aparatva*)*
Conjunction or contact (*saṃyoga*)*
Disjunction or separation (*vibhāga*)*
Distinctness (*pṛthaktva*)*
Size (*parimāṇa*)*
Number (*saṃkhyā*)*
Fluidity (*dravatva*)

Particular
Touch (*sparśa*)*
Smell (*gandha*)*
Taste (*rasa*)*
Colour (*rūpa*)*
Sound (*śabda*)
Merit (*dharma*)
Demerit (*adharma*)
Desire (*icchā*)*
Aversion (*dveṣa*)*
Effort (*prayatna*)*
Knowledge (*buddhi*)*
Pleasure (*sukha*)*
Pain (*duḥkha*)*
Viscosity (*sneha*)

3 **Activity** (*karma*)

Upward
Downward
Contraction
Expansion
Horizontal

4 **Universality/Generality** (*sāmānya*)

Higher – existence-ness
Lower – the 7 *padārthas*

5 **Particularity** (*viśeṣa*)
6 **Inherence** (*samavāya*)
7 **Non-existence** (*abhāva*)

The first three categories of *substance*, *quality* and *activity* represent the phenomenal objects of the world that are subject to impermanence, to cause and effect, individuality and generality, but which are perceptible. They are still given particular existence and reality, despite their finitude. The last four – *universality*, *particularity*, *inherence* and *non-existence* – are independent, eternal and non-causal in nature. Knowledge of them is dependent on inference, or intuitive perception and logical analysis, for they cannot be known by the senses. The last category here, non-existence, was added later. All the categories are given the characteristics of *existence*, *knowability* – either directly, or through inference – and *nameability*.

Substance (dravya)

Substance is a crucial category for existence, for it is through substance that both quality and activity or motion are able to exist, and which can combine both. It is only possible to have knowledge of a quality or an activity *of something* – in other words, of a substance. But, similarly, we cannot have knowledge of a substance unless we are able to define its qualities or activities. Then, too, it is only substances that are able to come into contact with each other, and this is termed *saṃyoga*. Thus there is a certain relational connection between substances, in that they have a certain impact one with another, and between all three categories in that qualities and activities inhere in the substances. A particularly neat definition of *dravya* is given by Sharma as "the substratum where actions and qualities inhere and which is the coexistent material cause of the composite things produced from it".[24] And while the compounds, the particular things that are formed from it, are transient – "transient constellations" as Halbfass terms them[25] – the nine basic and indestructible components of substance listed above are eternal and permanent, and different from one another. These nine kinds of substances, then, are the basic components of all existence.

The first five substances – earth, water, fire, air and *ākāśa* or ether – are physical substances because each of these is characterized by a quality that is perceptible to the senses,[26] and is characterized by motion. The remainder – time, space, soul and *manas* or mind – are not regarded as physical and perceptible by the external sense organs. *Ākāśa*, time and space are all-pervading, and are the media in which all other substantial things exist. Earth, water, fire, air and mind, are atomic substances ether, space, time and Self or soul are not, and so do not combine to produce anything in existence. While qualities of atoms may be perceptible to the senses, the basic atoms are not. It is the *combinations* of atoms informing the objects of existence that are perceptible but, unlike the basic atoms, the combinations of them are non-eternal and exist only as long as the composite atoms that inform them are combined together. In reducing the universe to nine basic substances, however, there can be no unity underlying reality, though there is an interconnection of the many things that arise from them. The nine basic substances are eternal, independent and individual, and they are uncaused and indestructible. In contrast, the objects that derive from the atomic substances are the objects of causation and dissolution, and are therefore dependent and finite. But it is because of the relative stability of substances that continuous identity is possible, while qualities and activities might change.

So all the things that we see in life, including our own physical, bodily selves, are made up of many parts. But each object can be broken down into its fundamental or ultimate atomic structure – its *paramāṇus* (*āṇu* = "atom" and *para* = "ultimate, supreme, higher") – and this structure will be a composite of the basic indivisible atoms that have no parts and which cannot, therefore, be broken down any further. The objects that we experience in the world are composites of the four basic atoms of earth, water, fire and air. And within each elemental substance, like earth, for example, there will be an infinite number of similar atoms, but they are never identical to one another. Each of these basic atoms will be associated with different qualities, and these qualities will inform the object that is caused. All these basic atoms provide an unchanging and constant substratum to the transience and flux of existence. Thus, the elemental substances are both eternal (*nitya*) and non-eternal (*anitya*) – eternal in their basic state, and non-eternal when combined and derivative. Conversely, what is combined can be broken apart, but this process can only go as far as the fundamental elemental atoms: there is a limit to division. Ether, time, space, souls and minds, however, retain their eternal, non-composite and independent natures; the ultimate, natural Self, always remains a separate substance.

Since, then, there are different, indivisible and fundamental atoms that inform all existence, there is never a time when nothing at all exists. Atoms combine and disintegrate to form both microcosmic phenomena, and macrocosmic universes, in endless cycles – a process sensitively described by Radhakrishnan:

> The components which unite to form a whole, and therefore were previously able to exist apart from such combination, possess the capacity for independent existence and return to it. Fabric after fabric in the visible world up to the terrestrial mass itself may be dissolved, but the atoms will abide ever new and fresh, ready to form other structures in the ages yet to come. The individual atoms combine with others and continue in that co-operative existence for some time and again disintegrate into their original solitary being to form new combinations. This process of grouping and separation goes on endlessly.[27]

The relevance of this particular Vaiśeṣika theory to modern scientific views is reflected in the words of Professor Robert Winston: "Atoms are only borrowed for the brief spell of our lives, to be recycled – used again and again by myriad life forms."[28]

Whatever entity results from combinations of atoms, it is given reality because it becomes a *whole* that is more than its atomic parts. Any compound substance is named and knowable as such by its whole composite nature. The buttercup is the *whole* flower and is something new and different from its parts. If this were not the case, then we could never know anything at all, we could not give names to anything because things would only be combinations of imperceptible atoms without wholeness, without distinct and individual identity. We could never know what a table is, a pen, a desk – anything. The whole, then, the *avayavin* as it is called, is of a different nature to its parts, or even the sum of its parts.[29]

The four supra-sensible elements, the *mahābhūtas* – earth *kṣiti* or *pṛithiv",* water *ap* or *jala*, fire *tejas* and air *marut* or *vāyu* – are known collectively as *paramāṇus* or primary atoms. Though there are an infinitesimal number of them in any one element, each one – each earth atom, for example – is a whole that has no parts and cannot be destroyed nor produced. Without combination with other atoms it has no magnitude, does not exist in time, which is a separate substance, and does not take up space, from which it is also separate. However, since the nature of mind is also a *paramāṇu* then it seems logical that the mind, because of its very nature, can conceive of the super-sensible atoms.[30] Importantly, every sense that we possess is a quality that is dependent on one of the elements, as the chart on p. 105 illustrates. Although qualities and activities are themselves fundamental categories that inform all existence, they cannot exist without the substratum of substance. Substance provides the medium for their manifestation, by being the material cause of all things that have qualities and activities. And yet, since independent substances have their own particularity, their own *viśeṣa,* then it could be claimed that no substance can exist without the qualities and activities that make it distinct from other substances – earth from air, for example. Indeed, it is problematic to suggest that substance can exist at all in a particular sense without special characteristics. But Vaiśeṣika believed that in *essence*, substances, in fact, are devoid of qualities. Radhakrishnan wrote of this enigma:

> At the first moment of creation the substance is said to be without any qualities, the suggestion being that the metaphysical identity of a substance is not the same as the permanent identity of its properties. The essence of a substance, which makes it what it is, has little to do with the permanent qualities which are characteristic of and peculiar to it. The permanence of the qualities is not essential to its remaining what it is. The special qualities of substances are regarded as effects, *i.e.* qualities are derived from substances . . .[31]

And yet, denial of quality must still be denial of particularity, for particularity must have some particularity of *essence* that distinguishes one substance from the next – earth from soul, for example. If not, then there is a unified quality-less basis as the substratum of all. The relation between substance and qualities in Vaiśeṣika suggests that one cannot exist without the other. This is a relation of *samavāya*, or inherence, a separate category that will need to be examined below. Nevertheless, substance still remained for Vaiśeṣika the independent category on which all other categories depended,[32] despite the difficulties presented by positing different substances that were fundamentally devoid of qualities.

Ākāśa, ether, is the unique substance that is the medium of the quality of sound. Hearing is another sense quality, and must, in the Vaiśeṣika view, belong to a substance. But because sound did not seem to belong to the other elemental substances, this fifth category of *ākāśa* was inferred as the substrate for sound. As a substance *ākāśa* is both imperceptible and infinite. It is also indivisible and, therefore, non-atomic. Because of its infinite nature, it is not composed of an infinite number of indivisible atoms, but is essentially one, indivisible, substance. Its non-atomic nature means that it has no atoms to form aggregates with other atoms, and so nothing can be formed from it. It is one (*eka*), and all-pervading (*vibhu*). The rejection of air as the substance in which the quality of sound is perceived is because the special quality of air is touch, and this sense faculty is not perceived by the organ associated with sound, the ear. Indeed, colour, taste, smell and touch are qualities that are always absent from *ākāśa*. Thus it was believed that sound could exist without the elements and, similarly, the elements could exist without the quality of sound. So the special non-atomic substance of *ākāśa* became the substance by which the quality of sound can be known. And like the substance in which it inheres, sound was believed to be an eternal quality, capable, like its substance, of arising anywhere, and of extending out in any direction.

How, then, does *ākāśa* differ from space, *dik*? Space is not seen as the material substance of the quality of sound. Rather, it is a locational substance, that which is responsible for the relation of one thing to another. It is *relative* space as opposed to the all-pervading nature of *ākāśa*, so it is concerned with what is north, south, right, left, up, down, near, far, and so on. It is thus space that conditions and temporarily holds all things in relation to other things. This is reflected in the meaning of the Sanskrit root *diś* "to show, point out", from which the term *dik* is derived. Yet, while space may seem to be divided in conventional language, it is *eka*, one, indivisible, eternal and all-pervading. Space, too, then, is a non-atomic substance. As such, it is separate, like *ākāśa*, from the primary, elemental substances, earth, water, fire and air.

Like space and ether, time, *kāla*, is one, *eka*, eternal, and indivisible. While it is imperceptible, it can be inferred from the effects that it has on all life and phenomena. For time is a causal factor in the existence of all things; no atomic aggregate can exist outside it, but is always subject to it. Like space, then, time conditions all relations, and all atomic aggregates that exist within it. While we refer to beginnings and ends, to past, present and future, to now and then, a minute and an hour, young and old, and so on, we refer only to the temporality of atomic aggregates and not to the infinite all-pervading, and non-atomic nature of time itself. The primary substances are outside time, in the same way that they are outside space, but non-eternal atomic aggregates are subject to the causal nature of time, to coming into being and to dissolution. The change and impermanence of life and all things are the effects of time, as are the movements of all things. Souls stand alongside time, and are not contained in it. Even though their temporary qualities and activities take place within it, the ultimate substances that are the real nature of souls are eternal and separate from time. Thus: "Time," writes Halbfass, "is an entity, not the horizon in which entities exist nor the abyss in which they disappear."[33] Space and time are eternally and equally present everywhere. They are not substances in which objects move and exist, but allow for relational knowledge.

The remaining two substances are Self or soul, *ātman*, and mind, *manas*. These are two important categories that I intend to deal with in considerable detail at a later stage in this chapter. Here, it needs to be pointed out that, in line with the pluralistic realism of Vaiśeṣika, souls are also plural – there is a separate one for each individual. As a substance, the soul will have its particular qualities, and these were stated as desire, aversion, knowledge, pain, pleasure, volition, and so on. While the *ātman* is not atomic, mind is, and is the medium through which memory is possible. It acts as the link between objects of the senses and the Self or soul.[34]

Quality (guṇa)

The qualities, as listed in the table on p. 105 are 24 in number, 10 being of universal nature, and 14 of particular nature. Many of them are subdivided into other qualities: colour, taste and smell, for example, are needful of such division. Some of the qualities warrant comment at this point. Of the universal qualities, *tendency* or *saṃskāra* is of three kinds:

- velocity, by which motion is maintained
- elasticity, by which something returns to its natural state after being stretched
- mental impressions that occur from experiences.

Distance and *proximity* are qualities that can relate to space or time. *Conjunction* is the bringing together of two or more things, like paper, pen and desk. Importantly, these things can exist separately, so conjunction has nothing to do with cause and effect. The difference between *disjunction* and *distinctness* needs to be noted. Disjunction is the separating of things that have been brought into contact with each other, whereas distinctness does not suggest any prior conjunction; it is the difference between a jar and a stone. At a deeper level, conjunction and disjunction account for the transient combination and later disjunction of atoms. They are the foundation of change in the universe. Of the particular qualities, *merit and demerit* will need to be discussed below in the context of causality. Knowledge, also, will require further discussion. Suffice it to say here, that knowledge is a quality of the *ātman* and is consciousness, or *buddhi*. Effort is subdivided into striving towards, striving against and vital effort.

Qualities, as has been seen, cannot be known without reference to the substances in which they inhere; they cannot exist independently. Nor can qualities have their own qualities or actions; they may have *modes* – sound may be quiet or loud, for example – but they can only be qualities of substances. They can also have nothing to do with conjunction and disjunction. They are not causative in that they define the nature and character of substances, but have nothing to do with the actual *existence* of them. Yet qualities can be the cause of other qualities, and the cause of activities: such qualities would be effort, impetus, merit, demerit, weight, fluidity and contact. Although they are dependent on substances, we can have knowledge of qualities – mental or material – can think about them, and name them, as if they were independent of substances. I can, for example think of the colour blue independently of a substance in which it might inhere. Thus, qualities are independent realities, even if they do not possess the eternal nature of substances. Some qualities would inhere in a number of substances; sound, as has been seen, relates only to one.

The distinction between universal qualities (*sāmānyaguṇa*) and particular qualities (*viśeṣaguṇa*) is that the former are qualities of two or more substances, and are therefore general qualities, while the latter are the more distinctive characteristics of one particular substance. Each self, for example, will have a number of particular qualities, like knowledge, desire, aversion, pleasure, pain, merit, and demerit, as well as some general, universal qualities like humanity, man-ness, woman-ness, etc. Qualities like merit or *dharma*, and demerit, *adharma*, are not at all perceptible; others are. Qualities are eternal in the elemental atoms – which, again, suggests that substances are as much dependent on their qualities for their existence, as qualities on substances – but are non-eternal in aggregates of atoms. Eternal substances have their specific qualities, their *viśeṣaguṇas*. The relationship between qualities and the substances in which they inhere is known as *samavāya*, and this quality of *inherence* is, itself, one of the seven categories.

Of all the qualities, *saṃyoga*, conjunction, is one of the most important. For it is by the process of the conjunction of atoms that the aggregates of atoms make up the objects that we know in the phenomenal world. This cannot take place in non-atomic substances like time, space, ether and particular souls, but it can certainly do so in the elemental atomic substances. *Saṃyoga* is a quality, therefore, that characterizes all the elemental substances. But if we think of conjunction, it really has to involve some kind of *activity* by which two or more substances combine together. So for conjunction to be a *quality* it has to be something that transcends the actual *movement* of two or more things that come into connection, otherwise it would belong to the category of activity rather than quality. This suggests that *saṃyoga* is an *effect* of movement, of *karma*. So when pen and desk come into contact temporarily, the quality of conjunction, *saṃyoga*, obtains *after* the activity that brings them together. And it can only relate substances, particularly ones that would normally have no relationship – like the pen and the desk. However, in the case of something inextricably linked, like clay and a clay jar, the relationship between jar and clay is more than conjunction, for the clay inheres in the jar, and is its causal material: the jar could not exist without the clay. Whatever aggregate of atoms makes up a new object, it is the atoms as substance that are regarded as the real cause; in this case, the activity of the atoms is a facet that inheres *in the substance*, just as the qualities do. This relationship between things that can never be separate is not conjunction, but *inherence*, itself one of the Vaiśeṣika categories that will be examined shortly. So conjunction remains a quality of the substances, without any inherence of the separate objects that are temporarily conjoined to each other.

Activity (karma)

Activity, action, motion, is the third of the Vaiśeṣika categories. It can relate only to substance, in which it inheres, and is the dynamic process by which things come into contact; it is the cause of all conjunction and disjunction. However, activity can only pertain to the elemental substances – earth, fire, water and air – and the mind. It cannot subsist in the non-atomic substances of ether, space, time and *ātman*. The category covers five kinds of activity – upward, downward, contraction, expansion and simply going. Unlike qualities, which may be eternal, activities are temporary. They may happen in one moment, or in a continuous series, as would happen in the case of something travelling directionally for some time. But sooner or later, activity ceases, either because of conjunction or disjunction, or because the substance relative to the action ceases to exist. Going covers many movements. According to Kaṇāda:

> Throwing upwards, throwing downwards, contracting, expanding, and going – these are the only actions. . . . all such actions as gyrating, evacuating, quivering, flowing upwards, transverse falling, falling downwards, rising and the like, being only particular forms of going, and not forming distinct classes by themselves.[35]

This category, then, is the rationale for all movement of atomic, finite substances. However, it would normally be accepted that an efficient cause of movement is needed: activity cannot cause itself, though it is the cause of active modes of substances. This will be the role of the divine, a topic to which I shall return later. The admission of activity as a category is also an admission of inactivity as a possibility: there is no suggestion that substances must constantly be in motion. Atomic substances may, therefore, be static at times, and activity is as much the cause of inertia as it is of conjunction and disjunction. It has no qualities, only modes – like fast or slow. Activity is not, itself, the cause of other activities. It is the cause of activity of substances, but never of substances themselves.

Universality/Generality (sāmāṇya)

Kaṇāda differentiated between qualities that have a universal character in that they inhere in things generally, and qualities that are particular, because they are the particular distinguishing qualities of one thing, and serve to differentiate it from all others. We automatically make the distinction in everyday life when we refer to something like the term "humanity" to refer generally to the "human-ness" of all human beings, and a "man" or a "woman" to refer to the particular. The former, the universal or general, tends to obtain irrespective of the particular. It is best depicted by the addition – if ungrammatic – of the suffix *-ness* to the particular, like cow-*ness*, tree-*ness*, and so on. Thus, cow-ness obtains irrespective of cows; so cow and cow-ness are two separate realities. And we could perhaps talk of dodo-ness, despite the extinct nature of the species. A universal serves to link a number of related but different entities in which that universal inheres, but is ultimately eternally present even if one or all of these entities cease to exist. Tree-ness is thus a fact irrespective of the number or future non-existence of all trees. The universal bears the particular sameness, the commonness, that unites all things of a class and allows commonality between things to be perceived. For instance, if there are two brown cows, the colour brown that is common to them is known through the universal, not through the quality of the colour brown that is an attribute of each: it is the universal brown-ness of the quality brown that is perceived.

Frauwallner considers the category of universality to be a very early philosophical one, pre-dating Kaṇāda considerably.[36] Indeed, the most obvious universal is that of *existence-ness*, and this is a metaphysical postulate that intrigued many Indian philosophers. This is the only universal that is *ultimate*, and that is reality, *existence-ness* itself, for it is pertinent to *all* substances, qualities and activities not, like non-ultimate universals, exclusive to a particular class. Obviously, universals must inhere in substances, qualities and activities without the possibility of separation: cow-ness can only inhere in cows, and with no knowledge of cow-ness, there can be no full understanding of what a cow is. In other words, we need the universal in order to recognize sameness in things and to classify them. *Substance-*

ness, *quality-ness* and *activity-ness* are the known universals that inhere in substances, qualities and activities respectively, and each is different. Then, again, *existenceness* or *being* is the universal of the three. The universal, then, is that identical or recurrent "something" that is present equally and completely in all things of the same type. In fact, it is the universal that allows us to relate two or more similar particulars, like two or more cows; we identify the particular through knowledge of the general. This is put succinctly by Phillips:

> Whereas perception is a causal process invariably involving individuals – no universal can be perceived unless an individual in which it resides is perceived – universals are nevertheless epistemically prior in that only by means of lawlike causal relations – with universals responsible for the lawfulness – are we able to recognize an individual. Devadatta cannot be known except through general features he exhibits, such as being a human being, being male, etc. – features that regularly give rise to our experience of him.[37]

But while we may accept that there is some kind of abstract universal by which we recognize particulars, we might not want to give that abstract universal any reality. Vaiśeṣika, however, does just this. Universals are *nitya*, eternal, real, and exist separately from particulars, though they inhere in them. It is from this one general essence informing all particulars, that we can have concepts of sameness between members of a class of substances, qualities or activities. Real knowledge would not be possible without such real universals. So all universals are integral to their respective particulars and relate to them by means of inherence, *samavāya*, but they are also indivisible, eternal and exist separately from the finite particulars in which they temporarily inhere.

Nevertheless, there are certain criteria for universals to obtain. To begin with, single phenomena, qualities or activities cannot have universals. So time, space, and ether, for example, have no universals. Two universals cannot refer to the same particulars, nor can they overlap each other in reference to particulars, otherwise things like cows could end up being sheep as well. Thus there can only be one universal for a particular class of things. Universals should not lead to infinite regress, like cow-ness, cow-ness-ness, and so on. Neither can ultimate particulars have their own universals; nothing can have a universal if it exists in isolation. Negations also cannot have universals because there is nothing that inheres in a class of things. Like particulars, universals are not causal and not effects.

What results from the *Vaiśeṣika* analysis is two kinds of universals, higher and lower. Existence-ness, noted above, or being-hood (*bhāva* or, later, *sattā*), is the higher, for it inheres in all. All other universals inhere in only some things, qualities or actions, and are of the lower kind; though universals like substance-ness are sometimes referred to as intermediate universals[38] to distinguish them from the even lower universals of more limited finite articles, like the jar-ness of jars. Of the fundamental higher universal of existence-ness, Halbfass writes:

> The concept of existence/reality reflects and expands, but also transcends and supersedes the first historical layer of the Vaiśeṣika system. *Bhāva/sattā* is the common denominator, the one universal ingredient of all concrete and particular entities. It circumscribes the totality of entities at the cosmological level of enumeration and classification, and it is added to these entities as if it were an enumerable, cosmological entity itself. It appears among

those entities that constitute the second level of enumeration and classification, as a universal among other real universals.[39]

This *reality-ness* that is characteristic of substances, in particular, imparts to all reality – all the collocations and compounds of elemental atoms that make up the entities in the universe – a subsequent and pervasive reality. Important to note is that universals are not just the collective names of classes, like animals, cows or jars. They depict the common *nature* of animals, cows and jars; that is why the suffix *-ness* is more appropriate. And while each universal is essentially one, it inheres in many. But if the many were to disappear, the universal remains – a particular weakness of this category. As Matilal observes, "the particulars provide a 'home' for the universal. The only mystery in this is that when the 'home' is destroyed, the universal is rendered 'homeless'; but it is not destroyed thereby! It maintains a 'homeless', i.e. unmanifest existence."[40] This problem is more pertinent if we consider that universals can *only* be known through the particulars – the very cows and jars – in which they inhere. But Vaiśeṣika, as Nyāya, insisted that universals are only located in particulars, but that the particular is not really the "home" of the universal at all. It is just a means by which it is known, and it does not cease to exist without that revelation.

Particularity (viśeṣa)

The important facet about the fifth category of particularity, *viśeṣa* (from which the word Vaiśeṣika is normally taken to be the adjective), is that it is a relational concept. Nothing can be particular unless it is so in relation to other things. Murti, then, defines a particular as "that in whose composition all other entities enter with varying degrees of relationship and significance. Taken by itself, no entity is particular."[41] But if particulars are relational, they are also independent of other particulars. By their very nature, they lack commonness and universality, and are, in their primary sense, necessarily infinite. Particularity, then, is the opposite of universality, though in terms of what we perceive in life, universality inheres in particularity, like cow-ness in cows. But by particularity, *viśeṣa*, Vaiśeṣika is not referring to the individuation that exists through the aggregates of atoms – cows, sheep and so on. It is referring to the particularity of the many basic primary atoms and substances. Each of the primary substances – earth, water, fire, air, ether, souls, minds, space and time – has its particularity that is independent of others and of all else. Yet it is because of *viśeṣa* that we perceive all the diversity in the world, and that we can differentiate between one thing and another. This is because whatever exists in life has its own particular combinations of atoms that are informed by primal differentiation.

Every one of the basic atoms that combines with others to make up the many animate and inanimate objects of existence has its own particularity that gives it its uniqueness. A composite object, then – the physical body, a jar, an animal – is composed of already unique atomic parts, for each atomic part is both quantitatively and qualitatively different from others. Each is what Chakrabarti terms "an ultimate differentiator".[42] Two physical selves, or two jars, may look alike, but they can never be the same. And this is because the ultimate atoms of which they are composed have their own ultimate particularities. *Viśeṣa*, then, refers to the particularities that subsist in primary, indivisible and eternal substances, differentiating each from the next.[43] It is this category of *viśeṣa* that is the hallmark of the school, that gives it its name, and that is the special contribution of Kaṇāda to it.

While particularities inhere in primary substances, just like qualities and activities, they remain a separate category. And were there to be no differentiation between the basic atoms of, say, earth or water, then all earth things would be the same as all water things. And if there were no particularity between *any* of the basic atoms, so that there were no earth or water atoms, then nothing could exist at all. *Viśeṣa* is the imperceptible *basis* of differences in all things, and is rooted in the differences in primary atomic substances. Ordinarily, however, the individual objects and physical selves in the world are differentiated one from another by the differing parts that make up the whole. But *viśeṣa* itself has nothing to do with parts, it is applicable only to what is partless. And yet primary atoms are the substances of all phenomena, so when a composite object is broken down into its many parts, the process ceases at the level of the indivisible particularity of the atoms. Praśastapāda wrote: "Individuators (proper) are the final differentiae of their loci. They occur in substances which are beginningless, indestructible, and eternal, such as atoms, *ākāṣa*, time, place, selves, and internal organs."[44] Halbfass, along with critics past and present, finds this category, and that of inherence, "the most peculiar and idiosyncratic Vaiśeṣika categories". "They appear," he writes, "somewhat marginal and controversial." The reason for this is, as he points out, the dispensable and redundant nature of "particularity" alongside the specific nature of ultimate substances.[45] In other words, why should an independent category of particularity be posited over and above the already differentiated substances. This is doing the same thing twice.

Inherence (samavāya)

The sixth Vaiśeṣika category is *inherence*, *samavāya.* I have already dealt with some aspects of it above, in connection with the qualities of conjunction and disjunction. It is a relational concept, but only of entities that are logically, coherently and necessarily inseparable. All particulars of qualities and actions, and all universals, are related to substances by means of *samavāya.* It is what Hiriyanna terms an "intimate" relation between relata,[46] and when separated, then one of the relata ceases to exist. Such *samavāya* relation is of five kinds – substance and quality, substance and action, particular and universal, primary atoms and particulars, and whole and parts. Thus, quality inheres in substance, action in substance, universals in particulars, particulars in primary atoms, and parts in the whole. In many instances, *samavāya* is the relationship between cause and effect. Separation in these five types of *samavāya* results in destruction of one. So if parts are separated from the whole, for example, the whole ceases to exist. *Samavāya* underpins interrelatedness of things in the world. As Halbfass points out, "because of *samavāya*, we can speak about the world in sentences and not merely in isolated words".[47]

Samavāya is extremely important to this school of thought. Indeed, Sharma considers it to be "the pivot of the Vaisheṣika system".[48] Kaṇāda dealt with the category more in the context of causality, while Praśastapāda concentrated on its nature as inseparable relationship, and this extended *samavāya* beyond causal relationships. Praśastapāda thus defined inherence in the following way:

> [intimate union, coming together inseparably] is the relationship subsisting among things that are inseparable, standing to one another in the character of the container and the contained, – such relationship being the basis of the idea that "this is in that."[49]

It is thus the relationship of one thing subsisting *in* another, and this is what distinguishes *samavāya* from *saṃyoga*, conjunction. Neither is *samavāya caused*, in the same way as two entities are caused to come into contact with each other. Conjunction is an accidental and temporary quality of whatever is brought into contact, like water in a jug, but *samavāya* is a permanent and necessary relationship between one entity and its subsistence in another, like the thread in cloth. But whereas Nyāya believed that such inherence was perceptible, Vaiśeṣika believed that it was not, and that it could only be inferred. Inherence was accepted as a distinct category because it was clear that it was needed to explain the necessary relation between aspects of the different categories. And since it was as relevant to qualities as to the other categories, it followed that it must be separate, since a quality can only inhere in a substance, not in another quality. Inherence, then, could not be a quality.

Non-existence (abhāva)

Non-existence is accepted as a category in its own right, and there are four kinds of such negation:

- The non-existence of something before it comes into being (*prāgabhāva*), like a pot before the potter has made it. Before it exists, there is no beginning, no cause, though there will be an end, an effect. If this state of non-existence of cause before it becomes effect were to be denied then all things would have no beginning.
- The non-existence of something after it has been destroyed (*dhvaṃsābhāva*), like a smashed pot. In this case the non-existence of the pot occurs when it is destroyed, and it can never come into being again. But this is a state of non-existence that has been produced, or caused. The non-existence has a beginning, but in view of its non-existence in the broken pieces, cannot have an end, unless the non-existent pot can be recreated. It is the *non-existence* of the jar that cannot be destroyed in this case, unless the jar is put back together again. If this state of non-existence of the effect were to be denied, then all things would have to be eternal.
- Mutual negation (*anonyābhāva*), like the cow that is not the horse or the horse that is not the cow. If this were to be denied, then all things would be the same; nothing could be differentiated from anything else.
- Absolute non-existence (*atyantābhāva*) is the total absence of any connection between things through all time. As the absolute non-existence of something, there is neither cause nor effect, no beginning and no end. If this absolute non-existence were to be denied, then things could exist eternally and everywhere.

Such negation is dependent on cognition: if I look for a horse and it is not there then the non-existence of the horse at that time, or in that space, is known. The non-existence of anything else – of which I am unaware, and have no knowledge of at that time, or in that space – is not *abhāva*. Absences have no *svarūpa* "existence" or "own-being". But, as Potter puts it, "each and every absence is the absence of some positive entity which does have a *svarūpa*".[50] This, however, as most came to accept, was knowledge gained by direct perception.

Since Kaṇāda did not mention *abhāva* as a separate category, it is probable that it was a later addition to the earlier Vaiśeṣika categories.[51] It is an interesting category, for it suggests that reality and existence are not synonymous. For the Vaiśeṣika school, what is cognized has validity, but to cognize the absence of something – the absence of the pot on the table – is real knowledge, and yet the non-existence of the pot accounts for that knowledge. Existence and reality cannot, therefore, be synonymous.

The self

Having looked at the seven *padārthas*, or categories of knowledge, I now wish to return to the concept of the self, the *ātman*, which, in its ultimate state, is eternal, and a primary substance. Strictly speaking, the self is not elevated to any greater level of importance than other substances in the Vaiśeṣika system, and it is somewhat contrived, therefore, to single it out here, for special mention. However, given the *Vedāntic* emphasis on the self, and its crucial importance in Indian philosophy generally, I have treated this topic at some length in all the systems. But it should be noted that the self – or, more specifically, the soul – is not singled out in the Vaiśeṣika structure of the universe, as more important than any of the other entities that compose it. Neither is its Sanskrit term *ātman* indicative of the same kind of force that it has in many *Upaniṣadic* sources, or in other Hindu orthodox *darśanas*. It simply refers to the bound *karmic* self, as well as the natural, liberated Self that is its particular primal substance.

The *ātman* is a non-atomic substance that possesses such qualities as consciousness, knowledge, desire, aversion, pleasure, pain and volition. It is qualities such as these by which the soul is inferred, for the soul is, *per se*, not an object of perception except to *yogins*. Thus, Jayanārāyana in his gloss of Kaṇāda's *sūtra* III:ii:4 wrote:

> Pleasure and the like also are to be regarded, like cognition, as marks of the Soul. Thus pleasure and the like must reside in some substance, because they are things which are produced, or qualities like colour, etc. Hence an inference by analogy, accompanied by an exclusion of other possibilities, takes for its subject inherence or residence in a Substance other than the eight substances.[52]

Like the substance of *ākāśa*, ether, the soul is infinitely large, and universally pervasive, given the amount of knowledge and experience of which it is capable.[53] There is a plurality of selves in a plurality of different bodies. Such plurality of souls is evidenced by the varying experiences of pleasure and pain that are products of each one. Vaiśeṣika, therefore, rejects any unifying concept of a single essence of *ātman* that unifies all selves as one. For Vaiśeṣikas, each *ātman* is characterized by a particularity, a *viśeṣa*, that differentiates it from all others. Importantly, the eternal *ātman*, is a separate substance from the mind, which is also eternal. It is the self that cognizes through the medium of the senses not the mind.

But it must be separate from the senses, because it is capable of experiencing more than one sense impression, such as touching and perceiving the same object at the same time. Similarly, we might *see* something that looks tasty and this will affect the *taste* organ of the tongue. This suggested to Vaiśeṣika that the self exists separately from the sense impressions to which it is exposed.

The self is inferred through the act of knowing, as well as through its internal sensations of pleasure and pain, though later Nyāya-Vaiśeṣika came to accept the self as perceptible by the mind. The selves of others are inferred from the activities and cessation of activities of their bodies, the differences in their states, and the testimony of scripture. There is, then, an "I" that is known intuitively through sense experiences. The fact that I can say "I know" and "I know that I know", as well as "I know that I am seeing", or "I know that I have a body", would seem to support this. Again, this suggests that the self is something different from sense perceptions, and from the physical body itself, for it has consciousness of all these. The *ātman* is the knower, the *jñātā*, and the cause of all activity in the body. It is the substance in which qualities of feelings like pain and happiness occur. All knowledge, feelings and experiences, therefore, are qualities of the substance of the self, and the existence of the self is inferred from these qualities. The medium of their perceptibility is the mind, the *manas*. The real state of the eternal substance of the self is one devoid of its qualities, that is to say, devoid of sense perception, the activities of the mind – which is a separate substance – and of consciousness and all knowledge. In other words, the self as a substance is primary, indivisible, but with its own *viśeṣa* that separates it from all other primary self substances. Knowledge, consciousness, feelings, experiences and volition only obtain as long as the body does, and as long as the mind is in contact with the self.

Consciousness is not believed to be a property of the body, the sense organs, *or* the mind. It is something that exists only through the substance of the *ātman*, though the *ātman* does not need it, and it is not a permanent quality of the self. Consciousness is not a facet of the sense organs, since it remains even when one is destroyed as, also, when the object of consciousness is no longer in contact with the senses. But consciousness is also not seen as belonging to the mind, because if it did, it would be able to function independently of the senses, and the mind would not then be a mere instrument used by the self as a medium of sense perceptions and inner-self experiences and feelings. Consciousnes could only belong to the self. In short, the self is seen as an agent that uses the function of the mind to apprehend sense perceptions, but which has the quality of consciousness that allows it to have knowledge of non-perceptible emotions and feelings. Consciousness, as far as Vaiśeṣika is concerned, has to be consciousness *of* something. Yet consciousness is not an agent, and it needs an agent to respond to it, work with it, make decisions as a result of it, and so on. This agent is the self, and consciousness is a quality of that self because it is perceptible to the self. Consciousness is not the essence of the self; the self is more than consciousness. The separability of consciousness from the self is evidenced by its loss in deepest sleep. In its natural, and certainly its liberated, state, the self has no consciousness. It is only when the self comes into contact with sense stimuli, the body, and the mind that acts as the mediator for them, that consciousness adventitiously becomes associated with it. Consciousness, which is mainly synonymous with knowledge, has no substance, and the self, to a considerable degree, controls what it wishes to be conscious of.

As something of an anomaly in the Vaiśeṣika system, mind, *manas* is an eternal substance. It is also atomic and, therefore, imperceptible, but it does not combine with other atoms, as do the elemental atoms. There are a multiplicity of minds, each having its own *viśeṣa*, and each associated with a self. This, said Kaṇāda is proved: "From the non-simultaneity of volitions, and from the non-simultaneity of cognitions."[54] The mind, then, is not an object of perception;[55] it can only be inferred. As the agent of the self, it acts for the self if needed, though it is quiescent in times of deep sleep, for example. Without the mind as a medium for sense perception the self would be bombarded with all objects of knowledge simultaneously. The mind prevents this happening by limiting the impact of the senses. *Manas* refers not just to the processing of sense data, but to all mental powers – the whole intellect and its various modes. It is because it is imperceptible that the existence of the *manas* has to be inferred, and it is inferred from the fact that it acts as an internal organ that can perceive the self, knowledge, feelings and volition that have nothing to do with external stimuli. Then, too, whereas the eye can only apprehend visual light stimuli, the ear sound, and so on, something is able to synthesize these senses so that they are presented to the self one after another, and not, confusingly for the self, all at once. If we think of our immediate environment, we don't see or hear *everything* in it: we see or hear only what we require to, and have to "turn our minds" to focus on what is necessary. Although the senses are in contact with so many other things in the environment, unnecessary objects are blocked out. Indeed, Vaiśeṣika believed that the mind could only process one sense at a time, and this is because it is an atomic unity and indivisible. Were it to have a number of different parts, those parts could function separately from each other, apprehending many and varied sense contacts at the same time. But its unitary atomic nature prevents this, and it acts as the internal sense organ that organizes data for the self.

Nevertheless, the functional role of the mind has nothing to do with knowledge or consciousness. It is exclusively the self that possesses knowledge as a quality. The mind may be the tool by which knowledge is acquired but, like consciousness, knowledge needs an agent, a knower, a subject, in order to be manifest. Since the mind is small and atomic, and can only process one thing at a time – though in rapid succession – omniscience is impossible for the self. Knowledge can only be partial, and pertinent to the specific mind—self contact in the limitations of time and space. So the limited sphere of the mind limits the knowledge the self can have. Like consciousness, with which it is virtually synonymous, knowledge cannot be identified with the mind because the mind is a tool, like a pot. Neither is memory a quality of the mind, for Vaiśeṣikas believed it to be a quality of the self. Again, the self has to be in contact with the mind in order to remember something that is necessary, that it wishes to recall, or that is needed in connection with other knowledge. Clearly, the sense organs are not always necessary for the presence of memory and recollection, so memory must have some involvement with the internal organ of the mind, but is nevertheless a quality of the self as agent, in the same way as consciousness. The mind, then, is inferred as that instrument by which the self relates to the objective world. In the words of Kaṇāda: "The appearance and non-appearance of knowledge, on contact of the Soul with the senses and their objects, are the marks (of the existence) of the mind."[56]

This is all very well, but there is a problem with making the mind the internal organ for the self, in the same way as the eye or ear are external organs. For the Vaiśeṣika concept of mind is of an eternal substance rather than a composite, atomic, non-eternal one. The reason for its non-composite and unitary atomic nature has been noted above – its function must be limited by its minute atomic size and inability to apprehend more than one sense perception at a time. But need it be eternal? And what is the mind when it is not connected to the self? Without the self it is inert – indeed, redundant. But it is the contact of the self with the mind that causes the transmigrating self – something that will need to be analysed more closely below in connection with causality. If the mind were not of some eternal substance, then a different mind would be associated with the self in the next life. So, whereas the body and the sense organs, being non-eternal atomic substances, are different from one life to another, the eternal nature of the self and the mind permits *karmic* continuity from one life to the next. Here, the eternal nature of the mind remains functional. However, like the self, as will be seen, when its function is over and the self is liberated from its qualities, the mind is of no use in the atomic structure of things.

It is the connection between the self and the mind, the *ātman* and the *manas* that lends *karmic* individuality to each self, causing each self to reap the negative and positive results of all modes of its actions. But *particularity* of each self and each mind is something that informs each in its primary nature. And when each self is liberated, devoid of all its qualities of consciousness, knowledge and memory, it still retains its *viśeṣa* – whatever that may be – in its liberated state. But with absolutely no consciousness at all, not even a pure, undifferentiating consciousness, it is difficult to concede any value to Vaiśeṣika views of the self. It is a conception of the self that one writer terms "the most absurd and degrading in the whole field of Indian Philosophy".[57]

Causality

The Vaiśeṣika view of causality is that effects come into being as a result of the different aggregates and collocations of elemental atoms. Effects necessarily follow their atomic causes. At the level of primary substances, it could be said that nothing changes at all; each has its own particularity that never changes and never disappears. It is only when such basic atoms come into contact with other atoms that change seems to have taken place, but it is transient change that produces finite objects.

The important question that arises from such an atomic view of causality is what makes the atoms combine in the first place? Vaiśeṣikas believed that there were some common causes, or *sādhāraṇakāraṇa*, of effects. These are the hidden power of *adṛṣṭa*, which will be discussed below, God, and the substances of space and time. They are occasional causes, like the potter that makes the pot, along with the tools that he uses. These causes are different from the more specific causes, *asādhāraṇakāraṇa*, which are the more material causes like the clay from which the pot is made. Some causes were believed to be independent of any other causes in the production of effects, while others were dependent on other criteria for effects. In the life of any individual his or her respective qualities of merit (*dharma*) and demerit (*adharma*), serve to act as determinators of the particular *karmic* effects that an individual will reap in his or her life.

The Vaiśeṣika view of causality is one of *asatkāryavāda*. That is to say that all collocations of atoms are completely new effects, and that only immediately antecedent causes are relevant to effects, not remote causes. But this is a difficult point, since the particularity of all things is dependent in part on the particularity of the original primary atoms. The *individuality* may be the result of the particular collocations of atoms, but not the particularity. It would seem, then, that primary – and therefore remote – causes must inform *something* of the effect, as well as the more immediate ones. But Vaiśeṣika maintained that while effects naturally presuppose causes, they are not present in their causes, and are in no way identical with them. Whatever arises as the result of atomic combination is different from, and independent of, the primary elemental atoms. This seems a separation of cause and effect to the extent that it could be claimed that anything could produce anything, but this is prevented by inherence, *samavāya*. For effects inhere in their material causes, like the pot in clay, and there is a particularity about both that makes cause and effect related and yet not the same: the particularity of the effect will have something similar to the particularity of its cause, though not identity. Importantly, as noted earlier, Vaiśeṣikas accepted that the *whole* has an independent reality from the parts that compose it: "I" am more than the sum total of the bodily parts of which I am composed. This reiterates the *asatkāryavāda* stance, for the whole – that is to say the effect – is something different from its parts, and is completely new.

As far as the individual selves are concerned, they are eternal. It is because of *dharma* and *adharma* that atomic combinations occur to provide them with the means of reaping the results of both – a theory that has much to say for a stronger link between cause and *related* effect, than *asatkāryavāda* permits. This *dharmic*/*adharmic* balance in the life of any individual is important to the spiritual quest of Vaiśeṣika (though its outcomes, as will be seen, fall short of a lofty spiritual goal). Material atomism is not the whole point of the Vaiśeṣika system, and the goal of *yogic* penetration of the real nature of life and the self is the aim of its philosophy. There is a moral purpose in the whole process of atomic collocations, and that is for individuals to pursue their moral destinies. Creation and dissolution of the universe are beginningless and endless. The purpose of creation is to provide a world where the individual *ātmans* can spiritually progress. The purpose of dissolution is to give them some respite from such long-term progression. So the universe is subject to never-ending cycles of creation and dissolution. In the process of creation and dissolution of the universe, it is a creation of the "wholes" that takes place in creation, and a breakdown of them in dissolution. A sensitive translation of Praśastapāda's account of the creation and dissolution of the world through the power of God is given by José Pereira:

> Afterwards the Supreme Lord wills to create, so as to make experience possible for living creatures. Atoms combine with all the souls, through the karma – whose powers have been restored – implanted in those souls. Activity begins to stir in the *aerial* atoms, and, through a sequence of dyads and other atomic combinations, a mighty wind is generated, filling the sky with its gusts.
>
> Later in the same wind the *watery* atoms combine in the same sequence and generate a vast sea that floods space with its billows. In the same sea the *earthy* atoms draw close together to form the great mass of earth. In that very sea the *fiery* atoms next combine in dyad and other sequences, erupting in a mighty blaze, which, unquenched, stands there flaming.

> And now that the Great Elements have arisen, the atoms of fire, solely through the Supreme Lord's will, combine with those of earth, and a great egg starts to form. The Supreme Lord then creates in it the four-faced Brahmā, the Grandfather of the worlds, his every face as lovely as a lotus. Together with Brahmā he creates the worlds too, enjoining Brahmā with the creation of living things.
>
> Commanded by the Supreme Lord, Brahmā, endowed with surpassing knowledge, dispassion and sovereignty, creates as his sons, the Lords of Creatures, and mind beings, and multitudes of progenitors, gods, sages and ancestors – furnishing them with faces, arms, thighs and feet – and the four castes and other beings, high and low. He then associates them according to their karmas, with the qualities of merit, knowledge, dispassion and power.[58]

It is thus Īśvara, God, who sets in motion the process of creation, through the cause–effect process of *adṛṣṭa*, the unseen power behind all creation, and the means by which it can be brought about.

Dissolution is initially brought about by the suspension of *adṛṣṭa*. And if the cause–effect process ceases, then the finite "wholes" can no longer exist. As a result of the quality of activity, disjunction or separation, *vibhāga*, of the atoms takes place, counteracting the connection, *saṃyoga*, that was necessary for creating effects for creation. All is dissolved into the atoms, and then the elements disintegrate in the order of earth, water, fire and air, to their basic primary states – a different order to the creative process. All that remains are the four kinds of atoms in their primary and isolated states. The process of creation and dissolution depicts a universal dissolution, when all things revert to their primal states. It is a *mahāpralaya*, a "great" dissolution. But within this cycle of universal dissolution there is also a more intermediate dissolution[59] represented by the cosmic day and night of the deity Brahmā. Here, creation lasts for a hundred cosmic years, and dissolution lasts for another hundred cosmic years of Brahmā: one such cycle of creation and dissolution is a *kalpa*.

Adṛṣṭa

The unseen power that operates between cause and effect is *adṛṣṭa*. It is that potency that is produced by the actions – verbal, physical and mental – of human selves, and is the power that links the causes of those actions, to their appropriate effects. Thus, it is the power that informs the law of *karma*. Radhakrishnan pointed out that whatever cannot be explained in Vaiśeṣika philosophy is done so with reference to *adṛṣṭa*.[60] Whereas Nyāya does not make use of the term, as Potter notes: "Kaṇāda makes extensive use of the notion to explain a variety of things: magnetic attraction, the initial motion of atoms, falling downwards, as well as transmigration."[61] Thus, the simplicity of the concept is clear in its earliest stages. The *Vaiśeṣikasūtras* illustrates this in such words as: "The movement of the jewel [towards a thief], and the approach of the needle [toward a lode-stone], have *adriṣṭaṃ* as their cause."[62] It is in its later phase that *adṛṣṭa* becomes, more widely, the potency that links human good and bad *karmic* actions to their appropriate results. But later Vaiśeṣika philosophy saw the drawbacks of assigning the mysterious relationship between cause and effect to the inexplicable, mysterious power of *adṛṣṭa*, and posited a divine being as the agent that controlled it. It is a valid criticism of Kaṇāda's metaphysics that he left too much to be answered by the nebulous concept of *adṛṣṭa*. Kaṇāda connected the effects of *adṛṣṭa* very clearly with obedience and conformity to *Vedic* injunctions, rather in the same manner as the Mīmāṃsā philosophers. Conforming to *Vedic* injunctions promoted *dharma*, and this was the aim of life. Thus, in its earliest phase *adṛṣṭa* was concentratedly applicable to *Vedic* ritual, and only later extended to wider human action. Then, whether life were lived according to *dharma* or *adharma*, it was *adṛṣṭa* that was the unseen power that brought about the appropriate negative or positive effects, to suit the causes. Whatever befell the self in life was attributed to this force. According to Praśastapāda, dreams do not involve the sense organs at all. It is *adṛṣṭa* that causes the dreams we have, along with dispositional traces in the memory and defects in the body. Good or bad dreams are the result of *dharma* and *adharma* respectively, and *adṛṣṭa* the means of bringing them about. Even the creation and dissolution of the universe were the result of its particular potency. But when the self is liberated, *adṛṣṭa* no longer operates. "In the absence of *adṛṣṭa*, which causes transmigration, there is the absence of contact of the internal organ with the self (which results in life), and also non-appearance of another body: this state is liberation (*mokṣa*)."[63]

Inevitably, the explanation of causal relationships as the workings of an inexplicable, unseen and imperceptible cause, ran counter to the whole attempt at a logical explanation of the universe. *Adṛṣṭa* was an unintelligent force, and it is difficult to see how, as such, it could create logical connections between causal processes. It was inevitable, therefore, that later Vaiśeṣika philosophy should create God, Īśvāra, as the agent that was to be the director of *adṛṣṭa*. God became the efficient cause of causal relationships, the power that directed all appropriate effects to suit their respective causes, positive and negative. God became the intelligent agent that was responsible for intelligent direction of cause–effect principles in existence. He was an agent sufficiently omniscient to be able to direct a whole atomic process and to oversee the fate of individual selves in the light of the positive and negative *karmas* that each had accumulated. This concept was a later addition to the original beliefs of the Vaiśeṣika school.

The concept of God

Kaṇāda did not articulate any clear concept of acceptance of God in his *Vaiśeṣikasūtras*,[64] and it is likely that it was left to later developments to posit a theistic God as controller of the results of the merit and demerit of all beings – in short, of *adṛṣṭa*. But since, for Kaṇāda, *adṛṣṭa* was an unintelligent and impersonal law that operated independently of any agent, and operated in conjunction with the accordance or discordance of a person with *Vedic* injunctions, there seemed no need of a God. But the denial of testimony as a valid means of knowledge would inevitably prove problematic to stringent analysis. Not that the positing of a divine agent in control of *adṛṣṭa* particularly solved any philosophical flaws, but it at least served to explain how cause and effect could operate in such an orderly manner in the universe, and why each person received his or her just deserts. It was Praśastapāda's *bhāṣya* that took up the idea of God and his role as creator for the first time. Even so, Potter notes, "one may safely say that God is not much on Praśastapāda's mind".[65]

Like each self, God, called Īśvara, is depicted as an *ātman*, but is distinguished from all the other selves in the world by being a supreme self, *paramātman*. Like all selves, God is eternal but, unlike ordinary selves who possess the qualities of consciousness and knowledge intermittently, God's consciousness and knowledge exist eternally, and he is omniscient. He is the efficient cause of both the creation and the dissolution of the world in its many cycles, and both creation and dissolution, as noted above, are for the sole purpose of assisting the bound, *karmic* selves.

The Vaiśeṣika God was not, primarily, the God of the *Vedas*, a God who is revealed through scripture and valid testimony. Rather, he was *inferred* teleologically, from the orderly manner of the causal processes that inform the world, and by the necessity of an agent that would control that order. Thus, as an agent who directed creation, the omniscient and omnipotent God is the cosmological, efficient cause of all effects, is the controller of the moral destiny of all people according to their deserts, and is the director of the physical laws that provide order in the universe. And to avoid infinite regress, a First Cause as an agent of all effects seemed necessary. Since in the state of dissolution there is *nothing* that can motivate itself to begin creation, a motivating principle that is separate from the rest of the eternal substances is needed. The primary, elemental atoms, however, always remain the *material* cause of the universe, even if they are directed by God to combine in certain ways. Indeed, how primary atoms could combine to form any kind of logical universe without some intelligent force, was a criticism levelled at Kaṇāda's atomic theory, and was a forcible reason for the later acceptance of God as causal agent.

As an efficient cause of the original combinations of atoms it might suggest that the Vaiśeṣika God is somewhat deistic – setting the atomic processes in motion and then retiring. But this would not explain the *karmic* mechanism of individual lives, and might suggest the need of an ongoing agent, sustaining the causal process in a more involved way, unless, of course, the destiny of an individual self were set for an entire *kalpa*. However, clearly the character of the world that is created by God is shaped according to the relative merits and demerits of the *karmic* selves waiting in the atomic wings for entry onto the world stage. If the fruits of their actions in past cycles of creation were to be determined for an entire *kalpa*, this would make nonsense of any real spiritual, evolutionary, development of an individual self. Importantly, however, God cannot step outside the real governing force of the universe, which is *adṛṣṭa*. He cannot interfere in its workings, he can only apply the quality of motion to set its mechanism working. The crucial question that Vaiśeṣika does not answer is the particular balance between the automatic working of *adṛṣṭa*, once it is set in motion, and the ongoing direction of it by God.

So however much God is or is not involved in the world, he can only direct its causal functions – and that through the medium of *adṛṣṭa*. Ultimately, he is separate from individual selves as much as from the primary atomic substances, which are the causal stuff of the world. There is no question of any connection between the liberated self and God. Indeed, Sharma makes the valid point here that, if liberated selves are devoid of their qualities of consciousness and knowledge, God, as eternally conscious and eternally possessing knowledge must, in some ways, be eternally bound.[66] And though he is not subject to cause and effect himself and is unlimited and perfect, the eternal and separate nature of each soul, each mind, the infinite number of atoms, time, space, ether – all limit whatever perfections

Īśvara might have. The Vaiśeṣika concept of God is a weak one, something of an appendage to the system.

Liberation

The Vaiśeṣika view of the *karmic* individual self is in line with most Indian thought in seeing the personality self as being bound through its own ego to transmigrate from one life to the next. Tied up with its physical body and its desires and aversions in relation to all it encounters in life, notions of "I", "me" and "mine" promote causal actions of word, thought or deed, that have to reap their effects for that same individual in the present life or a future reincarnated one. Where such actions are right and good, they are *dharmic* – particularly so if they are in line with *Vedic* injunctions. For Kaṇāda: "*Dharma* (is) that from which (results) the accomplishment of Exaltation and of the Supreme Good."[67] And when they are not right, and against *Vedic* injunctions, then they are *adharmic*. Either way, reincarnation, *saṃsāra*, is inevitable, because both *dharma* and *adharma* are qualities, normally imperceptible,[68] of the self, and to be liberated, the self has to lose all qualities.

While good deeds will bring pleasure, and bad deeds pain, both necessitate reincarnation, perhaps in the realms of the gods, or in one of the hellish realms like that of ghosts, or as animals. Suffice it to say that any egoistic action, thought or word must have its *karmic* effect at some time in the future. And while the individual is rooted in ignorance of the real nature of its own self, there can be no end to the reincarnating cycles. It is *adṛṣṭa* that is constantly operating to provide the appropriate results for all causal actions, and that provides the repeated birth circumstances in divine, animal and human existence, depending on the respective merit or demerit of the individual.

While liberation involves the loss of both *dharma* and *adharma*, the pursuit of *dharma*, especially through obedience to *Vedic* injunctions, is the beginning of the path to liberation. Thus, Praśastapāda said:

> The means of *dharma* consist in various substances, qualities and actions, laid down in the Veda and the Law-Books, – some as belonging in common to all men, and some as pertaining specially to distinct castes and conditions. Among the common ones we have the following: faith in *dharma*, harmlessness, benevolence, truthfulness, freedom from desire for undue possession, freedom from lust, purity of intentions, absence of anger, bathing, use of purifying substances, devotion to deity, fasting, and non-neglect (of duties).[69]

Disciplined separation of the mind from contact with the *indriyas*, the external sense organs through *yoga* became an important means to liberation, bringing about ceaseless *samādhi*. Only when the very last effect of good *dharma* has been experienced – the last ounce of happiness – can the self be liberated. It is assumed that no *adharma* remains to be worked off. Merit is, thus, an important means to liberation and it exists right up to the time when liberation is attained. The methods of acquiring merit vary according to one's class. Importantly, meritorious actions should be done without desire for their fruits. Acting purely, and disinterestedly, without desire or attachment to the fruits of actions accrues no *karma*. What brings an individual to this point is knowledge, which is also, like *dharma*, a means to liberation, but a quality to be discarded at the liberated point. And once *dharma* and *adharma* are eliminated in the self, *adṛṣṭa* is no longer operable in ensuring appropriate effects – the self is free. This is a negative view of liberation because in losing all its qualities the liberated self is devoid of all knowledge and consciousness.

The more spiritually evolved a person becomes, the greater the ability to understand the true nature of the atomic combinations that make up the reality of the world, and the true nature of the self as natural and devoid of any qualities of consciousness or knowledge. Through meditation and adherence to *Vedic* injunctions, *dharma* assists the individual in providing the right kind of environment for progression by birth into a pure family, the guidance of a teacher and holy surroundings: *adṛṣṭa* operates towards liberation. True knowledge removes the veil of ignorance, and gradually freedom from desires and aversions and their respective emotions occurs, so that production of *dharma* and *adharma* lessens until it finally ceases. Then, there is no further need for *saṃsāra*. The mediator of sense perceptions to the self is, of course, the mind, the *manas*. But when liberated, the atomic mind is separated from the self, and both exist eternally without relationship with each other, for the mind is the medium of the qualities that the self no longer has.[70]

The greatest problem of the Vaiśeṣika concept of liberation lies in the loss of all the qualities of the self. And since it seems that the *mahābhūtas*, the primary atoms, have eternal qualities, why should the selves have to lose theirs at liberation? The condition of the liberated self is incomprehensible. And this is not the "positive" incomprehensibility of a *neti neti* state of unified non-duality – unity with an ultimate and indefinable Absolute, it is an incomprehensible petrified self that makes little sense as an ultimate goal of countless lives in the *saṃsāric* cycle. The opponents and contemporaries of Vaiśeṣika had a field day criticizing its ultimate goal. Indeed, it seems something of an appendage – like the concept of God – which does not do justice to its more common sense attempts to portray an orderly, atomic universe. As Hiriyanna states of this Vaiśeṣika concept of liberation, the self without its qualities "will then be devoid of thought, feeling and will; and *mokṣa* thus becomes a condition of perfect gloom from which there will be no re-awakening".[71] Radhakrishnan stated of it, "the released soul, rid of all qualities, is a unit devoid of any internal variety, and is therefore not real at all. The object swallows the subject".[72] Realization that the self does not need body, mind, knowledge or consciousness may well be the aim, but the ultimate liberated self "retains its own peculiar individuality and particularity and remains as it is – knowing nothing, feeling nothing, doing nothing".[73] It is perhaps for this reason, as well as its minimalized concept of deity, that this *darśana* rates so low in Hindu philosophy.

5
Nyāya

Background to the school

The hallmark of the Nyāya *darśana* is its highly developed epistemology, theory of knowledge, and the basis this supplies for Indian philosophical inquiry. Logical proof is developed to an art. So influential was this, that even Buddhist monks of Tibet spend about four years in the study of Nyāya. In particular, its careful analysis of, and rules for, logical argument provide a useful tool for any philosopher. It is essentially a scientific investigation of knowledge and the means by which logical arguments can be regarded as valid. But it is not only a theory of knowledge since its remit includes a psychological analysis of the self, consciousness and mind, as well as theology and metaphysical inquiry. Broadly, its theories are realist, pluralist, theistic and atomistic. The school believed that it had set out logical means by which true knowledge of the self can be gained and by which the ultimate aim of *mokṣa* can be realized. Fallacies of argumentation have all been set out systematically by Nyāya so that illogical assembling of statements that lead to false conclusions is easily identified. Nyāya, then, is a science of reasoning, Tarkaśāstra or Tarkavidyā, a science of logic and epistemology, Pramāṇaśāstra, a science of debate and discussion, Vādavidyā, a science of causes, Hetuvidyā, and a science of critical study, Ānvīkṣikī. All these are alternative names for the school.

Nyāya is the Sanskrit term for logical investigation, for "going into a subject" as Bernard translates it,[1] or "that by which the mind is led to a conclusion", as Radhakrishnan put it.[2] These meanings reflect the school's concern with valid and invalid argumentation, with correct and not fallacious reasoning: it insists on knowledge that is right in terms of its premise, its argument and its conclusion. Nyāya is therefore concerned with common sense, analytic philosophy rather than speculative inquiry, though it is an inquiry that extends to metaphysics as much as statements of everyday perceptual knowledge: reason is applied to all claims about knowledge in a very scientific manner. The methodology of the school became a response to the Buddhist process views of life – the view that all is in a process of becoming and is therefore empty of "own being" and any permanent essence. Nyāya sought to ground the self in a substance view of an eternal and permanent soul. The newer phase of Nyāya is known as Navya-Nyāya,[3] "new Nyāya", and it is this that was conjoined with Vaiśeṣika. Of the differences between the old and new Nyāya, Chatterjee writes: "The old Nyāya gives us what may be called philosophical logic, while the modern Nyāya is formal logic and dialectic."[4]

The related school of Vaiśeṣika is conjoined with Nyāya, the two schools accepting mutual views from a very early period. Both schools rely on the teachings of the other to a considerable extent, and the concepts of the soul and of *mokṣa* became synonymous. Most sources thus treat the two schools as one but, since the overall focuses were different, despite convergence of views, there are some grounds for treating the two separately. Nyāya is mainly concerned with epistemology and logic, with valid knowledge as a means to establish what is real, and it accepts four *pramāṇas* or valid means of knowledge. Vaiśeṣika is more concerned with the metaphysics of reality *per se*, and it accepts only two *pramāṇas*, perception and inference. The *Vaiśeṣikasūtras* reached its final form much earlier than the *Nyāyasūtras*[5] so independence of philosophical inquiry preceded the coalescing of the two schools. This chapter will concentrate primarily, though not exclusively, on the contribution of the earlier phase of Nyāya.

The ultimate aim of Nyāya is *mokṣa* – liberation from all pain and suffering. Knowledge is the means to achieve it, for it is through knowledge of the real nature of the world that the endless chain of reincarnation can cease and allow the self to be free. Like most Indian thought Nyāya accepts that it is attraction to the world that causes the self to reincarnate. The stimuli of the world create the desires and aversions that promote most actions, thoughts and speech in the self – all of which are causes that must result in their appropriate effects. The world thus deludes us, entangling us in phenomenality that impedes the progress of the self to the point of liberation. Given a correct perspective of the world – *real* knowledge – the self is able to transcend the delusions of the world and be free. Thus, as Bernard puts it: "The Nyāya is founded on the belief that only by the thorough examination of the modes and sources of correct knowledge can the ends of life be truly accomplished; therefore, what has been supplied to us by the traditional teachings and by evidences of the senses must be submitted to critical inquiry."[6] Thus, Nyāya is ultimately concerned with *mokṣa*, even if its inquiry appears to be based on the means of knowledge, objects of knowledge and valid and invalid argument. It may seem to be involved with the phenomena of the world and our perceptions of it, but its deeper and ultimate concern is with the liberated self.

The origins of Nyāya lie in the intricate debates and discussions of the years that preceded the school, "from the dialectical tournaments, the sound of which filled the durbars of kings and the schools of philosophers".[7] It was out of a need to formalize such debate that Nyāya arose. The purpose of the earlier phase of Nyāya, then, was to formulate the grounds on which such debate could be logically conducted, setting out what is logical in argumentation and analysing what is fallacious. But the early period and origins of Nyāya are shrouded in obscurity, though they are likely to have predated the time of the Buddha.[8] When the ideas of the early school were first systematized, they were concerned far more with logic as a means of answering some of the fundamental questions about life itself and were concerned with objects of knowledge. Later proponents of the school emphasized the means of knowledge.

Main proponents and commentators

The name associated with the beginning of the school in its real sense is Gautama, also known as Gotama, Akṣapāda,[9] and Dīrghatapas. It was he who gathered together the various traditional strands of philosophical debate about epistemology into one composite work. Gautama's date is uncertain. He may be dated as early as the sixth century BCE and would, thus, have been contemporaneous with the Buddha, or he may have lived centuries later. Anything up to the second century CE is possible. Little is known of his life. It is Gautama's *Nyāyasūtras* (Aphorisms on Logic) that forms the foundation and earliest systematized philosophy of the school, but whether it was the result of a former oral tradition or whether Gautama himself wrote the *Sūtras* is unknown. Potter favours a more gradual compilation of the *Sūtras* in which Gautama's works may have had some contribution, but he suggests that several other contributions and stages brought about the *Sūtras* as we know them in about the second century CE. In fact, he adds: "One may sum up the situation pretty safely by saying that we have not the vaguest idea who wrote the *Nyāyasūtras* or when he lived."[10] Some suggest that at least the first book of the *Nyāyasūtras* was composed by Gautama, while others, though recognizing the problem of authorship, see the necessity of retaining the composite view of the material. Indeed, as Sinha commented, "you cannot retain the first book, and reject the others, without mutilating the system".[11] The aphorisms or *sūtras* attributed to Gautama are as cryptic as those in other philosophical circles. It is worthwhile reiterating that their format was prescribed. They were to be composed of minimal letters, yet their content had to be beyond doubt and contain the briefest possible essential material. This material had to be diverse, non-repetitive – both overtly and by implication – and devoid of any clarifying examples. In focusing on knowledge and logic, Gautama's *Sūtras* made no mention of *Vedic* ritual. This earned the school considerable disrespect in its early years, and the accusation of being non-orthodox.

The *Nyāyasūtras* is divided into five books, each of which contains two chapters. In the first book we find a general treatment of the sixteen categories that will occur in the other four books. It is these sixteen categories that will provide the format for the treatment of the school in this chapter, though with considerably more attention paid to some of the topics than others. The second book deals with the first category of *pramāṇa*, the means of right knowledge, and the third book, and some of the fourth, with *prameya*, the objects of knowledge. These will be the main categories for attention in this chapter.

The earliest and outstanding commentary, *bhāṣya*, on the *Nyāyasūtras* was written by Vātsyāyana many centuries later. Potter dates his *bhāṣya* somewhere between 425–500 CE.[12] Vātsyāyana's *bhāṣya* became the basis for a large number of other sub-commentaries. Later commentators of the school include Uddyotakara, who wrote a commentary on Vātsyāyana's commentary, dated possibly to the sixth or early seventh century CE, and Vācaspati Miśra, who commented on Uddyotakara's commentary in his *Nyāyavārtika* (approximately ninth or tenth centuries CE), and who is reputed to have been the master of all philosophical systems. Udayana (eleventh to twelfth centuries CE) possibly did much to lay the foundations of the Navya-Nyāya school, and the coalescing of the Nyāya and Vaiśeṣika. Another well-known proponent was Gaṅgeśa, who marked the final consolidation of ancient and modern Nyāya, probably in the thirteenth or fourteenth centuries. He has earned the title of the father of modern Nyāya, and his *Tattvacintāmaṇi* has been described as "the centrepiece of the period, and indeed of Navyanyāya through the centuries".[13] The school of modern Nyāya still obtains today in Bengal.

Reality: the Nyāya view of the world

Reality is truth or *prāma*, and what is true is so, irrespective of whether we know it is, or are aware of that truth. Something is not just true because we prove it to be so, it is proved to be true because it *is* true: it exists independently of our knowledge and perceptions of it and, therefore, *before* we verify it. The Naiyāyika has a pluralistic view of reality and a realistic one – a common-sense view of the phenomena of the world, or logical realism. The world is real, as are the selves that compose it; it is a world of substances, an independent reality. It is the things in the world that provide us with knowledge, so what we have in our subjective minds corresponds to the objective realities found in the world. Perception of the world is the basis of all our knowledge, so this makes the Naiyāyika a thorough empiricist. Truth must be in line with the facts of existence. Knowledge of an object must correspond with the character and qualities of it that are factually in place, though we do not always need to test this correspondence. I do not have to know that I am working at a desk, but the practical use of it permits a correspondence between me as subject and the desk as an object of knowledge. But this is not to say that the test of true knowledge lies in its practical use. As Chatterjee succinctly put it: "Knowledge is made true by its correspondence to some reality or objective fact. It is true not because it is useful, but it is useful because it is already true. Hence truth consists in correspondence and is tested by coherence and practical efficiency."[14]

The Naiyāyika accepted the equivalent of the Vaiśeṣika view of the world as consisting of combinations of eternal atoms that are uncaused, and that are not subject to change; it is the combinations of them that give rise to the varied phenomena in existence. Like atoms, the substances of ether (*ākāśa*), time and space are also eternal and uncaused; nothing can destroy them. All that we see is a combination of atoms, existing in eternal time and eternal space. Importantly, the world to Nyāya is not the result of chance combinations of these atoms. This is because the cause–effect process is so clearly discernible in existence, and conforms to some kind of established pattern; the acorn becomes the oak tree and nothing else. While atoms combine to form an entity, that whole entity is not simply the sum total of its parts but is something *extra* to its parts, something that is inherent in the totality of those parts. A flower, then, is something more than its constituent parts, and if we did not know it as an object apart from the parts that compose it, we would be unable to recognize it as belonging to a class of things.

Like Vaiśeṣika, Nyāya accepted the composition of the universe as informed by *dravya* substance, *guṇa* quality, *karma* activity or motion, *sāmānya* universality, *viśeṣa* particularity, *samavāya* inherence, and *abhāva* non-existence, negation. The three *dravyas*, *kāla* time, *dik* space, and *ākāśa* ether are considered to be eternal and independent of each other. The four elements of earth, fire, water and air are the basic, eternal, atomic substances from which all the things in the world, and all their qualities, are made. Qualities inhere in substances, but can also be distinct from them. There are twenty-four basic qualities. The remaining two substances are selves, which are eternal and non-atomic, and mind, *manas*, which is atomic. All atomically composed substances and their qualities exist in the eternal substances of time, space and ether. But as atomic substances they exist only in so far as the atoms that compose them are combined together: their atomic *structure* is thus impermanent.

It is the atomic structure of things that provides the apparent diversity of an object. Like Vaiśeṣika, Nyāya accepted that each object is a *particular* that is separate from other particulars. It is also a whole that is accepted as being different from, and more than, the parts that compose it. A cloth, for example, is more than the parts, the threads, from which it is made. So a whole, then, is a new entity, though it stands in relation to its parts by inherence. Inherence, *samavāya*, is that which occurs between two things when the destruction of one (parts or whole) means destruction of the other, even though the whole is different from its parts. The fact that wholes are more than their parts means that effects are not identical to their causes. Ultimate atoms may, then, form the basic causal stuff of a material object, but that object is a different effect, is more than the material parts from which it is made, and more than the basic elements that make it possible. Ultimately, however, the effect has no permanent reality, unlike the causal atoms. Despite the difference between parts and wholes, it is the wholes that are the cause of incorrect perspectives of reality. We desire, or have an aversion to, the whole, without seeing the parts of which it is composed. Getting rid of desire for wholes, and attachment to them, are the means to liberation. It is by concentrating on the parts that the self will be dislodged from *karmic*-producing desires and aversions.

All things, then, are informed by the unity of identity and particularity in relation to all other things, and this is an atomic composition that, despite its finitude, is given the status of reality because of the reality of the underlying atoms that compose it. Basic, indivisible atomic substances are what lend reality to all in existence, and what give the same identity to each object, irrespective of any changes in its qualities. The atomic particularity of *man* as an individual is present at the same time as the atomic universality of the man as belonging to *men-ness* in general. The particular *and* the universal are both objects of knowledge at the same time and the universal inheres in the particular. And at the same time we are able to observe in an object of knowledge the particular *relation* of the object to other things: relational characteristics also inhere in the object of knowledge.

Abhāva, non-existence or negation, is included in the structure of the universe. It refers to three aspects:

- What something is *not* – for example, this jar is *not* blue, or the absence of clouds in the sky and strong winds from which it can be inferred that there will be no rain.
- What existed in the past and no longer exists.
- What will exist in the future, but does not exist now.

Padārthas: categories of reality

Nyāya sets about establishing knowledge of sixteen categories that lead the self to a position of valid knowledge. The first two of these, the means of valid knowledge and the objects of valid knowledge – *pramāṇa* and *prameya* respectively – will be important in the following analysis, and both will be dealt with under separate headings below. The third to fifth – doubt, purpose, familiar example and established tenet – I shall deal with only briefly. The seventh category, concerning the parts of a syllogism, is a very important facet of Nyāya; it will be dealt with in some detail in the context of the *pramāṇa* of inference. The eighth to sixteenth categories – confutation, ascertainment, discussion, wrangling or controversy, cavil, fallacy, quibble or equivocation, futility and occasion for rebuke or disagreement in principle – will be mentioned only cursorily. Gautama lists his categories and defines them in the *sūtras* of book one, then examines them in the following three books. Gautama's categories are what he considered to be the true nature of things. By knowing the categorical structure that he presents, the ensuing true perspective of reality would lead to liberation – release (*apavarga*) from rebirth.

The third of Gautama's categories is *Doubt*, *saṃśaya*, uncertainty. Doubt occurs when there are conflicting possibilities with regard to the object of cognition. It is not a case of error or absence of knowledge, but neither is it certain knowledge: it is what Chatterjee and Datta depict as "a positive state of cognition of mutually exclusive characters in the same thing at the same time".[15] An important word here is "positive", for doubtful knowledge has positive value. In a way, doubt is knowledge that is only partially invalid. Even though, like error in knowledge, doubt does not proceed to successful action unless it is solved, it is nevertheless the means by which we usually proceed to further investigation. It is doubt that usually precedes inference and it is regarded as valid knowledge in one way in that one has to *know* that one has doubt about something. Chakrabarti puts the nature of doubt succinctly when he writes: "Gotama's point is that doubt arises when we are faced with two or more incompatible alternatives with regard to the same object and that the doubt may be removed if we find any distinguishing factor that makes only one of the alternatives applicable to the object, to the exclusion of others."[16] There is a recollection of differentiating characteristics but perception is obscured sufficiently to apply such differentiation. So doubt cannot be valid knowledge because there is no definite perception of an object as it truly is, but it provides positive incentive to acquire correct knowledge.

The most common kind of doubt arises through perception as, for example, in the perception of a tall object in the distance that could be either a post or a man, or a rope that looks like a snake. A more complex example is in a case where something like sound is seen to be uncommon to humans, animals or plants which are finite, and yet is also uncommon to atoms which are infinite: doubt arises, then, about the eternal or non-eternal nature of sound. Sometimes doubt arises where verbal testimony from a reliable source or sources differs, such as the conflicting philosophical arguments about whether an eternal self does or does not exist. Doubt may also occur through irregularity in perception, such as when we are unsure whether water in a tank is real as opposed to that in a mirage. Or there may be doubt whether water exists in a plant or vegetable or in earth, when in none of these cases is it actually perceptible. The remaining categories dealt with in the *Sūtras* are:

- *Purpose*: that which promotes action.
- *Familiar example*: common opinions about things that are shared by ordinary and wise people alike.
- *Established tenet*: dogmatic assertions of one or more schools of thought, some of which may be hypothetical theses and others implicitly understood rather than explicitly stated.
- *Members of a syllogism*: these will be examined in detail in the context of inference.
- *Confutation*: conjecture to show the absurdity of alternative arguments.
- *Ascertainment*: the removal of doubts by examining counter-arguments. This is known as *tarka*, "reasoning" or "argumentation". Nyāya includes this as a separate category. It is deliberation and reasoning about a doubtful or false hypothesis to test the validity of another statement. It exposes fallacies in argumentation. So, if someone claims "whatever is fiery is smoky" (as opposed to "whatever is smoky is fiery"), *tarka* is used to demonstrate false argumentation. *Tarka* begins with a false hypothesis and demonstrates its absurdities in order to prove the opposite. It is a useful tool in logic by which hypothetical contradictions are raised against a proposed conclusion to see if that conclusion can be broken down. If it cannot, then the conclusion is more likely to be true. It is useful in cases of doubt, and can serve to assist means of establishing valid knowledge, though it is not a means *per se*.
- *Discussion*: putting tenets to the test by submitting one's views to others.
- *Controversy, wrangling*: a polemical defence of one's claim irrespective of the validity of it.
- *Cavil*: frivolous carping at one's opponents in order to prevent their pursuing their argument – a useful device, Gautama believed, when one's opponent was opinionated and objectionable!
- *Fallacy*: categorized into five types – *erratic* in which the reason leads to more than one conclusion; *contradictory* in which the reason opposes what is to be proved; *equal to the question* in which the solution is provoked by the reason; *unproved* in which the reason and the proposition are without proof; *mis-timed* in which the reason is belatedly applied.
- *Quibble, equivocation*: the deliberate suggestion of an alternative meaning to prevaricate: thus playing on words, for example, when one word has two meanings, deliberately taking the opposite to the one the opponent means; the denying of the particular in one thing because the universal does not have that quality, e.g. a cow cannot be black because all cows are not black; the taking of a metaphor literally.
- *Futility*: argument where there is no universal relation between the middle and major terms (these terms will be clarified below in the context of inference).
- *Occasion for rebuke* or *disagreement in principle*: the ending of an argument because the opponent has no understanding. Such cases arise, for example, when the opponent shifts, opposes or renounces his or her own proposition; shifts the reason or the topic; states things that are meaningless, unintelligible, incoherent, inopportune, repetitious, evasive or ignorant; or when the opponent says too much or too little.

Epistemology

Nyāya does not accept the intrinsic validity of all knowledge, as does Mīmāṃsā. Most knowledge is not valid until it is proved to be so, although truths remain true, irrespective of whether we know them or not. However, some knowledge is sufficiently evident as valid without such proof, for example when I know that I am conscious of, perceive, or have knowledge of something. Nyāya has a remarkably optimistic and positive view of human knowledge. Junankar comments, "the Naiyāyika affirms his complete confidence in the faculties of man to know the world. He even goes further and asserts that not only is there nothing which is unknowable, but also, given a proper method of knowing, there is nothing which cannot be known by men".[17] Such words emphasize admirably the Nyāya focus on knowledge and the power of logic in coming to know the nature of reality.

Consciousness, intellect, knowledge and perception are all identical as far as Gautama and later Nyāya were concerned. Knowledge is not self-revealing. Knowledge can make objects manifest, but is not self-manifesting. It is the mind that is the medium for the perception of all cognitions and consciousness. Consciousness, intellect, knowledge, perception, then, are all absent in deep sleep. They are non-causal qualities, attributes, of the self – "knowledges" that the self has adventitiously. To be conscious is to be conscious *of* something, to have knowledge *of* something, to perceive something. Knowledge must always have an object; it occurs when the mind focuses on some sense data. But since knowledge is a quality that cannot be perceived, it must belong to an equally imperceptible and immaterial substance – and this is the self.

Knowledge may either be presentative when objects are presented truly to us, or it may be the result of memory. Presentative knowledge is either valid knowledge, *pramā*, or invalid, *apramā*, but memory – of which more below – is invalid. For valid knowledge to occur, there must be a subject (*pramātā*), an object (*prameya*) and a valid means (*pramāṇa*). But it is this last that is the reason for, or *karaṇa* of, knowledge – that which makes valid knowledge the logical outcome. For any object of knowledge to provide a valid cognition the cognition has to agree with it: if you mistake salt for sugar you will have experienced false knowledge when the initial knowledge proves to be false in practice. If knowledge is true it will lead to a successful outcome, if false to failure in outcome. Valid knowledge, *pramā*, is thus true, unerring knowledge that is presented to the senses, and *pramāṇa* the means and cause of it. It is this latter – the first of Gautama's categories – that must absorb some detailed examination at this point.

Pramāṇas

The means of valid knowledge, *pramāṇa*, is the first of the topics dealt with in Gautama's *Nyāyasūtras*. He accepts four: *pratyakṣa* or perceptual knowledge, *anumāna* or inference, *upamāna* or comparison, analogy, and *śabda* or verbal testimony. *Prāma*, as noted above, means truth, so the *pramāṇas* are the means by which we are able to ascertain that truth. In Nyāya philosophy, such *pramāṇas* reveal objects of knowledge as they really are. Justifiably, Chatterjee and Datta regard *pramāṇa* as the most important aspect of the Nyāya epistemology. They say: "Pramāṇa is the way of knowing anything truly. It gives us true knowledge and nothing but true knowledge. It thus includes all sources or methods of knowledge."[18] We need, therefore, to examine the four categories of *pramāṇa* that Nyāya accepts.

Perception (pratyakṣa)

Nyāya accepts that perception is the primary *pramāṇa*, for the other three must, in some way, be based on it. Inference must be preceded by it; comparison relies on perception of similarity; and testimony, on audial or written perception. Perception is the means by which maturation in knowledge can occur. Junankar states:

> According to the Naiyāyika the method of acquiring knowledge of the world of things and persons is the method of cumulative evidence. The foundation of this method is perception and on this foundation we can raise a pyramid of knowledge with the help of inference, analogy and verbal testimony. This method demands that whatever passes for knowledge must be confirmed or confirmable by perception, and underlies the doctrine of the convergence of the pramāṇas.[19]

All our knowledge, then, relies in some way on perception, as will be seen in the analysis of the other three *pramāṇas* below.

Basic valid cognition, according to Gautama, is that which involves direct cognition of objects through the senses. He said: "Perception is knowledge which arises by the contact of a sense with the object. This knowledge is determinate, unconnected with name, and non-erratic."[20] The object should be perceived determinately; that is to say, we can determine exactly what it is. It should not be connected with a name, that is to say the object of knowledge can be valid irrespective of our knowing its name, or of its having a name. It will also be well defined; it will not, for example, be a mirage, nor will it be "erratic". Rather, it will correspond to what is true. This, then, is ordinary perception – when the self connects with the mind, the mind with the sense organs and the sense organs with the objects. The self is the most important factor here in that, without its contact with the mind, cognition cannot take place, the mind being the connecting factor between sense organs and self. It is the self that is the cognizer, and knowledge is a quality of the self. Such a simple definition excludes any extraordinary, intuitive perception, especially *yogic* perception that is independent of sense organs and their perception of objects. Later Naiyāyikas, therefore, defined perception in a way that would include intuition. The wider definition saw perception as *direct* and *immediate* cognition that is not dependent on the process of any other cognition: it is independent knowledge that takes place immediately without our having to draw on anything else like previous knowledge or some sort of reasoning process to establish the knowledge. It is a definition, then, that can include intuitive knowledge, the extraordinary perception that came to be accepted by Nyāya. No previous experience informs direct perception, whether it is ordinary or extraordinary.

Pratyakṣa, then, is any immediate and direct perception that, for Nyāya, can be through the senses or without the senses. When the senses are involved, and directly bring about knowledge through contact with an object of the senses, *ordinary* or *laukika* knowledge occurs – the usual form of our knowledge of the world. Ordinary perception can be definite and indefinite. Definite perception is that in which the senses apprehend something and we are immediately certain of its identity – knowledge has directly occurred. Indefinite perception occurs when the cognition is more doubtful, for example when I see what could be a post or a man at a distance.

Like other schools, Nyāya divides the process of cognition into two, *indeterminate* and *determinate* knowledge. Indeterminate knowledge is *nirvikalpaka* and it represents the very first awareness of an object via the senses, and a "prejudgmental state".[21] Although we see the object, we don't classify it in any way; we simply see it. And this kind of indeterminate perception informs much of our daily life and never proceeds any further: we may be aware of a number of things in a room in the sense that they are in our vision, but we do not bother to take that awareness any further. So in indeterminate perception not even the *name* of the object of the senses enters into our minds, but it is the beginning of the process of cognition. It is the stage when we see something but have not yet assigned it to a class, differentiated it from other things, related it to something in our memories and analysed it. All the things that we may come to know about the object are still *there*, they are still real and existent, it is just that they have not yet been determined by the cognizer. So, in essence, this indeterminate knowledge is not separate from its later determined character. Sharma puts this well when he says:

> As bare awareness, as mere apprehension, we *sense* indeterminate perception, we *feel* it, but the moment we try to *know* it even as 'bare awareness' it has passed into conception and has become determinate. Hence all our perception being a cognition is determinate and is a perceptual judgement. We can separate indeterminate from determinate perception only in thought and not in reality.[22]

Thus, indeterminate perception is inferred from the later stage of determinate perception but is not separate from it. How far indeterminate perception has awareness also of the particular qualities, the class and name of an object, has been a matter of debate amongst Naiyāyikas. When, at the indeterminate stage, I see an orange, for example, can I also have the same undifferentiated awareness of its colour, its fruitiness, its texture, even its name, although that perception is still at the stage of basic awareness, even though I haven't synthesized the information to bring about full cognition? Some Naiyāyikas accept that such qualities, class and so on, are not present until the later stage of full cognition and, in fact, it is these characteristics that serve to move the perception to a more determinate stage. Others believe they are all present at the indeterminate stage but the relation between these qualities is not synthesized, and neither the universality of the object nor its particularities are determined. This was more the case with Nyāya-Vaiśeṣika, which accepted that at the *nirvikalpaka* stage of perception, the universal and the particular are manifest – even the particular characteristics – but they are not related to a specific class, and are not named: "it is a simple apprehension of the existence and attributes of an object without any corresponding judgment of it in words, or by way of predication", wrote Chatterjee.[23] *Nirvikalpaka* perception is thus "a real but not a perceived fact (*atīndriya*). It is a conscious, but not a self-conscious state".[24]

Determinate perception or *savikalpaka*, then, is that stage of full cognition when we are able to assign to the object of the senses clear characteristics – its class, its name, its relation to other things, its differentiation from other things, its colour, and all sorts of qualities. And all these different aspects I *relate* together, I *synthesize* them, in that cognition, so that I know both the particularities of the object and, at the same time, its universality, its relation to other objects of the same class. A third stage of the cognition process is usually that of recognition or *re-cognition*, that is, the relating of the object to things that have been previously cognized. This stage tends to qualify the determinate perception by relating it to former cognitions.

In the process of direct and immediate indeterminate and determinate perception it is the senses that are the organs of knowledge. Five – smell, taste, sight, touch and hearing – are external, and the mind, *manas*, came to be thought of as an internal sense.[25] The senses and their respective sense organs are each connected with one of the five elements and have their respective qualities. They inform all external, ordinary (*laukika*) perception:

Sense	***Sense organ***	***Element***	***Quality***
Visual	eye	light	colour
Auditory	ear	ether	sound
Olfactory	nose	earth	smell
Gustatory	tongue	water	taste
Tactual	skin	air	touch

Mind as the internal organ can perceive qualities of the self such as desire and aversion, volition, pain and cognition, and it is the mind that is the medium for experience of sadness, pleasure and pain – feelings that do not involve the external organs. Unlike the other senses that are connected specifically to certain organs, elements and qualities, the mind is a common organ for all kinds of knowledge, external and internal. No perception at all is possible without the mind, for it is the mediator between the senses and the self. It relays information like rapid pulses to the self, so that cognition is possible. The self and the mind are not always in contact with each other as, for example, in deep sleep. Every time cognition takes place, this contact of the self with the mind occurs. Older Nyāya believed contact of the senses was the cause, or *kāraṇa*, of perception, whereas later Naiyāyikas held the cause to be the sense organ. Older Nyāya believed that colour in an object was essential for external, ordinary perception, though later Nyāya rejected this view because it would exclude air.

Navya-Nyāya, as was noted above, also accepts that perception can be supersensuous, that is, knowledge that is not dependent on the senses but that is still perceptual knowledge, is still direct and immediate. This is *extra-ordinary* or *alaukika* knowledge. One kind of extraordinary knowledge is the intuitive knowledge attributed to the great seers. It is called *yogaja* perception. Nyāya accepted the abilities of the seers to acquire direct, intuitive knowledge in, for example, deep meditation, and this kind of knowledge they regarded as the highest knowledge of all. There are, then, two levels of knowledge, the higher, intuitive, extraordinary knowledge, and the lower, ordinary knowledge of the senses. This higher extraordinary knowledge of *yogic* intuition, says Radhakrishnan, "apprehends reality as it is in its fullness and harmony".[26] Intuitive knowledge does not involve the external senses at all, but is brought about through the internal sense of the *manas*, the mind, through psychic means.

There are two other kinds of extraordinary perception in which the senses are only partially involved. The first is called *sāmānyalakṣaṇa* perception and the second *jñānalakṣaṇa* perception. *Sāmānyalakṣaṇa* perception is concerned with classes or universals of things like, for example, the extraordinary knowledge we have of knowing the *class* of men when perceiving just one man. We know there is something *universal* such as the universal of *menhood* when we perceive one man, even though we could never have a perception of every man, present, past or future. So when I have a perception of one *man*, I can hardly do so without having also an extraordinary knowledge of the class to which he belongs – the universal behind the particular. These universals are extraordinary perceptions that are not directly dependent on the senses. Such universals are real and inhere in the objects of perception. An orange, then, can only be an orange because the universal of orange-ness as a fruit inheres in it, just as the cow-ness in cows, or the tree-ness in trees.

Jñānalakṣaṇa is the kind of extraordinary perception that allows us to know something additional to that directly perceived, such as the *softness* of grass, the *hardness* of stone, the *coldness* of ice, the *smell* of a rose. While we see the object, we also have an extraordinary perception of the qualities of softness, hardness etc., without actually involving the appropriate sense organ. This is really applying a past cognition to a present perception, and might be suggested as knowledge from memory if it were not for the fact that the present perception is the immediate source of the cognition. The *association* of the two – the sight of the rose and the past cognition of the smell – has not arisen through memory and it is the association that provides the cognition.

Error

Nyāya claims that *jñānalakṣaṇa* covers cases of illusion, invalid knowledge (*apramā*) or error. Error is perception of an object as something other than what it is. Thus, a rope that is mistaken for a snake is really a visual perception combined *incorrectly* with a past cognition. Similarly, in the case of a shell that is mistaken for a piece of silver, the past memory of the silver is incorrectly synthesized with the perceived object of the shell. Both the shell and the silver are real, but the synthesis of the two is incorrect: similarity is the cause of the incorrect cognition here. It is the universal of silver-ness that is incorrectly imposed on the shell.

Clearly, it is at the determinate stage of perception, that is to say in the classification and analysis of the object that occurs following the indeterminate stage of perception, that invalid knowledge may occur – perhaps through some defect in the sense organs or the environment, as well as incorrect synthesizing. Memory is always an invalid means of knowledge because it does not involve immediate and direct perception. Memory is just residual knowledge, things left by former cognitions, and really only serves to reproduce in the mind something from the past that no longer exists, like a star, unreal and long burnt out, that is still visible light years away. However, though not valid knowledge, memory can have its basis in what was originally valid knowledge, and the converse is also possible. Dreams are, like memory, erroneous cognitions. They are the result of past *karma* and, like memory, are not presentative at the time of occurrence: no *real* presentation of the object to the self is occurring.

Additionally, doubt, error and hypothetical reasoning (*tarka*) are conditions of invalid knowledge. Doubt, as was seen above, is only partially invalid, unlike error, which is the total misapprehension of, say, a rope for a snake. Hypothetical reasoning (to which scholars are rather prone!) begins with a proposition that is conjectured – *If* there is a snake on the road – and then proceeds to subsequent argumentation in order to demonstrate that there is *not* a snake on the road. Logicians use such reasoning as a tool, though it is not unusual to find those elsewhere who forget sometimes that their original premise was a hypothesis, and who proceed to unreliable and invalid fact! Some invalid knowledge arises because of illusions. Again, this may be because of some defective sense organ like a jaundiced eye, or it may be an obscurity in the object of the senses, perhaps only a part of the object being visible. On the other hand, it may be because the memory insists on relaying habitual false impressions.

Error always lies in the cognition itself, that is to say, it is the subjective self that makes the mistake and there is nothing wrong with the object. Error is the perception of something as different to what it really is. The test of valid knowledge is usually pragmatic: if knowledge works in practice then we are fairly certain that it is right, and experience normally reinforces its validity over a longer term. Importantly, invalid knowledge occurs as a result of deficiency in conditions *beyond* knowledge itself; it is not an attribute of the knowledge but is inferred from its effect, its outcome. Thus, we may think we are seeing silver, but on close examination come to know that it is, after all, a shell. Nyāya, then, does not link truth or falsity with knowledge *per se*. In fact, until knowledge is tested practically, it will retain an element of doubt. We don't need to know whether knowledge is true or false until we act on it; then it is put to the test. As Chatterjee states: "All that is necessary for our actions is that we must *believe* in what we know, and not that we must *verify* it as true before we proceed to act."[27]

Inference (anumāna)

Inference is critical to Nyāya logic, and its syllogistic inference will need to be examined in detail. It was a major contribution of Gautama, and was developed considerably in the evolutionary processes of the school in the years that followed him. Potter comments that: "The science of reasoning (*nyāya*) is alluded to in very early Indian texts, and the name of the Nyāya school indicates that Indian intellectuals looked to this school as the authority in matters of detail connected with logic."[28] It is in its theory of inference as a *pramāṇa*, that this is particularly so. Inference is knowledge that follows other knowledge (*anumāna* means "after knowledge", *anu* "after" + *māna* "knowledge"): it is knowledge that is preceded by perception. Chatterjee defines it succinctly as "the knowledge of an object, not by direct observation, but by means of the knowledge of a *liṅga* or sign and that of its universal relation (*vyāpti*) with the inferred object".[29] The *liṅga* or sign is perceived knowledge, and what comes after it is the additional, inferred knowledge, the "after" knowledge. So when I see heavy clouds, I think that it is going to rain.[30] This is inferring from lesser to greater, from cause to effect or *a priori*, and is termed *pūrvavat* in Sanskrit. Conversely, I may perceive that the roads are wet, or that the river is swollen, and infer that it has rained. This is inferring from effect to cause, or *a posteriori*, and is termed *śeṣavat* in Sanskrit. There is an element of commonality or universality about the relationship between a wet landscape and rain, a swollen river and rain, or clouds and rain, so inference suggests a *universal relationship* between two aspects. The perceived knowledge through the senses is related to the inferred knowledge, and the relationship between the two is a universal one – in all cases of A, we can infer B. Importantly, the cognition occurs not by the particular perception, but by the *mark* or property – the *liṅga* that is possessed by the object of perception. It is this mark that is universally related to the inferred character. The classic example is the perception of a hill on which there is smoke, and where one sees smoke, there must be fire: the hill is the object of perception that possesses the mark or property of smoke. Smoke always possesses another property, that of fire, so fire is the inferred character. The universal relation between smoke and fire is invariable. This *vyāpti*, or *universal pervasion*, is essential to inference, and is supplied by the memory. By it the cognition "that there is fire" is not directly perceived, but is the inferred knowledge. Thus, through inference something that is beyond the immediate senses can be known, and knowledge can be acquired through the medium of a precedent knowledge. Universals, of course, are reinforced by experience and by the uniformity of occurrences – in all cases of smoke there is fire. It is the universality of this, and not the *a priori* causal relationship, that is the inferred knowledge. The *vyāpti*, the universal relation between two things like smoke and fire, must exist without any conditions whatsoever – an *unconditional* universal concomitance. Despite such universal concomitance, however, the older school of Nyāya believed that all inference occurs through an element of doubt: it is this doubt about something that causes us to proceed to inferential knowledge for explanation.

Another form of inference is *sāmānyatodṛṣta*. According to Nyāya, this is the perception of an object, like the sun, in a different place from where it was previously perceived. From this it is inferred that the sun has moved, though its actual movement is imperceptible. However, the universal concomitance of the changing positions of the sun still obtains, as in other cases of inference such as the fire that is inferred from smoke. Chakrabarti defines *sāmānyatodṛṣṭa* as "the inference of something imperceptible on the basis of a general connection established by experience",[31] and it is the "general connection established by experience" that provides the universal concomitance necessary for inference. In this kind of inference, then, causal uniformity is absent, unlike cases of *pūrvavat* and *śeṣavat*.

The syllogism

A syllogism sets out the logical steps to establish inferential knowledge. It is a form of reasoning in which a conclusion is drawn from two propositions or premises. These two premises contain a common or middle term that is not present in the conclusion. An example given from Aristotelian logic is:

Whoever is a man is a mortal.
Socrates is a man.
Therefore Socrates is mortal.

The Nyāya syllogism has not three but five parts, members or *avayavas*.[32] It is called the *pañcāvayavanyāya*, "reasoning with five members". Gautama's *sūtras* referring to it are brief.[33] The classic example of a Naiyāyika inferential syllogism is the following:

> The hill is on fire
> Because it has smoke
> Whatever has smoke has fire, like an oven
> This hill has smoke that is always associated with fire
> Therefore the hill is on fire.

Each of these five statements represents an *avayava*, and each is logically characterized as follows:

(i) ***Pratijnā*** *the proposition to be proved: The hill is on fire*

The proposition is the knowledge or statement that has to be proved. It may be stated affirmatively or negatively. It states the problem and the limits of the inquiry. It contains a subject, *the hill*, and a predicate, *is on fire*. The subject is called the *minor term*, the *pakṣa*; it is the subject under consideration and has to be real. The predicate is called the *major term*, the *sādhya*. It is the object, it is that which has to be proved by inference, the *anumeya*; it is what we want to know in relation to the hill, and must be a property of the *minor term*. The syllogism sets out to prove that the subject, the *minor term* or *pakṣa*, has as a property, the predicate, object, and *major term* or *sādhya*. It is important that the *minor term*, the *pakṣa*, is present in the *major*, the *sādhya*.

(ii) ***Hetu*** *the reason: Because it has smoke*

The *hetu* must come second, for the analysis of the *minor term* must follow the proposition. The reason, the *hetu*, is the means of the inference, the means of proof, or *liṅga*, of the proposition. It is a *mark*, characteristic or sign, in this case *smoke*, that is present in the *minor term*, *the hill*. It is the reason for relating the *sādhya* to the *pakṣa*, *the fire* to *the hill*. This *mark*, the *smoke*, is referred to as the *middle term*, and it must occur at least twice in a syllogism, relating to both the *minor* and the *major* terms. It is the means by which the conclusion can be proved, and is connected with the *major term*, the *fire*. The connection here between the two has to be invariable – a universal – and this invariable concomitance, as noted above, is called *vyāpti*. Unless the universal concomitance between the *middle term* and the *major term* can be established, the conclusion cannot be stated. The *middle term* is that which proves, and the *major term* that which has to be proved. There are five conditions for the *middle term*:

- It must be present in the *minor* (a characteristic of the hill).
- It must be present whenever the *major term* is present (in all cases of smoke there is fire).
- It must be absent when the *major term* is absent – this is a second type of inferential reason by which the *middle term* is universally absent when the *major term* is absent. In this case the *vyāpti*, the universal concomitance, is negative rather than affirmative.

- It must be non-incompatible with the *minor term* (it must not, for example, prove that fire is cold).
- It must not contain contradictory and counteracting reasons leading to a contrdictory conclusion.

Inference must contain the three terms – *minor*, *major*, and *middle*, for logical inference. The *minor term* is that about which something is to be inferred, the *major term* is what is inferred in the *minor*, and the *middle term* is the means by which the *major* is inferred to be true of the *minor*. Both the *pakṣa* that represents the *minor term*, and the *hetu*, the *major term*, must be perceived. Vātsyāyana also made it clear that inference must result from two perceptual aspects of knowledge – previous perception of the relation between the reason and what is inferred and, also, perception of the reason itself. That is to say, the knowledge of the universal concomitance between smoke and fire (supplied by memory), and the smoke. While the older school stressed the *hetu*, the *middle term* as the reason for the inference, Navya-Nyāya made the *vyāpti* the cause.

(iii) ***Udāharaṇa*** *the example: Whatever has smoke has fire, like an oven*

This gives the universal concomitance between *middle* and *major* terms, with the addition of an example. The universal that is given is an object of perception, is the means of inference, and is the major premise of the syllogism. It shows the relation between the *minor* and *major* terms, and that relation will indicate a universal between the *mark*, the *smoke*, and the inferred character, the *fire*.

(iv) ***Upanaya*** *the application: This hill has smoke that is always associated with fire*

Upanaya is the application of the universal concomitance to the present argument. It indicates a comparison that is universally so, establishing the presence (or absence in a negatively formulated syllogism) of the ground suggested in the *minor term*. It thus demonstrates the presence (or absence) of the *middle* (smoke) in the *minor term* (hill).

(v) ***Nigamana*** *the conclusion: Therefore the hill is on fire*

Nigamana is the conclusion that restates the proposition and that brings the four previous parts together, interrelatedly, to conclude in valid inferential knowledge. Most make the conclusion a virtually straightforward restatement of the original proposition. *Therefore the hill is on fire (or fiery)*. Some, such as Chakrabarti, however, consider that the conclusion does not, in fact, restate the proposition, but should always include the *middle term*. If this were the case, then the conclusion would be: *Therefore the hill has smoke that indicates it is on fire*. It does not merely repeat the proposition but includes the *middle term*, the reason.[34] Here, the conclusion is a summary of the whole syllogism.

Inference, then, arrives at its conclusion through knowledge of a *mark* that has a *universal relation* to the character inferred: so the mark is the *smoke* that has an invariable and universal relation to the character inferred, the *fire*. And it is not enough that the universal occurrence of smoke infers that fire is present, it is also necessary to infer that there is also no smoke where there is no fire. Important to note is that, in the above syllogism, the converse is not the case. Proving that where there is smoke there is fire does not mean to say that it is also proved that where there is fire there is smoke. Only in some cases of inference is the *vyāpti* equally concomitant between the two terms, and concluding conversely is possible.

Inference, as noted above, can be used to infer what will be – an unperceived effect from a perceived cause, as when we infer heavy rain from stormy rain clouds, or what has been – an unperceived cause from a perceived effect, like a wet landscape that infers it has rained. In both these cases there is a *causal* relationship between the perceived and unperceived aspect, and this causal relationship is universally concomitant. It is clear from these examples that Indian inferential logic can be both inductive, that is to say the inference of a general law from particular instances, or deductive, the inference of a particular instance from a general law. The Nyāya syllogism is both inductive and deductive, whereas the Aristotelian example that was given is purely deductive. Sharma points out that to Nyāya, induction and deduction are both inseparably related, and that inference is not actually from the universal to the particular or the particular to the universal, but from the particular to the particular *through* the universal.[35]

Not all inferential knowledge contains this cause–effect relationship as a universal concomitant, however. We may, for example, infer that an animal has a cloven hoof because it has horns, and there is no causal connection between the two facts. This is a case of coexistence rather than a relationship of causation. Thus, while causal relationship is not essential in inference, the *vyāpti* or universal concomitance of the *mark* and the inferred character, and the presence of a *minor term*, are.

Fallacy occurs in inference when the *middle term*, the *hetu*, appears to be a reason but is in fact not one. It is usually the *middle term* that provides the ground for fallacious argumentation, particularly if it is not universally related to the *major term*. Thus, the logical processes for exposing false inferential reasoning became highly developed in the various branches of the school.

The following example of the five-membered syllogism comes from Vātsyāyana:

Proposition	Sound is non-eternal (sound is the subject, the *minor term*)
Reason	Because it is originated (originated is the *middle term*)
Example	What is originated is non-eternal, like a plate (non-eternal is the *major term*)
Application	Sound is originated
Conclusion	Therefore (since it is originated) sound is non-eternal

Put negatively, the syllogism becomes:

Proposition	Sound is non-eternal
Reason	Because it is originated
Example	What is non-originated is well known to be eternal, like the soul

Application	Sound is not so non-originated
Conclusion	Therefore (since it is originated) sound is non-eternal

Where other *pramāṇas* are accepted by other schools, Nyāya usually considers these to be cases of either perception or inference, rather than being separate *pramāṇas* Thus, the absence of something is often a case of inference. It is simply the contrast between what does exist and what does not exist – implied through inference – which results in the conclusion that something does not exist. Vātsyāyana accepted the absence of something as a valid means of perceptual knowledge. Thus, if we are told to leave items marked *x* in place, but to move any that have no *x* on them, we need to perceive the *absence* of something to carry out the appropriate action. In this case, such absence supplies valid perception. *Arthāpaṭṭi* or implication as a separate *pramāṇa* is also rejected by Naiyāyikas and its examples considered to be explained by inference. Thus, the implication that the fat man who is not eating by day, and yet is getting fatter, is therefore eating by night, is turned to knowledge by inference by the Naiyāyika:

> All fat people who do not eat during the day eat during the night.
> Devadaṭṭa is a fat man who is not eating by day.
> Therefore Devadaṭṭa is a fat person who eats during the night.

While Gautama set out the basic principles of inferential knowledge, it was left to his commentators and their commentators to develop them. The intricacies of the development of inferential argumentation in the school are considerable,[36] however, as Chakrabarti comments: "From the point of view of the historical development of Indian logic the pentapod reasoning was certainly the single most important logical contribution of Gotama."[37]

Analogy, comparison (upamāna)

Upamāna is a compound of *upa* "similarity" and *māna* "knowledge", and it is the *similarity* between two pieces of knowledge that is the key to this *prāmaṇa*. Gautama's *sūtra* defines it thus: "Comparison is the knowledge of a thing consequent to its likeness to another thing which is familiar."[38] It is knowledge that is acquired through the relation between a word and what it denotes. The word is told to a person and is then applied later to what is perceived. For example, if you are told that in India there is an animal called a *gavaya* that is like a cow, and then you visit India and see an animal that you recognize to fit the description, this is a case of *upamāna* or comparison, analogy. You will thus have learned what the word *gavaya* denotes. Analogy for Nyāya, then, is relating a word to its denoted object. Important in the cognition is the *similarity* that is used between two related objects in order for the cognition to take place – here, the *gavaya* and the cow. This was an aspect stressed more by the later Naiyāyikas, but was important because it is the validity of knowledge through *similarity* that serves to differentiate analogy more clearly from inference.

Later Naiyāyikas also stressed that analogous knowledge is knowledge of a *class* of objects (*gavayas*) through the prior authoritative knowledge that a *gavaya* is similar to a cow.

Early Nyāya accepted the authoritative description of a *gavaya* as like a cow, to be the cause of knowledge by analogy, but this could be accused of being verbal testimony. Gautama argued that analogy is not perception because the linguistic referent, the *gavaya* is imperceptible. Neither is it inference, since we can verify inferential knowledge through perception. Then, too, the universal concomitance is absent in cases of analogy. *Similarity* usually remains the novel means of knowledge here – something absent from the original perception of a cow, and only evident when the *gavaya* is seen.

Testimony (śabda)

Testimony comes from the authority of others, and a good deal of the knowledge that we have in life is gleaned in this way. Indeed, if we had to rely solely on our *own* knowledge we would not be able to function in the world. *Śabda* is verbal knowledge (the word literally means "sound"), so it is dependent on the words, and the meanings of words, combined into sentences. But, of course, verbal knowledge or testimony can only be valid when its source is a trustworthy person, and it can only be regarded as *knowledge* when the receiver actually understands what is imparted. If there is no understanding then there is no knowledge. Sometimes testimony is based on what has been perceived and what is readily perceptible. At other times, according to Vātsyāyana, it may be based on what is imperceptible, like the presence of atoms, of God, heaven, and so on. The sources of such knowledge may be highly reliable people, experts, or even prophets, saints and the scriptures.

To Gautama, no special validity was given to scriptural testimony. He said: "Verbal testimony is the precept of reliable person. A reliable person is one who has got intimate knowledge of the subject on which the testimony is to be given."[39] And in the following *sūtra* he said: "It (verbal testimony) is of two kinds, viz., that which refers to the seen, and that which refers to the unseen."[40] Some later Naiyāyikas differentiate between scriptural testimony that they consider is the word of God and therefore infallible, and secular, ordinary testimony that may turn out to be invalid. But even where later Naiyāyikas accepted that it was God who created the particular meanings of *Vedic* injunctions, since the recounting of such meanings is humanly conveyed, the reality and truth of the injunctions is subject to deterioration.[41] Nyāya certainly does not confine valid verbal testimony to scripture. If words are true, and the knowledge they supply is valid, then no differentiation is made in the *validity* of divine words as opposed to valid testimony from a person. All testimony, whether the source is human or divine, is personal.

Words are related to the objects they denote and are symbols of them. Like Mīmāṃsā, Nyāya accepts that the relationship between some words and that which they denote is fixed and eternal: each word can then only denote something that is exclusive to it. Some later Naiyāyikas believed that the correlation – the *śakti* – between a word and that which it denotes is determined by a divine being, by God, and that this assists us to ascertain order in the phenomenal world. Others accepted that the usage of a word came about by tradition and convention rather than by divine cause. In this case, the relationship between a word and its meaning is non-eternal and changeable. It was certainly the view of Gautama. He said: "There is no perpetual uniformity of connection between a word and its meaning."[42] Similarly, some words have more than one meaning and are clearly, therefore, non-eternal in terms of the relation between word and meaning. By no means, then, do Naiyāyikas take the relationship between word and meaning as fixed and eternal, in the same way as Mīmāṃsākas. Moreover, that words are conventionally originated is evidenced by terms invented by medics and grammarians. The overall thinking of Nyāya, then, is that words and their meanings come about through convention.

The power of a word to denote its meaning is its *śakti*. A word is a whole that is more than the letters that are its parts. The whole possesses a meaning that is the essential nature of the word. To Naiyāyikas each word has a meaning that is independent of sentence meaning: it is like a little sentence in itself. Spoken words rely on audial perception, written words on visual perception. Each word normally connotes both the particular and its universal. It is, therefore, indicative – like the sentences that it composes – of determinate knowledge. But words normally have to be combined with other words, forming a sentence, in order to provide valid knowledge. They also need to be combined in such a way that they do not contradict each other – so that they are *mutually fit* for each other. Additionally, for a sentence to be intelligible and clear the particular proximity of the words is extremely important – they would not be understandable if they were separated spatially or in time. Gaṅgeśa additionally considered that the meaning intended by a word has to be clear from the intention of the speaker or writer, and this is important where one word can denote two different meanings, like the English word *bat* or the Sanskrit word *saindhava* which can mean both salt and horse. In the combining of letters into words and words into sentences, we have to rely on memory to absorb one letter or word before we proceed to the next, and so on, until the last word. It is then that we are able to ascertain what the collected words mean. This is verbal understanding or *śabdabodha*.

Nyāya believed that a word has the power to denote three things, the individual object it denotes, its form, and its genus, its universal. An orange, for example, can be a particular orange (perhaps one I want to eat), the form of an orange (one I generally have knowledge of) or the genus, the whole class of oranges. It would depend on my particular intention in using the word, which of the three properties of the word would be important.

Prameyas

Having dealt in detail with the first of Gautama's categories, *pramāṇa*, the means of valid knowledge, I now need to look briefly at the second, the objects of knowledge, *prameyas*. But since these are concerned mainly with the self, I shall return to examine them in more detail in that context. Here, it needs to be said that Nyāya defines the most important objects that can be known as the self (*ātman*); the body (*śarīra*); the senses (*indriyas*) and their sense objects (*artha*); cognitions or knowledge and the faculty of intelligence (*buddhi*); the mind or intellect (*manas*);[43] activity of body, thought and speech (*pravṛtti*); mental defects like delusion, attachment and hatred (*doṣas*); afterlife and rebirth (*pretyabhāva*); the fruit of actions in the experiences of pleasure and pain (*phala*); suffering (*duḥkha*); release (*apavarga*). Although there are other objects of knowledge, these are the ones that Nyāya consider are essential to understand in order for the self to proceed to liberation. Of the twelve, mental defects or faults need some comment at this point, for it is these that provide the stimulus for all our activities. They consist of the basic drives of attraction, aversion and delusion, and it is these, especially delusion, which prevent the self from attaining its true nature. Reality consists of the combination of basic atoms that compose each entity within it. The reality of each object, then, is a diversity of atoms that informs the whole. There is no *unity* to the atomic reality of the universe and all combinations of atoms are temporary and finite even if the basic atoms that form them are themselves eternal. The self becomes attracted towards, or has an aversion to, the whole or just one of the parts of the whole. But if the true atomic nature of an object were known, there would be no tendency to isolate one aspect or another for egoistic like or dislike, and no tendency to make the whole the real as opposed to its atomic make-up. The outcome of any attraction and aversion is rebirth, or reappearance, as a result of the *karmic* energies that have accumulated by attraction and aversion. It is, therefore, by more detailed analysis of the self, and the way in which these *karmic* forces impede its progress, that the *prameyas* can be better understood.

The self

The self or soul is the first in Gautama's list of *prameyas*, or objects that can be known. In commenting on it, Vātsyāyana states that "the Soul is the perceiver (of all that brings about pain and pleasure), – the experiencer (of all pains and pleasures) – the knower of all (pains, pleasures and their causes) – who gets at all things".[44] The self is a substance that, when associated with the body, takes on the qualities of consciousness and intelligence. Thus, it is the ground of consciousness, knowledge and cognitions, but not any of these in its essence. On this view, the self is a *thing*, an object – though an immaterial one – and consciousness and intelligence are no more necessary to it than the colour of a cloth. Other qualities such as desire and aversion, pain, pleasure and effort inhere in the self, and are just as adventitious – qualities the self occasionally has, but can do without. Indeed, at liberation they are lost to the self, for they are only associated with *karmic* bondage. It is from such qualities, or marks, that the self can be inferred as an independent substance, that which is the "I" that knows the qualities in itself. Thus, Gautama said: "The marks of the soul are desire, aversion, volition, pleasure, pain and intelligence."[45] Consciousness, then, is not eternal, it is that which arises through cognitions when the mind comes into contact with the objects of the senses; it is therefore accidental, and merely an attribute of the self. But it has to be an attribute of the self and not the body because it doesn't last as long as the body – unlike colours, for example, that last in things – and it is not perceptible in the body.

The substance of the self is also inferred from the fact that it tends to desire what has brought it pleasure in the past, and avoid that to which it has grown averse. Here, memory feeds such continuity of each distinct self, and promotes further *karmic* activity. Memory and activity keep the self in bondage, and infer the presence of a continuous self. Thus, Junankar comments: "The Nyāya case for the eternality of the self, everlasting in time and not in the sense of timeless eternality, rests largely on the psychological theory of memory and the doctrine of moral responsibility and deserts."[46] So patterns of human behaviour suggest remembrance and recognition of the past – even of past lives, Nyāya suggests, in respect of fear of death. Gautama even believed that because a new-born infant could experience joy, fear and sorrow without having the opportunity to perceive occasions for these in its present life, then it must be through recollection of the experiences in its past life. The doctrine of *karma*, too, must presuppose continuity of the self in past time.

While being an immaterial and eternal substance, the soul is different from all other souls. Its independence is inferred from the unity of memory and consciousness that belong to it alone as qualities. The eternal nature of the self, the soul, is also inferred from its lack of parts, making it a basic primal substance like primal atoms, though the way in which atoms and selves are related in Nyāya is one of what Junankar justifiably terms "a bundle of mysteries".[47] The eternal self is also inferred because its characteristics or marks are present when the self is present, and absent when the self is absent. However, such characteristics, properties or qualities of the self are not permanent: they are not of the essence of the self, there can be no universal concomitance between the self and its marks, and they cease to exist when the self is liberated. Universal concomitance between the self and its qualities thus only pertains to the *karmically* bound self.

Against the Buddhist process view, then, the Nyāya view is that the self is more than the body, sense organs, mind, consciousness and sense experiences, for it is the substance that possesses these. The self can, for example, have a single cognition as a result of two different sense organs, so the self cannot be just the product of sense impressions. Indeed, memory functions separately from sense perception, and Nyāya considers it to be a tool of the self. But it can only use this tool for itself, it has no power to recollect or recognize others' experiences. Of course, it might be claimed that recollection and memory are mind functions, not those of a separate self. On this point, Nyāya, as most schools, is clear that the mind, the sixth of Gautama's *prameyas*, is simply an internal sense that functions as a synthesizer of the stimuli from other senses. It is, however, eternal and atomic, unlike the external senses.

Buddhi is the fifth of Gautama's objects that can be known. As reiterated above, it is a quality of the self that is thoroughly transitory. In fact, it would be more correct to speak of *buddhis* for, in the process of cognition a series of activities takes place. Vātsyāyana explains Gautama's example of perception, or cognition, being like a series of lamp flames:

> When the flames of a lamp appear in a continuous series, every one of the perceptions thereof is evanescent; as also is every one of the individual flames perceived; and inasmuch as every perception pertains to its own individual object, there exist as many *perceptions* as there are *flames*; and yet in this case we find that the perception of each of these flames is quite distinct.[48]

Vātsyāyana's comment demonstrates well the synonymy between perception, intellect, knowledge and consciousness, and these belong to the self and not the body. The body (*śarīra*) is the second of Gautama's *prameyas* and is concerned with the senses, the third *prameya*. Made from the atomic material elements the body is also conditioned by the balances of merit and demerit of former lives. But Gautama is anxious to show that the self is more than the body, senses and mind. It is the self, not the body or mind, that makes sense of sense impressions, and it can do so with more than one sense, synthesizing sight, sound, touch in a special way. The self still exists when not cognizing things, as a substratum for knowledge and consciousness. It is the response of the self to its fleeting cognitions that inhere in it, that produces the causes that must result in appropriate effects through the law of *karma*. All such *karma* must, therefore, be self-determining, so it is only the individual self that can bind itself to the chain of reincarnation.

But to lose *karmic* bondage, the self has to lose its qualities of *buddhi*; it has to lose consciousness. This is a difficult point, and it seems, as Radhakrishnan considered, that consciousness was not thoroughly worked out by Nyāya.[49] Some continuity of consciousness has to be presumed because there must be something that unifies our consciousness and enables us to remember things about our childhood, as well as something that allows us to identify ourselves as the same person from youth to old age. But if consciousness is intermittent and fleeting, how, it can be asked, is it able to promote recollection and recognition after periods of unconsciousness as in sleep? One answer to this might be the link between causes and their effects, the resulting effects from causes made before a period of unconsciousness flooding onto the substratum of the unconscious and providing both recollection and recognition. But Nyāya does not suggest this, despite the problem of denying continued consciousness. Nyāya was more interested in logic than in the problems adventitious consciousness posited.

Since knowledge is always a quality of the self, unlike Mīmāṃsā, Nyāya does not accept the validity of all knowledge. We can never know immediately whether our cognitions do or do not match reality: we have to infer this as a second stage when we test out the knowledge pragmatically. So the self is able to *infer* the validity of knowledge through relating the cognition to life itself. Again, however, if "I" know this knowledge, there must be an "I", a self, that is separate from the knowledge itself or the mind that relays it, a self that exists, too, when the mind is not operating. Early Naiyāyikas believed that the self could not be known to the self and that it could only be known through testimony or inference because something had to experience desires and aversions, happiness and sadness. Later Naiyāyikas accepted a kind of internal perception by which the self could be known to the self, either through some direct perception of the *pure* self, a conception that "I am", or, as a mental perception of the self during the process of cognition "I know that I am cognizing this book".

Activity is the seventh of Gautama's objects that can be known. It is that which motivates speech, the body and *buddhi*, and is the root of *karmic* merit and demerit. Each self, though non-atomic and eternal, passes through the *saṃsāric* cycle of births as a result of its past actions until it liberates itself through knowledge. As a new life is taken up, the appropriate body is connected with the self, a body that suits the *karmic* activities that were causes made in the previous existence. The body in the next life is, thus, created by the present existence. It is a reassociation of the self with its *karmic* physicalities. The self in life is rarely at rest in itself, and it is its activities in the form of desires and aversions that create the causes that must be followed by results. The complex web of causes accrued in any one lifetime takes endless lives to come to fruition. All activity is the cause of *karma*. Thus, despite its view of atomic reality, Nyāya still has to accept that the material world is the cause of suffering, and that it has to be transcended, and this might suggest some separation of the world as a lower reality from the pure self as a higher one.

The eighth object that can be known is defect, *doṣa*. Defects – the mental defects or faults noted earlier – are caused by activity. They are of three kinds – delusion, desire and aversion – and each of these is a *karmic* cause in itself. Delusion is misconception, misapprehension, stupidity, and of it, Gautama said: "Of the three faults stupidity is the worst because without it the other two do not come into existence."[50] It is delusion that is responsible for the way in which each self views reality, and it underpins behaviour in terms of our likes and our dislikes. Ultimately, all three kinds bind each self to *saṃsāra*. Only when the correct perspective of reality is obtained can the activities causing the *doṣas* cease. The correct course, then, is to gain true knowledge that prevents desires and aversions and their concomitant effects. Without this knowledge, results (*phalas*) – the tenth of Gautama's objects that can be known – occur in the form of pleasure and pain. Pain, or suffering (*duḥkha*), the eleventh *prameya*, is endemic to all life, brought about even by the pursuit of its opposite, pleasure. Thus, clearly, according to Nyāya the misapprehension of reality is the root of the problems of the self. But how did it originate in the eternal self? Nyāya considers that such delusion is without beginning, but we are left wondering about its primal causal connection with eternal substances as selves – another item in the "bundle of mysteries".[51]

Each self in its unconscious and non-cognizing state is indivisible and all-pervading, a unity, and separate from body, mind and senses: this, indeed, is its natural and liberated state, the state of release, *apavarga*, and the twelfth and last of Gautama's *prameyas*. In ordinary existence, however, the self engages via the mind and sense organs with all the phenomenality of the world. Although the liberated self is superior to the non-liberated self, and to the body that houses it, the non-liberated self and the body are still a reality for Nyāya. The body is a lower level of reality than the self, but a reality all the same. The real problem with *apavarga* as an *object* is its existence alongside a self that is devoid of consciousness. How can this last *prameya* be valid when the self loses all its consciousness and cannot subjectively experience it as an object? And if the self cannot, then what can? Release here is an anomaly that Gautama certainly left unanswered, as many that followed him.

Causality

Causes are antecedents of their effects invariably and unconditionally. And a specific cause will produce a specific effect and no other, and a specific effect is produced by a specific cause. Nyāya denies that there can be a plurality of causes for an effect because an effect, then, could not be reciprocal to a cause. But it does accept that a cause can be an aggregate of a number of conditions. Nyāya rejects remote causes. It also rejects any qualities contained by a cause as causes *per se*; the colour of the pencil I use is not the cause of the writing. Because remote causes are excluded, causes have to be fairly immediately antecedent; thus the potter who makes the pot is the cause of the pot, not the father of the potter as the cause of the potter, and so on. Any cause of a cause, like the father of the potter, is not unconditional. Something may be the cause of a number of things, like the potter who is the cause of different pots, or is the cause of very different things from pots.

All these effects produced by the potter are not causally related; effects can only be related to specific causes. Eternal substances such as space are also rejected as causes, as are any unnecessary factors associated with a cause, like something that happens to be present at the time of a cause.

These principles of causality belong to the theory of *asatkāryavāda*, the theory that effects do not pre-exist in their causes. Vātsyāyana gives a very clear analysis of the theory of *asatkaryavāda* in the following words:

> When we see that a new Substance, in the shape of *Curd*, is produced through a fresh re-constitution or re-organisation of the component particles, – this 're-constitution' being the form of coagulation, – we infer from this that the previous substance, Milk, has been 'destroyed' through the disruption of its component particles; just as when we see the new substance – Saucer – being produced out of a fresh re-arrangement of the component particles of the Clay-lump, it is inferred that the Clay-lump has been 'destroyed' through the disruption of its component particles. And the constitutional contiguity between Milk and Curd is similar to that between Clay and things made of Clay; [that is, the component particles of the Milk continue to subsist in the Curd, just as those of Clay do in the thing made of Clay]; if there were a complete destruction of the Milk (along with its component particles; if it were completely burnt to ashes, for instance), the production of the new substance (Curd) would never be possible, – there being no connection possible (between this production and any existing substance).[52]

Since a cause must be an *antecedent* to an effect, then the effect cannot be produced *at the same time* as the cause. Every effect, then, is something *new* that is produced by a precedent cause, and that effect does not exist until it is manifest as an effect. Different combinations and conditions that combine as an aggregate in one cause are the antecedent of an effect that is totally new, only to separate and recombine in another cause to produce another effect. Again, Vātsyāyana said, "when the composition of the particles becomes disturbed, the previous combination ceases and another combination takes its place; and it is out of this latter combination – and not out of *negation* – that the next substance is produced".[53] The antecedent cause is not, then, utterly destroyed in the production of the new effect, it is simply a new atomic arrangement, a new effect that is different from, though still related to, its cause. The theory of *asatkāryavada* makes some sense in a scientific world in which we find ever more complex results arising from simple causes, effects that are different from the causes that made them in the sense that they are more evolved ones. Just making a pot from clay is an elaborate effect that stems from a simple cause, and life seems to reflect such new effects emerging from their basic causes. Every effect, then, is a completely new creation, the result of a cause but not a transformation of that cause and in no way identical to it. It is an entirely new combination of atoms.

The causal relation between things is something that Nyāya believed we know intuitively and accept as self-evident in the world in which we live. The fact that certain causes produce certain effects is born out by experience and, conversely, the absence of a cause means the absence of the effect: there cannot be effects without their causes. And it is this cause–effect principle that is at the same time the principle of all the change that happens in existence. Life is characterized by the combining together and coming apart of atoms, and it is the cause–effect process that brings this about. This is a continuous process in existence, a continuous dynamism that informs all life, "a mere redistribution of energy" as Radhakrishnan called it.[54] This tends to lend to the world of causal change a degree of unreality and transience in comparison to the unchanging basic atoms that inform all existence. All causes and their effects exist in time and arise and decay. However, there can never be a universal destruction and final annihilation of all things, since atoms are eternal and, ultimately, indestructible because they are not divisible.

In terms of ordinary existence human beings are the cause of their own lives. Human agency as the cause results in *karmic* merit and demerit as effects for each individual. Certainly for early Nyāya this *karmic* agency is the linchpin of cause–effect processes in relation to the self. As Junankar comments: "The karma doctrine permits no escape from the total settlement of accounts in terms of what is due to oneself, whether it be pleasure or pain."[55] As was seen in the above section on the self, activity is the cause of the three *doṣas*, delusion, desire or attachment, and aversion or hatred – all *karma* producing. Causally, the three *doṣas* are productive of each other, but it seems the "concatenation of aberrations", as the *Nyāyasūtras* terms the incessant *doṣa*-producing activity in humans, are without causal beginning. Thus, Vātsyāyana said, "as a matter of fact, the concatenation of aberrations is without beginning; and what is beginningless can never be destroyed".[56] By this he meant that the innate tendencies of human beings to maintain the *doṣas* is perpetual. But this is not to say that the antecedent cause, activity, cannot cease, in order for the self to be liberated. When incorrect perspectives of what is real are eradicated, then the causes of the *doṣas* disappear and they, as results, cannot occur.

Nyāya identifies three kinds of causes. The first kind is the inherent cause or the material cause and therefore is the material, the substance or *dravya*, out of which an effect comes into being, like the clay that makes the pot. Thus the clay, as the material from which the pot is made, *inheres* in it. The second kind of cause is a *non-inherent* cause. This is not a substance but a quality (*guṇa*) or action (*karma*), which is inherent in the *material* of the cause, like the colour of the clay that makes the pot. The third kind of cause is the efficient cause, which can be a substance, a quality or an action, and which is the *power* behind the production of the effect. In the case of the pot, this would be the potter and anything the potter uses, like a wheel or water (the aggregates that make up the cause). The creation of the world itself was assigned to an unseen power by Nyāya and, being theistic, the direction of this special power that combined the atoms in such a way that creation began, or separated them so that the universe was dissolved, was assigned to God. Basic atoms, however, as well as souls, were regarded as eternal, and therefore as separate from God, and beyond any power he has. Nyāya did not accept an ultimate material cause of existence – if it did, then it would have to admit that effects can be traced back to a primary cause, and this would be *satkāryavāda*. Instead, the material cause of existence lies in the plurality of elemental atoms.

The concept of God

Nyāya is a theistic system of belief that, over the years, developed from a vague belief in God to a more systematized one. Indeed, Nyāya was always more interested in logic than in metaphysics, and a belief in a divine being of some kind was less clearly formulated. But God certainly came to be posited as the efficient cause of the world and as he who directs the combinations of atoms that make up the variety of effects in the universe. Such direction involves the combining of atoms in such a way that they bring about the appropriate lives of individuals according to their past actions. It is God, then, who is the efficient cause of the direction of atoms that produce *karmic* effects of pleasure and pain, joy and sorrow. The negative and positive residues as a result of desires and aversions in life reside in the self as a force, *adṛṣṭa*, and it is this that will result in merit or demerit. It is God who was felt by many Naiyāyikas to be the guide of *adṛṣṭa*, though he is neither the creator of it nor does he have power over it sufficient to change it. Importantly, it is *adṛṣṭa* that is the cause of the appropriate effects of actions, and there is no sense of a God who is responsible for our initial actions; human beings are the efficient instrumental causes of what they do or do not do. So while God does arrange the atoms, he does so only in so far as they comply with *adṛṣṭa*.

Many writers consider that belief in God was peripheral to the early phase of Nyāya. Sinha, for example, notes that the system "had no relation with the topics of the Vedic Saṃhita and Brâhmaṇa. At this stage the Nyâya was pure Logic unconnected with scriptural dogmas".[57] Given the early rejection of *Vedic* words and their meanings as God-given and eternal, there is much to support this, positing the few aphorisms that relate to God in Gautama's *Nyāyasūtras* as later interpolations, or as signifying a divine entity that is no more than a supreme kind of substance-self. But, as Sinha pointed out, *Vedic* authority came to be accepted by Nyāya – indeed, it was in this way that the school earned respectability amongst the orthodox systems.[58] Gautama's three *sūtras* that refer to God are difficult. It was common in the *sūtras* of the schools to present opposing argument, and at least one of the three *sūtras* does this. Potter, for one, thinks it likely that the three aphorisms – in which God, Īśvara, is mentioned explicitly only once – may have been part of an opponent's argument.[59] Vattanky is one who takes the opposite view, positing Gautama as a thorough-going theist. He translates the three *sūtras*, 4:1:19–21as follows:[60]

19. God is the cause because we find fruitlessness in the actions of men.[61]
20. It is not so because no fruit appears without the actions of men.[62]
21. This reasoning is not correct since it (the actions of men) is influenced by him (God).[63]

Translations vary according to the way in which one understands the verses. Compare, for example, Bahadur's obvious theistic slant:

19. Some say that, because man's acts do not bear the expected results, fruits are due to God.
20. Others may deny this, because in the absence of man's actions there are no fruits.
21. Since fruits are dispensed by God, man's actions cannot be their sole cause.[64]

The clear acceptance of Gautama as a theist is reflected in Bahadur's comment on these *sūtras*: "Actions are lifeless and so they cannot confer any fruits by themselves unless God too wills it. Without His grace and encouragement fruits are not possible. Hence man's acts cannot by themselves give fruits."[65] However, as will be seen below, God has no ability to operate outside *karmic* merit and demerit. "Grace" is not an option for God, and there is no other evidence in Gautama's work to suggest such a concept for God.

It is likely to remain unclear how these three aphorisms are to be interpreted. Do 19 and 21 represent the Nyāya view and 20 the objection to it? Or is it the other way round? On balance, the former seems more likely. Vattanky is one who favours the former, pointing out that this is the view taken by all the commentators on Gautama's work.[66] Vattanky writes:

> The intuition of Gautama that God is to be considered the cause of the world has remained the corner stone of Nyāya-theism and for this reason alone Gautama deserves to be called the father of Nyāya-theism. Further, his reference to God as cause has the implied meaning in the context of *sūtra* IV:1:19 that God actually confers to man the fruit of his endeavours. Therefore God stands supreme not only over the world but even over the inexorable law of karma, at least in some sense. This would point out that the God of the Nyāya-system is at least by implication a transcendent God.[67]

But this is something of an overstatement. Nothing is suggestive in Gautama's work of such a developed theism, and even later commentators portray the Nyāya God with considerable limitations. Early Nyāya concentrated on logic: if there were any sense of God it was a pale and underdeveloped one. And certainly in the earlier stages of Nyāya, there is no evidence that God can operate outside the inexorable law of *karma*.

It is the later Naiyāyikas that elaborate more on the concept of God, and it is here that belief that it is only through God's grace that liberation can be realized, can sometimes be found.[68] The eternal atoms, space, time, ether, minds and selves are the raw material out of which God fashions the universe. He is the efficient cause, setting up a system in which humans are able to act and reap the appropriate results of their actions through the divine ordering of atoms that makes this possible. As the efficient cause he is also the cause of the dissolution of the universe. Because of his role outside and beyond the universe, God is greater than the universe but is not panentheistically related to it since he is not the material cause, he is only the efficient cause. Although souls and atoms, too, are eternal like God, they do not play any role in creation at all, and they cannot affect each other: only God can do this. But at liberation, souls, God, atoms are all separated and exist independently of each other – a truly pluralistic view of liberation in which the individual soul in no way participates in the being of the divine, or is linked with any other soul.

God became for Nyāya the Supreme Soul with omniscience and omnipotence, though not over the liberated self from which he was separate. This is a predicable, anthropomorphic God, depicted as majesty, almighty, glorious, beautiful, omniscient and completely free. He is thus a tangibly describable deity and became, for the later Naiyāyikas, a personal, theistic God. He became a father-like deity, a supremely self-sufficient, eternally intelligent being who creates the world out of compassion, but who allows humans to make their own choices in life through his own self-limitation in a way that permits their evolutionary development. God is an uncaused cause, despite the general Nyāya view that all effects must come from some antecedent cause. Indeed, it is its theology that is its weakest point.

It is Vātsyāyana who first provides a more developed sense of God. Answering the question What is God?, he wrote:

> God is a distinct Soul endowed with certain qualities; for as a being of the same kind as 'Soul' He cannot be put under any other category; hence God is defined as a particular Soul endowed with such qualities as – (1) absence of demerit, wrong knowledge and negligence, and (2) presence of merit, knowledge and intuitiveness, and to Him also belongs, the eight-fold 'Power' – consisting of 'minuteness' and the rest – as the result of His Merit and Knowledge; – His 'Merit' follows the bent of his Volition; – he controls the activity of the residuum of Merit and Demerit subsisting in each individual Soul, as also that of earth and other material substances; and he is Omnipotent in regard to His creation, not however, failing to be influenced by the results of acts, done by the beings He creates; – He has obtained all the results of His deeds; [and continues to act for the sake of His created beings, because] just as the father acts for his children, so does God act father-like for living beings. There is no other category except the category of 'Soul' to which God could belong; for (as in the case of Soul so) in the case of God, no other property, save *Buḍḍhi*, Cognition, can be pointed out as being indicative of His existence.[69]

From this it is clear that God is a substance, like other selves. Moreover, he does not transcend *karma*, and he, himself, is subject to it, albeit having extensive and solely good merit. But unless *karma* is to operate as an independent and autonomous, impersonal law, some entity must control the fruition of effects from their respective causes. Simply, a pot cannot become a pot without a potter. An efficient cause to operate *karmic* cause–effect processes was thus necessary – and all Naiyāyikas saw the need for this. However, Vātsyāyana makes *karmic* cause and effect dependent on human effort *and* divine operation, but does not permit God to operate outside the law of *karma* even if he is the efficient cause of things. God is not free; he can only operate under the constraints and parameters of *karma*, and those constraints are orientated in human actions to which there must be necessary effects. As Bulcke rightly comments: "Īśvara can exert his lordly powers only according to a rigid law, conceived as existing independently of Him. It is therefore not Īśvara but karma which rules the universe."[70]

Indeed, the Nyāya concept of God is a very functional one, and it is difficult to see what role God plays beyond such functionalism, particularly if it is human activity that is the real shaper of the universe. Then, too, God is still subject to desires, albeit good and benevolent ones. But he cannot overcome evil and suffering if these are the just fruits of previous actions. He can only operate within, and not beyond, the cause–effect process. It is interesting that Uddyotakara in his *Nyāyavārṭika* sees the need for God as the efficient cause that combines unconscious atoms into their effects, and arranges the appropriate deserts for humanity. But Uddyotakara is one Naiyāyika who stresses that God *has* to create, and *has* to operate *karma*; he cannot be independent in any way of these processes. This, then, is hardly a transcendent God. It is a limitation of the concept of the divine that caused later Naiyāyikas to posit God as beyond *karma*. But for the most part we are left with God as a sort of Super-soul, not subject to the pleasures, pains and aversions of human souls or the impressions, the *saṃskāras*, that inform memory in ordinary selves. God's knowledge, his intellect and consciousness are eternal and omnipresent and not adventitious as in ordinary selves. God's knowledge, then, transcends the *pramāṇas* essential for human knowledge; his knowledge is supra-sensual, being founded on pure, intuitive, direct perception. It is from this that God's desire to act comes about. But placing God in the same substance category as selves is bound to limit the concept of deity. Junankar points out that by doing so, God should be subject to the same limitations as the self, for both really have the same, or similar, properties. And if they haven't the same properties, and God's are fundamentally different from those of the self, then "it is not reasonable to say that God belongs to the same category as the self".[71]

Nyāya argues its case for the existence of God primarily on the case of causality. Because the world is composed of things that are combinations of atoms, these things are effects, and effects must have their causes. Some things in existence are infinite substances that are eternal and have no prior cause. The substances of the self, space, time and ether are of this nature. Other substances are basic atoms that combine to make up things but are themselves indivisible and eternal. Such atoms are the elements of air, earth, water, light, and also the mind. All other things are composites of the atomic, elemental substances, but the particular composition of them all, as effects, is so orderly, so co-ordinated, that some extra cause must be responsible for the particular combination of atoms in such an orderly manner. Only an intelligent and omniscient being could be the cause of this, for the knowledge of the particular, infinitesimal atoms, the knowledge of their particular combinations, and the knowledge of the particular effects of those combinations, is essential to the world as we know it. Only a being such as God can be the cause of this. But God does not create the eternal selves, or the atomic elements that compose life. He is not the material cause of existence in any way.

Then, too, all the variety of life has to be explained by something, and the Naiyāyika explains this with reference to the law of cause and effect, of *karma*. It is asked why good actions should produce good effects and bad ones adverse effects? The concept of *adṛṣṭa*, the unseen power that stores the fruits of a cause until it is effectuated, is the immediate answer to this question. But since *adṛṣṭa* is an unintelligent principle, and an impersonal one, then there must be some intelligence that directs its operation, and provides motion for the essentially passive atoms. Such direction, moreover, conforms to a *moral* order and not a haphazard one and a generally immoral one. The intelligent agent, says Nyāya, is God, who oversees the law of *karma* by directing specific effects as the result of specific causes, and who causes both the creation and the dissolution of the universe.

As noted above, Gautama did not mention *Vedic* authority. It was Vācaspati Miśra who was the first to do so. Thus, unlike Mīmāṃsā, Nyāya came to consider that the *Veda* is not authorless but has God as its author. Nyāya states that since the *Veda* contains knowledge of supersensuous and transcendent material it cannot be the result of human authorship, but must be divine. This is a problem for Nyāya when it is remembered that extraordinary, intuitive knowledge is accepted on the human level, suggestive that human and not divine authorship of the *Veda* is possible. But Nyāya cites as additional evidence for the existence of God the fact that the *Veda* itself bears testimony to this. And if God is the highest premise to which the *Veda* points, then he cannot have any antecedent premise on which he can be deduced. Of course, here it could be claimed that the presence of the *idea* of God does not suggest that he really exists. But the Naiyāyika insists that it is *experience* of God that supports his existence and verifies *śruti* texts, and this experience of God is that beyond the perception of the senses. Certainly, a more developed theism, in line with acceptance of *Vedic* authority, were the keys of this school to orthodox acceptance. But perhaps, as Bulcke suggests, the Nyāya concept of deity was borrowed from Yoga,[72] and this is why it seems more of an appendage to the system than an integral part of it.

Liberation

Release, *apavarga*, is the twelfth of Gautama's *prameyas*, or objects that can be known. Gautama described it as the "absolute deliverance from pain"[73] – a terse aphorism on which his commentators have had much to say. Deliverance from pain is deliverance from countless transmigrations brought about by the egoistic self that is subject to the defects, *doṣas*, noted above. The basic defect is a misconception about the way the world really is – an incorrect perspective of reality. The objects of the senses encourage such misconceptions, leading to desires and aversions. To be delivered from pain, all this must cease, and the primary means to such cessation is knowledge.

It is in the means to release that more overt analogies to *yogic* practice are seen. Gautama recommended meditation as a means to lose the "I" that is so subject to world involvement. Commenting on meditation, Vātsyāyana wrote:

> When the Mind having been abstracted (withdrawn) from the sense-organs, is kept steady by an effort tending to concentration, – the contact that takes place between this Mind and Soul, and which is accompanied by a conscious eagerness to get at the truth, is what is called 'Meditation.' During this meditation, no cognitions appear in regard to the objects of the senses. From the practice of the said Meditation proceeds True Knowledge.[74]

Thus, meditation is an important means of promoting the kind of knowledge necessary for release. Gautama said that: "Pain, birth, activity, faults, and false notions – on successful annihilation of these, beginning from the last, release is obtained."[75] The last, the misconceptions about reality, then, are the root of pain, and are inimical to release from it.

Like Yoga, discipline, control of the mind, and non-attachment to the things of the world are essential means to liberation according to Gautama. But he also believed that knowledge exercised in dialogue with others could serve the same purpose – hence the emphasis on correct and logical argumentation in order to arrive at knowledge of what is real. Liberation is impossible without knowledge of the real nature of the world. Potter comments: "Given that intellectual doubts about liberation are obstacles to progress toward human perfection, it becomes clear why the Naiyāyika believes that nothing short of a full-scale account of the nature of the external as well as the physical world will do. Both these parts of the world must be shown to be such as to allow the possibility of liberation."[76] This is not, then, a system that advocates introspection about the nature of things; it advocates *debate* as a means to eradicate the kinds of doubt that impede the soul's progress to its destiny. Gautama said:

> In order to achieve liberation and to know the soul one must take shelter of yoga practices, because without this knowledge, knowledge of Reality is not obtained.

> And one should acquire knowledge and remove doubts by consulting with those learned.
> One should discuss these things with learned persons who are without fault, as a student seeking guidance of his preceptor.
> The seeker of knowledge should even seek counsel without taking a side.
> Wranglings and cavils may be used not for their own sake, but for the desire for truth; as thorny branches are used to protect growing seeds.[77]

These aphorisms put the categories, the *padārthas*, in a clearer perspective, demonstrating how important it is to see them in the light of the final goal of release. The balance is between *yogic* practice and a certain isolated withdrawal from the world that is concomitant with it,[78] alongside engagement of the intellect in worthwhile debate with others in order to enhance true knowledge. Yoga, however, is a key means to release for, according to Vātsyāyana, it produces the kind of good *karma* that stays with one in successive lives. Gautama mentions, especially, the "restraints" and "observances" of the internal discipline of Yoga.[79]

Naturally the most important knowledge has to be of the nature of the self, and Yoga anchors the self in itself. Knowledge of *saṃsāra*, *karma*, and suffering, knowledge that activity and defects need to be abandoned, knowledge that liberation is all that is to be gained, and knowledge of the true nature of things as the means to attain it, are the ways to overcome the bondage of the self. Desire and its resultant attachment for the things of the world – the objects of the senses – can only be overcome through knowledge.

Liberation is the final end for the Naiyāyika. As total absence of pain, it is, therefore, total divorce from the material body and the senses – the end of suffering. All experience of consciousness disappears and the self which, we should remember, is a substance, exists in its state of pure substance, devoid of cognition. Change, death, fear are absent in this pure substantive state. It is immortality and, for some Naiyāyikas, bliss. As in the state of deepest sleep, the self is separated from the *manas*, the mind. According to Gautama: "As one who is in deep sleep is not vexed with dreams, so for one emancipated there are no miseries."[80] The self, then, loses all its qualities at liberation, and Nyāya, therefore, mostly has a view of liberation as a negative state. God has no role in liberation. He is not working for the soul, encouraging his devotees in response to their prayers and praises. Nor is he one with whom the soul merges, or is in relationship with, at liberation. His role, if anything, in the process towards liberation is instrumental: "It is God," writes Junankar, "who ensures that before any self attains its liberation it has settled its moral account. It must have experienced every pleasure and pain due to it before it can be eligible for salvation."[81]

There have been many criticisms of this concept of *mokṣa* as a negative state that is without quality and consciousness and, for many Naiyāyikas, a state without bliss. Thus, Sharma says that "the soul liberated is the soul petrified".[82] Radhakrishnan was equally critical:

> The critic feels that the mokṣa of the Naiyāyikas is a word without meaning. There is not very much to distinguish the Nyāya philosophy from materialism. . . . The peace of extinguished consciousness may be the peace of death. The sleep without dreams is a state of torpor, and we may as well say that a stone is enjoying supreme felicity in a sound sleep

without any disturbing dreams. The state of painless, passionless existence, which the Nyāya idealises, seems to be a mere parody of what man dreams to be.[83]

At release, the self is distinct from the senses and the mind, and scriptural testimony, Nyāyā believed, supports this. When all the past *karmic* causes have come to fruition, then no new causes are produced in the self in order to require further reincarnation; the self becomes free. Rebirth was one of the objects of knowledge, one of the *prameyas*. This suggests that, like many objects of knowledge, it is an atomic combination that can cease. It is not the self that ceases, but the consciousness that binds it to existence. But we are left mystified at the final state. As Junankar comments concerning the Nyāya state of release: "It says what one will not have but is silent on what one will have. But one will always be what one had always been: the original self will recover itself, without so much as a trace of all that has happened to it since it was thrown into the orbit of *saṃsāra*. The beginning may be shrouded in mystery but the end is crystal clear."[84]

Despite the limitations of its philosophy of God, and its goal of liberation, the contribution of the school to Indian logic is considerable and impressive. While Gautama's theories came under fire from all quarters of Indian logistic philosophy, it caused the school to rise to its own defence through an even more refined presentation of its views. Its theory of knowledge became respected and taken up by other schools. Nyāya is an attempt to view reality, and an attempt to provide the answers to life, through logic. Its path is one that searches for truth through stringent logical analysis and masterly reasoning.

6

Sāṃkhya

Background to the school

While Sāṃkhya today is scarcely evident as a practising school[1] it has had considerable influence on Hindu and, indeed, Indian philosophical thought. It is not an easy school to study in depth because of its variety of interpretation and, therefore, its contradictory teachings. Furthermore, its beginnings do not stem from a single tradition or even homogeneous traditions. It is not, says Larson, "a monolithic system stemming from ancient times . . . One finds, rather, a kind of slowly growing organism which has assimilated a variety of traditions over a period of centuries".[2] While its roots stem back to ancient times, making it in some senses the oldest of the schools,[3] Sāṃkhya as an independent *darśana* did not obtain until much later. It is this, independent, school – known as *classical Sāṃkhya* – with which the present chapter will be concerned.

The term *sāṃkhya* is usually taken to mean "enumeration" or "number" from the Sanskrit *saṃkhyā* (*khyā* with the addition of the prefix *sam*). Since this can also mean "calculation" or "summing up of", *sāṃkhya* can mean the enumeration of the principles found in material existence, for which it is so well known, or it can also have a more philosophical meaning of calculating, analysing and discriminating in a more reflective sense. Indeed, the term probably had a variety of meanings. But while the most consistent one refers to its enumeration of the factors that compose the material world, the idea of discrimination is crucial to the philosophy of Sāṃkhya. This is because the summation of its knowledge lies in the utter discrimination between Self and matter.

While classical Sāṃkhya is an atheistic system, its purpose appears a religious one, for Sāṃkhya is concerned solely with the liberating of the Self from the suffering of life, and its philosophy is strictly soteriological. All its philosophy aims at separating the true Self from the material world and it is this discriminative knowledge that underpins the entire principles enumerated by the school. In order to provide this discriminative knowledge that frees the Self from suffering, Sāṃkhya pins everything on three important principles – an unmanifest and a manifest material world (*avyakta* and *vyakta* respectively), and a pure subject or knower (*puruṣa* or *jña*). The soteriology of Sāṃkhya, then, is one of knowledge; it suggests a way of release from the sufferings of life by an alteration in one's perspective of it, and it sets out valid knowledge to prove that the final goal of *mukti* is realizable. The major fundamental work of classical Sāṃkhya, the *Sāṃkhyakārikā*, begins with the statement that suffering is characteristic of all existence, that Sāṃkhya is the way to overcome it, and that the means to overcome it is knowledge. Such knowledge, as will be seen, is concerned with the distinct duality between the ultimate Self and the completely material world. It is a knowledge that in many ways offers a *practical* means to liberation in that it is not so much passive knowledge that is required but *dynamic* and powerful knowledge that overcomes the ignorance of the human state.

While Sāṃkhya can be analysed as a distinct school of thought, and has been articulated as such by some of its main proponents, it is frequently to be found conjoined with the school of Yoga. The usual differentiation between the two is based on the acceptance that, while Sāṃkhya is concerned with theory, Yoga accepts most of its tenets and concentrates on practice. While perhaps somewhat oversimplified – particularly in the light of the theistic stance of Yoga as opposed to the atheistic one of Sāṃkhya – there is some measure of sense in this view, and the *Bhagavadgītā* certainly accepts such a basic distinction. But this is a distinction that is generally more one of emphasis than of basic doctrine, and the similarities between the two *darśanas* are sufficient to combine them into one school. My purpose here, however, will be to treat the two schools separately, concentrating on classical Sāṃkhya that became independent of its associative partner of Yoga. Like Sāṃkhya, Yoga was a very early phenomenon, and the traditions of meditation and discipline of the body and senses have been pervasive in Hinduism, stretching back possibly to the Indus Valley civilization which has evidence of *yogic* figures on a few important seals. But classical Sāṃkhya shows little interest in such physical or mental discipline; its focus is on knowledge as the medium for liberation and there are strong suggestions that such knowledge in itself is sufficient. Such knowledge is *itself* a *yoga*, a discipline, and is a different path from the one of egoless action and meditation that the adherent of Yoga emphasizes. Yoga is a pervasive phenomenon; classical Sāṃkhya is more specific. Both Sāṃkhya and Yoga, however, probably originated as rather general terms. Harzer suggests that at the beginning of the first millennium, "the names *Sāṃkhya* and *Yoga* might not refer at this time to philosophical schools. *Sāṃkhya* may be a name for any system of metaphysics, knowledge of which leads to liberation. *Yoga* may be a name for any system of meditative practices that lead to liberation".[4] But if there were times when both terms were used generally, the synonymy of ideas between the developing schools brought them together. The long spell of association, however, was broken by a period of classical separation, and it is this more independent aspect of Sāṃkhya that forms the basis of the school.

Because Sāṃkhya may have originally been a very general term, and because elements of it can be found in diverse sources, it is really impossible to establish its origins. It is also impossible to trace its development through to its classical expression, though it is possible to claim that its roots are ancient. As Larson points out, while there is certainly no evidence of any *system* of Sāṃkhya in the earliest literature of the *Ṛg Veda*, the *Atharva Veda*, the early *Upaniṣads* and the *Brāhmaṇas*, there are certainly ideas in these texts that have been taken up or developed by the later systematized school.[5] Ideas of creation emanating from one source, and the importance of overcoming ignorance through knowledge, for example, are ideas likely to have been attractive to Sāṃkhya proponents. The *Kaṭha* and

Śvetāśvatara Upaniṣads, in particular, contain many concepts that are important to Sāṃkhya teaching, though the implications are more applicable to what Larson terms "a kind of undifferentiated *sāṃkhyayoga*".[6] But the technical terms to be used by Sāṃkhya proper were certainly in place from an early period, and primitive Sāṃkhya seems to stem back to some of the oldest *Upaniṣads*.

Two parts of the lengthy epic the *Mahābhārata* (fourth century BCE–fourth century CE), namely the *Mokṣadharma* and the *Bhagavadgītā*, deal at some length with Sāṃkhya and Yoga as two interrelated traditions.[7] As Harzer notes, however, at this time they were "trends" rather than established schools,[8] and while all the ingredients for classical Sāṃkhya were present, the complete articulation of them had not been synthesized. And it is clear from texts like the *Gītā* that the specific doctrine of the self, for which classical Sāṃkhya is renowned, still lay dormant.

Classical Sāṃkhya is articulated in the *Sāṃkhyakārikā*, but it is likely that many of the doctrines it expounds had been formulated in a pre-classical period throughout the various traditions and schools of thought. The emphasis placed on suffering might suggest some influence of Buddhism in the formulation of Sāṃkhya concepts. But it is equally the case that Buddhism in its early literary period owed something to Sāṃkhya. The *Buddhacarita* of Aśvaghoṣa contains a fairly detailed account of both Sāṃkhya and Yoga, and while Aśvaghoṣa does not refer to Sāṃkhya specifically, he does refer to the traditional founder of Sāṃkhya, Kapila.[9] But what Aśvaghoṣa has included is not an account of *classical* Sāṃkhya, but a similar kind of system that prefigures it.

It is clear, then, that prior to the *Sāṃkhyakārikā* there simply was no one major completed tradition of Sāṃkhya and it was the *Sāṃkhyakārikā* that systematized ideas of a number of traditions and schools (the latter in a very minor sense) into a coherent system. What emerged "is a derivative and composite system, a product of speculations from a wide variety of contexts, both orthodox and heterodox."[10] But if there are problems related to the pre-classical origins of Sāṃkhya, there are also problems for the classical Sāṃkhya that emerged many centuries after the *Sāṃkhyakārikā*. Disentangling the various theories that are the product of much later sources from the watershed of classical Sāṃkhya as expounded in the *Sāṃkhyakārikā* is something that most writers have not done, and so contradictions in doctrine abound. But Larson's treatment of classical Sāṃkhya purely from the *Sāṃkhyakārikā* is both clear and devoid of the contradictions of doctrine that emerge in much later expressions of the school.[11]

The *Bhagavadgītā* contains, clearly, a combined, theistic *Sāṃkhya-Yoga*. Larson believes that the Sāṃkhya-Yoga of the *Gītā* is an attempt to speak out against a process of differentiation between the two at a time when an increasing individualism for them was emerging.[12] The *Sāṃkhyakārikā* represents the culmination of a separating process, when what was hitherto the discipline or *yoga* of Sāṃkhya becomes Sāṃkhya proper: it becomes the school of knowledge as opposed to the *yoga* of knowledge, the discipline of knowledge. And Sāṃkhya was probably only one aspect of *yoga*, for *yoga* was a term that could be applied to any system that demanded its discipline and control. Yoga could thus stand on its own as a system of meditation and egoless action, or it could be allied to any other system as an epithet of discipline – as in *sāṃkhyayoga*. Thus, claims Larson, "*sāṃkhyayoga, karmayoga, dhyānayoga*, and so forth, seem to be divergent trends within the context of a general, undifferentiated Yoga tradition".[13] So it is possible that the Sāṃkhya-Yoga of the *Gītā* either represents a synthesizing of two separate traditions or, it represents a reinforcement of a combined tradition that was beginning to show signs of separation. Larson believes that it is the latter that characterizes the *Gītā*. Both traditions have an ancient past, one in ideas and the other in meditative practice; a neat alliance of Sāṃkhya to Yoga, rather than a complementary development, is perhaps unlikely. Dasgupta believed that Patañjali, the traditional founder of the school of Yoga, grafted a compilation of Yoga ideas on to the doctrines of the Sāṃkhya school[14] – and this is suggestive of Sāṃkhya pre-dating Yoga. However, Dasgupta favoured the equating of Patañjali with the grammarian Pāṇini, and dated the *Yogasūtras* of Patañjali to about the second century BCE.[15] Few, today, accept this identification and, thus, the dating of Patañjali. This, therefore, leaves the chronological relationship between Sāṃkhya and Yoga very much open. It is best to see both systems as complementary developments arising from ancient ideas about knowledge and meditative means to liberation of the self, and in pre-classical Sāṃkhya times, both having the ability to lend their ideas to others.

Classical Sāṃkhya extends from about the first century CE to the tenth, with a later resurgence from the fourteenth to fifteenth centuries. It is a credit to its metaphysics that it survived so long, for it had no attracting theism and no identifiable *means* by which its knowledge-based doctrines could be put into practice: it was Yoga that supplied this gap. It can be differentiated from the early diverse traditions that served to point towards it by its more systematized metaphysics. Classical Sāṃkhya moves to a new viewpoint on a number of doctrines such as its theory of causality and its view of the *guṇas*, the three basic constituents of existence. Its dualistic theory of a division between independent selves and material reality is developed meticulously and becomes the hallmark of the school.

Main proponents and commentators

There are no texts at all that emerge from pre-classical Sāṃkhya, and it is, therefore, the *Sāṃkhyakārikā* that emerges as the foundational and authoritative text. It was compiled by Īśvarakṛṣṇa, and has become the most important source for the study of this school. If there were other texts of the same period, they are no longer extant, so Īśvarakṛṣṇa's work is the earliest. There is no early collection of *sūtras* in Sāṃkhya like many other schools;[16] however, there is mention of some previous tradition in the form of a *ṣaṣṭitantra*, "system of sixty topics", of which the *Sāṃkhyakārikā* may have been a summary.[17] The *ṣaṣṭitantra* may have been the true foundation of the school. But since it is not extant – even if it could be assumed that it is a text – the *Sāṃkhyakārikā* remains the earliest known account of classical Sāṃkhya. Suffice it to say that it is not improbable that Īśvarakṛṣṇa's work was summative rather than foundational in presenting the views of the school. The evidence, then, though scant, indicates that there were a number of earlier proponents than Īśvarakṛṣṇa.

The first commentary on the *Sāṃkhyakārikā* was Paramārtha's Chinese version somewhere in the middle of the sixth century. Later major commentaries on the *Sāṃkhyakārikā* that are extant are Gauḍapāda's *Sāṃkhyakārikābhāṣya*, the Vedānta scholar

Vācaspati Miśra's *Tattvakaumudī,* Vijñānabhikṣu's[18] *Sāṃkhyapravacanabhāṣya* and *Sāṃkhyasāra*, and Aniruddha's *Sāṃkhyapravacanasutravṛtti*. A commentary called the *Yuktidīpikā* is also an important commentary – perhaps the most important – but its author and dating are unknown.[19] While commentaries are valuable, noteworthy is the failure of commentators to plumb the depths of Sāṃkhya. This was perhaps because they took fundamental issues for granted or, because a break in tradition resulted in an inability to understand and convey original teachings.[20] Tradition generally assigns the founding of the school of Sāṃkhya to a sage called Kapila, but this is a somewhat legendary tradition for there are no sources that can be related to him. As Frauwallner says of Kapila as founder of the school: "The name is the only thing that appears reliable in this tradition. Everything that is otherwise reported about him is completely legendary."[21]

While the *Sāṃkhyakārikā* makes mention of Kapila as the founder of Sāṃkhya philosophy, sources also refer to one Āsuri, and to a Pañcaśikha.[22] While information on these is scant, they serve to show that Sāṃkhya tradition(s) certainly predate Īśvarakṛṣṇa. New sources have also come to light[23] suggesting, again, that Īśvarakṛṣṇa's *Sāṃkhyakārikā* was summative rather than formative of early Sāṃkhya tradition, and likely to have been based on some fairly substantial earlier works. Dating of Īśvarakṛṣṇa varies. Dasgupta favoured a date of around 200 CE[24] while Larson considered a much later date of somewhere between 300 and 500 CE,[25] narrowing this down to about 350–450 CE, probably nearer the former.[26] What we have with Īśvarakṛṣṇa's *Sāṃkhyakārikā* is an explicit separation of Sāṃkhya as a distinct school from Yoga. At this point it is characterized by independently defined doctrines, and specific terminology. But as it stands, it is in need of explanation on a number of issues, and it is in such cases that the later commentaries are particularly helpful. Larson, however, believed that there are differences in the *Kārikā* and the presentation of Sāṃkhya doctrine in later commentaries. This makes a textual analysis of sources a challenging one.

The *Sāṃkhyakārikā* is composed of seventy-two verses or short sections. It is thus a very short text. It is set out poetically and, unlike more formal *sūtras*, makes use of similes and metaphors to portray ideas. Potter and Larson write:

> If the term "darśana" is to be taken in its original sense as an "intuitive seeing" that nurtures a quiet wisdom and invites ongoing thoughtful meditation, then surely the *Sāṃkhyakārikā* must stand as one of the most remarkable productions of its class, far removed, on one level, from the laconic sūtra style that glories in saying as little as possible and presupposing everything, and even further removed, on another level, from the frequently petty and tedious quibbling of Indian philosophy.[27]

The text covers the nature of life as suffering; knowledge as the means of release from suffering; twenty-five principles that can be known through knowledge; the means of knowledge, the *pramāṇas*; causality and the *guṇas*; the nature of material matter or *prakṛti*; the nature of the Self or *puruṣa*; the evolution and evolutes of *prakṛti*; the nature of reality as threefold; liberation; and the tradition of transmission of the doctrines.

Classical Sāṃkhya is a departure from mainstream *Upaniṣadic* thought, for there is no concept of a totally transcendent and unifying Absolute at all. And we might, with Śaṃkara, be right in criticizing the school as very *unorthodox* in its rejection of the major doctrine of orthodox *brahmanism*, the concept of Brahman. The Sāṃkhya conception of *puruṣa* was of a distinct soul suspended in its own timeless essence and separate from all other souls. It is a far cry from the unifying *ātman* of the *Vedānta*. Dasgupta, therefore, suggested that the pre-classical stages of Sāṃkhya posited some identification of *Puruṣa* as the unmanifest aspect of material existence.[28] Although a more orthodox idea, it is not one that is acceptable in the *Kārikā*. There are similarities with the concept of *ātman* in that *puruṣa* is also an egoless consciousness that is liberated from the *karmic* effects of existence, and is no longer bound to *saṃsāra*. But each *puruṣa* is distinct, and there is absolutely no monistic identity of it with anything. Śaṃkara's criticism of this school as rejecting Brahman – and, therefore, as having no grounds for orthodoxy – is somewhat apt, despite the fact that Sāṃkhya claims to base its teachings on *Vedic* authority. Such a claim, to Śaṃkara, was anathema.

Reality: the Sāṃkhya view of the world

The Sāṃkhya view of the world is essentially dualistic, but in that it accepts the reality of all things that we perceive in the world, it is also, in a sense, pluralistic and realistic. It is its dualism that is the most important factor and the two components of this dualism are considered to be totally separate. They are, on the one hand, *puruṣas*, the true Selves of pure consciousness, each being a *jña*, or "knower", and on the other both unmanifest (*avyakta*) and manifest (*vyakta*) material, unconscious existence called *prakṛti*. *Puruṣa* is an ontological principal while *prakṛti* is a teleological one. The dualism of self and the world is not unknown to *Upaniṣadic* thought, the Self being equatable with ultimate Reality and the world being a lower level of reality. But the dualism of Sāṃkhya sees no unity to the ultimate reality of all Selves. It does, however, accept the unity of the material world, of *prakṛti*. While there is a certain interaction between *puruṣas* and *prakṛti* – a critical issue that will need examination below – these two aspects remain dual. "The fact of consciousness and the fact of the world are two irreducible realities in constant interplay with one another."[29] Reality is thus divided into two – non-material, inactive consciousness, and material unconsciousness that is both potentially active and really active. Sāṃkhya metaphysics, then, can be termed dualistic realism.

Puruṣas and *prakṛti* are the two real categories or *padārthas* of the Sāṃkhya system. But Sāṃkhya also refers to a set of fifty categories. These are different kinds of ignorance, inability, complacency and spiritual attainment. They amount to:

- 5 kinds of ignorance or misapprehension
- 28 inabilities
- 9 complacencies
- 8 spiritual attainments.

What these categories represent is a total analysis of the kinds of mental and physical life-conditions and tendencies of all human nature. They will be dependent in each person on the particular dispositions that are accrued through *karma*.[30]

Prakṛti[31]

It is *prakṛti* that constitutes the whole theory of evolution in the Sāṃkhya system. In its basic state the whole world is a totally unconscious, unmanifest potentiality. As will be seen when the concept of the self is examined later, it is the *proximity* of the *puruṣas* that causes this unmanifest potentiality to evolve into its manifest form. In its unmanifest state *prakṛti* can also be termed *pradhāna* and *avyakta*. Both refer to the primordial source of all existence, that from which all matter emerges. Strictly speaking, the term *prakṛti* should be used more in the sense of an uncaused cause and the term *pradhāna* as the primordial principle. The term *avyakta* refers to the unmanifested effects of *prakṛti* – the state of unmanifest potentiality. Here, however, I shall use the term *prakṛti* to refer to the world of matter – unmanifest and manifest – that is one aspect of the dual reality that Sāṃkhya accepts.

Prakṛti, then, is the ultimate material cause of all things in existence and of every single aspect of the manifest universe. All things in existence inhere in this ultimate cause of *prakṛti* and will return to it. Jacobsen puts this superbly:

> *Prakṛti* expresses the unity and interdependence of the worlds of gross and subtle matter. It denotes the innate nature of living beings, the world's innate nature, and the material world in its totality. It therefore expresses the correlation of the micro- and macro- cosmos. It is the creative stuff of the world, the generative principle, that from which the world is produced, and that into which it will dissolve, in the eternal rhythm of death and rebirth, withdrawal and manifestation.[32]

So really, manifest existence – despite its differentiation – is a unity, just like all things made of clay are different in appearance but are ultimately of the same substance. There is, thus, a certain *samanvayāt* or homogeneity, sameness, about manifest existence, because it all comes from the same source. So whereas *prakṛti* and *puruṣas* form a distinct duality, and *puruṣas* are plural, *prakṛti* is the one aspect of Sāmkhya metaphysics that is unified. There is no transcendent deity or Absolute that is given the function of a First Cause from which all emanates, there is nothing conscious that creates the world through idea, volition, or as material cause. The world simply evolves from an unmanifest state of *prakṛti*.

There are, therefore, two forms of *prakṛti*: the unmanifest form termed *avyakta*, and the manifest form termed *vyakta*. *Avyakta* is unformed *prakṛti*, often termed *mūlaprakṛti*, and is the substratum of evolution, but is non-creative in its unmanifest form. The creative and created aspect of *prakṛti* is *vyakta*. It is this manifest aspect of *prakṛti* that is the effect of *avyakta*. As an effect, it infers its cause, but this cause, *avyakta* or *mūlaprakṛti*, is itself uncaused and eternal. *Avyakta*, then, although unmanifest, contains within it as the first cause, the *potential* for everything in existence: all the effects are held in an unmanifest state in *mūlaprakṛti*. The one thing, however, that the *mūlaprakṛti* cannot contain potential for are the *puruṣas*; these must always be separate. Sāṃkhya posits five reasons for inferring the existence of *prakṛti* in its unmanifest state:

- All things are limited, finite and dependent, but must stem from an unlimited, infinite and independent cause.

- The similarity and interrelatedness of things in existence suggest a common source. The three constituents of all life, the *guṇas*, produce the basic modes of pleasure, pain and indifference, but must have a related cause.
- Something must be the cause of the generating of evolutionary existence. All that is seen in the world is but the effects of some prior cause.
- Effects are limited and cannot create themselves; they must be implicit in an original cause. Just as many things may be created from clay, and return to the basic substance of clay when they are destroyed, so existence has its ultimate cause from which it as an effect emerges, and to which it will return.
- There is a unity to existence that suggests it has a single cause.

All this points to "one unlimited and unconditioned, all-pervading and ultimate cause of the whole world".[33]

While *avyakta* is uncreated and unmanifest it is dynamically so, for the potential for existence is held in three substances called *guṇas*. These will be examined in detail below, but in this context it is necessary to point out that there are three basic kinds of *guṇas*. They are *sattva* the subtle substance of intelligence, light and evolution; *rajas* the subtle substance of energy and activity; and *tamas* the subtle substance of mass and materiality. While the *Sāṃkhyakārikā* implies that there are only three such subtle substances later Sāṃkhya came to accept a multiplicity of each kind of *guṇa*. It is the many possible combinations of such *guṇas* that will produce the material world. In the state of unmanifest *prakṛti*, that of *avyakta*, these *guṇas* are dynamically vibrant, but in total equilibrium – an equilibrium that cancels out each of the others so that one cannot dominate over the others. Dasgupta said of this state of the *guṇas*:

> This is a state which is so absolutely devoid of all characteristics that it is absolutely incoherent, indeterminate, and indefinite. It is a qualitiless simple homogeneity. It is a state of being which is as it were non-being. . . . This is a state which cannot be said either to exist or to non-exist for it serves no purpose, but it is hypothetically the mother of all things. This is however the earliest stage, by the breaking of which, later on, all modifications take place.[34]

The "modifications" to which Dasgupta refers are the *tattvas*, the evolutes that emerge from the *mūlaprakṛti*. And it is a disturbance, a quiddity, in the *guṇas* that brings this about. What causes this disturbance, though in a passive way, is the sheer proximity of the many Selves, the *puruṣas*. It is the activity *guṇa* of *rajas* that is the first to be disturbed by the proximity of the *puruṣas* and, in turn, *rajas* disturbs the other *guṇas* of *sattva* and *tamas*. As a result of this disturbance the *guṇas* are able to combine into the differentiated material entities that compose the world: evolution begins. Importantly, as Jacobsen puts it: "*Prakṛti* is a mutating absolute principle. Movement is inherent in it, and no agent is necessary at any stage to move it."[35]

The evolution that occurs as a result of the disturbance of the *guṇas* by the *puruṣas* is first of psychical evolutes and secondarily of physical ones. So evolution takes place from the subtle evolutes to the grosser ones. The psychical ones are intellect (*buddhi*), ego (*ahaṃkara*), mind (*manas*), and ten organs of sense. Bridging the psychical and the physical are the five subtle *tanmātras* from which evolve the five gross, physical elements, the *mahābhūtas*. From the moment the *guṇas* are disturbed, *prakṛti* begins to produce its evolutes until twenty-three *tattvas* or principles have evolved all the way from the subtle to the gross. The twenty-five principles of the Sāṃkhya system, then, are as follows.[36] *Puruṣas* as the independent and separate principle are the first, and are differentiated from all the others. But though the *puruṣas* are separate, they passively witness all the *guṇic* evolutes that emerge from *prakṛti*. It will be in this witnessing that they become enmeshed in the world of matter. The other twenty-four principles are all *prakṛtic*. The second one is unmanifest *prakṛti* from which evolution begins. The third and fourth – the first two manifest aspects – proceed "vertically", *buddhi*, intellect, first, from which evolves *ahaṃkāra*, ego.

2 Unmanifest *Prakṛti*

3 buddhi*

4 ahaṃkāra*

From the ego, *ahaṃkāra*, evolve "horizontally" and simultaneously the mind or *manas,* five capacities for sense, the *buddhīndriyas*, five capacities for action, the *karmendriyas* and five subtle elements, the *tanmātras*. These, then, are as follows:

5 manas	*6–10 buddhīndriyas*	*11–15 karmendriyas*	*16–20 tanmātras*
	hearing	*speaking (mouth)*	*sound**
	feeling	*grasping (hands)*	*touch**
	seeing	*walking (feet)*	*form**
	tasting	*excreting (anus)*	*taste**
	smelling	*generating (genitals)*	*smell**

The five gross elements, the *mahābhūtas*, evolve directly from the *tanmātras*:

Mahābhūtas

ether (akāśa) associated with sound
air or wind associated with touch
fire associated with form
water associated with taste
earth associated with smell

* = created and creative in nature.

The whole of material existence, then, is composed of twenty-four *tattvas* "reals" or principles all arising out of an unmanifest state of the first one that is *prakṛti*. Unlike the unmanifest aspect of *prakṛti*, *avyakta*, the manifest aspect of *vyakta* according to the *Kārikā*, is caused, finite, non-pervasive, active, plural, supported, mergent, composite, and dependent.[37] It is the five gross elements that form the world as we know it. These elements are dependent on the previous sixteen, but emerge from the *tanmātras*. Thus, seven of the *tattvas* – *buddhi*, *ahaṃkāra*, and the five *tanmātras* – are themselves created but are also creative: all the rest – the five *buddhindriyas*, the five *karmendriyas* and the five *mahābhūtas* – are simply created.

Buddhi or mahat[38]

Buddhi or *mahat* is the first of the evolutes to emerge from unmanifest *prakṛti*. Its synonym *mahat*, meaning "great one", suggests its pre-eminence among all the *tattvas* and its function as that from which everything else emerges. In a sense, then, it is an all-pervasive cosmic principle that becomes more specifically defined as *buddhi* or "intellect" in individuals. Thus, it is possible to see some differentiation rather than synonymy between these two terms *mahat* and *buddhi*. The former is its cosmic dimension, the latter its psychological one. The main characteristic of *buddhi* is *sattvic* reflective discrimination. And since all creation emerges after it, it has the potential to discern all that is created, and reflects all of it in its potential state. It is in this sense that it is *mahat*.

It is in the human being that *buddhi* functions as that which enables the individual to ascertain, to discriminate and to differentiate. In essence it is a *sattvic* principle, having arisen mainly from the *sattvic guṇas* of the *avyakta*. So in the human being, it can lead potentially to qualities that are good, that promote the evolution of the self to liberation, that are *dharmic* and that facilitate true knowledge, *jñāna*. Conversely, the *buddhi* of the human being also includes *tamasic* qualities causing orientation towards what is not good, to what is *adharmic*, to ignorance and to attachment to the world rather than detachment from the world as a more *sattvic buddhi* would dictate. The *buddhi* contains eight[39] such possible *bhāvas* or dispositions and it is these that will determine the life of the individual. The four that are related to *sattva* are *dharma*, *jñāna*, *virāga* and *aiśvarya* – what is right, true knowledge, non-attachment and power respectively. The other four *tamasic bhāvas* are the opposites of these. Frauwallner points out that the eight dispositions of the *buddhi* cover all possible psychological temperaments. He writes:

> The group of knowledge and ignorance embraces all knowledge-processes. In the group of Power and Powerlessness are summarized every psychical efficiency and practice. Finally the group of Passion and Passionlessness contains all will-impulses. Besides in merit and guilt are included all moral factors and the effect of action (*karma*) in the sphere of psychical occurrences."[40]

The Sāṃkhya conception of the *buddhi*, then, covers the whole realm of human emotion and activity – all possible combinations of human disposition. It is the gene-house of experience.

Only one *bhāva*, *jñāna*, "knowledge", is the medium for liberation. All other *bhāvas* lead the individual to rebirth. It is the *bhāvas* that determine how a person will behave in respect of past *karma*. They are therefore predisposed to operate in conjunction with *karma*, the *sattvic* person behaving in one way and those disposed to other *guṇas* in other ways. The *bhāvas*, then, are closely associated with the transmigrating, subtle body, the *liṅgaśarīra* as it is called. They will dictate those drives and dispositions applicable to each individual as a result of past actions, causing the particular composition and personality of each one in the present existence. So although the *buddhi* is essentially *sattvic*, when it is individualized in each person, affected by *rajasic* and *tamasic karmic* residues, and by *rajas* as the dominant *guṇa* of all human life, its *sattvic* nature is temporarily minimized; reality becomes blurred by *karmic* involvement with life. Hiriyanna very pertinently remarks that "the phase of reality which reveals itself to us is always relative to our standpoint",[41] and the particular "standpoint" will depend on the *karmic* make-up of each individual. Importantly, such *karma* can only accrue to the *buddhi* and not to the Self, the *puruṣa*, which is always a separate reality.

Despite the fact that it is the *buddhi* that carries *karmic* dispositions, it is *always* unconscious matter. As such it cannot have any consciousness whatsoever. But what each *buddhi* can do is reflect the consciousness of an individual *puruṣa*. Its proximity to *puruṣa* enables it to reflect the consciousness of *puruṣa* in such a way that the *buddhi* itself *seems* to be conscious and intelligent. It *seems* to be a subject and not an object, and it *seems* to be the true Self. The greater the predominance of *sattvic* dispositions in the *buddhi*, the more able the individual will be to gain the kind of knowledge that overcomes this misapprehension about the real nature of the *buddhi*. Importantly, too, *buddhi* always *precedes* ego, *ahaṃkāra*, and, indeed, the entire gross world. This suggests that it is impersonal in its natural state, when it is not reacting with the ego and the mind. This is why *buddhi* is that aspect of the ordinary self that can transcend the phenomenal world and the desires and aversions of the egoistic self. It is the *buddhi* that is the medium for liberation of the Self, but it is left behind by the Self when liberation is finally revealed.

Unlike the pure spirit of *puruṣa*, *buddhi* is composed of the three types of *guṇas*, so while it is the closest to *puruṣa* in that it is, as the first evolute, the subtlest of substances, it is still transient and changeable, unlike the *puruṣa* that it reflects. But this proximity of *puruṣa* and *prakṛti* tends to bring about the apparent identity of the one with the other, so that *puruṣa*, in witnessing *prakṛti* in the form of *buddhi*, has a tendency to see itself as *buddhi*, just as *buddhi*, in reflecting *puruṣa*, seems to be pure consciousness and the real Self. Since it is the *buddhi* that is capable of being predominantly *sattvic*, and therefore of the quality of light, it has the capacity to reflect the *puruṣa* in a way that gross matter, for example – which has minimal *sattvic* content – does not. And since the *buddhi* is the direct evolute of unmanifest *prakṛti* it has within it the potential for all knowledge. When knowledge takes place, the *puruṣa* illuminates the *buddhi* with consciousness in respect of the particular cognition, and the ego and the mind – the later evolutes of *buddhi* – co-operate to bring about the relational and differentiating processes that we use in our view of the world around us.

The *buddhi*, then, is concerned with knowledge of the ordinary facts of the world, as well as knowledge that brings release from attachment to the world and that frees the individual *puruṣa* from all *prakṛtic* existence. But it must always borrow its consciousness from *puruṣa*. Somehow, the *buddhi* must come to realize intuitively that the consciousness it thinks it has belongs to something separate from itself and from all matter – *puruṣa*. However, for the most part the *buddhi* is involved with the phenomenal world and the objects that fill it. It becomes modified to suit the form of an object conveyed to it from the senses via the mind, and *transforms* itself into the necessary forms. When *puruṣa* informs it with consciousness, experience results. Because of its nature of reflective discrimination, each *buddhi* lends this *sattvic* characteristic to the *puruṣa* that is reflected in it, so that the *puruṣa* becomes aware of the world and reacts to it. But involvement with objects is not of the nature of *puruṣa*, for Sāṃkhya places such activity firmly as part of the materialism of *prakṛti* – the *buddhi*.

Ahaṃkāra

Ahaṃkāra, or ego, evolves directly and vertically from *buddhi*. Like *buddhi*, the ego is material and unconscious. The word *ahaṃkāra* is probably a composite of two words, *kāra* meaning "acting", "making" or "working", with the addition of the prefix *aham* meaning "I". But it is a difficult word to translate. The *Kārikā* does not tell us a great deal about it, other than to say that it is both self-awareness and self-conceit, and that from it creation emerges as the "eleven" (the *manas* and the five *buddhīndriyas* and the five *karmendriyas*) and the "five" (the subtle elements of the *tanmātras*). Weerasinghe describes it as "the uniform apperceptive mass as yet without any definite personal experience but with an obscure feeling of being Ahaṃ or 'I'".[42] This suggests that in reality the ego is unconscious and material; it imagines itself otherwise, considering itself to be the real agent of all actions, desires and aversions. It is associated with "me" and "mine", it owns things and people, makes choices, acts for its own ends and relates to the whole world from its own egocentrism. Later commentators claim that, like *buddhi*, it is characterized by one of the three types of *guṇas* that will be predominant over the other two. If the ego is *sattvic*, then it will be concerned with knowledge, with evolution of the self and with the subtle in life. If, on the other hand, it is a *tamasic* ego, then it will be concerned with the dull, the material and the gross. The *rajasic* ego is that characterized by excessive motion and activity. In developing from the intellect, the *buddhi*, the particular balance of *guṇas* in the *ahaṃkāra*, will match the same kind of balance of *guṇas* associated with the *bhāvas*, the dispositions, of the *buddhi*. It is *karma* that will dictate these predispositions. In other words, each human being creates for him or her self the *guṇic* dispositions of the intellect that predispose him or her to a particular type of ego in the next existence. All this is part of the cause–effect process. *Ahaṃkāra* is the "I-ness" by which *puruṣas* become enmeshed in the activities of *prakṛti* – and each becomes diferently enmeshed. This suggests that the world-picture that each *puruṣa* "sees" is different – dependent on dispositional tendencies of the intellect, as well as the individual impressions that affect the ego.

It is from the three types of *guṇas* of the *ahamkāra* that all except the gross evolutes emerge. Although there are some variations it is generally considered that from *sattva* emerge the mind, the five *buddhīndriyas* or organs of perception, and the five *karmendriyas* or organs of action. From *tamas* emerge the five subtle elements, the *tanmātras*. It is *rajas* that provides the motivating energy for both kinds of *guṇas* to create. The *guṇas* inform both cosmic evolution and individual personality. Such cosmic and psychological effects they create are the following, all from the *ahaṃkāra*:

	Cosmic	**Psychological**
sattva	produces mind and *indriyas*	goodness in personal action, thought and speech
tamas	produces the *tanmātras*	idleness, dullness, ignorance, indifference
rajas	produces energy for evolution	evil and suffering

The fact that these evolutes of mind and the facilitators of sense perception and action evolve *from* the *ahaṃkāra* suggests that pure *ahaṃkāra* is a state of self-awareness, of "I"-ness, that exists prior to any sense impressions, or to a mind that acts as the synthesizer and conveyer of them. It is a kind of "pure self-awareness" as Larson terms it.[43] He likens it to the state of dreaming sleep, or daytime fantasies, or the child that is becoming aware of his or her self; in such cases one is aware of oneself as having some identity, but ordinary experience is quite separate. Yet all three of Larson's examples rely on perception in some way, and perception is an evolute of the *ahaṃkāra*, suggestive that the pure self-awareness that precedes it in evolution is devoid even of the perceptions we can have in dreams.

Manas

From the *ahaṃkāra* emerge the *manas*, the *indriyas* and the *tanmātras*. The *manas*, the mind, is that which constructs and arranges the sense impressions that reach it from the senses and the organs of action, the *indriyas*. It performs an analytic function, providing sensible explanations of the sense data that it organizes, and its functioning feeds both the ego and the intellect, and links the two. Again, it is *prakṛtic* material, finite and unconscious. It is, in fact, an *indriya*, a sense organ, but in that it is connected so intimately with the higher subtle evolutes of intellect and ego, it is often classed with these two as an "internal organ", while the other *indriyas* are the "external organs". The mind is a sense that is of the nature of both the sense organs and the organs of action because, as the *Kārikā* states: "It is characterized by reflection (or synthesis or construction) and it is a sense because it is similar (to the senses)."[44]

Since the mind is not atomic and, therefore, composite, it is capable of synthesizing many different senses at the same time. It interprets all the perceptions of the senses, which will remain at the indeterminate level of knowledge until the mind synthesizes them. The ego then reacts to the determinate knowledge that the mind has presented and such reaction may be positive or negative or even neutral. But the *guṇic* dispositions of the ego will determine to a great extent just how the ego will react to the sense stimuli conveyed to it by the mind. The role of the intellect is in the level of choice about the conveyed impressions, and it is the intellect, therefore, that provides the resulting volitional activity of mind or body.

Buddhi, *ahaṃkāra* and *manas*, then, are collectively the "internal organ" or *antaḥkaraṇa*, and each of these three supplies a different characteristic for collective functioning:

buddhi	knowledge, volition, feeling
ahaṃkāra	desire to act
manas	means to act

It is this collective, but totally material functioning of the three as the *antaḥkaraṇa*, that is the means for discrimination and determinative knowledge, of "I-ness" and the attachments that arise from it, and of intention. But *buddhi*, *ahaṃkāra* and *manas* are *objects*; the only subject is *puruṣa*. And as material objects, they are incapable of consciousness – only the Self has this. So intellect, ego and mind are the internal organ that supplies agency for actions and thoughts, though with reflected, borrowed consciousness from the *puruṣa*.

The indriyas

The *indriyas* are the organs associated with sense, and with action, and there are five of each. All stem from the ego, *ahaṃkāra*. The organs of sense are the *buddhīndriyas*. They are not so much *organs* of the senses, like the eyes, ears and so on, for these are really gross objects that are composed from the gross physical elements. Rather, they are the capabilities of the senses, like seeing and hearing.[45] Each of the *buddhīndriyas* is associated with a particular quality – hearing with sound, feeling with touch, seeing with colour, tasting with taste and smelling with smell.

The *karmendriyas* are the organs of action – speaking, grasping, walking, excreting, generating. They are the active facilitators of speech, grasping and seizing, movement, excretion and reproduction respectively. The organs associated with the *karmendriyas*, like the other *indriyas*, are not the real mediums for sense perception and action. These were believed by Sāṃkhya to come from an imperceptible power or *śakti* that could be inferred. It is this inferred power, rather than the perceived organ, that is the *indriya*.

The tanmātras

The *tanmātras* are the five subtle elements that are created from the *ahaṃkāra* like the *manas* and the *indriyas*. The term means "only so much or so little", "rudimentary", or "trifle".[46] The *tanmātras* are particularly created from the *tamasic ahaṃkāra* unlike the eleven *indriyas* and the *manas* that are produced simultaneously from the *sattvic ahaṃkāra*. The *tanmātras* are, therefore, predominantly *tamasic* in nature, and the dominant *tamas* influence that produces them is usually termed *bhūtādi*. The *tanmātras* are both created from the *ahaṃkāra* and are themselves creative in that the gross, physical elements are created from them.

The *tanmātras* are an interesting, subtle aspect of creation. They are "pure" elements, non-particular, and so are imperceptible and only able to be inferred, unlike the gross, physical elements – ether, air, fire, water and earth – that are created from them. The *tanmātras* are extremely important since they are the medium by which the previous evolutes are connected to the physical world; they link, in particular, the ego with the gross world. All the evolutes that precede them, and the *tanmātras* themselves, constitute the *liṅga* or *liṅgaśarīra*, the subtle body of the individual, mentioned above, that is able to create and accrue fruitive *karma*. There are some indications from verses 32 and 33 of the *Sāṃkhyakārikā* that the *tanmātras* are not part of the subtle body. But verse 40 seems to suggest otherwise. Larson certainly accepts this by the comments in parentheses in his translation: "The subtle body (*liṅga*), previously arisen, unconfined, constant, inclusive of the great one (*mahat*), etc., through the subtle elements (i.e., inclusive of *buddhi*, *ahaṃkāra*, *manas*, the ten senses and the five subtle elements), not having enjoyment, transmigrates, (because of) being endowed with *bhāvas* ('conditions' or 'dispositions')."[47] It may be that the intention of Īśvarakṛṣṇa was to posit a thirteen-fold *liṅga*, *plus* the five *tanmātras* that act as a sheath or support for the *liṅga*. Thus, verse 41 of the *Kārikā* states: "As a picture (does) not exist without a support or as a shadow (does) not exist without a post, etc., so, too, the instrument (*liṅga* or *karaṇa*) does not exist supportless without that which is specific (i. e., a subtle body)."[48] This, then, suggests that the *liṅgaśarīra* consists of the subtle entity of the first thirteen evolutes, enclosed in the sheath of the five subtle elements, thus making it eighteen-fold in all.

It is the subtle body that transmigrates, permanently accompanied by the *puruṣa* through its respective reincarnations – indeed, until the *puruṣa* separates from *prakṛti* in the enlightened state. In Weerasinghe's words: "It is this subtle body that goes on from birth to birth as the basis of the reincarnated *Puruṣa* or the personality. It departs, so to say, from the sheath of the gross body at the time of death and then determines the nature of the next existence, for in it are left traces, like scars or furrows, of all our actions, desires and inclinations."[49] Thus, the nature of the subtle self is dictated by the *bhāvas* of the intellect, and by the predominant *guṇas* of the ego. These dispositions and tendencies will predispose the subtle self to respond to life according to its *karmic* nature. At the same time, however, the subtle self is able to influence the distribution of *bhāvas* and egoistic *guṇas* in the future, by the kinds of choices in the present. Acquiring the right kind of knowledge about, and reaction to, the world, would be important in creating a better *karmic* existence for the future. Since each *liṅga* is dependent on its own particular combination of *guṇas* it will differ from others, in addition to being different in each existence as a result of the *karmic* residues that have been built up. The *liṅga*, then, is what supplies our personality, our particular character and the happinesses and sorrows of life. It also dictates where life will be – in plant, animal, human, divine or hellish realms. The subtle body is the only means by which the dispositional tendencies can find an outlet. Given the intimacy of each link in this evolutionary theory, it would be logical to accept some kind of subtle elemental substance that is coded with the necessary *guṇic* dispositions and *karmic* residues that will inform each physical body that is yet to evolve. Then, what that physical body does in its life has a subtle medium to store the residues of those actions even when the body ceases to exist.

Coming from *tamasic* origins it seems natural to assume that the *tanmātras* would be of the *tamasic* qualities of dullness and mass. But they are not, and are subtle, in contrast to what is created from them – the gross elements. Dasgupta overcomes this anomaly with his description of the *tanmātras* as "subtle matter, vibratory, impingent, radiant, instinct with potential energy".[50] He goes on to say that: "The tanmātras possess something more than quantum of mass and energy; they possess physical characters, some of them penetrability, others powers of impact or pressure, others radiant heat, others again capability of viscous and cohesive attraction."[51] This very neatly depicts both the subtle aspects in the potentialities of the *tanmātras* and their associative aspects with physical matter. But each of the *tanmātras* has only one special quality or essence to inform the gross elements that will emerge from it. Unlike the gross elements that proceed from them, the subtle elements are always unchanging, remaining "non-specific" in themselves, each with its separate quality that has a special effect. The gross elements, however, combine in many different and finite ways. This special essence of each *tanmātra* is depicted perfectly by Larson:

> The subtle sound element itself is not any particular sound. It is the generic essence of sound,

the presupposition for all particular sounds, the universal possibility of sound-as-such. Similarly, the apprehension of a specific contact is only possible if there is an undifferentiated generic receptivity for touch, the universal possibility of touch-as-such, namely, the subtle touch element and so forth."[52]

These descriptions of the *tanmātras* as "generic presuppositions" or "generic essences" are particularly apt. Because they are subtle elements, the *tanmātras* are indeterminate; it will be their further differentiation in gross matter that will transform them into what is capable of being determinately perceived.

The mahābhūtas

The *mahābhūtas* are the five gross or physical elements (*pañcabhūtāni*) that result from the creative differentiating potentials of the *tanmātras*. These gross elements are those evolutes that form the physical world, the previous ones being of subtle, though still material, nature. Ether, air or wind, fire, water and earth are the traditional elements that inform all existence, but here they are the medium for the gross world and not for the more subtle aspects of the manifest universe. Gods, humans (in their gross physical forms), animals, creatures, insects, vegetation and minerals are all present at this gross, physical level. And each of the physical manifestations is characterized by a predominant *guṇic* type. Those *sattvic* in nature are in the more subtle realms of the gods; humans are characterized by *rajas*, and the sub-human world by *tamas*.

From the *tanmātras* the *mahābhūtas* are created progressively. Each one has certain qualities, and when the next one is created it adds to it the quality of the former. Thus:

Tanmātra	**Addition of**	***Mahābhūta***	**Quality**
Sound		*ether or ākāśa*	*sound*
Touch	*sound*	*wind or air*	*sound* *touch*
Form *(sight)*	*sound* *touch*	*fire or light*	*sound* *touch* *colour*
Taste	*sound* *touch* *colour*	*water*	*sound* *touch* *colour* *taste*
Smell	*sound* *touch* *colour* *taste*	*earth*	*sound* *touch* *colour* *taste* *smell*

While the *tanmātras* are imperceptible, the gross elements are not, and are normally found to be pleasurable, painful or neutral. It is to these that the subtle body, the *liṅgaśarīra*, reacts, desiring some things and having an aversion for others. The way in which it reacts will be *karmically* predetermined in so far as the nature of the individual is already set by the *bhāvas* of the intellect and the appropriate *guṇic* make-up of the ego. But freedom of desires and aversions is nevertheless possible, despite the individual's propensities. All these physical aspects of the world are real; they represent different combinations of elements, each entity informed by a different combination than the next, so that we have real diversity in the world. This diversity and differentiation in existence is, however, evolution from, and composed of, the unitary principle of *prakṛti*.

Thus we have the Sāṃkhya theory of evolution. It is not difficult to see that its perception of reality is, despite the designation of Sāṃkhya as orthodox, a total rejection of Brahman as the ultimate Reality and cause of manifest existence. Śāṃkara, the founder of the school of Advaita Vedānta, in particular, criticized the idea of a first cause as *avyakta* that was itself unconscious. And since Śāṃkara was very orthodox, the positing of a first cause that rejected *śruti* authority and its clear acceptance of Brahman was anathema. In this respect Śāṃkara objected, also, to the considerable reliance of Sāṃkhya on the *pramāṇa* of inference for proof of the existence of *prakṛti* (and, as will be seen, of *puruṣas*) as opposed to the *śruti* evidence for the existence of, and identity of the self to, Brahman. Śāṃkara also maintained that it is impossible to accept that the whole of animate and inanimate existence – all of which is so intricately designed in a way that it is impossible to conceive of – could come about through an unconscious cause. He argued that there would have to be an intelligent and conscious agent to be the efficient cause of the universe, just as we would need a potter to turn clay into its end products.[53] Indeed, Radhakrishnan wrote of *prakṛti*: "It is the symbol of the never-resting, active world stress. It goes on acting unconsciously, without regard to any thought-out plan, working for ends which it does not understand."[54] But, as will be seen below, it does have a purpose in relation to the *puruṣas* that become so involved in the *guṇic* interplay that is *prakṛti*.

The guṇas

The word *guṇa* means "thread" or "cord", and in *Sāṃkhya* it aptly refers to the three threads *sattva*, *tamas* and *rajas* that make up the unity of unmanifest and manifest existence, though the word can have several nuances of meaning.[55] In normal usage in Hinduism the *guṇas* are *qualities*; however, Sāṃkhya views the *guṇas* as *substances*, even though they are subtle substances. The *guṇas* are the "cosmic constituents"[56] of all manifest existence, and even in the unmanifest state of *prakṛti* they are indestructible potentialities. Each entity in existence is composed of them in some proportion in the same way as a rope is composed of its respective strands. They are the basic constituents present in the unmanifest *prakṛti* that are transformed into the increasingly differentiated evolutes of manifest *prakṛti*. Since they serve to bind individuals to material existence, and are also the substances that create happiness, pain and dullness, the analogy of a rope that ties the individual to the world is an apt one. As noted in the introductory section, though the *Sāṃkhyakārikā* mentions just *three guṇas*, later Sāṃkhya came to accept an infinite number of like *guṇic* substances that inform each of them. In this case it would be more accurate to speak of the *sattvic class* of *guṇas*, or the *rajas* or *tamas* classes of *guṇas*. The three *guṇas* inform each entity in existence with varying proportions that account for the differentiation of matter (which is why a multitude of each type of *guṇa* came to make more sense). They are completely dependent on each other, and account for the interconnectedness of all things in the universe and, reciprocally, the interconnectedness accounts for the evolution of all things from primal, unmanifest *guṇas*. The *Sāṃkhyakārikā* states: "The *guṇas*, whose natures are pleasure, pain and indifference, (serve to) manifest, activate and limit. They successively dominate, support, activate, and interact with one another."[57] Each entity in existence has a predominant *guṇa* giving it its more general characteristic, but all three are present in everything, which again, accounts for the unity and interconnectedness of existence.

Sattva is the substance of purity, of light, of goodness, is associated with pleasure and happiness, and is buoyant and shining. It is associated with whiteness, permits striving forward, and is inimical to darkness and ignorance. Because it is light, it is the most subtle of the *guṇas*, and has an illuminating character. It characterizes the inhabitants of the heavenly world. It is *sattva* that is best able to reflect the conscious *puruṣa*. *Buddhi*, as the first evolute of *prakṛti*, is predominantly *sattvic* and acts as the medium most affected by the *puruṣas*. The four positive *bhāvas* of the *buddhi* – virtue, knowledge, non-attachment and power – are *sattvic* dispositions. The full potential of this *guṇa* is well described by Chatterjee and Datta:

> The manifestation of objects in consciousness (jñāna), the tendency towards conscious manifestation of the senses, the mind and the intellect, the luminosity of light, and the power of reflection in a mirror or the crystal are all due to the operation of the element sattva in the constitution of things. Similarly, all sorts of lightness in the sense of upward motion, like the blazing up of fire, the upward course of vapour and the winding motion of air, are induced in things by the element of sattva. So also pleasure in its various forms, such as satisfaction, joy, happiness, bliss, contentment, etc. is produced by things in our minds through the operation of the power of sattva inhering in them both.[58]

It is the "tendency towards conscious manifestation in the senses" that makes the *sattvic* nature of the *buddhi* important in its association with the conscious *puruṣa*. Thinking is of the nature of *sattva* and it is, thus, seemingly conscious, though it remains *prakṛtic* and, therefore, material. But the *sattvic guṇa* resembles the *puruṣas* closely enough to reflect the pure subjective consciousness of them and to identify thought with consciousness and intelligent agency. The *sattvic guṇa* is of the nature of discernment, that is to say, of reflective determination. As the first of the evolutes to become manifest, *buddhi* is essentially *sattvic* and has all the potential for discernment in whatever direction its predispositions will take it. But it is the *sattvic* element with its pure, reflective perception, that is the only means of liberation.

The *tamas guṇa* is opposite in nature to *sattva*. *Tamas* is characterized by dullness and indifference, by restraint, obstruction and heaviness. Its restraining aspect opposes activity of the *rajas guṇa*, so it opposes all movement, rhythm, activity of the mind, and promotes ignorance, bewilderment and confusion. It is a *guṇa* associated with darkness. It is heavy and of the nature of inertia, and is negative as opposed to the positivity of *sattva*. When we are sleepy, drowsy and lazy, we are *tamasic*. *Tamas* has more to do with materiality and is the *guṇa* that predominantly composes the *tanmātras* and *mahābhūtas* of *prakṛti* – the subtle and gross elements of life respectively. It is therefore mainly concerned with what is physical, gross and, thus, with mass and matter – quite the opposite of thought. So if the individual is preoccupied with the *tamasic* elements of life he or she is a long way from the thought processes that lead to liberation, and is enveloped in ignorance. It is a *guṇa* that characterizes the sub-human realm in particular.

Whereas *sattva* is associated with joy, pleasure and happiness in life, *tamas* is associated with the kind of inertia that is the potential for pain and sorrow because it is gross, material, and promotes ignorance. The particular blend of sorrow and happiness in life was as evident to the ancient mind as it is to the modern one. It often seems that the moment one seems to relish a time of happiness, life brings the sorrows from round the corner very quickly! But the converse never seems to be quite the case even for the most positive of people. Sāṃkhya answers this paradox of life from the perspective of the *guṇas*. The *Sāṃkhyakārikā* begins with the statement of the nature of life as suffering, and if this seems a pessimistic view of life it is supported logically by the particular *guṇic* pattern of the evolutes in Sāṃkhya philosophy. *Sattva*, being light and very subtle, is barely evident in gross matter; whereas *tamas* is present in every evolute of *prakṛti*, but particularly in the whole of the physical world in which the human being is involved. Thus, *tamas* pervades the world at all levels and makes life proportionately more inert, an inertia that makes one more sorrowful than happy because it is involved in ignorance. "The wiser the man," said Dasgupta, "the greater is his capacity of realizing that the world and our experiences are full of sorrow."[59] If this were not so, then there could be no striving for the freedom that *mukti* brings; *saṃsāra* would be a delight. The more *sattvic* the individual becomes, the more subtle the sorrow, and the more potent the desire for release.

Rajas is the class of *guṇas* that is involved with action, movement and stimulation, with energy and passion. *Rajas* is an aggressive *guṇa* and is therefore associated with redness. It operates particularly in conjunction with both *sattva* and *tamas guṇas* to create the differentiated universe. "It is on account of rajas that fire spreads, the wind blows, the senses follow their objects and the mind becomes restless."[60] While *tamas* leads to pain through ignorance, *rajas is* pain, *duḥkha*, and since it is the stimulator of the other two types of *guṇic* substances, which cannot operate without it, it is present in every single evolute of life in some degree, and characterizes the human race in general. *Rajas*, according to the *Sāṃkhyakārikā*, characterizes worldly creation "from Brahmā down to a blade of grass".[61] This is another reason why pain and sorrow are proportionately greater than happiness and joy; indeed, with *two guṇas* operating to cause pain and suffering, the happiness in life can be very little and always tinged with sorrow. But "wherever there are guṇas there are pains"[62] for to be involved with any of the *guṇas* of *prakṛti* is to be bound in suffering and rebirth.

The three *guṇas* are, in their unmanifest state, the *mūlaprakṛti*. Here, the *guṇas* are in equilibrium, but in this state, they are still dynamic, still changing, but *homogeneously* so, only in themselves. It is only when evolution begins that they interact *heterogeneously* with each other. Then, they pervade the entire *vyakta* or manifest evolutes of *prakṛti*, constantly in co-operation, opposition and tension with each other, resulting in all kinds of collocations and modifications, and this causes the multiplicity of differentiation that obtains in the world. What results will depend on the predominance of one *guṇa* over the others. Because of the interplay of the *guṇas* there is continual transformation and change in all existence, in all *prakṛti*. And yet, while subject to change in the world of matter, the *guṇas* are eternal substances which, when not manifest, simply reside in unmanifest equilibrium. It is the *guṇas* that provide the unity of the Sāṃkhya system, for it is these that inform both unmanifest and manifest *prakṛti*. In terms of experience for each *buddhi*, they will create happy and satisfying, uncomfortable or confusing experiences. But they are unconscious matter and completely separate from the *puruṣas*, though as will be seen below, they "function for the sake of the *puruṣa* like a lamp".[63]

In terms of each human being, then, he or she is a composite of the three kinds of *guṇic* substances at a different number of levels – intellect, ego, mind, and subtle and physical bodies. As has been seen, the composition of intellect and ego will be determined by dispositions created from *karma* accrued in previous existences. The human being, too, will be subject to the pleasure, pain and indifference that the *guṇas sattva*, *rajas* and *tamas* create in the material self. And what brings pleasure for one will bring pain or indifference for another, for whatever exists is composed in varying measures of these three basic substance types, each capable of eliciting different responses. The *guṇas*, then, "mingle, combine and strive in every fibre of our being".[64] Transcending the *guṇas* to become *nirguṇa*, and of the nature of the *ātman*, was the goal of much *Upaniṣadic* thought, but for Sāṃkhya the goal is to leave the whole of the *guṇic* world behind in order to be the individual *puruṣa* that one really is. The medium for this liberation is knowledge.

While substances and not qualities, the *guṇas* cannot be known through perception; they can only be known through inference. It is the *guṇas* as effects that are observable in the world and, since Sāṃkhya accepts that effects pre-exist in some cause, and are of the same nature as that cause, the eternal nature of the *guṇas* in *mūlaprakṛti* as a first cause is posited. The entire universe is thereby reduced to a unified composite of three substances that are interdependent and that must exist in all things in various combinations. So even where one of the *guṇas* may not be particularly evident, it is merely subordinate and minor; but it has to be present. In constant transformation and change, the *guṇas* underpin the entire universe and are always dynamic, even in the state of *avyakta* where they are constantly dynamic and changing within themselves, though not affecting each other.[65] Here, they neither combine nor oppose, but are inherently changing in their own natures. It is only when the *rajas* substance becomes disturbed by the proximity of *puruṣas* that the equilibrium is broken and the *guṇas* become interactive, integrating and differentiating to form manifest existence. Hiriyanna has pointed out that, if the *guṇas* were not constantly dynamic and active, it would be difficult to explain how they suddenly could become so.[66] But, then, isn't it as difficult to explain why they should suddenly interact? The Sāṃkhya response to this will be examined below in the context of the Self, *puruṣa*, but it would be logical to accept that some *active* agent needs to be posited to bring this about.

Śaṃkara was very critical of the Sāṃkhya theory of *guṇas*, accusing the school of incorrect logic because the *hetu* or "middle term" (the *guṇas*) is not universally and invariably perceptibly visible in the major term (the universe). And neither do the *guṇas* when manifest in objects cause the same effects; they can cause pain for some, and pleasure or indifference for others: one man's meat is another man's poison. But, more obviously, Śaṃkara criticized the idea that there could be a material cause without an agent to cause it to manifest itself in a particular way. And even *puruṣas* could not fulfil this role of agent since they are essentially *inactive* and cannot *do* anything. Śaṃkara believed it was impossible to claim that the *puruṣas* could motivate both the evolution of *prakṛti* and the dissolution of it after a certain time, as opposed to a continuous differentiation and evolution. But if these are weaknesses in the Sāṃkhya philosophy, the theory of the *guṇas* was one that was to be very influential in Hindu belief in a variety of contexts.

Epistemology

Before examining the nature of the Self – the other aspect of the Sāṃkhya duality – it is necessary to pause here to examine the theory of knowledge. Sāṃkhya ideas of *pramā* or valid knowledge are somewhat different to those of the other schools of philosophical thought, because the mind, the intellect and the senses that apprehend objects of knowledge are all part of the unconscious material *prakṛti*. The only *conscious* elements in any valid knowledge are the *puruṣas*. It is the *reflection* of the *puruṣas* in the intellect that allows any form of *pramā* to occur – and it is only because the *puruṣas* are reflected in the intellect (*buddhi*), that anything can be known. While its epistemology was not finely developed, early classical Sāṃkhya based its fundamental dualism on the concept of a knowing spiritual subject and an unconscious, material object. Since subject–object interaction is the basis of knowledge, and of any understanding of what is real, this was projected to the ultimate level of its metaphysics. It was well in line with much *Upaniṣadic* teaching; that is to say, with the concept that the real Self is that which is separate from the objective and phenomenal world.

For knowledge to occur, first the senses are excited by an object. This is indeterminate perception. The *manas* then shifts the perception to the determinate level and channels the object (or inferred sign) to the *buddhi*. The *buddhi* becomes modified to correspond with the form or mode (*vṛtti*) of the object, and the *ahaṃkāra*, the ego, relates the perception to "I-ness". The *puruṣa* reflected in the *buddhi* illuminates the form or mode, and lends consciousness to the intellect, ego and mind. Then, the fatal mistake occurs. The *puruṣa* thinks it is the "I" of ego and becomes enmeshed in the results of knowledge – worldly activity. *Puruṣas* are not omniscient in this process: they can only know that which they perceive in the particular *buddhi* to which they are related. Importantly, subjective knowing can only pertain to the *puruṣas*: knowledge – all of it – is purely material, purely *prakṛtic*. There is a complete separation between subject and object, knower and what is known, Self and matter. This is *Upaniṣadic* orthodoxy of the separation of spirit and matter *par excellence*. While all knowledge is *prakṛtic*, it can be world bound or reach the kind of level that enables the true nature of the separation of *puruṣa* and *prakṛti* to be realized.

Pramāṇas

Three *pramāṇas* are accepted by Sāṃkhya – perception (*pratyakṣa*), inference (*anumāna*), and reliable testimony (*āptavacana*). The *Kārikā*, however, does not seem to be particularly interested in any systematized analysis of the *pramāṇas*; it merely states cursorily what they are.

Perception

Perception, or *dṛṣṭa*, is the kind of immediate knowledge that occurs when the senses come into contact with sense objects. The intellect (*buddhi*) is the major means of determinate perception, aided by the mind and by the ego. The intellect, the *buddhi*, reflects the consciousness of *puruṣa* so that the intellect has the means of perception – rather like a mirror reflects an image, or the moon can be reflected in water. Reality and image are totally separate, but they *seem* to be combined, and so the *buddhi seems* to be conscious of an object perceived, whereas in fact it is the *puruṣa* that is the conscious witness of the perception.

Perception is both indeterminate and determinate. *Indeterminate* perception, *nirvikalpaka*, is simply the moment of contact of the senses with an object without any analysis or synthesis of information about the object – a bare awareness. When this is followed by interpretation, analysis and synthesis, then perception moves to the *determinate* level, *savikalpaka*. This is a valid cognition that can ascribe to an object qualities and relations to other objects. It is the *manas*, the mind, that serves here to provide this relational and synthesizing analysis, and that serves to alter indeterminate perception to the determinate level.

Error

Error in perception, according to verse 7 of the *Kārikā*, arises from all sorts of conditions. Perhaps the object is too far away for determinate perception to be accurate, or it may be too close. The sense organ may be injured and impede perception, or the intellect may be inattentive. Sometimes the objects of perception are too subtle to be determined, or something may intervene between sense organ and object. Then, again, correct perceptions may be suppressed, as when in daytime we cannot see the stars because of the light, or things may look so much alike that we cannot see what is real. Error really breaks down to two fundamental issues. The first is mistaking a part for a whole. This is what ignorance causes the individual to do, that is to say, ignorance causes the mistaken view that one part of *prakṛti* is real and to be desired or avoided, whereas the whole unity of matter is not apprehended. The second issue here lies in not recognizing the distinction between two things like shell and silver or, more importantly, between *puruṣa* and *prakṛti*. In both these examples the two are real, but are incorrectly related.[67]

Inference

The *Kārikā* mentions three kinds of inference, *anumāna*, but does not say what they are. Inference is not immediate knowledge but mediate knowledge, that is to say it cannot be direct. Much of what Sāṃkhya teaches is inferred knowledge; its positing of *puruṣas* and *prakṛti* both falling into this category. Inference is defined, as in Nyāya, as a characteristic "mark" inhering in something, as smoke in fire. So it is possible to have inferred knowledge of something that is not perceived, like fire, from something that is perceived, like smoke. But a universal relation or *vyāpti* is essential between the "mark" and that in which it inheres. While inference is not dealt with in any depth in the *Kārikā*, elsewhere it is divided into affirmative inference that is related to positive universal inferential knowledge, and negative inference based on universal negative propositions. Positive inference may be gained through direct observation, as when one sees smoke and infers fire, or through similarity, or through the elimination of a number of impossibilities to arrive at the only thing that can be possible. In the main, the syllogism of Nyāya has been accepted by Sāṃkhya. Since the two critical principles that supply the Sāṃkhya dualism – *puruṣa* and *prakṛti* – are ultimately unmanifest and, therefore, imperceptible, they can only be known through the means of inference. Thus, inference is the superior *pramāna.*

Testimony

Sāṃkhya accepts reliable authority, *śabda* or *āptavacana*, as valid knowledge. Īśvarakṛṣṇa did not stress the importance of the *Vedas*, of worship of God, or of concomitant rituals. It was later Sāṃkhya tradition that felt the obligation to accept *Vedic* authority. Here, the *Veda* was accepted as not composed by human hand and, therefore, as self-valid. But while this assisted its orthodoxy, as Radhakrishnan commented concerning the school, "it discards many an old dogma and silently ignores others. It, however, never openly opposes the Vedas, but adopts the more deadly process of sapping their foundations".[68] And the most conspicuous of such "foundations" must surely be seen as the transcendent Absolute, Brahman, which does not feature in the Sāṃkhya scheme of things at all. The testimony of ordinary people is not accepted because it is based on the other *pramāṇas* of perception and inference. But *Vedic* authority and that of the sages is different in that it can provide knowledge that is beyond the senses.

The Self: *puruṣas*

We must turn now to examine the second fundamental aspect of reality – *puruṣas.* Each *puruṣa* is pure consciousness, and this is a consciousness that is not subject to change, is permanent, is inactive, and is pure consciousness, pure subjectivity, "something like a mirror without any reflection in it or a light that illuminates nothing".[69] Each *puruṣa* or Self is not an effect of anything; it is uncaused and therefore eternal, and it is devoid of *guṇas.* The self that we think we know – that which is active, impermanent, subject to change, and the one who experiences pleasures, pains, joys and sorrows – is not the real Self. It is a reflection and superimposition of a material, *prakṛtic* combination of *guṇas* on the pure *puruṣa*, so that the two cannot be distinguished. It is the separation of the two that brings about liberation from *saṃsāra. Puruṣas* are all different and individual, but despite being pure consciousness, they have no sense of "I"; they are not *personal.* The personal self that we experience is the result of the three *material* aspects of *prakṛti* – intellect, ego and mind, *buddhi*, *ahaṃkāra* and *manas* respectively. And these three material components of *prakṛti* will reflect, or superimpose themselves on, the pure consciousness of the *puruṣa* in different ways – in fact, in as many ways as there are individuals: thus, there are many *puruṣas.*

Sāṃkhya's adoption of the term *puruṣa* was not new. It is an ancient term that generally referred to the mortal human being, but it came to be used as the ultimate essence of the human being that is equated, either partially or wholly, with Brahman. As such, the term became synonymous with *ātman*, but this term was also at one time the general term for the ordinary human self. Thus, in pre-classical Sāṃkhya usage, *puruṣa* can mean both the ordinary self and the true Self. But *puruṣa* was also used in the *Ṛg Veda*[70] to refer to the primeval sacrificial being from which all things in existence were generated. This suggests that it can be conceived of as the source of all existence, the fundamental essence from which all emerges and which is, therefore, the common subtle substratum that unites all manifest existence. As such, *puruṣa* here is very much equatable with Brahman as the unmanifest and transcendent Reality that underpins the manifest world. Classical *Sāṃkhya*, however, has a distinct conception of *puruṣas* as plural, and denies any concept of Brahman.

Each *puruṣa* is the *jña*, or "knower"; that is to say it is the pure subject by which all the objectivity of the material world can be known. Yet it is itself separate from knowledge. Knowledge, intellect, ego and the mind cannot exist without the pure consciousness of each *puruṣa*, but the Self is not connected in any way with the emotions, the self-identity, or the personality that is each human being. Within the process of knowledge, if the *puruṣa* comes to accept itself as having knowledge, it becomes bound. "Losing the peace of eternity, it enters the unrest of time."[71] *Puruṣas* cannot know themselves, but they can be known by way of the *buddhi*. It is only through the *buddhi* that the intuitive knowledge of consciousness as a separate reality beyond its own materiality can be gained. The *puruṣa* has no volition, so it cannot decide to act or to think; it cannot reflect on itself for it is simple consciousness. Larson depicts it as the "fact of consciousness". He says:

> Impersonal yet individual, it is the fact of man's experience which renders him able to become a man. It is the fact of man's experience which provides the basis for his freedom precisely because it is not a part of or determined by the world. By referring to *puruṣa* as the simple fact of consciousness apart from all thought, feelings, etc., this also brings to mind such terms as "transparent" or "translucent." It is only by the "light" of *puruṣa* that one sees the world, and it is only the fact of the world which renders *puruṣa* aware of itself. The fact of consciousness and the fact of the world are two irreducible realities in constant interplay with one another.[72]

Larson refers here to *puruṣa* as being "aware of itself" but this is not in any sense of subjective awareness of the Self as an object. The key term here is "transparent", which suggests a passive essence that is simply located in itself, independent of objectivity and yet the observer of all objects – the material world. The *puruṣa* is thus like a witness, the subject viewing the object, but passively so. The self we associate with the material world we view as being actively and egoistically aware, and this is an awareness that gets bound up in emotions and intellect; it has *content*. Real *puruṣa*, on the other hand, has awareness without content, like a tube that allows all to pass through it without affecting or being affected by the content. Thus, the *puruṣa* is often referred to as "contentless consciousness" or "characterless consciousness". In essence, it remains passive to all the material cause–effect processes of the world.

Puruṣas can never become objects of knowledge, if they did so they would be definable with certain qualities and characteristics. Because the Self *is* consciousness,

consciousness is not a quality of it, as it is in some of the orthodox schools where the self is seen as a substance. This idea of the Self as pure consciousness is far from alien to *Upaniṣadic* conceptions of the *ātman*, and both concepts view the egoistic self as the source of suffering in the *saṃsāric* cycle. The world in the context of both the *Upaniṣadic* concept of *ātman* and the Sāṃkhya concept of *puruṣa* is that which ensnares the real Self and obscures what is ultimate and permanent in life. Sāṃkhya is, thus, not too wide of the mark in its evaluation and identity of the true Self. It is the multiplicity of Selves rather than the unity of essence of the Self that is the major departure from *Upaniṣadic* thought. But both *ātman* and *puruṣa* are, ultimately, the passive essences of pure consciousness that are distinct from the change and transience of the material world: both witness the world but are separated from it. Yet both the *Upaniṣadic ātman* and the *puruṣa* of Sāṃkhya are necessary for the material world to obtain, *ātman* as its fundamental essence, and *puruṣa* as that whose very proximity motivates the evolution of the material world. The consciousness of *puruṣa*, then, is necessary for the evolution of the unconscious matter of existence, and yet it is the opposite of material existence. And while *puruṣas* are necessary for material existence to come into being, they cannot be said to be the cause of it since they are neither causes nor caused. The *Kārikā* says of the real Self that it is a witness (of *prakṛti*), it is isolated and free, it is indifferent to the world, it is a spectator that simply views the world, and it is inactive.[73] While it witnesses the change of the world and its cause–effect processes, the Self does not *actively* affect the world, yet it affects it by its very passivity, its proximity.

Because the true Self is the passive, permanent pure consciousness of *puruṣa*, there is no such thing for Sāṃkhya as a self that is bound up in *saṃsāra*. The *Kārikā* clearly states: "No one therefore, is bound, no one released, likewise no one transmigrates. (Only) *prakṛti* in its various forms transmigrates, is bound and is released."[74] The self that we normally know, then, and the self that is subject to *karma* and *saṃsāra*, does not really exist. It is just a material conglomeration that acquires a false and transient consciousness that is not its own, through ignorance of the real Self, *puruṣa*. *Puruṣas* are reflected in the world, just as the moon is reflected in water, but they are not of the world at all. And just as the ignorant see the moon in the water and believe that it is really there, so the ignorant in life experience the reflected *puruṣa* in the intellect of the egoistic self and believe that the transient self is the real Self. It is the reflection of the pure consciousness of the real Self that makes the material, unconscious being *seem* conscious and real.

The entire psychical and physical self that we ordinarily experience in life, then, is totally material. It is subject to change and to transience, to rebirth and to death, in a way that the real Self is not. After each life, the subtle body, the *liṅgaśarīra*, will be composed of the *karmic* dispositional residues that will dictate the nature of the next life. The *liṅga*, then, is a "permanent annexe"[75] to each self, transmigrating according to the nature of the dispositions of the intellect. Larson explains this in modern terms:

> The "essential core" (liṅga) or the subtle body carries a particular constellation of these predispositions as it proceeds in the process of rebirth, and a particular sentient being, which becomes enlivened by the coalescence of a liṅga with a gross body, is, as it were, "coded" or "programmed" at birth by these tendencies and, hence, predisposed to a certain life trajectory.[76]

This, indeed, is how *karma* works, for the predispositions of the self are set up according to the actions, behavioural drives, desires and aversions in past existences. Ignorance makes us think that this is the real Self and that it is a conscious entity that is capable of knowledge, whereas in fact it is unconscious and incapable of knowledge: it is *puruṣa* that is consciousness and is the *jña*, the knower. Since the combinations of evolutes that make up any individual are different in each individual, there are real differences between individuals, even if, ultimately, they all stem from the same source – *prakṛti*. There is absolutely no inner *ātman* to unite them.

It is the subtle body, the *liṅgaśarīra*, then, that carries all the ingredients for each reincarnating self. The subtle body is primeval, emerging with the initial manifestations of *prakṛti*. It is permanent, though dispositionally changeable, and is connected with a particular *puruṣa* for its entire transmigratory experiences. This inseparable connection remains until the *puruṣa* knows itself as free. The *Sāṃkhyakārikā* graphically describes the associative relation between the *puruṣa* and the subtle body: "This subtle entity, motivated for the sake of the *puruṣa*, appears like a player (who assumes many roles) by means of its association with efficient causes and effects (i.e., by means of its association with the *bhāvas*) and because of its association with the power of *prakṛti*."[77]

While *puruṣas* are not a cause, it is their proximity to unmanifest *prakṛti* that causes manifest existence to occur. And like the analogy of light applied to a dark room, one cannot be illumined and manifest without the association of the other. So the world can only exist in so far as it is made manifest through the consciousness of the *puruṣas*. The reflection of each *puruṣa* is different, just as different lights illumine different rooms. The result is the variety of reality that we perceive in the phenomenal world. It is *puruṣas* that enable sense to be made of the world because of the reflected nature of consciousness: they *intelligize* existence.

The presence of *puruṣas* is posited by the *pramāṇa* of inference. Without pure consciousness Sāṃkhya believed that there could be no knowledge. To use the analogy of light again, just as the light illuminates a dark room, pure consciousness is necessary to allow aspects of knowledge. But just as the light is separate from the room, so pure consciousness is separate from that which it illumines. All knowledge, then, needs the light of consciousness in order to exist, as does the whole material world, and this includes intellect, ego and mind. Consciousness, therefore, has to be inferred for knowledge to occur. And what would happen without consciousness? There could be no differentiation of matter in such a case; therefore, consciousness has to be inferred in order for the sensible world to be meaningful. However, this rather suggests that the absolute dualism that Sāṃkhya posits is impossible considering the mutual dependency of spirit and matter – something also evidenced in the rationale for the existence of *puruṣas*, in the following points.

The *Sāmkhyakārikā* gives five reasons why *puruṣas* must exist. First, because the combinations of elements (*guṇas*) in the evolutes of *prakṛti* must exist for something beyond themselves, and secondly, this something must be separate from the *guṇas* that compose life. Thirdly, this separate aspect must be the controlling one, presumably not as an active control but as a consciousness that permits subjective knowledge; matter cannot control itself. Indeed, the need for an "enjoyer", a subject, an experiencer, for the whole of unconscious material existence is the fourth reason provided for the existence of *puruṣas*. The fifth reason is suggestive of the whole of *prakṛtic* existence being solely for the liberation of each *puruṣa*.[78] This is the teleological *raison d'être* for *prakṛti*. Later commentaries expand on these basic reasons in a highly teleological way. All objects in existence are believed to be means for the ends of the multiplicity of *puruṣas*. The *puruṣas* are the experiencers of the pleasure, pain and indifference in the world, for only they have the consciousness in order to do this, but such experience is ontologically motivated to move towards liberation by transcending the materiality of *prakṛti*. Something in the self is aware of this. As Davies puts it: "We are conscious of a nature within us, which feels joy or woe; and this we infer is something different from matter, for we cannot conceive of mere matter as feeling or thinking."[79] But the true nature of the Self is not an agent, or even an experiencer of joy or woe. Verse 19 of the *Sāṃkhyakārikā* tells us:

> And, therefore, because (the *puruṣa*) (is) the opposite (of the unmanifest), it is established that *Puruṣa* is a
> (a) witness;
> (b) possessed of isolation or freedom;
> (c) indifferent;
> (d) a spectator;
> (e) and inactive.[80]

The plurality of *puruṣas* is argued for in that each ordinary individual is different and so must reflect a different *puruṣa* than that of others. People obviously live and die at different times and in different ways, and if the pure consciousness of *puruṣa* were single, then one birth or death would have to be the birth and death of all at the same time. Or if one person were blind or lame then all would have to be so. And one consciousness would necessitate activity for all at the same time; one could not be sleeping while others were active. Then, too, distinctions between gods, humans and animals could not possibly obtain if one consciousness were common to them all. But it is this issue of the plurality of *puruṣas* that is one of the problematic areas for Sāṃkhya. Sharma is rightly critical of this plurality, claiming that the arguments put forward to infer them might just as well apply to the already accepted plurality of *jīvas*.[81] It is difficult to see how, if all *puruṣas* are different, they can have the *same* effect on *prakṛti*, by causing it to begin to evolve. If it is to be claimed that different individuals must be informed by different consciousnesses, then it would also have to be argued that the causal proximity is different and that they therefore cannot have the same effect of bringing about evolution. Ultimately, of course, *puruṣas* are causeless, but *prakṛti* cannot evolve without their causal proximity. But the *puruṣas* do not appear to be any different from each other than numerically so. And, as Sharma rightly comments: "Numerical pluralism is sheer nonsense."[82] Without difference in essence, the characterless consciousness of each *puruṣa* cannot really differ from the next one. This makes Sāṃkhya's move away from a unity of liberated Selves a very difficult issue.

The interaction of *puruṣas* and *prakṛti*

As has been seen, *Prakṛti* is an unconscious material principle that cyclically evolves into an equally unconscious material universe, and then involves. But, as Chatterjee and Datta pertinently point out with reference to Sāṃkhya: "It is not the dance of blind atoms, nor the push and pull of mechanical forces which produce a world to no purpose."[83] The whole purpose of *prakṛti* is to serve the *puruṣas*, and thus *prakṛti* is a teleological principle or, perhaps, "quasi-teleological" to use Hiriyanna's term,[84] because it is not consciously teleological. Yet it is perhaps this area of the interaction between the two aspects of the Sāṃkhya dualism that is its most problematic one. It is the *relation*, the *proximity* between *puruṣas* and *prakṛti* (and I believe it is important to remember that *puruṣas* are plural in this context), that causes the process of evolution to take place. What, then, causes involution, when all *prakṛti* returns to its unmanifest state? Are the *puruṣas* no longer in proximity? And if they are not, then what causes this spatial change, for they are inactive in themselves? Furthermore, all *puruṣas* must exercise an identical influence on *prakṛti*, otherwise some would cancel out the proximity of others. Then, too, any suggestion that *prakṛti* is guided by *puruṣas* in some way, makes the *puruṣas* active and not passive, and it is difficult to avoid the suggestion that the proximity of the *puruṣas* is causal. The *Sāṃkhyakārikā* likened the interaction of the two to a blind man and a lame man who co-operate with each other to get out of a forest,[85] *prakṛti* being the blind man for it is incapable of perception, and *puruṣa* the lame one because it cannot act or move. But this is not an adequate example for both the blind and the lame man are of similar substance – they are both *prakṛtic*. Other examples given in the *Kārikā* to explain the separation of *puruṣa* and *prakṛti*, and yet the purposeful nature of the latter, are that of milk streaming into the udder of a cow for the purpose of the calf – something that occurs without any causative effort on the part of the calf. Another simile is that of an actress (*prakṛti*) who performs for a passive spectator (*puruṣa*). But such examples do not suggest the disparity and duality between blind and lame man, or actress and spectators, to the degree that these exist between spirit and matter.

Nothing that is material – that is to say the whole of *prakṛti* – can be known at all without the proximity and presence of *puruṣas*. And the *puruṣas* are somehow trapped in *prakṛti* and need it in order to be liberated. The *Sāṃkhyakārikā* states: "Because of the proximity (or association) of the two – i.e., *prakṛti* and *puruṣa* – the unconscious one appears as if characterized by consciousness. Similarly, the indifferent one appears as if characterized by activity, because of the activities of the three *guṇas*."[86] This, too, is a problem, for how can a totally separate and inactive consciousness get bound up in matter in the first place? Sāṃkhya's answer lies in the fact that the *puruṣas* are the only conscious Selves, so only they can experience the effects of *prakṛti*, experiencing the three feeling substances of the *guṇas* – pleasure, pain and indifference or dullness, interacting with all the *prakṛtic* evolutes. It is in this sense that they become "trapped". The whole of *prakṛti*, on the other hand, serves the entire purpose of trying to free the *puruṣas* from matter: every single transformation and modification of the *guṇas* takes place for this sole teleological purpose of liberating them. But this tends to suggest that *puruṣa* and *prakṛti must* interact, for matter has no spirit and consciousness, and spirit has no efficient action. Without interaction there is no point to evolution, or no evolution at all. On this point, Radhakrishnan's following words are more than pertinent: "If an error of judgment had not thrust the *puruṣa* into the playhouse, and if our deluded minds had not watched the performance of *prakṛti*, there would be no action of *prakṛti* at all."[87]

Even more of a paradox is the apparent accumulation of *karma* by the Selves. Since they alone are capable of experience, only they can react to the material world in positive, negative and indifferent ways. Sharma comments: "Poor Puruṣa suffers for no fault of its own. Prakṛti performs actions and Puruṣa has to reap their fruits good or bad. And Prakṛti knows how to make delicious dishes, but not to enjoy them!"[88] But reaction is action, and it would have to be claimed that there is a dimension of the Selves that is not pure, inactive consciousness, but is active consciousness, otherwise it cannot be the recipient of fruitive *karma*. Presumably it is the *collective karmas* of the Selves rather than the pure Selves that create the proximity that brings about the evolution of matter, and the same *collective karmas* that cause manifest *prakṛti* to return to the unmanifest state.[89] Either way, it is difficult to maintain that the Selves are not in some way the cause of these processes, particularly if it is all for their own ends. On the other hand, if it is claimed that *prakṛti* has a teleological purpose that is aimed at liberating the Selves then this can only be an *unconscious* purpose, since it is all matter. And it is difficult to accept how unconscious matter can itself decide to evolve into manifest form for the sake of a totally separate principle that it cannot really know, especially if all knowledge is of material nature and objective. And yet, the way *prakṛti* is in any one evolutionary process must be determined by the *guṇic* necessities engendered by the *puruṣas'* involvement in the previous evolutionary world-process. *Prakṛti*, then, is conditioned by the needs of *puruṣas* and the *karmic* natures they have built up. It does not evolve without a blueprint for its nature, it can only evolve the way it is meant to. In this sense it really is unconsciously quasi-teleological.

Because the individual Self is reflected in the *buddhi* the world appears to it from an individual perspective, and it thinks it is active and actively engaged in the world. What results are the individuals of human existence which are really material evolutes with a separate pure consciousness. But since the separate consciousness becomes so intimately associated with the intellect the whole world is viewed from the point of view of a conscious intellect, ego and mind. Yet it remains paradoxical to claim at the same time that there is no relation between *puruṣas* and *prakṛti* and that they are totally independent and separate realities. Sāṃkhya would claim that the *puruṣas* are *witnesses*. They are immanent in the world via their association with *buddhis*, and by this witnessing nature. This is to say that they *are* conscious of the world and therefore are not separate to the extent that the world cannot be the object of consciousness. So it is as if one is observing a reflection in a mirror and gets carried away by the reflection, forgetting that it is simply that. Vācaspati Miśra, in particular, stressed this principle of reflection (*pratibimba*), to explain how each *buddhi* could be capable of experience in existence, by way of the reflected consciousness of a *puruṣa*.

The purpose of *prakṛti* is to provide the objective knowledge that will enable each Self to realize its true state, preventing it from thinking that the reflection in the mirror is real. Essentially it is the *buddhi* of each individual that is capable of this liberating knowledge for the *puruṣa*, just as it is the evolute that is able to reflect the real Self. *Puruṣa* is the knower that appropriates the knowledge supplied by the *buddhi*. The separation of knower and knowledge, of subject and object, is the reverse step that the *buddhi* has to present to the *puruṣa*. Really speaking, however, it should be impossible for the *buddhi* to infer the presence of *puruṣa*, since what is objective cannot infer what is subjective. It is nonsense to claim that the material object can ever have knowledge of the subject. However, the Self becomes liberated through the knowledge it can have of itself in *prakṛti*; it can *witness* the knowledge that is the truth. So between *prakṛti* and *puruṣa*, there is "a reciprocal dependence, a tie of mutual interest".[90] It is an intimacy depicted poetically in the following verse of the *Sāṃkhyakārikā*: "(She) (*prakṛti*), possessed of the *guṇas* and helpful in various ways, behaves selflessly for the sake of him (*puruṣa*) who is without the *guṇas* and who plays no helpful part".[91] In the succeeding verse the same genderized metaphor depicts the enlightened *puruṣa* and the separated *prakṛti*: "It is my thought that there is nothing more delicate than *prakṛti*, who (says to herself) 'I have been seen', and never again comes into the sight of *puruṣa*."[92] Here, using the analogy of a shy maiden with a lover, the *Kārikā* explains how the *buddhi* comes to recognize itself as non-consciousness. *Puruṣa* in turn sees *prakṛti* with the full understanding of what she/it is. The two become separate though proximate.[93]

Knowledge is matter, but since it is of the nature of thought it is predominantly *sattvic* in substance. And since it is *sattvic* it has the translucence necessary to reflect the *puruṣa* through the medium of the *buddhi*. Thereby the *puruṣa* believes itself to know all sorts of things and, similarly, the *buddhi* comes to regard itself as subjective consciousness. So everything that we think, all our reactions to the world, all our choices and emotions, are really unconscious matter. We *seem* to be the conscious subject of those thoughts and emotions, and so on, because the *buddhi* reflects the consciousness of *puruṣa*. And the *puruṣa seems* to be the one thinking and making choices. The two separate aspects of *puruṣa* and *buddhi* have enough similarity to become so incorrectly superimposed one on the other, that reality is blurred. It is the separation of this reality into its accurate dualities that is the whole goal of Sāṃkhya, and that amounts to the liberation of the Self in *mukti*.

This goal is the *raison d'être* of unconscious *prakṛti*, the very existence of which serves the *puruṣas* in every way. *Prakṛti* is a *puruṣārtha*, that is to say what exists for the end achievement of something. Hinduism has four general *puruṣārthas* – *artha* wealth, *kāma* pleasure, *dharma* what is right, and *mokṣa* liberation. These are themselves intrinsic goals for life, but they are also a means to liberation itself. It is in this latter sense that the term is used in Sāṃkhya in order to depict all *prakṛti* as that which serves the purpose of the *puruṣas* in bringing about their liberation. It is for this reason that *prakṛti* is a teleological principle. But *prakṛti* cannot function at all without the proximity of *puruṣas*, so the whole process of evolution and involution of the manifest world is dependent on the conscious *puruṣas*. Sāṃkhya claims that *puruṣas* are not actually the *cause* of *prakṛti*, but *prakṛti* cannot have any meaning and cannot be understood without *puruṣas*.

These are difficult aspects of Sāṃkhya philosophy, particularly the attempt to assign some kind of blind purpose to unconscious matter on the one hand, and to suggest that something that is already separate and pure consciousness can be trapped in such unconscious matter on the other. It seems futile for *prakṛti* to be purposefully (and yet unconsciously) operating for the freedom of that which is already free. Radhakrishnan commented that "The sāṃkhya cannot get across the ditch which it has dug between the subject and the object."[94] This is indeed true. *Puruṣas* and *prakṛti* can be either separate or interdependent, but they cannot be both; to be interdependent is not to be distinctly separate. Śāṃkara certainly pointed out such anomalies in the Sāṃkhya philosophy, and it has to be admitted that there is little defence against them. Sharma appropriately remarks that: "To dig a chasm between them is to undermine them both. And that is what Sāṅkhya has done."[95] Indeed, without a third principle that causes the proximity of the *puruṣas* and *prakṛti* for the process of evolution, and that pulls apart such proximity for cosmic dissolution or *pralaya*, it is difficult to see what creates the proximity in the first place. It is also difficult to see what causes the interdependence, if neither aspects of the duality are causal to the other. How can *prakṛti* have any teleological purpose if it is unconscious matter? It is difficult to accept that all the evolutes of *prakṛti* are so designed to transform and combine to provide sufficient experiences for each *puruṣa* to free itself from the *saṃsāric* cycle *without* some designer or efficient cause to make it all so. The dualism of Sāṃkhya is certainly compromised by the interdependency of the two principles and, as Hiriyanna points out, "puruṣa, were it not for its association with *prakṛti*, would be hardly distinguishable from nothing".[96]

Causality

Causation is an extremely important concept in Sāṃkhya philosophy, because the theory of the unitary nature of all evolution is dependent on it. The entire Sāṃkhya metaphysics relies on the acceptance of its theory of causality. Sāṃkhya posits the theory of *satkāryavāda*, the view that all effects exist latently in their causes; in other words effects exist even before they are manifest. The term *satkāryavāda* can be broken down into *sat*, meaning "true", "real", or "existent", *kārya* meaning "effect", and *vāda* meaning "theory". In practical terms it maintains that the phenomenal world as an effect was already existent in its cause – *prakṛti* – before the various *guṇic* combinations combined to produce it. So nothing new can come into being; everything exists potentially in its cause. As Dasgupta said, "just a little loosening of the barrier which was standing in the way of the happening of such a change of arrangement will produce the desired new collocation – the effect."[97] So when an effect comes into being, there is no *material* change, only a modification of the material. Since we cannot have something from nothing, there must be a causal material in which effects inhere, that is to say, *prakṛti*. *Prakṛti* is the cause from which everything in the universe is an effect: the effects are but transformations of the basic stuff of which all existence is made. This is called *pariṇāmavāda* and, despite periods of quiescence when the *guṇas* of *prakṛti* are in equilibrium in *avyakta*, the process of collocations of cause and effect is beginningless and endless.

Verses 5–16 of the *Sāṃkhyakārikā* give five reasons for positing *avyakta* as the unifying cause. These are:

- because finite things of the world need a cause
- because of the similarity of things in the world
- because evolution implies a powerful cause
- because effects are modifications of some cause
- because of the unity and uniformity of the world.

If there were no primal cause – itself uncaused – then effects would be traced back to causes *ad infinitum*, a position of infinite regress. *Prakṛti* is eternal, without beginning, without end, and so uncaused. When involution occurs, the retirement of all things takes place through a change back to their imperceptible, latent states, just as things made from clay revert to their natural and unrecognizable, natural states. So from one primal cause everything develops and then is enveloped back into that cause. Evolution and involution follow each other in eternal cycles. *Prakṛti* is, therefore, termed *pradhāna* "primordial matter", that from which all effects emerge, and to which they will return. There is no creation as such for there is no real beginning, no ultimate dissolution, only perpetual transformation to effects and back to cause.

The theory of *satkāryavāda*, then, is based on the idea that any effect must be existent in some way or other in its cause. If this were not so, it would be possible to create an effect out of nothing, or even create an effect that is different from a cause, like creating cheese from clay instead of milk. So really any effect has to be implicit in, or inhere in, its cause, it just needs the right kinds of conditions in order to become an explicit manifestation of its cause. But it must be *related* to that cause; any amount of effort cannot produce an effect that is different in nature from its cause, and gold cannot produce the effect of milk, though clay can produce the effect of a clay pot. The interrelation and uniformity of things in the world are put down to the interaction of the manifest *guṇas* in the immediate sense, and the presence of the same *guṇas* in the non-interactive unmanifest state – the first cause. Verse 14 of the *Sāṃkhyakārikā* states that: "The unmanifest is . . . established because of the *guṇa*-nature in the cause of the effect (or because the effect has the same qualities as the cause)."[98] *Mūlaprakṛti* is the cause (*kāraṇa*) of all the effects (*kārya*) of existence, and all these effects inhere, or pre-exist – albeit as potentials – in the unmanifest state. All that happens when evolution unfolds is that the pre-existent effects are transformed into their manifest forms.

Potentiality is important in the cause. It is the potential of clay to produce effects that are made of clay, or gold to produce effects that are made of gold, and it is this *potentiality* that supports the view that all effects inhere in their causes. Indeed, it would be difficult to claim that effects are totally unlike their causal materials. Effects are but explicit manifestations that were once implicit in their cause. Such transformations of cause to effect are, for Sāṃkhya, *real* changes.

In contrast, as will be seen, the school of Advaita has a slightly different view of *satkāryavāda*, believing that the transformations from cause to effect are only *apparent*, and the cause is not really transformed at all. Verse 9 of the *Sāṃkhyakārikā* gives five reasons that neatly summarize the Sāṃkhya position on *satkāryavāda*. Expanded a little here they state that effects inhere in their causes:

- because you cannot have something from nothing; that is, if the effect does not pre-exist in the cause it cannot occur
- because an appropriate material cause is needed; that is, by appropriate, it must be invariably connected with an effect
- because you cannot have everything coming from anything, so things must be implicit in their appropriate causes

- because things can only produce certain things: the potential for something is, again, implicit in its cause, otherwise you could have gold from clay
- because the effect is not different from the cause.

The whole of the phenomenal world, then, is but a transformation, *pariṇāma*, of the unmanifest *mūlaprakṛti* or *avyakta* as a cause, into its modifications as effects. There is nothing new that comes into being. The Sāṃkhya concept of creation is therefore one by which there is more and more differentiation from the first cause as the evolutes are produced. This is a differentiation that is changeable and finite, that is, a coming together of the *guṇic* substances in one group and then their separating and reuniting. Dasgupta put this well: "Varying qualities of essence, energy, and mass in varied groupings act on one another and through their mutual interaction and interdependence evolve from the indefinite or qualitatively indeterminate the definite or qualitatively determinate."[99] But all this increasingly differentiated matter is but the effect of one cause, the *mūlaprakṛti*. All the effects are parts of *one*, unified whole, a whole that is divided into parts or, a cause that is transformed into effects. The eternal existence of the *guṇas* and their constant interdependence maintains the whole. It is through *puruṣas*' witnessing of parts that their knowledge of the whole is impaired, and they become bound.

There is no conscious first cause, only the material and unconscious first cause of *prakṛti* in its state of *avyakta*. Presumably the *puruṣas* would have to be as much conscious of, and a witness to, unmanifest *prakṛti* as of its manifest evolutes, otherwise they would be at some times conscious of objects and at other times not conscious of them, and therefore changeable. The difficulty is, as was raised above, that if the *puruṣas* affect the *avyakta* to promote creation, how, then, do they affect creation to cause *pralaya*, dissolution, when evolution ceases and there is a movement backwards until the *guṇas* return to their unmanifest state? Latent *karmas* of the *puruṣas* are believed to be held in the unmanifest state of *prakṛti*, that is to say, all the different *buddhis* containing reflected *puruṣas* that have been trapped in the world through their misconceptions of, and involvement in, it are suspended. So how can they then affect the *mūlaprakṛti* to cause creation without some kind of change or activity in themselves? The *puruṣas* are conscious but only witnesses; they cannot *do* anything. Can they then "require that there should be a temporary cessation of all experience", as Dasgupta suggested?[100] This cannot be, since it suggests causal activity and *puruṣas* can be neither causal nor active. What happens to the *puruṣas* during this "temporary cessation of all experience"? Do they no longer have any effect on *prakṛti* or do they no longer witness anything? After all, there is no *buddhi* in unmanifest *prakṛti* that could present anything for the *puruṣas* to witness. Sāṃkhya gives us no answer here.

The problem of wanting to see the relation between *puruṣa* and *prakṛti* as cause and effect is difficult to overcome. Radhakrishnan, for example, wrote of the effect of *puruṣas* on involution: "When the desires of all *puruṣas* require that there should be a temporary cessation of all experience, *prakṛti* returns to its quiescent state."[101] But this belies the so-called passivity of the *puruṣas*, and overtly presents them as the conscious cause of involution. Yet it is really the only logical outcome to the question of what causes involution, and yet, wrote Radhakrishnan, *puruṣa* "does not desire or hate, govern or obey, impel or restrain".[102] The problem is that we cannot speak of the interaction between *puruṣa* and *prakṛti* without compromising the strict dualism of the school. It is *buddhi* as a material concept that is a particularly problematic area, for its nature appears so subjective that it is difficult to view it as a material object. It is the *buddhi* that "desires", not the *puruṣa*. In particular, it is the discriminative and reflective discernment of the *buddhi* that is so close to – indeed, barely different from – the nature of consciousness, creating tensions in separating *buddhi* as matter, and spirit as consciousness, in any ultimate sense.

When *prakṛti* evolves from *avyakta* to *vyakta*, the first evolute is the reflected *puruṣas* in the *mahat* or *mahat buddhi*. *Mahatbuddhi* and all other evolutes are effects of the same unmanifest cause and all effects serve the ultimate purpose of liberating the *puruṣas*. The theory of causality unites a single cause with the variety of effects that are essential for the experiences of *puruṣas* in moving towards freedom. Thus: "Identity is fundamental, while difference is only practical."[103] The whole of manifest matter evolves according to the theory of *satkāryavāda*, modifying and differentiating itself in a very dynamic way. As a cause, *prakṛti* in its foundational state informs all existence, dynamically energizing the entire interconnected effects that evolve from it. But are all the evolutes really effects if they already exist in their cause? How can an effect be produced if it is already in existence? And could it not be said that a pot is not the same as the clay from which it is made? It may be of the same basic substance, but as an effect it is quite different from its causal substance and clearly distinguishable as such. Even if it is claimed that the pot is simply a modification or change in form of the original clay, there is a good deal about the pot as an effect that the clay doesn't have – sufficient to claim that they are different. Then, too, ultimately, there is no agent that affects any stage of the cause–effect processes in the Sāṃkhya system. From our general observations of life we know that an agent or efficient cause is needed to transform a substance into a particular effect: pots don't become pots on their own; they are transformed from the original clay by the potter. Sāṃkhya is a system, however, that eschews any kind of divine agency.

Atheism

Classical Sāṃkhya is an atheistic system, possibly influenced by Buddhism and Jainism. Yoga, on the other hand is theistic, and the combined *sāṃkhyayoga* usually supports a theistic stance, as exemplified in the *Bhagavadgītā*. This is not to say that classical Sāṃkhya rejected all ideas of Hindu gods. Indeed, the deities of Hinduism were accepted, but they were simply redundant in a school of thought that saw knowledge alone as the means to liberation, and that accepted an unconscious first principle that was the cause of all things. Gods are demoted from the spiritual to the material – caught by their respective *puruṣas* in the materiality of existence, albeit a divine one. There was no room for a transcendent Absolute, and no need for it, even if, at an earlier stage, *sāṃkhya* may have originally linked what later came to be individual *puruṣas* as one. A more overt linking of this one *Puruṣa* with the unmanifest aspect of *prakṛti* was also probable in pre-classical Sāṃkhya.[104] Again, it was the increasing emphasis on knowledge as the means to liberation that supplied the root cause for the move to atheism, but it is unlikely that it was either a consistent developmental shift or a regular one; the steps towards it are obscure. The emphasis on knowledge meant that it would be impossible for Sāṃkhya to accept that knowledge could ever be of a transcendent God. Knowledge occurs only when the *buddhi* formulates an object for the *puruṣa* as subject to see. And it could not formulate an imperceptible, inconceivable God.

The resulting denial of a concept of Brahman in classical Sāṃkhya, however, was a considerable departure from *Vedāntic* thought and was a clear rejection of theism and monistic absolutism. Brahman is rejected because what is permanent and unchanging cannot be the cause of what is constantly impermanent and changing. Of what point, Sāṃkhya claimed, is a totally transcendent Absolute that is beyond all action and non-action, and is completely unmanifest. How could this Brahman *involve* itself in material manifestation? And if it did, for what purpose? Why would such an Absolute create a world full of evil and suffering? Then, too, as far as the individual self is concerned, if it were partly or wholly that Absolute it must have some divine powers. But we know that individuals do not have such powers. And if the individual self is non-divine and simply created by God, then why would God want to create something that is finite and subject to destruction? Thus Sāṃkhya's dualism saw no need for a transcendent deity to which the universe owed its existence, and which provided the rationale for liberation. *Prakṛti* could operate by itself, and knowledge could prove to each *puruṣa* that it is, in reality, already free.

Liberation

Given the material nature of every component of the human being it is real in one sense and unreal in another. It is real in that it is a collocation of *guṇas* at all its composite levels, but it is unreal in respect of its false consciousness of itself as a subjective agent in the *prakṛtic* world. It is this latter aspect that is the *avidyā*, *ajñāna*, the "non-knowledge" or ignorance that binds the *puruṣa* to the world, for it is the reflection of the *puruṣa* in the *buddhi* that creates this individual and unreal self. It is the failure of the *puruṣa* to see itself as separate from material existence that is the root of *ajñāna*. It is too intimately connected with the *buddhi* to see the truth, and it is ignorance of this truth that causes the self to suffer or, rather, causes the individual *puruṣa* as the subjective consciousness to be the one who experiences suffering. It is the non-discrimination (*aviveka*) of itself as separate that is the problem and which causes the binding of the real Self to a material world. Discriminative knowledge (*vivekajñāna*) of the separation of the two is therefore essential.

The means to freedom of the Self are referred to in verse 51 of the *Sāṃkhyakārikā* as eight spiritual attainments or perfections: "The eight perfections are proper reasoning, oral instruction, study, removal of the three kinds of suffering, friendly discussion and generosity. The previous threefold division (i.e., ignorance, incapacity, and complacency) hinders the perfections."[105] The resulting knowledge, or *jñāna*, that is needed for liberation of the Self is not everyday knowledge of the world but knowledge of the true nature of that Self as separate from it. It is a knowledge that transcends worldly knowledge in that it is, according to the second verse of the *Sāṃkhyakārikā*, "the (discriminative) knowledge of the manifest (*vyakta*), the unmanifest (*avyakta*) and the knowing one (or knower – i.e., *puruṣa*)."[106] It occurs with loss of "I-awareness", and with release of the Self from the *buddhi* and the evolutes that emerge from it. It is the *jñāna* of the *buddhi* that is the means for realization of this discriminating knowledge. It is the *buddhi* that distinguishes the subtle difference between *prakṛti* and the *puruṣa*.[107] It is the *buddhi* that has to detach itself from involvement with the rest of *prakṛti* – this is the knowledge that is the means to liberation. It is knowledge of the materiality of its own nature and of all that exists.

What sets the Self free is the self itself, matter cannot do this but the Self in conjunction with matter can. The *puruṣa* sees what the *buddhi* presents to it: its involvement or detachment from the material world is, as a result, its own affair. True knowledge is that which brings release from suffering and liberation from *saṃsāra*, for the *real* Self is free from time, space, and cause and effect processes. Intellect, ego and mind are the only aspects of the human being that can be associated with the material effects that create happiness or sadness and that relate to the world positively, negatively or indifferently. But they can only do so through the reflection of the real Self in the *buddhi*. Separate the reflection between the two and there is no suffering, no positive and negative response. All that we see in the world, and that to which we daily react, are the effects of causal processes, but the real Self is neither cause nor effect, it is eternal and unchangeable. Knowledge on the part of the *buddhi* for the *puruṣa* is only a means to release; the liberated *puruṣa* becomes devoid of connection with knowledge for it has become separate from the *buddhi* that conveys the objects necessary for knowledge.

The liberated *puruṣa* is in a state of *kaivalya*, total isolation, passivity, aloneness, suspended in its own eternity. There is total dissociation from *prakṛti* and total isolation from all other Selves – "translucent emptiness", as Larson terms it[108] – in which consciousness lacks even the witnessing of *prakṛti*. This is the Sāṃkhya *mokṣa* or *mukti*, total liberation. It is the revelation of the *puruṣa* as it has really always been. As noted earlier, according to the *Sāṃkhyakārikā*: "No one therefore, is bound; no one released, likewise no one transmigrates. (Only) *prakṛti* in its various forms transmigrates, is bound and is released."[109] In reality nothing has changed in the nature of *puruṣa*: it has always been free, always eternal and always separate from the *prakṛtic* world. Now it becomes totally isolated. But this isolation was a perspective of liberation that was not without its critics past and present. It is a "most uninspiring"[110] end to the trials and tribulations of poor *puruṣa*. There is a problem, too, in the natures of this plurality of Selves. Why should they be plural? What is it that makes them so? Hiriyanna justifiably comments: "In their liberated state there is absolutely no difference; and to postulate numerical difference between entities, when there is no distinction whatever in their intrinsic nature, seems unwarranted."[111] The lack of differentiation between the *puruṣas* is also surprising in that *mokṣa* is not something that can only be realized after death, for Sāṃkhya recognizes that one can be a *jīvanmukta*, one liberated while still in the body, awaiting *kaivalya* after death. Here we have a liberated but seemingly differentiated *puruṣa* still engaged with physical and subtle bodies that are different from all others. A *jīvanmukta* is accepted because of the *prārabdhakarma* that is already on its way, but no new fruitive *karma* is formed. The *buddhi* has seen the light of the *puruṣa* and is the cause of its release, but past impressions are the causes that compel the free *puruṣa* to dwell until death, reflected in the physical body. When death occurs, the Self becomes free from all matter, free from all sense of "I", free from all happiness, sorrow, joy and pain. The Self becomes empty of subjective awareness of matter, suspended in its own timeless, and spaceless essence. *Prakṛti* withdraws: the shy maiden never permits the man to see her again; the dancer, having performed for her audience, leaves the stage.

How, then, do we view this atheistic and yet orthodox system? It is precisely its lack of belief in a divine of any kind that moves some of its critics to see little sense in its ultimate goal. Davies hints at the lack of theistic anchorage in the following words:

> The grandeur of the soul, in Kapila's system, is unreal and useless. It has no moral elevation. It knows nothing of virtue and vice as connected with itself. It has no purpose beyond itself. It directs in some undefined degree, but it never condescends to work, either for itself or for others. It has no sympathy. Its highest state is one of perfect abstraction from matter and from other souls; a self-contained life, wherein no breath of emotion ever breaks in on the placid surface.[112]

It is perhaps for reasons such as this that the somewhat cold philosophy of Sāṃkhya in its entirety failed to endure the tests of time. And yet, so many of the individual concepts of Sāṃkhya found their way into Indian philosophy, to the extent that its basic notions were disseminated widely, albeit separately. When we study Hinduism at any level, the influence of Sāṃkhya will always be found.

7

Classical Yoga

Background to the school

Classical Yoga is a practically orientated *darśana*, presented in *sūtra* form by Patañjali, and is underpinned by the philosophy of Sāṃkhya. In its broadest sense *yoga* has been a varied phenomenon in Indian practice from the earliest of times and has become allied to different perspectives of Hinduism, as much as to the other schools of philosophy, in one form or another. In this same, broad, sense, Yoga is a philosophy for the living of one's life in its practical dimension. One is reminded here of the Buddha's tenet that by *actively* engaging in the "Eightfold Path" the truths of life will follow, rather than becoming immersed in the contradictions of philosophy. Yoga is similar, though in its narrower sense of a specific school of practice, it is by no means to be undertaken by the faint-hearted and unmotivated. In all its aspects, Yoga perceives that the Self that is real in the deeper levels of our consciousness transcends the empirical self that we know, and it provides the practical means for its realization. It is thus pervasive in Hinduism.

Although Yoga is concerned with the practical means by which it is possible to become liberated, it would be a mistake to see it as so practically orientated that it must rely completely on Sāṃkhya for its underlying metaphysics. For basic to Yoga is a philosophy of life, of its suffering, of the humanistic heights possible for human beings, and a thorough understanding of the nature of the mind. It is especially the last of these, the psychology and philosophy concerning the mind – particularly the way in which the mind impedes or impels each individual on the spiritual quest – that is the legacy of Yoga, even today. Had it no philosophy *for*, and *of*, life, it could not have survived. *Yogic* practice is not taught at the expense of theory, and theory can never be separated from it without destroying the ethos of what Yoga really is.

The ultimate goal of Yoga is the cessation, *nirodha*, of the "modifications", *vṛtti*, that constitute the mental functioning of the mind, *citta*. *Vṛttis* are literally "whirls", a word that provides a very graphic image of the human mind, and the thoughts that whirl into the mind in day-to-day life, even in the dreams we have when asleep. Combining these three Sanskrit terms, then, we have the Yoga goal of *cittavṛttinirodha* which, in Patañjali's words means, "the restriction of the fluctuations of mind-stuff"[1], and can only be achieved by immense discipline of the mind. This is essentially what the word *yoga* as a concept means, being both an aim and a practice. In general, the word is associated with the kind of discipline of the mind that takes place in meditative practices on the one hand, and through austere practices, on the other. The actual meaning of the word is derived from the Sanskrit *yuj* "to yoke", "to bind together", and this is suggestive of yoking the senses so that the "fluctuations of mind-stuff" are stilled.[2] To the extent that one is able to still the mind there will be a corresponding transcending of the senses and the usual mind patterns. This brings about what Karel Werner has described as a very different perspective of being and existence: "The whole personality becomes transformed and can function in a new dimension hitherto unknown or inaccessible to it. Knowledge is widened, deepened and increased and there is a sense of communion with the infinite or with the essence of all things or with reality as a whole."[3] But the sense of communion – indeed any sense at all – is completely quelled in the classical expression of Yoga, when the mind becomes totally still. Here, personality is lost and all sense of duality and objectivity. The Sāṃkhya goal of *kaivalya*, isolation of the self in its pure consciousness, is the ultimate goal of classical Yoga, and it is therefore something of a "science" that sets about providing a technical means for the achievement of its goal. The aim, then, is the silence of the mind. This, as one writer depicts it:

> is the prerequisite condition for the mind to be able to reflect accurately the objective reality without introducing its own subjective distortions. Yoga does not create this reality, which is above the mind, but only prepares the mind to apprehend it, by assisting in the transformation of the mind – from an ordinary mind full of noise, like a whole army of frenzied and drunken monkeys – to a still mind.[4]

As a very varied phenomenon, Yoga has not only been adopted by many different proponents of Hinduism, it is also characteristic of both Buddhism and Jainism. And each time it is adopted it is given a new dimension and expression. So in terms of Hinduism itself, we find Yoga affiliated to many different religious expressions. The *Bhagavadgītā*, for example, highlights this well, emphasizing *karmayoga*, *bhaktiyoga* and *jñānayoga*. But underpinning such different expressions of Yoga is the same idea of the yoking of the senses, the same discipline of the mind. In *karmayoga* this takes the form of egoless action, that is to say acting without any selfish expectancy of the consequences, though always in line with the personal, the social, and the universal *dharma*, what is right. Again, the mind has to be stilled for this kind of almost meditative *action*. Then, too, *bhaktiyoga* is the Yoga of devotion to a personal deity. Here, too, the self is lost in ecstatic devotion and total surrender to the divine. There is here the discipline of focus on the deity to the exclusion of all other things with which the mind may be concerned, and the deity becomes the filter through which all aspects of life are perceived and through which all actions in life are undertaken. *Jñānayoga* comes closest to the classical expression of Yoga in that it emphasizes the path of intuitive knowledge and the discipline of deep meditative practice by which it is promoted. It is a path often associated with ascetic practice, as is classical Yoga. In each of these examples of Yoga it has adjusted to a specific path or *mārga*, and has been adapted to provide varied religious expression. Whicher rightly warns us: "There can be no totalization of Yoga for in all its rich diversity Yoga proper is not a uniform whole. Even just a cursory look at Yoga in its historical context reveals that methods/techniques/practices and philosophies of Yoga can vary from school to school and from preceptor to preceptor."[5]

The very general nature of Yoga is its most prominent characteristic and in a multiplicity of forms it has had a long history in Indian religious praxis. What is important about its classical expression is that, in this context, it became systematized sufficiently to become a philosophical *darśana* in its own right. But in other contexts Yoga maintains an individuality that only loosely associates it with a specific type of religious belief. It virtually carries with it the connotation of "mysticism" because of its transcendent goal – the pure Reality that is ultimate, whether divine or not. It is this mystical character that made it somewhat separate from orthodox, *Brahminical* Hinduism in its formative period, but its pervasiveness was also to penetrate orthodoxy.

Given the pervasiveness of Yoga in the Indian tradition as a whole, it is impossible to trace in it a neat evolutionary development. Karel Werner points out in this context: "There are changes only in the form of transmitting the Yoga experience, changes in description and interpretation and in the exposition of what can be called the path to the Yoga accomplishment."[6] The origins of Yoga go back into distant antiquity and were perpetuated by groups of mystics – wherever, in fact, there was inquiry into the depths of spiritual consciousness behind ordinary mortal thought. Classical Yoga itself reflects this long pre-history. We find some evidence of *yogic* practice on the Indus Valley seals. These seals show seated deities in *yogic*-type posture, heels brought together and drawn up towards the body, the back erect, and the arms stretched out so that the hands rest on the knees – not unlike, though not identical to, the classic "lotus" posture of *yogins.*[7] Additionally, identical, nude, bearded and upright male figurines have been found, also suggestive of a standing ascetic pose associated with some Indian ascetic traditions. The use of *soma*, a potent hallucinogenic substance, in *Vedic* ritual suggests that the more transcendent and subtle heights of expanded consciousness characteristic of *yogic* practices could not have been unknown in the context of *Vedic* ritual.

One hymn in the *Ṛg Veda* depicts the traditional ascetic sage, the traditional *yogin*, or *muni*, with long hair and naked body:

> He with long loose locks supports Agni, and moisture, heaven, and earth:
> He is all sky to look upon: he with long hair is called this light.
>
> The Munis, girdled with the wind, wear garments soiled of yellow hue.
> They, following the wind's swift course go where the Gods have gone before.
>
> Transported with our Munihood we have pressed on into the winds:
> You therefore, mortal men, behold our natural bodies and no more.[8]

These ascetic sages were *keśins*, those with uncut hair, and their esoteric and mystical means to go where the Gods have been before, beyond where the mind of ordinary mortals can go, are clearly implied in the hymn. Some of the earliest *Upaniṣads* also include references to *yogic* practices such as contemplation (*dhyāna*),[9] and a much more developed account of Yoga occurs in both the *Kaṭha* and the *Śvetāṣvatara Upaniṣads.* In both of these texts some of the specific terminology articulated in classical Yoga occurs, suggesting on the one hand that there may have been some more independently developed tradition or traditions, and on the other hand presupposing Yoga as an already present phenomenon in early Hinduism.

Early traditions of Yoga are also to be found in ancient societal practice. Wandering ascetics such as the *vrātyas* feature in the *Athārva Veda* as those who practised breath control and special meditative trances. They were also believed to have practised such austerities as standing for a whole year. Similar, though more endemic and longer lasting, were the *śramaṇas*, spiritual wanderers who undertook extreme ascetic practices in order to promote their spiritual consciousness. The Buddha in his early ascetic years is likely to have been such a person. Alhough often outside the Āryan fold, there was much of such *śramaṇist* tradition that eventually gained ground in orthodox Hinduism. Then, too, the very pattern of societal life with four stages (*āśramas*) of life, has *yogic* characteristics. Only the second stage, the *gṛhastha*, or householder stage, lacks some emphasis of ascetic denial. The first stage, *brahmacarya*, is the stage of the celibate student, the stage of being assigned to a *guru* and the stage of religious study. The third stage of *vānaprastha* is one of partial spiritual renunciation of the world, and of asceticism, the time for withdrawal from society. The final stage is the *saṃnyāsa āśrama* when the remainder of life is spent divorced from society as a wandering ascetic, deep in meditation of the ultimate source and Reality that underpins all existence. Given such traditions, it is easy to see how Yoga penetrates to so many aspects of Hindu life.

It is not my purpose here to dwell further on these broader characteristics of Yoga. Suffice it to say that the classical Yoga that comprises the orthodox philosophical school is only one dimension of Yoga. But it is an important one that serves to systematize a variety of trends that had been present in the centuries before the advent of Patañjali's work. He wrote at a time when Yoga traditions had infiltrated many aspects of orthodox and unorthodox Indian society. Patañjali's system of Yoga is very closely allied to the philosophy of Sāṃkhya. But there are differences, particularly considering Yoga's acceptance of a divine being, and of a theistic, devotional approach to him, which we shall examine in due course. But it is not necessary to discuss the same twenty-five principles of Sāṃkhya in the context of Yoga, since there are no real differences. However, classical Yoga has a very different ethos to Sāṃkhya. And it is what it *does* with the Sāṃkhya metaphysics that makes this so. Yoga even has different terminology for the evolutes of *prakṛti*. Important to note, too, is that Yoga emphasized mind control, rather than solely emphasizing intellectual discernment, as does Sāṃkhya.[10] Yoga aims at a practical means for liberation in addition to a theoretical philosophy, and it uses the philosophy for its praxis. It is in this sense that it provides complementary teaching to that of Sāṃkhya.[11]

From what has been said it is obvious that Patañjali was not the founder of Yoga; he was simply one who drew together a number of important threads into a composite philosophical and practical system. As Mircea Eliade comments: "He merely rehandles the Sāṃkhya philosophy in its broad outlines, adapting it to a rather superficial theism and exalting the practical value of meditation."[12] Although this is a somewhat pejorative comment, it would be true to say that it is the steps and stages of Yoga as a path to liberation that interest Patañjali. But like Sāṃkhya, Yoga begins with the fundamental life condition of the suffering and disharmony of each individual and with what Werner terms "the solitude and self-enclosedness of the human heart".[13] Like Sāṃkhya, then, classical Yoga aims to direct the Self to the point at which its distinction from material existence – and that includes intellect, mind and ego – is realized and the *puruṣa* is liberated into pure, isolated consciousness. Classical Yoga aims at presenting the means by which the individual is able to transcend the functions of mind and ego that bind the Self to the world of matter. Yoga "is not an artificial attainment, the opening of a door into another life, but a great change in attitude toward oneself and the world".[14] In particular, it is the suppression of the "modifications" of the mind that brings about liberation. Once these fluctuations of the mind cease, the Self is prevented from attaching itself to them, and all suffering ends. "All life," claim Chatterjee and Datta, "is a quest of peace and a search for the means thereof. Yoga is one of the spiritual paths that leads to the desired goal of a total extinction of all pain and misery through the realization of the self's distinction from the body, the mind and the individual ego."[15] The *yogic* path to such realization is not an easy one, for it demands chastity, discipline, solitude, control of the body, of the breathing and of the mind, as well as single-pointed concentration – all in opposition to the normal patterns of life and behaviour. It seeks to enable the individual to control the psychological, physical and mental dimensions of normal personality, with the aim of experience of the true Self.

Main proponents and commentators

Although associated with the school of classical Yoga and the compiler of the foundational *Sūtras* of the school, Patañjali was neither a founder nor an innovator. Yet Dasgupta described his *Sūtras* as "a masterly and systematic compilation, supplemented with certain original contributions".[16] What he did was to present in his *Yogasūtras* a very systematic and succinct account of the practice of Yoga – "a codifier of what was best in the Yoga practice and knowledge of his time".[17] But we know little of him. Although some have favoured identifying him with the grammarian Patañjali who lived in the second century BCE, there is much about such an identification that is problematic.[18] Woods points out that the philosophical concepts of the two Patañjalis are different, and demonstrates this at some length.[19] He dates the author of the *Yogasūtras* much later, to some time in the fourth or fifth centuries CE. Some date the *Sūtras* much earlier, perhaps to the second or third centuries CE.[20] But dates are widely given, and it would be difficult to substantiate clearly any particular one. In short, we do not know exactly when Patañjali lived. Equally debated is whether the text is a unitary one, for some see Patañjali as merely a redactor.[21]

The Yoga that is presented in Patañjali's *Yogasūtras* is often referred to as *rājayoga* "Royal Yoga", and *rājamarga* "Royal Path", is one of the four major paths to liberation in Hinduism. The *Yogasūtras* itself is highly condensed and consists entirely of aphorisms. This was an advantage in memorizing and transmitting the material from one generation to the next. The *Yogasūtras* is divided into four parts or *pādas*. In the first *pāda*, entitled *Samādhipāda*, Patañjali dealt with the subject of concentration, dealing with the modifications or fluctuations (*vṛtti*) of the mind (*citta*), the nature of these fluctuations and the approaches one might take to restrict them. In this first section, too, Patañjali discusses the nature of Īśvara, the supreme, divine *Puruṣa* that provides the focus of theistic devotion in the Yoga system. The second *pāda*, *Sādhanapāda*, deals with the means of attaining liberation and the hinderances to these means, and the third, *Vibhūtipāda*, with the supernormal powers that accompany advanced *yogic* practice. The fourth *pāda*, *Kaivalyapāda*, concentrates on liberation itself.

While Patañjali's *Yogasūtras* is the foundational work of the school, this has been supplemented by a number of later commentaries. One, the *Yogabhāṣya*, was written by a so-called Vyāsa somewhere between the seventh to ninth centuries CE, and was the earliest commentary. A sub-commentary on this, the *Tattvavaiśāradī,* was compiled by Vācaspati Miśra in the ninth century, and another, the *Yogavārttika*, was compiled by Vijñānabhikṣu in the sixteenth century. It needs to be remembered that these commentators were not proponents of Yoga themselves, and their commentaries, although helpful, may not always be an accurate analysis of Patañjali's *Sūtras*. Another commentary, the *Rājamārtaṇḍa*, was written in the eleventh century by King Bhoja. It was he who was the first to equate Patañjali with the grammarian Patañjali – a theory mainly rejected in modern times.

General features of the school

The main characteristic of classical Yoga is an emphasis on practice, a practice that "becomes confirmed when it has been cultivated for a long time and uninterruptedly and with earnest attention", says the *Yogasūtras*.[22] But in emphasizing practice, classical Yoga turns its attention to the analysis of the mind – one that, I believe, holds as good for modern times as for the centuries past. In holding the fluctuations of the mind in check, the *Yogasūtras* recommends concentration on one single object, what is termed *ekāgra*. This object can be physical, such as the tip of the nose, the navel, the middle of the forehead, or subtle, like the *sattvic* substance of the "Lotus of the Heart", or the light within the head. Or, it can be mental, such as a particular idea or thought. It can also be concentration on God, on Īśvara. Even an object perceived in a dream is a possible focus for concentration; in fact, in the early stages of *yogic* practice, any object one wishes.[23] In other words it is concentration on a single object as opposed to the normal mind fluctuations of multiple perceptions and thoughts. So until the final stages of *yogic* practice, classical Yoga does not suggest that the mind is emptied, as much as controlled by single-object concentration. If the focus of the mind can be maintained on just one thing, then all the other thoughts are constrained, and all the stimuli that promote such thoughts will remain unnoticed. Breathing is particularly important in promoting such concentration with emphasis on the inhalation, retention and exhalation of the breath.

Two principles in particular are important in Yoga: *viveka*, which is "discriminative discernment", and *vairāgya*, which is "detachment", "dispassion", "renunciation". *Viveka* refers to the kind of discernment that enables the distinction between the consciousness of *puruṣa* and the materiality of *prakṛti* to be realized, and the true and permanent nature of the former, as opposed to the impermanent, finite and changeable nature of the latter, to be recognized. *Vairāgya* is what Taimni defines as "the deliberate destruction of all attractions and the conscious mastery over the desires".[24] All the thoughts that invade the mind as a result of sense perceptions serve to promote a personality that, in constant reaction to these sense stimuli, becomes tied to the world of matter. It is the desires and aversions of the individual in response to such stimuli that are *karmic* and that bind the individual to the process of rebirth. *Vairāgya*, then, is dis-desire, non-passion, dispassion, and suggests the training of the mind to restrain it from reacting to the stimuli of the world. Closely connected with the strenuous exertion to free the mind of all desires is the asceticism associated with Yoga – hunger, thirst, cold, heat, standing or sitting for long periods, immobilization and fasting.

Patañjali refers to Yoga as "the Yoga of action", and this, indeed, is what it is, not a still and passive contemplation, but a very vigorous striving to restrain the fluctuations of the mind, intensive study, and equally intensive devotion to God. It is a strenuous path, for the mind is not easily controlled. The state that is aimed for is the still mind, the state of restriction, *niruddha*, when all desire is quelled. Thus there is a certain similitude and equilibrium in attitude to all things that needs to be generated in the mind of the *yogin*. As the *Yogasūtras* states: "By the cultivation of friendliness towards happiness and compassion towards pain and joy towards merit and indifference towards demerit [the yogin should attain] the undisturbed calm of the mind-stuff."[25]

Reality: the view of the world in classical Yoga

In the fourth *pāda* of the *Yogasūtras* Patañjali tells us that: "The that-ness of a thing is due to a singleness of mutation."[26] This is to say that each entity in the phenomenal world is a particular combination of the three substances accepted by Sāṃkhya, the *guṇas* of *sattva*, *rajas* and *tamas*. Since these three *guṇas* are eternal substances, they lend reality to the phenomenal world, even if that reality is a changeable one in terms of the coming together and breaking apart of the various combinations of the *guṇas*. The *guṇas* are not part of *prakṛti*, they *are prakṛti*, and underlie and inform all change in the cosmos. They ground all entities in a real unified whole. As Dasgupta put it: "The changes come and go, the combinations break and form but the reals remain ever the same, though they may seem to appear in diverse characters. The characters and qualities are the results of the diversity of their combination. Thus the totality of the mass and energy also remains constant if we take account of both the manifested and the unmanifested, the actual and the potential."[27] The "reals" here, are the evolutes, the *tattvas* of the Sāṃkhya school, though classical Yoga preferred different terms for some.[28] So, like Sāṃkhya, Yoga accepts the realism of the world, along with the same division of reality into the pure consciousness of the *puruṣas* on the one hand, and the unified *prakṛtic* matter on the other.

Prakṛti, then, is a constantly changing reality. There are four states of it in the Yoga scheme of things:

- **The non-designated** – ultimate, unmanifest *prakṛti*, termed *aliṅga* in classical Yoga.
- **The manifest differentiator, designator or indicator** – *buddhi*, termed *liṅga* or *liṅgamātra*. This is the source of individuation in the entire universe.
- **The six unparticularized, undifferentiated or undiversified** – egoity or

asmitāmātra, and the five *tanmātras*, all of which are causative, creating other *prakṛtic* evolutes. The six altogether are termed the ***aviśeṣa***, indeterminate.

- **The sixteen particularized, differentiated or diversified** – the ten sense potentials or *indriyas*, the mind sense or *manas*, and the five gross elements. None of these is creative. Together they are termed ***viśeṣa***, determinate, qualified.

Feuerstein has some attractive terms for the *aviśeṣa* and *viśeṣa* aspects of reality. The former, being non-visible and subtle, he terms "deep-structure", and the sense potentials, mind and gross elements he terms "surface structure".[29] These definitions are novel, but divide reality rather appropriately. Feuerstein also uses the useful analogy of a triangle, with *aliṅga* being the apex, and the base the phenomenal world. In between are the subtle *aviśeṣa* aspects and *liṅga*.[30] Throughout this entire *prakṛtic* scheme are the changing collocations of the three *guṇas*, except in the unmanifest state, where they are as much real but do not interact.

Reality, then, is *prakṛtic* reality as much as the reality of the other dual principle, *puruṣa*. The nearer mind functioning comes to this fact – that is to say, represents matter truly – the more the mind is dislodged from involvement with *prakṛti*. But there has to be a realization of the difference between the permanent, changeless reality that is *puruṣa*, and the permanent but changing reality that is *prakṛti*. It is this that is *satya*, Truth.

It is exactly because the *guṇic* reality is a changing one, and because each individual is a codified blend of *guṇic* dispositions that are different from all other individuals, that each individual perspective of reality is different. As Jacobsen puts it, "the experience of reality is conditioned by the capacity of the species of the experiencer as well as by individual capacities. Reality, as humans experience it, is conditioned by our nature",[31] and the senses by which we view the world "are narrow portholes allowing us a fragmentary and deformed glimpse of the reality outside".[32] Inevitably, then, the human mind is trapped in its own specific kind of reality, programmed to be receptive to certain stimuli and to repel others according to the individual *guṇic* composition of its higher subtle faculties of intellect and ego. Inevitably, too, there can be no true perception by anyone other than the liberated *yogin*, so all perspectives of reality, other than the liberated one, are false: empirical truth is always tainted. And since *prakṛti* is without beginning and without end, human bondage, the *karma* that produces it, and the ignorance that sustains it, will always be characteristic phenomena of manifest *prakṛti*. Thus, *stilling* the mind, *controlling* it, is the only possible solution to a myopic, ignorant and individual perspective of reality. The *yogin* has to still the mind in order to view matter as it really is. Feuerstein sensitively writes:

> A thorough reflection upon the meaning of suffering in Indian thought is a prerequisite to any study of Yoga, for the painful impermanence of all things is nowhere experienced more intensively than in Yoga, where the adept, by constant efforts in changing his personality, lifts himself out of the valley of ordinary life with the aim of calmly and objectively examining the flux of empirical existence. As one who has, at least partially, overcome the whirlpool of human and cosmic affairs, the yogin's view penetrates the misleading façade of life and beholds the things as they really are: impermanent, painful, sorrowful.[33]

Needless to say the path of the *yogin* is a long and arduous one. There are many levels, many classifications on its route, many different depths of devotion and aptitude.

Epistemology

Knowledge of the phenomenal world occurs when the senses convey impressions to the mind and the mind "comes into a state of balance", as the *Yogasūtras* puts it, with the object. It tunes itself in to the appropriate object of perception. But it is the pure consciousness, or pure awareness, of the *puruṣa* of the individual that is the real subjective knower, not the mind. It is the association of *puruṣa* and *prakṛti* that results in *karmic* bondage of the Self, and the dissociation of them that results in liberation. Knowledge is critical to liberation, but as Berry rightly remarks: "The supreme difficulty of man lies in his lack of understanding."[34] When *puruṣa* is associated with *prakṛti* the combined effect produces knowledge and all experience, *bhoga*. But when knowledge is of the discriminating kind, it leads to the dissociation of *puruṣa* and *prakṛti* – and that is liberation. In the Yoga view, the knower, *puruṣa*, that which can be known, *prakṛti*, and the instrument of knowledge, *citta*, are three different entities. The last two, however, are both matter and must, ultimately, be separate from the changeless, pure consciousness of *puruṣa*. Both what can be known and the instrument of knowledge are subject to *guṇic* change. Each cognition that occurs is a single and particular modification, *vṛtti*, of the mind. Thus change is of the nature of the mind, as it is of the intellect and, mostly, of the ego that responds to sense stimuli.

Yoga accepts the extra-ordinary knowledge that states of *samādhi* can bring. This is knowledge of subtle levels of *prakṛti* that could never be known via the ordinary means of knowledge. The process of acquiring *discriminating* knowledge (*vivekakhyāti*) is essential to the *yogin*. It involves a regression from ordinary perception through the senses, to the deeper knowledge of the subtle evolutes of *prakṛti* – a journey of knowledge of ever finer *prakṛtic* evolutes. This is an important point that I shall return to later. The *yogin* has to understand thoroughly the true nature of *prakṛti* but, as Jacobsen succinctly puts it, "the purpose of understanding matter in Sāṃkhya and Yoga is not to use matter, but to get rid of it".[35]

Pramāṇas

Yoga accepts three *pramāṇas*, or valid means of knowledge, perception, inference and testimony.

Perception

Patañjali defined perception as "that source-of-valid ideas [which arises as a modification of the inner-organ] when the mind-stuff has been affected by some external thing through the channel of the sense-organs.".[36] In other words the mind becomes subject to modifications in order to "come into a state of balance with" the object. This process is direct and immediate. Perception is the superior *pramāṇa*, because of the particularities it conveys in cognition. Inference and testimony can only convey generals.[37] Ordinary perception inevitably involves the senses, but the *yogin* has to transcend all the sense stimuli of ordinary perception for extra-ordinary perception that penetrates directly to the subtler states of *prakṛti*. Eventually, the *yogin* reaches that finely subtle state of *sattvic* knowledge pertinent only to the intellect, *buddhi*. Such *yogic* perception that is extraneous to the senses is not subject to *karmic* results.

It is the modifications of the mind that bind the *puruṣa* to the world of matter. For instead of being a mere observer of an object, the *puruṣa* becomes involved with it. It lends consciousness to predications that are made about the object – it is this or that, it is something to be liked or disliked, it is a source of pain or joy, and so on. Thus, objects are not perceived as they are, but are reacted to. It is this reaction and the subsequent modifications of the mind in the perceptive process that have to be controlled. Instead of perceiving external gross objects, the *yogin* attempts to perceive the essence of them, the subtle *tanmātras*. Then, without any subsequent reaction related to such objects, they remain such as they are – *prakṛtic* matter, and no more. This, said Vācaspati Miśra, is the "super-deliberative balanced-state."[38] It will be the means that Yoga recommends for the process of concentration and meditation. This is the concentration on, and identification with, the "wholeness" or essence of an object in such a way that apparent subject–object differentiation is transcended. One "becomes" the object, losing all aspects of memory and differentiation associated with it. In effect, this is a transcending of normal mind processes and a perception of the subtle "thusness" of an object without relational predication.

Error

Error in perception occurs when the mind fluctuations, or modifications of the mind, do not come into a state of balance with the object of perception. So whenever we see something but fail to perceive it accurately, the mind's analysis and synthesis of the perception will not correspond to the real thing. Error, then, is perception that is incorrect. For Yoga, it has nothing to do with memory of a past, similar object, for example silver that is incorrectly imposed from memory on the present perception of a piece of shell. It is ignorant perception – knowledge of something as being different from what it really is. The ultimate error in knowledge is put succinctly in the *Yogasūtras* 2:5: "The recognition of the permanent, of the pure, of pleasure, and of a self in what is impermanent, impure, pain, and not-self is undifferentiated-consciousness."[39] The real error, then, lies in the lack of discrimination between the real Self of pure consciousness and the whole of *prakṛtic* matter, including any notions of the egoistic and thinking empirical self.

Inference

Similar to the other schools, inference is mediate knowledge that occurs when we see one thing and relate what we see to a particular class. Thus there is a relation between the object seen and the class that is remembered, and this relation is uniquely characteristic to the two. Inference occurs where relationship between things universally occurs. Thus, to see one is to know that the other is present, though not necessarily *vice versa*. In classical Yoga the ultimate goal of liberation is never something that can be inferred; it has to be experienced.

Verbal testimony

The third *pramāṇa* accepted by the school of Yoga is verbal testimony – the knowledge conveyed by a reliable person. While scriptural testimony is accepted as reliable and as revealed by Īśvara, it is ultimately of the world of *guṇic* matter. Verbal testimony and inference will always be inferior to the true knowledge gained in higher stages of *samādhi*.

Citta

In the Sāṃkhya analysis of *prakṛti* outlined in the last chapter, three "inner" evolutes are initially present. The first is *buddhi* or "intellect", the second is *ahaṃkāra* or "ego", and the third, along with the organs of sense and activity, is *manas* or "mind". While Yoga accepts the twenty-five principles of Sāṃkhya, it is a school that prefers the use of *citta* to refer to the mind. But in many cases, it seems this term *citta* covers also the principles of *buddhi* and *ahaṃkāra*. *Citta* in the Yoga system is "mind-stuff",[40] that is to say, all that goes on in the substance of the mind, the sophisticated organ of sense.[41] But since the *buddhi*, the intellect, synthesizes the mind-stuff, there is a certain overlap in the use of the term *citta* as bridging the two. And since the ego is that which relates so readily to the objects conveyed by the sense organs to the mind, then mind-stuff is intimately connected with that also. Gaspar Koelman, therefore, defines *citta* as "mind-complex", and considers that the term is akin to *manas* when it is linked more with the physical aspects of the functioning of the mind, and is akin to *buddhi* when it is more concerned with the psychical aspects. He considers that the term *citta* covers the three aspects of intellect, ego and mind because it refers to the individualized thinking and experiential self. It is, he says, "individualized cognitive nature with its set of incommunicable experiences, dispositions and inclinations. It is the whole individual psychical and psychological and moral prakritic individual."[42] Larson, too, is definitive that *citta* is the collective term for intellect, egoity and mind.[43] On the other hand, Radhakrishnan identified Yoga *citta* with Sāṃkhya *mahatbuddhi*, though stating that in Yoga it includes ego and mind.[44] But Yoga primarily focuses on *mind* in particular, intellect being drawn into the mind functioning. If anything, Yoga *citta* is Sāṃkhya's *manas*, though encompassing the necessary intellect and egoism for efficient functioning.

Citta, then, refers to the psychological individual that is motivated by his or her dispositional intellect and ego, and that thinks and synthesizes sense impressions in his or her own unique way. The term *citta* is, thus, a very comprehensive one, and it is one that may be synonymous with *manas* in some contexts and with *buddhi* or *ahaṃkāra* in others, and sometimes may refer to all three. In what follows, I shall use the term *citta* to refer to the collective functioning of intellect, ego and mind. This corresponds to the Sāṃkhya *antaḥkaraṇa* that combines the three. It is highly likely that Patañjali understood the term *citta* in this way, though some writers will disagree.[45] Incorporating the three aspects of intellect, ego and mind, the *citta* acts as the medium between *prakṛti* and *puruṣa*.

If, however, *citta* is mind-stuff, then it has the potential to be the mind that is free of the fluctuations that pervade it – the still mind-stuff, the substratum of the intellect, ego and mind that is like an empty screen on which no images are placed. It is only in this sense that *citta* has the potential to be like the Sāṃkhya *mahatbuddhi*, the pure *sattvic* intellect that is unrelated to either ego or mind. The whole purpose of Yoga is to restrain the fluctuations of the mind so that it becomes still in this way. But in ordinary life the *citta* is disposed to react according to its own combination of *karmic guṇas*. It reacts to the stimuli that invade the senses and cannot be still. It is "an arena of conflicting forces",[46] "bubbling in a hundred places with disturbing visions excited by uncontrolled emotion or worrying thought".[47] It classifies everything into categories of pleasure (*sattva*), pain (*rajas*) and indifference (*tamas*), and so reinforces the *karma* of its nature. But really, the *citta* is pure substance, as is all that takes place in it, and it is only the pure Self, the *puruṣa*, that lends it a sense of subjective consciousness that it can reflect but never be. The *citta* is dependent on both *puruṣa* for its proximity to give it a false consciousness, and on *prakṛti* that fills its substance with sense impressions from the gross world of physical forms; it could not exist in the ordinary sense without both. But once the mind fluctuations cease, then the *citta* is simply just aware of *prakṛtic* existence, and it no longer *reacts* to it. It is then in a position to perceive the reality of the separation of the *puruṣa* from the world of matter, or, to put it more appropriately, the *puruṣa* is simply reflected in the *citta* as its pure Self, as pure consciousness, and as totally separate from the *prakṛtic* world of matter.

The mind has been called "the great architect of all one's sorrow and glory".[48] In other words, it makes us what we are, and is the medium by which our future *karma* is mapped. The modifications or fluctuations of the *citta*, *cittavṛttis*, are all the responses to the stimuli that we are bombarded with in daily existence. To the extent that the *citta* is subject to one fluctuation after another, no two fragments of thoughts are really the same – a theory not unlike the Buddhist momentariness. But substantiality pervades reality in Yoga in the form of *prakṛti*: it is only the *vṛttis* of the mind that are insubstantial as far as Yoga is concerned. Most of our mind modifications, our *cittavṛttis*, are concerned with encouraging what brings pleasure and discouraging what brings pain or distaste. And all our efforts in these directions are dictated by the impressions built up by previous actions stored in our conscious and unconscious memories. This is an important point that will need to be taken up below in relation to the concept of the self.

Yoga classifies mind fluctuations into five categories:

- right knowledge (*pramāṇa*)
- incorrect knowledge (*viparyaya*)
- fancy, imagination, conceptualization or mental abstraction (*vikalpa*)[49]
- sleep (*nidrā*)
- memory (*smṛti*).

In considering carefully the things that fill our mind, this is a good analysis of its content. The human mind is particularly prone to existing outside the moment, projecting its thoughts to images of yesterday, to tomorrow, to the next event, the next thing to do, creating images of the past or future. Alice Bailey wrote of such thought, "these images have no real existence in so far as they are conjured up by men themselves, constructed within their own mental auras, energized by their will or desire and are consequently dissipated when attention is directed elsewhere".[50] Memory aids this process. Rohit Mehta, taking his cue from Patañjali, stated, "the memory is the effort of the human mind not to allow the experienced events to be stolen away".[51] Thus, we cling to the memory of what we are, and the memory of past experience that fuels what we want to do, to be, to happen. The five kinds of mind content can be either afflicted (*kliṣṭa*) or unafflicted (*akliṣṭa*). If the former, then the mind content is *karmic*, but the latter creates dispositions that will counterbalance the afflicted, *karma*-producing tendencies. Thus, Vyāsa described the content of the *citta* as like a river that could flow in opposite directions, one to good and the other to evil:

> Now when it is borne onward to Isolation [*kāivalya*], downward towards discrimination, then it is flowing unto good; when it is borne onward to the whirlpool-of-existence, downwards towards non-discrimination, then it is flowing unto evil. In these cases the stream towards objects is damned by passionlessness, and the stream towards discrimination has its flood-gate opened by practice in discriminatory knowledge. Thus it appears that the restriction of the mind-stuff is dependent [for its accomplishment upon means] of both kinds, [practice and passionlessness].[52]

So the *citta* can turn towards the world, or away from the gross to the subtle, to calmness, tranquillity, stillness – all in the direction of discriminative *sattvic* experience.

Additionally, the *citta* is said to be capable of five states:

- wandering, restless, through too much of the *rajas guṇa*
- delusive, through excess of *tamas* and, therefore, indolent and sleepy
- unsteady, and therefore, distracted one minute and attracted the next, thus flitting from one thing to another
- one-pointed, single in intent and *sattvic*, the concentrated mind in the state of *ekāgra*
- ceased – *nirodha*, the state of cessation of mind activity.

The first three are the states of the ordinary mind, representing the pull of the *rajasic* and *tamasic guṇas* in various proportions. The last two represent the more controlled *citta* of the *yogin*. Singleness of intent, *ekāgra*, is that state of concentration in Yoga that focuses on one particular object or thought, as noted above. *Ekāgra* is a stage of consciousness that is much more concentrated and which is wholly *sattvic*. Because it is characterized by focus on *one* object or thought, it is still suggestive of an activity of the *citta* and there is a clear consciousness of the object or thought on which the *yogin* focuses. At a higher stage of *ekāgra* there is total fusion of the *yogin* with the object of concentration. Cessation of the *citta* fluctuations is *nirodha*, the state in Yoga when the mind is completely still. Here, fluctuations of the *citta* have ceased entirely and the mind no longer knows anything at all. This has been described as "the trance of absorption in which all psychoses and appearances of objects are stopped and there are no ripples in the placid surface of the mind",[53] and is a state of higher *samādhi*, the goal of *yogic* practice.

Each modification or *vṛtti* of the *citta* corresponds to some object of knowledge, so the *citta* is constantly changing or fluctuating in order to match, and take the form of, each object of experience. Because the *puruṣa* is so intimately reflected in the *prakṛtic* make-up it thinks it is changing and fluctuating and becomes over-involved with the objects of perception processed in the *citta*, instead of just witnessing them in its true, independent nature. Vyāsa in his *Yogabhāṣya* referred to the mind-stuff as a "magnet" that aids the *puruṣa* simply by its proximity to it, "and thus the relation between it and the Self is that between property (*svam*) and proprietor (*svāmin*). Hence the reason why the Self experiences (*bodha*) the fluctuations of the mind-stuff is its beginning-less correlation [with the thinking substance]."[54] The Self, then, incorrectly thinks that it experiences pain or sadness, joy, happiness or indifference, and so it suffers. The Self is always pure subject and the mind-stuff pure object; one is the experiencer the other the experienced. But if the experiencer detaches itself from identity with the mind fluctuations it will be sufficiently discriminative to experience itself such as it is, separate from the objective *citta*.

The mind of the ordinary mortal, then, is constantly in a state of fluctuation. The nature of the mind will be dictated by the *guṇas*. It is the three *guṇas* that permit mind sensations – reflection, volition and feeling. These are all states of knowing with borrowed consciousness from the *puruṣa*. Because the *guṇas* inform mental states, each mental state will contain the characteristics of the three *guṇas* in varying proportions – pleasure, pain and indifference. Patañjali believed that even sleep is a fluctuation of the mind and, although *tamasic*, this fluctuation allows us to assess that we have slept deeply, dreamlessly and well, or that we have slept too deeply and too heavily. Some kind of separate conscious judgement of ourselves in the state of sleep must, therefore, be presupposed.

The goal of Yoga is the passionless mind, the mind free of desires that bind it to the world. The practice that pervades the *Yogasūtras* is that which seeks to restrain all mind fluctuation. It is a practice that encourages a state of the mind that is one of pure *sattva*, when the *guṇas* of *rajas* and *tamas* are dormant. *Sattva* signifies clearness, lightness and a pellucid steadiness. In this state the *yogin* is able to perceive things such as they are without subjective attachment or aversion to them. The *citta* at this level is unified and not diverse, the *prakṛtic* world is simply witnessed in its unified wholeness without relational attachment of the Self to it. It is a balanced state when memory drops its relational discrimination of, and reaction to, all things. It is pure witnessing, pure seeing, without reaction to what is seen. But eventually even the *sattvic* intellect has to be lost. As Vyāsa put it, the *guṇas* "like rocks fallen from the top of the mountain peak, without support, of their own accord, incline towards dissolution and come with this [thinking substance] to rest".[55]

It is its emphasis on the philosophy and psychology of the mind that makes classical Yoga stand apart from Sāṃkhya. Yoga is concerned with an analysis of the nature of the conscious and subconscious, and the interaction between the two that binds each individual in his or her own mental pathology. Indeed, as Feuerstein states, "Patañjali operates with a remarkably sophisticated concept of mind which bears a close semblance to certain modern psychological theories. According to him, mind represents a system of dynamic relations which have as their mainstay the complex neurophysiological (= objective-*prakṛtic*) organism."[56] It is the complex nature of the mind I want to take up for further analysis in the context of the nature of the self, later in the present chapter. For the moment, it is pertinent here to pause and look at the means by which the *yogin* learns to "tame his instincts, his worldly inclinations, his desires, and channel the forces they embody toward a new goal".[57]

The eight *aṅgas* of Yoga (*Aṣṭāṅga* Yoga)

To turn, now, to the practices by which the goal of liberation is achieved, it has to be asked, How much is the aim to turn away from life entirely? There are those who see the accomplished *yogin* as having an aversion to involvement or participation in life, preferring the route of harsh ascetic practice and isolation. It is perhaps the more common view of the *yogin* – one deep in meditation without care for the world. Others are more sceptical about such traditional views of withdrawal, and have a view of the *yogin* as a more compassionate being. I shall have occasion below in the section on liberation to discuss Whicher's view of the fully-liberated *yogin*, who may, as a *jīvanmukta*, become re-immersed in life, but a point of Feuerstein's is worth noting here. He observes, "the yogin to whom conditioned existence becomes transparent and who is able to discern the subtle workings of, and relationships in, nature, does not display a fanatic thirst for life, but rather refrains from getting too much involved in its enticing-dangerous play".[58] But the real point of *yogic* practice is to withdraw the senses from *karmic* mind fluctuations that lead to increased bondage. The *controlled* mind should have no fear of falling into the "enticing-dangerous play" of ordinary *prakṛtic* existence. Of certainty, however, is the fact that: "The path is steep and studded with obstacles, and the goal is distant",[59] and this means that throughout the long journey there will be times when removal from external existence is exigent for spiritual progress.

The practical dimension of classical Yoga is formulated into eight *aṅgas*, a word meaning "parts", "limbs" or "individuals". It is worth noting that they do not represent the major part of the *Yogasūtras*, only one section of it, despite being frequently, and mistakenly, considered as the sole contribution of Patañjali. Unlike the Buddhist *Eightfold Path*, which is a simultaneous practice of all components, except, perhaps for the contemplative and meditative aspects, the Yoga *aṅgas* are progressive.[60] They deal with the outer body and response to life as much as the inner spiritual individual. They are the means by which the final discipline of Yoga can be realized, and provide a technique for release of the Self from *prakṛtic* existence. These eight *aṅgas* are *yama*, which is restraint; *niyama*, discipline; *āsana* bodily postures; *prāṇāyāma*, which is rhythmic control of respiration; *pratyāhāra*, which is the withdrawing of the senses from the external world of sense stimuli; *dhāraṇā*, focused concentration and attention; *dhyāna*, meditation; *samādhi*, which is deep and unified concentration and the medium for liberation. *Dhāraṇā*, *dhyāna*, and *samādhi* are more directly concerned with Yoga, the former five being external aids to it.[61]

Yama

Yama, or restraint, constitutes the basic requirement for any would-be ascetic, and while it is not in itself Yoga, it is a means to, and a preparation for it, as is the second *aṅga* of *niyama*. Both terms stem from the Sanskrit root *yam* "to control". *Yama* is of five kinds. The first is *ahiṃsā*, which is abstention from injury and violence to any form of life. And this is not qualified by species, by place, by time or exigency. In other words fishing is wrong even though the fisher only harms fish, and it is still wrong to kill even if one claims exceptional circumstances of time, place or need, such as in war, or if non-harm is only practised in sacred areas or on sacred days.[62]

It is not by accident that *ahiṃsā* is the first of the restraints and the first practice of all on the *yogic* journey. It is impossible to be a living being without causing harm. Whatever lives, does so because it feeds off something else. Thus, this sheer interdependence of all things must necessitate the causing of pain or disharmony. The only way to overcome this is to separate the Self from matter, to be independent of it. Jacobsen makes these important points and states that: "Permanent freedom from interdependency is the goal of Sāṃkhya and Yoga because only permanent freedom from interdependency can guarantee permanent freedom from pain."[63] As Jacobsen notes, as far as Yoga is concerned, the presence of the three *guṇas* in all things must temper good actions with some pain, because what is good to one causes pain to another, as the food chain so aptly illustrates. *Sattvic* goodness must also contain some *rajasic* energy that is pain, as well as the inertia and stupefaction of the nature of *tamas*.[64] No action, then, can be wholly good if it is *guṇic* bound, and there can be no real happiness in any part of *prakṛtic* matter: "The ethics of non-injury toward all beings is therefore a result of the knowledge of the painful nature of existence and the idea that the true identity of all beings totally transcends nature."[65] So by attempting to uphold *ahiṃsā*, the first step in extracting the Self from its links with *prakṛtic* interconnected unity is being taken.

The second aspect of *yama* is *satya*, which is truthfulness in mind and speech – an abstention from any kind of falsehood. This encourages sound actions and their consequences and is the hallmark of a person on whom one can depend. The third, *asteya*, is abstinence from theft, or the appropriation of things that are valued by another person. According to Patañjali, wealth automatically comes to those who do not take from others. The fourth aspect of *yama* is *brahmacarya*, which is sexual control and celibacy. It was believed to promote energy, sexual activity dissipating it. The word *brahmacarya* means "dwelling in Brahman" and is indicative of the strength and energy one acquires through the spiritual rather than physical aspects of life. The final aspect of *yama* is *aparigraha*, which is the non-acceptance of gifts, especially since such things lead to attachment to objects. Its observance encourages a state of mind in which nothing is owned, and Werner notes that this means one's own body or even one's own life,[66] for the physical body becomes insignificant, not needing the gratifications of ordinary mortals. With truthfulness, the *yogin* acquires the power of making his words come true. When he abstains from theft, he acquires all, and when he is adept at continence he acquires supra-human powers. Through non-acceptance of gifts, those objects that are desired are no longer wanted. It is detachment from accepting of the things in life that the body normally needs that permits the expansion of knowledge to more subtle dimensions.

Niyama

Niyama is the kind of discipline that is concerned with five areas – purification, serenity and contentment of mind, ascetic practices, study, and devotion to Īśvara, God. Purity is *śauca* and involves cleanliness of the body and in the partaking of pure food into the body. Such external aspects of purification are balanced by internal emphasis on the purification of the mind, and the cultivation of good states of mind such as compassion and joyfulness, as well as indifference to the more negative sides of life and the negativity in others. The aim of *śauca*, however, is not to take pride in a pure body. On the contrary, the *yogin* needs to gain disgust of it, in order to lose attachment to it. Aversion to one's own physical body promotes aversion to the physical bodies of others and, therefore, no attachment to others. But the focus is on changing the mind, not on attention to the body. This is Yoga in its full sense of yoking and disciplining the senses. Importantly, purity is not something gained by constant cleanliness, and the body can be impure despite outward cleanliness. Purification of the mind is the necessary corollary of purification of the body.

Serenity and contentment of mind is *santoṣa* and it is the kind of contentment that accepts things such as they are without reacting to them either negatively or positively. Thus, an indifference to failure or success, praise or blame, is acquired. And when such indifference is acquired, true contentment and serenity is experienced which, says Patañjali, surpass anything one could experience through the medium of the world. But balanced with such contentment is *tapas*, austerity, or ascetic practice, and this really creates the ability to be content in mind even while enduring physical hardship. It also serves to bring the body to a state of physical perfection – denying it will promote its well-being. Thus extreme heat or cold, excessive fasting, or the taking of vows that are concerned with long penance, are all aspects of *tapas*. Again, however, there is control of the physical and mental being through such practice. Feuerstein considers *tapas* to be probably the oldest characteristic of Yoga, and connected to the *Vedic yajña*.[67] Importantly, he later notes that *tapas* is to do with *perfection* of the body, "not its mutilation and destruction".[68] Such practices are a distortion of the true practice of Yoga.

Regular study, *svādhyāya*, is also an important aspect of *niyama*, and because this study is of a religious nature, it is designed to bring the *yogin* into contact with his chosen deity. *Svādhyāya* means *self* study, and so it is devoted to the raising of the consciousness and mental faculties of the individual. It is also closely linked to the fifth aspect of *niyama*, which is devotion to Īśvara, to God, through *Īśvarapraṇidhāna*, which is meditation on, and surrendering to, Īśvara, a surrendering of the self to God in the process of meditation. This is something that is said to promote a breadth of intuitive knowledge. Such surrender to the divine is not occasional but constant, and in these early stages of the Yoga technique is meant more in the sense of training the *yogin* in focus on the divine. Only at the later stages will a more explicit fusion with the divine as object take place.

Āsana

The discipline of the body also extends to bodily postures, of which there are many. The aim here is to free the body of its constraints, so that the inner, mental self can also be free. Removing such constraints frees the body of disease and preserves its vital energies. Again, there is control and harnessing of the body in order to promote the equilibrium of the mind. Eliade links this physical activity with the one-pointed concentration that will come with later stages. He writes:

> On the plane of the "body", *āsana* is an *ekāgratā*, a concentration on a single point; the body is "tensed," concentrated in a single position. Just as *ekāgratā* puts an end to the fluctuation and dispersion of the states of consciousness, so *āsana* puts an end to the mobility and

> disposability of the body, by reducing the infinity of possible positions to a single archetypal, iconographic posture.[69]

These words get behind practice *per se* to the deeper experience that takes the *yogin* further on the journey to the ultimate goal. Postures should always be stable and easy, despite the complicated nature of some. There should be no effort that impedes the balanced state of the mind. Concomitant with such a balanced mind, perfection in *āsanas* makes the *yogin* immune to opposites (*dvandvas*) in life, like heat and cold, happiness and sorrow. The most well-known *āsana* is the lotus posture, which is sometimes the basic position from which other *āsanas* are derived. But each posture is a unified one, and, as Eliade points out, a "concentrated" single position. He writes of this:

> Thus, one arrives at a certain neutralization of the senses; consciousness is no longer troubled by the presence of the body. Furthermore, a tendency toward "unification" and "totalization" is typical of all yogic practices. Their goal is the transcendence (or the abolition) of the human condition, resulting from the refusal to obey one's natural inclinations.[70]

Again, this is typical of Patañjali's Yoga in that outward praxis has a corresponding deeper experience that assists progress – a unique blend of praxis and philosophy.

Prāṇāyāma

Regulation of breathing, *prāṇāyāma*, is a very important aspect of the practice of Yoga. It is a regulation that covers the inhalation, retention and exhalation of breath. Since breath is vital to the body, the way in which we breath affects the internal state of the physical body and the mind. We have only to think of the way our breathing changes with our emotions to see that this must be so. The technique slows down the process of breathing so that, while inhalation, suspension and exhalation are equal, the equal length of time taken for each becomes increasingly longer, and one single process of breathing may last many minutes, and for the more adept *yogin* much longer. But it is particularly the effect rhythmic breathing has on the mind that is important to the *yogin*. Feuerstein brings out the deeper implications of this rhythmic emphasis rather well, when he writes that *prāṇāyāma* "endeavours to restore the primeval rhythm and cosmic harmony as manifested in man, the microcosm. The rhythmisation of breath (which, in the end, is also a unification) is considered to be the most effective method of inducing the re-establishment of the harmony of the microcosm as an exact replica of the all-harmonious macrocosm".[71] His words suggest experience of the unity of matter, of balancing the *prakṛtic* matter that is the self with the *prakṛtic* matter that is the universe.

The suspension of breath, especially, is believed to promote intense concentration. Breathing tends to fluctuate with the mind fluctuations, so if it is controlled, then so is the mind. And if the mind is controlled then *karmic* thoughts are under control too. In the ordinary person discriminative knowledge is prevented by the countless actions of thought, speech and body that are world and *karma* orientated. Such *karma* spreads a thick veil of ignorance over the kind of knowledge necessary for liberation of the Self. *Prāṇāyāma* causes such *karma* to dwindle away, allowing the light of true knowledge to shine through. The aim of breath regulation is to slow the process sufficiently to gain access to areas of consciousness that are not normally experienced, such as the kind of consciousness we have in sleep. Such access gives the *yogin* a highly concentrated and unified deeper consciousness. There is an anchorage of the self in its own energy, a point put lucidly by Eliade: "Through *prāṇāyāma* the *yogin* seeks to attain direct knowledge of the pulsation of his own life, the organic energy discharged by inhalation and exhalation. *Prāṇāyāma*, we should say, is an attention directed upon one's organic life, a knowledge through action, a calm and lucid entrance into the very essence of life."[72]

Pratyāhāra

Pratyāhāra is the withdrawing of the senses from the sense stimuli of the environment. The senses are restrained from reacting to the world around and the mind is closed in on itself, shut off from objects of the senses. As Vyāsa put it in his commentary on Patañjali's *Sūtras*: "Just as when the king-bee flies up, the bees fly up after him; and when he settles down, they settle down after him. So when the mind-stuff is restricted, the organs are restricted."[73] *Pratyāhāra* is the control of the fluctuations of the mind that occur when the senses are in contact with sense objects and relay the impressions to the mind. The process is cut off, and the mind is alone. The senses are brought back into the mind instead of out into the world, and in such a state the *yogin* is believed to be able to have knowledge of objects at a different level – not the outward *form* of the objects, but the inner *essences* of them. What occurs is apprehension of objects irrespective of the fact that they are divorced from their external stimuli.

With the withdrawal of the senses we find the first control of the mind that is foundational for the more intensive practices that come with the last three *aṅgas*: *dhāraṇā*, *dhyāna*, and *samādhi*. It is these last three stages that are most important, and they are collectively given the name *saṃyama*. They are linked by single-pointed contemplation, concentration and meditation on an object, so they really form three parts of one process to the ultimate stages of *samādhi*. Further, their boundaries merge as the *yogin* moves from one stage to the next, so there is no clear demarcation between each one. It is a question of the depth of practice that makes one stage glide into the next.

Dhāraṇā

Coming from the root *dhṛ* "to hold fast", *dhāraṇā* means to hold the *citta* firmly in concentration on one particular object. This may be some part of the body like the navel, the tip of the nose, or the point between the eyes, or it may be like the subtle effulgence of the lotus of the heart, or it may be on the image of a deity. The lotus of the heart is an inner light, visualized as an inverted lotus with numerous symbolic aspects. At this stage we have the real one-pointedness of Yoga, *ekāgra*, "a motionless meditation, a silent collecting together of the mind's powers".[74] The mind is still withdrawn from external sense objects of the world; it is an *inner* focus on an essence of an object in the mind, not a return to the external world.

Dhyāna

Dhyāna is the stage of meditation when there is an even-flowing current of thought between the object of meditation and the mind, without any disturbance, change or interruption of concentration. So intense can this become that the object is known to the mind in its entirety and it can be materialized by the *yogin*. The entire essence and reality of the object is cognized in a stage of deep meditation. For it to occur there is total, effortless absorption in, and meditation on, the object, though the mind does not even think that it is concentrating on an object.

Samādhi

Samādhi, sometimes translated as "enstasis", and meaning "settling down",[75] is the last of the eight *aṅgas* and itself consists of several stages grouped under two kinds, *saṃprajñāta samādhi* and *asaṃprajñāta samādhi*. Importantly, the stages are fluid: they merge into each other, and there is no abrupt change from one to another, just a deepening of the experience and an intensification of the process. But each stage is purer and subtler than the previous one, and the mind becomes more and more refined. At these stages, the *yogin* has to take care that no sense of ego intrudes into these successively refined experiences. There must be no thought of the gains acquired through such heightened consciousness: utter detachment (*vairāgya*) must accompany each stage. Importantly, the higher stages of Yoga that lead to *samādhi* are *voluntarily* entered into. That is to say, the *yogin* can enter such states at will. So any chance, ordinary, states where mind fluctuations cease, are not Yoga. Intense discipline of the self is essential in *yogic* practice, and its higher states cannot be realized without it.

It is at this stage that awareness of the subjective self is lost in concentration on the object. In *samādhi*, writes Āraṇya, "meditation becomes so deep that forgetting everything, forgetting as it were one's own self, the mind is fixed only on the object contemplated upon".[76] The *yogin* is not aware of the process of meditation, he is not aware of the stage at which he is, only the object of concentration is in the mind. This is the deepest layer of consciousness; it is consciousness that is pure and free, devoid of any fluctuations of the *citta*, any sense of "I". Vyāsa in his commentary on the *Sūtras* wrote of *samādhi*: "When the state of meditation (*Dhyāna*) becomes so deep that only the object stands by itself, obliterating, as it were, all traces of reflective thought, it is known as *samādhi*."[77] Yet *samādhi* is not in itself liberation, but the phases to it. These now need careful analysis, an analysis perhaps facilitated by laying out each stage, beginning with sense withdrawal. Between each stage, the mind swings or "oscillates", as Dasgupta termed it,[78] before taking root in the next stage. The stages of *samādhi*, then, are as follows:

Pratyāhara	Withdrawal of the senses.
Dhāraṇā	Concentration.
Dhyāna	Meditation

Saṃprajñāta samādhi

Saṃprajñāta samādhi is a cognitive stage of *samādhi*; that is to say, the mind is still engaged, even though one-pointed, *ekāgratā*. It is *samādhi* "with support", or *bījā samādhi*, *samādhi* "with seed". But it is a state of pure cognition, with no egoity, no subjectivity, no separation from the object of cognition. It is "seeing with the soul when our bodily eyes are shut".[79] In *saṃprajñāta samādhi* an object of concentration is still required, albeit one with which there is unity. But the mind is, in some minute way, still subject to a single modification, a single *vṛtti*. This may be refined, subtle and wholly *sattvic*, but it is insufficient for liberation, because the mind is still engaged. Four stages of *saṃprajñāta samādhi* occur:

Savitarka samādhi Here, in the lowest stage, there is some conceptualization of the word and cognition related to the object, even though the mind is not engaged in ordinary perception, and so is not classifying and analysing. It is a stage associated with the sixteen *viśeṣas*, thus using gross objects as aids. While there is direct perception of the object as it is in the present and as it was in the past – all taking place as a completely internal perception – the mind has not yet gone beyond ordinary consciousness.

Nirvitarka samādhi is the next stage, when verbal conventions of the previous stage are lost. Words and memory that aid the internal perception of an object are abandoned. The object is seen without any name, relational appendage, or even as an object. However, the objects used as aids are still from the gross phenomenality of *prakṛti*. Āraṇya gives the example here of the luminosity of the sun, which becomes the sole object of concentration to the extent that all other characteristics of the sun are excluded, as well as the "I" that is concentrating on its luminosity.[80]

Savicāra samādhi is the stage where the *yogin* is at one with the very essence of the object, and is able to exercise total detachment and dispassion (*vairāgya*) in the process of merging with its nature, though the image of the object remains. It is a stage associated with the five *aviśeṣas*. Thus, gross aids are now abandoned and only subtle aids are used. It is meditation on the subtle potentialities and sources of gross matter, on the *tanmātras*. The *yogin* must go beyond words for this experience.

Nirvicāra samādhi is the final stage of *saṃprajñāta samādhi*, when the imagery of the former stage is lost. There is meditation on the *tanmātras* in such a way that they remain unclassified. There is no assistance of thought or words, and there is a unity of essence with the *tanmātras* that transcends time, space and causality. "Thought becomes one with these infinitesimal nucleuses of energy which constitute the true foundation of the physical universe."[81]

Ānanda samādhi It is not clear whether *ānanda samādhi* is a higher stage again or part of the experience of *nirvicāra samādhi*. It is an experience of supreme bliss, and seems to have been added by commentators. Patañjali does not mention it. Associated with the experience of pure *sattva*, it is also experience of pure I-ness, the sixth of the *aviśeṣas*. Stages beyond this become blurred and are differently viewed.

Asmitā samādhi may be part of the experience of *nirvicāra samādhi*, like *ānanda samādhi*, and is a later addition, not mentioned by Patañjali. Here, the I-ness of pure ego is transcended in order to dwell in the vast subtlety of the *asmitāmātra*, the *mahatbuddhi*, which is the very first evolute of manifest *prakṛti*, the subtlest, and the most refined. It is only at this stage, where *puruṣa* lends consciousness to intellect, that discernment between *puruṣa* and *prakṛti*, the "seer" and the "seen", can be possible. The *yogin* here is poised in an omniscient sense of being one with the whole *prakṛtic* world. He has a vision of cosmic Truth. However, "seer" (*puruṣa*) and "seen" (*prakṛti*) are not yet separated. The potential for their separation exists, but is not realized until the next stage.

All these stages are prior to the separation of *puruṣa* and *prakṛti* and are therefore involved faintly with cognition. Cognition is knowledge, and knowledge is *prakṛtic*. Only *puruṣa* is the knower, is pure consciousness. The seeds of *prakṛtic* ignorance have not been fully eradicated, and latent impressions in the subconscious, are waiting to be burnt up like roasted seeds.

Whicher writes of cognitive or *saṃprajñāta samādhi*: "The essence of cognitive *samādhi* is the centering of our diversified, fractured being leading at its most profound or advanced level into an organic and spiritual reunification of our individuated sense of self with the universal matrix (*mahat*) of manifest *prakṛti*."[82] At this stage, then, the *yogin* is at one with all *prakṛti*.

Asaṃprajñāta samādhi

While some *yogins* pause at the highest stage of cognitive *samādhi*, as if it were the end of the journey, this is, in fact, to become *attached* to liberation, and to miss the final higher supreme detachment (*paravairāgya*). At first, only glimpses of this highest state are experienced until the adept remains longer and longer in *asaṃprajñāta samādhi*. Here there is total cessation of mind *vṛtti*, there is *cittavṛttinirodha* – no thought at all. *Buddhi*, ego, sense-reaction and mind-fluctuations are completely still, leaving only the pure awareness that is *puruṣa*. It is the pure substratum of consciousness devoid of any ripple on the surface of it. However, it is a state into which the *yogin* slips but does not remain. It is a state that has to be worked at.

But in total liberation what is left is the pure consciousness of *puruṣa*, a state that is no longer a state of experiencing the *prakṛtic* world. The Self is free and delivered, *mokṣa* is realized, and the *puruṣa* is in a state of autonomous isolation, *kaivalya*. This is the final goal of the *yogin* when, says Vyāsa, "the mind-stuff resolves itself into its own primary matter".[83] *Prakṛtic* mind has become separated from the pure consciousness of *puruṣa*, and *puruṣa* can abide in itself. According to Vyāsa, for such separation and isolation to occur the *citta* has to be in that state that is purely *sattvic* and devoid of the *guṇas* of *rajas* and *tamas*. The *citta* then is in equal balance with the subtlety of the Self, and the true separation of the two can occur.[84] But when that separation does occur the pure *sattvic* mind that was the bridge to it is separated. The world of *guṇas* no longer enslaves the *puruṣa*. When this final goal of *kaivalya* is realized, all latent past *karma* is destroyed, and the *yogin* lives in the world as a *jīvanmukta*, one liberated while still confined to the physical body. Lost to ordinary consciousness, in this final state: "We pass in it to the realm of mysticism."[85]

During the higher stages of the practice of Yoga, the *yogin* is said to have extraordinary powers. These powers constitute knowledge of the past and the future, friendliness, joy and compassion for all things, and knowledge of the constitution of the planets and stars. It is also knowledge of the internal constitution of the body, the ability to go without food and water for extended periods, the ability to become motionless, to have omniscience, or to make the body as light as air so that it can float. These and many other powers are the *siddhis*, and they are practised in order to promote final *samādhi* rather than to be used as powers *per se*. It would be a mistake to assess the *siddhis* as "the popular cult of magic" that "is mixed up with the religious scheme of salvation in the Yoga", as Radhakrishnan has done.[86] More accurately, Feuerstein states of the *siddhis* of the *yogin*: "The powers are the inevitable by-products of his prolonged struggle towards this lofty goal. They cannot be separated from the profound transformation which he has to undergo in order to realise the Self. Viewed differently again, they are signposts along the way or, in contemporary parlance, confirmative evidence that he is on the right track."[87] Each *siddhi* is different, requiring *saṃyama*, "combined practice" (*dhāraṇā*, *dhyāna* and *samādhi* collectively), on a specific thought or object to accomplish it. For Yoga, such powers are the natural concomitants of higher states of consciousness. More empathetically, Radhakrishnan commented: "They are the flowers which we chance to pick up on the road, though the true seeker does not set out on his travels to gather them."[88] Also in the highest stage, according to *Yogasūtras* 3:51, celestial beings tempt the *yogins* into the delights of heaven. This is reminiscent of the Buddha's temptation by Mara, the foe of *dharma*. If the ultimate goal of *kaivalya* is to be reached, the *yogin* must allow such temptations to pass unheeded.

Samādhi is the long, last stages of the *yogin's* journey, what Feuerstein called "the final phase of the long process of de-humanisation".[89] It is a point, he says, when: "The yogin then takes the last step to outstrip his human limitations, to change his very nature by transforming his empirical consciousness into a supramental consciousness."[90]

The self

The liberated Self is that which is separate from suffering and reincarnation, and is beyond the mind–body unity that we normally know. Strictly speaking, there is no other self at all, but we all experience an ordinary *jīva*, the ordinary personality that exists in the causal network of life. What, then, is this self? It is the bound Self that exists only because the *puruṣa* becomes so intimately involved with *prakṛti*. In so far as the self functioning in the world can have no experience or knowledge at all without the ongoing presence of *puruṣa*, the self might be said to be a composite of both *puruṣa* and *prakṛti*. Because the *puruṣa* cannot separate itself from *prakṛti* it believes that *it* is initiating and reacting to all the mind fluctuations of the *citta*. And so it becomes involved in the world of choices, desires and aversions, in a world of birth, decay and death, in a world of suffering, sorrow and joys – in short, it becomes the empirical self that does not really exist. For every fluctuation or modification of the *citta*, there is an involvement of the *puruṣa*, for it is reflected in the whole mind process and cannot free itself from it.

In ordinary existence the self is subject to what are termed *kleśas*, "afflictions" or "hindrances", and there are five of them, all influenced by the *rajas* and *tamas guṇas*. Whicher calls them "the motivational matrix of the unenlightened mind".[91] The first is ignorance, *avidyā*, of the true nature of existence. It is *undifferentiated consciousness*, that is to say the inability to see consciousness as pure and separate from matter. It has been called a "congenital infection located within our psychophysical being".[92] It is also the inability to recognize impermanence in all life, and to see what is impure. Assigning permanence to what is not permanent, or believing the impure body to be pure when it is not so, are the examples cited by Patañjali.[93] It is the undifferentiated consciousness that believes itself to succeed or fail, that owns things, that likes and dislikes, and so on. *Avidyā* is a fundamental misconception, a misidentification, of Reality.

The second *kleśa*, *asmitā*, is the false identification of the Self with the material mind, intellect and ego, and is closely linked to the first. It is the false conjoining of the Self with the means of thought that produces what we call personality, and the failure to recognize that the Self is separate from the thinking process perpetuates that personality. The third *kleśa* is *rāga*, which is the attachment to, and desire for, pleasurable things and happiness. The fourth is the opposite of *rāga*, *dveṣa*, which is the aversion to anything painful in life, the disposition that causes anxiety about so many things. Vyāsa's comment on aversion is particularly clearly translated by Āraṇya: "Aversion is the feeling of opposition, mental disinclination, propensity to hurt and anger towards misery or objects producing misery, arising out of recollection of the misery experienced before."[94] The fifth is the fear of death, *abhiniveśa*. This, said both Vyāsa and Vācaspati Miśra, occurs because, while the living being can have no real experience of death in this life, the fear of it comes from the experience of it in past lives. It creates the will to live, the will to avoid that which is the ultimate in pain – death.[95]

The common denominator of the five *kleśas* is the ignorance that maintains them, so that the first *kleśa* of *avidyā* underpins the other four, and is responsible for all erroneous perception. Without the afflictions, moreover, there will be no self-assertive "I" that relates to the world in terms of I, me and mine. It is the correlation between the *puruṣa* and the whole thinking process of intellect, ego and mind that causes all the ignorance that brings about the bondage and concomitant suffering of the self. And it is the correlation between the Self and *prakṛti* that results in the kind of fruitive *karma* that necessitates rebirth in order to reap the results of it: this is what is meant by bondage. The Self, too closely involved in *prakṛti*, comes to desire what is pleasurable and has an aversion to what is not. It therefore becomes increasingly involved in the world, all the time lending the intellect, mind and ego a consciousness that they do not really have. Thus, the *kleśas* are responsible for creating the *karma* that binds the self to the world, for creating a personality that differentiates between this and that, desiring one thing and being repulsed by another, and all the associative life conditions and modes that occur as a result. But the empirical self relates to the effects of his or her own *karma* with the same degrees of desire and aversion, the same ignorance and will to live, and thus perpetuates his or her own specific *karma*. Vyāsa described this *karmic* being as one

> who casts off the pain received time after time which has been brought upon him by his own karma, – and who receives the pain cast off time after time, – and who is as it were permeated through and through from all sides with fluctuating mind-stuff complicated from time-without-beginning with its subconscious-impressions, – and who under [the influence of] undifferentiated-consciousness (*avidyā*) conforms [himself] to the 'I-substance' and to the 'Of me-substance' with regard to those very things which are to be rejected, – upon him, born again and again, the triple anguishes from both kinds of causes, both inner and outer, sweep down.[96]

Vyāsa's words are a very graphic description of the bound Self, the bound and *karmic*-producing *puruṣa*, which lacks the discriminating consciousness that can separate itself from *prakṛti*. The liberated Self is, on the other hand, pure consciousness, consciousness devoid of any reaction to the world of matter. It is a Self that is free from the fluctuations of the mind, the *citta*. Only when the ripples of consciousness within the *citta* become still and calm can the *puruṣa* experience itself such as it really is.[97]

Karma

Karma is critical to Yoga because it is that which impedes discriminative knowledge. It is the cause of the ignorant self, and it is what subjects *puruṣa* to bondage in the world of matter. All *karma* stems from the five afflictions. We are, then, thoroughly responsible for what we are, for how we behave and for what befalls us in life. The intricate balance between *karma*, the subconscious impressions (*saṃskāras*) that are left in the memory and subconscious as residues of human living, and the forming of habits (*vāsaṇās*) in each individual, is critical to the Yoga system, and we need to examine each in turn, beginning with *karma*.

There are three kinds of *karma*. ***Prārabdhakarma*** is *karma* that has already been accumulated and is beginning to take effect in the present life, or is waiting to come to fruition in the present life. It will already have determined the nature of the physical and mental person in the present existence. It cannot usually be changed, only used up. ***Sañcitakarma*** is *karma* that is beginning to mature from past or present life. It is in the process of being formed and has not yet produced any effects, nor will it in the present existence. ***Āgāmikarma*** is *karma* that is being formed now in the present existence and still has to mature.

Karma acquired through thought is ***mānasakarma*** "mental action/reaction". More active *karma* of speech and physical action is ***vāhyakarma***. All action is black, white, or black and white. Black *karmas* are evil ones and are *adharmic*. White *karmas* are meritorious and are associated with those who practice austerities, who study and meditate. When carried out by advanced *yogins*, they are wholly *sattvic*, for the *guṇas* of *rajas* and *tamas* will be quiescent through practice of *samādhi*. Black and white *karmas* are both good and bad, and are the kinds of actions of ordinary individuals. Being thoroughly *guṇic*, any good actions of such people may be *sattvic*, but never wholly so, for they must contain some elements of *rajas* and *tamas*. Equally so, evil, *tamasic*, acts can never be wholly evil but must contain elements of the other two *guṇas*. Thus, actions of ordinary individuals are black and white. The balance between good and bad actions produces the particular nature, or *karmāśaya*, of an individual, as human, or cat, for example. Those who perform all actions for God, for Īśvara, so having no actions of their own, and therefore having no fruits of their actions, are said to have neither black nor white *karma*. Those in the final phases of *samādhi* will also have no black or white *karma*, nothing that might cause the need to be reborn.

All actions inform two kinds of *karma* in an individual. Actions undertaken through individual free will, through personal effort, form ***puruṣakārakarma***. Unconscious, innate actions form ***adṛṣṭaphalakarma***. The way in which an individual acts, thinks and speaks, will depend a good deal on the innate tendencies – the coded genetics of character, temperament, propensities and dispositions. This is *adṛṣṭaphalakarma* operating. But each individual also has the free will to counteract his or her natural tendencies – the *guṇic* combinations that make up each person. Although it will be difficult to offset the experiences due in each life that are the effects of previous causative actions, free will permits some degree of control over the manifestation of such effects.[98] *Prakṛtic* materiality, as Jacobsen puts it, "can flow into any form".[99] Thus, each thing that exists, whether plant, creature or human, carries the *guṇic* potentiality to be something else in existence. And as Jacobsen notes, all living beings physically consist of the same gross elements. The possibilities for rebirth are, therefore, countless. And whatever rebirth occurs, the physical body – whether human or animal – is given the mind and senses appropriate to it by the *prakṛtic* order of things, that is to say, the nature of causes created by that individual or creature in past experiences. But having at least some free will to affect the future life is essential to the liberating process.

Saṃskāras

Why is it that we cannot still our minds for anything more than brief moments? And if we could, through constant practice, would we then become liberated? Is that all we would have to do? What prevents a simple affirmative answer here are the complexities of the human subconscious. While consciousness in the sense of mind fluctuations may be suspended for a short (usually very short) time in ordinary existence, it is from what Eliade terms "the immense reserves of latencies in the subconscious"[100] that new activity is immediately relayed to the mind. The subconscious is a dark, unknown world that is stocked full of the residues of past experiences of countless lives, and is continually being replenished by present consciousness. The process is graphically described by Dasgupta:

> This lower region is a store-house of experiences of the most varied kinds in a latent state. The door of that treasure house which is also a work-house is locked, so far as the conscious experiences of the purusha are concerned. The senses are like the chinks and crevices through which there is a constant coming and going, and the manufactured products of the lower world are continually returning to the upper plane of consciousness and once more entering into the train and sequence of what we call active life; both the invisible processes of this life as well as their root cause are as active as the visibles but from which these are

> derived. There is a continual movement from below upwards. A never-ending train of images, memories, and ideas keeps emerging into the light.[101]

It is this lower world of the subconscious that normally lies beyond our control and yet influences the way we think and the way we behave as human beings.

All actions leave subtle, but dynamic and latent, impressions in the self. They are the "latencies" of which Eliade wrote above. It is these that are called *saṃskāras* and they feed the faculty of memory. Feuerstein calls them "subliminal-activators",[102] and "a vast, inexhaustible pool of stimuli".[103] The impressions are stored in the mind following any experience or memory activity that we have. In many ways they are difficult to separate from the self, because they inform so much of each individual's character, behaviour and outlook on life. In psychological terms, they condition action, thought and speech. Humphries compares the *saṃskāras* with the Freudian *id*, "that repository of chaotic instinctive drives which have to be lived with and controlled if civilization is to survive".[104] *Saṃskāras* gather homogeneously deep in the self. Every time the mind is active or recalls a memory it creates further *saṃskāras*. It is the five afflictions that will dictate the kinds of memories an individual will wish to recall.[105]

Saṃskāras are not only effects of actions, but are also causative in that they condition the self in each rebirth. It is specifically the five afflictions – ignorance, desire, aversion, sense of I and fear of death – that cause the latent impressions, the *saṃskāras*, to be built up in the subconscious. In ordinary humans, where ignorance prevails, the mental activity of each individual will be informed by these subconscious impressions rising to the surface consciousness, and will lead to related actions in the present life. Immediately, other impressions of the same type are sown back into the subconscious, and older ones are reinforced. There is thus a continuous cycle of subconscious impressions conditioning all actions, speech, thoughts and habits, and these in turn build up more of the same kinds of subconscious impressions. Rebirth is inevitable. The continual building up of impressions will result in the energy necessary for continued lives, the energy that feeds ignorance and attachment to egoistic identity and the world of matter. At the end of each life the balance of negative/positive *saṃskāras* will dictate the kind of character an individual will have in the next life.

Vāsaṇās

While the term *vāsaṇās* is sometimes used as a synonym for *saṃskāras*, it is likely that there is a difference between the two, for *vāsaṇās* are more passive and latent in the mind.[106] They are the deep-rooted habits, the traits and tendencies brought about by *saṃskāras* that gather together homogeneously to form them, so that "the mind is pervaded all over with them like knots of a fishing net".[107] Feuerstein calls them "subliminal traces".[108] *Vāsaṇās* are acquired from the experiences of *all* previous existences. They are like containers, whereas *saṃskāras* are like the materials by which the containers are filled. Such habits or traits, as we know so well, are very difficult to counteract – we are creatures of habit, and habit is mostly beyond our control. While overlapping somewhat with the meaning and nature of *saṃskāras*, Eliade gives a very lucid description of just how *saṃskāras* and *vāsaṇās* affect the psychological and behavioural beings that we are. He points out their intrinsic nature of potentiality – a potentiality that is waiting to be activated:

> Thus the yogin – even if he has long years of practice to his credit and has passed through several stages of his ascetic itinerary – is in danger of finding himself defeated by the invasion of a powerful stream of psychomental "eddies" precipitated by the *vāsanās* . . . Life is a continual discharge of vāsanās, which manifest themselves through *vṛttis*. In psychological terms, human existence is a continuous actualization of the subconscious through experiences. The vāsanās condition the specific character of an individual; and this conditioning is in accordance both with his heredity and with his karmic situation. Indeed, everything that defines the intransmissible specificity of the individual, as well as the structure of human instincts, is produced by the vāsanās, by the subconscious.[109]

Here, then, is the reason why we are unable to still the mind, why we are more subject to the dictates of our minds than we are able to exercise control of them. The human being is bound by the particularities of the mind's subconscious characteristics that will cause him or her to act and react in certain ways. This, in turn, reinforces and builds up the same or similar characteristics. It is in such a way that the human being is bound. Control of the subconscious, then, is the key to control of the mind.

Saṃskāras are separated in time, space and many births, but gather in their patterns, *vāsanās*, to inform present behaviour, personality and also memory of the individual. And all the time new impressions are forming new *vāsanās*, collecting together in like-with-like fashion, building on previous impressions – in short, formulating the person of the future. Memory reinforces the impressions, for the memory of a particular happiness or a particular sorrow will feed the *karmic* accumulation of the same related impressions. And it is the fluctuations, the *vṛttis*, of the mind that perpetuate the memories and impressions. In this manner, the Self is trapped in *prakṛti* until it can discriminate between knowledge that is binding it to the world, and the knower, *puruṣa*, that is separate from all knowledge.

From what has been said it can be seen how intimately *saṃskāras* and *vāsanās* are connected with the formation and working out of *karma*. Whicher puts this well in the following words:

> The *vāsanās* lie dormant in the mind until the fruition of *karma*. The impressions (*saṃskāras*), that combine into habit patterns (*vāsanās*) are thus the very substance of the karmic residue. The action one performs proceeds according to the residue of past actions. The presence of a *saṃskāra* begins to produce certain mental tendencies, attitudes, thoughts, desires, images, and so forth even before the fruition of karma. Thus saṃskāras provide a certain momentum toward the external decisions one makes. These decisions – which appear to be conscious, but are in fact propelled by the dominant and unconscious residue of action – expose one to situations that are then credited with or blamed for one's fortune or misfortune, merit or demerit. Past actions stored in the residue of *karma* continue to affect present actions even if those actions are not remembered.[110]

In Sāṃkhya an individual is a coded entity with a psyche that exists by reason of the particular distribution of dispositions in the intellect. Similarly, in Yoga, the pre-coded character of each individual is also accepted – a character coded by that individual's own actions in previous existence(s). It is the *mind* that is the medium by which such a pre-coded character is formed, and is the means by which it can be changed for the future.[111] However, the emphasis is on mind control in classical Yoga, and its praxis for overcoming the limitations of the mind, far outweigh anything Sāṃkhya had to offer.

Karmāśaya

The collective *saṃskāras* of a particular type – accumulated from all kinds of different places, different times, and in different births – will form the *karmāśaya*, the "potential energy" [112] that will become a specific *karmic* effect as one individual. There is, so to speak, a thread that unites similar residues of actions into a connected cause or causes and this thread will, one day, in one particular birth, come to full fruition when sufficient strength of cause has accumulated. It is this *karmāśaya* that will determine the particular kind of life an entity will have – human or animal, for example – as well as the time of that life and the pleasurable and painful experiences in it. *Karmāśaya* will be the result of all kinds of previous actions formulated into a particular combination that will result in a unique individual in the next existence. Āraṇya describes it as "the aggregate of manifold latencies of Karma",[113] in other words, an aggregate of *saṃskāras*. Some *karmāśaya* comes to fruition in a present life, some in a future life, and some in the very distant future. Even death is no chance event, for the *karmāśaya* of the present existence will determine the length of life and the death that will end it. Then the particular nature and balance of other *karmāśaya* will determine the nature of a being in the next existence.

Vāsaṇas that stretch back through countless previous lives stimulate *karmāśaya*. The term "potential energy" is an apt one, for it is a dynamic energy that is subject to continual change through the activities of the mind. Changing the *karmāśaya* in an attempt to alter the patterns of the next existence is no easy task. Since we usually follow our individual natures in our response to the world in which we live, there is a tendency for the potential energy of the *karmāśaya* to be *reinforced* rather than changed, though all the time, it is being modified by present activity. But the complex matrix of *karmic* causes that result in *karmāśaya* stretch back over countless lifetimes – even to those in animal form – and are being slowly modelled and formulated to account for just one particular life. Vyāsa, commenting on *Yogasūtras* 4:9, gave the example of birth as a cat. He wrote: "The fruition of actions involving birth as a cat, when put in motion by the causes of their manifestation, will take place simultaneously even though they might have taken place after an interval of a hundred births, at a great distance or many eons before, because, although separated from each other, all actions of the same nature involving birth as a cat will be set in motion." [114] So because *karmas* are constantly being built up, they will not ripen fully for a long time. It is as if each individual fills many vessels with the residues of a myriad actions. Only when a vessel is full of the same propensities and characteristics will it brim over into fruitive effect in the life of the individual.

The yogin response

From all that has been said here on the nature of *saṃskāras*, *vāsaṇās*, *karma*, and *karmāśaya*, it is obvious that stilling the mind is not going to prevent the subconscious from presenting images and thoughts to it, nor will it overcome the accumulated impressions of innumerable lifetimes. What, then, can the *yogin* do? How can liberation of the *puruṣa* be secured when an individual carries within the baggage of lifetimes of causes that are continually being formulated into effects?

The *yogin*, too, is subject to subconscious impressions, but through discriminative knowledge and not ignorance, is able to tread a different path from that of ordinary mortals. The *yogin* begins with the five afflictions, the *kleśas*. The effects of the afflictions, the *saṃskāras*, are like seeds that will eventually ripen in the fruits of new actions and new experiences. So as long as the *yogin* refrains from being subject to the afflictions, no reinforcing or new negative and *karmic*-producing *saṃskāras* are generated. Just as roasting seeds destroys their ability to germinate, so discriminative knowledge can rid the *yogin* of involvement with the afflictions and, at the same time, counteract the *saṃskāras* already in the subconscious. The way to do both is to control the way the mind operates – its fluctuations. Constant effort, *abhyāsa*, will be needed to control the mind. Mental activity in the *yogin's* case counteracts the five afflictions and their negative *saṃskāras*, and promotes good actions. *Saṃskāras* are not evil; they can entrench an individual in ignorance or assist on the path of discriminative knowledge. New *saṃskāras* that are acquired by the *yogin* work towards fuller discriminative knowledge. The *yogin* tries to programme the mind so that whatever fluctuations take place, they are of an opposite nature to the afflictions and deposit impressions that rise to the surface consciousness as discriminative knowledge. But even these impressions, while positive, have themselves to be burnt out in the final stages of *samādhi*.

The destruction of the afflictions necessitates the loss of the mind modifications, the *vṛttis*, that impede liberation. So there is a choice: the *saṃskāras* can either be built up as a result of the afflictions or they can be of the nature that builds up discriminative knowledge. It is only this discriminative knowledge that will counteract the impressions that bind the individual to *prakṛti*. It is these positive types of *saṃskāras* that need to be developed by the *yogin*; it is these that will burn up the negative ones like roasted seeds. This is "comparable to a millstone which grinds itself away for lack of grain",[115] or "a culture of antagonistic bacteria which gradually destroy each other".[116] One-pointed concentration prevents the kind of mental activity that creates new *saṃskāras*, and disallows old ones ever becoming manifest.

The *yogin*, then, fills the subconscious – the "lower region" as Dasgupta put it – with positive impressions stemming from truer knowledge and from calmness and stillness of mind. Then, the impressions already in the subconscious will undergo change, and will become weaker when counteracted by the newer ones. If, and when, they rise to the conscious level, they will do so in a form that enhances and not impedes the *yogin's* progress. Needless to say, the process of changing the habitual tendencies of the subconscious mind is a long one, and demands intensity of effort (*abhyāsa*) to keep the mind in control. This is what Yoga is all about. The more advanced the *yogin* becomes the more he is able to acquire the supra-normal powers that will permit perception of the latent impressions that have accumulated in his own previous lives, and this knowledge will help his mastery of them. Through concentration on these subliminal impressions, their nature, as well as the place, time and way in which they were acquired, will be evident to the *yogin*. But through effort, gradually there is less and less in the subconscious to form effects of actions. In promoting a mind that is dispassionate, in ridding the self of desires, aversions and ego-identity, fruitive *karma* is burnt up. "As a wheel set in motion keeps on rotating for some time out of its own inertia, so also the Karma of such a person having started fructifying, gradually becomes attenuated and then vanishes for ever."[117] As to the rest of humankind, we are how our minds work, and it would appear that we are trapped in our own natures, bound by our archetypal tendencies as much as by our present actions rooted in lifetimes of habits. This rather pessimistic view is reflected in Whicher's following words:

> Psychologically, in such a fractured or fragmented state of self-hood (*cittavṛtti*), the network of impressions (*saṃskāras*), habit patterns (*vāsaṇās*), and *vṛtti*-identifications continues to sustain and reinforce a predominantly afflicted human nature. The power of consciousness potentially present to all is forgotten and concealed within this framework or "wheel" (or "whirl") of misidentification and spiritual ignorance. Life is experienced through a repetitive or seemingly unending generation of habit patterns (*vāsaṇās*) rooted in dissatisfaction (*duḥkha*) and affliction (*kleśa*)."[118]

The pessimism here lies in the "repetitive" characteristics that beset human nature, the difficulty in overcoming habitual patterns of behaviour, habitual responses to situations, habitual thoughts, actions, manner of speaking, and *karmic* lives. But it must not be forgotten that Yoga is a soteriological school. It does not suggest that human beings are doomed to be trapped in their own *karmic* personalities for endless lifetimes. Āraṇya makes the pertinent point that: "A storm in the sea is not caused by an individual's Karma but the decision to sail or not to sail in such a storm lies with him alone."[119] Āraṇya's words are indicative that we should not sit back and accept the way we are and what befalls us in life. *Karma* is what we make of it. Yoga accepts that it is essential to strive to overcome the mental forces that bind the Self to perpetuated ignorance of the kind that impedes soteriological progress.

Causality

Like Sāṃkhya, Yoga accepts the theory of *satkāryavāda* – the belief that effects inhere in their causes. All existence is but the effects that inhere in the original primal cause of unmanifest *prakṛti*. It is a relationship that brings about a unity between cause and effects, a unity that is strengthened further by the belief that all effects will eventually dissolve back into the unmanifest *guṇas* from whence they evolved. As to an efficient or instrumental cause of evolution, this must be put down to the proximity of the *puruṣas*, a point that Vyāsa accepted in his commentary on *sūtra* 1:45. But *prakṛti* is clearly the *ultimate* principle, a first cause that is independent of any prior cause. Only its manifest effects are dependent on its unmanifest potential.

The unity of cause and effect, of potentiality and actuality, is never compromised. Potentiality is but a collection of *guṇic* energies that, given the right conditions, will become actualized. Vyāsa gave the example of a farmer who, needing to irrigate a part of his land, simply removes obstacles that prevent water from one area reaching another. Such is the nature of effects in life. In Yoga, it is Īśvara who came to be the one who removed obstacles so that effects could be actualized.

Given the unity of *prakṛti* and the theory of *satkāryavāda* there can be no real difference between a whole and its parts. Thus, the many *buddhis* carrying different *guṇic* combinations that give rise to all the different individuals are really no different from fundamental *prakṛti*. Dasgupta conveyed this point graphically when he wrote: "Just as portions of the ocean are transformed into foam while still the great ocean lies within itself, or just as a tree grows up knot by knot, so this universal pure being as stuff of consciousness contains within itself as inherent in it many buddhis or individual conscious planes which form its part."[120] The unity of unmanifest and manifest *prakṛti*, of cause and its effects, of potentiality and actuality, is the outcome of the theory of *satkāryavāda*. Effects exist *before* they are manifest. As one writer puts it: "At this very moment everything, an infinite number of worlds, that was, is and will be, the unmanifest and the manifest, is in existence, and is held together as causes and effects, within this immense material power."[121] The "immense material power" that is *prakṛti* simply maintains what is subtle and what is gross simultaneously. Vyāsa stated: "Cause can only bring forth to the present what is already in existence; it can never produce what is altogether non-existent. Only a present, i.e. existent cause can bring out an effect in its present perceptible form, it cannot produce anything non-existent."[122]

The *satkāryavāda* theory of causality is critical to the praxis of the Yoga school and its many branches. Just as the ultimate subtle cause of manifest existence causes evolutes to emerge from the subtle to the gross, so the *yogin* reverses the process in practice, refining the mind from attraction to the gross world, to concentration on the subtler stages of *prakṛtic* evolution. Thus, the gross effects in the form of the world are left behind for concentration on the subtle elements (the *tanmātras*) from which they emerge. Then, since the subtle capacities for organs of action and senses (*indriyas*) along with the subtle elements (*tanmātras*) and the mind all evolve from I-ness, the *asmitāmātra*, the *yogin* learns to settle concentration in this pure egoness. Once this is accomplished the mind is no longer subject to the fluctuations stimulated by the outward, gross world: it has transcended gross matter and is still. From there, the *buddhi* – the intellect that holds the key to discerning knowledge of the separation of *puruṣa* and *prakṛti*, knower and knowable, subject and object – will be the highest plane to which the *yogin* can aspire with the exception of liberation itself.

The process of reversal from gross to subtle could not occur if effects were not real transformations of their causes but in a way that made a cause and effect of the same nature, and simultaneously existent in both latent and manifest forms. This is called *pariṇāmavāda*. Whicher notes the same idea in the third chapter of the *Kaṭha Upaniṣad*. He writes: "By understanding spiritual practice as a return to the transcendent origin of being or retracing in consciousness, in reverse order, of the various stages of the evolutionary unfoldment of manifest existence only to arrive at the origin of it all, the *Kaṭha* distinguishes seven levels that comprise the hierarchy of existence."[123] It is exactly the same concept that is to be found in Yogic praxis. However, the ultimate state of liberation transcends all cause and effect and all the by-products of *guṇic* interaction, including unmanifest *prakṛti* itself.

The concept of God

From an examination of the *Yogasūtras* of Patañjali, it would seem that the concept of God, Īśvara, does not play a major role, despite the characteristic theism of the school in general. Indeed, Radhakrishnan wrote very disparagingly of the concept, "we cannot help saying that the Yoga philosophy introduced the conception of God just to be in the fashion and catch the mind of the public".[124] Yoga is a practical rather than a theoretical *darśana*, and God, therefore, serves a practical purpose as an object of *yogic* concentration. But it is also evident that there are other means of concentration than Īśvara, and so it is difficult to claim a major role for the concept of God in Yoga. In fact, as Gaspar Koelman remarks: "It is striking how the mention of the *Iśvara* in the Yoga Sutras is quite casual."[125] Devotion to God is *one* method of Yoga but is not the only one. As Koelman comments, devotion to God serves not the function of submission to, and adoration of him, but only as a focus for single-mindedness – a means to still the fluctuations of the *citta*. And he therefore suggests that the theistic sections of the *Sūtras* could very well be taken out without any detriment to the overall coherence of the teaching.[126]

Yet it would also seem that devotion to God is the best means of concentration.[127] For God is more than an object of concentration, and is the Supreme Lord, Īśvara, that is able to assist in the ridding of obstacles on the path to liberation of his devotee, in particular, the hindrances, the *kleśas*. This, then, renders single-pointed focus on God as rather different from the same kind of focus on any other object, and there was a tendency in later Yoga to emphasize this theistic path. Āraṇya makes this clear:

> Placing one's own mind in the tranquil mind of God is placing self in God and God in self. By thinking that all unavoidable efforts are being done by Him, as it were, one can give up all desires for fruits of action and thus be able to completely surrender all actions to God. Such a devotee considers himself as established in God in all his actions and thus is perfectly at peace and continues his physical existence in a detached manner until his senses stop their functions.[128]

Such words are very much in line with the thought of the *Bhagavadgītā*, and are typical of the later theism. But such thoughts do not feature in the *Yogasūtras* itself. Yet the idea proposed by both Feuerstein[129] and Eliade,[130] that some vision of Īśvara was part of *yogic* mystical experience, and that it is here that the God of Yoga has its origins, is certainly possible.

Focus on the divine, even if it is not pervasive in Yoga, lends the school a definite orthodoxy in its support of *śruti* testimony to a Supreme Being. The school of Yoga, as most Indian schools of philosophy, accepts the existence of minor gods who are fellow travellers in *saṃsāra*, albeit having reached a plane of existence that surpasses, temporarily, the earthly one. But, when their good *karma* – which is what has placed them in a heavenly realm – has been exhausted, then they will return to the *status quo* of life in human form. In contrast, Īśvara transcends such *karmic* existence as the Supreme Self that is purely *sattvic* and that is beyond the world of matter.

There is no sense of Īśvara being an omnipotent creator of the universe. Yoga does not abandon the concept of the evolution of the world from unconscious matter, *prakṛti*, and God remains separate from the world as neither its material nor efficient cause. Īśvara is, like all conscious Selves, also a *puruṣa*, but one that has never been bound in *prakṛti* like all other Selves. As such, Īśvara stands as an inspiration to the *yogin*. Īśvara is thus the Supreme *Puruṣa*, superior to all other *puruṣas* because he has been, and always will be, eternally free from the *kleśas* that cause fruitive *karma*.[131] He is the God of theistic Yoga, the eternal Perfect Being who has omniscience, omnipotence and omnipresence. Therefore, unlike the liberated Selves, God is able to exercise a permanent control over the world of *prakṛti*, directing its course by sheer will. It is he that is the source of the wisdom of the *Veda* and who has imparted that wisdom to the ancient sages, and it is he who is expressed in the mystical syllable of *Aum*. *Aum* became both a symbol of Īśvara and a focus of concentration.

Both Vācaspati Miśra's and Vyāsa's commentaries[132] refer to Īśvara as wholly *sattvic*. This is because Īśvara has the excellence of perfection that is associated with the *sattvic guṇa*. In a way, Vācaspati Miśra tells us, the *sattvic* quality of God is an assumed one for the benefit of the world, rather like an actor who assumes a certain role but always knows his real identity. God's *sattvic* identity is therefore one that is not *prakṛtic* but is merely eternally adopted, and there is no question of this divine Being having any trace of the ignorance of his true nature that would bind him to the world. It is a perception of the divine that gave credence both to Īśvara himself as divine and omnipotent, and to the scriptures, the *śāstras*, of which he came to be known as the source. But Koelman argues that the God of Yoga must have need of the *prakṛtic* world of matter in order for consciousness to function in it. This would necessitate an intellect, mind and ego by which to have such involvement, and by which a recognition of his self as affecting the world can be known. Even though the purely *sattvic* nature of God means there is no element of either *rajas* or *tamas* to cause an imbalance in his perfection, Koelman argues that God must have a *prakṛtic* body in order to exercise guidance, compassion, to impart knowledge, and to communicate with the world.[133] And if God has a body – albeit a subtle, *sattvic* one – he, too, must be dependent on the duality of *puruṣa* supplying consciousness and *prakṛti* reflective analysis and all material characteristics. But, strictly speaking, Īśvara is an addition to the evolutes of *prakṛti* and the other *puruṣas*. He is not fully *puruṣa* nor fully *prakṛti*, but transcends both.

What we have here, then, are many of the characteristics of a theistic divine being, one to whom devotees are able to relate and focus their attention. Yoga is, therefore, basically theistic, and it would be difficult to argue otherwise in view of the clear statements of devotion to God as a means for liberation. But it should be remembered that it was left to Patañjali's commentators to provide the anthropomorphic descriptions of Īśvara by which he became a devotional focus. It is also wise to remember that Yoga is allied with the atheistic system of Sāṃkhya, and that fact in some measure limits an all-out theism. Theistic devotion is *one* means to liberation, as was stated above, but it is by no means the only one. There is no suggestion that *kaivalya* as a goal of isolation of the Self is ever compromised to allow fusion with God or even awareness of God in the liberated state. God is only a *means* by which the *yogin* is aided to final liberation in the functioning world of *prakṛti*, and a supreme example of what the *yogin* can achieve – in short, a model to emulate.

The God of Yoga, then, does not cause the world to be. *Prakṛti* still operates in its cycles of evolution and involution. But Yoga solves at least one problematic area of

Sāṃkhya philosophy. For it sees God as the agent that causes the proximity of *puruṣas* to *prakṛti* that enables the world to evolve. It is also God who dissociates them so that the evolutes of *prakṛti* will break down into their primal unmanifest state. At least this explains why two principles that are unrelated to each other can so affect each other, and it also explains why a process of increasing evolution should suddenly cease and dissolve. The relationship between causes and their effects – that unseen and mysterious power of *adṛṣṭa* that operates to make one, particular effect emerge from a particular cause and no other – is seen as under the power of Īśvara. And this is so, not only of the cosmos itself, but also in relation to the cause–effect principle that governs individual life – *karma*. God, then, is the director of *adṛṣṭa* at all levels, and directs it in favour of the liberation of the Selves. However, theodicy is not a problem for the God of Yoga, for evil is part of *prakṛtic* matter and God is independent of all *prakṛti*.

It is as a focus of meditative devotion, however, that Īśvara is important in this tradition of classical Yoga. For if God is pure *sattva* in his operative sense in the world of matter, then each Self, each *puruṣa*, is more intimately similar to God than to any other object of concentration, whether gross or subtle. The liberated Self, the true Self, is of the same nature of pure consciousness as Īśvara, making God by far the most appropriate object of single-pointed concentration and meditation. Yoga also accepts that God is of service to the *yogin* in aiding his journey, even to the extent of causing a leap in practice on what would normally be a progressive path. God is seen as the *ultimate* Self, the Self at its greatest limits, and as such is the "archetypal yogin".[134] Īśvara is a deity for *yogins* only, and is thus relevant only to one on the *yogic* path. Eliade thus diminishes his status considerably when he states: "All in all, Īśvara is only an archetype of the yogin – a macroyogin; very probably a patron of certain yogic sects."[135] A completely opposite view, however, is posited by Feuerstein, who writes, "any attempt to exorcise this concept would amount to a crippling of both the theoretical superstructure and the practical substructure of Yoga".[136] It has to be said, however, that Īśvara does not feature powerfully in the *Yogasūtras*: it is the commentarial literature that enlarges his image.

Unlike Sāṃkhya, then, Yoga is a theistic tradition, though it will depend considerably on its different branches how far that theism is taken; later tradition, especially, taking a firmer theistic stance. Considering the emphasis on orthodox scripture it is difficult to see how any so-called orthodox school could deny existence to some sort of transcendent divine being, particularly an impersonal Absolute. The God of Yoga comes nowhere near both these and often seems something of an appendage to the tradition. The concept of God in Yoga was sufficiently weak to allow all sorts of speculation concerning his nature and role in the commentarial literature. Somewhat disparagingly, Eliade writes: "Although it was Patañjali who introduced this new and (when all is said and done) perfectly useless element of Īśvara into the dialectics of the Sāṃkhya soteriological doctrine, he does not give Īśvara the significance that late commentators will accord to him."[137]

Liberation

Despite the remote nature of the final goal of Yoga, and the innumerable lifetimes that the Self remains bound by its own involvement with matter, the journey to the final goal is a positive, if arduous, one. It is a journey that sees constant effort to control the mind, and it is the mind that is the locus for the changes necessary to facilitate liberation. This is Yoga's positive message. Whicher's words put this point well: "By locating the cause and functioning of affliction within the mind (*citta*) itself, Yoga asserts that there is a way to overcome misidentification with the modifications (*vṛtti*) of the mind and 'achieve' emancipation from the afflictions that permeate our everyday minds of perception, experience (*bhoga*), and livelihood."[138] The more the *yogin* can remain in *samādhi*, the more ordinary states of knowledge become transcended for the wisdom of true knowledge. And all the time, the subconscious is being fed by the impressions (*saṃskāras*) that occur as a result of this higher knowledge and a still mind.

It is the overcoming of ignorance that brings about liberation, that is to say, the kind of ignorance that results in perpetual cognitions – modifications of the mind – each contributing to the causes that necessitate rebirth. It is also the overcoming of the ignorance that conjoins knower or seer as *puruṣa*, with knowledge or the seen, that is *prakṛti*. The outlet of ignorance in daily existence is expressed in egoistic desires, aversions, and a thirst for life that shuts out death. These are the practical dimensions of misguided knowledge and incorrect perspectives of the nature of the Self and the world of matter. Meditation is the important means to liberation, for through it these afflictions, the *kleśas*, are overcome. Faith (*śraddhā*) is also an important means for those on the path to liberation, for it suggests that belief in the ultimate liberated state must preceed practice. Jacobsen comments: "*Śraddhā* is certitude in the desire for the object of pursuit."[139] However, Eliade points out that it is more likely that faith comes after experience. Thus, it is only by experiencing the results of practice that the *yogin* would have the faith to continue on the path.[140] It is likely that both are right, some degree of faith being necessary to embark on the path, and praxis reinforcing faith through experience.

Yoga facilitates knowledge of the true nature of *prakṛtic* matter. It is a discriminative knowledge that proceeds from the gross to the subtle nature of *prakṛtic* reality. In the process of liberation, the *yogin* becomes adept at perceiving subtle matter and, as was seen above, attempts to transcend from the grosser elements of *prakṛti* to increasingly more subtle ones, *bhūtas* > *tanmātras* > *asmitāmātra* > *buddhi* > *aliṅga* or *avyakta*.[141] Thus, through discipline of the mind the gross elements (*bhutas*) that inform all phenomenal life, and that stimulate ordinary mind functioning, are no longer experienced in their gross forms, but in their subtle forms from which they proceed, the *tanmātras*. No *karmic* effects in the forms of happiness, sorrow or delusion are relevant to the self at this subtle level. But the *yogin* has to transcend even the subtle originators of gross elements. As was seen in the analysis of Sāṃkhya, the *tanmātras*, like the *indriyas* and mind, emerge from the pure ego (*ahaṃkāra*), and the *yogin* needs to be able to focus total concentration on this pure I-ness that precedes the later evolutes. The more the *yogin* is able to concentrate on the subtlest aspects of *prakṛti*, the nearer the goal of realization of pure *puruṣa*. Feuerstein makes the interesting point that the *yogin uses* the Sāṃkhyan layers of reality to progress to subtle states of consciousness.

He writes: "These models are used by the *yogin* to orient himself on his inward odyssey. They are primarily practical *maps* for the process of involution, and secondarily descriptive accounts of the gigantic process of cosmic evolution."[142] It is this subordination of metaphysics to praxis – yet the interdependency of the two – that makes the ethos of Yoga very different from that of Sāṃkhya.

When the *yogin* is able to reach the subtle aspects of I-ness and *buddhi,* this will inevitably involve a preponderance of *sattvic* characteristics in the nature of the *yogin*, though all *guṇic* characteristics are transcended ultimately. The heart is considered the centre of I-ness, and it is by concentration on the "lotus of the heart" – often called the "abode of Brahman" – that the *yogin* is able to experience this pure sense of I-ness that is thoroughly *sattvic* in nature. To reach this kind of level of concentration, detachment (*vairāgya*) from the world is necessary. The ability to be passionless – unperturbed by heat or cold, good or evil and so on – is essential. The result is real freedom from the stimuli of gross phenomena, and from the mental constructions associated with them. The intellect becomes controlled, balanced, and the *guṇas* of *rajas* and *tamas* have been transcended to leave, for a while, pure *sattva.* It is the *sattvic* character of the *buddhi* that facilitates detachment, its other *guṇic* nature being predisposed to attachment to the world. But it will be *supreme* detachment (*paravairāgya*) from any object whatsoever, subtle or gross, that is the highest *samādhi*, *asamprajñāta samādhi.*

In the process of inhibiting the *rajas* and *tamas guṇas*, there is a concomitant inhibition of the subconscious impressions, the *saṃskāras* in favour of *sattvic* impressions that counterbalance the ignorance impelled by the former with discerning knowledge built up by the latter. It is the subliminal impressions that pull the *yogin* back, time and time again, from the highest states of *samādhi.* Only by repeated perseverance can the *yogin* remain longer and longer in the advanced stages until, eventually, they can be achieved at will. There is, then, a counter-balancing process that takes place, rather than a transcending of all *guṇic* activity, even *sattva.* Impressions resulting from a still mind counteract those acquired earlier from the "whirls" of a mind functioning in relation to the gross world. Such a process will obtain until the very brink of liberation when all the *guṇas* are transcended.

To be liberated is to be free of the *guṇas* of *prakṛti*, for it is only the *guṇas* that combine to bring experience of pain, pleasure or stupidity. In whatever combinations they exist in ordinary life – even if predominantly *sattvic* – the less dominant *guṇas* must also be present. So there can never be true happiness, true pleasure, at the gross, phenomenal level of life. But when the *rajas* and *tamas guṇas* are transcended in the move towards the subtlest aspects of *prakṛtic* matter, pure *sattvic* experience is possible. What this process does, is to destroy the afflictions, the *kleśas*, that perpetuate *guṇic* activity in the mind, thus inhibiting *karma.* In the pure *sattvic* state of the mind, a particular balance between the *sattva* of the *buddhi* and *puruṣa* occurs. It is this that is the impetus for liberation, as *sūtra* 3:55 tells us: "When Equality is Established Between Buddhi-Sattva And Puruṣa In Their Purity, Liberation Takes Place."[143] Vyāsa's comment on this *sūtra* reads thus: "When Buddhi-sattva being freed of all Rajas and Tamas impurities, is occupied with only discriminative discernment of Puruṣa and thus comes to acquire the state where seeds of afflictions become roasted, then it becomes like Puruṣa on account of its purity."[144] Here, discriminative knowledge prevents any further misidentification whatsoever. The afflictions, the *kleśas*, are burnt up like roasted seeds, the *guṇas* and the knowledge they represent are no longer presented to the knower, *puruṣa.* As Vyāsa put it, "Puruṣa shining in His own light becomes free from dross and all contacts".[145] While the *yogin* comes to know that the discriminative knowledge necessary for liberation is a characteristic of the *sattvic buddhi*, it also has to be realized that the *sattvic buddhi* is itself an object that is separate from *puruṣa*. The experience of *buddhisattva* is a desirable and blissful one, but it is *guṇic* and, until the *guṇas* recede into their causal state, separate from *puruṣa*, liberation cannot be complete.

The liberated *yogin* is sometimes termed a *muktakusāla*. He has no "I". His actions do not belong to him any more than worldly objects or people. The *puruṣa* that he is remains separate from all *prakṛtic* existence. What can be known is no longer of relevance to the liberated *puruṣa*: it no longer needs knowledge of the world, and it no longer wants involvement with *prakṛti*. Complete annihilation of the subconscious impressions, the *saṃskāras*, has occurred, so there is no fruitive *karma* remaining. Any *karmic* forces already in motion have been prevented. There is nothing left of the *guṇic*, empirical self; it has been absorbed back into unmanifest *prakṛti*, leaving the *puruṣa* alone. "At the peak of the ultra-cognitive enstasy, the *yogin's* individual cosmos comes to a standstill."[146] But *prakṛti* only ceases to be for the single *puruṣa*, whose objective *prakṛtic* constituents have dissolved into their unmanifest cause. For all other bound *puruṣas prakṛti* continues – and will eternally do so. Just one tiny fraction of *prakṛti* ceases to be in its manifest form. The Self that never really was bound, that never really changed, is now free. Feuerstein puts this well:

> Throughout the ups and downs in the life of the *yogin*, no change took place on the level of the Self. What seems like an unsurpassed achievement from the perspective of the finite consciousness, is an absolute non-event from the Self's viewpoint. For, the Self is by definition free, autonomous, sheer awareness and quite unaffected by any loss of identity or by any form of limitation.[147]

Usually, Patañjali's Yoga is associated with the goal of world denial. That is to say, the ultimate goal of Yoga as the thorough separation of *puruṣa* and *prakṛti* is suggestive of the need to transcend the gross physical world – even the subtle aspects of *prakṛti* – leading eventually to a total divorce from matter. Indeed, this is especially so when it is remembered that Sāṃkhya dualism is normally considered to underpin the *Yogasūtras* of Patañjali. This would present no problem, except for one significant factor – the acceptance of *jīvanmukti* by the Yoga schools. The acceptance of a *jīvanmukta*, one who has become liberated while still alive, still having a physical body, is hardly consonant with the total divorce from matter that liberation posits. And yet, since the Yoga *darśana* is a practically orientated school, it sets out a clear journey for the would-be *yogin* – a journey that does not end in some unknown state after death, but one by which the full dimension of the word "*yogin*" is commensurate with total liberation *in life*. India, indeed, rarely denies that there are enlightened living beings, and such beings are essential to the path of Yoga, where *gurus* are the medium by which others, too, may journey on the same path to the same end.

Feuerstein claims that the idea of *jīvanmukti* is not evident in the *Yogasūtras*, and that Vyāsa as the major commentator and an outsider to the school, imposed this alien concept on Patañjali's thought. Feuerstein writes, "whenever a liberated person takes on a body again, either composed of gross or subtle matter, he is no longer residing in freedom, but is again subject to the laws governing the machinery of the universe".[148] Feuerstein's deduction is sensible, and is suggestive that the Yoga adept stops short of the complete release from *prakṛti* while alive. If not, and the concept of *jīvanmukti* is accepted, then the radical dualism of Sāṃkhya cannot be the basis and aim of Yoga praxis. But to deny *jīvanmukti* to India's *yogins* runs counter to the, now established, tradition of the school.

My own inclination here is to maintain the strict duality of *puruṣa* and *prakṛti*, and to lay the concept of *jīvanmukti* at the feet of tradition – much as Feuerstein suggests. But a reverse side of the argument is put forward by Ian Whicher, who qualifies the radical dualism normally taken to underpin Yoga, by what he terms the "responsible engagement" of spirit (*puruṣa*) with matter (*prakṛti*) in the liberated, yet embodied, state.[149] This means that, far from denying worldly involvement, the liberated *yogin* turns *to* the world in altruistic, moral engagement. Whicher accepts what he calls a "sattvification" of the mind, through positive modifications of it – in other words, a process of refining the mind away from the *kleśas* towards a more *sattvic* nature. Whicher's thesis makes sense when it is remembered that it is the *sattvic* nature of the *buddhi* that permits the discriminative knowledge of the different natures of *puruṣa* and *prakṛti* that is penultimate to liberation – a point well in line with Patañjali's thought.[150]

But Whicher does not accept that suppression or restraint of the mind – let alone annihilation of the mind – are true interpretations of Yoga. He prefers to view the goal of Yoga as control over the *vṛttis* of the mind, not a complete annihilation of them. His view is that the mind of the *yogin* is not dissolved into the unmanifest state of *prakṛti* at the point of liberation. Only the *karmically* binding *vṛttis* are dissolved.[151] He is against what he calls "an anaesthetization of human consciousness"[152] at liberation in favour of "a state of utter lucidity or transparency of consciousness (mind) wherein no epistemological distortion can take place, yet *vṛttis* (e.g., valid cognition, memory, etc.) can still arise, can still function".[153] It is the misapprehensions that the mind carries that have to be negated, not the mind itself.[154] So according to Whicher, *nirodha* is not the cessation of all the *vṛttis* of the mind. It is the cessation of the "empirical limitations", "restrictions", "suppressions" in the mind, and "the removal of the *kleśas* and karmic barriers only to reveal the full-blown nature of *puruṣa*".[155] This means not aloneness in the sense of total separation of the *puruṣa* from *prakṛti*, but a *jīvanmukta* that can operate in the world. Whicher writes:

> The yogin therefore is not a mindless, inactive being. Rather, the mind has become an instrument of consciousness under the yogin's direction. The modifications of the mind may continue in day-to-day life but they no longer enslave the yogin, no longer divert the yogin's attention away from authentic identity. . . . [The yogin] can use the body and mind out of benevolence and compassion for the spiritual benefit of others.[156]

Here is an attractive view of the liberated state, one transcending by far the Sāṃkhya view of the total isolation and aloneness of each *puruṣa*. And it permits altruistic interaction with the world, counteracting the view of writers such as Radhakrishnan, who claimed that Yoga is an unethical system.[157] According to Whicher, "cessation results in our consciousness remaining unbound, nonenslaved, and transparent to things of a worldly nature while yet being thoroughly engaged in practical life".[158] Whicher's theory is that *prakṛti* goes on, but the liberated *puruṣa* simply observes, unaffected by the *guṇic* changes and the *vṛttis* of the mind. Thus, there is a *harmony* between *puruṣa* and *prakṛti* and not a separation of the two, and this is a harmony that permits world involvement. Whicher writes: "The yogin does not become a 'mind-less' (or 'body-less') being. Rather, the yogin is left with a transformed, fully sattvified mind, that, due to its transparent nature, can function in the form of nonbinding *vṛttis* – whether of a cognitive or affective/emotive nature – thoughts, ideas, intentions, and so forth."[159]

How far such an integrated *puruṣa* and *prakṛti* are possible in the liberated state is something of a problem. This is especially so for a school that accepts *kaivalya*, aloneness, of the liberated *puruṣa*, is fundamentally dualistic, and which upholds what seems to be a goal of cessation of all mind activity (*cittavṛttinirodha*). What Whicher proposes is a kind of qualified dualism that sees spirit and matter operating together, providing the former misidentification of the two has been annihilated. The idea that the *yogin* can participate fully in the world without ego, seeing and experiencing the world of matter but detached from it, is not unlike the *karmayoga* of the *Bhagavadgītā*. Here, such a unity of spirit and matter is also possible, providing there is no egoistic attachment of the former to the latter. But it is doubtful whether Patañjali had this conception of the liberated *yogin* in mind, even if tradition has overlaid his perception with a more attractive picture of a liberated *yogin* with emotions, feelings and thoughts, "vital, creative, thoughtful, empathetic, balanced, happy, and wise".[160] It must be remembered, too, that there is much in the nature of Yoga that advocates withdrawal from the world of matter while on the long path to the final goal. As Eliade notes, the liberated *yogin* has achieved the final goal through techniques that are deliberately "antisocial" and "antihuman".[161] He considers Yoga to be an opposition to life,[162] not an altruistic engagement in it. It is unlikely that the goal would reverse the trends to be found in praxis. And as Feuerstein points out, once liberation takes place, "the *yogin* in fact ceases to exist as a human being. His body may live on for a period of time, though in a state of catalepsy, and before long goes the way of all finite things".[163] Thus, attractive as Whicher's thesis is, my own view is that Patañjal's *cittavṛttinirodha* referred to a *complete* cessation of all mind activity – a separation of mind from spirit after death.[164]

What Whicher depicts as the liberated *yogin* is more akin to what are termed *prakṛtilīnas*. These are almost-liberated beings who achieve a lower form of *asaṃprajñāta*. This is called *prakṛtilaya*. It is the dissolution of the *prakṛtic* self into its causative state – the ultimate, unmanifest *prakṛti*. Those *yogins* who achieve such a state are at first beyond ordinary existence and ordinary worlds, living outside space and time in a state of subtlety unknown to normal experience. But while the *buddhi* is dissolved into its pre-existent state of unmanifest *prakṛti*, no concomitant discrimination between *prakṛti* and *puruṣa* has occurred. There is a detachment, *vairāgya*, from manifest *prakṛti*, but this lacks the supreme detachment (*paravairāgya*) for *puruṣa* from all forms of *prakṛti*. However, while reincarnation is suspended for the *yogin* who achieves the *prakṛtilaya* state, it is only temporarily so. While the released *prakṛtilīna* exist beyond the subtlest of realms, beyond the gods, they will eventually be reborn, for they are, ultimately, still *prakṛtic* matter. They will, in the words of Jacobsen, "like cosmic matter, which is eternally pulsating back and forth between manifestation and non-manifestation, have to become manifest again in material individual bodies".[165] On their return to worldly existence, they would presumably be in an advanced state of consciousness and able to take up an altruistic involvement in human life.

But is there just one, universal *puruṣa*, or are there a plurality of them? Feuerstein points out that "qualitatively there is no difference between the Selves (*puruṣas*) and the one Self (*ātman*) of Śaṅkara".[166] Some suggest that Patañjali did not advocate a plurality of *puruṣas*,[167] but if this were the case, then it is surprising that Patañjali did not make more of what was to be a Supreme Self, or even to project Īśvara to this end. But, to cite the Sāṃkhya argument, positing a single *Puruṣa* would not explain the differences in experiences of multiple Selves. Nor would Whicher's view of liberated Selves being active in the world be tenable. For if there were just one Self – albeit free of matter and in control of mind fluctuations – there could be no difference between one liberated *yogin* and another: they would have the same mind functioning, the same feelings and the same thoughts.

How, then should Patañjali be assessed? Is his work merely a contrived patchwork of bits and pieces from earlier sources as some suggest?[168] And if so, does this diminish his achievement? Berry claims that, "the work of Patañjali deserves all the praise lavished on it, for it is in truth one of the masterworks of the spiritual history of man".[169] Perhaps the truth lies somewhere in between these two extremes. Certainly, as Berry also points out concerning Patañjali's work: "It is so universal in its basic outline that it has proved wonderfully adaptable to the various religious movements in India throughout the centuries that have found spiritual support in the Yoga tradition."[170] For the most part, it must be said that Patañjali's contribution to Yoga is inestimable. Eliade rightly claims: "Patañjali's *Yoga-sūtras* are the result of an enormous effort not only to bring together and classify a series of ascetic practices and contemplative formulas that India had known from time immemorial, but also to validate them from a theoretical point of view by establishing their bases, justifying them, and incorporating them into a philosophy."[171]

It is to Patañjali's credit that Yoga is a living tradition that is still handed down by the great (and not so great) *gurus*. While Sāṃkhya had critics sufficient to make it obsolete as a system of practised belief, Yoga has never suffered from this. The fact that it is a word understood – admittedly not as it should be – by those westerners far removed from knowledge of Indian history or philosophy, shows how far Yoga has spread its influence in time and location. And whatever the philosophical tenets held by Indians, they accord the utmost respect to the *yogins* of the Indian culture. These *yogins* have climbed to the summit of Reality and have left behind the foothills of ignorance. Others may find different paths to the summit, but it is still the *yogins* who are living examples of the fact that such ultimate Reality is realizable in mortal state.

In contrast to Sāṃkhya, Patañjali's Yoga is "essentially psychological, warm and dynamic".[172] And there is an ethos to Yoga that counterbalances the turmoil of life. Radhakrishnan put this well:

> We discern in the Yoga those cardinal conceptions of Hindu thought, such as the supremacy of the psychic over the physical, the exaltation of silence and solitude, meditation and ecstasy, and the indifference to outer conditions, which make the traditional Hindu attitude to life appear so strange and fantastic to the modern mind. It is, however, conceded, by many who are acquainted with it, that it is a necessary corrective to our present mentality, overburdened with external things and estranged from the true life of spirit by humdrum toil, material greed and sensual excitement.[173]

The fact that forms of Yoga are becoming so popular in the western world is indicative of the strength Yoga contains to offer a variety of paths to searching souls in modern life.

8
Advaita Vedānta

Background to the school

Advaita Vedānta is a school that has been, and still is, of considerable influence. While it has had many expressions, it still obtains in one form or another in the monastic traditions of Hinduism and has absorbed numerous lay followers. Two fundamental questions pervade its philosophical inquiry, *What is the relation between the Absolute Brahman and the self?* And *What is the relation between the Absolute Brahman and the world?* It is the nuances of responses to these questions that serve to distinguish the various branches of Vedānta schools in general, and that have given rise to a prolific amount of philosophical literature within the various strands of Vedānta, both original in content and as commentaries on the works of others.

The schools of Vedānta, as the name suggests, are based heavily on the literature of the end of the *Vedic* period – the *Upaniṣads*. They are, thus, schools that break rather sharply from the older tradition of the Pūrva Mīmāṃsa, whose main emphasis was on the ritualistic portions, the *karmakaṇḍa*, of the earlier (*pūrva*) *Veda*, and which had, therefore, a tendency to exclude *Upaniṣadic* philosophy. The Vedānta schools are sometimes referred to as *Uttara* Mīmāṃsā, because they were occupied mainly with the latter (*uttara*) part of the *Veda*, the *Vedānta*, or end of the *Veda* and, therefore, with the knowledge portion, or *jñānakaṇḍa*.[1] This makes Advaita Vedānta, as well as other branches of Vedānta, different from the older Pūrva Mīmāṃsā. While there are some links, there is not a neat development from one to another, and very little in basic concepts to connect the two. But all of the Mīmāṃsā philosophers were exegetes, analysing, interpreting and commenting on the *Veda*.

One of the most important proponents of the Vedānta tradition was Śaṃkara, and the teachings related to him have witnessed centuries of impact. The *Upaniṣads*, as we know, put forward a thoroughly (if somewhat inconsistently) articulated concept of a transcendent Absolute as Brahman, and how Brahman might be known. It is these facts that make Śaṃkara's Advaita Vedānta essentially a path of knowledge – a knowledge that reveals ultimate consciousness and Reality. It is a search for the true Self, like the *Upaniṣads*, and came to be viewed by its proponents as the superior path to that of ritual action in the performance of religious duty. As a non-dualist, Śaṃkara believed that both ritual and knowledge portions of the *Veda* were aimed at different people. There was nothing in the *karmakaṇḍa* to suggest that it would bring someone to liberation, though it could prepare a person for the kind of moral restraint that underpinned the path of knowledge, and could be effected for the purpose of specific results. But, as far as Śaṃkara was concerned, no action could bring about liberation, only knowledge. Therefore, the actions of the *karmakaṇḍa* were bound to be seen by Śaṃkara as inferior to the *jñānakaṇḍa*.

Because Brahman is the centre of inquiry of the knowledge portion of the *Veda*, it is the schools of Vedānta that provide the most developed concepts of the divine of all the *darśanas*, and Śaṃkara's Advaita is no exception. Unlike the non-Vedānta schools, in basing its teachings very firmly on the content of the *Upaniṣads*, all strands of Vedānta rely on the same, traditional, foundational material, concentrating on the nature of Brahman and the Self. All Vedānta schools are based on three major sources, the *Upaniṣads*, the *Brahmasūtras* and the *Bhagavadgītā*. There was no need for Śaṃkara to gather together the respective strands of philosophical thought about the path of knowledge to provide the basis of his teachings, for the material was already in place. Some systematization and elaboration of ideas occurred, but it was not the aim of Śaṃkara to depart from what was revealed Truth. He believed, however, that those texts that dealt with the identity of Brahman and *Ātman* were superior to all others in the *Upaniṣads*.

Yet, as we shall see, the complexities of those two fundamental questions of the relation of Brahman to the self on the one hand, and to the world on the other, inevitably required differences in perspectives. Some Vedānta schools are absolutist. That is to say the underlying philosophy is based on the acosmic Brahman of the *Upaniṣads*. Others are theistic, resting their cases on the *Upaniṣadic* cosmic Brahman as a describable God. These differences are well exemplified in the major branches of Vedānta with the proponents of Śaṃkara, Rāmānuja and Madhva, to name only a few. This chapter, however, is concerned more specifically with *advaita* Vedānta, that is to say with the strictly non-dual approach to these two questions. In this approach Śaṃkara aimed to refute the doctrines of the other schools, which he felt had no support in the *Upaniṣads*. At the same time, of course, he had to demonstrate that his own interpretations were correct – and that often meant dealing with some very inconsistent material in the *Upaniṣads* themselves. A primary aim was to interpret the *Upaniṣads* as a single and coherent philosophy concerning Brahman. Four statements from the *Upaniṣads* informed Śaṃkara's views:

- Brahman is Consciousness, *prajñanam Brahma* (*Aitareya Upaniṣad* 3:5:3)
- I am Brahman, *aham Brahmāsmi* (*Bṛhadāraṇyaka Upaniṣad* 1:4:10)
- That you are, *Tat tvam asi* (*Chāndogya Upaniṣad* 6:8:7)
- This Ātman is Brahman, *ayam Ātmā Brahma* (*Bṛhadāraṇyaka Upaniṣad* 2:5:19).

Śaṃkara was not, however, the first to adopt the aim of demonstrating the consistent nature of *Upaniṣadic* thought. A systematization of the philosophical teachings of the *Upaniṣads* was undertaken by Bādarāyaṇa in his *Brahmasūtras*,[2] and many commentaries, *bhāsyas*, on it were undertaken, as well as sub-commentaries and independent treatises. When exactly Bādarāyaṇa compiled the *Brahmasūtras* is unclear,[3] though its refutation of most other Indian philosophy suggests that the last few centuries BCE is a possible date.[4]

As its name suggests, the *Brahmasūtras* was primarily concerned with Brahman, but was also concerned with the human endeavour to break free from the bondage of the world and the process of reincarnation. However, it seems that Bādarāyaṇa was probably a dualist rather than a non-dualist and, as Dasgupta has pointed out, many of those who used the *Brahmasūtras* to fuel their own commentaries were also dualists.[5] The exceptions are Śaṃkara and Gauḍapāda – of whom, more below. Dasgupta considered that the dualism that emerged in the later *Upaniṣads* came to be the more attractive course of thought, and that the rather loosely worked out monism of the *Upaniṣads* was somewhat put to one side. The dualism that is so rife in the other schools seems to support this view. But what we find in the traditions of Advaita Vedānta, is a return to the traditional monism of the *Upaniṣads*. Apart from commentaries on the *Brahmasūtras*, proponents of the different schools of Vedānta also wrote commentaries on a number of *Upaniṣads* and on the *Bhagavadgītā*. The literature of Vedānta is, thus, considerably vast.[6]

Main proponents and commentators

The names predominantly associated with the schools of Vedānta are those of Śaṃkara, Rāmānuja, and Madhva, each of whom is the major proponent of a particular school, but there are other significant contributors to this tradition who belong to other schools. In this chapter, and the two that follow, however, I intend to confine this examination of Vedānta to these three proponents, whose theories are known as non-dualism, qualified monism and dualism, respectively – a wide enough spectrum of philosophical analysis of reality to illustrate the broad remit of Vedānta. Śaṃkara, then, was the great proponent and traditional founder of the school of Advaita Vedānta. His name is frequently found suffixed with *ācārya*, "great spiritual teacher". Although the thinker mostly associated with Advaita Vedānta, there were several others of like-minded thought that preceded him.[7] Indeed, as Potter points out, Śaṃkara not only refers to his tradition, but cites earlier thinkers within it,[8] though there is little trace of an Advaitin tradition before the time of the *Brahmasūtras*.[9] While Śaṃkara's dates have been traditionally accepted as 788–820, some modern views are inclined towards a longer life for Śaṃkara and an earlier dating of about 700–750.[10]

One earlier proponent who is worthy of mention as the significant precursor of Śaṃkara, is Gauḍapāda. He may just have been a contemporary of Śaṃkara in that Śaṃkara's own teacher, Govinda, is said to have been a pupil of Gauḍapāda.[11] Certainly, Śaṃkara admits his debt to this great teacher. The debt of many commentators to Bādarāyaṇa was considerable but, as has been seen, he was probably more of a dualist than a non-dualist, and it is to Gauḍapāda that Śaṃkara owes the foundations of a developed emphasis on the non-dual thought of the *Upaniṣads*.

It was Gauḍapāda, in fact, who was responsible for the earliest known exposition of *advaita*, or "non-dualism", in his *Gauḍapādakārikā*. This was a commentary on the *Māṇḍūkya Upaniṣad*. So much of his teaching pre-empts that of Śaṃkara that it is clear his influence on the latter was considerable. Gauḍapāda taught of four phases of the self, the self that is awake, the dream-state of the self in sleep, the self in deep sleep, and the truly liberated Self. He also dealt at some length in the *Gauḍapādakārikā* with the world as illusion, as unreal, or *māyā*. It is a world incorrectly imposed on the consciousness of the true Self, the *ātman*. Then, too, Gauḍapāda taught that all the apparent dualities of the world and all the apparent multiple selves are really one, like the temporarily confined space in a jar that is the same as the space outside it. Reality exists solely as *vijñāna*, pure Consciousness and, just as a revolving firebrand *seems* to create a complete circular image, so the perceptions of the world reflected in the reality of pure Consciousness *seem* to make the plurality of the world real. Many of these ideas were to be taken up by Śaṃkara.

In Gauḍapāda's view, all perception is subject to a beginning and an end and is therefore insubstantial; it cannot really exist, and is but the creation of the mind. The ordinary self as different from all others and the perceiver of diverse things in the world is a misconception. When one goes beyond such apparent diversity and imaginary appearances of life then the unified pure Consciousness is what remains. So all the distinctions we make in life are falsely superimposed on this pure Consciousness, rather like our experience of dreams when we sleep. It is like a magic show, the real identity of the magician all the time being present, though the magician is, at the same time, the perpetrator of all the unreal aspects of the magical manifestations. Needless to say, being unattached to this world of unreality and apparent diversity was the means suggested to overcome *māyā* and realize the liberated state. Unlike the self that is in the waking state, or the self when dreaming or in deepest sleep, the true Self of pure Consciousness is indescribable – beyond all possible conception – except to say that it is essence in itself, it is one, and non-dual. Again, these were views accepted by Śaṃkara.

The ordinary self for Gauḍapāda, then, as it is for Śaṃkara, is an imaginary one; it isn't born, it doesn't suffer, and it doesn't die. It cannot do any of these things because it is *really* only Consciousness without perception. But by imagination, by illusion, the ordinary self seems to exist and seems to be involved in the world of diverse forms and plural selves. The Self of pure Consciousness is the only real Self. It is the *Ātman*: it is knower and known all in one without the normal distinction between the two.

As far as causation is concerned, Gauḍapada's views endorsed his perspective of the world as unreal. For if a cause–effect principle were to operate in the world then all effects must be the result of causes and all causes themselves must have causes, otherwise something can come forth from nothing. In this case, one would have to search for an ultimate cause *ad infinitum*. But, if there is an original cause that is itself unproduced, and that is not the effect of anything else, then it cannot itself produce an effect, otherwise it would be a cause, and causes must have causes. What is real, then, is real *in itself*, it is neither cause nor effect, but is beyond such dualities. This makes the world of effects only illusory – a world of apparent effects. It was to these fundamental views that Śaṃkara was indebted for his own articulation of the non-dual perspectives of reality.

According to tradition, Śaṃkara was a *Brahmin* and was born in southern India. He became a *saṃnyāsin* at an early age, and a disciple of Govinda. In his mature life, he is said to have been the founder of four *maṭhas* or monasteries, having been a prolific traveller.[12] His commentaries seem to suggest that Śaṃkara was a worshipper of Viṣṇu,[13] in the form of Nārāyana. This is a term for Viṣṇu that contains the word for human, *nāra*, and is indicative of the manifestation of the divine in the human – a concept close to Śaṃkara's thought, if only from the lower level of reality of the phenomenal world, as we shall see. Other traditions see him in the Śaiva religion, though there is nothing in his writings to connect him with the worship of Śiva. Those works that do connect him with Śiva are doubtfully authentic.[14] But, while not strictly atheist,[15] he was primarily non-theistic: his beliefs were rooted in one ultimate Reality of Brahman, a Reality so ultimate that it denied, as did Gauḍapāda, the world as we know it.

Śaṃkara was a prolific commentator, though there are many works attributed to him that are not authentically his. The *Upadeśasāhasrī*, the *Thousand Teachings* of Śaṃkara, is authentic, and is one of the few works that is not a commentary. The foundational commentary for Advaita Vedānta is his *Brahmasūtrabhāṣya*, his commentary on Bādarāyaṇa's *Brahmasūtras*. This, the most important of his works, has been described as "the single most influential philosophical text in India today, a status it has enjoyed for at least a century, possibly much longer".[16] Another writer believes it is a work that "is as remarkable for the charm of its style as for the logical consistency of its arguments".[17] Śaṃkara wrote a commentary on the *Gauḍapādakārikā*, and a notable commentary on the *Bhagavadgītā*. But he also wrote commentaries on many major *Upaniṣads*, and his theology and philosophy were, thus, particularly well related to *śruti* literature. The emphasis on the theological nature of Śaṃkara's religious career, as well as a number of his qualities, are depicted very well by Mayeda:

> Penetrating insight, analytical skill, and lucid style characterize Śaṅkara's works. He cannot be called a particularly original philosopher . . . but it has to be remembered that in India it is not originality but fidelity to tradition which is the great virtue. He was an excellent exegete, with an approach to truth which was psychological and religious rather than philosophical. . . . He was really not so much a philosopher as a pre-eminent religious leader and a most successful religious teacher.[18]

Of the many pupils that wrote commentaries on Śaṃkara's works, two stand out in particular. These are Padmapāda and Sureśvara. A notable later Advaitin was Maṇdana Miśra. Later Advaita became somewhat splintered in its views.

While the commentary on the *Brahmasūtras* is his most outstanding work, Śaṃkara's own views departed considerably from the views held there. If the *Brahmasūtras* are in any way monist, it is a limited monism that incorporates the theory of *bhedābheda* to explain the relationship between the divine and the world. This theory points to identity-in-difference, literally difference-and-non-difference. That is, the self and the world are monistically identifiable as Brahman, but seen as different from the divine in view of their many parts. The theory attempts to combine the two views of the *Upaniṣads*, one suggesting that Brahman and *ātman* are identical, and the other that they are dual and, therefore, different. Śaṃkara, too, attempts to unite these two perspectives but his views are very different from Bādarāyaṇa's as we shall see, and are closer to Gauḍapāda's. Despite being orientated towards the *Upaniṣads* themselves, and being deeply loyal to the *śruti* tradition of *Vedānta*, Śaṃkara, and certainly Gauḍapāda, may have been influenced by Buddhist thought and dialectic. There are strong similarities between Madhyamaka theories of *śunyata*, "emptiness", and some of Śaṃkara's thought. However, the differences are fundamental, and it is the differences that reveal his loyalty to *śruti* tradition.

But there is little to suggest that his views were original. He was not an innovator. As Das remarks: "For Advaitism truth has been already found and recorded in the Upanishads. What is left for Advaitic philosophy to do is to defend this truth against hostile criticisms and make it generally acceptable to our understanding by removing from our mind all doubts about it."[19] Śaṃkara was thus a prolific critic of the views of other schools – both unorthodox and orthodox – especially of orthodox schools that he felt fell short of a correct interpretation of *śruti* literature.[20] But despite such emphasis on correct interpretation much of his terminology is "recklessly used" to quote one author.[21] This is a factor that is not without its problems in analysing his views. Nevertheless, while he has had many critics, Śaṃkara was a remarkable philosopher, all the more so if his life were really so brief.

General features of the school

The non-dualism of Śaṃkara, and the qualified non-dualism of Rāmānuja, reject the atomic view of reality of the world put forward by the Nyāya-Vaiśeṣika schools. They also reject the dualistic division of the world by Sāṃkhya into a plurality of conscious Selves, and a unified and real world of matter. Both Śaṃkara and Rāmānuja believed that unconscious matter cannot evolve in such a way as to produce the supposed world. Ultimate Reality for both is Brahman, and this is the only single reality. The word "single" here is difficult. It suggests monism, the reduction of all in the universe – divine and worldly – to one principle. This is possible in the case of Rāmānuja, but in that of Śaṃkara, the principle of strict *advaita* is beyond all duality, and beyond even the concept of one. Yet, in that Śaṃkara accepted some single *identity* of all things in the essence or *Ātman* of pure Being, it might be claimed that his thought is pure monism. Certainly, he eschewed all sense of duality between subject and object, and between Self and divine. In a way, this reduces all to one essence, and is monistic. But in other ways, "one" is dual to two or many, and Śaṃkara, being true to *Upaniṣadic* thought, takes the principle of Reality beyond any definition. In this sense his non-duality is absolute (*kevala advaita*).

Śaṃkara was particularly critical of the Sāṃkhya idea that unconscious matter could produce interdependent evolutes neatly mapped out in a progressive evolution. He was equally critical of the idea that this unconscious material could in any way serve the purpose of the passive Selves that were trapped in it. Some conscious principle to guide such events would have to be posited for the Sāṃkhya theory to make sense. Nothing unconscious can be consciously purposeful.[22] The same can be said of the Vaiśeṣika theory of unconscious atoms all binding together in a logical way to produce the phenomenal world: a conscious motivator and guide for such combinations is necessary. To the Advaitin, the unseen, and again unconscious, force of *adṛṣṭa* cannot be the means of such effective combination. In both Sāṃkhya and Vaiśeṣika there is the need of an efficient cause to control the pattern of evolution and phenomenal creation as much as to cause its breakdown and dissolution. Śaṃkara's view of ultimate Reality and the world had to take into account these illogical presumptions of opposing schools. His solution, as that of Gauḍapāda, was to deny any reality to the world in any ultimate sense.

Śaṃkara, as noted above, drew his theories from the *Upaniṣads*. He sought to unite their somewhat disparate teachings into a cohesive whole that was comprised of what might be called core teaching of the identification of Brahman and *Ātman*, and provisional or supportive teaching, that spoke of the world from the viewpoint of the unenlightened. His aim in doing this was, like all the other orthodox schools, to find the means of liberation from suffering and reincarnation. It is this division of *Upaniṣadic* thought into two kinds; core teaching related to ultimate Reality and the acosmic Brahman, and supportive teaching to the lower reality of a cosmic Brahman – that is the key to the understanding of Śaṃkara's theories. It is a dual view of things, the enlightened one, and the unenlightened one. And this dual perspective of things underpins Śaṃkara's views of knowledge, the self, the world, causality and the divine. Since there are few who could perceive things from the enlightened level, he is forced to give much space to the unenlightened one. He has to teach *as if* the world is real, *as if* cause–effect exist, *as if* there is a self that is bound and transmigrates, *as if* there is a describable God. Ultimately, none of these obtains, but Śaṃkara cleverly applies the theory to the *śruti* texts themselves, which, to him, also contain supportive material that speaks *as if* dualities exist. This dual perspective of reality, then, needs to be kept in mind in the pages that follow.

Reality: the Advaita view of the world

Behind all the apparent plurality of the universe, Śaṃkara believed there was an underlying Reality. This we can call *Existence*, *Being*, *sat*, or Brahman. It is the common substratum or essence that runs through all things as *Ātman*,[23] but all such things are only an apparent, and not real, modification of it. Everything that we see, therefore, is *really* this same essence, which is the material cause of all we think we see. Chatterjee and Datta put this succinctly in the following words:

> Existence is thus found to be the one undeniable reality persisting through all states, internal and external. It can, therefore, be accepted as *the* substance, and material cause of which all determinate objects and mental states are the diverse manifestations.
>
> We find then that pure existence which is the common cause of the entire world is itself formless, though appearing in many forms; partless, though divisible into different forms; it is infinite, though it appears in all finite forms.[24]

The formless, infinite and indivisible essence that is Brahman remains despite all the seeming modifications of it. It is, therefore, a greater level of reality – indeed, the only Reality. In the *Bṛhadāraṇyaka Upaniṣad* 1:4:10 we find the words "I am Brahman", on which, Śaṃkara says of Brahman: "I am all, always pure, enlightened and unfettered, unborn, all-pervading, undecaying, immortal, and imperishable."[25] Brahman is an underlying and permanent essence, but not, like the Sāṃkhya or Nyāyā-Vaiśeṣika theories, an unconscious cause. For Śaṃkara, as Gauḍapāda, this pure Existence, pure Being, was self-illuminating Consciousness, a Consciousness that illuminates and reveals itself as just that. Existence, then, is both Reality and pure Consciousness. For anything to be "known" we have to assume that there is a reality that makes that knowledge possible. For Śaṃkara, reality is not the modification of reality but the Reality itself. It is not the clay pot, but the "clayness" that informs the pot that is real: the clay seems to have different forms, but its reality of clayness stays the same. Similarly, Existence or pure Being *seems* to become diverse, but it is the ultimate Reality of all things, the "things" only being of an apparent reality. Thus, "I" as a perceiver am really pure Consciousness, and "that" which I perceive is also pure Consciousness. Thus "I" and "that" are really the same, and cannot be said to exist apart from that essence of sameness, in any real or ultimate sense. The Reality of "me" and the Reality of the world are both the same, and this Reality is identified as Brahman. Thus the non-dualism of all things is established.

Reality, then, is something that *is*, that *exists* throughout all existence: it pervades, and persists in, all things. It is pure Subject, pure Consciousness, devoid of objects. In Śaṃkara's words: "As I am devoid of the life principle, I do not act. Being without intellect, I am not a knower. Therefore I have neither knowledge nor nescience, having the light of Pure Consciousness only."[26] Pure, subjective Consciousness is self-illuminating, and all-expansive, unlike ordinary consciousness that is limited, fluctuating and subject–object orientated. Pure Consciousness, then, has a thorough "autonomy of status".[27] What is not real – unreality – neither pervades all things nor persists in one or more things, and the phenomenal world that we know falls into this latter category. Reality, Dandekar summarizes, is: "that which is one without a second, which is not determined by anything else, which is not sublated at any point of time, which transcends all distinctions, to which the familiar categories of thought are inapplicable, and which can be only intuitively realized."[28] The description admirably fits many of the *Upaniṣadic* statements about Brahman: Reality is Brahman, and since it pervades all things, then all things are identical in their pure Being to Brahman. Reality as Brahman is Absolute and unchangeable and exists in itself without being caused. Śaṃkara depicted it thus:

> The highest [*Brahman*] – which is of the nature of Seeing, like the sky, ever-shining, unborn, one alone, imperishable, stainless, all-pervading, and non-dual – That am I and I am forever released. Om.
>
> I am Seeing, pure and by nature changeless. There is by nature no object for me. Being the Infinite, completely filled in front, across, up, down, and in every direction, I am unborn, abiding in Myself.
>
> I am unborn, deathless, free from old age, immortal, self-effulgent, all-pervading, non-dual; I am neither cause nor effect, altogether stainless, always satisfied and therefore [constantly] released. Om.[29]

While all this suggests that the world is to some extent unreal, Śaṃkara does not go as far as to say that it doesn't exist *at all*. We can see that the world exists, and we operate in it according to that perception of its "reality"; we believe what we see. If there were no reality at all, then there would be no value in any thought, for our minds would have nothing external to which they could relate. We *do* distinguish between objects, and we certainly know the difference between the illusory objects of a dream and those in our experience when we are awake. But just as the world we know when we are awake is a different level of reality than the world of our dreams – even though the latter may be the cause of "real" emotions – just so the pervasive Reality of Brahman is of a different level to the reality of the world. But this pervasive level of Reality that is Brahman is such that we can hardly call the lesser reality of the world "reality" at all. Śaṃkara preferred to describe the world as of the nature of *vivarta*, "appearance" or "apparent change". Just like clay can be changed in appearance to be a plate or a pot, but is *really* clay, so Brahman, ultimate Reality, "appears" to be the forms of the phenomenal world. In fact, the change is not a *real* one at all. Reality doesn't become transformed into something else, and the things of the world do not evolve into their present states as Sāṃkhya believed. Neither are they combinations of atoms. All things are simply apparent changes but not *real* changes; it is in this sense that they are illusory.

The world is the unenlightened view of reality. Reality, whether from the enlightened or the unenlightened perspective is Consciousness / Knowledge / Intelligence / Awareness. It can be ultimate, absolute, pure and objectless, or it can be empirical consciousness of objects, subject to change and apparent only. Between these two kinds of reality there is what Indich terms "a radical ontological discontinuity",[30] that is to say, they are totally dissociated from one another. Brahman is subjective Consciousness, the world is objective and unconscious – they cannot be the same. In the lower consciousness that belongs to the world, there is always contradiction, finitude and contingency. Raphael pointedly states: "Reality, fragmented into indefinable and fleeting phenomena, does not guarantee the stability and certainty of knowledge, but leaves it a prey to gnawing relativism, incapable of determination."[31] But the world and ordinary selves are not totally unreal like the horns of a hare; they are simply not ultimately real like the *Ātman* that is Brahman. Being neither real nor unreal, they have a vague reality, like an illusion. They are understood to be real for pragmatic reasons – just as a rope that appears to be a snake produces the appropriate reactions. Ignorance, nescience, is the cause of such illusion. The world must be taken as real until the time when ultimate Reality dawns. However, as Sharma puts it: "Thought reigns supreme in the empirical realm and its authority cannot be questioned here, otherwise the entire empirical life would be exploded."[32] Thus, the vague and apparent reality of the world lies somewhere between absolute Reality and absolute non-reality. This leaves us with three levels of reality.

- *Pāramārthika*: Reality that is absolute, ultimate and pure, and that cannot be contradicted by any other reality.
- *Vyāvahārika*: Appearance – the phenomenal world of the senses, and of ordinary selves, which can be contradicted or sublated.
- *Prātibhāsika*: Illusory impossibilities like the horns of a hare or the child of a barren woman.

Between these levels of reality there can be no relation.

The world, then, is not an effect that is any different from its cause: it is not a transformation of its cause but a rather unreal *superimposition* (*adhyāsa*) of names and forms on what is a substratum of Reality. What we live in is a world of illusory phenomena to which we give names, and to which we cling in the belief that they are real. It is the path of knowledge that leads one away from such an illusion to the ultimate level of Reality that is Brahman. *Ultimate* Reality is not open to any contradiction, but other levels are. When we wake up from a dream, we realize that what was so real in the dream was unreality. But since the things we dream about are the things we experience in waking existence, then waking existence must, to some extent, contain the same images as dreams, and so must be partly unreal too. When we wake up to ultimate Reality, we will then know that the experiences we had in the waking world are also unreal. Just as in dreams the senses are not operating, and only consciousness witnesses the images, so in the wakened state, consciousness is really the only thing operating. Ultimate Reality is just Consciousness alone – Consciousness not operating at all, and not reflected in anything else.

There is much in Śaṃkara's works to suggest that he was considerably influenced by Sāṃkhya philosophy. Potter considers it evident that "either Advaita takes over some of the Sāṃkhya psychology or that the two systems have a common source".[33] There are core beliefs that inform the two schools and, also, similarities with some elements of classical Yoga.[34] Śaṃkara was prepared to accept the Sāṃkhya *guṇas* of *prakṛti* – *sattva*, *rajas*, and *tamas* – as the constituents relating to pleasure, pain and indifference, but constituting the illusory world, not ultimate Reality. Śaṃkara had to exist in the world – apparent though it may be, and this means he was forced to depict the world in terms of its *guṇic* realities. As an orthodox *Brahmin*, it was necessary for Śaṃkara to present some sort of provisional reality that would endorse and retain the *Veda*, though recognizing that ultimate Reality transcended anything in the material universe, even the *Veda*.

Similar to Sāṃkhya, Śaṃkara posited that anything that was not the Self had no consciousness. The difference between the two, however, is that, whereas matter for Sāṃkhya was real, for Śaṃkara what was non-conscious was relatively unreal. Similar to Sāṃkhya, too, Śaṃkara believed that the pure Consciousness that is both *Ātman* and Brahman is reflected in the mind to create a personal identity. At the same time, the mind borrows its consciousness from *Ātman*, which is the only witnesser, and knower. Śaṃkara said,

> the superimposition of the object and its attributes, pertaining to the notion "thou", onto the subject, which pertains to the notion "I" and is of the nature of pure Consciousness, must be erroneous. And the opposite superimposition of the subject and its attributes onto the object must be erroneous too. And yet, though these two principles are utterly distinct in nature, there is a failure to distinguish one from another. And from that there results this natural worldly experience, based on wrong knowledge (mithyā-jñāna) and involving a synthesis of the real with the false, which expresses itself as "I am this" and "This is mine."[35]

Śaṃkara's view here is very similar to the Sāṃkhya theory of the interaction of *puruṣa* and *prakṛti*. The medium for the reflection of the light of Consciousness that is Brahman, should really be, as in Sāṃkhya, the *buddhi*, the intellect. Śaṃkara, it seems, sometimes suggests this, but at other occasions, he posits the mind, vital breath, or the subtlest self of *prajñā*.[36] But, as Indich points out, there is mutual superimposition between pure Consciousness and *ignorance*, not pure Consciousness and matter,[37] and this differs from the Sāṃkhya view.

So the important question of the relation between the infinity of the divine and the finitude and change of the world and selves is answered in two ways by Śaṃkara. First, he states that pure Consciousness, that is to say the Absolute, is the only Reality, in comparison to which all else is impure consciousness, erroneous and illusory. Second, he uses the analogy of the *reflection* of the pure Consciousness of the Absolute in the mind and intellect of each individual, like the moon reflected on the surface of water to account for selves and their perspectives of an apparent world. Both *separate* the ultimate Reality that is Absolute from the finitude of the world, from transmigration, suffering, evil, pain, joy – in short, from the whole manifest universe.

Brahman

Brahman is the ultimate focus of Śaṃkara's being, "the polestar to which he orients all his philosophical and religious endeavor".[38] Brahman, as the ultimate Reality of pure Existence that runs through all things, is the *Ground of all Being*, the substratum of Reality informing all the "appearances" that are contained in the world. It is unchanging, unlike the change that characterizes the world of appearances:

> And I am always the same to beings, one alone; [I am] the highest [*Brahman*] which, like the sky is all-pervading, imperishable, auspicious, uninterrupted, undivided and devoid of action. Therefore no result from your efforts here pertains to Me.
> I am one alone; No other than that [*Brahman*] is thought to be Mine. In like manner I do not belong to anything since I am free from attachment. I have by nature no attachment. Therefore, I do not need you nor your work since I am non-dual.[39]

So each time a particularity of the phenomenal world is perceived or experienced in some way, it is but an apparent form, the essence of which is pure Existence, pure Reality that is Brahman in all things. There can be no *categories* of reality for Śaṃkara, then, for there is only one Reality. Importantly, this absolute Reality, being itself unchanging, doesn't *do* anything. It doesn't change itself into the world, it doesn't emanate out into the world, and it doesn't create the world as an efficient cause of it. And yet Brahman is manifest in all things without any modifications of itself, just as clay does not modify itself to become the clay of pots but simply *is* the substance of the pot. The most important factor to arise from this is the total identification of the essence of the self, the *Ātman* with Brahman.

Brahman, then, is not the differing forms that appear in the world, or the different selves that inhabit it. Brahman is the same essence that underpins them and informs them. All the apparent forms of the world are incorrectly superimposed on this *Being* that is Brahman. So, while *Being* is the Ground or substratum on which all the appearances of the world are based, in their essence the appearances are really no different from their *Ground of all Being*. As will be seen later, a conception of a manifest "God" is added to the non-dual viewpoint of this school, but the real conception of the Absolute, Brahman, is of a totally *nirguṇa* principle, a "no-thing" that transcends all description and all analysis, and that can be only intuitively experienced. Again, this is in line with so much *Upaniṣadic* thought. Supreme Reality (*pāramārthika sattā*) is beyond the world as we know it and yet is the only means by which the world can be known.

So the nature of Brahman, if at all it can be depicted, is Truth, Reality, Being, Existence or *sat*, and pure Consciousness, *cit*. As pure Consciousness, Brahman is pure awareness, pure subject and the one that witnesses. Unlike ordinary consciousness, however, the Consciousness of Brahman is independent of any object whatsoever. It is never the object of another consciousness, nor does it have objects that it is conscious of. It is not the object of its own Consciousness. It is the differentiation between this and that, consciousness of dualities in the world around us, that makes our consciousness, our knowledge, always object-centered. This is where the self gets lost. As Das writes: "If we are to appreciate the Advaita position properly, we must fasten upon the utter distinction between the subject and the object and make the subject altogether free from the least taint of objectivity."[40] When the Self realizes this it becomes Brahman, for it *is* Brahman, and it is, at the same time, the essence of all things in the universe.

The famous words of the *Chāndogya Upaniṣad*, *tat tvam asi*, "That you are" depict the Self, the *Ātman* as identical to Brahman, and Advaita Vedānta is true to this teaching. Brahman as Absolute is without parts. This means that the Self, the *Ātman*, cannot be a part of Brahman, but must either be or not be Brahman. Since Brahman is also, according to the *Veda*, "One without a second", there cannot be a Self that exists secondarily to Brahman. When this truth is realized the world of appearances no longer has any reality, just as the dream has no reality in the waking world.

While primarily, the Absolute of Advaita is often referred to by Śaṃkara as pure Consciousness (*cit*) and, also, as we have seen, as Truth or Being (*sat*), later proponents were to add the third quality of Bliss (*ānanda*), the three being referred to as *saccidānanda* when combined. Śaṃkara does not combine these three, however, and it is only pure Consciousness and Being that feature as the nature of the Absolute in those works of his that are authentic: the concept of the Absolute as Bliss is rare, though evident.[41] Bliss might have been seen as too qualitative for Śaṃkara, but where he did use it he was keen to separate its nature from anything experienced in the empirical world.

Māyā and avidyā

What we need to turn our attention to now is not the ultimate Reality that is Brahman and the true Self, but the world, its "unreality", and its illusory nature that is known as *māyā* – "the warp and woof of the world of appearances".[42] If the world is a lower level of reality from the ultimate Reality of Brahman, and sufficiently so to give it an "unreality" and make it of the nature of "appearance", how, then, did this come into being? Why should we have a world at all? And why should the real Self or *Ātman* not be so readily perceptible? The answer the Advaitin gives to the first of these questions is the rather unsatisfying one that the world has always been so. The *Upaniṣads* accepted mainly that existence was one, and that the plurality we normally know of in the world is a mistaken view. Śaṃkara went further and said that the world itself was illusory. But from the unenlightened view Śaṃkara, as *Upaniṣadic* thought, accepted that the world exists timelessly in its cycles of manifestation and dissolution. Thus, illusion is timeless. It is a fact that is accepted, rather than logically worked out. As far as the second question is concerned there is a rather delicate balance between answering it totally negatively and suggesting that the world doesn't exist at all but is merely an illusion, or, by depicting it as a lower level of reality that has only an apparent existence, like the apparent existence of the world of the dreamer. But in both cases it would have to be asked who or what creates the illusion and who or what creates the dream? So pressing was this question that some Vedāntins made Brahman the substance from which the appearances of the world came into being – a material cause.[43]

Māyā is the principle of illusion, it is that which obscures unified Reality. But, while it is beginningless and endless, in itself it has no reality. It acts as a kind of veil over the real essence of things, the *Ātman*, and represents error in true perception. As such, it is very close in meaning to ignorance, *ajnāña* or *avidyā*. Indeed, as far as Śaṃkara was concerned, these terms were synonymous. *Māyā* is not seen as something that opposes Reality and, therefore, as something dualistically juxtaposed to Brahman. It is, like ignorance, a misconception, a lack of the appropriate knowledge of Reality. We cannot say *why* ignorance occurs, or what it really is. We only know that it obscures the truth and real knowledge, and lasts only as long as the truth is not perceived. So, just like ignorance, when illusion is removed and the truth is realized, it ceases to exist. Illusion, like ignorance, is not deliberately created, it is simply there when the truth is not known. Neither does it affect the truth; the truth still exists and is not affected in any way by ignorance, just as Brahman is not affected in any way by the *māyā* of the world. Thus, *māyā* "is not conceived as utter non-being, but only as deficient in being".[44]

The inscrutable nature of the term *māyā* is reflected in the *Ṛg and Atharva Vedas* where it was used in the sense of supernatural power. But it was not a prominent feature of the *Upaniṣadic* texts, where it was more implicit than explicit in their thought. There, too, it tended to be used in the sense of a mysterious power. But it was to be taken up by a number of thinkers before both Gauḍapāda and Śaṃkara. Alston notes that Śaṃkara uses the word sparingly, except in his commentary on the *Gītā*.[45] It eventually came to mean something like "magic" and the kind of illusory effects that can be produced by magical skill. Śaṃkara writes of *māyā* in the same sense as magic. Just as the performer of the Indian rope trick hypnotizes his audience *en masse* so that everyone thinks there is someone climbing up the rope, so the power of illusion, ignorance or nescience traps each individual in a phantasmagoric world of magic, albeit one in which there seems to be an interrelation of causes and effects. Śaṃkara equates the power of the Absolute to create the illusion of the world, with the power of the magician to delude his audience without any effort. In both the truth is hidden, and yet is evident for the enlightened. And the world is no more real than the figure at the top of the rope in the Indian rope trick: it only appears to be so by the deluded. However, just as the vision of the figure at the top of the rope cannot exist without the magician, so the illusory world cannot exist without the existence of the Absolute: "The magician himself is in no way affected in past, present or future by the magic display he has spread forth by his hypnotic power (māyā), as it is nothing real. And in just the same way, the supreme Self is unaffected by the magic display of the world of transmigratory experience (saṃsāra-māyā)."[46]

Such are the difficulties presented by this key concept of *māyā* in the thought of Advaita, that it has been variously interpreted in order to solve some of the complexities inherent in it. In particular, the whole question of the relation between *māyā* and God, Īśvara, will be examined below. Suffice it to say here that projecting Brahman as the cause of the illusion in the world would do much to explain away the difficulties, but Śaṃkara does not really do this: it would be an unenlightened rather than an enlightened perspective. Śaṃkara sometimes referred to *māyā* as the *creative* and, therefore causative, power of God, just as the power to burn is inherent in fire, but he would never have accepted that any change took place in Brahman to create an illusory world. Nothing could be said of the relationship of Brahman to the world because questions about it were non-starters and illegitimate. It is impossible to speak of difference when they are the same. *Māyā* is, therefore, representative of the supposed changes that we see in the world when the truth of the unified and changeless Reality that underpins it is not experienced. It is referred to as the creative power of God, Īśvara, the creative power that appears, from the perspective of nescience, to bring about the effects that are the material world. Only in this sense, then, is *māyā* the material cause of the world. But since Īśvara is also a superimposed reality on the ultimate Reality, and an unenlightened view, the creative power as *māyā* is itself unreal.

The world to Śaṃkara was one in which what seems to be real at one moment is contradicted in the next. Indeed, our views about the world are constantly changing, and can be subject to contradiction time and again, if not in the present, then in the distant future. So one particular existent is likely to be contradicted by another in time. This is bound to make truth illusive, and present knowledge illusory. The empirical world is "real" only in so far as it serves our immediate purposes, a world that is *ultimately* and unchangingly real would not serve the practical purposes of daily life. But it is attachment to the practical and not the real that necessitates the reincarnation of the empirical self – illusory or not.

It is the plurality and particularity of the world that is the substance of illusion; it is a perception of the world that is erroneous, and error has nothing to do with truth and is itself only apparent. Error is only real for as long as ignorance of perception maintains it, just as a dream lasts only as long as we are asleep. Real knowledge nullifies all ordinary knowledge as erroneous. But without real knowledge the world becomes *māyā*. Objects in the world have no reality in their particular forms, but they *do* have reality in their *essential* natures. So the *particular* that we see is something that is neither real nor unreal; it is neither one thing nor the other. And being neither real nor unreal it is contradictory in character and can only have the character of illusion. Thus, what we experience when we see particulars is the same as seeing a piece of conch shell as silver, or a rope as a snake; the perceptions are erroneous because we fail to see what is real: "the world is quite real so long as true knowledge does not dawn".[47]

The illusory nature of the world of appearance, the world of names and forms, is essential for a truly non-dualist philosophy. For if the world is accepted as real then so is its impermanence, its change, its constant cause–effect processes, and the reality of all this has to be the same Reality as Brahman. This would necessitate Brahman being changeable itself – at least in terms of the world that is composed of It – and if Brahman is changeable then it would have to be asked what causes the change? Then we are into the quest for a cause beyond the cause *ad infinitum*. But if the world is a kind of illusion it has no effect on the ultimate nature of the Reality of Brahman, the unity of Reality is safeguarded, and there is no duality of cause and effect. Nevertheless it is an unsatisfactory solution that resorts to a mysterious manifestation of an illusory power that exists indefinitely (and therefore is permanent!) without original cause. It leaves us begging the question of how pure and real Existence can appear to be manifested as a plurality of different forms. Das concurs: "Advaitism is unsatisfactory as philosophy mainly on account of its self-contradictory notion of *maya* which defies all logical treatment."[48] While *māyā* serves to explain the apparent nature of the world, it lacks substance on the one hand, and is not a quality on the other. The *Upaniṣads* solve the problem by making God the supreme magician that brings the illusion of the world into effect, the world then being a great conjuring trick that is allowed to remain "real" through the ignorance of its audience. But this analogy is not a good one in that there is no real mystery here. To the enlightened of the audience both the real and the trick become known: yet *māyā* remains a mystery, even if it is a level of reality left behind, we never know just how it is related to ultimate Reality, to Brahman. And if Brahman were to be the creator of *māyā*, we would be left asking why this should be, and to what purpose? We are left with the view that *māyā* is not really a cause, it simply *is* when we misperceive what is real. In the words of Vivekananda:

> Thus we find that *māyā* is not a theory for the explanation of the world; it is simply a statement of facts as they exist – that the very basis of our being is contradiction, that wherever there is good, there must also be evil, and wherever there is evil there must also be some good, wherever there is life, death must follow as its shadow, and everyone who smiles will have to weep, and whoever weeps must smile also. Nor can this state of things be remedied."[49]

One partial solution to the nature of *māyā* lies in the separation from, and yet relation between, *māyā* and ignorance, *avidyā* or *ajñāna*. *Avidyā* is ignorance or nescience. It was a term widely used in the *Upaniṣads*, where it designated the opposite of knowledge, *vidyā*. Clearly it was a fundamental principle in Śaṃkara's thought, though here, too, as Potter comments, Śaṃkara sometimes "confesses inability to explain the mysterious ways of *avidyā*".[50] It was certainly propounded by Advaitins before Śaṃkara.[51] But while before the time of Śaṃkara there seems to have been a distinct difference between *avidyā* and *māyā*, as far as Śaṃkara was concerned, there seems little to differentiate them. After him, and more logically, the former came to be viewed as "a small parcel of Māyā pertaining to an individual".[52] If *avidyā* is the general ignorance in human perception of the world, while *māyā* is the apparent result of that perception – the illusory world in which the effects of the perceptions are worked out – it would solve some of the issues. I do not think that this does any violence to Śaṃkara's general position. He is not clear in his use of the terms but at least positing ignorance as the individual perception of a dual and differentiated world would make *māyā* its concomitant result – an illusory world of perceived effects.

Sharma reflects this nuance of meaning in the two terms when he writes: "Ignorance is the stuff illusions are made of. Ignorance (*avidyā ajñāna*) is not merely absence of knowledge, but also positive wrong knowledge (*bhāva rūpa*). And it is this positive aspect of ignorance which contains the sting of illusion."[53] *Avidyā* is, thus, endemic to human nature, and illusion, *māyā*, the collective superimposed experience that makes up our view of the world. The separation of the two terms, found in later Advaita, is reflected in Sharma's neat definition of them: "Brahman reflected in Māyā is the Īshvara and Brahman reflected in Avidyā is the Jīva."[54] It is a definition that brings out well the general cosmic nature of illusion and the personal nature of ignorance. After Śaṃkara there was a tendency to make Brahman the basis of *māyā* and the latter the more obvious cause of the world. Yet there are problems here, too. Rao contends that, if effects are the same as their causes as Śaṃkara maintains, then matter can only be caused by matter, and neither Brahman nor *māyā* is so,[55] unless the world of matter has some concealed sentiency.[56] He concludes that the universe is not inherently insentient.[57] Indeed, it would amount to a duality of consciousness and matter were this not so. Thus Brahman is the inner sentience of matter, but not the appearance of outward, gross forms. His view clearly illustrates the inner essence of *Ātman* as Consciousness that is all things, but does not explain why we should view all things as illusory. Another solution was to understand *avidyā* as "a power inherent in the *Brahman* . . . In other words, *avidyā* belongs to *Brahman*, as only a conscious being capable of knowledge can be ignorant".[58] In this case, "*ajñāna* or nescience exists in the pure self which is its locus".[59] This is a logical assertion, but not one that Śaṃkara would have accepted.

Clearly, however, ignorance is not something usually imposed from without, but is inherent in the self; it is one's own fault. Śaṃkara said: "Everything comes from nescience. This world is unreal, for it is seen by one who has nescience and is not perceived in the state of deep sleep."[60] Here, there is no cause of error other than *individual* false perceptions of reality. So, despite the use of *māyā* and *avidyā* as one and the same – and in some senses they are – there is some measure in making sense of non-dualism in terms of the latter. Ignorance suggests a more personal condition of error in perception of reality. Thus, as Das comments, "we cannot think of an impersonal ignorance, of ignorance which belongs to nobody. Ignorance is not a self-subsistent entity".[61] But *māyā* tends to suggest a more general life-condition; it is, thus, that we tend to question the source and cause of *māyā* rather than *avidyā*. This nuance of difference in meaning is perhaps implicit in Alston's definition of *avidyā*. It is, he writes, "the fateful condition (avasthā) of ignorance of the true nature of the Self, followed by false superimposition, that gives rise to a world and worldly experience. It is the precondition for the possiblity of *any* appearance, including that of a material cause".[62] Ignorance has a power, a *śakti*, to maintain illusion, and it is this that keeps the world processes in existence – albeit in its cycles of evolution and involution. Yet it is not real because it is sublated by correct knowledge, and is not completely unreal because of its power to maintain the illusion that is the world. But it is ignorance rooted in individual misconceptions that maintains the power of illusion.

The point about ignorance from the level of the empirical self is that it conceals (*āvaraṇa*) and distorts (*vikṣepa*) the Reality that is Brahman, causing that Reality to be, as in the philosophy of Sāṃkhya, confused with the world of forms. *Avidyā* wrote Radhakrishnan, is "the force that launches us into the dream of life", and "the mental deformity of the finite self that disintegrates the divine into a thousand different fragments".[63] In this case, the *Ātman*, too, becomes falsely conceived of as involved in the world, through ignorance. Thus, as Dasgupta pointed out: "We not only do not know what we ourselves really are, but do not also know what the world about us is."[64] But ignorance is illusion in the sense that it is a veil that hides Reality. It is in this sense that illusion is unreal; it isn't really there, but is just a mind blockage, a refusal to see Reality. The pure Consciousness, the *cit* of the true *Ātman* is there, and the ignorance of the mind is the veil, the illusion, that hides it. Thus, all life is lived in ignorance. In the words of Vivekananda,

> ignorance is the great mother of all misery, and the fundamental ignorance is to think that the infinite weeps and cries, that it is finite. This is the basis of all ignorance – that we, the immortal, the ever pure, the perfect Spirit, think we are little minds, we are little

> bodies. It is the mother of all selfishness. As soon as I think I am a little body, I want to preserve it, to protect it, to keep it nice, at the expense of other bodies. Then you and I become separate.[65]

Like the rope that is perceived as a snake through ignorance of the real nature of the rope, the world of forms is seen as real through the same kind of ignorance that blinds the individual to the *sat*, the pure Being that is Brahman in all things. This is a projection or superimposition of something that is unreal on what is real – the medium of which is ignorance. Śaṃkara called this *adhyāsa*, "illusory superimposition". Of it he said: " This whole [universe] is qualification, like a beautiful ornament, which is superimposed [upon *Ātman*] through nescience. Therefore, when *Ātman* has been known, the whole [universe] becomes non-existent."[66] Pure Consciousness is overlaid by ignorance and a resultant association with the forms of the world occurs, lending to them a reality that is false. It is this superimposition that creates illusion. Ignorance veils the pure Consciousness that is the only source of what is real and the only means by which the realization of *Ātman* can be possible. Ignorance, like the pure Consciousness of Reality, is timeless and beginningless, but is not associated with pure Consciousness. Rather like Sāṃkhya where the *puruṣa* lends consciousness to the unconscious *prakṛti*, so in Advaita, pure Consciousness is reflected in the ordinary perceiving consciousness, but by doing so, gives that ordinary consciousness the power of an illusory perception of reality. Neither the ordinary consciousness nor the illusion can be real – only pure Consciousness, pure Being, *Ātman*, can be real. Once *Ātman* is realized, all the illusion will vanish and the unreal is left behind for the real.

Therefore, *avidyā* according to Śaṃkara neither exists nor does not exist. It is certainly not of the nature of the Absolute, and therefore cannot have existence-ness as its true nature. If it were real, it would depict things truly, and then it wouldn't be ignorance at all. It would also be a dual concept in opposition to the Absolute. But if it does not exist at all, then the *Veda* has no purpose in overcoming it. Nor would we experience it in life. But there can be no *real* nescience. It is the perception of the unenlightened; lift the veil and Reality is there all the time. It is merely a reason why the world exists, not the gross materiality that forms it. In the words of Lott, ignorance "is the essential principle of explanation for the discrepancy between the one-ness posited of transcendent Reality, and the multiplicity of common experience".[67] Thus, Radhakrishnan was right to claim: "Unreal the world is, illusory it is not",[68] but not in line with Śaṃkara's thought to claim that it is the "phenomenal truth" of Brahman.[69] Śaṃkara would never have connected the gross world to Brahman in such a way.

Śaṃkara's acceptance that the phenomenal world continues for the enlightened one is problematic – an anomaly the concept of the *jīvanmukta*, one liberated in life, poses. It would be expected that, having woken up to Reality, a liberated one would transcend the world entirely. But the self is already liberated in the here and now. Alston puts Śaṃkara's view clearly on this: "The Self only *appears* to be deluded and only *appears* to be liberated. It is not that time is a reality and that liberation is a real event involving a real change taking place at a fixed point in time. Nor can we say that nescience is anything real or that the Self undergoes a change from bondage to liberation, as if the latter were two separate real states."[70] In other words: "Enlightenment does not so much destroy nescience as reveal that it never existed."[71] Neither is nescience a characteristic or quality of the self. It is misperception of reality, a misapprehension of the way things are, false- or non-comprehension. In this case, once the misapprehension is removed, nescience disappears. However, the world of forms does not then disappear for the *jīvanmukta*; it is just that only the *essence* of it all is experienced, and all dualities and differentiation are abandoned.

In later schools of Advaita, *avidyā* was to become a cosmic power that, while neither real nor unreal, was the eternal primary substance from which the world sprang. It was not real, for it lacked the ultimate Reality of Brahman, but it was not unreal in that it had a measure of reality. This would have been an abandoning of true non-dualism for Śaṃkara. He did not work out the difficult problem of the origin and nature of *avidyā* very well, and as Mayeda points out, it was "the most crucial problem which Śaṅkara left for his followers".[72] It was the beginningless nature that was posited for it that was particularly problematic, for it suggested a degree of reality and permanence.

Epistemology

Knowledge, which is synonymous with consciousness, is of two kinds. Real knowledge, real consciousness, is the pure Consciousness of the enlightened state. The other kind of knowledge or consciousness is that of the unenlightened state. Real knowledge is the "higher knowledge", *parāvidyā*, which is Brahman realization. Unenlightened knowledge is "lower knowledge", *aparāvidyā*, the knowledge of the phenomenal world. Indich describes the higher knowledge as "a fully autonomous state of being in which the identity of the all-pervading consciousness underlying the apparently distinct subject, object and means of knowledge is realized".[73] As we have seen above, however, the lower knowledge is not absolutely unreal; it is simply unreal in relation to *parāvidyā*, higher knowledge. Indeed, as Radhakrishnan commented: "If not, Śaṃkara's elaborate and even passionate discussion of the lower knowledge will border on the grotesque."[74]

Knowledge, *vidyā* – of the deep intuitive type – is critical to the soteriological quest of Advaita. It is the opposite of *avidyā*, ignorance, which is completely dispelled once true knowledge is acquired. This pure Knowledge or pure Consciousness is passive. So it is not an action, and it has no object; it simply *is*. Thus, "no *action* can remove *avidyā*; the only thing that can remove *avidyā* is knowledge, and knowing is not an act".[75] Pure Consciousness is Self-knowledge and transcends all dualities that are normally associated with knowledge. It is knowledge that *is* the *Ātman*, in which subject and object is one. Śaṃkara said: "Thus, with concentrated mind, one should always know everything as *Ātman*. Having known Me to be abiding in one's own body, one is a sage, released and immovable."[76]

Like Mīmāṃsā, from which Advaita developed, there is a common acceptance that all knowledge is self-valid. Knowledge is direct and immediate consciousness that needs no other knowledge to illustrate it. Yet there are differences. Whereas ritual action was so important to Mīmāṃsā, and therefore the validity of knowledge was tested in activity, it is intuitive knowledge that is the focus of Advaita. Importantly, it is not activity that is the test of accurate knowledge for Advaita, but knowledge that is not contradicted by other knowledge. It is this conception of valid knowledge that really eradicates any ordinary knowledge from being valid, since any knowledge may be contradicted in the near, or very distant, future. Indeed, whatever exists in the phenomenal world now, will not always exist, and therefore our knowledge of it is going to be contradicted at some point. The contradiction of one knowledge by another is referred to as sublation. The term suggests a hierarchy of knowledge that transcends ignorance – an increasing removal of veils of ignorance. Only Brahman realization, *ultimate* knowledge or pure Consciousness, is non-sublatable. Thus, Indich says, "the less capable something is of being sublated, the truer it is, the more real it is, and the more highly is it to be valued. Following this logic, reality, or Brahman, is that experience or state of being which is non-sublatable and ultimately valuable."[77] But, as Indich later notes, if there is a complete distinction between pure Consciousness and the consciousness or knowledge at the level of the phenomenal world, how can consciousness depict both?[78] The answer lies in the *reflection* of pure Consciousness in ordinary consciousness. And, just like the moon reflected in water is totally different from it, so pure Consciousness is different from empirical consciousness.

Memory is excluded as a valid means of knowledge for it is considered that cognition has to be of something that was not previously known. So true knowledge, or *pramā*, must be on the one hand new knowledge, and on the other, not contradicted by any other knowledge. But since Brahman is the *ultimate* truth, any knowledge we have in the empirical world – even if it is new knowledge – is bound to be contradicted by Brahman realization. In this case, there really is no valid knowledge at all in the world as we know it. This reinforces the idea of the world as a lower level of reality in which "truths" are but temporary and cannot be said to be real. The only truth that we can know in the world is that of our own Consciousness which, as we have seen, in its pure state is Brahman.

From the unenlightened view, Śaṃkara conceded that knowledge/consciousness is that *of* something. It must have an object. However, the *antaḥkaraṇa* (intellect, ego and mind) is a limited consciousness that is affected by the physical self, the body and the particular dispositions of the egoistic self. How can it have a *true* perception of what it sees, when it is so limited? No object can reveal itself, it has to be revealed by the subjective consciousness of a perceiver, so it is known only by the level of consciousness that perceives it. And that level of consciousness is not pure, unless it is the pure Consciousness of the liberated Self. When knowledge is knowledge *of*, that is to say is focused on an object, it is always *aparāvidyā*, even if the object of knowledge is Brahman. As Sharma says: "Thought cannot reveal Reality; it necessarily distorts it".[79] Thus, what we perceive is done so with the limitations of our empirical consciousness and, when pure Consciousness is realized in the state of liberation, it will contradict all our knowledge and perceptions from the limited consciousness that we once had: thus, our present knowledge must be illusory. There is a distinct difference between pure Consciousness and the objects that are in the world. The outward *forms* of objects are simply superimposed on pure Consciousness like images on a screen, and they are dependent on the screen, the pure Consciousness, for their manifestation. But, just like the images on the screen, the objects of consciousness have no real existence, they are limited in existence, unlike the infinite pure Consciousness that is all-pervading. In comparison to pure Consciousness, then, such objects, such forms, have no reality, and the empirical self that perceives them is living in a deluded state ignorant of its own true identity:

> The states of the mind, the intellect, and the sense-organs, which are aroused by actions, are illumined only by Pure Consciousness as a jar, etc., are illumined by the sun.
> Since this is so, the Knower, which illuminates the notions [of the intellect] by Its own light, and of which they are the objects, is called the agent of those notions [of the intellect] only by the deluded.
> [Only to the deluded], therefore, is [It] also all-knowing since [It] illuminates everything by Its own light. In like manner, as [It] is the cause of all actions, *Ātman* is all-doing.
> The *ātman* thus described is [the *ātman*] with adjuncts. [But] the *Ātman* without adjuncts is indescribable, without parts, attributeless and pure; neither mind nor speech reaches It.[80]

Thus, the self that says "I know this", and "I know that" is deluded because the real *Ātman* is *passive* Consciousness. It is devoid of any object of knowledge that creates duality between subject and object. But as long as the self is unenlightened it will be involved with the world of objects. Sharma puts this well when he writes: "The tragedy of human intellect is that it tries to know everything as an object. But whatever can be presented as an object is necessarily relative, and for that very reason unreal. The knower can never be known as an object. Ultimately there is no distinction between the true knower and pure knowledge."[81] Thus, Śaṃkara says: "he who has fallen into the rivers of births and deaths can never save himself from them by anything else but knowledge".[82]

At times it seems as if Śaṃkara portrays the *Ātman* that is Brahman as the Knower: "Just as a light on a stand can illumine without any effort everything that its light reaches, so the Knower sees without any effort the notions [of the intellect] in the forms of sound, etc., which It reaches".[83] Similarly, Śaṃkara says: "As the sun always shines, without destroying or creating [anything by its rays], so does [It] always know all, being all-pervading, all-seeing, and pure",[84] and: "As a killer of the unreal thus covers himself with the truth, 'I am the Real-*Ātman* and the Knower, but, like ether, I am empty of anything else,' he is not bound [again]."[85] But the knower is a pure Knower, without knowledge! When the intellect superimposes itself on the *Ātman* and absorbs the Consciousness of the *Ātman* erroneously as its own, then *Ātman* might be said to be the knower. But, strictly speaking, the *Ātman* can *do* nothing at all, not even know, and in the state of pure Consciousness, when everything simply *is*, there is no objective reality at all to be known: "As Knowledge is the very nature of *Ātman*, It is constantly applied figuratively to the intellect. And the absence of discriminating knowledge is beginningless; this and nothing else is taken to be transmigratory existence."[86]

Ordinary knowledge is an attribute of the mind and intellect, not of the self. Since the true Self, the *Ātman*, is pure Consciousness, or pure Knower – devoid of any ripple of knowledge from the mind the knowledge held in the mind of the empirical self is that which makes the self bound:

> In this way, everyone naturally says "he knows" as if it were a real act. Superimposing onto the Self the agent properly pertaining to the intellect, we say of the Self "he knows" and call it the knower. And superimposing onto the intellect the consciousness (that pertains properly to the Self) we speak of the intellect also as the Absolute. . . . Therefore, the words of phrases like "he knows", the (apparent) experience (corresponding to them), and the (apparent) memory of that experience, all proceed from failure to distinguish from one another consciousness, its reflection in the intellect and the intellect.[87]

Śaṃkara's view of knowledge, then, is twofold. It is an acceptance of false knowledge for the pragmatic existence of unenlightened beings, on the one hand, but this knowledge is to be retracted on the other in the enlightened state by pure Knowledge devoid of objects. It is the superimposition (*adhyāsa*) of objects – name-and-form as Śaṃkara termed them – on the pure Consciousness that is *Ātman*, that binds the self to transmigration. Radhakrishnan rightly commented: "That particular application of adhyāsa which inclines us to break up the nature of one absolute consciousness into a subject–object relation results from the very constitution of the human mind,"[88] and; "The reality of an ordered world exists only for mind and in terms of mind."[89] It is thus our slavery to sense perception, and our ego-involvement with what we experience, that cause us to impose differentiation and duality on a non-dual Reality.

Pramāṇas

In line with Pūrva Mīmāṃsā Advaita accepts six *pramāṇas*, or means of valid knowledge, perception (*pratyakṣa*), inference (*anumāna*), testimony (*śabda* or *āgama*), comparison (*upamāna*), presumption (*arthāpaṭṭi*), and non-apprehension (*abhāva* or *anupalabdhi*). It is not a particularly developed epistemology in comparison to that of other schools, and we find Śaṃkara being dependent on the ideas of other schools for the basis of his own views. He seems to refer to only three of the *pramāṇas* – perception, inference and testimony, and these he does not really discuss in depth. Because the world is a lower level of reality, valid means of knowledge cannot be found at the ordinary level of existence. Whatever we perceive is informed by ignorance, so it cannot ultimately be real. For this reason Śaṃkara was not interested in analysing the nature of perception, because there can be no valid means at all of knowing the Self that is the Absolute. Only when nescience disappears is the Self left as it really is, and Reality experienced. There is always a complete contrast between the stillness of pure Consciousness and the activity of the mind-complex in any individual. Consciousness is the substratum on which all perceptions are superimposed. These superimposed perceptions are *limiting adjuncts*, or *upādhi*, that obscure the stillness and ultimate identity of the Absolute and the Self as pure Consciousness and pure Being. Such limited – indeed false – knowledge can only occur as a result of the reflection of pure Consciousness in the mind, Śaṃkara said:

> A reflection (pratibimba) of the Spirit (puruṣa) enters, as it were, into the "mirror" arising from its own contact with the intellect and, through that, with the elements. The process is like the reflection of the sun and other luminous bodies "entering" into water and other reflecting media. This contact of the Deity of infinite and unthinkable power with the intellect and the rest constitutes a reflection of consciousness arising from a failure to discriminate the true nature of the deity, and it gives rise to a variety of false notions such as "I am happy" "I am miserable" and "I am bewildered." Because the Deity only enters as the individual soul, as a mere reflection, it is not itself in any way connected with bodily characteristics such as pleasure and pain.[90]

Śaṃkara very neatly removes the totally transcendent Absolute or the *Ātman* from any involvement in a finite world of change. Ultimate Reality, pure Being and pure

Consciousness is without any modification. Its reflection is no more real than the reflection of the moon in water, and the receptacle of that reflection, the mind-complex, is matter. This leaves no room for a personality self that transmigrates from one life to the next, it makes the self we think we know, unreal. To use an analogy mentioned earlier, the ordinary self is like the ether in a jar, which is just the same as the cosmic ether, as will be evident when the jar breaks. Likewise, the real Self is the same as the Absolute, as will be evident when the ignorance that holds it otherwise, is removed. It is the desires and aversions of the intellect, mind and ego – all the time being given a false reflected consciousness – that bind the self to transmigratory existence.

Perception

In the process of perception the senses relay information to the *antaḥkaraṇa*, which projects itself in order to become transformed, to match, or take on the form of, the object of the particular sense, whether in the waking or dreaming state. This object may be external to the physical body, or it may be internal, as in pain, happiness, and so on. As in Yoga the modification or transformation of the *antaḥkaraṇa* is a *vṛtti*, though Śaṃkara preferred to use the term *pratyaya*. As in Sāṃkhya and Yoga, the intellect, ego and mind are unconscious matter, and they can only be the objects of knowledge and not the subject, the knower, for they have no consciousness. It is the *Ātman* or *Puruṣa* within that is the witness, the perceiver, and whose proximity within lends the *buddhi* a reflected consciousness – a concept very similar indeed to the Sāṃkhya theory of *puruṣas* and their relation to the *buddhi* of matter. And just like the *puruṣas* of Sāṃkhya, the *Ātman* is passive in the process, it doesn't do anything. It is the pure subject, the pure Consciousness, the passive witnesser that is changeless. So the consciousness that *appears* to characterize the intellect, the *buddhi*, is an illusion; it is a consciousness that is nothing more than the *reflection* of the *Ātman*, just as a reflection in a mirror is unreal. Like Sāṃkhya *puruṣas*, then, the *Ātman* is really separate from the whole, gross material world. Unlike Sāṃkhya, however, the world is given no formal reality, so what the *buddhi seems* to perceive, does not exist ultimately: only the *Ātman* is real. This makes all perception ultimately false.

It is the pure Consciousness of *cit* that illuminates the object in order that it can be perceived, and at the same time illuminates the object in the mind. Ignorance creates the supposed diversity of all objects and selves instead of their unity. When the *cit* illuminates the object, the veil of ignorance is partially removed and the object is recognized such as it is – its essence only – but not wholly removed so that the distinction between subject and object is obliterated. "Intellect being pervaded by the reflection of Pure Consciousness, knowledge arises in it; and so sound and other [objects of the sense-organs] appear. By this people are deluded."[91] In reality, there is no distinction between perception and perceiver.[92]

Inference

Since Śaṃkara was not concerned with establishing any means of knowledge beyond the ultimate identification of Brahman and *Ātman*, he did not expand on the acceptance of inference as a means to establish knowledge in the ordinary world.

Testimony

Śaṃkara accepted both *Vedic* testimony and reliable testimony extraneous to the *Veda*. But testimony, in the form of *śruti*, was the primary, indeed only, means by which knowledge of ultimate Reality could be developed, because this was the only source dedicated to providing evidence that Brahman and *Ātman* is one. Śaṃkara said: "There is no other attainment higher than that of *Ātman*, for the sake of which [attainment] exist the words of the *Vedas* and of the *Smṛtis* as well as actions."[93] For Śaṃkara, therefore, the *śruti* texts contained infallible knowledge – the identification of *Ātman* and Brahman: "It is indeed declared to us in the *Śruti* that knowledge is the notion of the oneness [of *Ātman* and *Brahman*] and nescience is the notion of the difference [of *Ātman* and *Brahman*]. Therefore knowledge is affirmed in the scripture with all vigor."[94] For those locked into the ways of the world and the desire for some things and aversion for others, Śaṃkara said: "The scripture gradually removes his ignorance concerning this matter."[95] Yet ritual actions were regarded by him as merely supportive to the primary teaching of the *nirguṇa* Brahman and the identity of Brahman and *Ātman*. Such a denial of the primary importance of *Vedic* ritual as the means to liberation was, as Atmananda comments, one of "the boldest steps taken by Sankara".[96] Once again, we find the dual views of the enlightened and unenlightened presented, the primary teaching that leads to enlightenment, and the supportive teaching for the unenlightened.

Yet all language is another part of the phenomenal world that is, when all is said and done, also an object of nescience, and this includes even the *Vedic* core of teachings of the identity between Brahman and *Ātman*. Something beyond these words and language was needed for true realization, and this would be the depth of understanding that could bring truth to a level that made all other knowledge superfluous. Śaṃkara divided the *Veda* into three groups of texts, those dealing with ritual, those dealing with knowledge of the Self, the Absolute and liberation, and those dealing with meditation. But the key to all *śruti* lay in the words of the *Chāndogya Upaniṣad* 6:8:7, *Tat tvam asi*, "That you are". These words, which identify the innermost Self with Brahman, are analysed at length by Śaṃkara. Lott considers Śaṃkara's interpretation of such key texts of the scriptures to be "probably the most subtle aspect of his system",[97] and there is certainly much penetrating commentary to be found in Śaṃkara's exposition of such texts. Most other teachings in the *Veda* Śaṃkara believed to be subordinate to this central statement. They were supportive texts that would assist in the growth of knowledge by making ultimate Truth initially easier to understand. In the last event, however, it would be the experience within that would transcend all knowledge for Brahman realization. Thus, *Vedic* revelation supplied the initial impetus for the disciple, followed by reasoning and debate; to acquire understanding. But it was meditative experience at the very depths of the self that would bring liberation.

It is this emphasis on intuitive knowledge that accounts for the vagueness of Śaṃkara's terminology. Isayeva notes the tendency of Śaṃkara to use language to direct individuals towards ultimate Truth without ever being specific about it. She writes: "We were not told (and so we cannot, in turn, tell) everything; that is why, according to Śaṅkara, we are always trying to catch this being at its word, to apprehend it through fragments, through scraps and broken phrases, where one can still discern the echo of the true word, unpronounced and ineffable."[98]

So despite Śaṃkara's acceptance of the *Veda* as essential for the spiritual evolution of the self, he overcame the dual concepts of Brahman presented in the *Upaṇisadic* texts – the cosmic and acosmic perspectives of the Absolute – by eschewing neither. This was so even though he believed that the *Veda* was ultimately part of the illusory world, and that it would be transcended at liberation. He could uphold both views, and the necessity of the *Veda*, exactly because of his acceptance of an ultimate Reality on the one hand, and an apparent reality on the other. For the unenlightened, transmigrating self, the *Veda* provided the best means of knowledge. But it had to present that knowledge at different levels. Cleverly, Śaṃkara interpreted *Upaniṣadic* texts that appear to separate Brahman from the self, or that speak of Brahman as having qualities, as the *Vedic* method of "false attribution" in order to offset incorrect knowledge. So if the self is depicted as something that can be "attained", this is only to demonstrate that it cannot be realized apart from knowledge. Or if the Absolute is referred to as a "Knower", this demonstrates that only the Absolute is worth knowing, and so on.[99] In other words supportive material in the *Veda* was concerned with the means of assisting the experience of ultimate knowledge itself.

The ultimate Truth was of the acosmic Brahman that is totally identifiable with the *Ātman* of all, and that Truth is for the liberated or nearly liberated only. But for the rest of those who were permitted access to the *Veda*[100] the *sṛuti* texts provided a more acceptable philosophy and theology. It would depend on one's level of consciousness just what would be absorbed, and what left behind. Either way, Śaṃkara endorsed the *Veda* as the best possible means of knowledge. Although the *Veda* did not always portray the truth, it was the best preparation for it. But once liberation was attained, the *Veda* was rendered useless. Ultimately, no words could ever describe the Absolute, but the *Veda* could speak of Its existence in negative terms and still point in Its direction through language appropriate for those still bound by nescience. It was particularly those parts of the *Veda* that referred to Brahman in negative terms that Śaṃkara accepted – the *nirguṇa* Absolute, devoid of all qualities. "The Absolute is that in which there is no particularity. There is no name, no form, no action, no distinction, no genus, no quality. It is through these determinations alone that speech proceeds, and not one of them belongs to the Absolute. So the latter cannot be taught by sentences of the pattern 'This is so-and-so.'"[101] This did not prevent Śaṃkara from accepting the *Veda* on a variety of levels. Halbfass demonstrates well how Śaṃkara viewed the *Veda* "as a complex, differentiated structure of discourse, speaking at different levels and with different voices.[102] So however he viewed *śruti* literature it was not without the application of reason. And where *śruti* contradicted experience, experience could override it. Yet reason alone was impotent without *Vedic* revelation.[103] Ultimately, he had utmost veneration for *śruti*.

Error

Error is *avidyā*, ignorance, by which the nature of one particular thing is superimposed on another. It is, thus, "illegitimate transference".[104] In Śaṃkara's words: "It is the false appearance in one place of what has previously been seen at another place, of the nature of a memory".[105] So just as the qualities of silver are erroneously superimposed on a shell, so that the shell is mistakenly believed to be silver, the empirical, ordinary self and all its experiences are superimposed on the *Ātman*. Thus, the real nature of the *Ātman* is obscured. Error, or superimposition of the qualities of one thing onto another, is the ignorance, nescience, *avidyā*, that is endemic to life. It is a lack of discrimination between what is real and what is unreal. Nescience colours all perception, inference and testimony – all knowledge in ordinary existence – simply because only the *Ātman* as pure Consciousness is real. When there is consciousness *of* something, *of* an object, this can only be because superimposition occurs. Only the Absolute exists, and is One without a second: there can be no dualism of subject *and object*, no experience of any object in the liberated state.

Mīmāṃsakas denied error in perception, claiming that all immediate perception is valid. Thus, the rope that is mistaken for a snake to Mīmāṃsakas is taken as a mixture of perception and memory, two processes, in which the perception is valid but the memory wrong. Advaita, however, sees such error in perception as a *single* act of cognition, because in seeing a rope as a snake there is, at the time of perception, only *one* perception, *one* cognition. So, unlike the Mīmāṃsakas, Vedāntins accept perceptual error.

Similarly, Nyāya-Vaiśeṣika explained such error as the rope seeming as a snake by the power of a *real* memory of a snake imposing itself on the present idea of the rope. This suggests that the memories we have of the past are *real* and, therefore, that the world is real – a tenet that would be anathema to the Advaitin. So the Advaitin claims that the rope perceived as a snake must be erroneous perception because what comes into the mind is the *that* of the past, and not the *this* of the present perception. So what is actually perceived remains enigmatic. There is really no relation between the memory and the presently perceived object: it is ignorance that supposes so. And through ignorance the perception is given the *appearance* of something else, an appearance that is later contradicted by other knowledge; the cognition of the rope as a snake is therefore invalid and erroneous – in short, apparent reality. Such misapprehension is positive error. One only has to remove the misapprehension and reality is there. So there is some truth in all error. When we see a rope and believe it to be a snake, there *is* an object of perception (the rope) but it is misapprehended as a snake.

In every perception, a double error takes place, a misapprehension of an object that is different from all other things, and the misapprehension that that object is real. When a piece of rope is misidentified as a snake, the memory of the snake is superimposed incorrectly on the rope. But the rope is needed as the substance on which the memory can be imposed. So, too, Brahman is the foundation on which the world is superimposed, from memories and misapprehensions.

The self

Each individual consists of a physical body, a subtle body, vital breath or air, five organs of action, five senses, and the *antaḥkaraṇa*, the intellect, ego and mind. These are all aspects of the self that exist only because of *avidyā*, ignorance. The *real* Self is the *Ātman*.

And since it is passive Consciousness, the *Ātman*, the real Self, is never born, is never bound, and never dies. Like the Absolute that it is, it is not subject to any modifications at all. It is pure Being, Existence-*ness*. There is, then, a Self and a not-self. Alston writes of these: "From failure to apprehend the true nature of the Self arises, by way of unwitting superimposition or projection, a not-self. And then comes that 'failure to discriminate' (aviveka) the Self from the not-self which is the proximate cause of our self-identification with the body and mind and thus of our painful experiences in the realm of saṃsāra".[106] In Śaṃkara's words: "The notions 'oneself' and 'one's own' are indeed falsely constructed [upon *Ātman*] through nescience. When there is [the knowledge of] the oneness of *Ātman*, these notions certainly do not exist. If the seed does not exist, whence shall the fruit arise?"[107]

It is Brahman as *Ātman* that is the real essence of all things, so all Selves are identical.[108] It is only through ignorance that the illusion of the diversity of forms in existence, and the diversity between one individual and another, are present. As *Ātman* the Self pervades all things as pure Existence, pure Being. What constitutes the self is really Consciousness – that factor that unites all aspects of an individual – and it is Consciousness that, for Advaita, is not an attribute of the self, but the real *essence* of the self. The true Self is characterized by *pure* Consciousness, whereas the unreal, empirical self, is characterized by consciousness that is subject to ignorance and illusion. But this inferior consciousness can only exist by reason of the pure Being of *Ātman* as the substratum of pure Consciousness. Sinha writes: "Transcendental consciousness is to be conceived as the foundation behind the conscious life, beyond which there can be no further background – at least within the realm of personal experience."[109] Consciousness, then, is the essence of the real Self and the means of existence for the empirical self. Then, too, in sleep, consciousness remains as the essence of the self, for even in deepest sleep we have awareness that we slept deeply, for example. But what we are talking of here is not consciousness that exists just when there is something of which to be conscious. On the contrary, the Consciousness that is the essence of the self for Advaita is that which is not dependent on any objects for its manifestation, but which makes possible the consciousness of objects that characterizes the empirical self.

Thus the individual, empirical self that we ordinarily know is not the real Self, for it is changeable, finite and illusory in comparison to the *Ātman*. The *Ātman* is merely the passive observer. The *Ātman* is not at all involved in the experiences of the empirical self, even though it is present in every reincarnation. It merely observes, and is the "innermost nucleus"[110] of all cognition. As the witness the *Ātman* within is the *sākṣin*. It is Consciousness, rather like the *puruṣa* of Sāṃkhya, which becomes involved with the world through the mind of the empirical self. The *sākṣin* here is the *Ātman* bound, rather than the *Ātman* free. Yet it is different from the ordinary self, which is altogether of the world of appearance.

All the reactions of the empirical self to the world, which create a fluctuating consciousness, are illusory perceptions of reality. The *real* Self is devoid of subject–object differentiation, devoid of perceptions that are unreal, and aware only of its own self-luminosity that runs through all things. The self – whether empirical or real – can never be an object, for it is consciousness that reveals objects and it cannot itself be an object of itself.

And if consciousness *were* to be an object, then it would require something else to make it an object, and that would require something else, and so on *ad infinitum*. The self-luminous and independent nature of pure Consciousness means that any knowledge is dependent on it, but the non-liberated self remains bound to the objective world, and rarely glimpses the Reality beneath it.

This self that is so involved in the world is the *jīva*. It is the self that transmigrates, that is involved with the world in every way; it is the thinking and egoistic self. Śaṃkara depicted it as a sad self:

> But those who take part in the round of transmigration revolve round the midst of ignorance, of thick darkness, swaddled in the bonds of a thousand longings for sons and cattle and worldly goods. Thinking themselves to be wise and to be great experts in the secular and sacred sciences, they pursue a crooked and devious course. Lacking true discrimination, they wander about afflicted by old age, death and disease, like a large crowd of blind people being led by others as blind along a rocky road leading to a great disaster.[111]

These words of Śaṃkara vividly depict the bound self that is unaware of its true nature. It is an apparent, material self that is difficult to escape.

Apart from the gross body, the *jīva* functions by means of the intellect (*buddhi*), the mind (*manas*), the ego (*ahaṃkāra*) and consciousness (*cit*): collectively, the *antaḥkaraṇa*. However, Śaṃkara is not specific about his use of the terms *manas*, *buddhi* and *citta*, which can sometimes be used synonymously. And although the *antaḥkaraṇa* normally refers to intellect, ego and mind collectively, it is not clearly defined by Śaṃkara; its usage has been described as "unorganized and ambiguous".[112] It is also uncertain whether he considers the *manas*, the mind, to be a sense. Thus, there are a number of departures from Sāṃkhya usage, though he agreed that the mind was both material and unconscious. But there is a certain looseness of analysis of these aspects of the self. Śaṃkara was not really interested in the nature of such things that were, when all is said and done, aspects of material matter that were far removed from the Reality that was Brahman.

Each individual *jīva* is "but the reflection (pratibimba) of the Infinite Consciousness on the finite mirror of ignorance (avidyā) and compared to one of the many reflections of the moon cast on different receptacles of water."[113] Thus, pure Consciousness is seemingly sullied by the specific nature of the ignorance of the individual. It is the difference in this ignorance, operating through the *antaḥkaraṇa*, that makes one person appear different from another, and that makes Brahman appear as different in different selves. Like the moon or the sun reflected on water, which are really separate from it, they appear to take on the character of the water as moving or still, as rippled, murky, or clear, and so on. Potter describes such reflection analogies as "the most complex and sophisticated of the models offered by Śaṃkara and his contemporaries" to explain the apparent differences between the selves and the divine.[114] But a particularly good analogy is that noted earlier, of the *jīva* being like the space in a jar. This space is really no different to the space in other things, and no different to the space outside it. But the *jīva* ignorantly sees itself as different, and sees Brahman as confined in various forms like the space. When the jar disappears, like ignorance, the space inside becomes the space outside – which it always was – just as the self becomes the pure Existence and

Consciousness that it has always been. No modification of the original space has taken place at all, just as no modification of Brahman takes place for the illusions of the world.

The *jiva* lives life after life forgetful of its true nature as Brahman, and is constantly involved in the world and relates all things to its own ego – owning things, liking things, disliking things, and experiencing appropriate joys and sorrows. It treats others as different and as beings to be liked or disliked or indifferent to, and thus the veil of ignorance prevents *Ātman* realization. However, the egoistic self can only exist because of the pure Consciousness of *cit*. In fact, it is the association of *cit* with intellect, mind, ego, body, senses and the resulting experiences of life that makes the illusory world possible. But the pure Consciousness is there all the time, and this always lends to the self a degree of Reality that combines with the unreality of ignorance. The *antaḥkaraṇa* not only perpetuates this ignorance through its involvement in the world but, also, is that which stores past memories and past *karmic* dispositions. In a way, then, *avidyā*, ignorance, surrounds the *Ātman* layer by layer, and the veil that obscures it is constantly thickened. This answers a question I raised above in the introductory sentences about *māyā*: Why is the *Ātman* not readily perceptible? It is the *jīva* that prevents its realization because of its being bound by ignorance. Deussen poignantly remarked: "No man, whatever he may do, can get out of his own Self; everything in the world can only arouse our interest, nay, only exists for us, in so far as, affecting us, it enters the sphere of our 'I,' and so, as it were, becomes a part of us."[115]

In line with the *Taittirīya Upaniṣad*, Advaita accepted "five sheaths" or "five selves", that make up what we know as the self. Symbolically, these are like five layers of an onion. They are, first, the gross physical body (*annamayakośa*), pervaded within by the second sheath or layer, its subtle replica as vital breath or energy (*prāṇamayakośa*). The third is the subtler mind-self (*manomayakośa*), the fourth, the even subtler "knowledge-self" (*vijñānamayakośa*), and the fifth, the subtlest "bliss-self" (*ānandamayakośa*). All these are composed of the elements; they are all material, and non-conscious, though increasingly subtle. The true Self as pure Consciousness, as far as Śaṃkara was concerned, transcends all five. Each of these selves lies within the former one, and the more adept the student, the more the inner selves will be experienced. The bliss of the inner self comes from treading the path of greater control of the mind, of following the *Veda*, and practising celibacy and meditation.

Although the *Ātman* is passive and does not do anything, from the level of the ignorant self, it is said to be in three states. These – the waking, dreaming and deep sleep states – were of particular interest to Śaṃkara because of the light they cast on the question of consciousness. The true pure Consciousness that is the natural state of the Self is known as *prājña*. It becomes involved with matter, and through nescience seems to exist in the dreaming and waking states. *Virāj* or *vaiśvānara* is *prājña* in the waking state, when the senses are focused externally. In the *Māṇḍūkya Upaṇisad* it is associated with the syllable *a* of the symbol *Aum*. *Taijasa* is *prājña* in the dreaming state, when subconscious impressions come to the surface in dreams, and the effects of *karma* are worked out. In the *Māṇḍūkya Upaṇisad* it is associated with the syllable *u* of the symbol *Aum*. Here, the senses are inactive; it is only the internal organ, the *antaḥkaraṇa*, that is functioning, and that is creating the appearance of dualities. All perceptions in the dreaming state are erroneous perceptions. However, the *Ātman* is purer in this state than in the waking state, for it is not subject to the external sense stimuli and the desires and aversions that these involve, it is simply observing-consciousness. But both the waking state and the dreaming state are determined by past *karma*. If the external senses are withdrawn in the dreaming state, then this leaves only the light of pure Consciousness to view the dreams, via the intellect. Śaṃkara maintained that consciousness in dreams is no different from consciousness in the waking state. In the latter, like the former, it is merely witnessing. This renders all perception as imaginary and illusory.

Prajñā (wisdom), *avyākṛta* (unmanifest) or *tamas* (darkness) are the terms given to the *Ātman* in deep sleep, when even the *antaḥkaraṇa* is not operating. In the *Māṇḍūkya Upaniṣad* it is associated with the syllable *m* of the symbol *Aum*. It is a state in which there is total non-perception. The *Ātman* here is "a mass of mere consciousness"[116] with no sense stimuli and no activity of the intellect, mind or ego. All is still, and there can be no emotions, no experience of happiness, pain or sorrow – just consciousness. Śaṃkara believed that in this stage of dreamless sleep, the individual ceases to exist and becomes identical with the Self of all. He said: "And this same soul, embraced by its own Self in the form of Consciousness in its real natural state of transcendent Light, becomes a perfect unity, the Self of all, with no internal differentiation, and knows no other object outside itself, and no distinction within itself, such as 'This am I, happy or miserable (or whatever the case may be).'"[117]

This state of deepest sleep, then, is the closest the individual can come to the enlightened *Ātman*. The Self is united with pure Being. We might note here with Indich this hierarchy "based on increasing degrees of interiorization or unification of modified consciousness within itself".[118] But, even though the purity of it underpins deep sleep, as also, the dreaming and waking states,[119] a metaphorical "seed" of nescience remains. The *Ātman* or *sākṣin* is coalesced with nescience. Once the individual moves again into the dreaming or waking states, this "seed" will permit the subconscious impressions to influence the mind once again. The mind is simply not ready for the enlightened experience, and the Self will fall from its true nature. Thus, Śaṃkara also equates the state of deep sleep with darkness and ignorance. This is seen in his following words which, incidentally, also show that he equated *avidyā* and *māyā*:

> That which is called deep sleep is darkness or ignorance (*ajñāna*), the seed of sleeping and waking awareness. It ought to be completely burnt up by Self-knowledge like a burnt seed that does not mature.
>
> That seed, called *māyā*, evolves into three states that succeed each other over and over. The self, the locus of *māyā*, though without change and single, appears as many like reflections in the water.[120]

The only constant factor between waking, dreaming and deep sleep states is the unifying *reflected* Consciousness that is supplied by the *Ātman* that is Brahman. Beyond these three states is *turya* (*turīya*), Śaṃkara's fourth state, the final, enlightened Reality. It is the stage of spiritual intuition and knowledge of the Absolute and of the Self as that Absolute. It is consciousness of the Absolute unlike the state of dreamless sleep where the Self is at one with the Absolute, but has no consciousness of the fact. It is a knowledge that is final, eternal and infinite. Reality perceived here shows the former states of waking, dream and dreamless sleep to be unreal, though the real Self, *prājña*, remains the same through these three states.

The nature of the self in Advaita is, thus, a complex of three aspects, the real Self, the *Ātman*; the *jīvātman*, that is the *Ātman* limited by a false conjoining of it with the empirically conscious self associated with experiential existence; and the *antaḥkaraṇa*, that is the sum total of all experiences of the past, and is the cause of the reincarnating self. These last two selves are superimposed on the true self, the *Ātman*, and thus consciousness experiences joys, sorrows, suffering and the bondage of reincarnation, and identifies with the illusory phenomena of existence. *Ātman* and matter are *mutually* superimposed. Overcoming this superimposition – caused by ignorance, and overcome by knowledge – is the key to liberation.

At times it seems Śaṃkara makes the *Ātman* the agent of action. Thus, Śaṃkara wrote: "The intellect and so on are non-*Ātman* since they are by nature [objects] to be rejected or accepted. *Ātman* is the agent which rejects or accepts; [*Ātman*] is neither to be abandoned nor taken."[121] But it is really the material mind that is the cause of the self being bound to the external world, and this is not given any reality at all by Śaṃkara:

> In essence you are non-existent in this world, O Mind, since when scrutinized through reasoning [you] are [found to be] non-existent. Now there is no destruction of what is existent, and there is no origination of what is non-existent. Both [destruction and origination] belong to you. Therefore you are not accepted as the existent.[122]

Since it is only Consciousness that can perceive, the mind and intellect are not perceivers at all. It is only in this way that the *Ātman* seems to be an agent. The *Ātman* is not an agent of action, but is the "agent which rejects or accepts", purely because it lends intellect and mind the light of consciousness. So it underpins agency but is not in itself an agent. Consciousness is reflected in the many minds of the selves. And just as light sometimes seems to be broken up and diffracted as it passes through something, so Consciousness appears to be divided up into units – the many selves in existence. All the entities that Consciousness reflects are its external adjuncts (*upādhis*). Memory and subconscious impressions feed the ordinary self with reinforcements of previous desires, aversions, attachments and fears. Through nescience the self feels "I am happy, sad, intelligent" and so on. All these factors are but mind-functions, rooted in apparent matter, but not reality. Puligandla writes:

> The mind can grasp neither itself nor reality. It can only function by drawing distinctions, and for it to grasp itself it should function without drawing distinctions – a self contradiction. In a word, the mind cannot catch itself, just as a knife which cuts everything cannot cut itself. The mind can't grasp reality, because reality wholly transcends the realm of the mind – the realm of distinctions.[123]

All these attributes drawn up in the mind are assigned to the self and superimposed on the *Ātman* that is the real Self, by means of the Consciousness that is *Ātman*. But *that* Self has *no* attributes, and it can never be known as an object, only intuitively realized. In the words of Vivekananda:

> That Self cannot be known; in vain we try to know It. Were It knowable, It would not be what It is; for It is the eternal Subject. Knowledge is a limitation; knowledge is an objectifi-

> cation. It is the eternal Subject of everything, the eternal Witness of this universe – your own Self. Knowledge is, as it were, a lower step, a degeneration. We are that eternal Subject already; how can we know it?[124]

This pure Subject is Reality. It is the real Self that is Brahman. The self that we know is merely an apparent self invented by the material mind. Raphael depicts the other end of the scale from Vivekananda's words above, when he writes:

> In our mind we can conjure up an ideal, a passion, etc., and identify with it to such an extent as to forget that we are individuals above and beyond passions and ideas. We can dream while wide awake . . . and identify with our dreams to such a degree that we lose our identity. This happens to the majority of people; in fact, they are not persons but teachers, politicians, tradesmen, fathers, mothers, children etc.; they are everything and anything but entities aware of their true and profound reality.[125]

Śaṃkara believed that the presence of the Self was self-evident and had no need of proof. No one thinks "I do not exist". The problem is the *nature* of the Self and the false attributes we give it, not whether it exists or not. The Self, bound or liberated, is always the subject, never the object, for it is the knower, the experiencer. It is impossible to see the seer who is seeing, or to know the knower that is knowing. Śaṃkara refers to the Self as a "knower" only to portray the fact that the Self is never an object, and not to suggest that the Self is an agent in the process of knowledge. The Self is always inactive.[126] It needs nothing. In the words of Raphael: "The *ātman* or pure Spirit, being the Absolute in us, cannot seek experience because it is not subject to the law of *necessity*. The complete-in-itself cannot be in need of anything. The sun does not need or desire light seeing that it is itself light. In the same way, the knower cannot desire knowledge if he himself is knowledge."[127]

So any characteristics given to the Self are the results of erroneous superimposition. All its pain, suffering, joy and sensations are the result of false identification with the intellect and ego. Humorously, Śaṃkara stated: "Whoever wishes to characterize the nature of the Self in this way is like one wishing to roll up the sky like a piece of leather and climb up on it as if it were a step. He is like one hoping to find the tracks of fish in the water or of birds in the sky."[128] The Self can never be known by the mind, it can only be realized at liberation. Thus, it would be impossible to claim "I know the Absolute". That is something that can only be experienced when ignorance is removed. It is like finding you are wearing something you have been searching for, or like ten people crossing a river and the leader finding only nine at the other side – for he forgets to count himself. "Here, within our own Self, we gain an infallible guide to the absolute Being which we are seeking."[129]

Is there, then, any distinction between selves and matter? Hiriyanna affords *jīvas* a greater level of reality than the world. After all, it is selves that reflect the Consciousness that is *Ātman*. He writes: We cannot therefore say that the individual self is false (*mithyā*), as we may that the world is false."[130] But *Ātman* is the essence of all things, from Brahmā to a blade of grass. To say that the ultimate essence of *jīvas* is different from the ultimate essence of matter is to create a duality. What constitutes *jīvas* is the materiality of the intellect, ego and mind – much like the Sāṃkhya view. But there can be no difference between the *Ātman* of the self and that in a blade of grass, or any material object, otherwise non-duality is compromised.

Ultimately, then, Śaṃkara's view of the self is, again, twofold – the enlightened self that is real, and the unenlightened self that is only apparent. And Śaṃkara has to work with the latter in order, ultimately, to transcend it for the former. This gets to the centre of the way Śaṃkara taught, something brought out fully in Satchidānandendra's analysis of the method of Vedānta. He writes: "Whatever characteristics are attributed to the Self as a means to awaken the student to ultimate reality are always finally denied. This is the heart of the method."[131] Deussen called Śaṃkara's view of the two selves – the Self and the not-self – the "double fundamental view of the Vedānta".[132] The view of the liberated Self he refers to as the "esoteric" doctrine, and of the empirical self the "exoteric" doctrine.[133] It is the "exoteric" view that permits the plurality of selves in the world. So a dual perspective, as noted earlier, runs through Śaṃkara's philosophy of world, self, causality and the divine. We now need to see how it is worked out in relation to the third of these, causality.

Causality

Vedānta accepts the theory of *satkāryavāda*, as does Sāṃkhya, but whereas the latter believed that effects were transformations of their prior causes, the Advaita school believes that only the cause is real, and any apparent effects, *kārya*, exist only in the cause. In this case, no transformation occurs, and nothing new comes into being: the pot is still the clay from which it originated, just as the world is still Brahman as its Ground and Cause. This is really *satkāraṇavāda*, the belief that cause alone exists and is real, while any effects do not really exist and are illusory. The modifications of the cause are therefore of the nature of appearance only, or illusory, and is termed *vivarta*. It contrasts with the Sāṃkhya belief of the *real* transformations of cause as unmanifest *prakṛti* into the evolutes of manifest *prakṛti*, which is known as *pariṇāma*. So whereas Sāṃkhya has a theory of *satkāryavāda* that posits real effects inhering in, and evolving from, a real cause, Śaṃkara takes this theory further and relates cause and effect completely so that they are identical and non-dual. The similarity between the two schools lies in the fact that both agree that effects inhere in their causes. For Advaita it is impossible to identify the real nature of something without referring to its cause; thus the pot can only really be known in terms of the clay of which it is composed.

An effect, then, is really its cause, and if this is the case, then nothing new has come into being. Moreover, even if we take into account an efficient cause of something, like the potter who turns clay into the pot, the potter does not make anything new; the pot still remains identifiable by its clayness, and is therefore no different from its cause. "We never build anew; we simply rearrange."[134] Whenever we wish to know the basic nature of something, we have to look to its cause. For Śaṃkara a change in form was not a change in reality. Each individual as a baby, child, youth or old person changes *form* but not identity; there is no change here in *reality*, so we cannot say that the effect is different, a different reality, than the cause. And if we could separate the clay as cause, from the pot as effect, we could never have any real knowledge of an object. Brahman is, however, the cause of the universe in the same way that a rope is the cause of a false impression of it as a snake. This is because the Consciousness that is Brahman and *Ātman* underpins the perceptions we have of the world by reflecting Consciousness in the intellect–mind complex of the empirical self. But, just like the rope, no change takes place in it to become the snake, though it is the basis of the misapprehension. Just so is Brahman the non-transforming basis of the world of appearance. This, too, is *vivarta*, a cause producing effects without undergoing any real change. Brahman changes neither wholly nor partially and, as Deussen neatly puts it: "A transformation resting merely on words can alter nothing in the indivisibility of the Existent."[135]

The theory of *vivartavāda*, the belief that the world we see is but a false appearance and illusory, is unique to Advaita Vedānta. Śaṃkara described it thus:

> For pairs of opposites, like heat and cold and their causes, are not found to be real when critically examined through (perception, inference and other) recognized means of knowledge. For they are modifications and every modification is subject to change. Every formed object, like a pot, is unreal because, when it is examined through the eye, nothing is found apart from the clay or other material cause. And similarly every other modification is unreal because it is not found to be anything over and above the causal substance from which it is composed. Moreover, it is not apprehended at all before its production or after its destruction. Even the material cause itself, clay, together with its own material cause, are not found to be anything over and above the causal substances from which *they* are composed, and are hence unreal.[136]

From the standpoint of non-duality, the enlightened view, Śaṃkara had no choice but to deny that effects are non-different from their causes, otherwise the duality of cause and effect would obtain, and non-duality would be compromised. Similarly, there can be no whole and parts. Thus, the Absolute could not really emanate into the parts that form the world, "that which is partless and unborn (like the Absolute) cannot undergo real change or modification in any way whatever".[137] But from the viewpoint of nescience, the unenlightened view, Śaṃkara had to accept causality to explain the relationship between causes and their effects in the empirical world in which we live. As Alston points out, positing no causality at all would be of little help to the, as yet, unenlightened disciple: "What he then needs is not a negation of causality but a rationally defensible theory of causality which will enable him to accept and make sense of the Vedic texts at the level of ordinary subject–object experience, while at the same time leaving the window open looking out onto the vistas of infinity in which causality is finally transcended."[138]

The dual perspective of an enlightened and unenlightened view is also applicable to the creation and dissolution of the universe as much as to the ordinary world of forms that we know, because it is something that is accepted only by the unenlightened. Creation is an *apparent* and not real evolution of the world from Brahman. Brahman as Cause does not change, and the world as effect always remains grounded in the Cause. The *apparent* changes are the illusory power of *māyā*, but in so far as the world is experienced as one of effects – as one with objects like selves and pots – *māyā* has a creative power to manifest itself in all things from the subtle to the gross to all those who are not enlightened to the

Reality behind it. Cause and effect are one, so there is no difference between Brahman and the world of effects, but the effects as we mistakenly know them – the pot devoid of its causal substance of clay – are superimposed incorrectly on their cause. So the forms of things are given differentiated reality, while the *substance* is disregarded. The link that unites all things as their essence is missed for the illusory effects. In other words, Brahman as the true Cause is overlooked, and through ignorance, *ajñāna* or *avidya*, all appearances in the world are given reality.

Śaṃkara's theory of creation solves one of the major difficulties that were highlighted in the discussion concerning the nature of reality in the *Introduction.* This difficulty is how to relate a world of change and finitude to the Absolute, ultimate Reality that is unchanging and infinite. Once it is claimed that the world emanates forth from Brahman, then it has to be conceded that *part* of Brahman – the world – is changeable. This is somewhat contradictory and also inimical to the concept of the Absolute, permanent Cause. And yet, if the world with all its finitude exists separately from Brahman, then the nature of Brahman is limited or, to really maintain its *absolute* nature, Brahman must be both change and permanence. Śaṃkara solves all these difficulties through the theory of *satkāraṇavāda.* The world of change is not real; it only appears so through ignorance. There are no changes, for the effects are the same as their cause and are permanent; the changes are apparent and not real. And the world does not exist separately from Brahman: it is, in its essence, identical to Brahman, it is an apparent effect that inheres in its cause and is identical to its cause. Once Brahman is identified with the world – either wholly or partially – then the permanent and unchanging nature of Brahman is compromised. Śaṃkara's theory of causality being one of apparent and not real modification from cause to effect, avoids this difficulty.

All this does not really explain how the world of forms – apparent or otherwise – actually takes shape for each and every individual, and why the possibility of so many apparent effects, unreal as they may be, can be present. In the *Upaniṣads* it is clear that the world *does* come forth from Brahman, and this would seem to offer it a degree of reality. Indeed, such a partial reality of all creation is a feature of Rāmānuja's *viśiṣṭadvaita.* As noted above, to overcome the difficulty *māyā* is the power of illusion and ignorance in creation that, after Śaṃkara, came to be credited to Brahman. So while Brahman does not actually change, *māyā* is the power that is within Brahman just like the power to burn is inherent in fire. In this case, creation is not an independent or dependent effect of Brahman, it is Brahman with a veil of ignorance thrown over it to make it appear as diverse effects. The difficulties of the projection of *māyā* into creation are manifold, and have resulted in various explanations in Vedānta as a whole.

So whereas the *Upaniṣads* tend to present creation as an emanation of the Absolute, Brahman, as does the *Brahmasūtras*, Śaṃkara could not bring himself to link the world so intimately with the divine in the sense of a finite and impermanent world emanating from the eternal Brahman. The concept of an Absolute that was active in a world of suffering and change was impossible to Śaṃkara. And yet, since the average individual – even the disciples of Śaṃkara – was far from the end of the spiritual journey, positing a Creator of the world had some value for those still within the bounds of an egoistic existence. As Alston points out, "the conception of the Absolute as the Creator and Controller of the world, endowed with omniscience, omnipotence, compassion and other superabundant excellencies, is for most people the best that is available".[139] So Śaṃkara has two concepts of creation: first, the enlightened view, that it does not exist at all, it has never happened; and second, that for those entrapped in nescience, there is no harm in accepting the divine as a Creator and Sustainer of the world. It is only the liberated one who continues to live in what Alston terms "a kind of twilight existence" until death.[140] Creation here exists only in so far as the enlightened one has a physical body that encases the true Self that is Brahman. All else ceases to have effect on what is now a Reality that transcends "creation".

For those not liberated, it makes sense to understand the divine in the same kind of dual sense that one understands the rest of life. Thus, as Śaṃkara stated, "the 'Lordship' of the Lord, as well as His omniscience and omnipotence, exist only in relation to external conditions (*upādhi*) which are (illusory because they are) of the nature of nescience".[141] Thus, it is through such "Lordship" that a divine creator can be posited. So Śaṃkara does not devote his energies solely to the enlightened view of Reality. He writes of creation, of duality, of an omnipresent God, and of the world of varied effects that rise from the single Absolute of Brahman – all of which is ultimately unreal when intuitive knowledge reveals the *Ātman* as Brahman. And it has to be said that Śaṃkara writes *extensively* of the world of nescience and of the unreal God that creates and sustains it.

Thus, in his commentary on the *Brahmasūtras* Śaṃkara appears to accept Brahman as both the efficient and the material cause of the world, accepting the *pariṇāma* or transformation of Brahman into the effects that are the universe. This makes God the creator, maintainer and dissolver of the universe, and the inner controller, or *antaryāmin*, of all existence – even if all this is far from the Truth. But these concepts are taught "as a preliminary device to help induce the mind to understand the unity and sole reality of the Self."[142] In considering the *Upaniṣadic* texts, Śaṃkara believed those passages that taught of the creation-through-emanation theory, were deliberately directed to those who, in their world of nescience, could only think in terms of causality. The higher wisdom of Brahman as separate from the world, as non-Creator and Consciousness only, the identity of Brahman and *Ātman*, and the illusory nature of all else, were aspects of the *Upaniṣads* pertinent to *ultimate* and non-dual Reality. Only the liberated *Ātman* could experience this higher Reality. Ultimately, the Absolute is not subject to any modification at all. Thus, commenting on the *Brahmasūtras*, Śaṃkara stated:

> But the Absolute becomes subject to modification and to all empirical experience through distinctions consisting of name and form, manifest and unmanifest, which are imagined through nescience and are indeterminable either as being the reality itself or as being anything different. But in its ultimately true form it remains beyond all empirical experience and not subject to modification (pariṇāma).[143]

It is also from the viewpoint of nescience that Brahman is said to be he who metes out the respective rewards and punishments according to the *karmic* merit and demerit of each individual. But since that *karma*, too, is illusory, the Absolute remains the inactive pure Consiousness at all times, experienced only by the liberated, but believed to be the controller of the world and all that is in it by those still bound by nescience. The acceptance of these two aspects of Brahman neatly reflects the dichotomy of the cosmic and acosmic views of Brahman in the *Upaniṣads*, but Śaṃkara's attempts to solve it are not wholly successful. He gives so much space to the world of dualities that it is difficult to see how he can ultimately deny it. He can even posit a very tangible theory of creation.

Śaṃkara's reliance on Sāṃkhya philosophy is seen in his positing of a primary unmanifest matter that he calls "unmanifest name-and-form". It is the seed from which the whole cosmos evolves, and is analogous to the Sāṃkhya *avyakta*. However, unlike Sāṃkhya, unmanifest name-and-form is said to have emerged directly from Brahman. The first evolute of unmanifest name-and-form is ether, and from ether comes air. Fire comes from air, water comes from fire, earth comes from water. In this way the five gross elements that form all matter and life emerge, starting with the subtlest, and ending with the grossest. When the universe is dissolved, the elements recede in the reverse order from that of evolution. Śaṃkara also accepted (from the viewpoint of nescience) the cyclical *kalpas* written of in much *smṛti* literature. These are periods of the world's manifest existence interspersed with its quiescence – evolution and involution. But it is unmanifest name-and-form that runs through all things. Importantly, unmanifest name-and-form, though originating from Brahman, has no substantiality to be an emanation of Brahman. It is mere potential, so Brahman is separated from ether and all that emerges from it. While Brahman pervades all that has name-and-form as *Ātman*, It remains separate from every created substance, whether subtle or gross, but It is identical to the innermost essence of all things. However, name-and-form is illusory, composing the world through the nescience of the beings within it:

> He for the sake of attaining whom the whole discipline of Advaita is undertaken: He to whom agency, action and its results are falsely attributed through natural ignorance: He who is the cause of the whole universe: He who is the real nature of that unmanifest name and form which come to manifestation like cloudy foam from clear water: He who is different from that (manifest) name and form, by His very nature eternal, pure, illumined and free: He, bringing into manifestation unmanifest name and form, which were really none other than Himself, entered into all these bodies from Brahmā to the nearest clump of grass.[144]

Mayeda points out two difficulties that this cosmological view of Śaṃkara's poses. The first is the problem of the material evolute of ether arising from Brahman as pure Consciousness, and the second is the dualism that ensues by separating pure Consciousness and material evolutes.[145] To overcome this, Śaṃkara depicted Brahman as the clear water that underpins dirty foam, the latter being analogous to name-and-form. Clear water overlaid with dirty foam cannot be separated, and yet the dirty foam can never be the same as the clear water.[146] But, as Mayeda notes, the theory of unmanifest name-and-form – peculiar to Śaṃkara – was sufficiently problematic alongside a doctrine of an illusory world, that his followers did not take it up. Indeed, it is difficult to see how Śaṃkara could deal at length with a world of illusory matter witnessed only through the ignorance of the unenlightened, and an evolutionary name-and-form world that Brahman motivates – albeit indirectly. Lott, justifiably, considers that Śaṃkara found causality "extremely difficult to fit into his concept of the transcendence of the supreme Being".[147] It will be the *saguṇa* concept of Brahman as Īśvara that will fulfil this function in overcoming some of the difficulties.

The collective *karmas* of all individuals – the myriad impressions built up by a humanity trapped in nescience – are what cause the particular nature of the next world appearance. The power of ignorance to produce this is *śakti*. Through nescience an individual has a misconceived perception of causes and effects, and a relational desire for certain effects and an aversion for others. The world of appearances does not disappear when I am not perceiving it myself, for it exists for the effects of the collective *karmas* of other individuals also. It is an apparent plurality that is particularly difficult to explain away, especially considering the amount of space the Advaitin affords it in discussion. Individual *karma*, and the transmigration necessitated by it, are determined by the subconscious impressions (*saṃskāras*) and habits (*vāsanās*) that are built up over countless past lives, all carried forward to the next life by the subtle body, the *liṅgaśarīra*.

Śaṃkara followed much of the traditional *Upaniṣadic* view of the cause–effect process that brings about reincarnation. It occurs roughly according to the following process. At death, speech, followed by the functions of other organs, is absorbed in mind, then all is absorbed into *prāṇa*, breath, which is then absorbed into the self, with its *karmic* residues and impressions from past actions. This self then becomes associated with the subtle elements, the *tanmātras*, which provide its subtle body. This collocation of subtleties, including all the codes for the new being that will link the immediate past life to the next one, then resides in the heart, before leaving the physical body for good. Two paths are then available for the subtle bodies. The "northern path" is for those who have knowledge of Brahman. It is the way of the gods, and will lead to light, to the sun, and liberation. Here, meritorious *karmic* residues will be used up, and the reincarnating life, if it exists at all, will be in divine form, enough to acquire the knowledge of Brahman necessary for liberation at the end of the *kalpa*, when the universe is withdrawn. The "southern path" is for those who have followed *Vedic* rituals carefully, but who do not have knowledge of Brahman. It leads through smoke to the moon. Through the acquisition of merit, a happy existence will be the fate of those on the southern path in the specific heaven of their chosen deity. But when that good *karmic* merit is used up, a return to a human birth will occur. Deities assist these subtle selves on the stages of their respective journeys. Those who are not suited for either the northern or southern paths are reborn in plant, insect or minor animal forms.

The subtle bodies of those who are destined to return to earth, those who reached the moon, pass through ether, air, smoke, mist, cloud and rain, back to the earth. This is the reverse order to their ascent to the moon after death. The subtle body is no larger than a grain of rice and, as such, its fate on the earth is a hazardous one. It may take a long time before it is ingested by an animal or human, is passed into the blood and semen, and is then reborn with a physical body. The newly-born is not starting anew in character, type of birth, birth circumstances, and so on. All these factors, and those that befall it in life, will be determined by past *karma*, specifically *prārabdhakarma*.[148]

The cause and effect process that results in transmigration has nothing to do with the *Ātman*. It only *seems* as if the self is born time and time again, and that it experiences the joys and woes of existence. In reality the cause–effect process also does not exist, but through ignorance, nescience, we experience ourselves as mortal beings with all the trappings that mortality brings. Ultimately, the Absolute remains *neti neti*, "not this, not this", neither manifest nor unmanifest, always beyond all dualities. Bearing in mind the Advaita view of causality as a particular kind of *satkāryavāda* whereby effects are non-different from their causes, true modifications of the cause into effects cannot occur. The diversity that seems to exist in all creation, cannot have any reality, for "this pluralistic universe, consisting of experiencers and their objects of experience, is nothing other than the Absolute".[149]

The concept of God

Śaṃkara wrote of two concepts of God, the concept held by the liberated Self, and that held by the non-liberated. As far as he was concerned, this reflected the teachings of the *Upaniṣads* where two kinds of Brahman are dealt with, the *nirguṇa* Brahman without attributes, the "higher Brahman" and the *saguṇa* Brahman, the "lower Brahman", who has attributes and is that from which the whole world comes forth. As *nirguṇa,* Brahman is the ultimate Reality and essence that pervades existence: It is *sat* and *cit.*[150] Anything beyond this is unreal. Śaṃkara's supreme Brahman, the higher Brahman or *Parabrahman*, is the *nirguṇa* Brahman about which nothing can logically be conceptualized: no distinctions can be made about It. It is therefore indeterminate. Even descriptions such as infinite, pure Consciousness, ultimate Reality, and so on, cannot in any way depict this totally transcendent Absolute. Assigning attributes or qualities would only serve to limit It in some way. It is, thus, non-predicable in every sense. However, it is an utter denial of any qualities for Brahman that is not without its critics. Lott writes:

> There is no denying the determination with which Sankara sets out to protect the absolute nature of the knowledge of Brahman. The skill and the consistency with which he maintains its transcendent nature is impressive. The question is, however, whether this does not result in a loss of viability as a theological descriptive method. He can allow no statement about that supreme Being to stand without radically stripping it of all those positive meanings normally associated with such statements.[151]

This is perfectly true, but Śaṃkara counteracts negative statement of Brahman with the fully describable Īśvara.

Thus, in contrast to the *nirguṇa* Brahman is the *saguṇa* aspect of Brahman. It is the *saguṇa* Brahman who is equated with the ocean, the Ground from which the changing waves that form its surface exist. But, always, it is the *nirguṇa* Brahman that is the *ultimate* Reality, and it is that which the Self really is. As Arvind Sharma puts it, "Advaita accepts one God as the ultimate *empirical* reality, but not as the ultimate *absolute* reality".[152] It is only in the latter case that the waves *are* the ocean, not an extension of it. It is the *saguṇa* aspect of Brahman that becomes Īśvara, "Lord", or "God". It was the aspect of the divine particularly developed by Rāmānuja. Īśvara is the perspective of God held by the empirical self. As such, it is a perspective that must be seen only through the veil of ignorance that is the characteristic of all knowledge other than Brahman realization. As Chandradhar Sharma says, "the moment we speak of Brahman, He ceases to be Brahman and becomes Īshvara".[153] This is because, being *saguṇa*, Īśvara has qualities. These are qualities normally associated with supreme divinity – omniscience, omnipotence, omnipresence, Creator, Sustainer, Dissolver. It is Īśvara that can be the focus of worship but, in so far as it is ignorance that sustains the view of him, when liberation occurs, Īśvara will cease to exist, for the real essence of Brahman is the *nirguṇa* totally transcendent Absolute. Īśvara, then, is only *apparent*, like all the other illusory phenomena in the universe. Thus: "Transcendental absolutism becomes when it passes through the will of man's mind an empirical theism, which is true until true knowledge arises, even as dream states are true until awakening occurs."[154] In some ways, then, Īśvara is identifiable with the empirical self, for both are identified with *māyā*. As controller of the grosser aspects of *māyā* as creation, Īśvara is termed *Virāṭ Puruṣa* or *Vaiśvānara*. Yet, Śaṃkara's position is undermined somewhat by his use of the terms *Parābrahman*, *Paramātman*, *Parameśvara* and *Īśvara* as synonyms, for this suggests a blurring of the distinctions between the *nirguṇa* and *saguṇa* Brahman.

When he writes of the *saguṇa* form of Brahman, Śaṃkara states that the *ātman* and Brahman are dual, "the Lord is something more than the embodied soul if the latter is considered *qua* embodied",[155] because he is writing for those who are still bound by nescience. Any differentiation at all – whether between worldly phenomena or between Brahman and *Ātman* – is ignorant perception. It is only when he writes of the *nirguṇa* Brahman that he writes of the non-duality of all things and identifies the *Ātman* as Brahman. "Brahman cast through the moulds of logic is Īśvara", wrote Radhakrishnan: "It is the best image of the truth possible under our present conditions of knowledge."[156] And in Śaṃkara's own words:

> (The Absolute is that which ultimately has to be known.) So, in order to show that it exists, it is first spoken of in its false form set up by adjuncts, and fancifully referred to as if it had knowable qualities in the words "with hands and feet everywhere." For there is the saying of those who know the tradition (sampradāya-vid) "That which cannot be expressed (in its true form directly) is expressed (indirectly) through false attribution and subsequent denial."[157]

It is *śrūti* that provides knowledge of the omnipotent, omnipresent and omniscient God, the cause of the universe, as much as of the indescribable Brahman.

Īśvara is thus intimately connected with *māyā* and is as unreal as *māyā*. As Dasgupta pointed out, "he is but a phenomenal being; he may be better, purer, and much more powerful than we, but yet he is as much phenomenal as any of us. The highest truth is the self, the reality, the Brahman, and both jīva and Īśvara are but illusory impositions on it."[158] Brahman is like a magician or actor, and Īśvara like the role of the magician or actor on stage. The real person is not the one that we see and the degree to which we identify with the roles is the degree to which we are ignorant of the real nature of the magician and the actor. Thus, to the discerning, Īśvara lacks any reality. If we want to view the magician as real, or Īśvara as real, or the rope as a real snake, then, bound by our own ignorance, we can do so. But Reality is not affected by such ignorance. The magician is really someone else, and neither Īśvara nor the rope are really what we think they are just because we see them so. Brahman is not a Creator, the quality of being such is not a part of the *nirguṇa* essence of Brahman: the apparent association of creation with Brahman is only the result of our illusion and ignorance.

It is not difficult to see that a *nirguṇa* Brahman is removed from any taint of involvement in the *karmic* world. It is only at the relative level of reality that good and evil obtain, and that Īśvara might be said to be responsible for both. But at the point where all dualities cease to exist – Brahman realization – there can be no good or evil. In any case, at the empirical level it is the *karmas* of individuals that bring about resulting good or evil. So, in the long run, divinity is removed from evil (or good), at both the relative and absolute levels.

One problem that emerges with the concept of Īśvara is his relation to the individual *jīvas*. According to Chandradhar Sharma, *jīvas* are Īśvara in the same way that space in jars is really all the same. But Hiriyanna's perspective is more pertinent. He considers that,

> saguṇa Brahman cannot be the same as any of the jīvas with its fragmentary experience. Nor can it be regarded as a collection of all of them, for that would give us only a collection of individual experiences and not, as required, an integral one which alone can serve as the ground and explanation of the whole universe. That is, we cannot identify the saguṇa Brahma with either any of the jīvas or with the totality of them. Equally imposssible is it to think of it as altogether different from or outside them, for in that case there would not be that intimate connection between the two which is implied in the description of the whole as a system.[159]

Hiriyanna's views are sound, for Īśvara is qualified by very different limiting adjuncts or *upādhis* than finite *jīvas*. But what has to be remembered as far as Śaṃkara was concerned is that both Īśvara and *jīvas* have the same degree of reality, and that is a reality totally sublated by the higher reality of Brahman. We can posit what we like at the empirical and experiential level – ultimately it is all false.

Yet, despite the relative unreality of Īśvara he serves the purpose of directing the steps of the individual to the higher planes of the evolution of the self. He is "an empirical postulate which is practically useful",[160] who points the way forward to the more ultimate level of Reality. Vivekananda depicts this well: "The God of heaven becomes the God in nature, and the God in nature becomes the God who is nature, and the God who is nature becomes the God within this temple of the body, and the God dwelling in the temple of the body at last becomes the temple itself, becomes the soul and man."[161] Īśvara can therefore be viewed as a means to the ultimate goal of liberation. So Śaṃkara was not totally non-theistic in his approach to that goal. He recognized the role of Īśvara, and even of many deities, in the progressive path to *mokṣa*.

To Śaṃkara, the pre-eminent deity was Viṣṇu, whom he preferred to call Nārāyaṇa or Vāsudeva. Thus, he did not eschew the vast *smṛti* literature that dealt with the God Viṣṇu. Deities such as Viṣṇu, in particular his *avatāras* of Rāma and Kṛṣṇa, were an important focus for those on the path to liberation. Frequently, too, Śaṃkara equated Viṣṇu with the Absolute, whereas all other deities have vicarious roles and proceed from the great creator deity Brahmā, he who holds all aspects of creation, and all *karmic* dimensions of the human self in his mind. All these deities other than Viṣṇu are finite and transient, and every one is ultimately illusory. The great creator God Brahmā, also called Hiraṇyagarbha and Prajāpati, is the world-soul, the divine being at the apex of all divinity and humanity. While the distinction between Īśvara and Brahmā is sometimes blurred in respect of their functions, Brahmā seems to have been equated with the Cosmic Intellect, consisting of the totality of past experiences of all beings. This brings about a certain identity between all beings, and an interconnectedness of all experiences.[162] But Brahmā is still part of the illusory nature of the world, though posited as the active creator by those bound by nescience. From this nescient point of view, Brahmā also reflects the Consciousness of the Absolute, and is thus able to function in his own specific way as creator.

If there is a divine creator, and creation is an illusory appearance of effects, then it follows that God is also the creator of *māyā* – an illusory creator creating an illusory world. Dandekar calls *māyā* "the potency imagined of *brahman* for cosmological purpose",[163] and Hiriyanna depicts it as "a mere accessory to Īśvara" in his role of creation, a "self-consciousness or self-determination".[164] As noted earlier in this chapter, Śaṃkara was justifiably critical of the Sāṃkhya theory of an unconscious material cause producing such a logical world of effects. Only an intelligent cause can do this – in this case, Īśvara. But there is only a need to posit such a material or efficient cause if the effects that are the world are real. In Śaṃkara's case, ultimately, they are not. Īśvara is removed from the scene as material and efficient cause once the higher Reality is experienced. An elaborate theory of Īśvara's role in creation and control of *māyā* seems, therefore, somewhat contrived, even if it is the empirical world itself that assigns to Īśvara the potency to create it, and Brahman ever remains *nirguṇa*, pure Consciousness and pure Essence.

It is this acceptance of the *saguṇa* aspect of Brahman – albeit from the view of ignorance – and the many words that are used to portray his character, his involvement in the world process, his grace to his devotees, and so on, that belies the Advaitin standpoint of the world as only apparent. It is all very well to give analogies of a rope that appears to be a snake or, even more appropriately, that of the image in a mirror that is taken to be real, but to waste so many words on the snake and the mirror image, is illogical. Potter states:

> What is difficult to comprehend from the standpoint of ordinary theism is that the Advaitin can say all this about God and yet view Him as conditioned by ignorance. Brahman is the Supreme, the texts say, and yet in the same breath they affirm that He is not only not the Highest, His properties are unreal, false attributions of our ignorant superimpositions.[165]

Thus, the Advaitin is open to a good deal of valid criticism concerning the world of illusion in which he lives so enthusiastically. And as Potter later remarks: "Whatever the uninitiated may make of this apparently ambivalent attitude to the deity, it is undeniable that some, including Śaṃkara, are able to work up a fervent devotional attitude toward God despite His involvement with ignorance."[166] Ultimately, the Absolute does not act, does not change, does not exercise power. It is not unlike the single *puruṣa* of Sāṃkhya, the impassive witness, consisting of pure Consciousness, although for Advaita there is only *one* essence, one Consciousness that is every *Ātman*. But if this is the Real, why waste so much space on the unreal? Radhakrishnan has one answer. According to him, the difficulty of the relation between the unchanging Brahman and the changing world can only be solved by Īśvara. He wrote:

> The only way is through the recognition of a saguṇa brahman or changing Brahman, and Īśvara who combines within himself the natures of both being and becoming, the unattached Brahman and the unconscious prakṛti. The indeterminate for thought becomes the self-determined. The primal unity goes out of itself and produces a manifestation relatively independent of it. The pure, simple, self-subsistent Absolute becomes the personal Lord, the principle of being in the universe, binding all things to each other in binding them to himself.[167]

Radhakrishnan's view is legitimate, providing Śaṃkara's dual perspective of the enlightened and unenlightened concept of divinity is maintained. Śaṃkara struggled to overcome the dual portrayal of an acosmic and cosmic Brahman in the *Upaniṣads*, not to maintain them. The "radical ontological discontinuity" of which Indich wrote was clearly a problem for Radhakrishnan.[168] Linking the finite with the infinite would not have been possible to Śaṃkara, but it is interesting that even Śaṃkara himself focuses so readily on the *saguṇa* God. It is small wonder that later Advaitins found the issue of Īśvara, to use Sharma's phrase, "a taxing problem".[169]

Liberation

Liberation is what results when the involvement of the *jīva* in the illusory world ceases and pure Consciousness shines through. Potter puts the Advaita position on liberation succinctly in the following words: "The Advaita view is simple to state and devastating in its implications. Liberation is nothing more nor less than being, knowing and experiencing one's true Self. In this disarming statement we can find the key to many of the Advaita teachings."[170] Liberation is not a change from an unenlightened state to an enlightened one. It is simply the removal of the misconceptions about reality, a different perspective of reality that is not coloured by error. The Self that knows itself as the Absolute is the same Self that is the essence of the ordinary self; it is just obscured. Thus, Śaṃkara stated: "There is no real distinction between a (supposed) liberated and a (supposed) non-liberated state, for the Self is ever identical."[171] So liberation cannot be reached, found or acquired. It is not a result of some action. Nothing happens to the *Ātman* at liberation. It is as it always has been. Śaṃkara said: "It is also unreasonable that [final release] is a change of state [in *Ātman*], since [It] is changeless. If there were change [in *Ātman*, [It] would have parts; consequently [It] would perish, like a jar, etc."[172] Śaṃkara said that when nescience disappears and the Self becomes liberated, "empirical existence just disappears, swallowed up in the Self, like the squall of wind accompanying a stroke of lightning that vanishes into the sky, or the fire that sinks down into the burnt-out fuel".[173]

As far as the means to liberation were concerned, the life of the monk is the ideal according to Śaṃkara:

> The true discipline is to become a monk and give up the three desires for a son, wealth and a "world" (after death) and then to cultivate the qualities of wisdom . . . child-like simplicity and sagehood (mauna). Psychological defects like attachment, aversion, infatuation and the like have to be ironed out. The monk must know from the beginning what he has to reject, what he has to know, what he has to cultivate and what he has to eliminate, as this is the means to success.[174]

Śaṃkara saw meditation, *upāsana*, as an important part of the *Veda* and seems to have differentiated it from both ritual and knowledge.[175] While meditation would be expected to be meritorious in connection with ritual practice, it also brought spiritual knowledge. But it is meditation on the Absolute in its associated forms of particular deities, a practice that was believed to bring about liberation gradually, that was specifically taken up by

Śaṃkara. Since the Absolute could not be accessed *directly* through such meditation, the finite forms of the Absolute provide an appropriate intermediate focus. The advantage of such meditation was that, after death, the practitioner could enter the abode of the deity on whom he had focused, there to await the end of the aeon, when he would become Brahman and transmigrate no more. While recognizing that meditation on a finite form of a deity was still an action undertaken from the point of nescience, its ultimate result, according to Śaṃkara, was a transcendence of nescience to become Brahman. He stated: "Such meditations (Upāsanas) contribute to the final understanding of the metaphysical truth by purifying the mind, and are in this sense auxiliaries to knowledge of non-duality: and because they offer a definite conception for the mind to hold on to they are easy to practise."[176] Thus, a gradual path to liberation seems to have been accepted by Śaṃkara – one that leads to the heaven of Hiraṇyagarbha/Brahmā. Śaṃkara said:

> The unenlightened man is eligible for the ritual laid down in the Veda, which may be performed with or without accompanying symbolic meditations and which varies according to caste and stage of life. On this path (i.e. of ritual) he may rise higher and higher from the condition of man up to that of Hiraṇyagarbha. If, however, he ignores the injunctions and prohibitions of the Veda and acts merely according to his natural inclinations he will sink from the human level to that of vegetation.[177]

The real point of meditation is put clearly by Alston:

> In Advaita teaching there is ultimately no duality. All deities, therefore, are reducible in the end to the non-dual Self. In their own true nature, they are identical with the true nature of the person meditating on them. It is therefore possible for a meditator to reach through meditation an intuitive awareness of his identity with the deity on whom he is meditating, and that awareness may have different degrees of intensity, ranging from a full sense of identity to a mere sense of proximity, according to the degree of intensity with which the meditative path is pursued.[178]

Meditation that informs the gradual path, however, is surpassed by that which is more directly intuitive. This is *nididhyāsana* "deep" or "sustained meditation". It is "fixing the mental gaze on the principle of reality to determine its true nature, like one examining a jewel".[179] It is associated with the higher Brahman. *Upāsana*, on the other hand, is "maintaining a stream of identical images of which the form is (not dictated by one's knowledge of any reality but) prescribed in the Veda",[180] and is associated with the lower, *saguṇa* Brahman. Meditation by *yogins* is *nididhyāsana*. It places them on the "northern path", mentioned above, and is meditation on the sacred syllable of *Aum*. These are the *yogins* for whom liberation will be the result in life. Others, who are destined to be reborn, follow the "southern path" of meditation. The crux of Śaṃkara's teaching on meditation, however, comes with his words on *adhyātma yoga*, meditation on the supreme Self. Through constant hearing of the knowledge that the *Veda* presents,[181] constant reflection on what has been heard, and constant meditation, that moment of direct intuitive knowledge (*anubhava*) of the identity of the Self with the Absolute and with all, occurs. Some of Śaṃkara's own writings, as exemplified in the *Upadeśasāhasrī,* were clearly used for meditation, and reflect the striving for intuitive discernment. The following, sensitively translated by Alston, is an example:

> I am the Absolute, the all, ever pure, ever enlightened. I am unborn and am everywhere beyond decay, indestructible and immortal. In all beings there is no other knower but me. I distribute the rewards of merit and demerit. I am the Witness and illuminer, eternal, non-dual, without empirical qualities. I am neither being nor non-being nor being and non-being combined. I am the Alone, the Transcendent. I am that eternal Witness in whom there are neither day nor night, neither dawn nor dusk. Like the ether in being subtle and free from all form, I am one without a second. I am the non-dual Absolute, void even of the ether.[182]

There is much in the discipline and process of meditation that is reminiscent of classical Yoga, though Alston is of the opinion that Śaṃkara puts forward a *yoga* that is different from the *rājayoga* of Patañjali.[183] Yet it seems Śaṃkara endorsed the meditative process of extracting the mind from its involvement with sense stimuli, the dissolution of the mind into the *buddhi* and *antaḥkaraṇa*, then into "the great Self" of Hiraṇyagarbha, presumably, the equivalent of the Sāṃkhya and Yoga *mahatbuddhi*. It is at this point that the true Self can be realized.[184] Thus, Śaṃkara quotes the *Kaṭha Upaniṣad*: "The wise man should dissolve the senses in the mind and should dissolve the mind in the higher mind [the *buddhi*]. The higher mind he should dissolve in the great Self [*mahatbuddhi*] and he should dissolve that in the Self that is pure peace."[185] This correlates particularly well with the Yoga view of liberation. The similarities to Patañjali's Yoga are also clear in the following words of Śaṃkara, referring to the final discriminating knowledge that brings liberation: "When this clear knowledge arises, the pure intellect becomes capable of apprehending the Absolute. The meditator then perceives the Self in contemplation, devoid of all distinction, being himself possessed of truthfulness and other helpful virtues, with mind one-pointed and senses withdrawn from objects."[186] Like classical Yoga, the path to liberation is arduous: "Only those who possess the kind of buoyant will that would be capable of draining the ocean with the tip of a piece of grass can acquire rigid control of the mind."[187]

The influence of Yoga is certainly evident in Śaṃkara's advocating of one-pointed meditation as a means to liberation: "Because the Self is Consciousness unassociated with objects, it is supremely peaceful. Being Consciousness-by-nature, the Self is eternal light. It is called one-pointed meditation (samādhi) because it can only be known in the high state of consciousness (prajñā) attained in one-pointed meditation (samādhi)."[188] And yet, Śaṃkara's view of Patañjali's Yoga seems to be that it is devoid of Self-knowledge, and involves action.[189] This is true, but like Advaita, the liberated Self passes beyond all the action that is involved with material *prakṛti*. As I see it, there is little difference between the *yogin* of Yoga and the *saṃnyāsin* of Advaita in the state of *jīvanmukti*, other than one is insular and the other unified with Brahman. However, unlike classical Yoga, where liberation has to be worked at, ultimate knowledge of the Self as Brahman is, at best, instantaneous. "Once it dawns, it dawns for ever and at once removes all ignorance and consequently all bondage."[190]

Of all meditations, that on the symbol of *Aum* is the superlative. Śaṃkara said of it:

> It is a symbol, like the image standing as the symbol of Viṣṇu or some other deity. When it is meditated on as the Absolute with deep reverence, the latter manifests "grace" and reveals itself to the meditator. This is so in the case of the unconditioned Absolute, and it also holds true of the conditioned Absolute. Hence the text identifies the sound OM with the uncon-

> ditioned and conditioned Absolute by way of a figure of speech.
> Therefore, he who knows this attains either to the unconditioned or conditioned Absolute through meditation on the syllable OM, this means of attaining to the Self. For the syllable OM is the closest symbol of the Absolute there is.[191]

In the *Upadeśasāhasrī* Śaṃkara says that the means to liberation should only be taught to one with faith and desire, and,

> if he is dispassionate toward all things non-eternal which are attained by means [other than knowledge]; if he has abandoned the desire for sons, wealth, and worlds and reached the state of a *paramahaṃsa* wandering ascetic; if he is endowed with tranquility, self-control, compassion, and so forth; if he is possessed of the qualities of a pupil which are well known from the scriptures; if he is a Brahmin who is [internally and externally] pure; if he approaches his teacher in the prescribed manner; if his caste, profession, behavior, knowledge [of the *Veda*], and family have been examined.[192]

While Śaṃkara conceded that *śruti* ritualism was essential for those on the lower slopes to liberation, and potential disciples of his would certainly be expected to be well versed in walking the path of *Vedic* morality and ritual, such ritualism was activity, and all activity is of the nature of illusion, not of the Consciousness that is Brahman. For this reason, action could not ultimately procure liberation. But tradition endorses *dharmic* activity in obedience to *Vedic* injunctions, and this must involve ritual activity. There are occasions, then, when Śaṃkara is prescriptive about the means to liberation, as Mayeda notes in his analysis of Śaṃkara's *Upadeśasāhasrī* 1:17, 21–3. Here, much akin to the initial *aṇgas* of Yoga, Śaṃkara advocates restraint, non-violence, truthfulness, non-theft, continence, non-possessions, austerities, concentration, bodily emaciation, and performance of obligatory *Vedic* duties.[193] Śaṃkara believed it important to maintain such practices until ignorance was removed – until the point of liberation. In the *Upadeśasāhasrī,* Śaṃkara says that "the use of rituals and their requisites is prohibited, if the identity [of *Ātman*] with the highest *Ātman* is realized",[194] and "since all the rituals and their requisites such as the sacred thread are the effects of nescience, they should be abandoned by him who is established in the view of the highest truth".[195] But the following extract suggests the necessity of action up to the point of liberation: "When the mind becomes pure like a mirror, knowledge shines forth; therefore [the mind should be purified]. The mind is purified by abstention, the permanent rites, sacrifices, and austerities."[196] Ultimately, however, Śaṃkara said: "Actions result in things being produced, obtained, changed, or purified. There are no results of action other than these. Therefore one should abandon [actions] together with [their] requisites."[197] Potter summarizes the issue succinctly: "In short, it is Śaṃkara's view that Self-knowledge and action are entirely incompatible – the conditions for the presence of one constitute the conditions for the absence of the other. Of course, prior to gaining Self-knowledge, the seeker practises action combined with meditation; but once true knowledge is gained, no further action is possible."[198]

Thus, non-active, intuitive knowledge is the key by which freedom becomes possible. But as a preparation for the path to *mokṣa,* and for final liberation of the Self, knowledge of the *Veda* was considered essential, and this certainly necessitated action.

Brahmins were expected to maintain their class duties and those relevant to their stage of life. The earlier Mīmāṃsā aims are accepted here, and it would be expected that in this, or a former, life the obligatory rituals and duties as laid down in the *Vedas* be maintained, as well as avoidance of prohibited actions, and observance of any optional duties that promote selflessness. As Pūrva Mīmāṃsā accepted, such a path leaves one without fruitive *karma.* Yet knowledge of Brahman and Its identity with *Ātman* remains the key to liberation. It is knowledge at the deepest levels of the self, and can only come about when activity ceases, even if that activity is obedience to *Vedic* injunctions, moral action, or ethically necessary action. This knowledge is directly opposed to the kind of ignorance, nescience, that characterizes the ordinary self, and *all* activity is an expression of such ignorance.

> Only knowledge [of Brahman] can destroy ignorance; action cannot [destroy it] since [action] is not incompatible [with ignorance]. Unless ignorance is destroyed, passion and aversion will not be destroyed.
> If you have come to know that the notions "mine" and "myself," efforts and desires are by nature void in *Ātman*, continue to be self-abiding. What is the use of efforts?[199]

> Whoever sees *Ātman* as devoid of duties remaining [undone], devoid of action itself and of the result of the action, and free from the notions "mine" and "myself," he [really] sees [the truth].[200]

So no amount of effort can secure the knowledge necessary for liberation in this school. Deussen stated, "liberation consists only in Knowledge, but in Knowledge of a special kind, in that there is no question of an object which investigation could discover and contemplate, but only of that which can never be an object, because in every cognition it is the subject of cognition".[201] Deussen reiterates what was said in the section above on epistemology. But to embark on the path to liberation the disciple will need to cultivate knowledge that can differentiate between the real and the non-real. He will be detached from all the experiences that occur in the physical body, both in the present and in the future. He will have the equanimity that comes from having been an adept in all the required moral restraints, and he will be thoroughly focused on liberation. It is not that there is an increasing knowledge, as much as a "desuperimposition" process, as Indich terms it.[202]

The liberated person, the *jīvanmukta*, is sometimes equated, as far as Śaṃkara is concerned, with the *saṃnyāsin*, one at the fourth and final stage of life.[203] If the two are equated, then it seems that the *jīvanmukta* can either lose the Self in Brahman or turn towards a world as a *saṃnyāsin* that is no longer characterized by perspectives of life that are dual. The goal of liberation does not exclude *egoless* action, and the *mukta* is capable of service to others through such action. Śaṃkara follows the *Bhagavadgītā* in his emphasis on the kind of actions that are devoid of thought of either success or failure, but that are performed without attachment. Indeed, Śaṃkara himself travelled widely in India teaching and founding monasteries. Only when actions are selfless and performed without attachment to their results can they bear no fruitive *karma.* Interestingly, Śaṃkara does not seem to exclude women from the liberated state. He said: "If there should be some few souls, whether they be men or women, who acquire a fixed conviction about the existence of the unborn, all-homogeneous principle of reality, they alone will be the people of true metaphysical knowledge."[204] Śaṃkara accepted that those of lower castes and even outcastes (as they were then termed) could attain to liberation through the gradual path – though probably because they had had experience of the *Veda* in a previous life.

Advaita, then, accepts the concept of *jīvanmukti*, the belief that liberation can occur whilst still confined to the physical body. While after death there will be no *karma* left to render another birth necessary, the *prarābdhakarma* that created the present life will still have some *saṃskāras*, latent impressions from past actions, that need to work themselves out. But there will be no more fruitive *karma* for the liberated one that is devoid of egoistic identity and that no longer relates to the sensory world. Any *karma* in formation will be burnt up and eradicated since the liberated Self is no longer connected with it, and has acquired the kind of knowledge that destroys formative *karma*. The *jīvanmukta*, the liberated one, is no longer an agent or experiencer of the world.

Śaṃkara described liberation as the non-rebirth of the mind. It is what happens "when the mind stops trying to grasp its own tail".[205] The liberated mind is not subject to sensory impressions; it is still. "It is eternal, identical in all states, featureless and without subject–object duality", said Śaṃkara in his commentary on the *Gauḍapādakārikā* 4:77.[206] The mind, he said, is,

> unborn, unproduced, constituting all reality and non-dual even before (the appearance called liberation supervened). For even before enlightenment duality and birth were mere visions of the mind. The mind (in its true nature) is unborn and ever the whole of reality. Its "not being produced" is its continual true state, void of subject and object duality. There is no question of it sometimes existing and sometimes not existing: it is ever the same.[207]

The *jīvanmukta* enjoys blissful pleasure in the remaining days of what have been long journeys in countless reincarnated lives. He becomes the all-pervading Absolute, living in a state of total bliss that is totally divorced from the world of matter and the senses that perceive it. He experiences everything as his own Self. Any actions that he performs are *inactions* in so far as they are not performed by a self, and there is no attachment to actions or the fruits of them. Actions of the liberated one do not *belong* to anyone. The dualities of life have disappeared; pain and pleasure, gold or a piece of earth, are the same. It is as if he were disembodied, though he still has a physical body. He sees all beings and all things as his own Self, and that Self and all beings as the Absolute. In his commentary on the *Bṛhadāraṇyaka Upaniṣad*, Śaṃkara stated:

> Since this glory of the Brahmin (who has realized the Self) is unconnected with action and transcendent in nature, it follows that one who has this realization becomes "peaceful" (śānta), which means desisting from the activities of the external senses, "controlled" (dānta), which means above the thirsts of the mind, "withdrawn" (uparata), which means a renunciate (saṃnyāsin) who has given up all desires, "ascetic" (titikṣu), which means able and willing to bear extremes of the pairs of opposites such as heat and cold, "concentrated" (samāhita), which means concentrated in one-pointedness after withdrawing from all movement of senses or mind.[208]

To the *jīvanmukta* there is no more identity with the physical self or the physical world as such: the illusion of it will have vanished, and all that remains is *Ātman* Consciousness. While active service to others is still maintained, the *mukta* will continue only so long as is necessary for the final working out of *karma* and then, once the physical body is left, will become *videhamukti*. Liberation, then, is the dispelling of ignorance, the ridding of illusions that veil the truth. It is what Dasgupta termed "the dissociation of the self from the subjective psychosis and the world."[209] The ignorance of the world, its illusory nature, however, has to continue, for it is beginningless and timeless, just as consciousness is. But the liberated Self is divorced from it, having realized the higher Reality that is Brahman, and having experienced the bliss of pure Consciousness that is the Essence of all selves and the universe:

> There is no need for taking active steps to achieve peace (liberation) in the Self. All souls are eternally at rest, unborn, and completely withdrawn by nature, homogeneous and non-different from one another. That is, the Self, as a metaphysical principle, is unborn, homogeneous and pure, and hence there is no need to *produce* the state of blessed abstraction or liberation. Action can have no effect on that which is eternally of the same nature.[210]

Much has been written about Śaṃkara's contribution to Indian philosophy, some negatively, and much positively. Undoubtedly, his contribution is considerable, indeed, to the extent that he has been depicted by one writer as "an epoch-making reformer of the Vedānta school of philosophy".[211] This is especially true in that Śaṃkara is faithful to the *Upaniṣadic* concept of a totally transcendent Absolute that is Brahman. It is this that informs all Vedānta inquiry, whether that inquiry remains monistic or diversifies into more qualified monism or dualistic panentheism. While other schools diminish the concept of deity, Vedānta schools enhance it to its ultimate levels, and it is to Śaṃkara that such a trend partly owes its foundation. By positing a dual perspective of reality in which the inferior was sublatable, Śaṃkara attempted to unite the disparate trends of the non-dual absolutism and the dualistic theism of the *Upaniṣads*. Some measure of success must be granted given the influence of Advaita up to, and including, the present day.

Regarding the prevailing influence of Advaita, Smart commented that: "Śankara's metaphysics is *par excellence* the theology of modern Hinduism as presented to the West; and is the most vigorous and dominant doctrine among Hindu intellectuals."[212] There are a number of possible reasons for such an appeal. To begin with, Śaṃkara relates primarily to the bound, empirical self. Radhakrishnan wrote of him: "Religion for Śaṃkara is not doctrine or ceremony, but life and experience. It starts with the soul's sense of the infinite and ends with its becoming the infinite,"[213] – a remarkably all-embracing, almost universalist perspective. As Radhakrishnan also pointed out: "In Śaṃkara we find one of the greatest expounders of the comprehensive and tolerant character of the Hindu religion, which is ever ready to assimilate alien faiths. This attitude of toleration was neither a survival of superstition nor a means of compromise, but an essential part of his practical philosophy. He recognised the limitations of all formulas and refused to compress the Almighty within them."[214] Such a view has been echoed very recently by Ninian Smart.[215] There is also a definite attractiveness in the idea that all is ultimately divine, and ultimately equal. In the last resort, seeing all others as one's own self must lead to the ultimate kind of altruism, "for a true elimination of delusion will also eliminate all those self-centred ways of thinking that motivate selfish behavior".[216]

As far as his philosophy is concerned, Śaṃkara has been described as "the most remarkable rationalist India has ever produced".[217] But it has to be said that it is his denial of reality and, therefore, the absence of any *real* focus of devotion, that suggests an ultimately limiting aspect of the concept of deity for the devotee. And some have appended to this a lack of emphasis on moral requirement and ethical values. Mayeda is one, however, who defends Śaṃkara against such an accusation. He makes the valid point that:

> Śaṅkara is primarily concerned with the salvation of people who are suffering from transmigratory existence here in the present world and not with the establishment of a consistent philosophical system. . . . Śaṃkara's view of ethics may be vague or self-contradictory, but this is because its real aim is the highest possible effectiveness in leading his pupils to the final goal.[218]

In positing Reality that is ultimately non-dual, morality has to transcend the self. As Deussen poignantly said, "in truth morality lies beyond Egotism, but therefore also beyond causality and consequently beyond comprehension".[219]

In examining Śaṃkara's theories, it seems that he owed a considerable debt to Sāṃkhya for his main theory of the mutual superimposition of *Ātman* on the world, and the world on *Ātman*. And this motif is repeated as the basis of all his other theories. Potter justifiably writes: "Listening to an Advaitin is deliciously, or irritatingly, repetitive, depending on one's receptivity to the message."[220] But Larson is highly critical of Śaṃkara's borrowing of the concepts of others. He writes: "Vedānta, stripped of its scripture-based monistic *brahman-atman*, is in many ways a warmed-over Sāṃkhya ontology and epistemology spooned up with the philosophical methodology of the old negative dialectic of the Mādhyamika Buddhists."[221] But it is the major difference from Sāṃkhya that makes Śaṃkara's work so valuable – the identity of all Selves as one *Ātman* that is Brahman, rather than the plurality and isolation of the individual *puruṣas* of Sāṃkhya, which left no room for the divine, as well as the challenges to the reality of phenomenal existence. Yet the charge that Śaṃkara was a synthesizer and copyist is partially justified. He owed a considerable debt to other philosophical systems for major concepts, even if, as Isayeva observes, "he bore full responsibility for the specific way in which these blocks were fitted into the balanced structure of Advaita".[222]

It is the lack of a *real* world, and the mysteries of ignorance, *avidyā*, and the power of illusion, *māyā*, that are problematic areas for Śaṃkara, and were pursued by his successors. The same questions with which Śaṃkara dealt – the relation between Brahman and the self, and between Brahman and the world – were taken up by other Vedāntins who posited different answers. It is these that will occupy the remaining chapters of this book. Sinari thinks that Śaṃkara "sidetracks" the issue of the relationship between Brahman and the finite world,[223] and there is a measure of truth in this, since the linking factor of *māyā* remains ever mysterious. As far as I can see, Śaṃkara rejects relationship between the two by a theory of two distinct realities that pervade his philosophy – the enlightened and unenlightened perspectives of what reality is. The unenlightened view is always devoid of proper reality. It is a dual view that is evident in all his themes:

- liberation and bondage

- higher knowledge and lower knowledge
- reality and appearance
- Brahman and Īśvara
- cause only and the cause–effect processes.

But while he accepts such dualities at the level of the empirical world, he then denies them in order to transcend the world and keep Reality non-dual.

Sometimes criticized for its cold metaphysics, there is certainly a warmth in the presenting of Advaita Vedānta by its more modern proponents. Vivekananda thus got to the heart of Śaṃkara's teaching when he said: "The highest heaven, therefore, is in our own souls; the greatest temple of worship is the human soul, greater than all heavens, says Vedānta; for in no heaven, anywhere, can we understand Reality as distinctly and clearly as in this life, in your own soul."[224]

9
Viśiṣṭādvaita Vedānta

The overriding characteristic of the Viśiṣṭādvaita strand of Vedānta is its devotional theism – a theism rooted in the reality of life itself and directed to a personal, loving God of grace. The outstanding name associated with the school is Rāmānuja who, along with Śaṃkara, is the greatest philosopher of the Vedānta tradition. They were very different men, with very different perspectives of reality and the nature of the divine, and it has been well said that "the best qualities of each were the defects of the other".[1] Both were highly influential in the effect their respective philosophies had on subsequent Hindu thought and practice. But whereas Śaṃkara's philosophy was more rooted in *Upaniṣadic* thought, it might be claimed that Rāmānuja's was primarily rooted in a religion that was fully established in his day – Vaiṣṇavism. Indeed, it was the grafting of *Upaniṣadic* credence on the Vaiṣṇavism of his time for which Rāmānuja is so well known, and it is this that hallmarks a major contribution of his as a philosopher and theologian. There are many who see his contribution to Indian thought and religion as greater than that of Śaṃkara, mainly because his ideas were so effective in influencing the rise of devotional movements,[2] and some claim that he is more faithful to *Upaniṣadic* thought than Śaṃkara.[3] Be this as it may, both turned their considerable intellectual skills to answering the problem of the relationship between the finite world of change, and the ultimate and changeless Brahman as its cause. Their responses to the problem were thoroughly at variance.

Background to the school

Viśiṣṭādvaita is generally translated as "qualified monism". *Viśiṣṭā* means "particularity", "distinctness", indicating what is qualified, or determinate, and *advaita* "not dual". It is a term that is designed to suggest two things: first, *identity* and *non-duality* of the world and selves with the divine and, second, a certain *difference* between the world, selves and the divine, because there are qualifications that inform that identity and non-dualism. It is ideas such as these that are crucial to Rāmānuja's thought, for he sought to retain the differentiation of all things, and yet their dependence on Brahman as the changeless Ground of all. "Qualified monism", or "qualified non-dualism", are two terms that are not actually identical in that monism reduces everything to one, whereas non-dualism is beyond even one.[4] For this reason, it is the former that is more appropriate to the teachings of Rāmānuja, and that permits of a unity of reality that is qualified by differentiation of its individual aspects.

There is, thus, a oneness and wholeness that is characterized by distinctiveness of all its modes – a theory that would have been unacceptable to Śaṃkara. And it is God that creates and sustains the whole unity of reality, because its interrelated parts are, in fact, the attributes of God himself. God is the *viśesya*, the substantive element to which the *viśeṣaṇas*, the subordinate particulars or attributive elements in life, are subject. Yet the whole is a single unit, a *viśiṣṭa*. Thus, the "particularity" or "distinctness" refers, on the one hand, to the pluralistic realism of the world. But from another perspective, the term *viśiṣṭā* refers, also, to the *divine* as qualified. Unlike Śaṃkara's Brahman that is without attributes, Rāmānuja's Brahman has an abundance of characteristics and qualities – "particularities" – both in his own being and in the form of the whole universe that stems from him. To sum up, then, "qualified monism":

- is a unity in which God and the universe is one, but there is a differentiation between the aspects or modes of the whole.
- God is one and non-dual, but is qualified by the attributes he has.
- The attributes that God has include all that exists in the world.

These nuances of meaning in the term *viśiṣṭādvaita* are intricately dependent on each other because the differentiated parts of the universe *are* the attributes of God and, therefore, are inseparable from his nature. In all the attributes – in all things in existence – Brahman is the underlying Reality that unites and sustains, but allows plurality. Everything is thus dependent on Brahman for its existence, is interrelated through Brahman, but has a certain independent reality from anything else. All that we see in life reflects this kind of oneness between something and its properties. A jar, for example is one whole, but it has the attributes of shape, texture, colour and so on. Each of these attributes is part of its "oneness" but is not its "oneness" *per se*. And the shape, the colour, and so on, are independently different. Such inseparability between the whole and its qualities is termed *apṛthaksiddhi* – unity that contains inseparable, different and dependent attributes.

These are important issues that I want to develop throughout this chapter. But to return to more general issues that relate to the school, it should be noted that the term *Viśiṣṭādvaita* was not coined by Rāmānuja, and has been somewhat anachronistically attached to his name: in fact its usage post-dates him by some four centuries.[5] Neither were the ideas of the school embryonic to Rāmānuja. The origins of Viśiṣṭādvaita certainly predate him, for he quotes a variety of earlier sources that are no longer extant. As a system of philosophy it is likely to have originated with Nāthamuni in the tenth century,[6] though his works, also, have not remained extant. However, the works of his grandson Yāmunācārya give us some insight into the school before Rāmānuja's more systematic development of its tenets.

The aim of the school – particularly of Rāmānuja – was clearly to counteract the colder metaphysics of Śaṃkara's school of Advaita. This was done in accordance with the authority of the *Upaniṣads*, but the essence of the *Upaniṣadic* teaching was seen as *bhakti*, and as a dualistic monotheism between devotee and the divine. Rāmānuja outlines his aims and how he interprets the *Vedānta* at the beginning of his *Vedārthasaṃgraha*:

> In truth, all declarations of the Vedānta are meant to set forth the knowledge of the proper form and nature of the individual soul which are different from the body; the proper form and nature of the Supreme Spirit who is the inner Ruler of the soul; the worship of the Supreme Spirit; and the apprehension of Brahman as perfect boundless bliss which presupposes the revelation of the proper form of the soul that results from the worship of the Supreme Spirit. By setting forth all this the declarations of the Vedānta serve to remove the danger of rebirth.[7]

The whole aim of life, according to Viśiṣṭādvaita, was to realize the perfect subject–attribute relationship between God and the self. These aims were set in the context of Vaiṣṇavism. There is a clear purpose to bring together the philosophical and metaphysical teachings of the *Upaniṣads* on the one hand, with, on the other, the powerful expression of loving-devotion to a personal God that so characterized the *bhakti* movements. It was liberation through love, not just knowledge, and yet a deliberate attempt to formalize and systematize this powerful, emotive expression of devotion is evident. That Rāmānuja did not kill it dead in the process is a measure of his remarkable achievement. And that he was able to authenticate the path of devotion in the face of the acclaimed metaphysics of Śaṃkara is a hallmark of his greatness. Radhakrishnan wrote of the difference between *bhakti* and Advaita:

> The Absolute of Śaṃkara, rigid, motionless, and totally lacking in intitiative and influence, cannot call forth our worship. Like the Taj Mahal, which is unconscious of the admiration it arouses, the Absolute remains indifferent to the fear and love of its worshippers, and for all those who regard the goal of religion as the goal of philosophy – to know God is to know the real – Śaṃkara's view seems to be a finished example of learned error.[8]

Given such an ethos, it was necessary for Dvaita to present the validity of its philosophical thought, and to point out the errors of others – particularly those of the Advaita of Śaṃkara. The process began in the south in the tenth century and was taken up in earnest by Rāmānuja.

The blend of philosophy and practical expression of religion was no easy task, yet in its systematization the school achieves precisely this. There was no attempt to deny the ritualistic portion of the *Veda* in favour of the knowledge portion or *vice versa*. Rather, the aim was to synthesize both, and to synthesize these, in turn, with the profound theism so characteristic of the school. But I do not see that this categorizes Rāmānuja as a theologian, as opposed to a philosopher, any more than it could be said that those aspects of the *Upaniṣads* that relate to the *saguṇa* aspects of Brahman are wholly theological and devoid of philosophical speculation. But clearly there is a blend of the two: the colder philosophical inquiry is not divorced from the religion of intuitive emotion in Viśiṣṭādvaita. And the fact that the school arises from, and stands firmly in, the Vaiṣṇava tradition ensures that its philosophy is merged with a thoroughly practical religious expression – what one writer terms "a very powerful correlation of theism and philosophy".[9] Yet it was inevitable that in time the theological aspects, in conjunction with the Śrī Vaiṣṇava faith, obscured the clearer philosophical basis that informed the early systematization of the school under Rāmānuja.

Rāmānuja lived at a time in which devotion to a personal God flourished, and had inherited a long tradition of powerful devotional literature that gave expression to the relationship between the divine and the human being. Great theistic movements and thinkers had preceded him and influenced his thinking – in particular, the Āḷvārs, the mystic poets, and the Ācāryas, the great theologians and teachers. These human influences, combined with classical devotional literature and *Upaniṣadic* theism, are the clear elements that inform Rāmānuja's philosophy. The beliefs of the Āḷvārs are certainly evident in Rāmānuja's thought. The Āḷvārs – twelve of them, including one woman – were the great saints of southern India, whose devotional poetry spoke of mystical communication with, total surrender to, and entire dependence on, God. They *ecstatically loved* God with their entire being, and could not bear the pangs of separation from him at those times when their communication with him was lessened. They span the sixth to eighth centuries,[10] and their hymns have been recorded in what is called the *Nāḷāyira-divya-prabandham* – an important enough work to be given the same credence as the *Veda* by Viśiṣṭādvaita. It is composed of twenty-four *prabandhams* each of widely different length. The Āḷvārs came from low and high castes and walks of life. And this is a point worth noting. For it is one that gave credence to two important ideas. First, caste was largely irrelevant in surrender to God and, second, as Kesarcodi-Watson rightly states, such a tradition "rigorously acknowledged *achievement in devotional practice*".[11]

While, surprisingly, Rāmānuja never mentioned any of the Āḷvārs in his works, the close correlation between the fundamental beliefs of the Āḷvārs – particularly Nammāḷvār – and the philosophy of Rāmānuja, suggests that he was certainly systematizing philosophical and religious ideas that had been long in currency.[12] And these were ideas that had been fed to the ordinary person in the vernacular of Tamil and, in the context of Vaiṣṇavism, the worship of Viṣṇu. Such is the richness of the religious devotion and intuitive experience of God contained in the *prabandhams*, that they are still a part of Vaiṣṇava worship of modern times. Chari's recent work on the Āḷvārs demonstrates well that these devotional mystics were not divorced from the philosophy of the *Vedānta*, and that, far from teaching only a devotional means to liberation of the self, they sought to teach *Vedānta* philosophy to the common person in his – or, in the case of Viśiṣṭādvaita, her – own language.[13] Yet the interpretation of such philosophy was of its theistic strands – those that inspired *bhakti*. The Āḷvārs were also inspired by other, Vaiṣṇava, devotional literature – the *Bhagavadgītā*, the *Vaiṣṇava Purāṇas* and the *Pāñcarātra Āgamas*. From such scripture they taught of the nature of ultimate Reality, of a personal God with attributes and of his consort, Śrī, and the *avatāras* of God.[14] They taught of the nature of the self, the means by which it can find liberation, the nature of that liberation, and the doctrine of *prapatti* "surrender" as a means to it. They taught also of the grace of God, *bhakti* and *bhaktiyoga*. And all these ideas were gleaned from the theistic elements of traditional scripture, and were incorporated and systematized by the school of Viśiṣṭādvaita. Indeed, emotional, mystical poems could hardly present deliberate and formal theology, but their content was important enough to be taken up in more systematic expression. Since the correlation between the ideas of the Āḷvārs and Viśiṣṭādvaita is so obvious in fundamental issues, such synonymy of ideas will need some comment throughout this present chapter.

The Ācāryas were the more systematic thinkers who propounded their beliefs in traditional philosophical and theological modes – the academics of the religious world. Both Śaṃkara and Rāmānuja were Ācāryas, the latter, according to tradition, having descended in direct line from the first Ācārya, Nāthamuni, and his grandson Yāmuna. So Rāmānuja – and, hence, the Viśiṣṭādvaita school – stands fairly firmly in a long tradition of theistic devotion. There will, thus, be much in the school that has been inherited from the past, even if it was not clearly articulated in the centuries before the advent of Rāmānuja.

Rāmānuja was not just a great Ācārya, but came to be *the* Ācārya of the Śrī Vaiṣṇava sect. Thus, Viśiṣṭādvaita is set in the Śrī Vaiṣṇava tradition: the ultimate Reality is Viṣṇu, or Nārāyaṇa, which is the preferred name of the sect. Other deities such as Śiva and Brahmā are accepted as manifestations of Viṣṇu. Viṣṇu's consort Śrī or Lakṣmī, is also accepted alongside Brahman as ultimate Reality. It is precisely this kind of religious belief, involving a good deal of anthropomorphic theism, that lifts Viśiṣṭādvaita from strict Vedānta philosophy to a level of workable devotion. But the roots of Viśiṣṭādvaita lie in the *Vedānta* tradition, the *Upaniṣads*, and it is on such a basis – indeed on the composite *Veda* itself – that it partly builds its views. And yet, while Viśiṣṭādvaita should be set against the philosophical traditions of its ancient past, it is Vaiṣṇavism that has also informed the devotional poetry of its mystical saints and great religious teachers. Viśiṣṭādvaita, then, is founded on these two gigantic pillars of philosophical tradition and religious devotion to a personal God. And the latter might be said to be the greater influence for, while aspects of the former may have been disregarded as subservient to theistic ends, Vaiṣṇava religious concepts were accepted wholesale. What emerged was a school that systematized a doctrine of devotion to, and grace from, a personal God.

Viśiṣṭādvaita bases its views on scripture rather than on logic, and theistic sects like the Vaiṣṇavas have their own scriptures termed *Āgamas* that they venerate alongside the *Veda*. The Vaiṣṇava *Āgama* is called the *Pāñcarātra Saṃhitā*, a scripture whose authority is accepted by all Vaiṣṇava schools but which, for Rāmānuja, is believed to have been revealed in the same way, and with the same claim to antiquity, as the *Veda*. It was Rāmānuja's predecessor, Yāmuna, who aimed at demonstrating that the *Pāñcarātra* scriptures were in line with *Vedic* teaching.[15] Much other literature is also accepted by the school – portions of the *Mahābhārata*, the *Viṣṇu Purāṇa* and the *Bhagavadgītā*, as well as the works of the Ālvārs and Ācāryas.

As a school, Viśiṣṭādvaita has had a number of different strands of philosophy. But two major divisions took place centuries after Rāmānuja. These were the Vaḍagalais (Northern Tamil) and the Tengalais (Southern Tamil) schools. The Tengalais school, whose greatest proponent was Piḷḷai Lokācarya, accepts only the Tamil *prabandham*, rejecting Sanskrit traditions. It also is prepared to involve God in condoning the sins of the world in order to allow a greater medium for his grace. Surrender, *prapatti*, is the key concept of this school, sometimes known as the Passivist school, which is symbolized by the kitten that is carried around helplessly in its mother's mouth, utterly passive in the care of the mother. Such is the way the devotee should be in relation to the grace of God. *Mokṣa* for this school does not permit the blissful enjoyment of the being of God, unlike the view of its rival school. Then, too, the Goddess Śrī is not given equal status with Viṣṇu in this school: she is seen only as a subordinate consort.

The Vaḍagalais school boasts a great founder in Vedānta Deśika, also known as Veṇkaṭanātha, who is reputed to be one of the outstanding thinkers of Viśiṣṭādvaita in the centuries following Rāmānuja. The Vaḍagalais school accepts the authority of both Tamil and Sanskrit writings of the Āḷvārs. But it believes in some self-effort alongside *prapatti*, symbolized by a monkey that is carried by its mother, but needs to cling on in the process. Thus, it is the Activist school. *Prapatti* for this school is only one way to God, and more of an end product of the means to *mokṣa*. Here, the Goddess Śrī is given equal status with God as an integral part of him. With the exception of the last point, these ideas might be said to be more in line with Rāmānuja's. As time went on, the divisions between the two schools widened sufficiently for them to become very different sects.[16]

Main proponents and commentators

One of the precursors of Rāmānuja, who had been, for a time, his guru, was Yādavaprakāśa. He was a proponent of the theory of *bhedābhedavada*, the theory that Brahman is changed into the world of spirit and matter but, at the same time, remains unchanged in his essential nature. Thus, *bhedābhedavāda* means "difference and non-difference", "non-difference in difference" or "identity in difference". It was not a view that Rāmānuja was to accept without some nuances of changed meaning, and such challenges to his *guru* over this and other concepts earned Rāmānuja the hatred of his teacher. It was the ideas of Yāmuna that were more acceptable to Rāmānuja. As van Buitenen comments: "Much of what we see blossoming into full maturity in Rāmānuja's works we see budding in Yāmuna's writings."[17] Yāmuna set out to prove the existence of the true Self as separate from the body, as a knower, as conscious of itself, and as the very "I-ness" to which consciousness, knowledge, experience and perception are related as qualities. And just as the world is the perceived object of the "I-ness" of the self, so the world is an effect of God, who perceives it with his intelligent, all-knowing attributes. Yāmuna posited three categories of what is real – selves, the material world, and God. Though he was never to meet Yāmuna,[18] Rāmānuja did not find much to be critical of in his theories: but he was to take Yāmuna's ideas a far greater distance, and in many directions.

Of Rāmānuja, much has already been said. Kesarcodi-Watson finds in this great philosopher "a person exhibiting a far more subtle, pluralistic depth, reflecting life's complexities and nuances, through a sager age" [19] than Rāmānuja's rival Śaṃkara. There will always be divisions as to whom is the greater of these two thinkers, but there is some measure in accepting these particular words of Kesarcodi-Watson. Rāmānuja's dates are normally consistently given as 1017–1137 CE, accepting a long life of one hundred and twenty years. He was a Tamil and a *Brahmin*, was married at sixteen but, being disenchanted with married life, became a *saṃnyāsin* in his early thirties. He lived at Śrīrangam, converting many people to the Vaiṣṇava religion. He also travelled to Benares in the north and throughout southern India, restoring temples. Tradition believes Rāmānuja to be an incarnation of Lakṣmaṇa, the brother of Rāma. Kesarcodi-Watson describes him as "a *bhakta* to the core. This was his atmosphere, his family, his nature; the being he began with, not something he set out to absorb".[20] Clearly, there were many influences that propelled this profound background to the philosophical and religious heights found in his writings, and his debt to the earlier Āḷvārs and Ācāryas was considerable. The writings that he produced amounted to his *Śrībhāṣya* on the *Vedāntasūtras* (*Brahmasūtras*) and eight other works, including a commentary on the *Bhagavadgītā*, and the *Vedārthasaṃgraha*, his "philosophical debut",[21] which forms the essence of his beliefs.

While there were obviously a number of important exponents of Viśiṣṭādvaita apart from Rāmānuja, one name stands out as exemplary, and that is Vedānta Deśika or Veṇkaṭanātha, dated to the thirteenth century (1268 CE). He was a prolific writer of great ability, writing over a hundred works, and capably articulated sound arguments against the Advaita of Śaṃkara as well as the views of the other schools. He also systematized the important views of his own school, laying out the Viśiṣṭādvaita doctrines in a way that clarified them against opposition. Hiriyanna describes him as "one of the most learned scholars which medieval India produced",[22] and Chari refers to his contribution as "unique and unparalleled in the history of Indian Philosophy".[23] In all, the literature of the school of Viśiṣṭādvaita is extensive,[24] but it is to Vedānta Deśika of the Vaḍagalais school that one must look for the lasting quality of literary output.

Reality: the Viśiṣṭādvaita view of the world

The Viśiṣṭādvaita definition of reality is a pragmatic one. The world *seems* real, and when we react to that reality in practical daily life, testing it, whatever works we can accept as real. This can only happen when reality is the object of a valid way of knowing. For Rāmānuja, therefore, the world of matter is real, as are the selves within it, and the God who creates and sustains it. But what distinguishes God from matter and selves is the fact that he is the only one that is an *independent* Reality – the other two kinds of reality (world and selves) are dependent on God. But, all objects perceived by the self are absolutely real, and they also exist independently of the subjective selves that perceive them. In terms of its practical outcome in religious expression – and in ordinary living – the world should not be denied, or renounced. The critical question here, however, is in what way is God related to a reality that involves finitude, transience, evil and impermanence? The answer to this underpins the whole philosophy of Viśiṣṭādvaita, as we shall see below.

In the main, Rāmānuja is able to accept the *prakṛtic* structure of reality posited by the school of Sāṃkhya, with slight variance in the creation of the evolutes, and with the important exception that independent *puruṣas* are rejected for selves and a world dependent on the will of God. The world of *prakṛti* is also a separate reality from the selves that inhabit it, and is not an infinitely self-evolving complex. It always remains dependent on God for the manifestation of its evolutes. And whereas Sāṃkhya believed *prakṛti* to be composed of the three *guṇas* as substances, for Viśiṣṭādvaita they are its qualities that are inseparably bound to it yet do not constitute it – rather like a red pot that is inseparable from its redness, and yet the quality of the redness is not the same as the pot. Such inseparable relation, or *apṛthaksiddhi*, will exist between God and selves, between God and matter and between substance and quality or attribute. The reality of the material world serves a soteriological purpose: the real world is the field in which selves evolve towards liberation from *saṃsāra*.

Padārthas: categories of reality

Substances and their attributes

Viśiṣṭādvaita maintains a substance philosophy, accepting a reality that is subject to changing attributes or qualities as far as matter and selves are concerned. It rejects the Advaita view that the world is illusory and is neither real nor unreal, as nonsense: either something is real or it isn't, but it cannot be anything else. There are mainly two fundamental categories of reality, substances and attributes. The school accepts six substances or *dravyas*, a substance being that which serves as a substratum for modifying changes. These are:

- *Prakṛti*, which is unconscious (*acit*) and material. In the *Gītābhāṣya* 7:4–5, Rāmānuja informs us of a higher and lower *prakṛti*, the higher being sentient beings and the lower insentient objects, the elements, the senses and the mind.
- *Kālā* "time", which is unconscious (*acit*) and material. It is an independent *dravya*, not being part of *prakṛti*, but existing alongside it. Time has no beginning and no end. As a fundamental substance, qualities of past and present inhere in it. So an object with the quality of past existence can also have the quality of present existence but remain the same substance. This would refute the Buddhist theory of momentariness.
- *Cit* "spirit", which is conscious (*cit*) and non-material, and is the self, the *jīva*.
- Īśvara, God, who is conscious (*cit*) and non-material.
- *Dharmabhūtajñāna*, knowledge or consciousness, which is immaterial, self-luminous, eternal, all-pervasive, and both substance and attribute or quality (*guṇa*). It is one of the difficult areas of Viśiṣṭādvaita metaphysics, and will, therefore, be found variously explained. Presumably, by making knowledge a separate substance, it prevents it ever being of the real nature of the Self. Thus, the Self cannot be pure Consciousness, pure Knowledge, as it is in Advaita. It is often referred to as the *essence* of the Self, but this is always in the sense of an attributive essence of the Self, and not the Self *per se*. As a substance it is knowledge potential, that which makes knowledge possible. In God it is pure attributive essence, as it is also in liberated Selves. But in bound selves it is obscured, and expands and contracts to cause change. It is when it is the substratum for such change that it is a substance. But the expansion and contraction that engender change make it the attribute that belongs inseparably to its substance nature, like rays of light belong to light. And just as rays of light are always dependent on the light itself, so is knowledge dependent on God or selves, and is their attribute.

- *Śuddhasattva*, "pure *sattva*", or *nityavibhūti*, which is an unconscious, immaterial and transcendental substance and is composed of pure *sattva*. It is of this substance that liberated souls are composed, that forms the body of God, and that constitutes Vaikuṇṭha, the heaven of Viṣṇu. Special images of Viṣṇu are also said to be made of this pure *sattvic* substance. It also exists for the purpose of the conscious substances.[25]

Anything in evolution that is not a substance, a *dravya*, and can never be a substance, like colour, is a non-substance, an *adravya*. And such *adravyas* are dependent attributes or qualities of substances. Viśiṣṭādvaita posits ten fundamental kinds of them:

- The three *guṇas* of *sattva*, *rajas* and *tamas*.[26] These are the three essential qualities that characterize the whole of *prakṛti*.
- The five qualities of the five gross elements – *śabda* sound; *sparśa* touch; *rūpa* colour; *rasa* taste; *gandha* smell.
- Potency (*śakti*), which is the characteristic of a substance that produces an effect, like the burning effect of a fire.
- Conjunction (*saṃyoga*), which is the external relation between things, as a jar on a table.

These sixteen *tattvas* or "reals" represent the categories that constitute reality in the Viśiṣṭādvaita system, that is to say, those "reals" that it is prepared to prove by its accepted *pramāṇas*, its means of valid knowledge.[27] While these sixteen basic *dravyas* and *adravyas* are mutually exclusive, *derivative* substances and their attributes are not, and such substances may, in certain contexts, become attributes, or attributes may become substances. For example, the light of a lamp is its attribute, and yet the rays of the light as the attributes of light, make light a substance.

Broken down, these sixteen categories of substance and non-substance amount to three "reals" – the non-sentient world (*acit*), the finite selves (*cit*) and God (Īśvara). But of these, only God is ultimately Real; the rest are dependently real, and cannot exist without God as the inner controller and sustainer of all. As a result, Brahman is threefold, too. He is the controller and sustainer of the individual selves, that is to say of sentient substances; he is the controller and sustainer of insentient substance – thus far, being indirectly involved in the world and all its change and finitude. But God is also something beyond both these activities, for he exists in his own being, beyond all other substances, as the only eternal and self-dependent "Real". God is thus *ultimate* Reality. Viśiṣṭādvaita thus removes God from the world and selves, and yet does not deny his involvement in, and harmony with, both.

All substances, then, exist only in so far as they are related to, and dependent on, God. Viśiṣṭādvaita posits that they are *attributes* of God through the inseparable connection of *apṛthaksiddhi*. God's attributes are, thus, the world of matter, and the conscious selves that inhabit it. But both the world and selves are also substances in so far as they serve as substrata for modifying change, forming the triune reality – a concept evidenced in the *Upaniṣads*. For example, the *Śvetāśvatara Upaniṣad* states:

> That Eternal should be known as present in the self
> Truly there is nothing higher than that to be known.
> When one recognizes the enjoyer, the object of enjoyment and the Universal Actuator,
> All has been said. This is the threefold Brahman.[28]

Essentially, the three "reals" are a unity – hence the monism of the system – but not in the sense of identity. The differences between the three "reals" cannot cease to obtain, though the three are organically inseparable. As ultimate Reality, God would be utterly unknowable without some attributes, and is only knowable through the world and the selves that he supports and controls as the attributes of his own self. It is the *inseparability* of substance and attribute that is crucial to the Viśiṣṭādvaita view of reality. Indeed, there is nothing that we can know unless it is qualified by some kind of attribute(s). Thus, God, too, cannot be known without the medium of the real world and real selves as attributes. A substance can have an independent existence, but an attribute must always be dependent on a substance. So if God controls and sustains the world and selves, they are dependent, and therefore of the nature of qualities, attributes, in relation to God. But because they have their own changeable attributes, they are also the substances for those attributes.

Strictly speaking, there is no reason why one *substance* should be dependent on another. But in the case of the three "reals", the dependency of matter and selves on God means that they cannot really have *ultimate* reality. They will always be attributes of that which *is* the only independent real. So while matter and selves can be both substance and attribute at the same time, God is never an attribute of something else: he has attributes that depend on him, but he depends on nothing. However, as an attribute of God, the self does not become a fundamental *adravya*; it is a different kind of attribute that does not, in any other context, become a quality of something else. The whole world, and the selves that are in it, have substance–attribute relationships, but in the view of Īśvara, it is all but modes, qualities that belong to him, but do not change his being.

What we have so far, then, is a theory of substances that are defined by the fact that they are the substrata for modification and change, and inseparable attributes that can only exist in so far as they inhere in a substance. Between substance and attribute there is an inseparable unity – like the quality blueness in a blue lotus – but both substance and quality/attribute are different from each other. No substance can exist without qualities, and no quality can exist without a substance. God is a substance that both changes and does not change, and has inseparable attributes of unconscious matter and conscious selves. The three form a unity, but are different. The self can never *be* God: Rāmānuja could never concede that the divine should be limited by identity with the depth of the self, nor that each individual soul should be annihilated in complete identity with an absolute, indescribable Brahman.

The body–soul doctrine

The example used by Viśiṣṭādvaita to explain the inseparability of substance and attribute is the soul and the body, the soul being the substance to which the body belongs.

This is because the soul controls the body and not *vice versa*. This is a particular example of *apṛthaksiddhi* that is central to the philosophy of the Viśiṣṭādvaita school as will be seen in what follows. For just as the human soul is superior to the body, is responsible for it, sustains it and directs it, just so, Brahman is the Supreme Soul that is immanent in the self, the *jīva*, and in the world. God, Īśvara, is the Ground of all that exists, controlling and sustaining both *cit* and *acit* as the only substance that has ultimate Reality. The self that each person is, is the same regardless of the changes that take place in the material body: as Radhakrishnan put it: "The dark shadows of materiality do but hide its glory, but do not destroy it."[29] Similarly, the world, and the selves that inhabit it, are from God, are the qualities of God, but do not change God. They are his body, standing in inseparable and organic relation to him – and thereby in unity with him – but remaining different from him.

Rāmānuja defined a body, *śarīra*, as that which is controlled, supported and for the purpose of, a soul, a *śarīrin*. And since the world and the *jīvas* are controlled, supported and used by God, then together, they must also be a body – the body, *śarīra*, of God. Here there is an inseparable relationship, *apṛthaksiddhi*, between two substances, just as the body and soul inseparable relationship is between two substances. But the lesser substance becomes the attribute – the body of the soul, and the self of God, because soul and God provide the substratum for modifying change. Once the soul is withdrawn, the body cannot exist: indeed, what possible purpose could a body have without a soul? Similarly, once God is withdrawn, *jīvas* and the world also cease to exist, and have no purpose whatever without the God who controls, supports and has a purpose for them. Īśvara is the Soul of all. Rāmānuja wrote:

> This entire universe, composed of spiritual and non-spiritual entities, is pervaded by God who is its inner ruler. God pervades the spiritual and non-spiritual entities of this world by being their inner ruler, and He does so in order to reign and maintain them, although they themselves are unable to see him. In this way all beings depend on God because they constitute his body. But God does not depend on them for they serve no purpose in maintaining his being; nor does God contain these beings like a jug contains water.[30]

The body–soul doctrine – *śarīra-śarīri-bhāva* – is the central doctrine of Rāmānuja's teaching, and of Viśiṣṭādvaita in general. The idea of the *jīva* being the property and glory of God, and that it exists in order to serve God, was one taught by Nammāḻvār, and one accepted in Vaiṣṇava theology.[31] Whether Rāmānuja was influenced by Nammāḻvār's analogy of the body–soul to depict the relationship between the self and God, and the world and God, as some suggest,[32] is debatable, for Rāmānuja makes no mention of the Āḻvār. But their thoughts are so similar on a number of points that some legacy of the analogy from Nammāḻvār is not out of place. Essentially for Rāmānuja, the body–soul doctrine solved two issues. First, the need to remove God from the world sufficiently to avoid compromising the divine nature and, second, the need to involve God sufficiently in the world for the human soul to remain in a personal relationship with the divine. Thus, the essence of God is the Supreme Soul and the efficient cause of all things, yet remains unchanged. It is the *body* of God – the world of *cit* and *acit* – that is concerned with change, and which is the material cause of existence. And all is organically united as the body of Brahman because, as Rāmānuja put it, "the entire aggregate of things, intelligent and non-intelligent, has its self in Brahman in so far as it constitutes *Brahman's* body".[33] Thus, the world can only be understood in relation to God. Always keen to support his philosophy with scriptural authority, Rāmānuja frequently referred to the *Bṛhadāraṇyaka Upaniṣad* to uphold the body–soul theory: "He, who, dwelling in all things, yet is other than all things, whom all things do not know, whose body all things are, who controls all things from within – He is your Soul, the Inner Controller, the Immortal."[34]

So despite the whole of existence having as its identity the body of Brahman, there is no sense of a unifying *ātman* that denies reality to all things and all beings. In the world of *cit* and *acit* everything has its own identity that is different from the next thing. Each is a distinct mode of the whole, just as the many parts of the body are distinct from each other, and yet are inseparable from the unity of the whole. Souls and matter may well be qualities or attributes of God, but each has its own characteristics, its own differentiating attributes. Yet each stands in inseparable relationship to God, who is sustainer of the sustained (*ādhāra–ādheya*), controller of the controlled (*niyantā–niyāmya*), and is self-subsistent master, as opposed to his dependent creation (*śeṣī–śeṣa*). The *śeṣī* (master, owner) and *śeṣa* (that which exists for another) description is a prominent means by which Rāmānuja portrays the relationship between God and self. And in existing *for* God, the whole purpose of each self is to serve God. Passages such as that from the *Bṛhadāraṇyaka Upaniṣad* above are cited by Rāmānuja as evidence that God indwells all things and all selves, which all take their name, form and special being by way of that immanence – all is the body of Brahman. Brahman thus becomes the *Ātman* of all things and all beings. They are all *modes*, *prakāras*, of Brahman and, as such, are real, with real differences of being. But it is Brahman who is the possessor of those modes, the *Prakārin*. Yet Rāmānuja was keen to stress that, whereas the self *needs* its body to function in the world, Brahman does not need its modes of *cit* and *acit* at all: they are not necessary to Brahman in any way, and are subordinate to him, like slaves to a Master. It is this subordination of the self to God that permits the personal devotion of the *bhakta* to the Lord, to Īśvara – and that is the *raison d'être* of Vaiṣṇava religion and worship.

It is, then, the body–soul theory by which Rāmānuja overcomes the difficulties of limiting Brahman through involvement in the world. But it must be pointed out that there are many anomalies in the analogy, not least the fact that the soul is accepted as surviving beyond the body. The analogy breaks down because the body ceases to exist in the soul–body relationship, whereas the soul is eternal in the Brahman–soul one. There is also the difficulty of accepting that the whole can exist without its parts, or a substance without its qualities. And that suggests that Brahman without modes, without attributes, cannot really obtain – despite the positing of an ultimately unchanging essence. As Rāmānuja often stated, nothing can exist unless it has qualities and attributes, and Brahman must be, in some way, an object of knowledge in that he can be known. Existing without his modes would make this impossible. Then, too, the true Self, the soul, really does need to be subject to changing modifications in order to evolve through the countless existences of the *saṃsāric* cycle. Is the liberated Self the same as the self that begins this journey? If it is, then, as Sharma points out succinctly: "It can never become the object of experience and cannot be called finite and individual. How can then it be identified with the empirical 'I'? How can it be dragged to the level of a finite object? How can it be a real agent and a real enjoyer?

How can its plurality be proclaimed?"[35] Indeed, without the Self's intimate connection with the empirical "I", the *reality* of finite selves is severely compromised.

But the world is given firm reality by the Viśiṣṭādvaita school, and the plurality within it is accepted as real and differentiated. In Rāmānuja's words: "So, since the sum-total of all entities, animate and inanimate, constitute the Lord's body, their proper forms have real existence as the modes of the Lord."[36] All human consciousness witnesses plurality and difference in the universe, appropriates different sounds to differentiate between this and that, and differentiates via its means of perception. There is an eternal nature to such plurality according to Viśiṣṭādvaita. The body of Brahman in the form of the world is eternal, for *prakṛti* is never destroyed; it merely passes through stages of evolution and dissolution. This rather suggests that Brahman is never really without the modes and attributes that make his body, for they are either manifest, or in an unmanifest but potential state (*pralaya*), where everything exists subtly. So just as modes have no existence apart from a mode possessor, something without any modes – and that must surely be true of Brahman – can hardly be said to have reality at all. And if the world is real only because it participates in the reality of Brahman, then it must always be so – as must be the different modes of the empirical and egoistic self.[37] Clearly, the Viśiṣṭādvaita view accords reality to change and finitude – both accepted as facets of the qualities of God. And there must be a certain permanent character to all the aspects of the body of Brahman, despite their change from gross to subtle, from creation to dissolution, otherwise some attributes of Brahman would disappear forever! This is why an eternal *prakṛti*, but one that is always controlled and sustained by God, has to be posited. The plurality of manifested effects in the universe "are nothing but the spillings of His being which is eternally expanding and retracting, eternally creating and dissolving".[38]

The One and the many

The body–soul theory is an extension of the important concept in all Hinduism of the relationship between the One and the many – the One being Brahman, and the many being the plurality of the world. The body–soul theory of Viśiṣṭādvaita is designed to explain this in a particular way, the One, containing the many. It is the oneness, or unity, of all things in Brahman that leans towards the monism characteristic of much *Upaniṣadic* thought. But this is a oneness characterized by internal diversity, in other words Brahman with distinguishing characteristics. Dasgupta explained this well: "The 'difference' and the 'unity' are not two independent forms of things which are both real; but the 'difference' modifies or qualifies the nature and character of the 'unity,' and this is certified by all our experience of complex or compound existence."[39] In Viśiṣṭādvaita the One becomes the many – or Brahman becomes the world and the *jīvas* – because, as Chari puts it, "Brahman as associated with *cit* and *acit* in their subtle form becomes Brahman with *cit* and *acit* in their manifest form".[40] The change from subtle to manifest means God and the world and selves form an organic whole, but the multifarious parts of that whole are dependent on the "whole" itself for existence. And there is no limit to the forms that Brahman can take.

The concept of the One and the many occupies much *Upaniṣadic* thought and is of particular interest in so much of Hindu philosophy. Indeed, it could be said that the *Vedānta* upholds *both* these concepts independently, as well as the fusion of them. Thus Rāmānuja accepted the unity, non-difference, or *abheda*, of all, since Brahman is the controller and sustainer, the One without a second, that unites all. Yet he permits difference, *bheda*, in the plurality of reality observed at the microcosmic level of human existence and experience. In Viśiṣṭādvaita the oneness, the monism, is exemplified in the dissolved state (*pralaya*) of the world, in which is inherent the potential for the many. Carman puts this well. He writes that in the state of *pralaya*, "intelligent entities and non-intelligent matter were pressed so closely together and so inseparably united with the Supreme Self that their distinction from one another and from Him, though real, could not be expressed by name and form. Therefore in this state one can speak of Brahman *ekam-eva* (one only), whereas in the state of creation the differences have become manifest".[41] Carman's words neatly express the solution to the problem of the One and the many in the Viśiṣṭādvaita school. So in the main the solution lies in the concept of *bhedābheda*, *bheda* "difference" and *abheda* "non-difference". It is a term that can have a number of nuances of meaning, which may be why Rāmānuja was keen to refute the use of it on some occasions, and yet seemed to advocate it on others. Indeed, the term *viśiṣṭādvaita* serves to offset the difficulties which that of *bhedābhedavāda* brings out.

Bhedābheda

At first glance it seems that the theory of *bhedābheda* "difference in non-difference" is appropriate to Rāmānuja's philosophy, for the plurality, the *bheda*, is upheld through the distinction between *cit* and *acit* and the distinction between these two and Īśvara. Then, because all *cit* and *acit* are the modes and attributes of Īśvara, they cannot be separated from him. Thus, through inseparable relation, *apṛthaksiddhi*, there is a fundamental non-difference, *abheda*, because all attributes stem from the same substance, the same source. The desire of Brahman to move from the One to the many is stated in the *Chāndogya Upaniṣad* with the words "Would that I were many! Let me procreate myself" (6:2:3).[42] The words suggest that existence is unified by its source, but that there are "many" aspects to manifest existence that come from that source – the plurality of effects that are related to, and come from, a fundamental cause. Rāmānuja explained passages in the *Upaniṣads* that seemed to deny plurality[43] as indicative of the One without a second – that is to say One without any rival reality – who is the source of all. He did not suggest that such passages taught the reality of Brahman to the exclusion of the world, but that the plurality of the world was real because of its relationship to Brahman. Radhakrishnan put this neatly:

> From Rāmānuja's theory of knowledge, it follows that the real cannot be a bare identity. It is a determinate whole, which maintains its identity in and through the differences. While Rāmānuja is clear that there exists an absolute self, he is equally clear that every finite reality is an expression of this self. To make reciprocal interaction among a plurality of existents possible, the constituent elements of the world-whole must have a common bond of unity and interdependence, which must be a spiritual principle.[44]

It is the "common bond of unity" that is important here, for reality is to be understood in terms of an organic unity related by a central source and core. And there is no time when the world and selves do not subsist in Brahman – whether during manifest existence, or during the periodic cosmic dissolution of *pralaya*. But, just because there is a central source to which manifest existence is subject, there must be some form of duality of status to existence – God on the one hand, and the manifested world of matter and selves on the other. Given this basic duality – albeit organically unified – plurality is not a problem providing that unity is not compromised. As Bhatt puts it: "So all the time unity is there, but sometimes in a homogeneous state and sometimes in a heterogeneous state. Both these states are equally real and none is false or unreal."[45]

But strictly speaking, *bhedābheda* upholds the *equality* of reality between identity and difference – that is to say between matter and selves on the one hand (the difference) and Brahman on the other (identity). Rāmānuja was not able to accept this because it would have given attributes the same status as the substance in which they inhere. And since attributes cannot have an independent reality, they must be inferior to the substance. Difference only obtains as a modifier or qualifier of a substance. Just so, the world and selves as the body of Brahman remain inferior, and not equal to, the Brahman that unifies them. They are, to use Bhatt's expression, "as moments in the life of God".[46]

Another way of expressing the theory of *bhedābheda* is by the term *identity-in-difference*, or *identity-and-difference*. But, the word *identity* here would not be acceptable *per se*. It is clear that Rāmānuja would have rejected any suggestion that identity causes only *apparent* differences in the manifest world and not real ones, as Śaṃkara believed. For Rāmānuja, *identity-in-difference* meant one substance of Brahman creating, sustaining and controlling all of the different modes of his own being. But no part can *become* the whole, so there can be no *identity* between the part and the whole, between one manifested phenomenon of *cit* or *acit* and Brahman as the Ground of all. In summation, it is a *relational* identity, but not a complete identity. Thus *unity-in-difference* might make the theory clearer to the reader. Then, too, the *difference* of the phrase, being only relational, indicates that the more the self moves towards the liberated state, the less *difference* is experienced between the self and God. Not that the two ever become exactly the same, but the move towards greater *identity* means the experience of the self as the body of God. The whole point of Vaiṣṇava worship is to bring the self to this kind of realization. Things and selves are characterized by *difference* because they are attributes of the substance and not the substance itself. And as attributes of a substance, of God, things and selves can never exist independently of that substance. They are always the *prakāra*, the dependent types, or modes, of the substance in which they inhere, which is God, who is the *Prakārin*. There is some measure, then, in accepting Radhakrishnan's view that *identity* to Rāmānuja meant *apṛthaksiddhi*, inseparable relation.[47] Sharma makes the point that Rāmānuja's view of *identity-in-difference* is something like "identity *in and through and because of* difference".[48] This serves to keep the essence of Brahman differentiated from the differences that are, and the changes that occur in, the manifested attributes that are his body. Essentially, *identity* and *difference* are opposite concepts, and the only way that they can be reconciled is relationally, that is to say, when the differences are modes that are dependent on a substance for their very identity. *Identity* then becomes the key issue that is qualified by the *difference(s)* that belongs to it. Such differences have reality and individuality, but subsist only in the substances that support them. The complexities of the concept of *bhedābheda* cause some to reject it in the context of Rāmānuja's thought.

Bhatt, for example, says that Rāmānuja, "throws away both the concepts of bheda and abheda and institutes instead the concept of Viśesaṇa (predication)".[49] The idea of predication is a sound one, the predicate as the selves and the world being intimately linked with God as the substrate and subject, but it does not suggest so strongly the inherent inseparability of the two.

Avidyā and māyā

While accepting that ignorance, *avidyā*, causes the inability of the self to understand that it is the body of Brahman, that it causes a false belief in the independence of the self from Brahman, and that it causes the self to become over-involved with the world of matter, Rāmānuja contested the Advaita view that ignorance deludes us into thinking the world is real. Nothing, he believed, can be really relational to ignorance. Śaṃkara characterized it as indefinable, and neither real nor not real – a category, according to Rāmānuja, that is illogical and cannot obtain. Rāmānuja believed that it is the effects of *karma* that cause the self to be deluded about the world, not some timeless substrate of ignorance that pervades all creation. *Avidyā* is simply a lack of appropriate knowledge, it is misapprehension, and is generated by the involvement of the self in the world. If it existed, it would have to exist as an attribute of something, just as its opposite of knowledge, and that something could not be selves, since they, and their individuality, are said to be the *result* of *avidyā* in the Advaita school. Neither could it be associated with an Absolute that is pure Consciousness, as Advaita suggested, since pure Consciousness could not contain ignorance. In a varied dialectic, then, Rāmānuja refuted this key doctrine of Advaita, accepting it as illusion – but one in the mind of the Advaitin.[50]

Similarly, Rāmānuja rejected the Advaita concept of *māyā* as illusion. He preferred to view it as the marvellous power of God in the cosmos. God is described in *Upaniṣadic* thought as one that wields magical power, but for Rāmānuja this is merely the miracle of *prakṛti* under the control of Brahman. So, far from seeing *māyā* as an indefinable and delusory "something" that is neither real nor non-real, Rāmānuja makes it thoroughly real – the whole unfolding of Nature as the magical effects and attributes of God. Rāmānuja wrote, "this one Being has an infinite and wonderful variety of forms and still retains His uniformity in this infinite and immeasurable diversity".[51] Thus, Rāmānuja was critical of the Advaita theories of *avidyā* and *māyā*. If they are neither real nor non-real, they cannot be verified by any means of knowledge.

Epistemology

What emerges in Viśiṣṭādvaita, then, is a very real world, and Rāmānuja assigns to all aspects of life knowledge of what is real. Dreams, too, are considered to be real in the sense that they are the result of past *karma* and, therefore, provide very real means by which the effects of one's previous causes can be worked out according to one's merit or demerit. For Rāmānuja knowledge is always of the real, and knowledge is essential for the path to liberation – in particular, knowledge of the true nature of the Self as the body of Brahman.

Viśiṣṭādvaita accepts three *pramāṇas*, perception, inference and testimony, this last being of primary importance in the context of scriptural testimony. These are the valid means by which knowledge can reveal an object. All knowledge must have an object in the Viśiṣṭādvaita school, and the objects are revealed to a conscious self, to a subject that possesses the knowledge. Knowledge itself can know nothing, it is not itself conscious, but simply illuminates an object for a conscious subject. Further, according to Rāmānuja, knowledge involves discrimination; it means recognizing something as different from something else, distinguishing one thing from another. As was highlighted above in the context of substances and non-substances, *dharmabhūtajñāna* is an immaterial substance that is, in fact, differentiated from both *cit* and *acit*. It is self-luminous, and therefore needs no other means to validate it. So knowledge stands somewhere between spirit and matter, and really links the two, since spirit – the self – needs it to make matter manifest. While knowledge cannot know itself, just like a light cannot know it is lighting up a dark room, the self can know nothing without it. The essence of the self is as a knower, that is to say, it is the substratum on which knowledge or consciousness, as a quality or attribute, is based. It is the difference between knower as a principle, and knowledge of something. Thus, Chethimattam refers to the "bi-polar conception of consciousness as a knower and knowledge, as the one basic and lustrous substance and the shining quality".[52] So the self has the attributive essence or nature of knowledge, and is therefore self-luminous. And yet, the self is not *pure* consciousness; it is not, itself, knowledge in its purest form. For the knowledge, or consciousness, that belongs to the self is always an *attribute* of the self as a subject. When subject to change, through expansion and contraction, knowledge always points to an object. So it has different, but real, modes, like love, hatred, pain and pleasure, indicative of its changeable and not *pure* nature.

Thus, Viśiṣṭādvaita accepts that all knowledge is true; there is no grand illusion, no *avidyā* or *māyā* that informs all existence. Even things we see that are misapprehended, are true in the sense that they have meaning to the self, just like the perceptions in dreams have reality in terms of being related to past *karma*, and so have some purpose for the self. So even if we see something that is not, subsequently, what we think it is, at the initial perception of it, knowledge takes place, though it may well, later, be shown to be erroneous. Knowledge must reveal objects as they are, even if we misapprehend them. But two criteria for valid knowledge are identified in Viśiṣṭādvaita: first, that it should serve some practical purpose in life that indicates its common acceptability and, second, that it should reveal things as they really are. In both cases, the knowledge obtained is by means of attributes.

The purpose of knowledge, then, is to reveal objects in the external world to the self, the knowing subject. And it cannot do this if the objects in the world have no intrinsic reality. Since all matter is real for Viśiṣṭādvaita, it exists irrespective of knowledge revealing it to a conscious subject: it is there when we are not. Knowledge occurs through perception of the senses, or through memory of objects once perceived. It also takes place through inference, with the concomitance of two objects, or through testimony based on the particular relationship between words that denote objects. In fact, whatever comes into the mind must be the result of some kind of knowledge. Since objects have an independent reality in the world of matter, and since selves are differentiated one from another, knowledge is different from one person to another: the subject–object relation thus ensures differentiation of knowledge from one experience to the next, and between different subjects as the basis of knowledge. Knowledge, therefore, is not one but plural to the Viśiṣṭādvaitin, a point that is in line with its rejection of pure consciousness. Again, all knowledge must reveal an object to a conscious self; it cannot exist independently of either, even if it is self-valid.

Knowledge is eternal, because the self of which it is an attribute is an eternal substance in Viśiṣṭādvaita. Knowledge really has no limit to it and, while Īśvara's knowledge remains complete and total, the knowledge of the ordinary, bound self is subject to expansion and contraction; it rises, falls, disappears, and re-emerges, but always exists. And when the self becomes liberated its knowledge is expanded to the point of omniscience – though not to the same level as that of Īśvara. Knowledge is thus eternal because it is an inseparable attribute of the self: through such *apṛthaksiddhi*, it must remain as permanent as the permanent substance in which it inheres. As Chari explains, using an analogy of Vedānta Deśika's: "The lustre of the diamond remains permanently with the diamond since the two are inseparable. Even if it is eclipsed temporarily due to dirt, it is not lost but only eclipsed. In the same way, knowledge is not something which arises as a product as the Nyāya-vaiśeṣika believes but exists as a permanent attribute of the self."[53]

Of course, there are modifications to the knowledge of each individual *jīva*, and these are subject to change and finitude, but they belong to a foundational substance of knowledge potential, and that is permanent. Even in deep sleep, knowledge exists in an unmanifest form – otherwise we should know nothing when we wake. Knowledge can only be manifest when it comes into contact with an object, and this it doesn't do in deep sleep when it remains latent. Nevertheless, because knowledge is a dependent attribute, when it is a function of the self, it cannot have the same status as the substance to which it is inseparably related but on which it is dependent. The self, then, is something different – as a substance – from the attributive knowledge that exists for its purpose. But, at the same time, knowledge, *dharmabhūtajñāna*, is a substance in its own right, as one of the six *dravyas* of Viśiṣṭādvaita. It is its self-luminous status, and the fact that it is the basis for modifications, like other substances, that classifies it as a basic substance.[54] As attributive knowledge it is known as *dharmabhūtajñāna*, but as the essence of the *jīva*, as the knowledge principle, it is known as *jñānasvarūpa*, or *dharmijñāna*. This is a point that will be taken up below in the context of a separate section on the nature of the self.

Knowledge is self-luminous and reveals itself and its object without the need of any other knowledge to suggest that knowledge has occurred – otherwise we would be in a position of infinite regress. Light, for example, can reveal an object, but doesn't need another light in order for it to be revealed itself. So when we know something, we come to know both an object *and* that we have knowledge of it at the same time. All such knowledge is of a relational and differentiating kind between subject and object – including knowledge of God. However, it is important to note that there is no direct relation between the self and the object of knowledge; it is only *knowledge itself* that can possess this function *directly*. In the process of knowledge, the knowledge radiates out from the self to the mind, comes into contact with an object through the senses, assumes the form of the object, then relays the impression to the mind, again via the senses. Knowledge can also be an object itself. Were it otherwise, one person's knowledge could never become the object of another's, and communication of any sort would be impossible. It is also an object in the sense that the self is aware of it. Even in deep sleep, when no external knowledge is taking place, there is knowledge of the existence of the self – otherwise, we should not be able to say "I slept well", or "I fainted".

All this is in direct opposition to the Advaitin's view of the self as essentially pure Consciousness and as identical to Brahman as the same nature. Pure Consciousness can never obtain for the Viśiṣṭādvaitin since consciousness needs an object, and there is no valid means of establishing a pure Consciousness devoid of subject–object relationalism. In any case, pure Consciousness can only be proved if it has attributes that can qualify it as real – in which case it is no longer consciousness *per se*. But the self *is* consciousness, or knowledge, because it has the eternal capacity for being a knower in its essence, and yet is also the possessor of consciousness, or knowledge, because it uses it as its attribute. The self has to have consciousness as its essence because, as Lipner puts it, "the relation between the *ātman* and consciousness in its various ramifications may best be examined by a form of introspective self-awareness in which the knower catches itself at work, so to speak. For it is only in and through consciousness that the *ātman* can be present to itself, understand its essence and look into the grounds of its being".[55] What we have, then, is a substratum of expansive knowledge that is eternal and essential to the self, and attributive knowledge that rises and falls, originates and ceases in its involvement with the objects in the material world – knowledge that is *karmic* in nature. When this *karmic* knowledge ceases, the dust on the diamond is removed, and the expansion of knowledge in the self can take place. What these ideas will point to is a conscious Self at *mokṣa* that has knowledge of the bliss of communion with God. But the self is never consciousness or knowledge *per se*; the fact that it can say "I know", or "I am conscious" reiterates this, the "I" being the substrate for the existence and characteristic of knowledge.

Pramāṇas

As means to establish valid knowledge, Viśiṣṭādvaita accepts the three *pramāṇas* of perception (*pratyakṣa*), inference (*anumāna*) and testimony (*śabda*), as stated above. And all knowledge established by such means is real, is knowledge of real objects in a world where selves and matter have independent and differentiated reality. Viśiṣṭādvaita refutes the Advaita view that the world is illusory. Were it to be so, then there would be nothing real at all – including *pramāṇas* – to prove the existence of Brahman, who would be totally unknowable. Nor could metaphysical truths be proved in any way. The *pramāṇas* for the Viśiṣṭādvaitin are real means, resulting in real knowledge of real objects and truths.

Perception

Perception takes place when there is direct contact with an object via the senses and results in knowledge. If we fail to identify an object correctly through perception, we still have knowledge, even though it is subsequently shown to be erroneous: such misconceptions have to be the result of some particular cause – and that must be knowledge.

Importantly, when perception takes place it does so of an object *and* its inseparable attributes. In fact, as Vedānta Deśika made clear, it is the attributes by which we know the object of perception.[56] Knowledge, then, is always to some extent determinate. For Rāmānuja, indeterminate perception is perception of an object that is without qualifications, but not without *all* qualifications.

Thus, Rāmānuja accepted a difference between indeterminate and determinate perception. The former, in order to be knowledge, has to have *some* discrimination of the object, albeit one devoid of its fully differentiated nature. Rāmānuja believed that in indeterminate perception there is initial recognition of an object *and* its class nature. But it is only when the cognition, after a second or third apprehension, moves to the determinate level, that the object and its class character are related to the rest of its class. Full, determinative, cognition takes place when the object is finally related to prior, indeterminate, perceptions of it. The distinction is between particulars in indeterminate perception, and universals or classes at the determinate level. The universal character is known at the indeterminate stage, but not truly cognized until the determinate stage. It is past impressions of the same object that serve to bring indeterminate knowledge to the level of determinate knowledge. This makes indeterminate perception at some kind of mid-point between partially and fully true knowledge, and more complex than the indeterminate knowledge accepted by the other schools.[57]

Unlike so much other Hindu philosophy, Viśiṣṭādvaita accepts memory as a valid means of perception – an essential view considering its acceptance of the authority of "remembered" scriptures, as will be seen below. Rāmānuja also accepted *yogic* extra-sensory perception as a special kind of cognition, but Vedānta Deśika believed that such perception was not separate from that via the senses. If it were to be so, then it would be separate from experience, and therefore invalid. Vedānta Deśika's view gives *yogic* perception a more defined reality and suggests that the reality of special, evolved cognitions does not differ from ordinary cases of perception. Either way, the acceptance of *yogic* perception was important. In the words of Lott: "This opens the way for the very special 'divine-perceptions' granted by the Lord, in which the knowledge of himself is given as the culmination of all other knowledge."[58] Thus, *yogic* perception facilitates intuitive knowledge of God, which, wrote Radhakrishnan, "is religious experience or the immediate awareness of the infinite. The individual soul is *en rapport* with the ultimately real".[59] Meditation was the important means of development of such perception.

Error

In the case of illusion or erroneous knowledge, Viśiṣṭādvaita still accepts that some sort of knowledge has taken place. After all, when a piece of rope on a path is believed to be a snake, knowledge of some sort causes a very real reaction in the perceiver of it. Although illusory in some senses, the object *appears* as real. And in cases like the conch shell that looks like silver, there *is* an object present that the senses perceive, albeit with an incorrect analysis. But the object of deception does exist, so perception and knowledge occur. By a remarkable thesis, Rāmānuja argues that what we mistakenly see as silver instead of a conch shell is due to the similar preponderance of the elements in one object with the other.

Citing the evidence of scripture, Rāmānuja accepted that each object in the universe was composed of the five elements of fire, air, water, earth and ether. Some objects possess more of one of these elements than another, giving each its distinctive characteristics. But since all objects must have the same elements in some proportions, it is not impossible for a person to see the recessive elements in an object, instead of its dominant ones. And this would create the illusion that an object is not what it is – silver, as opposed to a piece of conch shell, for example. The theory would serve to maintain Rāmānuja's view that all knowledge is valid. In the case of the mistaken silver in the conch shell, the silver is *really* there, though not quite in the same proportion and reality as the perceiver thinks. But the knowledge does correspond to the object in respect of the silver element. Thus, the perception is not a total illusion, but is real. It is only the pragmatic test of it that will verify the partial nature of the knowledge. The knowledge we have turns out to be erroneous because the piece of conch shell is of no use to us, and because, on closer examination, it has no correlation to the rest of the knowledge we have.

Inference (anumāna)

Inference is accepted under virtually the same criteria as the Nyāya-Vaiśeṣika school. Thus it is possible for inferred knowledge to take place as a result of the universal concomitance between two things, such as the presence of smoke indicating that there is fire. But Rāmānuja insisted that where universal and logical concomitance is used to establish the particular, the fire from the presence of smoke, inferred knowledge can only occur from empirical, perceptible, sense objects and not from super-sensory ones. Inference, then, would not be a means of establishing the existence of God.

Testimony (śabda)

Two kinds of testimony are accepted. *Laukika* refers to the empirical level of life, and *alaukika* to the non-empirical. As far as the latter is concerned, Rāmānuja accepted that it was only through the testimony of scripture that God could be known. Thus, it is the most important of the *pramāṇas*. Reason, applied through the *pramāṇa* of inference, was incapable of supplying valid knowledge of God for, Rāmānuja believed, God is a being that differs from anything that could be cognized through the other two *pramāṇas*. Such a theory serves to keep the essence of God removed from anything that might limit it in the sense of ordinary perception and description: God could not be *like* anything else in the cosmos. Rāmānuja said:

> Hence only the śāstras [Scriptures in the broadest sense] are the authoritative source of knowledge concerning the Supreme Person, the Lord of all, who is the Supreme Brahman. There is no possibility for even a trace of any imperfection due to His similarity in nature to the things known by the ordinary source of knowledge, since the Scriptures declare Him to be entirely distinct in character from all the substances known by these other means of knowledge, to be an ocean of bountiful qualities which are immeasurable and of matchless excellence, such as possessing universal knowledge and having His will ever accomplished and being in essential nature radically opposed to everything defiling.[60]

Rāmānuja conformed to all Vedānta philosophy in accepting the infallibility of scripture which, he believed, had no beginning or end, was self-existent, and therefore had no human author. The two portions of the *Veda* – those of ritual, *karmakāṇḍa*, and knowledge, *jñānakāṇḍa* – were given equal importance and recognition as being complementary to each other. The ritual portion, Rāmānuja believed, taught the means by which God could be worshipped, while the knowledge portion taught of the nature of God himself. At the beginning of each cycle of creation, God teaches the sacred scriptures to the foremost of the divine attributes of his own self – in other words, to a deity – but he does not create the scriptures himself: they are self-existent and eternal. And during *pralaya*, the dissolved state of the universe, God holds the scriptures in his mind so that, in Lipner's words, they repose "deep within the consciousness of Brahman in potency proximate to their pre-established empirical form".[61] That is to say, the potential for the manifestation of the *Veda* is held in the essence of God until the time for its re-manifestation in its empirically known form.

Knowledge is acquired through a twofold process in the case of *śabda*. First comes the meaning of the words connected together in a particular way, and this is followed by knowledge of the objects that these words denote. Since the *Veda* is eternal, self-existent and self-valid, the particular *order* of the words, and the objects and concepts they denote, are also eternally determined. Thus, Rāmānuja stated: "In the Vedas the same words have their appointed place in that regular order only and are there alone used, whereas the words used elsewhere are used differently."[62] Further, all words serve the purpose of denoting Brahman, because everything leads to him as the ultimate essence. Rāmānuja wrote, "all Vedic words denote their proper meanings but as terminating in the Supreme Spirit. All words are Vedic: the Supreme Brahman has extracted them from the Veda and, after having created all the corresponding objects as He did before, applied these words as names to those objects, which terminate in the Supreme Spirit".[63] Conversely, words and their associative representations as objects, are the attributes of Brahman that constitute his body in both *cit* and *acit*. The theory of words and their associative meanings in relation to specific objects, further supports the differentiated realism of the school. All is real, and all knowledge has validity until it is proved erroneous. But scriptural testimony is regarded by Rāmānuja as *self-valid*; it cannot, subsequently, be shown to be erroneous, so it has supreme authority.

Viśiṣṭādvaita recognizes not only the *śruti* scripture of the *Veda*, but various *smṛti* texts, like the *Manusmṛti*, also. Such scriptures are also authoritative in that they explain and expound the *Veda*. The particular Vaiṣṇava texts, the *Pañcarātra Āgamas*, are also accepted as authoritative, as well as the *Vaiṣṇava Purāṇas*, and the Tamil *Prabandham*. These texts, which are extraneous to the *Veda*, are believed to be based on, conform to, and in harmony with, *Vedic* teaching, and they are thus a valid *pramāṇa*. But the *Pañcarātra Āgamas* are particularly favoured because they are said to have been composed by Īśvara because of his compassion for humanity. In accepting some *smṛti* or "remembered" texts as a *pramāṇa*, memory has to be given validity as a means of knowledge, and is, as noted above, an accepted means of perception.

These, then, are the three *pramāṇas* accepted by the school. Comparison, *upamāna*, is rejected as cases of perception involving memory, a case of inference or of testimony.

Arthāpaṭṭi, or presumption – as when Devadatta is said to be elsewhere because he is not at home but known to be alive – is considered as inference. *Anupalabdha*, non-apprehension, is rejected because nothing at all is perceived by the senses in the case of non-existence: non-apprehension is an instance of perception – perceiving the absence of something.

The self

Much has been written already above about the relationship between the self and the divine with reference to the body–soul theory of Rāmānuja. And in summation of this analysis, it must be said that there can be no complete *identity* between the self and God, as far as Rāmānuja was concerned. More certainly, there is *difference*, particularly in the sense that the embodied self of finitude and change is very different from the changeless essence of Brahman. Even when the self is liberated the differences between it and the divine are always sufficient to speak against complete identity. Yet, because God is the substance from which the self takes its whole being, there is an element of identity. What this suggests is put very clearly by Chatterjee and Datta:

> It is reasonable to conclude then that according to Rāmānuja, in different respects, there are different kinds of relations between the self and God. In so far as the self is finite and subject to imperfection, and God is just the opposite in nature, there is difference; in so far as the self is inseparable from God who is its inner substance (ātmā) there is identity . . . but as the self is a part of God, both identity and difference are tenable.[64]

The particular relationship between both identity and difference, however, is not, as was seen above, a straightforward *bhedabheda*, "identity-in-difference", nor is it identity-*and*-difference. It might be said that it is identity or unity *qualified-by*-difference, a view that is distinct to Viśiṣṭādvaita, and one that needs to be borne in mind in the examination of the concept of the self that follows.

Radhakrishnan described the true Self as a "reflex of the whole reality" and a "trinity in unity".[65] The Self consists of the very essence of Brahman in its *mode* quality – and that would be part (but not the whole) of the essence that characterizes all matter and selves. There are problems, however, with this particular aspect of a fundamental essence. Is it *identical* in all the different parts? If so, and, as Sharma points out, souls are *essentially* alike, but numerically different, then "quantitative pluralism is no real pluralism. The difference which makes no difference is no difference".[66] The only alternative is that Brahman has different essential modes in different beings, and this must, surely, be what Rāmānuja accepted, given his theory of dependent difference of bound selves. The Self in Viśiṣṭādvaita is atomic and, as such, very different from Brahman. Does Rāmānuja then posit a plurality of identical atomic Selves in the liberated state? There are times when it seems as if he does. Different classes of beings such as gods and humans are accepted by Rāmānuja as the outcome of *karma* and the particular working of *prakṛti*. But the *essence* of the Self Rāmānuja accepts as the same in all beings. He said that souls "are equal because, when they are free from the differentiations god, man etc., they all have the self-same form of knowledge".[67] Similarly, in his *Gītābhāṣya* Rāmānuja said: "The innate ātman cannot be destroyed, even if its body be destroyed. This nature is common to all embodied ātmans, so they are essentially equal and eternal; inequality and perishableness are brought about by the body."[68] And later in the same text he comments: "He who knows the proper form of the ātman will see that same form in the ātmans of all other creatures – however dissimilar these creatures may appear –, because all ātmans have only one form, knowledge . . . All ātmans are equal to one another, as long as the ātman-substance is not conjoined with prakṛti."[69]

Despite such evidence, there are a number of points that oppose the view of the identical nature of the *ātmans*. It is true that each has an identical *essential* nature that is characterized by the knowledge principle – they are knowers. Thus, van Buitenen writes: "Rāmānuja endorses the Sāṃkhya view that there is an infinite number of *ātmans* which although mutually distinguished, all have the same generic structure (*ākāra*) of unrestricted knowledge."[70] But the identical generic structure need not preclude individual knowledge *of* God in the liberated state. So while Rāmānuja wrote: "Though present in all beings, the ātman is undivided because its only form is being a knower",[71] in the *Vedārthasaṃgraha* he wrote of "spiritual entities themselves which are of an infinite variety, either bond (*sic*) or released".[72] Might it not be claimed, then, that Selves are ultimately of the same *rank*, the same generic nature, but are otherwise *various* and individual? Expanding and contracting consciousness belongs to the essence of the soul,[73] but expands and contracts only in *karmic* activity. When this ceases, the self is characterized as a generic knower that sees no differentiation between the generic nature of one self and another, yet sees others as different modes of the divine. It should be remembered that on the body–soul analogy each part is different within the whole. The true Self also consists of the knowing subject that is different from all other Selves together with the quality of functioning processes of consciousness. To make these identical is to rob the liberated devotees of any individual, personal experience of divinity, replacing this with a composite one.

The self is real; the knowledge it acquires is real; it is a real agent of action in the world; it experiences the real fruits of its own actions. Importantly, each self is of the nature of *cit* "spirit", and its fundamental state is an eternal substance with an independent and different reality from anything else. While subject to *karma* in its embodied form, the pure Self is really eternal, and so is really neither created nor destroyed. Even during the time when the cosmos is dissolved into Brahman, it exists in subtle potentiality. Being of the substance of spirit, *cit*, its fundamental state is an atomic essence, like a fine point of spiritual light.[74] This fundamental Self is untouched by the changes, joys and woes that *karmic* existence attaches to it. And this fundamental essence must surely be characterized by *difference* from all other Selves, just as *karmic* selves are also different. Plurality and differentiation, then, characterize both the gross, *karmic*, self, and the subtle, fundamental Self. What creates this is the "I-ness" of the combination of the subjective self, with the consciousness of knowledge. In the bound state this can, as it were, stream out in any direction to create unique experiences for the "I". Here it creates a self-awareness that cannot be communicated to any other, that is unique, and that necessitates the awareness of the same uniqueness of all others.

The self – either subtle or gross – is always a knowing subject, or *jñātā*. It is because

God pervades the self, controlling and guiding from within, that it always remains an accessory, a *prakāra*, of the divine – part of the body of the divine. Viśiṣṭādvaita has a number of terms to depict the embodied or the liberated self.[75] The general term, however, is that of *jīva*, which is synonymous with *ātman*, and sometimes combined as *jīvātman*. This latter term is not indicative of the personality self as opposed to the pure Self as *ātman*, but serves to differentiate any kind of self from Brahman as the Supreme Self or *Paramātman*. But the term *jīvātman* is not without its difficulties in the Viśiṣṭādvaita school, and this occurs because of its association with ego – in particular, the ego that pits itself wilfully against God, and that is drawn towards the world. In the Sāṃkhya analysis of *prakṛti*, which Viśiṣṭādvaita largely follows, *ahaṃkāra* "ego" proceeds from *buddhi* or "intellect" *before* the evolution of the senses, sense organs and active organs. These last three evolve from the *tamasic* and *sattvic guṇas* present in *ahaṃkāra*. Clearly, then, there can be no perception at the level of the *ahaṃkāra* and, indeed, no objects of perception to constitute knowledge. The *prakṛtic* self of Saṃkhya is essentially unconscious matter, but the self of Viśiṣṭādvaita is quite the opposite – conscious spirit. And the question has to be asked, conscious of what? At the pure level of *ahaṃkāra* it can only be of itself – for there is no external world to be perceived. While *guṇic* propensities are present in the *ahaṃkāra* and will develop exactly the kind of empirical self necessitated by past *karma*, at its pure level, the *ahaṃkāra* is devoid of such manifested character. The empirical, *karmic* ego is, then, yet to come, and it will be this empirical self that will find itself involved with the world of matter. Strictly speaking, then, the "I" is *ahaṃkāra* and might be called pure ego, the pure Self which, as eternal and unchanging conscious spirit, is aware of its own Self. The *karmic* ego, however, is a different matter. The "I", the pure Self, becomes the substrate for egoistic knowledge – that which makes us claim "I am male, female, a *Brahmin*" and so on.

There are three kinds of *jīvas* according to Viśiṣṭādvaita. First, there are those that are eternally free, called *nityamuktas*. These are the divine beings that have never been bound and who exist in the Vaiṣṇava heaven in divine service of Viṣṇu. Then there are those who have eventually left the cycle of reincarnation for ever, having become free because of their right actions, knowledge and devotion to God; these are the *muktas*. Those still left in *saṃsāra* are the bound ones, the *baddhas*. The Āḷvārs had also categorized *jīvas* into three such classes.[76] Such categories clearly lift the *jīvas* from any identification with the body itself. Indeed, the fact that the *jīva* can use such expressions as "*my* body", or "*my* self" suggests some kind of "I" apart from the body itself. Then, too, losing a part of the body does not suggest that the "I" is affected in its essential nature.

It is the body that is born and dies, but it is the eternal "I" that reaps the result of its *karmic* entanglements with the world. And the functions of the senses, the mind, the breath, and even the function of knowledge itself are but attributes of the *jīva* but not the *jīva* itself. The *jīva* is essentially *cit* "spirit" and knower, with the attribute of *dharmabhūtajñāna* "consciousness", "knowledge", eternally belonging to it. And yet the *jīvas* are never without a body in that, when the *prakṛtic* body ceases to exist, in their pure and liberated state the *jīvas* are attached to the transparent pure *sattvic* substance body composed of *śuddhasattva*,[77] and are of the nature of bliss. This is not something acquired by liberation. Rather, it is the natural state of the *jīva*, but this is obscured through the years of *karmic* transmigration. The body subsists and has its nature and its activities dictated solely by the volition of the *jīva*.

The *jīva* has control of it and supports it for its own purposes: the body, as the *śarīra*, is always subservient to, and dependent on, the sentient self. If the self departs from the body at death, or at liberation, then the body that is so dependent on it ceases to exist. This relationship, which is one of *apṛthaksiddhi*, inseparable relationship, between the *jīva* and its body, mirrors that between God and each individual *jīva*, as well as that between God and the world. But whereas God does not identify himself with the *cit* and *acit* that he supports, the *jīva* in its bound state identifies itself with its material body, satisfying the body's desires and avoiding its aversions.

In its enlightened and true state, the *jīva* has many similarities with Brahman. Of the nature of consciousness and of spirit, its character of bliss, knowledge and purity, and its eternal nature, are features it holds in common with Brahman. But Brahman is never bound, is never subject to expanding and contracting knowledge, and is never coated with the dust of ignorance. But at all times – whether in the liberated or bound state – the *jīva* is always like the servant to the master, respectfully distant, yet intimately bound. Thus, Rāmānuja saw any identity between the pure Self and Brahman in the *Upaniṣads* as relational: as a part of the whole that is the body of Brahman, the *jīva* is identified with Brahman, but remains different because it is only a part. And just like the master–servant relationship, God exists in and for himself, but the *jīva* exists for God.

The identity between the *ātman* and Brahman – so evident in much *Upaniṣadic* thought – is, then, qualified by Rāmānuja. He argued that it is tautological to say that two things are identical, for *this is that* suggests at least some qualifiable difference exists for a *this* to be identified with a *that*. As Radhakrishnan put it: "The negation of all difference renders impossible even the relation of identity."[78] Identity can only be identity *in and through* difference. And a *part* may be identical in some ways to the whole, yet, because it can never *be* the whole, it can never be wholly identical, but only qualifiably so. The *jīva* as a part of Brahman has a certain identity with Brahman as an integral part of him. According to Rāmānuja this is the identity of which the *Upaniṣads* speak, and is an identity of substance and attribute. But the attribute remains different as a part, as it is only an attribute of the whole. What Rāmānuja attempted to do, therefore, was to uphold the integrity of the *Veda* by justifying the Brahman-*ātman* identity passages as consonant with the more dual suggestions of difference between the two.

The statement crucial to the issue of absolute identity of Brahman and *ātman* is that famous expression *Tat tvam asi* "That you are" of the *Chāndogya Upaniṣad* (6:9:4) where "That" is Brahman, and "you" is the *ātman*. It, too, Rāmānuja saw as a "this is that" type statement, where identity cannot be absolute. Then, too, there is the statement "The self is Brahman" – another "this is that" statement. In Viśiṣṭādvaita both are interpreted in the sense of identity of part to whole, but qualified by the inseparable substance–attribute relationship. But a new nuance of meaning is added: the "you" in "That you are" refers to Brahman in his mode as the indwelling supporter and controller of the self, while "That" refers to the Primal, causal Brahman. In Rāmānuja's words:

> The word *tat* refers to Brahman as the One who is the cause of the world, the abode of all perfections, the immaculate and untransmutable One; whereas *tvam* refers to that same Brahman under the aspect of inner Ruler of the individual soul as being modified by the

> embodied soul. So it is said that the words *tat* and *tvam* both apply to the same Brahman but under different aspects."[79]

The identity here, then, is of two different aspects of Brahman, and of relationship of whole/substance to part/attribute. It is identity between Brahman unqualified and Brahman qualified, or qualified identity, qualified monism: "That" and "you" in Viśiṣṭādvaita are the same Brahman, but are qualified differently. Thus, there is oneness, but not absolute identity. This is implied in the words of Brahman: "May I be many" which are to be found shortly before the *Tat tvam asi* statement (6:2:3). And if Brahman does become many, then all things are ultimately relationally connected to him, as are all words and all terms – including the "That" and the "you".

As was seen above in the context of the Viśiṣṭādvaita view of the world, the "I" that is the *jīva* is self-luminous; it is the knower that is aware of itself as different from that which it knows, and needs nothing else to validate it. This comes about because of its fundamental consciousness – the fact that the "I" is conscious. It is not some pure consciousness that is common to all reality, but an *individual* consciousness, an individual "I"-awareness, that is different from that of other *jīvas*. It is this reflexive awareness of the "I" that is unchanging through transmigration and in the state of liberation. In its pure state it would permit all-pervading, omniscient knowledge, though it is tarnished by world involvement. Ordinarily, it is what enables us to know who we are when we wake from dreamless sleep, and to be able to say "I slept well". While the sense of the reality of the "I" will be blurred by the particular involvement of the *jīva* in the material world, yet in every cognition it will be aware of the "I" as the knower, and the fact that the "I" knows that it knows. In all situations, the "I" is the doer, the hearer and the knower. The self then is two selves; it is the real Self or "I", that is pure, and it is an empirical, egoistic self that is attached to the "I" as the result of *karmic* necessity, arising from all the previous modifications of knowledge. The more awareness of the former, the nearer the *jīva* is to liberation.

Then, too, as indicated above, the "I" is the substrate of all knowledge. While the "I" does not change, knowledge itself goes forth from it and expands and contracts to gain the empirical impressions about, and experiences in, the world. Knowledge is, thus, always a quality of the self. It is something the self uses in order to access objects of knowledge. So while the *jīva* can know itself, it can know nothing outside itself without the medium of knowledge. The self, then, has generic knowledge, the principle of knowledge, as its very nature – something reiterated by the *Upaniṣads*.[80] The knowledge or consciousness attributed to the *jīva* is also of two kinds. The *dharmabhūtajñāna* is the knowledge attribute of the self that it uses to apprehend objects: it is therefore subject to modifications of expansion and contraction. Then there is the *dharmijñāna* or *svarūpajñāna*, that is the knowledge which is the very *essence* of the Self and is unchanging, like the Self itself. It is the Self as generic knower, as essential knowledge. Of the soul, Rāmānuja said: "In essence it is only characterized by knowledge and beatitude. It can only be defined as essentially knowledge; and this essential nature is common to all souls."[81] Van Buitenen comments that this does not suggest that pure knowledge is of the real nature and essence of the Self, only that it is an attribute of the Self.[82] Likewise, of Brahman, Rāmānuja wrote: "Brahman's proper form is designated by knowledge as its defining attribute, but it is not mere knowledge itself . . .

knowledge is a property and not a substance."[83] In other words, Rāmānuja says that the Self is essentially knowledge, but that that knowledge is an essential property of the substance of the Self.[84]

So all acts of knowledge emerge from the *ātman*, the *jīva*, for it has the essential property of consciousness, of knowledge, and, at the same time, it uses this as an attribute for its processes of cognition. What we have, then, is an unchanging, knowing, conscious subject, and changeable, modifiable qualities of knowledge and consciousness. The relationship between these two kinds of knowledge/consciousness is not one of separation, but of intimacy; one is merely inward, and unchanging, and the other is outward and pragmatically modifiable. And because the *jīva* cannot exist without consciousness, nor *vice versa*, there is a certain synonymy and identity between the two, though it is wise not to press this identity too explicitly. It is the word "essence" that is suggestive of identity of the *jīva* with consciousness, but it should be remembered that it is always a *quality* of the *jīva* and, therefore, cannot really be the *jīva per se*.[85] Such identity was certainly refuted by Vedānta Deśika, for knowledge/consciousness can only show but never know.[86]

Having some similarity to Brahman, the *jīva* is eternal and unchanging. But as an attribute of God, and only a mode of God, it cannot be infinite, like the primal, causal Brahman. As the "you" in "That you are", Brahman indwells all *jīvas* and accompanies each in its *saṃsāric* wanderings. Rāmānuja described this indwelling of God in the *jīva*, as like a flash of lightning in the heart of a blue cloud. This does not suggest passivity; indeed, the *ātman* is not still and passive, but is characterized by activity that is informed from within by the will of God. And yet, each *jīva* is capable of more independent, self-willed action. Indeed, all the injunctions and prohibitions of *Vedic* scripture are designed to assist the best kind of activity for the path of liberation, and must indicate free human response to follow them, or they would be meaningless. God, in a way, *consents* to such self-willed response and action. However, Rāmānuja makes it clear that consent does not equate with involvement. For while God supports the activity of the *jīva*, he is separated from finite agency, and from any moral outcome that may ensue from it. The *jīva* is free to interact with the world, experiencing the realm of *prakṛtic* existence, reacting to it and acting in it through the expansion and contraction of its consciousness. Thus, the self is an active self, active in knowledge, devotion and meditation. Whereas to the Advaitin the self could not be an agent of action *per se*, Rāmānuja accepts the opposite.

In *saṃsāra* the *jīva* is limited by its particular *karma*. There are four kinds of such *karmic* individuals, celestial, human, animal and inert. Each *jīva* is really immaterial, but when it is connected with a body or a material substance as a result of its past actions, then it becomes so associated with substance and matter, that it seems to be such. These associations cause it to reap appropriate results in terms of material bodies that belong to a certain class and caste, and pattern of life. Some *jīvas* will search out enjoyment; others will orientate towards liberation. As the *śruti* texts were keen to reiterate, the *jīva* is the agent of actions and, therefore, will be the enjoyer of the results of such actions. *Vedic* injunctions tried to ensure that actions were of the right kind. The confines that the *jīva* finds placed on it in life are the results of what it has reaped in past existences. Such selves, wrote Radhakrishnan, "are like islanders who live unconscious of the sea".[87] The true nature of the pure Self being obscured, such bound individuals have little awareness of the God that is their ultimate ground and support. The world becomes all-important. So whenever there are results to be reaped from conscious activity, the *jīva* has to be reborn in order to experience those effects of its causal acts. Even though the self exists in its subtle state at the dissolution of the universe, the *karmas* associated with a *jīva* accrue to it, and cause its rebirth in the next evolution of manifest existence. Such *karma* is accepted by Viśiṣṭādvaita as beginningless, though liberation of the self can free it for eternity from *saṃsāra*. The body serves the purpose of associating a *jīva* with a material medium, as a means for working out fruitive *karma*. It is only a temporary union of the immaterial self with a material substance – a material substance that is destructible, unlike the eternal and changeless, real Self that pervades it.

In accepting the *Gītā* as valid testimony, Rāmānuja also accepted its teaching that it is actions that are engaged in without consideration of their respective results that cannot accrue fruitive *karma*. Thus, two individuals can do the same thing, but it is the *intention* behind the action that determines much of the nature and degree of the fruitive *karma*. The whole point of Viśiṣṭādvaita is to endorse the actions of an individual that are so dedicated to God, so intensely focused on love of God, that thought of personal gains from such actions cannot obtain. Such actions would thus be other-centred and pure in aim, not self-centred and engaged in from the level of the empirical self. Only in this way can the *jīva* transcend the cause–effect process of the *saṃsāric* cycle. This, indeed, was where the Self was meant to be – liberated into the divine. But Rāmānuja never eschewed correct *dharmic* actions as unnecessary. In other words, the ritual portions of the *Veda* were to inform the path of the self to final liberation. Ritual *karma* was the path of goodness; it was duty for the sake of duty. And this implies an important point, for the operation of *karma* is not an impersonal one. Just as God reveals the *Veda* at the beginning of each age in order to assist the right kind of actions and prohibit the wrong ones for the benefit of the evolution of the self, so *karma* is controlled by God for the same purpose. Thus, in Viśiṣṭādvaita it is God that initiates its functioning, and who ensures the appropriate results for causal actions. Such control of *karma* is also considered to take place in the dreams of each individual. As stated earlier, dream experiences supply an appropriate means for reaping the results of *karma*.

It is debatable, then, whether or not *karma* is irrevocable. It is in the control of God, but since the grace of God is a key feature of Viśiṣṭādvaita, does this mean that God's grace can overcome *karma*? Murthy suggests here – and the idea is a sound one – that the control of *karma* is a *means* for the operation of God's grace in the world.[88] Thus, it is irrevocable because God's grace is just, and each individual gets his or her just rewards. However, the actions that each *jīva* undertakes are his or her own, and not God's: inevitably just rewards and retribution will account for the varied pleasures and pains of all individuals. *Karma* is a means of bringing the self towards God. And the whole purpose of existence and the countless lives of any *jīva*, is devotion to, and utter concentration on, God as the Ground of all. These are all points that now need to be examined in length in the context of Rāmānuja's concept of God.

The concept of God

At the beginning of his *Śrībhāṣya*, his commentary on the *Brahma* or *Vedāntasūtras*, Rāmānuja wrote :

> The word 'Brahman' denotes the highest Person (purushottama), who is essentially free from all imperfections and possesses numberless classes of auspicious qualities of unsurpassable excellence. The term 'Brahman' is applied to any things which possess the quality of greatness . . . but primarily denotes that which possesses greatness, of essential nature as well as of qualities, in unlimited fulness; and such is only the Lord of all.[89]

The Viśiṣṭādvaita view of the divine stands clearly in the framework of theism. God is *accessible* to the devotee, though at the same time, he remains the Absolute of so much *Upaniṣadic* thought. This *absolute* dimension that underpins the Viśiṣṭādvaita concept of a personal God, is beautifully expressed by Dasgupta:

> The entire universe of wondrous construction, regulated throughout by wonderful order and method, has sprung into being from Brahman, is maintained by Him in existence, and will also ultimately return to Him. Brahman is that to greatness of which there is no limitation. Though the creation, maintenance and absorption of the world signify three different traits, yet they do not refer to different substances, but to one substance in which they inhere. His real nature is, however, His changeless being and His eternal omniscience and His unlimitedness in time, space and character.[90]

Such a description would not have been amiss in the teachings of the Āḷvārs. Nammāḷvār, too, spoke of the personal Absolute as without equal, as being of the nature of infinite bliss, as dwelling in all things and as controlling and supporting all things. Clearly, from the works of the Āḷvārs, the Absolute is a God of differentiated attributes, and this is very much the thought of Rāmānuja and of Viśiṣṭādvaita as a whole. The Absolute of the *Vedānta* is conceived of as the personal Nārāyaṇa by the Āḷvārs and Rāmānuja, with a spiritual "body" that lends itself to much anthropomorphic description. Yet, while pervading all, the utter transcendence of God is never compromised by the defects of the sentient and non-sentient attributes – the selves and matter – that are his body. Raghavachar writes of Rāmānuja's introduction to the *Gītā*:

> The fundamental factor in the situation is God. He is the supreme Reality and attaining Him is the Supreme goal. The nature of the supreme Reality is brought out in a systematic array of significant adjectives. That the infinite Reality is the object of all spiritual aspiration and endeavour is brought out in the very statement of the nature of God. God in His fundamental nature is beyond the reach of souls caught up in the meshes of Māyā.[91]

As pure Spirit, God – like the individual pure Selves, which are also of the nature of spirit, pure *cit* – is unchanging in his real essence. Again, these are ideas expressed by both Nammāḷvār and Rāmānuja.

In the hymns of Nammāḷvār and in the teachings of Rāmānuja, God, Īśvara, is the Ground, the *ādhāra*, or supporter of all that is – again, like the soul is the supporter of the body. Brahman is the substantial cause of the world, being the substance from which the world and selves – as effects – are produced as the attributes of God. Brahman ensouls all things entering into insentient matter as well as sentient beings. According to Rāmānuja he is "the material cause, the operative cause, the substratum, the controller and the principal of the entire phenomenal world of spiritual and non-spiritual entities".[92] As the Ground of all, then, there is a relational intimacy between Brahman and the attributes he generates. But by generating the attributes he is also their efficient cause – he is the Ground of all in the sense that he wills all to be. However, the ultimate transcendency of God never permits him to be merely the pantheistic whole that unites the parts: while causative, he panentheistically transcends all. Brahman is always the *Lord*, and thus the term for this, *Īśvara*, has particular meaning in that it expresses the Lordship of Brahman, of God, over all the body of his creation. In Rāmānuja's words: "In short, He is the core, whether manifest or not, of all beings in whatever condition they exist. The totality of beings, mobile or immobile, cannot exist apart from God who is the ātman within themselves."[93] Brahman is an independent reality that is supreme, and that is One without a second.

Whereas in some Hindu thought Brahman denotes a neuter "It", an indescribable Absolute that cannot be limited by any association with the empirical world, for Viśiṣṭādvaita, Brahman is a synonym for the describable God: no distinction is made between the two. The concept of a *nirguṇa* Absolute is rejected for the *saguṇa* God with an abundance of marvellous qualities. We have to remember that Rāmānuja asserted that what is known can only be so by virtue of its qualities, and a *nirguṇa* Brahman, therefore, could not be known at all, and could not be proved by any valid means. To Rāmānuja the *Upaniṣadic* idea of Brahman as One without a second is not indicative that he is One without any secondary qualities, but that he is One without any equal and rival reality. Rāmānuja believed that those texts referring to the indescribable *nirguṇa* Brahman as the unequalled, transcendent Absolute alluded only to the essence of God that underpinned his qualities. So where Śaṃkara stripped Brahman of qualities, Rāmānuja expressed them in abundance. And there was no question here of a "higher" and "lower" Brahman, the former being the undifferentiated ultimate Reality, and the latter a lower, qualified reality, Rāmānuja rejected the undifferentiated Brahman outright. Rather, he saw the higher Brahman as the transcendent Brahman that is the substance on which selves and matter depend. If any distinction is to be made, the attributes of his body – the selves and matter – are the lower Brahman, as the supported and controlled.

Rāmānuja, then, rejects the concept of a *nirguṇa* Brahman for a God that is determinate and qualified, individual and personalized. Both the acosmic and the cosmic Brahman feature in the *Upaniṣads*, the former without qualities (*nirviśeṣa* or *nirguṇa*) and numerous cases of the latter with them (*saviśeṣa* or *saguṇa*). Where reality of the world is accepted – as it is in the Viśiṣṭādvaita school – then the predicable reality of Brahman as the creator, controller, sustainer and supporter of the world, is essential. It is only where the reality of the world is denied, as in Advaita, that the *nirviśeṣa* Brahman is viable. Viśiṣṭādvaita sees the acosmic and cosmic portrayals of Brahman as two aspects of what is the One, Brahman, and that is a God distinctly *with* qualities. But what of the well-known statement in the *Bṛhadāraṇyaka Upaniṣad* that says Brahman is *neti neti*? This is usually taken to mean that Brahman is neither this nor that, and is, therefore, devoid of the differentiating dualities that would grant him qualities. In his *Śrībhāṣya* (3:2:23) Rāmānuja analyses the phrase in its context. He concludes that, since qualities of Brahman both precede and succeed the phrase, *neti neti*, "not this not this", is used to point out that the qualities that precede it are not the *only* ones that can be applied to Brahman. Further, Rāmānuja believed that the phrase served to state that only *some* qualities are denied Brahman – those that are negative, like evil, *karma* and change, for example. In other words, Brahman without qualities is Brahman without negative qualities, and not without all the positive qualities by which he is so often depicted in the *Upaniṣads*. According to Rāmānuja, then, the phrase *neti neti* is not meant to be indicative of a Brahman without qualities. Any thought of an indescribable Brahman in the *Upaniṣads* refers to the inadequacy of finite human minds to describe the ultimate and infinite nature of God. Rāmānuja, then, saw God's qualities as of two kinds, his positive perfections, and his utter lack of any imperfections.

The two dimensions of Brahman – the transcendent essence or "Soul", and the indwelling immanent Brahman or "body" – are reflected in words from the *Bṛhadāraṇyaka Upaniṣad*, favoured by Rāmānuja for its description of God: " He who, dwelling in the earth, yet is other than the earth, whom the earth does not know, whose body the earth is, who controls the earth from within – He is your Soul, the Inner Controller, the Immortal."[94] It is a verse that exemplifies rather well the way in which Rāmānuja sought to stay well within *Vedāntic* confines for his understanding of the concept of God. But Viśiṣṭādvaita also accepts the infinite attributes and wondrous qualities given to God in the *smṛtis* and the *purāṇas*. Scripture supplies knowledge of God's qualities – not a God devoid of qualities, but a God replete with them. This is certainly a God who can be the object of worship, and who is a means to the liberation of the self. God has the characteristics of knowledge, inexhaustible strength, sovereignty, immutability, creative power and splendour. To these are added also qualities that reach out to his devotee – compassion, grace, love that is forgiving and protecting, and generosity. These qualities thoroughly transcend their counterparts in humans; "because I possess such qualities as universal knowledge, creative power and untiring strength, I am superior, and there is nothing whatsoever distinct from Me which could be superior by possessing such qualities".[95]

For Advaita Brahman was of the nature of pure *sat*, *cit* and *ānanda*, Truth, Consciousness and Bliss respectively, and there was an absolute unity between the three. Rāmānuja, too, accepted these descriptions of the nature of Brahman, but as attributes of Brahman – and, therefore, not Brahman *per se*. He also regarded them as distinct attributes not unified ones. Such attributes inhere in Brahman and are inseparable from him, but are dependent on Brahman as the substance in which they inhere. It is for this reason, according to Viśiṣṭādvaita, that the real Self, and Brahman too, cannot be the pure consciousness that Advaita posits.

Brahman is both cause and effect. He is causal when both *cit* and *acit*, spirit and matter, exist in their subtle states. He is effect, when the subtle is transformed into the manifest world and the selves that inhabit it – all being the body of Brahman, and each entity being a part of Brahman and supported by him. But despite the change from cause to effect, Brahman is not changed at all by the manifestation of his attributes, the *vibhūti* of God: he transcends them and controls them, and also transcends his own causal and effected modes. But everything is intimately a part of Brahman. This is put beautifully by Rāmānuja:

> The supreme wonder in nature is its being the garment of God. All that seems ugly, trivial, or insignificant, acquires a new dimension of this view. Nature and finite souls are packed with God and are suffused with the hues of the Divine. . . . God is not merely a marvel in Himself but also He moulds nature into a wondrous manifestation of Himself.[96]

It is only the attributes of Brahman that are subject to change: his essence is unmoved and unchanging. Brahman is thus three-fold, unchanging essence, causal potency, and effected attributes. The "supreme wonder in nature" can only be linked with the attributes of God, the effects of God, not with the essence of God itself. Nevertheless, there is an intimate relationship between *cit*, *acit* and God. God is not distant from what he creates, but constitutes it as his own *vibhūti*, his own manifested body. He is always accessible, though there are dimensions of God as the One and not the many, that will always remain supremely apart from human understanding. Of this, Bhatt comments: "Like the Upaniṣads, Rāmānuja solves the problem of one and many not by denying many and affirming one, nor by denying one and affirming many but by making many the predicate of one. As a matter of fact one and many never posed any problem to him, because he starts with the position that one, by its very nature of immanent necessity, is impregnated with the many."[97]

Brahman, then, is a describable, predicable deity. He is God, or Īśvara. He is real, of the nature of omniscient consciousness, bliss, purity and infinitude. He has personhood and has many perfections such as Love, Beauty, Power and Goodness, and no imperfections. He has a supernal form, is male, and can be anthropomorphically depicted. He is the "Golden Person" of the *Chāndogya Upaniṣad* with a golden beard and golden hair, who is brilliant to the tips of his fingers (1:6:6), with eyes like a lotus flower (1:6:7). He lives in a divine abode and enjoys the pleasures that sense perception offers. But God's form is not of the same kind as human physical and *prakṛtic* form; it is a special, supernal form, which Rāmānuja graphically described:

> He who is always gloriously visible is the pre-eminent Person who dwells within the orbit of the sun. His splendour is like that of a colossal mountain of molten gold and His brilliance that of the rays of hundreds of thousands of suns. His long eyes are spotless like the petals of a lotus. . . . His eyes and His forehead and His nose are beautiful, His coral-like lips smile graciously, and His soft cheeks are beaming. His neck is as delicately shaped as a conch-shell and His bud-like divine ears, beautifully formed, hang down on His stalwart shoulders. His arms are thick, round and long and He is adorned with fingers that are reddened by nails of a most becoming reddish tinge. His body, with its slender waist and broad chest, is well-proportioned in all parts, and His shape is of an unutterably divine form. His colour is pleasing. His feet are as beautiful as budding lotuses. He wears a yellow robe that suits Him and he is adorned with immeasurable, marvelous, endless and divine ornaments – a spotless diadem, earrings, necklaces, . . . [98]

And so the descriptions continue. Rāmānuja is remarkably graphic and anthropomorphic about such characteristics of the divine, and this, it has to be said, rather detracts from his carefully formulated philosophy. Bhatt is one who is critical of this outright anthropomorphism with which Rāmānuja adorns his concept of God. He claims: "In this adulteration of anthropomorphism in the metaphysical truth Rāmānuja loses the severity of his metaphysical contemplation and gives vent to mythological fancy." He further comments, "such sentimental expressions are quite superfluous and unwarranted in his ontological set up".[99] There is a good measure of truth in this. Such anthropomorphism detracts from the concept of God rather than enhances it, opening up all kinds of problems in connection with the transcendent essence of divinity on the one hand, and the implications for theodicy on the other.

It is from the supernal form of God that the *avatāras*, the "descents" or incarnations, of God emerge – the ultimate in anthropomorphism. And it is the manifest form of the divine that is so readily approachable by his devotees, yet the abundant qualities of the supernal form of God are so infinitely wonderful that they can only be glimpsed, and not fully comprehended, by his devotees. But intimacy and union with his *bhaktas* is joy to God, and therefore his devotees experience his loving-kindness, his mercy and his love. The supernatural bodily form of God is for the benefit of relational devotion between human and divine.

Knowledge, consciousness or *dharmabhūtajñāna* is a particular attribute of God, as it is of selves. But it is not subject to the expansion and contraction that characterizes its presence in *karmic* humans, nor is it dependent on sense perception. God's consciousness is intuitional and eternally omniscient. Like selves, the consciousness of God is as much his essence as it is his attribute.[100] The essence or *svarūpa* of Brahman is, therefore, depicted as being knowledge. Four other aspects of his essential nature are also added – he is real, infinite, of the nature of bliss, and devoid of any imperfections. Together they form the five basic attributes of the essence of Brahman, and are called the *svarūpanirūpaka dharmas*. They depict the highest, transcendental Brahman, *para* Brahman, from which he manifests himself in four other forms. One of these is as Nārāyaṇa, Viṣṇu or Vāsudeva, the divine form that lives in the supernatural, pure *sattvic* realm of Vaikuṇṭha. Then, there is God in his creative, sustaining and dissolving role in the manifested world as his body, and his indwelling of all. Another form constitutes his *avatāras*, yet another is his presence in the sacred images in the special temples of his devotees.

Like Nammāḻvār, Rāmānuja characterizes God as Lord of the universe and its supporter and controller. The world and selves as the body and attributes of God are created, sustained and eventually dissolved by God, though being eternal, these attributes are merely undifferentiated potential in their dissolved, unmanifest state. From its unmanifest state, the world of matter, and the unliberated selves that inhabit it, are made manifest by God. The world is created so that the selves are able to reap the results of their former *karmic* actions, and so that they can have an opportunity to evolve towards liberation. For these purposes, they are deemed to need a physical body. Once the world and selves are manifest, God is manifest too as the inner Controller, the *antaryāmin*, of all. This was a concept thoroughly consonant with both *Upaniṣadic* thought and that of the *Bhagavadgītā*. But in whatever form God is manifest all his attributes remain – even if some are latent. Thus, his essential nature is present as much in the *avatāras* as in the images he indwells in the temples.

It is these last two aspects that are important in the life of the devotee. Although primarily inaccessible to all – even to deities such as Brahmā – God makes himself accessible to his devotees. The physical representations of the divine are the visible presence of

God in the realm of humankind. For Rāmānuja there was no question of this presence being an inferior reality of the nature of God, or a temporary, illusional one, that would cease to exist when the devotee transcended the lower slopes of devotion and knowledge. No, scripture attested to the reality of the divine form as far as Rāmānuja was concerned. It was this perspective of divine reality that was so essential to the heart of Vaiṣṇava religion in the richness of its thought and practice. There are a variety of names to refer to the person of God – Viṣṇu, Hari, Vāsudeva, Bhagavat, Puruṣottama. But the favoured name used by the school, and certainly by Rāmānuja, is Nārāyaṇa, for it is this name that appears to be the most inclusive of the whole nature of Brahman. Nārāyaṇa was a name particularly favoured by the Āḷvārs. Chari notes that it was one used in the *Upaniṣads* as synonymous with *Sat*, *Ātman* and *Brahman* to denote the highest form of divinity and ultimate Reality.[101] It is a term that depicts the Lordship of God, his attributes, and his status as the inner Controller of the whole universe. The term *Nārāyāṇa* contains the word *nāra* meaning "human" "humanity" (strictly speaking, the masculine "man"). The whole word expresses the concept of a highest, supreme God who, out of compassion to his creation, individualizes himself in human form, in order to become a focus for the devotion of humankind, so that individuals may evolve to the point of liberation. Nārāyaṇa is thus the supreme Reality, the supreme Brahman but, as such, is personal. It was probably one of the earliest Vaiṣṇava names for Brahman.[102]

Viṣṇu as the name for God, though rarely used by Rāmānuja himself, is synonymous with Nārāyaṇa and, therefore, with ultimate Reality. And both terms are used of the more anthropomorphic conception of God who sits on the serpent Śeṣa as his throne, in the subtle *sattvic* realm of Vaikuṇṭha with his consort Lakṣmī. His mount is the eagle Garuḍa. In the Vaiṣṇava faith, Viṣṇu is Brahman and is superior to Śiva. In the Śaiva faith, it is Śiva who is supreme, but for Vaiṣṇava belief it is Nārāyaṇa/Viṣṇu who is the creator, preserver *and* dissolver of the universe, thus taking on the role of Śiva. This certainly was the view of Vedānta Deśika, who believed that Nārāyaṇa was the creator of both Śiva and Brahmā – the other two members of the *Trimurti* or three forms of Brahman. According to Vedānta Deśika, both Śiva and Brahmā are subject to *karma* because they are part of manifest existence like all else that is created by Nārāyaṇa.[103] There is no thought here of equality between the triad, or of their being manifestations of an unmanifest Absolute that transcends them. Nārāyaṇa is Brahman, and the other two deities are inferior creations. Indeed, the whole pantheon of deities that feature in Vaiṣṇava belief is part of the body of God, of Nārāyaṇa, and all these deities are therefore controlled, supported by, and dependent on, him. However, since all other deities, such as Śiva, are attributes of Nārāyaṇa/Viṣṇu – part of his manifestations, his *vibhūti* – in the spirit of the *Gītā*, worship offered to them is, in reality, offered to Nārāyaṇa.

Given the considerable emphasis in Viśiṣṭādvaita on the dependency of the world and each self on God, and God's support and inner control of all things, it seems logical to suggest a firm determinism of all life. But this is not so. Human free will is essential to Viśiṣṭādvaita thought. So although God is the ultimate Controller of all life, a certain degree of control and self-determinism is given to each self, especially moral autonomy: the individual is free to choose between right and wrong. But there is no sense of withdrawal of the divine from the performance of human action. God always remains the inner

Controller, *permitting* actions to obtain as the result of individual desires. Thus, as Dasgupta commented: "This is a sort of occasionalism, which holds that, in every action which I am performing, I am dependent on *Īśvara's* will. I can move my limbs because He wishes it."[104] And yet, the grace of God will favour and support those who are devoted to him: as the desires of the individual become more God-orientated, so the reciprocal inner control of God, operating through the *ātman*, draws the devotee ever closer. Conversely, those antagonistic to God are pushed away. But, always, the control is there, permitting the freedom of action and adjusting the self, and its environment, to the life it creates through its own choices. Dependency of the *jīvas* on God never ceases, but: "They have a sort of secondary subsistence, which is enough to enable them to develop on their own lines."[105]

It is through the medium of *karma* that God manipulates the evil or good effects appropriate to the choices and actions of each individual *jīva*. So all operates according to the natural turn of events. According to Rāmānuja:

> When someone of his own accord has been active before in an extremely good action, then the Venerable Lord is pleased with him and by granting him a mental disposition for good actions helps him to be so active. When, however, someone has indulged in extremely inauspicious actions, then the Venerable Lord incites him to wicked activities by giving him a wicked disposition.[106]

It is the law of *karma*, then, that operates to bring about each person's just deserts, but it is God who is in control of its operation. Rāmānuja had effectively attempted to retain the unlimited nature of the divine alongside human free will. He removed God from the *actual* perpetration of *causes* of good or evil, but retained God's control over both by way of the more specific control of the *effects* of them. Rāmānuja wrote: "By stating the truth that Brahman is the Self of finite beings, we have not contradicted the truth that He is the very home of auspicious qualities and the antithesis of everything evil and defiling, for the imperfections [doṣa] adhering to the bodies, which are modes, do not affect the self who is the underlying substance [prakārī] of these modes."[107] Thus, although little can be done to avoid the effects God has set up according to his *karmic* law, causes remain the free choices of each individual.

The whole process of *karmic* desserts, then, is the effect of the *grace* of God in permitting freedom in human effort. It is particularly in the evolution towards liberation that God's grace is effective in removing obstacles on the path. It is a *love* of God for the devotee and the reciprocal love of the devotee for God that promotes God's grace – a concept repeatedly stated in the *Bhagavadgītā*:

> Hear again my supreme and most secret word of all: I love you dearly, therefore I shall speak to you what is for your good.
>
> Fix your mind on me, be devoted to me, sacrifice to me, bow down to me, then I promise you in truth you will come to me, for you are dear to me.
>
> Having abandoned all dharmas, take refuge in me alone. I shall liberate you from all evils; grieve not.[108]

For Rāmānuja, a certain balance of *effort* on the part of the *jīva* is necessary, along with *elec-*

tion on the part of God. But the human effort involved is that which is steeped in deep devotion and self-surrender to God. Ultimately, it is by God's grace that the law of *karma* operates, and yet God seeks to liberate the *jīva* from its bound state. Rāmānuja, then, does not remove God so far from human action that he becomes remote and impersonal:

> God of Rāmānuja is not an Absolute who is rigid, motionless, totally lacking in initiative or influence, who cannot comfort in stress and suffering when weak and erring human beings call from the depths, and who does not extend His helping hand but remains indifferent to the fear and love of His worshipper. He is a God of grace and favour, love and kindness, who is always at the disposal of His devotee, and who descends from the supernatural to the natural order to gratify this.[109]

But the problem of theodicy looms large in a system of philosophy that binds God so closely to witnessing human action – albeit that Rāmānuja posits an unchanging essence underpinning the modifications of Brahman. If Viśiṣṭādvaita accepts that God can make the ignorant knowledgeable and the weak powerful, if he can pardon the guilty and make the wicked good,[110] or if it pleases him one is good and another is evil,[111] then the very worst atrocities that human beings can commit can be prevented by God. However, if God acts only in conjunction with the law of *karma* – and this must surely limit his omnipotence – then he is removed from the taint of sanctioning evil. Viśiṣṭādvaita accepts that, while God may have the power to override *karma*, he does not violate his own laws: only in this way can he be guiltless of involvement in evil. Whatever the state of the world, it is a result of the individual and collective *karmas* of its past inhabitants. And since the world has no ultimate beginning and no end – only eternal cycles – there is no primal cause even of the process of cause–effect by which evil can originate. For Rāmānuja, since the world and the *jīvas* that inhabit it are the attributes of Brahman, the existence of evil might be said to be like the blueness of the lotus – a quality that cannot constitute the substance in which it inheres. God is impartial in permitting the good and evil actions of *jīvas*, and is really impartial in permitting the just deserts of those actions. As the inner Controller, according to Rāmānuja, "while observing the soul in its doings the Supreme Spirit Himself takes no sides".[112] Yet the tint of theodicy hangs on here, and I sympathize with the words of Keith Ward concerning the difficulties any theism will present in the solutions to the problem of evil and suffering in the world. Of this problem in relation to Viśiṣṭādvaita he writes:

> How can Brahman find sport in a suffering world? The doctrine that "all imperfections and sufferings belong only to the individual souls" . . . has just a hint of a sadistic God about it, rather than of one who truly cares for what is, after all, in some sense his own Body. If the souls are a manifestation of Brahman, then can one quite so confidently ascribe all suffering to their own fault, and not to the necessary self-manifestation itself? And can one talk of the Lord blessing and punishing, that is, reacting to specific events in time, while yet he "is in no way touched by imperfections and changes" . . . ?[113]

There is a good deal of sense in this statement, particularly considering the analogy of the *control* of the body by the soul and its utter dependence on the soul for all its actions. And yet, as the *Gītā* so frequently points out, the soul has a separate identity from the physical body that acts, performs, and desires fruits of its actions. In the last resort, it is this "in-itself-ness" that divorces the real Self from the world of evil and suffering, just as God's "in-itself-ness" divorces him from the temporary world and the selves that inhabit it. So despite the changes necessitated by a *karmic* world, Brahman remains unchanged in his essential self: only his attributes are subject to change, and it is only here that theodicy can be relevant.

Yet God becomes fully involved in the human world through his *avatāras* – a concept central to Vaiṣṇava religion. The word, as pointed out above, literally means "descent" and refers to the real manifestations of Viṣṇu/Nārāyaṇa on earth. The purpose of such descents is to restore the *dharmic* order when humanity moves too rapidly towards chaos, to be an accessible refuge to, and protection for, devotees, and to be a paradigm for moral being, that displays beauty and glory. Such descents are the result of the free will of God, and occur for the benefit of his creation. They thus arise from a compassionate desire of God to assist humankind and to perform miraculous acts in order to captivate humankind. In such manifest form, however, God is not subject to the *karmic* patterns of ordinary existence: he remains God, Viṣṇu and Brahman – as the *Gītā* constantly implies. Thus, the essential nature of God remains unchanged. Some *avatāras* may be partial: this is the case with the enlightened saints and teachers.

Śrī

The feminine aspect of the divine is a particular feature of Viśiṣṭādvaita, and of Vaiṣṇava religion. But as the consort of Viṣṇu/Nārāyaṇa, Śrī, or Lakṣmī, is not subject to the same depth of theological and philosophical discussion as her male counterpart in the works of Rāmānuja, though a developed theology was to occur later. Although Rāmānuja defends her reality, she has no real function, and any attribute assigned to her is also assigned to Nārāyaṇa. While possessing the very best of qualities, a glorious essential nature and exquisite beauty, not even her title as "Mother" is exclusive to her, for all her qualities and titles are equally applicable to Nārāyaṇa. Nor do we find in Viśiṣṭādvaita the kind of active/passive, male/female, unmanifest/manifest dualities of Nārāyaṇa/Śrī that characterize Tantric Hindu thought. Rāmānuja does not refer to Śrī as the *śakti* or power of Nārāyaṇa, though Vedānta Deśika does – an attitude that was typical of the Vaḍagalais school in general. Rāmānuja's concept of the divine feminine is of a creature of gentleness, mercy and femininity. But she is merely attendant to her consort and "suits his pleasure".[114] Certainly, the Āḷvārs appear to have given Lakṣmī the same status as her Lord,[115] but the lack of a developed theology relating to her in the early stages of formal Viśiṣṭādvaita, might indicate a more subservient role for her.

Despite the school being associated with qualified monism, there are some who find Rāmānuja's concept of God to be pantheistic.[116] My own view is that qualified monism and a dual relationship with the divine, where the soul never becomes the divine, can only be indicative of a concept of God that is panentheistic – a God that pervades all things and yet, ultimately, transcends them. This is especially so because each *jīva* is a *part* of the divine, and an inseparable part at that. But the part can never be the whole for it is an effect of God as the causal Ground of its being. The existence of God in himself regardless of the manifestation of his attributes, reinforces a panentheistic perspective: God is all his attributes, but as the Soul that controls them, is greater than them. Panentheism permits the intimacy between God and selves and God and the world, so evident in Viśiṣṭādvaita. Bhatt aptly comments, God is "the root of life as well as its fruit. He is the ground of existence and the goal of existence, the summum genus and the summum bonum",[117] but he is always much more than his created attributes.

Causality

The relationship between cause and effect is crucial to Viśiṣṭādvaita thought, for it is this that answers the relation between the One and the many, between God as the Soul and *cit* and *acit* as his body, between the Infinite and the finite. Causality in the Viśiṣṭādvaita philosophy is a transformation of what is subtle into gross form. It is the transformation of potentiality into actuality, of cause to effect. But no limitations must be placed on Brahman as the causal Ground of all that would suggest any transformation of the *essence* of the changeless God into a world of change. And yet, clearly, there must be a causal relationship between Brahman and the world and *jīvas*, for it is sensible to claim that all effects must have causes. How, then, do these effects come into being?

Viśiṣṭādvaita accepts the eternal nature of the three "reals" of God, souls and matter. But souls and matter, although eternal, do not always exist in manifest form. Rather, they are subject to endless cycles of manifest and unmanifest being, existing in cycles of actuality in the manifest state, alternating with cycles of potentiality in the unmanifest state. In the unmanifest and potential state, the world and souls exist in an undifferentiated state that is devoid of name and form; but they still exist as eternal substances. Causation is the process by which such subtle substances undergo modification that transforms them from the subtle to the gross. And as modified substances, such resulting effects are *different* from their causal states. The clay pot, then, is different from the basic clay from which it is made; it is a new object. This is a modified *satkāryavāda* by which, in one sense, effects pre-exist in their causes, but in another, they are different from their causes. They pre-exist in their causes in that they are the same substances, but it is the modifications, the attributes, the characteristics, that constitute real differences from the original causal substance. Underpinning this process of causality is Brahman who wills it to be the extension of his Being, becoming his body, *without any change to his essential essence*, as Soul, and by which the effects, being different, remove him from change and finitude. The *Bhagavadgītā* expresses this causative function of Brahman in the following words from 9: 7, 8:

> All beings, Kaunteya, go into my *Prakṛti* at the end of the *kalpa*. At the beginning of the *kalpa*, I send them forth again.
>
> Having animated my own *Prakṛti*, I send forth again and again this multitude of beings, all helpless by the force of *Prakṛti*.

It is by these means that the One becomes the many. Rāmānuja put the same thing in the following way. He says of Brahman:

> He conceives the thought "Let me become the world body, composed of conscious and

> unconscious beings, differentiated, as previously, in conceptual and corporeal fashion" – and then transforms Himself, in His world body, through entering one evolute of Matter after another. This is the doctrine of transformation in all the Upaniṣads.[118]

But in becoming the world body, Brahman as the Soul remains unchanged. Thus, in his *Gītābhāṣya*, Rāmānuja wrote: "Brahman is the material cause of the world, because Brahman, if modified by gross and subtle cit and acit is effect and cause respectively. Nonetheless it is clear that the natures of cit and acit on the one hand and the nature of Brahman on the other are not amalgamated only because Brahman is the material cause of the conjoined cit and acit . . . the Supreme Brahman, though entering the effect, is not transformed thereby, because his proper form does not change".[119]

So when the world and selves are held in the unmanifest state by Brahman, he is said to be in the causal state, *kāraṇāvasthā*. This is because he contains the potential for all things in existence – all latent in his Being. But when the world and selves are projected into their manifested forms, God is in his effect state, *kāryāvasthā*, and pervades all as the Indweller and inner Controller (*antaryāmin*). But it is not the essence of God himself that is subject to modification through transformation – only his attributes, his body, are the effects. All such projections, such transformations, are real, a concept known as *Brahmapariṇāmavāda*. Carman writes that,

> the causal relation in the strict sense is not, as we might expect, between God as cause and world as effect but between Brahman in His causal state as the cause and Brahman in His effected state as the effect. In both states, souls and matter form part of Brahman as His body and his modes. Causation is what is responsible for the universe in its present state, not for its absolute origination, since finite selves and the fundamental nonintelligent substance underlying material objects are coeternal with Brahman. While, strictly speaking, it is Brahman with His cosmic embodiment who is the effect, the essential nature of Brahman is unchanged in the latter state. It is finite beings whose state (in this case souls) or nature (in the case of material objects) is radically changed, since they are brought out of the darkness called pralaya into the ordered universe (sṛṣṭi) that the Supreme Person has created or projected.[120]

Thus, while Rāmānuja's thoughts on causality come under the category of *satkāryavāda*, the view that effects pre-exist in their causes, there are some nuances that suggest a modified *satkāryavāda*. And this is because effects are the same as their causes on the one hand, thus causing Rāmānuja to claim "there is no difference between cause and effect",[121] and different on the other. It is the acceptance of *real* change that necessitates the latter. Thus, there is both identity and difference in the relation between cause and effect and this allows for the continuity between the two that makes sense in day-to-day existence, and yet the independent plurality of all things. Identity is evident because the *essence* of the cause, its basic substance, is not changed, the cause just has different, but real states that are its effects. Cause and effect are different states of the same substance: "Causation makes explicit what is implicit in identity. The cause persists in the effect and the effect is latent in the cause", writes Bhatt.[122] So clay is a cause until it becomes an effect as a pot. The two are related, have continuity and are different; yet there is identity in the causal substance and the transformed substance as effect that it becomes. The former is the material cause of the latter. Rāmānuja said: "The Self with names and forms non-evolved is agent (cause), the same Self with names and forms evolved is object (effect). There is thus nothing contrary to reason in one Self being object as well as agent."[123]

So this is a *satkāryavāda* view by which effects do not *exactly* pre-exist in their causes, and in this sense are unrelated to their causes. A clay pot does not exist in the clay, the clay may be the antecedent material cause, but an instrumental cause like the potter's wheel is needed to transform the clay into a new and different effect. The clay, then, is only the cause of the pot *to an extent.* The pot is a modified state of the clay, the same in substance yet different in name and form. To achieve the effect, the substance of clay is not negated, but its characteristics are. These are modified to the extent that the effect is new and different. In this sense, effects cannot pre-exist in their causes. Again, this does not deny reality to the effects that are produced, and allows for the reality of the differentiated forms in existence.

The amended *satkāryavāda* theory of causality is important to Viśiṣṭādvaita because the identity between cause and effect on the one hand, and yet the separation of them on the other, is crucial in the context of the relation of *cit* and *acit* to the divine. Thus, *cit* and *acit* as effects are sufficiently separated from the causal divine to have a certain independent and plural reality, and for the divine not to be involved in the finitude and causal limitations and imperfections of worldly existence. There is identity but difference. In Bhatt's words, God "is above all, in all, and through all. All are in Him, out of Him and unto Him".[124] This illustrates causal connection, and at the same time the point that both causes and effects are true. The view of Śaṃkara that only the cause is true – and thereby denying any reality to the world of effects – is rejected by Viśiṣṭādvaita. So the transformations from causes to effects are also real and not apparent, in contrast to what Śaṃkara believed. Such effects may not be permanent, and they may be confined to a particular time and place, but they are nevertheless real. While the causal substance from which an effect is produced remains the same substance as that which is the basis of the effect, everything else about the effect is new, is real; there is a change of state that remains real until it is destroyed. Just so, Brahman as the causal substance transforms himself into the world, which will always have a degree of identity with its causal substance. And yet, the world and selves as effects have a reality and difference apart from the causal divine; they are states or parts of the divine body. Just as light is different from the lamp that emits it, the effects that are the world and selves are different from Brahman that causes them.

Since all things are the body of God, and effects to his cause, the body of God – that is to say his attributive Self – is the *material cause* of the universe. And since it is the Soul of God that wills creation to be, he is also the *efficient cause* of the universe. Important to note is that both world and selves are not created *ex nihilo*, for they exist in subtle and unmanifest form in the dissolved state of the universe. There is no time when they cease, entirely, to exist. God merely makes manifest what is latent. But because creation remains a manifestation of the attributes of Brahman and not the essence of Brahman, he remains removed from, and unaffected by, the limitations of creation, from its evils and its finitude.[125] And yet, as the substantial cause of the universe, nothing can exist without God as the substance; he is that in which all inheres. God does not become the world, or the *jīvas.* He is a substance that can never become an attribute of something else, which is what the world and *jīvas* are. As the whole, he can never become the parts, and as the efficient cause, he can never become the effects. These, too, are reasons why he is removed from the limitations of manifest creation. Chethimattam comments: "The key point of Ramanuja's solution to the problem of causality is the shift of emphasis from causality as a relation between two entities, cause and effect, to the view that it is primarily a relation between two states, the prior causal state and the posterior effected state. In both states, the cause remains immutable in the centre."[126]

In the dissolved state of the universe, or *pralaya*, *prakṛti* is totally latent, in a state of subtle potential without any differentiation. As the efficient cause, Brahman wills the subtle material causes of *cit* (selves) and *acit* (*prakṛtic* matter) which constitute his body, to be transformed into their gross and differentiated states with name and form – "Let me be many" he says. In so far as the body of Brahman is the substrate for *cit* and *acit*, then it is in this sense that he is the material cause of both. Commenting on the *Taittirīya Upaniṣad* and 1:4:27 of the *Brahmasūtras*, Rāmānuja depicted this in the following words. He described the state of *cit* and *acit* in *pralaya* as,

> in so subtle a form that they may be called non-existing; and as they are his body he may be said to consist of them (tan-maya). Then desirous of providing himself with an infinity of playthings of all kinds he, by a series of steps beginning with Prakṛti and the aggregate of souls and leading down to the elements in their gross state [Brahman] so modifies himself as to have these elements for his body – when he is said to consist of them – and thus appears in the form of our world containing what the text denotes as sat and tyat, i.e. all intelligent and non-intelligent things, from gods down to plants and stones.[127]

But the changes that take place in *cit* and *acit* are accidental and not related to the unchanging essence of Brahman. Commenting on the same verse, Rāmānuja said,

> all imperfection and suffering are limited to the sentient and non-sentient beings constituting part of its body, and all change is restricted to the non-sentient things which constitute another part. The highest Self is *effected* in that sense only that it is the ruling principle, and hence the Self, of matter and souls in their gross or evolved state; but just on account of being this, viz. their inner Ruler and self, it is in no way touched by their imperfections and changes.[128]

Brahman does not *need* to will the world to come into being, Rāmānuja states, but does so partly in order that the *karma* of individuals can be worked out. The state of the manifest world will be particularly related to the individual and collective *karmas* of its last manifestation. Once willed to transform from the subtle to the gross state, the unmanifest, subtle matter changes into the elements of fire, water and earth. From these elements the three *guṇas* of *sattva*, *rajas* and *tamas* emerge as qualities, and combine in all kinds of combinations to produce each entity in the world of gross forms. Brahman creates through the medium of *prakṛti* but is not himself characterized by its *guṇic* changes, differentiations and dualities such as good and evil. *Prakṛti*, then, becomes the body of God also. The substratum that is Brahman remains unchanged, and only his attributive aspect of *prakṛti* is changeable. Neither matter nor selves are really created; they simply change in state, from potentiality to actuality, motivated by the will of God. It is the function of the creator deity,

Hiraṇyagarbha, or Brahmā, the specific deity associated with the *rajas guṇa*, to direct the creation of the world. It is he that is given the *Veda* by God. While Brahman wills these things to be, and they are of his being, he is not involved directly.

During the process of manifestation of the universe, *jīvas* are appropriated to a physical body according to the nature of their accumulated *karma*, with its particular balance of merit and demerit. God is said to control events so that each *jīva* experiences what is appropriate to its nature. So individuals create themselves. Rāmānuja wrote, "it is the innate power of their previous karman which causes them to be the substances, god, man etc., which they are".[129] A certain *raison d'être* of creation lies in this point, for each soul is given its chance to evolve towards the point of liberation. This is described as the divine *līlā* "sport" of God but, given that God operates within the bounds of *karmic* retribution, the term does not have the capriciousness that "sport" might suggest. Rather, *līlā* reflects the unbounded joy, delight and freedom God has in the creative process. Carman goes as far as to say: "It is the Divine sport itself which is the purpose of God's creation. In this sense we may say that this universe was not primarily created for the sake of or in the interest of finite beings, for God's spontaneous self-expression in creation is an end in itself."[130] Such a view also highlights the *jīva* – as the whole of creation – as being the recipient who is utterly dependent on God's power and will. Rāmānuja wrote:

> He has as instruments of His sport [līlā] an infinite number of intelligent beings, both those bound in saṃsāra and those released from it, all of whom are parts of Himself. Likewise, He possesses all material things, which are subject to infinite, wonderful, and varied changes and which form the objects of enjoyment for intelligent beings. Since He is the Inner Controller of His whole creation, He has all things as His body and His modes.[131]

Dissolution is the reverse process of creation and is equally dependent on the will of God. Two kinds of dissolution are evident. The first is that which occurs at the cosmic night of the deity Brahmā, when Vaiṣṇava mythology depicts the world as dissolved into darkness while he sleeps, and being re-manifested when he wakes. The second dissolution is a greater one, and even Brahmā is reabsorbed into the totality of Brahman; nothing exists beyond Brahman in this state. When each self loses its gross form in the state of dissolution it reverts back to subtle, undifferentiated potential. Each effect reverts to its causal state and becomes, once again, the potential body of Brahman. There is no time, then, when the selves and the world are not the body of Brahman, and in their subtle state, *cit* and *acit* become attributes of the causal state of Brahman. This dissolved state of the *jīvas* and the world remains latent until God once more remembers to will that he becomes many.

Rejected by Viśiṣṭādvaita is the concept of *adṛṣṭa* as an impersonal potency between cause and effect – that which makes a particular effect related to a specific cause, and that ensures merit or demerit for individuals, according to their actions. *Adṛṣṭa* in Viśiṣṭādvaita is the disposition of God to reward or punish the deeds of individuals. It is a modification of God's attributive intellect that ensures the appropriate effect; it is purely the result of his will. *Dharma*, too, is considered to be the grace of God in rewarding the right actions of individuals. It is not an impersonal consequence of actions, or good actions themselves: again, it is subject to the will of God. *Adṛṣṭa* was a thoroughly impersonal potency without any intimacy in relation between cause and effect. The Viśiṣṭādvaita view is its antithesis. Bhatt writes:

> The absolute of Rāmānuja is a living reality with a creative urge. It is a synthesis which does not deny differentiations, but expresses itself through them only. It is a whole that does not deny its parts, a substance that does not oust its attributes, a ground which does not negate its consequent, an integrity that does not shut itself of fulness. It is the concrete Being which contains the finite as moments of Its own existence, through which it transcends its own initial abstract character.[132]

In any case, as will be seen in the examination of the nature of liberation, and as was mentioned earlier in this chapter, good actions must be so selfless and devoted to God that there is no thought of reward and personal *dharma*. All sense of rewards for good and right actions must be abandoned in devotion to God.

Liberation

The Viśiṣṭādvaita concept of liberation is the most developed of all the schools of philosophy, and it must command considerable space here. It is because the liberated *jīva* retains its personal relationship with God at *mokṣa* and because of the intensely theistic nature of Viśiṣṭādvaita, that the concept of liberation is such a graphic one. Essentially, the self comes to know itself as the mode of God. There is absolutely no sense of complete identity with an impersonal Absolute. On the contrary, the *personal* nature of the relationship between the liberated Self and the divine is stressed. Rather than *kaivalya* "aloneness" of the liberated Self, there is conscious and blissful relationship with God of a dualistic and personal nature.

Since the true Self has consciousness as its fundamental attributive essence, once fruitive *karma* is lost, and the self is no longer attracted to the world of matter but is thoroughly God-orientated, liberation is possible through the grace of God. But the consciousness that is experienced at *mokṣa* is not the same as that which is the essence of God. Knowledge or consciousness according to Viśiṣṭādvaita, it should be remembered, is always of an object, and this is no less true of liberation as it is of *saṃsāric* existence. With a consciousness that is different from God's, the liberated soul is able to experience the joy and bliss that communion with God brings – and this is essentially a dual experience. But, in that the liberated soul is still an attribute of the divine, there is a certain *identity* between Brahman and the Self, particularly because of the inseparable relationship, *apṛthaksiddhi*, between the two. It is this kind of identity, according to Viśiṣṭādvaita, that *Upaniṣadic* texts imply.[133] After all, the liberated soul has no powers of creation and dissolution of the universe, and it has been subject to bondage – two distinctive characteristics that can never be applied to God. In short, the soul is *always* dependent on God, but in the liberated state has some *equality* with God, but not total identity. Equality is evident in the omniscient knowledge that characterizes the liberated soul. Whereas such knowledge was subject to expansion and contraction in the bound state, in the liberated state it is unbounded consciousness, like that of God's, though not completely identical to God's. Such consciousness allows the liberated soul to enjoy the *vibhūtis*, the manifested attributes, of God, something that would be impossible if the two were identical. This is a very *positive* state of liberated existence; the omniscience attained through liberation permits the full comprehension of God by the soul. It is, then, a relational experience and not a fusing and identity.

The universality of liberation?

One of the pronounced features of the Vaiṣṇava religion is its classless nature. Viśiṣṭādvaita, too, has strong elements of such universality and equality. It was not unknown for leading Viśiṣṭādvaita thinkers to be in the company of Buddhists, *Śūdras* or even the, then, untouchables.[134] And yet, it also seems clear that Rāmānuja believed liberation was not for those who were unprepared, who lacked the *Vedic* knowledge that could prescribe correct ritual practice, meditation, and correct knowledge of Brahman. This, inevitably, included only twice-born classes, and excluded *Śūdras* and women, for whom study of the *Veda* has never been permitted.[135] And it would have to be said that if God abides by the law of *karma* then each individual is different because of his or her relative merits or demerits. The *Śūdra*, having no access to the *Veda* because of *karmic* dispositions, would not be able, therefore, to acquire the prerequisites for release.[136] Nevertheless, Rāmānuja spoke out against caste pride as a hindrance to devotional faith: "All beings who worship God by bhakti – whether they be of an exalted or a humble class – will at their desire foregather in God as if they share his virtues, and God himself will dwell in them as if they were more exalted than He."[137] It seems, too, that Rāmānuja was not averse to eating with *Śūdras*.[138] But it appears he never admitted that women should study the *Veda*, should be nuns, or should undertake devotional practice alongside men; he believed carrying out household duties was where their role in life should be.[139] We should remember in this context that he left his wife, whom he clearly did not like, but is reputed to have done so because she could not accept his lower-class associates. His teacher, in fact, was one such person. Ideas of universality and equality, then, did not overstep traditional boundaries in terms of scriptural tradition, but certainly broke away from established norms in other areas.

While *Śūdras* and women were largely excluded from the means to *mokṣa* through *Vedic* knowledge, devotional worship by-passed the priestly class with great appeal to the more ordinary person; at least the path to salvation was shown to be not just for a privileged few. And if the *Veda* were denied to certain sectors of society, the path of surrender to God was not. For all classes, for rich and poor, it was possible to turn to the refuge of God in self-surrender, particularly in starting out on the path to liberation. But Rāmānuja favoured a measure of conservative acceptance of *Vedic* injunctions as essential for the path of liberation, though he seems to have been open to the use of other means for those not qualified to engage in the accepted tradition. While the biographers of Rāmānuja are keen to illustrate his universality and brotherhood, it is likely that this may have been a somewhat intentional hagiographic portrayal.[140] But devotion is an approach to God that really needs no mediator, and it seems that for some, Rāmānuja encouraged the love of God through *bhakti* that was independent of scriptural prescriptiveness. All are fundamentally eligible for liberation, and all can set out on the path for it, progressing towards God in each birth. The initial steps on this path need not be the hearing of the *Veda*, but the opening and surrendering of oneself to God. But for those on the higher slopes, more prescriptive means were traditional.

Bhakti and bhaktiyoga

As far as the more conservative means (*upāya*) to *mokṣa* are concerned, there is a certain synthesis of the paths of knowledge, action and devotion, but not one that blurs the distinctions between them, as much as incorporates them into a systematized, and progressive, path. Knowledge and selfless action become the integrated prerequisites for ultimate devotion, while devotion itself pervades all stages. As a preparation for the final discipline of *bhaktiyoga* ordinary *bhakti*, too, is concerned with meditational devotion to God. But even for this there are stringent prerequisites – attention to the correct foods in order to purify the body; detachment from the world and continuous thought only of God; fulfilling one's moral obligations; truthfulness; integrity; compassion; benevolence; non-violence; being of good cheer; balance of mind. These are the necessary, albeit subsidiary, qualifications for one who wishes to embark on the path of *bhaktiyoga*. It is not difficult to see, then, that the path of *bhakti* is not just emotional devotion. He who embarks on the path is one equipped by *Vedic* study and is one traditionally accepted for the path to God. Lipner puts this pointedly: "Clearly, at the very least Rāmānuja implies that the one ideally qualified (i.e. the *adhikārin*) for embarking on the path to salvation in the present life is a pious Śrī Vaiṣṇava male, belonging to one of the twice-born castes, and duly initiated by the proper teacher into reflection upon the Vedas and into the performance of the ordained sacrifices."[141]

Bhaktiyoga is the key to liberation. It is "the ripened fruit of karma and jñāna".[142] It is the kind of love of, and devotion to, God that obliterates all else from the mind. Such concentration on God leads to a non-attachment (*vairāgya*) to the world so that the senses and mind are thoroughly controlled. All actions are done for God. *Bhaktiyoga* is not something that is acquired instantly, but is progressive. It is loving *meditation* on God, with the goal of bringing the individual to a point of perfection in devotion to God. Such *bhakti* is not really an emotion, for it is underpinned by a concomitantly progressive and continuous knowledge: at its height it will incorporate a state of knowledge, a state of consciousness. *Bhaktiyoga* is, thus, a highly disciplined path that is practised continually and scrupulously throughout life.

Since the soul is always subordinate to God, and is controlled by God, its true nature in existence is to see itself as the body of God, subordinate to God, and intimately and inseparably related to God. It is through *bhaktiyoga* that the soul becomes more and more conscious of this until, finally, it abandons itself completely to God. This is the highest *bhakti*, *parabhakti* – pure intuitive consciousness of God. At this stage, only the grace of God is required for final liberation. *Bhaktiyoga* is disciplined meditation in conformity with that laid down in the scriptures, but incorporates a love of the divine alongside total surrender to him. It is thoroughly informed by intuitive knowledge.

Karmayoga and jñānayoga

The paths of *karma* and *jñāna* are also necessary as subsidiary means to *bhaktiyoga*, and as complementary to ordinary *bhakti*. Scrupulous adherence to religious duties without thought to the fruit of one's actions, is the path of *karmayoga*. It is the surrendering of all actions *to God*. The performance of such rituals is always to be an important part of the life of the *bhakta*: renunciation of action was not acceptable to Viśiṣṭādvaita, and was not consonant with the concept of a personal God who wished for the moral and *dharmic* nature of humanity. *Karmayoga* is purificatory for the soul; it initiates the individual in discipline and, when the highest stage of *bhaktiyoga* is reached, action is always maintained but with more intuitive, internalized God-consciousness. Such continuance of *karmayoga* is especially important in respect of the *nityakarmas*, the obligatory rituals laid down in the *Veda*. Such observance also has the advantage of averting any evil that might ensue from neglect of duty and negative *karmas*. *Naimittika* rituals – those that should be performed only at certain times – also help to avert sin and evil.

But of crucial importance to the process of liberation is the discipline of knowledge, *jñānayoga*. Self-knowledge is critical to liberation, that is to say, knowledge of the nature of the self in relation to God. Since the self consists eternally of attributive knowledge, that is devoid of the dust of the world, it is this that characterizes enlightenment. Without *jñāna* the soul cannot experience this knowledge, its relationship to the world, and its inseparable relationship with God. But *jñāna* is not itself the final goal; it is only the means to the grace of God that brings full vision of the divine. There are two kinds of knowledge involved in the path to liberation. The first is the knowledge that is acquired through study of the scriptures. The second is the higher intuitive knowledge of God, experienced through constant meditation and devotion. However, while in the *Gītābhāṣya* 3:3 Rāmānuja commented that *karmayoga* is for those who are unable to withdraw the senses sufficiently, he said that, so difficult is *jñānayoga* that *karmayoga* is sometimes superior (3:7–8). It is because of the innate subconscious habits (*vāsaṇās*) that *jñānayoga* is difficult to practise. We must remember, too, that *activity* for Rāmānuja was an essential part of human nature – without it, there could be no praise of, or devotion to, God. And yet, Rāmānuja also said that disinterested action without thought of result, and without thought of the *prakṛtic* and *guṇic* world, is really "knowledge in the disguise of action" (4:20). While Rāmānuja often concedes that *jñānayoga* and *karmayoga* are both autonomous means of liberation, he believed there could be no *jñānayoga* without *karmayoga* (5:6).

Thus, both *karmayoga* and *jñānayoga* are important on the path to liberation. They are "the power which tears up our selfishness by the roots, gives new strength to the will, new eyes to the understanding and new peace to the soul".[143] In the thought of Rāmānuja there is a definite interrelation of *karma* and *jñāna* throughout the entire path to liberation, and both are supportive to ordinary *bhakti*, and to *bhaktiyoga*. This was important for the nature of *bhakti* as a means to liberation in the school, for it was devotion *complemented* by knowledge. Bhatt comments:

> Thus by equating bhakti with jñāna Rāmānuja gives to bhakti a predominantly meditative significance on the one hand, and on the other, regards the redeeming knowledge taught by

> the Upaniṣads as neither something purely intellectual nor as something to be accomplished once and for all, but as a meditative devotion daily practised and constantly improved by repetition throughout one's life, and culminating in a mystic intuition of the Deity.[144]

But *jñāna* tends to be more important than *karma*, for the higher knowledge of God, according to Rāmānuja, cannot but result in devotion and love of God, and ceaseless devotion and love of God brings that ultimate knowledge of God that has its end product in liberation. Knowledge and devotion are reciprocal, but knowledge should really precede *bhakti*, for it has to develop to the point that devotion and love of God are inevitable. What Rāmānuja has done in combining both *jñāna* and *bhakti* is to unite the metaphysics of knowledge in the *Upaniṣads* with the theism of the Vaiṣṇava religion. But he goes further in teaching of a higher knowledge that is the nature of continuous meditation on God, and it is this that provides the more direct means to *parābhakti*.

The ideal devotee, then, is the *bhakta* who is also a *jñānin*, one who has direct intuitive knowledge of the divine, and this intuitive knowledge is synonymous with constant and continuous love of, and devotion to, God. It is not so much an *emotional* love, as one characterized by intuitive vision of divinity. There is an increasing knowledge of the nature of the self, of God, and of the inseparable relationship between the two. There is blissful realization of the self as the attribute of God, an outpouring of love and devotion to God that is reciprocated by the grace of God, who loves his devotee. As the *jñānin* is immersed in higher *bhakti*, the world of *prakṛti* recedes from the mind, fruitive *karmas* can no longer bind him to the physical world, for thoughts have become totally God-focused and not self-centred, and so the *jñānin* is ripe for liberation. But even at this stage, ritual actions remain obligatory; *karmayoga* remains an essential subsidiary means to avert sin, evil, and obstructive *karmas*.

In summation, the individual begins the path to *mokṣa* by observance of ritual obligations as laid down by scripture – the path of *karma*. Then, at the next stage, while not ceasing in such ritual practice, the individual begins to acquire the knowledge that the *Vedānta* teaches – knowledge of the Self, of the divine, of Reality, and the true nature of knowledge. It is this knowledge that directs the individual on the path to liberation. But it is only a surface knowledge in the light of that which is to come. Total focus of the self on God in devotion is important at this stage, as well as pure and constant meditation on God. So far the devotee is at the level of ordinary *bhakti*. From here, at the next stage, the higher knowledge comes as an intuitive knowledge of the nature of God and the relation between the self and God. This is supportive to the highest *bhakti*, the direct means to *mokṣa*. Such *bhakti*, Rāmānuja said, "is a kind of knowledge that is so excellent, precious and exclusive that it robs everything else of its interest. . . . It is through bhaktiyoga, furthered at first by karmayoga that is daily intensified in the above way and subsequently by jñānayoga, that such knowledge in the form of supreme bhakti arises".[145] Here, the self rests in the bliss of the divine. The soul *enjoys* God. But the final goal is not yet reached, and the *bhakta* has only glimpses, visions, of God. When such visions are not experienced, an agony of separation occurs. God's grace is all that is then needed for the self to be totally, and permanently, liberated.

Meditation

Meditation, *upāsana*, is an important means to liberation. While it cannot avert *karma* that has already matured, that is, like an arrow from a bow, already on its way, *karma* that is still in the process of maturation can be eradicated. Meditation leads to knowledge, and knowledge to devotion. Merely hearing the knowledge of the scriptures is insufficient in the light of the necessity for that ultimate intuitive knowledge that brings one to the point of liberation. Linking meditation with *bhakti* was an unusual philosophical move on the part of Rāmānuja. Again, what we have here is the combination of philosophical knowledge with the emotion of devotional practice, though in linking *parābhakti* with intuitive knowledge, the emotional side of *bhakti* is much diminished. Knowing Brahman and meditation on Brahman were often synonymous terms in *Upaniṣadic* thought.

The grace of God

But it is God that has the final word in the process of liberation. For, while all humanity is loved by God, his devotees are particularly elected. Indeed, this is something that runs as a theme through the *Bhagavadgītā*. God is the ultimate means to *mokṣa* and favours his elect with the rewards appropriate to their righteous *karmic* activity. It is why observance of obligatory commands of the *Veda* is so important. The lesser deities that preside over aspects of the universe serve as guides to the would-be *mukta*, and God himself strives to bring the devotee to him – something, again, that the *Gītā* stresses.[146] All human action needs the grace of God to succeed. In the words of Rāmānuja: "So when people have taken refuge in God, then his grace will facilitate all their activities: they will no more be subject to the misconception that ātman is non-ātman."[147] God's grace is also crucial for the higher *bhakti* that is the penultimate point on the path of liberation. Carman notes this. He writes, "intimate communion with God is not something that man can gain; not even the advanced devotee who yearns desperately for this communion can gain it by his own effort. Salvation is God's election and God's gift".[148] Rāmānuja himself stated: "For it is only He, who is omniscient, omnipotent, and very generous, who having been worshipped . . . is pleased to grant different forms of enjoyment and final emancipation, which consists in attaining His own essential nature."[149] Yet such grace does not offend the law of *karma*, and it is not proffered without being justly deserved. God's grace has to be earned, for God does not operate outside his own laws. God effectively remains the inner Ruler, the *antaryāmin*, by nodding his head in agreement to the fruition of appropriate effects for individual human causes. Certainly for Rāmānuja the individual was expected to strive for liberation. Thus van Buitenen observes: "Whenever God's grace is mentioned, the personal efforts of the aspirant are stressed too. There is certainly no trace of that importance given to prapatti by later Viśiṣṭādvaitins. God's grace may crown the aspirant's efforts, but he first has to deserve it. Only when a man has devoted his life to exclusive bhakti towards God will He elect him to his beatitude."[150]

Prapatti

The doctrine of *prapatti*, surrender, in Viśiṣṭādvaita is highly important. It is a word meaning "to take refuge in", from Sanskrit *pra-pad*. The Northern or Vaḍagalai school that developed in the years following Rāmānuja believed that liberation necessitated effort on the part of the devotee. Co-operation, then, rather than total surrender, was necessary. The Tengalai or Southern school, on the other hand, favoured total, passive surrender of the self to God, making the role of the divine in liberation the overwhelming factor. Passive surrender to God was an alternative to the disciplined *bhaktimarga*, the path of devotion, which has been outlined above. Nammāḷvar was probably the first to see this path of total surrender to God as a legitimate path to liberation.[151] Clearly, Āḷvārs and Ācāryas were prepared to accept *prapatti* as an alternative path to liberation for all classes, castes, and even for women. It was a very *emotional* and *passionate* path. It is not one of intense discipline, but one in which God reaches out to his devotee if that individual is capable of total surrender.

But Rāmānuja favoured *bhaktiyoga* as the true path – a path that was more characterized by knowledge than emotion, though not entirely devoid of the latter. Although surrender of the self to the divine is an important ingredient of all Viśiṣṭādvaita teaching, as a means *per se* to liberation, it was less favoured by Rāmānuja. Bhatt points out that the word *prapatti* does not really occur in the *Śrībhāṣya*, *Vedārthasaṃgraha*, or the *Gītābhāṣya*. [152] It is a feature of Pāñcarātra doctrines, but not one that Rāmānuja would have espoused.[153] Van Buitenen, too, notes that the doctrine of *prapatti* as a means for liberation is absent in Rāmānuja's *Gītābhāṣya*[154] and, if anywhere, this is exactly where we might expect it to be. Although it is used as a means that leads to *bhakti*, and certainly as a means to transcend the *guṇas* that bind one to reincarnation, as a means to liberation *per se* Rāmānuja does not accept it. Rāmānuja does not suggest that such an act of total surrender can elicit the grace of God to raise the self from its *karmic* bondage. He did not regard it as *the* most appropriate means for *any* individual that wishes to tread the long path to release from *saṃsāra*.

It was later Vaiṣṇava thought that came to see *prapatti* as a superior path to those of *karma*, *jñāna* or *bhakti*, but for Rāmānuja it was primarily one criterion for liberation within the more disciplined approach to the divine that has been outlined above. Rāmānuja certainly never abandoned the necessity for moral action as a prerequisite for the grace of God,[155] even if he allowed that *prapatti* was an appropriate path for those who were denied access to *Vedic* knowledge. But given the overriding factor of God's grace, it is easy to see how the yearning soul that could abandon itself to God – irrespective of class, caste or knowledge might achieve liberation as a gift of God. Murthy writes:

> Grace is the uplifting force that comes to the rescue of the seeker when the spiritual equilibrium is lost. It throws new light on the soul when the soul struggles in darkness. Universality is the supreme merit of prapatti. It is suited to all castes and classes. It guarantees salvation to all souls who find it difficult to follow the precipitous and arduous path of Bhakti. It is easier to secure immediate effect by following the religion of Prapatti.[156]

Prapatti here is an abandonment of self-centredness and a thorough concentration on the divine. Given that most Hinduism accepts the loss of ego as indicative of enlightenment, it is not difficult to see how *prapatti* is synonymous with *mokṣa*. But it was a concept developed after the time of Rāmānuja.

The simple idea of surrendering oneself to God, and of being so totally dependent on him that egoistic attachment to the world is abandoned, is the message that emerges from Vaiṣṇavism, and later Viśiṣṭādvaita. Prior to Rāmānuja, self-surrender (*śaraṇāgati*) was certainly known as a direct path to *mokṣa*. It was the teaching of the Āḻvārs and many Ācāryas. Nammāḻvār as a *Śūdra* would have been excluded from a formal path of *bhaktiyoga*, though he advocated it.[157] Therefore *prapattimārga* was the means by which he sought liberation, recognizing God as his sole refuge, and the futility of any other means to God. For Rāmānuja, *prapatti* was mainly synonymous with ordinary *bhakti*, and was thus seen as a stage on the path to higher *bhakti* and the concomitant of knowledge that constituted the penultimate stage to liberation, though even in higher *bhakti* surrender of the self remained essential. For others, *prapatti* came to be *the* means to liberation, a means that meant abandoning oneself to the compassion of God, doing his will, believing in his salvific power as the means and end of salvation, turning to him for help, and yielding up oneself to God. Inevitably, surrender to God is necessary at any stage of the path to liberation, since God is the means and the goal. There is a universality about *prapatti* as a means to the final goal of liberation that the more arduous path of *bhaktiyoga* does not have. In the end, acquiring the intuitive knowledge that the self is but the inseparable attribute of God, is the same as surrendering the self to God as his property. Knowledge brings surrender, and surrender brings knowledge. But Rāmānuja favoured the traditional and more arduous means to *mokṣa*, leaving it to his followers to develop surrender as a path in its own right.

While the liberated soul is no longer subject to the law of *karma*, in the sense that no fruitive *karma* is being caused, Rāmānuja did not accept the idea of a *jīvanmukta*, one liberated whilst still in the physical body. Since some *karmas* must affect the physical self, total liberation is impossible until after death, when the body is discarded for all time. To have a body is to be bound in some respects, and that is not to be free. The released souls enjoy the bliss of the transcendental *śuddhasattva* realm of God, the place of pure *sattva*. They can assume bodies that are composed of this transcendental material if they so wish, (and hence must be individual), but for the purpose of serving God in their enlightened state. *Mukti* is a direct apprehension of God, and the knowledge of the self as inseparably related to God – as the *Tat tvam asi* of *Upaniṣadic* thought. It is a positive state of existence, of self-fulfilment, of communion with God. Knowledge is expanded to the point of omniscience in each soul. And Viśiṣṭādvaita makes no sense unless that knowledge is one that includes a *personal* identity for the soul. As each soul was individual in life, so it is logical for it to have particular characteristics that differentiate it from other souls in the state of liberation. But the point is never clear in Rāmānuja's works. It seems to me that, in line with substance–attribute relationalism, liberated Selves as substances are identical, but their attributes are different – again, identity qualified by difference. Bhatt is one who implies such individuality for liberated Selves, at the same time accepting "an equality with all other freed selves".[158] Puligandla, too concurs, "the liberated self, instead of losing itself in God, retains its individuality and consciousness and eternally enjoys the highest bliss in the infinite glory of God".[159]

The released soul becomes Brahman in the sense that there is so much similitude in the two essential natures. But individuality – and therefore some duality – remains between God and soul; identity is not absolute. There is proximity to God, and an inner Self that shines forth as an "I" by which there can be blissful experience of such proximity. But the liberated soul is still an attribute that qualifies God; it is still the body of God and not his essence. But being the body of God, the soul has the perfections of God, though not the powers of creation and dissolution. There is, too, a definite anthropomorphism about the nature of the Viśiṣṭādvaita afterlife, where souls dwell in a beautiful *sattvic* world with a visible God. This is something graphically described in Vaiṣṇava accounts – golden sunshine, gentle breezes, refreshing streams of water, trees laden with fruit, music, singing and feasting. There is a fellowship of liberated souls, each of the same nature of attributive knowledge and bliss, but subtly different from the next. And all are united in service to God. "The released soul becomes a piece of living poetry, beauteous in form, rhythmical in beats of living", writes Murthy.[160]

In conclusion, there is much that must have been attractive in the teaching of Rāmānuja. His is a philosophy that blends intuition and feeling with considerable subtlety, and Bhatt rightly remarks: "In Rāmānuja we find a sincere attempt to reconcile the demands of the religious feeling with the claims of logical thinking."[161] Viśiṣṭādvaita attempts to solve the problem of the intimacy of God with the world, without compromising God's absolute nature. There are problems with its solutions – not least its anthropomorphism and the panentheistic rather than monistic overtones.[162] There are difficulties in suggesting that divinity that is always qualified with attributes – the *saguṇa* Brahman – can ever be really unchanging in essence, without being fundamentally *nirguṇa*. Even the desire "let me be many" suggests a changeable basic essence. There are equivalent difficulties in suggesting that all selves can have the same – and therefore single – attribute of God as their essential natures, making them quantitatively and not qualitatively different. This, indeed, would so nullify the state of liberation that I cannot believe that Rāmānuja would have denied the fact of attributive knowledge *of* God for each released *mukta*. This robs the ultimate goal of all its warmth. However, it was the more developed ideas of a tangible ultimate goal, and warm religious practice, that were immensely attractive. In combining traditional philosophy with Tamil devotion, Rāmānuja's contribution to the Vaiṣṇava religion is immense, despite its problematic areas. He gave devotional religion scholastic and academic credence, and this gave an enormous impetus to the Vaiṣṇava religion, establishing it firmly in the bounds of orthodoxy. Sharma writes of Rāmānuja: "He has given us the best type of monotheism pregnant with immanentism. He has emphasized the religious side but not at the cost of the philosophical. His intense religious fervour and his bold logic make him one of the immortals in Indian Philosophy."[163] But it is the goal of Viśiṣṭādvaita that is its greatest legacy to Hinduism: "The end of knowledge is not an 'It', but first an 'I', the one who knows, and then finally the 'THOU', the Supreme Person in whom alone I find my fullness and fulfilment."[164]

10
Dvaita Vedānta

While somewhat upstaged by Rāmānuja and Śaṃkara as the giants of Hindu philosophy, Madhva, the founding proponent of Dvaita Vedānta, has important contributions to make to the collective philosophy of Hinduism. While he was dependent on earlier traditions, he was nevertheless sufficiently innovative to deserve space here. This is particularly necessary since the overt dualism of Dvaita Vedānta stands in contrast to the other Vedānta traditions of Advaita and Viśiṣṭādvaita. Yet Madhva's school of Dvaita is given less space elsewhere – and this is another reason why it deserves some recognition and analysis in this book.

Background to the school

Whereas the *Upaniṣads* were preoccupied with the real nature of the self, and its relation to Brahman, Dvaita begins with Brahman, and maintains it as the focal point of its philosophy. This was something stressed in Bādarāyaṇa's *Brahmasūtras*, and that influenced Madhva's conception of deity. Dvaita is a school that, like Viśiṣṭādvaita, stands firmly in the folds of religious devotionalism, and the influence of devotional scriptures like the *Bhagavadgītā* and the *Bhāgavad Purāṇa* is clear. Both these sources teach of the utter dependency of the world, and all creatures within it, on the divine. It is this eternal, causeless, ultimate Divinity that is absolute bliss, that exists separately in its own powers, and that is the cause, sustainer and dissolver of all things.

The dualism of Madhva is absolute, not in the sense that there is absolute distinction between Brahman and everything else, but in the sense that there is utter dependence of the world and selves on Brahman as the transcendent Absolute. The dualism of Madhva, then, is a dualism of dependence over and against independence – the world and selves over and against Brahman. But the dependent world and selves are real, even though they are limited by time and space. Thus there are two realities, one independent and one dependent, and since Dvaita stands clearly in a devotional framework, the school is thus characterized by *theistic realism.* One clear aim informs Madhva's Dvaita, and that is to promote the conception of Brahman as the ultimate Reality that gives reality to all else.

Brahman is the principle behind all existence, the only independent Real, or *svatantratattva*. But since Brahman gives reality to the world and to selves, such dependent reality cannot be denied, as the Advaitin wished, but neither could it be organically related to Brahman as the Viśiṣṭādvaitin posited. This theistic dualism and realism is what will be explored.

Main proponents and commentators

Madhva is the founder of Dvaita Vedānta. Some place his birth in about 1197 or 1199 and his death in 2176 or 2178.[1] Others place him much later, from the thirteenth to fourteenth centuries. Sharma puts his dates as 1238–1317.[2] He was born a *Brahmin* in southern India in a village near Udipi in the South Kanara District. At an early age he became a *saṃnyāsin* and spent many years in study, prayer and meditation as a Vaiṣṇava devotee. As a keen opponent of non-dualism, and living at a time when it was very influential, he later travelled widely teaching and debating his own position of dualism. Tradition has it that he could walk on water, and that he was the third *avatāra* of the *Vedic* god Vāyu, the god of the wind. In this manifestation, he believed he had taken on the role as a mediator between Brahman and humanity. He founded a temple to Kṛṣṇa at Udipi, where he was to spend the remainder of his days, dying at the age of seventy-nine. A recognized Ācārya, he is often referred to as Madhvācārya, but he is also known by the names of Pūrnaprajña, "Completely Enlightened", the name he was given at his sacred thread initiation, and also Ānandatīrtha, the name by which he liked to refer to himself. He became the first of a long line of Madhva *Gurus*, still extant.

Madhva wrote many works. Sharma wrote of him: "Madhva is the most prolific writer among the great Bhāṣyakāras of the Vedānta system. He surpasses them all in the variety and range of subject-matter of his works."[3] Outstanding amongst his works are his exegesis of the *Mahābhārata*, four works on the *Brahmasūtras*, including a commentary, and two on the *Bhagavadgītā*, a commentary and a companion volume to it. His greatest work was his *Anuvyākhyāna*, which accompanied his commentary on the *Brahmasūtras*. He also wrote works based on a number of *Upaniṣads* and the *Bhagavad Purāṇa*, and a number of minor works. All Madhva's writings are terse in thought and require a commentator for understanding. His main commentator was Jayatīrtha who expanded on and interpreted Madhva's writings, particularly the *Anuvyākhyāna*, in a work called the *Nyāyasudhā*. Another important commentator was Vyāsatīrtha, a great dialectician who wrote a number of major treatises on the Dvaita philosophical position. In his writings Madhva accepted Viṣṇu as the supreme deity of the scriptures. It is clear from his extensive works that he viewed Hindu scriptures as composite and integrated. In focusing solely on the *Upaniṣads*, Śaṃkara both effectively bifurcated the *Veda* and segregated the *Upaniṣads* from any interpretative literature that followed. Thus, as Sharma pointed out, Śaṃkara "cut off Hindu philosophy from its Vedic roots on the one hand and the cool sheltering foliage of the Epics and *Purāṇas*, on the other, with the result that it stood like a bare stump".[4] But Madhva sought to overcome this. He was even unique among the philosophers of the various schools in writing his *Ṛgbhāṣya*, a commentary on the *Ṛg Veda*. Such a task is thoroughly indicative of his efforts to retain the composite nature of the *śāstras*, the scriptures.

Reality: the Dvaita view of the world

As the term *dvaita*, "dualism", suggests, the perspective of reality of this school is distinctly dualistic in that it sees a separation between the temporal and divine. This is an unqualified dualism as opposed to the outright monism of Śaṃkara and the more qualified monism of Rāmānuja. Madhva's theories of reality, ontology, epistemology and causality are set out with minimum statement, but with an underlying depth of both realism and idealism. Because Brahman is his primary focus, it is Brahman that is the *ultimate* Reality, and the only *independent* (*svatantra*) Reality. Yet Madhva's philosophy is one, also, of focused realism, one that accords to all manifest existence, a secondary – if dependent (*asvatantra*) – reality. Indeed, it could be said that such realism is one of the most important doctrines of the Dvaita tradition. Madhva sees no problem whatsoever in the reality of what is impermanent, and finite.

Madhva defines what is real as that which can be an object of valid knowledge in a particular time and place, and which is not superimposed (like a picture on a screen, or silver being superimposed on a piece of shell). According to Vyāsatīrtha, the world is real because it could not be claimed that it doesn't exist at all, the *pramāṇas* prove it to exist, and it is pragmatically existent. In Dvaita Vedānta reality is diverse, with each object separate from the next, and each individual separate from any other. All objects can exist irrespective of experience and knowledge of them by a subject. The school is thus one characterized by pluralistic realism. Reality is not one but many, and the joys and sorrows, pains and pleasures experienced by humanity are as real as the more tangible objects in existence. But there are no degrees of reality. Reality is reality whether divine or human. Crucially important to the perspective of reality is the concept of a level of the self, the *sākṣin*, that is the ultimate determinant of what is valid knowledge. This is a concept that I shall return to in due course. With characteristic logic, Madhva asserted that things are either real or not real: there cannot be any other descriptors than these two. And what is real can be unchangeable, and independent like God, or changeable, and dependent like the finite objects in the finite world. What is changeable and dependent may only exist for a limited time, but the fact that it *does* exist somewhere and for some time, is sufficient to accord it reality. So whereas to Śaṃkara a finite object could always be sublated, contradicted, by a more permanent reality, Madhva accepted the reality of finitude. Sharma puts this well: "The world is factually existent. It is not necessary that it should also be eternal. The real *may be* eternal or non-eternal, as the case may be. A short-lived real is no less real than the long-lived one or even the eternal. A rose may blossom, exude fragrance and fade off, after a time. That is not to say that it is 'contradicted'."[5]

For Dvaita, then, existence (*satya*) is equated with reality or, at the very least, is one aspect of it. It is therefore quite erroneous to claim that objects of valid knowledge are illusory. Providing they exist at some time and in some place, they are real. What is unreal has no existence in time or place. Those *śruti* texts that point to the unreality of the world, Madhva interpreted as meaning a lack of reality in comparison to God's *independent* reality, not an unreality *per se*. As will be seen below, he was keen to separate the reality of the divine nature from that of the world and anything in it, and it was this kind of dualistic reality, he believed, to which the texts referred. But it is common sense to suggest that the world is real, for the pragmatic use we make of it suggests that it is so. Thus, the One and the many of which the *Upaniṣads* spoke are equally real, the many being different from, but just as real as, the One that is Brahman. Madhva stated:

> The knowledge of the many thro' the knowledge of the One, so prominently taught in the Upaniṣads, is to be understood in terms of the pre-eminence of the One; or in virtue of some similarity (of nature between them); or on account of the One being the cause (or sustaining principle) of the many and such other grounds. The teaching of the Upaniṣad does not support the deduction of the falsity (*mithyātva*) of the many. For, the knowledge of the One (real) is here, solemnly said to *produce* the knowledge of the many *and not to annul it.* On a monistic view, as the real and the false would be mutually contradictory and exclusive, knowledge of the One would *not produce* the knowledge of the many.[6]

In being thoroughly dualistic in his view of reality, Madhva rejected the inseparable substance–attribute relationship between God and the world, and between God and the self, that was proposed by Viśiṣṭādvaita. Thus he rejected, too, the idea of the world and selves as the body of God. Each entity, Madhva believed, exists as a substance in its own right, and is characterized by its own particular, real, attributes, or *viśeṣas*. Difference is essential to all things in existence, and provides each entity with its unique and separate identity. Like Rāmānuja, however, Madhva accepted the three eternal "reals" of God, matter and selves. But he emphasized the thorough independent nature of God in contrast to the absolute dependency of the world and selves on God. This is the dualism of an independent Real, and a dependent, but equally real, universe, the former being that principle on which everything else depends for its very being. Madhva wrote: "Whosoever realizes all finite reality to be essentially dependent on the Supreme is released from Samsāra."[7] It is this that underpins all else. Dependent reality exists only in time and space. It is a reality viewed by God in a way that no other being can imagine or accomplish, for every entity in existence is dependent on God for its own reality, existence and identity. Because the existence of individuals is grounded in the divine, Madhva depicted them as "reflections" or "images", even "shadows", of the divine, but never in any way identified with divinity. Nothing can come into being or can *be* without the independent Reality that is Brahman. All dependent reality, then, is an *object* (*pramitti*) as far as divinity is concerned, but each object has its own essential essence, its *svarūpa*, and its own particular effort or function, its *pravṛtti*. It is these three aspects – objectivity, essence and function – which connote *existence* and, therefore, reality in Dvaita philosophy.

The doctrine of five differences: pañcabheda

To Madhva, then, every thing in existence, and every person, is unique and different from anything else: difference is of the nature of reality. What a thing or a person *is* amounts to its, his or her distinguishing and differentiating characteristics. Whatever we perceive in life, whatever we recognize, we do so because of such recognition of the difference between one thing and another. In Madhva's own words:

> If difference were *not* the nature of things, then, when an object is perceived, its distinction from all else (in a general way) would *not* be known. In that case the perceiver himself might

> come to have a doubt whether he is his own self or the perceived object! But no one falls into such errors or doubts. This shows that difference is realized in the first perception of things, at least in a general way.[8]

Whatever exists, then, has its own subjective essence and nature, its *dharmisvarūpa*. But such "difference" is not something over and above its manifestation in a particular object or person. There is no *universal* of difference, only the difference that is the particular essence of each entity. Five such differences or distinctions, called *pañcabheda* obtain. (*Pañca* means "five" and *bheda* "difference"). They are:

- *Between God and selves*: The relationship between God and each self is depicted as *pratibiṃba* "reflection". Selves have some likeness to God, just as an image in a mirror reflects the real object. But this is as far as the likeness goes. *Biṃba* is the "principle" of Reality, Brahman, that informs all things, both conscious and unconscious. It is a concept that is crucially important for the theistic devotion that characterizes the school. As Narain pointed out: "The Vaiṣṇavite zeal for establishing the supremacy of 'devotion' (*bhakti*) over 'intellect' as a means to deliverance (*mokṣa*) can hardly find a philosophical justification unless difference between the Lord and the devotee is an ultimate fact."[9]
- *Between God and matter*: Because the world exists or may not exist only as a result of divine will, and because it makes no difference to God whether it exists or not, there is a fundamental difference between God and the world. Such difference is particularly so considering the dependence of the latter on the former. God wills a world to be, and it is a world that is different from his own nature.
- *Between selves*: Difference obtains between all individual selves; each has its own particularities that differentiate that self from others.
- *Between selves and matter*: The world is external to, and different from, the selves that inhabit it. It is a fundamental difference perceived by the *sākṣin*, the inner self that is capable of infallible, intuitive knowledge.
- *Between matter and matter*: Each material object differs in nature from all other objects, and has its own fundamental characteristics.

Such fundamental difference does not exclude the concept of dependency. Just as the body depends for its functioning on the conscious self, so the world and selves depend on God for their functioning and very existence. Because the world and selves exist only in so far as God wills them to be, the reality of both exists. Thus all the pleasures and pains of life, all its experiences, and the cycle of rebirth are real. God is the author of the universe, and it would make no sense to say that he creates what does not really exist. Pragmatically, we *know* the world exists, and that other selves exist in the same way as we do. And we know that each entity we perceive is different from all others. Because God, on the one hand, and selves and the world on the other, share the same characteristic of reality, there is a degree of *abheda*, non-difference, between the two – a degree of reflection of the same Reality of God onto the world. But for Dvaita, God remains the transcendent Real on which the world and selves depend: therefore, the *bheda*, the difference, is considerable.

While the doctrine of differences establishes the plural reality of all things, since all is dependent on God, it is he that lends to the universe a certain order, and the kind of unity that permits effective and pragmatic functioning in the world. To Madhva everything on earth is a living, animated organism. This is because all *prakṛti*, Nature, is considered an eternal principle that is activated and infused by the divine energy, an energy equated with the power of Brahman. Once produced, the world and its plurality of objects are perceived by selves, *jīvas*. Such perception is characterized by real subject–object differentiation, and real object–object separation.

The doctrine of viśeṣas

Narain calls the doctrine of *viśeṣas* "the backbone of Mādhva philosophy".[10] Not only are all substances different, but it is their particular attributes that make them so. Such relative particularities are known as *viśeṣas*, and they exist in all entities, eternal and non-eternal and in positive and negative being. It is *viśeṣas* that produce difference, *bheda*. Some *viśeṣas* are inseparable from the substance that they characterize; others are not. Each substance will have an infinite number of *viśeṣas* that distinguish that substance by way of their particular expression in it. *Viśeṣas* are the power, *śakti*, that expresses what something is. They are the particular *energy* of essence that is emitted exclusively from each entity. The particularity here is something innate to the object, and does not refer to the object itself, though it may be identical to it. It is the "me-ness" of me, and the myriad particulars that create that "me-ness". It is the "oak-ness" of a particular oak tree, the "divine-ness" of a particular deity. Madhva said: "This difference, tho' partaking of the nature of things, is yet colorfully identical with it and thro' such colorful identity it is mentally and linguistically differentiated from the object, wherever exigencies require it. *Viśeṣas* are the basis of such colorful identity."[11] The concept serves to separate attributes from their substances in a way that is quite dissimilar to Rāmānuja's theory of *apṛthaksiddhi*, inseparable relationship, and yet it retains the notion of identity – either temporary identity or permanent identity. *Viśeṣas* are thus the special characteristics of a thing or a person, or even a non-thing, but will always serve to differentiate one thing from another regardless of any apparent identity.[12] *Viśeṣas* will also co-exist with their substances, like the "oak-ness" of the oak, where the *viśeṣa* is identical with its substance. But it may also be more transient, like the "going" of a person from one place to another, or the ripeness of a fruit. Here, where identity with the substance is transient, there is more clearly both identity and difference. In eternal substances, then, like God and selves, *viśeṣas* are also eternal, but they can be non-eternal in finite substances.

It is the doctrine of *viśeṣas* that permits the separation of parts from wholes, qualities from substances and character from the thing that possesses it. As Sharma defines it, *viśeṣa* is "but another name for the potency of the thing in itself whereby it maintains its unity and continuity through all its modes, predications and aspects".[13] It is the "immanent dynamics of substance itself expressing itself through its essential properties".[14] *Viśeṣas* are thus what constitute the special nature of something, which are at once identified with that thing, but which also can be different from it, and which are peculiar to one thing and not to any other. Each thing is a unity of its own particularities, a unity of parts with the whole, or of attributes with substance. Its particularities are identical with the essential nature of the object, and yet are different from the object itself (like a large, blue, one-handled jug). This theory is known as *saviśeṣābheda*, but is close to simple *bhedābheda*, identity-in-difference. *Saviśeṣābheda*, then, is the identity between a substance and its attributes that is characterized and conditioned by *viśeṣas*, differences, "It is simply an expression of the idea that a substance is a unity in diversity in so far as it exists. Even the diversity in it is the expression of its unity."[15] *Viśeṣa* as a theory serves to maintain both identity *and* difference at the same time: "It is a pluralising or differentiating agency without actually splitting or cutting through the substance."[16] Differences/particulars, thus become a real category of reality as *viśeṣas*, the ultimate differentiators, or essential natures (*svarūpas*) of all entities. This, then, is a doctrine of *svarūpabheda*, differences in essential natures. Narain writes: "It is the paramount consideration and contention of the Mādhva school that the status of the reality of 'quality' is commensurate with the status of the reality of the 'qualified'. According to this school, no relation between 'quality' and 'qualified' is imaginable if the 'quality' belongs to a different order of reality from that of the qualified."[17] The attributes that are the *viśeṣas*, then, are as real as the substances to which they are related. Applied to Brahman, it was a theory that "justified the presence of absolute and non-contradicted qualities in Brahman and thereby outraged the Śaṃkarite proposition that Brahman is beyond all determinations and qualifications".[18]

In the schools of Nyāya and Vaiśeṣika, *viśeṣas* existed only in so far as they were associated with eternal substances. But for Madhva, *viśeṣas* are that which provide the essential nature of *all* things, irrespective of their transience and finitude: whatever exists in time and space – and whatever does not exist – can be defined by its special *viśeṣas*. Change is characteristic of all existence, but in the Dvaita school, such change does not exclude the idea of reality. The oak may change from seed to immense proportion, the baby to the old man or woman, but because they exist in *some* time and *some* place, they have real existence. It is the *viśeṣas* of each that provide their respective, different continuity. Thus, even pain, happiness, sorrow, transmigration and bondage have their own real characteristics and are real experiences in the same way that all objects are real. To Madhva it made no sense to believe that God had created an unreal world, and he believed the bulk of the four *Vedas* and the *Brāhmaṇas* supported its reality, even if some *Upaniṣadic* texts were interpreted otherwise by other schools. Madhva, of course, believed that the *Upaniṣads* taught of the reality of world, selves and a creator God. Dreams, too, are considered by Madhva to contain real emotions. He believed that they are created by God for the purpose of the selves. The unreal aspect of dreams is created by their later comparison with reality in the waking state, and by their being mistaken for the waking state itself. Madhva, in common with many, accepted that the content of dreams comes from the subtle tendencies that are embedded in each *jīva*. They are the residual impressions, the *saṃskāras*, that are called up in dreams, but are *real* impressions with their own space–time appropriateness that differs from waking existence. Dvaita, then, accepts the reality of all things, even dreams, by the distinct particularities that are the unique essence of each gross or subtle entity.

Avidyā and māyā

Avidyā, ignorance, is one of the substances of *prakṛti* in this school. It is that which prevents each self, each *jīva* from knowing its true nature as dependent on God, and from knowing God. It is an ignorance that is beginningless, real, and different for each individual: it is not some general veil that pervades all life but is specific to each *jīva*. It is a lack of knowledge, nothing more. Jayatīrtha saw *avidyā* as a kind of sheath that covered the true self. But just as the self is the basis of knowledge, it, and not Brahman, is also the basis of ignorance. In depicting it as a *prakṛtic* substance, *avidyā* becomes a positive entity and not an unreal abstraction. But if ignorance is beginningless, it is not endless for many *jīvas*. For the whole purpose of existence is to evolve to the point at which ignorance is overcome and the self is able to see itself as the dependent being of God. For some *jīvas*, however, ignorance is forever their fate and their destiny is never to be free – a point to which I shall return later. Clearly, however, just as God is the creator and controller of *prakṛti*, so it is by his will that he is the cause of ignorance. Madhva does not, however, explain why ignorance should have such a beginningless hold on creation, and we are left with the idea of a God that is thoroughly responsible for its presence in the first place. Madhva is content to put the problem of *avidyā* down to the mysterious power or *māyā* of God, and the overcoming of it, to his grace. By doing so, many implications are raised for the question of theodicy – the relationship between a good God and the manifestation of evil in the universe – again, a point that I shall take up below. But if ignorance is willed by God – for whatever reason – then it has to be real and not illusory. Just as Madhva accepted the reality of anything that has existence in time and space – however temporary – so he accepted the reality of ignorance. What is real does not have to exist eternally.

Māyā as illusion, is rejected by Madhva. It is impossible to have an illusion that a piece of rope is a snake unless *at some time* and *in some place* there has been some real perception of a snake. To say that the world is an illusion must then suggest that there is some world that is understood as real for the illusory one to be illusory. In Madhva's words: "If this universe is to be regarded as imagined by our delusion (as the illusory snake in the rope), it would require the acceptance of a real universe (as the prototype of the imagined one) and a real substratum . . . No theory of illusion can be demonstrated *without at least two reals*."[19] So when we have an illusion of a snake as a rope, we can only do so because *at some time* we have had a *real* perception of a snake. And to superimpose this on the rope, the rope must exist *really* in the present for the erroneous illusion to occur. And if the world *is* illusory, then everything in it must be so – including the very scriptural testimony that is supposed to be eternally real, and that provides knowledge of what is supposed to be ultimately real – Brahman. Hence, Madhva reasoned that the world is real. It will never disappear in the same way as the silver that is mistakenly thought to be the piece of shell, or the snake that is thought to be the rope.

To Madhva, *māyā* is the mysterious power by which God controls the universe, rather like Rāmānuja's interpretation of the concept, though he accepts its obscuring factor, like *avidyā*, as present in creation. Thus: "In Mādhva philosophy it is *Māyā* and not *avidyā* that is the driving force behind creation. *Māyā* has its seat in the Divine personality of God, whereas *avidyā* is always associated with the *jīva*."[20] Yet, since it is *māyā* that throws a veil over truth, then knowledge, ignorance, liberation and bondage must all, ultimately, originate by the will of God. *Māyā* is the mysterious power of God by which he creates, sustains and dissolves the universe. But it is also the means by which he veils the truth and causes the ignorance and errors of human living. *Māyā* is really *prakṛti*, the means by which God creates the universe, and so it is *prakṛti* that "presses down on the Jīvas from beginningless eternity and obscures their natures at the will of the Lord and not by its own power".[21] Bondage, then, occurs through the will of God operating through the medium of *prakṛti*, but does not come about directly from God. Thus, Madhva said: "The true and final explanation of bondage is therefore the Will of the Lord and not merely Karma, Ajñāna, Kāla, Guṇas, etc.; for these are insentient by nature and hence dependent on something else (viz., God)."[22]

Padārthas: categories of reality

God is the only truly independent Real. The rest of reality is dependent on God. Dvaita Vedānta accepted ten categories:

- **Substance** (*dravya*). Of these there are twenty – God; Lakṣmī; selves; unmanifest Space (*avyākṛtākāśa*) that is eternal and unchangeable through creation and dissolution;[23] Nature (*prakṛti*); the three *guṇas* of *sattva*, *rajas* and *tamas*;[24] cosmic intellect (*mahat*); ego (*ahaṃkāra*); intellect (*buddhi*); mind (*manas*); potential and actual senses (*indriyas*); the elements (*bhūtas*); subtle elements (*mātras*); ignorance (*avidyā*); sounds of speech (*varṇa*); darkness (*andhakāra*); residual tendencies (*vāsanās*); Time (*kāla*);[25] reflection (*pratibimba*).[26] To Madhva, a substance is a unitary whole composed of a number of particular parts. It is the substrate of qualities and the basis of change and manifestation.
- **Quality** (*guṇa*). This includes mental qualities like strength, beauty, fear and shame, as well as those in line with the Vaiśeṣika school. Some are inseparable from, and identical to, their substances; others are partly similar and partly different, yet related, like part and whole, cause and effect. Qualities cannot exist independently of substances.
- **Activity** (*karma*). Action is not a quality or a substance but is dependent on substances. Unlike qualities that are permanent aspects of substances, actions are only temporary. All action causes merit or demerit in some measure.
- **Resemblance** or **similarity** (*sādṛśya*). Similarities between things or selves are the result of *resemblance* not identity of class, because the doctrine of *viśeṣas* prevents any one thing from being exactly like any other. The uniqueness of each individual or each thing makes the acceptance of universals in the usual sense of the term impossible.
- **Universals** (*sāmānya*). Madhva accepted universals as an independent category but as existing in *one* entity – the cow-ness of a *particular* cow that is like cow-ness in another cow, and so on, but not the same cow-ness of all cows. There is resemblance in the latter case (hence the separate category), but not sufficient identity for

a universal class of cow-ness. Universals relevant to different finite entities are, like them, not eternal. But the universals of eternal entities like selves are also eternal.

- **Particulars, differences** (*viśeṣas).* These, as we have seen, obtain as the special qualities of each entity in existence, making that entity what it is.
- **Negation** (*abhāva*). This is of four kinds, that which is antecedent to being produced, that which is subsequent to something being destroyed, the negation of one thing being anything like another, and that which never occurs, like horns on a hare or a square circle. So the idea that *x* is not *y* or is not in *y*, is perception of an aspect of reality.
- **Power** (*śakti*). Not only the power of God is referred to here, but also the power of change that exists in so many facets of life, the power that is infused in a divine image through ritual installation, and the power of the spoken word. It is supersensuous and is sometimes latent and sometimes manifest, as, for example, God's power of creation that is latent during the unmanifest stage of the universe.
- **The qualified** (*viśiṣṭa*). These are the different aspects of an entity that contribute to its composite wholeness, but which are different from that wholeness. It is rather like all the parts that inform a whole, because it is the "qualified", that which something is when its substance and attributes are conjoined.
- **Whole** (*aṃśi*). This is the acceptance that the *whole* of something is different from its necessary parts.

A few points need to be mentioned here. First, the **Qualified**, **Whole**, **Power** and **Resemblance** are new categories introduced by Madhva. Second, while in the Dvaita school qualities or attributes cannot really exist apart from the substances that they qualify, they are given a distinct identity of their own through the doctrine of *viśeṣas*. The closeness of substance and quality, then, is never as inseparable in this school as in the case of Viśiṣṭādvaita.

Epistemology

To Madhva Brahman is the centre of his philosophy, and the content of scripture is used as the religious and philosophical base of his knowledge of God. The process of knowledge, the inquiry into what is ultimately true, is, he believed, a stage-by-stage process of discipline and self-realization: it is a spiritual journey. For Dvaita all knowledge is true; whatever we see in time and space is true, for what exists in time and space is reality. So valid knowledge is what we see, the comprehension of things as they are. Because of this realism valid knowledge is knowledge of a real fact, and there can be no shades of reality here; what is real fact is real fact. Truth is, therefore, intrinsic to knowledge.

Of course, to be valid, knowledge must occur through non-defective senses in the case of perception, through flawless reasoning in the case of inference, and through reliable sources in the case of testimony. Our knowledge should conform to, and not disagree with, other facts. And it should not fail us when we test it out pragmatically. Such theories suggest that there must be something beyond knowledge itself to which its validity is known. This, indeed, is the *sākṣin* – the self, the ground of our knowledge. It is something that will be explored in more detail later, in relation to the self. Here, suffice it to say that it is the self that validates such knowledge through experience. The self comes to acquire a body of knowledge that common sense tells us is necessary for efficient living in space and time. We come to know that certain things are true, and others false. But while all knowledge is true, providing there have been no flaws in the means by which it has come about, Madhva conceded that God's knowledge must necessarily be greater in quality (though not in reality) than that of the ordinary self as, also, is the knowledge of the *yogin*.

Knowledge is self-valid; it contains its own proof. But that self-validity (*svataḥprāmāṇya*) of knowledge is perceived intuitively only by the *sākṣin*. In Madhva's words: "The very validation of knowledge depends upon the *sākṣī* which is the ultimate principle that knows the knowledge."[27] The *sākṣin knows* intuitively when something is true. What is false or doubtful never reaches it, but is engaged by the mind. Sharma writes: "The approbation of the *Sākṣī* is the logical limit of all certainty, clarification and validation, as it is intuitive."[28] In short, when the mind is faced with knowledge acquired through perception, inference or testimony, that knowledge is tested against other knowledge, is assessed pragmatically, its universal concomitance is assessed, and so on, until finally it is accepted at a fundamental and intuitive level of the self as true. Once the *sākṣin* has intuited the validity of any knowledge, any further tests of its validity become unnecessary. The self-validity of knowledge, then, is dependent on the *sākṣin*. Knowledge cannot know itself because it is insentient. Importantly, once this validity of knowledge is demonstrated, it cannot be proved to be untrue – what is valid knowledge is always so. Moreover, because knowledge obtained by the *sākṣin* is always self-valid, the objects of that knowledge must be real. The *sākṣin* has knowledge of *ātman*, mind, pleasure and pain, ignorance, Time and unmanifest Space. Since the *sākṣin* has immediate experience of these, there is nothing outside it that is needed to validate either the experience itself, or the *sākṣin* as experiencer.

Dvaita Vedānta accepts sublation of knowledge though not, like the Advaitin, that sublated knowledge is rendered unreal. Knowledge in the ordinary world is bound to be contradicted by knowledge that is God's, but this will not render temporal and temporary knowledge unreal. God's knowledge and ordinary knowledge are different in nature, but the same reality in degree. Narain writes: "The meaning of 'reality' is always the same though the nature of its 'content' may differ. The 'reality' of the world though different in nature from God is none the less the same."[29]

Knowledge must involve an immaterial subject – the knower – and an object – the known. Knowledge always has attributes and cannot obtain without them. There can be no such thing as pure consciousness, pure knowledge existing in itself, since all knowledge must be of an object. And knower, knowledge, and object of knowledge are different and independently real. Knowledge is an attribute of the mind, in which some sort of modification or transformation must take place in order for the object of knowledge to be conveyed to the self. Mind, *manas*, is an *indriya*, a sense. It is the sense responsible for synthesizing sense data and for storing memory. And just as the eye may have distorted vision and incorrect perception as a result, so the mind often becomes so involved with desires, attachments and aversions that it makes erroneous judgements. It is here that the *sākṣin*, the intuitive element of the self, serves the function of recognizing only that which is true. What goes on in the mind as a result of sense impressions, is ordinary knowledge. The *sākṣin*, while being the medium for intuitive knowledge, also underpins the functioning of all other knowledge connected with the mind. It is different for each person. As a realist, Madhva accepted sense perception as the most important of the valid means of knowledge, for he believed that both inference and testimony – the only other two means of valid knowledge that he accepted – were ultimately dependent on perception in some way. So if scripture were ever at odds with commonly perceived facts, Madhva had no difficulty in rejecting it. As the intuitive organ of the self, the *sākṣin* is able to override *śruti* testimony, if the latter does not conform to perceptual experience. Thus, because universal perception suggests that there is a duality between subject and object, and a plurality of objects in the universe, any scriptural text that suggests monism would need to be carefully reinterpreted to bring it in line with universally perceived facts.

In the pursuit of knowledge four stages are identified. The first is the ordinary stage at which we acquire knowledge through perception, inference and testimony. The second stage is one in which reason is applied. The third stage is instruction in the scriptures and awareness of their, sometimes contradictory, nature. It is at the fourth stage of what is called *jijñāsā*, philosophical inquiry, that the knower begins to transcend empirical knowledge and understand the real and non-contradictory meaning of scripture, in particular, *śruti.* But unique to Dvaita is the concept of a gradation of conscious intelligence. That is to say, the innate dispositions of each individual predispose him or her to certain kinds of knowledge. Thus, those who aspire to liberation, to scripture, study, and the guidance of a *guru* have the kind of consciousness that is *muktiyoga*, disciplined for release. Others will be inclined to more deluded knowledge, or to doubtful knowledge. In these last two cases higher intuitive knowledge about the nature of the self and the dependence of the self on God will hardly reach the level of the fundamental intuitive *sākṣin.*

There is a very real relationship between knowledge and the object of knowledge as revealer and revealed respectively. Notably, the revealer is not the self, but knowledge. As an attribute of the self it brings the self into relation with the object. Thus, although an attribute of the self, knowledge is always different from the self. No change takes place in knowledge or the object of knowledge when knowledge takes place.

Pramāṇas

Madhva defined a *pramāṇa* as "what comprehends an object of knowledge as it is".[30] Similarly, Jayatīrtha said: "*Pramāṇa* is that which does not go beyond the object of knowledge and makes an entity an object of cognition as it really exists and not otherwise."[31] So *pramāṇa* is knowledge and the means to it. It is thus of two kinds – primary (*kevalapramāṇa*) and secondary (*anupramāṇa*). Primary *pramāṇa* represents true knowledge, and secondary *pramāṇas* the means by which it is obtained. Thus, the three *pramāṇas* accepted by the school – perception (*pratyakṣa*), inference (*anumāna*), and scriptural testimony (*śabda* or *āgama*) – are the secondary, *anupramāṇa*, means.[32] Primary, *kevalapramāṇa*, is differentiated according to the intensity of the quality in its manifestation. God's is first and foremost in quality, followed by that of Lakṣmī, who is dependent on God and therefore has an inferior quality of knowledge. But the knowledge of both God and Lakṣmī is not dependent on sensory knowledge. Their knowledge is beginningless, eternal and always correct. Then there is the knowledge of the *yogins*, and then the more inferior quality of the knowledge of the deities. Last, is the knowledge of other mortals. *Yogins*, deities and mortals are dependent on sensory knowledge.

Perception (pratyakṣa)

According to Madhva: "Perception is the *flawless* contact of sense-organs with their appropriate objects. Flawless reasoning is inference. Flawless word, conveying valid sense, is Āgama."[33] Flawless perception is only applicable to God, Lakṣmī and the liberated Selves, because their perception is not informed by materiality, unlike that of the rest of sentient beings. Thus, the possibility of flawed perception because of flawed organs of perception or objects of perception, cannot be ruled out for mortals. However, perceptions cannot be considered invalid except in the light of other, more appropriate, perceptions. And this really makes all perception valid until proved otherwise, for even if it is proved incorrect, something existed at the moment of perception. The only exception is if one or more of the seven sense organs (*sākṣin*, mind, eye, ear, nose, tongue and skin) are defective in some way. At the level of human knowledge, *total* knowledge of something – of every aspect of it – would be impossible, but this does not invalidate the limited knowledge acquired. The reality of knowledge and the reality of the objects of the world go hand in hand. Madhva wrote:

> Sense knowledge is its own standard of truth. It cannot be stultified by inference or scripture. The moon's limited size and such other defective perceptions are accountable as being due to distance and other abnormal conditions. But, in so far as the most rigorous tests could go, there is nothing to warrant a wholesale rejection of the evidence of sense-perception, regarding *the existence of a world outside our minds*.[34]

Memory is not excluded as a valid means of perception, for even though something may not exist now, the recollection of it at a specific time and place in prior experience validates the fact of it, regardless of any subsequent change in the object of knowledge. In true realist fashion, Madhva, and particularly Jayartīrtha, posited that sheer common sense and pragmatism in human experience of life shows us that we can rely on memory all the time for the purpose of functioning in the world. Memory is only to be discarded as invalid if we want to think that something that was there in the past is there now in time and space. However, memory is not given status as a *pramāṇa* on its own. It is brought under *pratyakṣa*. Indeed, any knowledge of the past must, according to Madhva, involve memory and, should it be rejected, this would invalidate all inference or past valid perception. Memory is the recollection of the perception of something in the past by *direct* means of the mind. Madhva accords to the mind as an organ of thought, this particular skill of projecting itself into the past, or even into the future. But something is added to the memory, and that is the further knowledge that what is recollected is something past, not, as originally perceived, as thoroughly present. Memory, thus, is a valid "mind-perception". In the same way, the mind-perceptions of dreams are valid in so far as the objects seen in dreams have past reality.

Dvaita rejects the concept of indeterminate perception. When first apprehended, some of the properties of an object are recognized – that it is an immovable substance, its action, or some particular quality like colour. Hence, all perception is to some extent determinate, *savikalpaka*. Indeed, difference, the *dharmisvarūpa* or essential different essence of something, is perceived at the same moment as sense perception takes place. Superior to all kinds of secondary perception, however, is the primary perception of *kevalapramāṇa* – the direct and intuitive knowledge of something that transcends the knowledge acquired through the medium of the senses. In particular, it has intuitive knowledge of Time and Space, and of the nature of its own being – the self, or *ātman* – that is independent of mind. It is through such intuitive knowledge that the *sākṣin* can know its own consciousness, knowledge, pleasure, pain, ignorance and, ultimately, God. Since it is a medium for such experience, the *sākṣīn* must, therefore, be considered as an organ of sense as much as sentience itself: as such, the mind or *manas* functions little more than a synthesizer.

Inference (anumāna)

For inference to be valid, it must be flawless. Universal and invariable concomitance (*vyāpti*) is essential, so every time there is smoke there must be fire, and that concomitance must be inseparable and invariable. Such concomitance can be the result of any of the three accepted *pramāṇas*. For Madhva, invariable concomitance is the crux of knowledge acquired by inference and the five-form syllogism of Nyāya is therefore unnecessary, but later proponents of the school adoted the five aspects of the Nyāya syllogism.

Testimony (āgama)

Testimony is of two kinds, personal (*pauruṣeya*) and impersonal (*apauruṣeya*). The testimony that is personal is from an *āpta*, a trustworthy person, who transmits correct knowledge. Impersonal testimony is that of the *Vedic śruti* scriptures. While the *smṛtis*, the *purāṇas* and some other literature related to the *Veda* are important, it is only the *Veda* that is absolutely self-valid, eternal and does not owe its origin to any source – divine or human. While not being divinely created, it is God who gives to the eternal words of the *Veda* – originally in "a confused and hotch-potch state without any system"[35] – their particular order and succession. It is the divine mind, then, that systematizes the word-order of the content of the *Veda*. However, Madhva believed that the authority of the *Veda* extends only to theological and philosophical matters related to the divine. As far as the empirical world is concerned, he was sufficiently a realist to claim that there is much that lay outside its domain. Where the *Veda* clearly contradicts common sense, then Madhva believed its interpretation had been misguided, and there were many occasions when he sought to make sense of the *śruti* texts to bring them in line with a thoroughly realist view of the world. As one writer put it: "While others fit truth to Vedic sayings, Madhva fits the Vedic sayings to truth."[36] The *Veda*, therefore, is eternally true, its entire content of words being prior to the facts that it asserts.

Despite the importance of perception in the school, it is only the *Veda* that can supply knowledge of God. Perception cannot do this until it reaches the purely intuitive level. Madhva believed that *śruti* evidence suggests a thorough difference between human and divine. Common sense demonstrates that we are not God and, therefore, Madhva eschewed any suggestions of identity of the *ātman* with Brahman that might have been implicit or explicit in the *Vedic* texts. He interpreted the scriptures to maintain the duality of the self and God, and God as the personal Viṣṇu. The *śruti* texts provide knowledge of Brahman conveyed in the timeless and perfect language particular to that knowledge. It is God speaking of himself, of his creation. Since all things depend on God, the very words of scripture express the divine nature, and all words, all sounds, point beyond themselves to God. It is up to the individual destined for *mukti* to understand their purport through the process of inquiry, *jijñāsā*. It was by this process that Madhva reinterpreted the ancient texts. He accepted much *smṛti* literature as valid – the *Pañcarātras*, the *Mahābhārata*, the *Rāmāyaṇa*, the *Brahmasūtras*, the *Vaiṣṇava Purāṇas* and the *Manusmṛti*. To Madhva, any *smṛti* literature that did not contradict *śruti* teaching of the *Veda* could be accepted as valid testimony and as infallible authority. In particular, the *Pañcarātra Āgama* was raised to the same level of reliability as the *Veda* itself. Rejected, was literature that clearly ran counter to his dualistic realism. The purpose of all scripture was to express the utter supreme nature of Viṣṇu as God, but it also provided the very foundation of morality, of *dharma*.

Error

Knowledge cannot always be right, and our experiences in life suggest that error in knowledge is a very real facet of existence. And considering the bound nature of selves and their subjection to countless lifetimes, it is obvious that knowledge is far from true in many instances. Yet error is the exception to the rule. The *sākṣin* is the final judge of what is true or false, and nothing that is erroneous as knowledge is accepted by it. Error takes place in the mind and not at the level of the *sākṣin*. It is usually pragmatic experience that exposes error. So the conch shell that is taken to be silver is a case of error that, when the shell is seen closely, handled and examined, will be corrected. The error, the illusion, is contradicted by better perception. The illusion of silver being the conch shell can only happen because both silver and conch shells have *really* existed or have been part of perceptual experience, just as the images in dreams. But it could not be claimed that the silver seen as the conch shell exists *now* in the perception of the shell. Such erroneous knowledge results from past impressions on the mind that are incorrectly combined with present perception. Neither the objects that are perceived incorrectly (like the conch shell) nor the objects imposed on them from past impressions (like the silver) are, and were, false or unreal.

What creates error in knowledge, then, is the defective apprehension of the object; it is distorted knowledge arising from defective combination of two pieces of knowledge. It is a misapprehension by which something unreal in a *present* time and place (like silver) is superimposed on what is perceived (shell), and is claimed to be real. Silver may well exist in all kinds of places, and may well have been perceived in the past by the subject. But not one scrap of this can be present in the erroneous perception of silver in the conch shell:

the error is the result of defective superimposition of a past impression that is thoroughly unreal in the present situation. Error is thus accepting what does not exist as existing and what does exist as not existing. Error is "the ill-directed interpretative activity of the mind".[37] Since valid knowledge is perception of things *as they really are*, error is simply perception of them *as they are not*. It is past *saṃskāras*, impressions in the memory, and defective sense organs, that are the inhibitors of knowledge.

The self

In concentrating on the supremacy of Brahman as the focus of his entire philosophy, there was no way in which Madhva could accept the kind of inseparable relationship between self and God that epitomized Rāmānuja's body–soul theory. Madhva had to distance the self and the finite world from God so, while never independent of Brahman, the existence of selves in time and space necessitated a separation from God in essence and nature. To Madhva, the "body" of God is more his will that functions in the world. The "body" of God, in the sense that Rāmānuja meant the word, is rejected by Madhva as the world, or the selves that inhabit it.

The Brahman-*ātman* relationship in Dvaita is one of *reflection*, *pratibimba*. God is the *original* the *Bimba*, of which the self is a reflection. This is called the theory of *bimba-pratibimba*. And since the self is but a reflection of God, Madhva believed it could never be identical to God. However, since God is eternal, the self as a reflection of God is also eternal. But its distinctive qualities, its *svarūpopādhi*, give it a separate existence from God, as well as from other *jīvas* both in the bound and in the liberated state. This doctrine of the contrast between God and the self has been described by one writer as "the heart of his thought",[38] and it is certainly central. But alongside this, and perhaps of greater significance, is the doctrine of the *dependency* of the self on God. Any *śruti* text that intimated identity of the self, the *ātman*, with Brahman was reinterpreted by Madhva in line with the numerous other parts of *śruti* that indicated their duality but independent–dependent relationship. It is an outright denial of monism. But neither did Madhva court pantheism, for though the self might be referred to as a "part" or "fraction" of Brahman, that "part" is but a reflection, like an image on water, and not a part in terms of identical essence. Always, the transcendent supremacy of God detracts from any over-identification of self and divine. But reflection does not mean illusion on the one hand, or *literal* reflection on the other. *Pratibimba* is a symbol for dependent relationship more than anything else, like the shadow that cannot exist without, is dependent on, and resembles, the material object that causes it. There is some similarity, but that is as far as the resemblance can be pressed. The analogy is also important in another way, for it indicates, too, that the object to which the shadow is attached is in no way dependent on its shadow. Thus, God is always the completely independent Reality – he is separate from the self and the world.

Each self, then, is dependent on Brahman but is not of the same substance as him. Just as a rainbow exists because of the sun's rays in the raindrops, but is not the sun, so the self exists only because of Brahman but is not Brahman. But Madhva, as we shall see, takes the concept of the dependent self to the point of fairly limited agency, like a puppet caused to act by forces other than itself. There are similarities to God – both are real, both have consciousness, and a natural, blissful nature. But the dependent nature of the self is such that it must always be separate from God, and any *śruti* text that suggested identity between the two, Madhva reinterpreted as indicative of a dependent belonging to God: he eschewed entirely identity of essence. Such dependence is absolute: it is characteristic of the liberated Self as much as the bound self. Indeed, the recognition of such absolute dependency is itself of the nature of *mokṣa*. The relationship of *bimba–pratibimba* between God and self is an eternal and inviolable one. And it is this *relationship* that is of the essence of the self, and is a relationship that can only be fully realized when the self is liberated from reincarnation.

Madhva believed that all our experience of life reveals that we have no identity with God: no-one *feels* "I am Brahman". Most experience of life and of God, he believed, pointed to God as supreme and transcendent to the self. As the absolute independent Reality on which all selves depend, it is impossible to *be* Brahman. Dependency is dualistic separation, and there can be no identity between the limited, powerless and imperfect selves and the perfection of Brahman. The fundamental natures of self and divine are *real* and *different*. The drop may eventually realize the ocean, but the drop can never *be* the ocean; it only resembles it in very inferior and limited ways. The difference that obtains between the bound self and Brahman cannot suddenly disappear when the self is liberated, and the nature of the self can never begin to compare with the infinite excellences of the attributes and nature of God.

So those passages of the *Upaniṣads* that speak of the soul as Brahman speak of resemblance and not identity in Dvaita thought. There is a sense that the released Self becomes one with Brahman or enters into Brahman, but this is an entering into the full dependent relationship with Brahman, like a drop in the ocean. While selves are eternal, they are only so because they are like God's shadow. The true nature or *svarūpa* of the self is one that is free of the impurities attached to the bound self. It lacks the pains and sorrows of life that *karma* brings to the bound selves, and enjoys unobscured reality, consciousness and bliss – though this will be graded according to its particular special nature, as will be seen below. But this liberated and atomic *ātman* is not the all-pervasive Brahman. While the true Self is of the nature of consciousness, there can be no consciousness, no knowledge, unless it is of an object. The true Self is very much an egoistic "I", for the *viśeṣas* that determine each self are never separated from it. Individuality, ego, albeit non-worldly in the liberated state, always obtains. Ego-consciousness and self-consciousness are identical. "It is the 'I' of each soul that proves it to be different from the other, and also from the Lord", writes Narain.[39] While the ego is normally associated with activity and enjoyment in life, it is not, then, dissociated from both at liberation. Consciousness continues, then, with God as its objective focus.

What, then, does Dvaita make of the established identity of the self *as* Brahman in the celebrated statement from the *Chāndogya Upaniṣad*, *Tat tvam asi*? Certainly, the interpretation would be more "That you are not", rather than "That you are". Of this, Madhva wrote: "Śrutis sometimes describes (*sic*) the Jīvas as non-different from Brahman, in virtue of some broad similarities of their attributes, or the outstanding prominence and metaphysical independence of Brahman (besides which naught else seems to exist *or matter*). Such descriptions should not, however, be understood literally, in terms of any identity of *essence* between them."[40] Similarly, of the statement "I am Brahman", Dvaita is adamant that this does not indicate identity of Brahman and *ātman*. Echoing the Dvaita texts, Raghavendrachar wrote: "In the light of the context it must be interpreted from the standpoint of the ground as 'my ground is Brahman'. Similar is the regard to all the statements that appear to teach the identity of *jīva* and Brahman."[41] But, in any case, and as Jayatīrtha was quick to point out, any text that appears to teach identity of the self with Brahman would be invalidated by the infallible knowledge of the *sākṣin* that experiences itself as other than Brahman. *Tat tvam asi* can, therefore, only be interpreted in terms of *bimba–pratibimba*, the self as a dependent reflection of Brahman. If there is any identification of the *ātman* with Brahman it is because Brahman is that which rules all things from within, and which pervades all. The phrase reflects harmony and similarity, but not identity.

As we have seen, Madhva subscribed to the theory of *svabhāvabheda* "real difference in being". That is to say, each self, each individual, is essentially different from all others: there is an infinite number of such selves in the universe – divine ones, human ones and demonic ones. Each has its own unique essence, and its own repertoire of experience that cannot be transferred to another. The essential nature of reality, consciousness and bliss is not common to all even at *mokṣa*, but is different for each individual. If there is any doubt whether Rāmānuja accepted qualitative differences between liberated Selves, there is no doubt whatever that Madhva believed in the quantitative *and* qualitative differences between all beings. It is the doctrine of *viśeṣas* that accounts for such differences. No two people past, present and future, can ever be the same according to this theory; each has both its individuality and its particularity. It is this theory that will necessitate a hierarchy of both bound selves and liberated ones and, importantly, a hierarchy that is imposed by the will of God. Raghavendrachar wrote of this innate difference in selves:

> Though it is difficult to define it clearly in the case of an individual at a given time, on the whole we have to admit that the experience of a knower is ruled by a general disposition of his. A deep insight into the behaviours of different individuals placed under the same external conditions reveals this fact. Whatever the circumstances may be, men are guided by their natural inclinations. To expect from all the same dispositions is impossible. In the presence of a particular disposition it is impossible to make a man conscious of other possibilities.[42]

It is the law of *karma* that presupposes different selves in the world, for it is this law that illustrates the inequalities in individuals – in their moral behaviour, their actions, their speech, thought, dispositions and propensities for experience. "The doctrine of multiplicity of selves is not open to any objections", said Madhva.[43] Selves must be plural Madhva believed, because we can never have *direct* experience of someone else's *karmic* experience. The law of *karma* operates so that just rewards and punishments are meted out according to the various merits and demerits of each individual. But in Dvaita, it is God that controls *karma*. Dvaita is alone in the orthodox schools in seeing the relative dispositions of a person – individual *karmas* – as pre-ordained. While *karma* suggests freedom of choice for any individual, Dvaita sees those choices as somewhat limited by the particular dispositions of the individual. And those dispositions are dependent on the unique essence of a person, the *svarūpabheda*, that is created by the special *viśeṣas* peculiar to him or her.[44] Sharma writes:

> It is accepted that the inequalities of individual equipment and endowment are regulated by one's past life and its Karma. But, by its very nature, the Karma theory would be powerless to explain the *why of such inequalities*, in the remotest past, without *recourse to the hypothesis of an intrinsic peculiarity* (*anādi-viśeṣa*) *that is uncaused.* It is this *anādiviśeṣa*, says Madhva, that distinguishes one soul from another.[45]

The self is an active agent, experiencer and knower in Dvaita Vedānta. Activity is not, as in Advaita, ignorant superimposition of an illusion on a passive *ātman.* Madhva said: "The Jīva must indeed be a real doer; otherwise, the Śāstra, which is addressed to those who want to achieve certain objectives by certain specified means and to avoid certain undesirable contingencies by not doing certain things, would have no scope."[46] In other words, scripture implies an active self in search of liberation. Yet how far the individual has self-determined choices in such a system is difficult to say. On the one hand we have a supreme God who is the inner Controller of all, who predetermines the particular natures of each individual, and who sets up the eternal system of *karma*, ensuring the appropriate results for each action. On the other hand, we have a *real* self with, presumably, some measure of *real* choice and real experience in life. The tension between the two is obvious, and we have to be left with a self-limiting God who permits some degree of choice in all individuals despite being the inner Ruler of all, the all-pervasive Controller. It makes no sense to be a realist if the self is not a real agent with self-determining power. Dvaita might not give to the self absolute independent agency, but some freedom is essential. But the constraining factor of a deep-rooted innate *and given* nature will only allow the individual to act according to his or her limited, or expanded, dispositions. Sharma is unequivocal that free will is granted to the self. He writes:

> The Jīva chooses out of his free will a particular line of action for good or bad with sufficient foreknowledge of its moral worth and has himself to thank for the consequences. He cannot, therefore, blame anyone, least of all God, for the unpleasant consequences of his acts, should he have chosen wrongly. He has freedom of choice within the realm of works. God does not throw the creatures blindfolded into an unknown region or set them adrift chartless on the high seas. Each is provided with a chart, a book of instructions of where lies the haven and how to reach it. This book is the Śāstra (*vidhiniṣedhātmakam*).[47]

But this will not do, for the raft each person has in life is a different craft; some have better crafts than others. And those not originally bestowed with the appropriate dispositions by God are not able to benefit from scripture in the same way as others. Indeed, they may be excluded from access to the *śruti* literature. Ultimately, in the Dvaita system it is God who is the inner Controller that ensures the right kind of result for any action of merit or demerit in the *jīva*: and the *jīva* cannot act at all unless it is by the will of God. If freedom is an expression of the innate nature of the self, as Sharma suggests,[48] and the *karma* of each individual is the result of that innate nature imposed by God, then it is freedom under constraint and, therefore, limited in character and causally regulated from the start. God may well permit freedom of choice for each individual but, since the starting point for each is differently determined by God, freedom is considerably compromised. I shall take up this point again in the context of the concept of God and the issue of theodicy, but one further point is relevant here. The self is always a *limited* agent, is always dependent on God, and this, in itself, presupposes limitation of the freedom of the self. Indeed, actions and the results of them are expressions and outcomes respectively of an individual's innate characteristics. Raghavendrachar, therefore, reminds us that the same action done by different people will reap different results, and will affect each one differently, according to one's innate dispositions.[49] Clearly, this view shows the force of the dispositional nature and the secondary nature of *karma*.

Madhva defined the self, the *jīva*, in the following words: "He who enjoys the happiness and suffers the ills of life, who is eligible for bondage and release, is the Jīva. He is indeed in a position to know himself, in all his states, as 'I am'."[50] The true self is the knower, the *sākṣin*, the inner witness, of which I have already written much, above. It is an inner sense organ that operates with the mind, but is not the mind or dependent on it. Thus, in deep sleep the *sākṣin* can exist without the aid of the mind, as it can, also, during the long time when the universe is dissolved. Aided by the three *pramāṇas*, the *sākṣin* is the inner arbiter of valid knowledge, even of scripture, but it is also the intuitive self that can understand such things as Time and Space, which are unavailable to normal means of knowledge. It is never wrong. Madhva is unique among the philosophical schools in positing such an inner arbiter for valid knowledge. The *sākṣin* is *the* self, the inner consciousness of each individual and is different in each individual. There is a slight tension between the *sākṣin* that intuitively knows itself as *ātman*, and the *sākṣin* as an attribute of the *ātman*. Sharma maintained that the *sākṣin* is identical to the self.[51] But he also shows how the two aspects are present: "Sākṣī, in Madhva's epistemology, is the name of the spiritual sense organ of the self through which it intuits its experiences. But this instrument of intuition is not something different from the self (*pramātā*). The distinction is only one of reference and not of essence."[52] The functioning of the *sākṣin* is a particular *viśeṣa* of the self, an aspect of it. The *sākṣin*, then, is the *ātman* that knows itself intuitively as "I" and is, therefore, self-luminous. But it is also the consciousness of the self. Such consciousness of the *sākṣin* is not static; it is constantly changing. It is a *process* of consciousness that takes place in the self – indeed, this must necessarily be so if the *sākṣin* is continually the arbiter of new knowledge. It is a novel contribution of Madhva, and it will be an important factor in the process by which the individual becomes liberated.

It is the inner *sākṣin* that comes to know the finitude of the transmigrating self, the dependence of the self on God, and the different natures of the self and God. It will know itself as reality, consciousness and bliss at liberation. It is the more external *jīva* that obscures such awareness through its involvement with the finite world, with the mind, the body and the reactions to the stimuli of the world around. This obscures the real *jīva* and the dependent nature of its agency in the world.

Given that Madhva accepted eternal differences in the innate natures of individuals, the logical outcome was to accept also a hierarchy of selves in both their bound and liberated states. Thus, Dvaita accepts three classes of selves. All are eternal. They are:

- Those that are eternally free (*nityamukti*). Such is Lakṣmī, the consort of Viṣṇu.
- Those that have become free (*muktas*). These are the gods and men who have found release from *saṃsāra*, the great seers or *ṛṣis*, and the "fathers", the *pitṛ* or ancestors such as great kings. Of the gods here, the creator God Brahmā is noteworthy as the

highest-ranking deity, with an extraordinary amount of merit. It is he that is responsible for the evolution of the material world.

- Those that are bound (*baddhas*). Some of these are capable of *mukti* and others are not. And of those who are not, some are destined for eternal reincarnation, others for hell. Demons and ghosts, in particular, are subjects for hell.

In the first two classes are the *sattvic* selves that are destined for release and for heaven. The bound souls are *rajasic*, and hence destined for eternal reincarnation, and *tamasic*, destined for hell. But in all three classes there is a hierarchy dependent on the quality of consciousness, power and bliss. Dvaita subscribes to a theory of predestination alongside one of the grace of God. And even in the state of release, such gradations occur, with the outcome that the vision of God will depend on the innate tendencies of the individual god, seer, father or human. The tripartite division of sentient beings into gods humans and demons is well known in Hinduism,[53] the *permanent* and *unchangeable* gradation of beings in each class, however, is innovative. It is God who pre-establishes by his creative will that the wise will be knowledgeable and the foolish ignorant. And he controls the law of *karma* to ensure the just deserts for actions that can only occur within the bounds of the particular innate tendencies of each being.

The bound self is one that does not know its true nature as dependent on God. It is the reaping of past *karma* that necessitates a material body by which the self can experience the pains and sorrows or joys that are its due. It is because the *jīva* imposes its own agency on its life and actions in it, and believes itself independent, that it remains bound. Instead it should understand God as the only independent agent. But it becomes attached to a personality that it thinks it owns, avoids what is distasteful to it, and desires what it enjoys. Each person has a proportion of each of the three *guṇas* and will relate to life depending on the particular balance of them – the good will seek good and the evil, evil. But each person is unique and will act, experience life and be of a kind of consciousness that is pertinent to him or her. It will only be possible to live, think and act within the boundaries of that nature. The material body that ceases at death, the spiritual body that transmigrates and the innate consciousness that is the self, are the three aspects of the self given purposefully by God to best suit each individual.

The Dvaita purpose of life is to evolve within the boundaries of such parameters, but only those destined for *mukti* will have the necessary prerequisites for the arduous journey of moral and spiritual effort and the developed knowledge to make it possible. According to Dvaita, this is the purpose of God's creation. Madhva never poses the critical question of *why* selves should have been so indiscriminately bound in the first place, and regards such bondage as beginningless, like the ignorance that accompanies it. But he does consider that it is their involvement with the stuff of the mind that conceals their ultimate natures. The best outcomes in life are only for the innately good:

> The good among the uncreated souls lying in the Womb of Prakṛti from the beginningless past are like impure gold which has to be dug out of the rocks and mines and duly processed before it could be converted into jewellery. They are like the veins of gold and nuggets imbedded in the rocks. They can be reclaimed only after they have been crushed, washed, sifted and melted down in the crucible. The same principle applies to the other categories

> of souls also, all of whom are to be brought to the surface of life from the depths of Prākṛtic stupor in which they have lain all along. God in His mercy provides them with the conditions suitable to their gradual evolution . . . [54]

These words are thoroughly suggestive of elitist theism, by which the grace of God works only for the elected. Those lacking such grace cannot evolve to the point of liberation and, were their innate natures to be highly *tamasic*, they cannot proceed very far at all. The *śāstras*, the scriptures, however, presuppose the possible response to, or rejection of, the relative requirements and prohibitions by each being. This must suggest some free agency. The purpose of life is, therefore, the evolution of each individual *as far as its innate potential will permit.* And for some, this will mean eternal damnation – a concept rejected by all other Indian philosophy. Ultimately, Dvaita tries to have it both ways: the self is controlled by God, but it is a free agent. It is also a free agent, but is limited by the innate being that God makes it.

Causality

It is the *will* of God that is behind every cause–effect process, for everything in existence – sentient or insentient – is dependent on God. Therefore, there can be no independent causal force other than God. The whole of creation is an eternally dependent effect of God's will, and cannot exist, or be sustained continually, without it. It is also through this creation that sentient beings have some concept of what God is. Thus, Madhva said: "The Supreme Being should be accepted as the Creator, sustainer etc., of this vast universe of stupendous organization."[55]

The theory of causation in Dvaita is referred to as *sadasatkāryavāda*. It lies midway between the *asatkāryavāda* doctrine of Nyāya and the *satkāryavāda* doctrine of Sāṃkhya. It is the belief that effects partly exist and yet do not exist in their causes. They partly exist in their causes because we can only have oak trees from acorns, or cloth from thread. In other words, effects arise from certain causes and not others. But once the effect comes into being – like the oak tree from the acorn – it is very unlike its material cause and, as such, cannot be said to have existed in its cause. It just depends whether one is viewing an object from the causal state or the produced effect – the acorn, or the oak. An effect is non-existent as such, when it is latent in the cause. When manifest as an effect, it no longer exists in the cause. Cause and effect are, then, related but different – there is identity and difference, or *bhedābheda*, although it is *saviśeṣābheda* that really explains the relationship between cause and effect. The identity and difference occur as follows:

- Effects are identified with their particular causes – so there is identity.
- Effects have characteristics that the cause does not – so there is difference.
- There can be no relation between cause and effect when the effect has not come into being – so there is difference.

To Madhva, the process from cause to effect suggests that something has changed, and such change is a change in the *viśeṣas* of the causal substance. The new effect cannot simply appear, it has to have a causal substance from which it is produced, and the effect that is produced occurs through a process of continuity of change from the causal state. But while the effect is ultimately linked to the cause it is different from it, for it has different *viśeṣas*. In some cases, the difference is minimal, in others the changes result in such difference that the effect does not seem to be linked to the cause at all.

But whatever causal processes are evident in the universe, Brahman is the fundamental Cause of all things: the world is the effect of God as the intelligent cause, and in line with *sadasatkāryavāda*, the world is a very *different* effect from its cause, God. God is the cause of every action, of every process of cause–effect, and of the bound and liberated *jīvas*. As Lott points out here: "In whatever way other Vedantins may have acknowledged Brahman's supreme control of the universe, none of them took it to be the principle by which to interpret the whole Vedantic system as Madhva did."[56] Yet this is in line with much *Upaniṣadic* thought. Importantly, however, Dvaita sees God as *efficient* Cause and not material cause. It is by his *will* that the causal process operates, and while God is immanent in the world, nothing of his essence or being emanates into the world that he wills to be. This is consonant with Madhva's clear separation of, and differences between, self and the divine, and the world and the divine.

The material cause of the world is *prakṛti*, which is motivated to produce its evolutes by the will of God. There is, thus, a very clear departure here from the body–soul/world relationship with God of Rāmānuja, by which God must be the material as well as the efficient cause of the world. Madhva could never have gone down such a route, since this would have jeopardized the transcendence and perfection of God. He keeps God substantially removed from the world. To Madhva it was illogical to accept that God could allow part of his own being to become the world of finitude and sorrow – particularly when the *śrūti* texts are so keen to stress the unchanging and immutable nature of Brahman. While maintaining the will of God as the efficient cause only, Madhva is able to stress the power and majesty of God as Ruler and Controller, without compromising the divine nature, and without permitting any aspect of the world's causal processes to be independent of that divine will. The theory of causality – as any other theory in Dvaita – points to Brahman as the independent and supreme Cause of all. As Lott aptly states: "It is through this sheer will, transcendent in its character, immanent in its operation, that Madhva feels best able to account for the coordination of the various sub-causes in his system, and to avoid making the Lord directly connected with the innumerable changes incurred in the creative process."[57]

As the material cause of creation *prakṛti* is eternal and insentient.[58] It exists in manifest and unmanifested states in alternating cycles. It is controlled by God, but separate from him. It differs, therefore, from the self-evolving *prakṛti* of the Sāṃkhya system, but makes sense of that system by positing an agent that causes it to unfold. But like Sāṃkhya, Madhva accepted the evolution of *prakṛtic* matter from its unmanifest state to the subtle and then gross states of manifest existence. The whole process is one of continued modification and change. Time, *kāla*, is the first evolute of *prakṛti*, followed by the three *guṇas* and then *mahat*, *ahaṃkāra* and so on. *Prakṛti* is the primal material cause of all manifestation in the universe, both subtle and gross. But it is not, as in Sāṃkhya, a unifying cause that makes all matter and all evolutes one. This is because of the doctrine of *viśeṣas* that makes each entity different from any other, and because Dvaita does not accept that effects are the same as their cause(s). At all times, however, *prakṛti* is dependent on the will of God. Creation, then, is not *ex nihilo*, and since *prakṛti* is eternal, it might be suggested that the basic stuff of which the universe is made has not been created by God in any way. But it is always dependent on the will of God in its cycles of evolution and involution. Yet, such is the will of God that Madhva believed it is not inconceivable that God *could* have created a world *ex nihilo*. Madhva also accepted the likelihood of a myriad of universes.

The creative will of God is part of his being, as is the dissolving will: when one is actualized, the other will remain in potential. These are just particular *viśeṣas* of God that are rhythmically active and latent. When creation takes place, Brahman takes on manifested forms in order to oversee the process of creation. A fourfold divinity – Vāsudeva, Pradyumna, Aniruddha, and Saṃkarṣaṇa – are responsible for redemption, creation, sustaining and dissolving, respectively. While fourfold in terms of function, there is ultimately no division envisaged here: the unity of God is always maintained. Through other such manifestations, God exercises the power of his will over the different stages of the evolution of the universe. Creation is, thus, a continuous process that is dependent on God for every moment of transformation and modification. In Madhva's words: "The Supreme Being, possessed of infinite powers, enters into various stages of evoluton of matter and brings about each and every such stage of such manifestation of things, Himself."[59] Eternal entities like selves, Time, Space and the *Vedas*, have no modifications to their fundamental causal states, unlike the rest of the evolutes of *prakṛti*. The eternal selves are the reason behind creation, for they need the manifest world in order to rid themselves of the accumulated *karmas* of their many existences. Madhva outlined a whole hierarchy of deities to preside over the individual areas of *prakṛtic* evolution. But God himself is always the controller of all these manifestations of his will – a will that is conceived of as the feminine aspect of him, as we shall see below – and of the multiplicity of deities that act in creation and dissolution. The purpose of such deities is to provide order and stability to both evolution and dissolution, to both of which there is no beginning and no end.

Eightfold causative determinants

The causal forces of God in the world, according to Madhva, are creation, preservation, dissolution, law and order, bondage, liberation, knowledge and ignorance. All the happinesses and sorrows of human existence are results of these eight causal determinants that come into effect by the will of God. They are appropriate to the specific *dharma* of each individual and of life as a whole. God, thus, is the controller of all *dharma*, as well as of the *karmas* of all beings. *Karma* is but the effects of previous causes, and God is he that ensures the appropriate effects to match those causes: he makes each *jīva* act according to his or her individual nature and just deserts. *Karma* is insentient, it cannot itself work out what is right for an individual; only an agent can do that. *Karma* is, thus, fully subordinate to God, for it cannot operate as a system without him. Dreams, too, fall into this category of God-controlled effects appropriate to each individual. But just as Nature itself is without beginning and end, so is *karma*: both are created and dissolved in a pattern that is infinite through the past and infinite in the future.

The concept of God

To Madhva, and in Dvaita as a whole, God is thoroughly *independent* (*svatantra*) of the entire world and *jīvas*. This is the central doctrine of Dvaita. God is a transcendent Absolute and is the only independent Reality, having being in itself; all else is dependent reality. In order to maintain the transcendence of God, Madhva maintained that he is *unmanifest* (*avyakta*). Strictly speaking, it might, therefore, be more pertinent to refer to God as the neuter "It" that the term Brahman presupposes, but Dvaita is theistic, and therefore believes that Brahman makes itself known to devotees as the more personal God. Because God has self-contained being in himself, he is not subject to any limitations, and is changeless. His essence is that of Reality, consciousness, and utter bliss.

But while God is so different from all dependent reality, he controls that reality by being immanent within it. Madhva wrote: "God is the Independent Being possessed of all adequate and unrestricted powers in regard to Cit and Acit and who is all-knowing. He is the One who controls Cit and Acit (sentient and insentient reals) which are of a different nature from Him."[60] Yet God always remains incomprehensible in his essential self. It is only through scripture that something of God can be known. He is, as Hiriyanna neatly states, "apprehensible but not comprehensible".[61] The *nirguṇa* concept of God is, therefore, rejected in favour of a *saguṇa* God who makes himself available to his devotees through his power and grace. Like Rāmānuja, Madhva interpreted any *śruti* texts that referred to a *nirguṇa* Absolute – one without qualities – as to one without *adverse* qualities. In any case, Madhva's doctrine of *viśeṣas* pointed to distinct qualities for God also – albeit totally different and independent qualities in relation to those of the world and *jīvas*. There were also, he believed, too many instances in the *śruti* texts that referred to the qualities of God. Vyāsatīrtha believed that the references to the *nirguṇa* Brahman referred to his transcendence and lordship over the three *guṇas* of existence, rather than to an indescribable, totally transcendent Absolute *per se*. That is to say, *nirguṇa* states that God is not *prakṛtic*, not *guṇic*. It was always the essential, incomprehensible nature of God that was paramount to Madhva. This is the *Ātman*, the unlimited essence that God is. As well as referring to the inner soul of the individual self in Dvaita, *Ātman* is also a term used to depict God as the "Pervader", he that pervades and controls all existence by his will. God is the Supreme Self, the *Paramātman*. For Dvaita, then, God is *saguṇa* because he possesses qualities, though distinct qualities that are different from any associated with the world and the human self. However, whatever the qualities and activities of God in the world, their independence of nature is firmly maintained. They are aspects of the essential, incomprehensible nature of a transcendent God, a God that is truly *neti neti*, "not this, not this", in the sense that he is very different from the whole of his creation.

Madhva reiterated the *Oneness* of God, and his non-dual nature. That is to say, there is no equal or rival to God. This, he claimed, is what the *Upaniṣadic* statement that God is One without a second means. And yet that Oneness that is God is not removed from the many that he wills to be. As Sharma puts it: "The Upaniṣadic Brahman would remain the One without a second – not in a dry numerical sense; but in a richer and deeper sense of being the active source of the rich multiplicity of finite reality and the sustaining principle behind it."[62] The *viśeṣas* that are the distinct characteristics of God exist harmoniously and, where they operate separately, such as in creation or dissolution, where one must be dormant while the other is active, they are merely expressions of the distinctive rhythmic balances that are part of the essence of God. But while the number of attributes of God is countless, the Reality of God is always unitary; it is one and undivided. It is the distinctive *viśeṣas* of the infinite attributes of God that serve to make up the unity of divinity. But, at the same time, each attribute is capable of being utilized separately from others, while remaining inseparable from the whole. In short, the attributes of God are a part of his essential essence, and not merely attachments to his divinity: divine substance and attributes are a unity. That is why worldly equivalents in name are but mere shadows of the Reality of the attributes of God.

While Madhva was keen to depict God in negative terms, he did not eschew the describable qualities of God that were readily available from scripture. God is a substance, because he is an object of knowledge known through the scriptures. It was important that Brahman was knowable. At the beginning of his *Brahmasūtrabhāṣya* Madhva wrote: "Having bowed down before Nārāyana who is full of virtuous qualities, is free from defects, is knowable and obtainable and the teacher, I begin to explain the meaning of the sūtra."[63] But he stressed that the attributes of God are limitless, and preferred to speak of the "fullness of qualities", the perfection and freedom from limitations, that characterized God, as paramount. Dvaita theories of knowledge claim that nothing can exist without qualities. And this is no less true of God than anything else. Even to describe God as *neti neti* is assigning a characteristic, just as it is to say that he is real. Thus Madhva claimed: "There cannot possibly be anything that is *utterly attributeless*."[64] Being a realist Madhva needed to explain the relationship between substances and the attributes they possess. In particular, his theistic vision necessitated a God with attributes that were at once identifiable with God and yet did not *per se* constitute the totality of God. It is by such attributes that God can be known to his devotees – albeit in a very limited kind of knowledge. Thus: "The conception is personal; but the personality, it is added, is of the absolute kind."[65] The attributes of God, his *viśeṣas*, are innumerable, just as each entity has numerous *viśeṣas* also. But God's attributes are only good. A substance that is a completely positive entity, like God, can only have completely positive and perfect attributes. No negative attributes can, therefore, be ascribed to God. As applied to God, the doctrine of *viśeṣas* allows many qualities for God, but no distinction between them. Thus, they are identical to God and yet different – identity-in-difference of the subject and its attributes. Madhva said: "The attributes and actions of Brahman are the same as itself. They are not different. There is no mutual difference, either, among them."[66]

The essence of God is Reality, absolute Truth, *sat*, that which is true being without dependence on anything for its own existence. As Raghavendrachar wrote of this Truth: "It is therefore not one among many truths. It is the Truth which includes all and transcends all."[67] This nature of *sat* is equated with pure goodness and that level of Reality from which the world and selves derive their own reality. God is also of the nature of a supreme bliss (*ānanda*) that is incomprehensible in comparison to the glimpses of it individuals may have in earthly bliss. Similarly, the consciousness and omniscience of God are unlimited, whereas at *mokṣa*, the liberated *jīva* has but limited consciousness in comparison to the divine. God's knowledge, being omniscient, is not subject to the *vṛttis*, the mind-modifications, that characterize ordinary knowledge. The "fullness" of God is fullness in every perfection, and utterly transcends human comprehension in its absolute, unlimited nature. And this is an absolute nature that is imperishable in every dimension of its attributes.

The dualism of the Dvaita system emerges from this utterly self-determining divine Absolute on the one hand, and the totally dependent, "other-determined", and limited freedom, of the *jīvas* and the world, on the other. This is the independent-dependent (*svatantra–paratantra*) dualism of the system. The contrast is one that Madhva constantly reiterates. While manifest existence and divinity are both real, the Reality assigned to God is the only independent one. Importantly, the dualism here is not a separation of reality into two totally separate kinds, for one is always dependent on the other for its very existence. It is in this sense that God is the Ground of all being – not in the sense of everything in existence being of the essence or substance of God, but in the fact that nothing can exist without him. Thus, God is the *independent* Ground of all dependent being.

The transcendent Absolute, however, is not the remote Brahman of Advaita. The God of Dvaita is one that pervades the world, and is immanent in it either through his will, or through his power. Indeed, the name of God as Viṣṇu is translated as the "All-Pervader", and was one used by Madhva to express this immanence, this subtle pervasion of the divine in the world. Without this presence of the will or power of God, nothing can exist. Another name by which Madhva liked to refer to God was Hari, "Lord", and this, too, expressed the idea of the lordship of God over the whole of creation, and that creation as the *līlā*, the effortless "sport" or "play" of the divine. But while God pervades the very soul of each human being, as the *Ātman*, as I noted above, the individual soul itself is not identified with God. It is God, as *Ātman*, who indwells the self as the motivator to action. The more the self is open to the agency of God in this way, the more that individual moves towards the dependency on God that results in the liberated state. Nevertheless, however much divine agency is evidenced in creation, God always remains completely separate and independent of all Nature.

God is the efficient cause of both ignorance and bondage, even if he is also the cause of knowledge and liberation. Ignorance arises in the self as the material cause of it, not in Brahman, but God creates the innate disposition for levels of ignorance in the first place. He has the power to create, preserve and dissolve the universe, to control, to give knowledge, and to obscure it. He can keep selves in bondage or he can liberate them. Translating closely from the primary texts, Raghavendrachar writes of God: "It knows all. It is all powerful. It is capable of doing any and every thing. Nothing is impossible for It. It favours good *jīvas*. It puts down the bad ones. If It likes it can make the bad good. It does not do so because that would not be to maintain the order in the world."[68] Moreover, human beings will always be in bondage when there is a lack of God's grace. And although they need to win his grace by right action and devotion, some will never do so.

But even the distancing of creation as different effects of an unrelated causal divine cannot avoid the issue of theodicy that still looms large in the system of Dvaita. For if God is the inner Controller and Activator, and is also omniscient and omnipotent, he surely stands by to witness the very worst of atrocities. And, as was seen above, the innate nature of each individual – and all that individual's propensities for good or evil – are predetermined. Hiriyanna pertinently comments on this last point that: "It not only means that the element of evil will ever persist in the universe, but also restricts the scope of human freedom and the power of divine grace."[69] The origin of suffering is more clearly traced to the will of the divine in Dvaita than in other philosophical schools. For, even though the good or evil that is done by any individual stems from his or her individual nature, it is God that bestows such a nature in the first place. And that means the bestowal of some natures to those who have the propensity for the very worst of evil activity. Radhakrishnan was right to point out that: "Unless we are in a position to believe in the spiritual possibilities of every one who bears the human form divine, we cannot have a really useful ethics."[70] And this is not "soft emotional thinking" as one author suggests.[71] Neither is it a solution to suggest that God causes bondage in order to be the source of our redemption,[72] or that evil assists the better class of *jīvas* to avoid its temptations.[73] These are fundamentalist notions that only serve to evade the issue.

Manifestations of God

Since the formless and incomprehensible God cannot be directly known, his manifestations are essential as a means to have some valid knowledge of what God is – albeit limited. To be knowable in this limited way is part of the perfect nature of God who, if totally unknowable, might be said to be less than perfect through the absence of one quality. Vāyu, the God of the wind, was the means by which God made himself known to individual *jīvas* and, as was noted very early in this chapter, Madhva himself was often equated with this deity. In this role he was believed to assist individuals on the path to liberation as the mediator of God. But apart from this particular deity, Madhva accepted the polytheistic tradition so evident in the *Vedas*.

But if the polytheism of Hinduism pervades the general praxis of Hindu worship, Madhva was particularly keen to emphasize the monotheism of Dvaita. He did this by stressing that all divine manifestations of God are thoroughly equal and not hierarchical.[74] God is exactly the same in an *avatāra* form, for example, as he is in his transcendent state.[75] None of the *avatāras*, therefore, is subject to *karma*: each is thoroughly divine, and thoroughly real. Such *avatāras* are God's chosen embodiments by which he protects his devotees and punishes those who are evil. He can assume any form, but always retains his essential being in such forms: there is no limitation on the nature of God by such material, embodied forms. But the hierarchy of deities from Śrī and Brahmā down to the most menial, including Vāyu, are characterized by different *viśeṣas* and are essentially different from God. These deities preside over both sentient evolutes and every aspect of insentient matter, but they are always dependent on God and separate from him, who is the only independent Reality. God empowers these deities to act: they are powerless without his activating will.

While God has no physical form, Dvaita accepts that he has a supernatural and subtle body. God, therefore, has personhood through his own particular subtle form and his distinct and independent nature. It is a personhood with the qualities of consciousness, experience, thought, action, control and volition. But because these characteristics are held in a formless God who is transcendent, Madhva's conception of the divine generally falls short of being anthropomorphic. Whatever "form" God may have, it is ultimately subtle and spiritual. Madhva wrote: "Brahman is 'Formless' because It transcends Prakṛti and others and controls them all."[76] Yet: "He enters into *Prakṛti* and energizes it to transform in various ways and assumes many forms to control such modifications."[77] And yet it is Viṣṇu who is the focus of worship, and here there is an abundance of anthropomorphic expression. Brahman is equated with Viṣṇu, and all other deities are non-Brahman. Madhva understands the term "Brahman" to mean what is perfect, and this is Viṣṇu, and no other. And in many cases he believed that references to *Vedic* deities such as Agni or Indra were really references to Viṣṇu. Lott, for example, refers to Madhva's "discovery of veiled references to Viṣṇu in all manner of texts, especially in the various names of deities".[78] His favourite names for God were Hari, Viṣṇu, Nārāyaṇa and Vāsudeva. The focus on Viṣṇu was immensely important not just because of the impetus it gave to Vaiṣṇava devotion. Sharma pointed out that Viṣṇu "had struck deep roots in the Indian spiritual soil and was the link that connected the Vedic with the Upaniṣadic and the Upaniṣadic with the Epic and Purāṇic phases of Hindu thought".[79]

The divine feminine force

The consort of Viṣṇu is Lakṣmī or Śrī. She is sometimes equated with *prakṛti* in the sense that it is she who energizes the primary matter of *prakṛti*, the material cause of the world, so that it produces the universe through its changing evolutes. "The intelligent *prakṛti* is not withdrawn into the Lord; for she is co-existent with the Person (the Lord) (in time and space), never subject to mundane bondage; and she is eternally blessed, but not in consequence of meditation."[80] Lakṣmī pervades *prakṛti* with her female power and energy, and it is in this way that *prakṛti* becomes personified mythologically as female. As female, it is regarded as a consort of God, and is rather like the manifest outcome of power in creation that proceeds from the will of God. As such, it is called *māyā*. But in the dissolved state of the universe it is *prakṛti* alone that exists, all being withdrawn back into its subtle, latent state. It is from it that God wills manifest existence to be, and it is this will that is epitomized as the active power of Lakṣmī. The first products of *prakṛti* are the *guṇas*, which are then stimulated to combine in their infinite variety to produce the world. While eternal, *prakṛti* is insentient, though its mythological identification with Lakṣmī gives it an apparent intelligence.

So it is the female energy in the universe that is assigned the more active roles of creation and dissolution. In particular, Madhva associated the three strands of *prakṛti*, *sattva*, *rajas* and *tamas*, with three female deities. These are Śrī, who is representative of the *sattvic guṇa* and is responsible for the creative evolution of life; Bhū, who is associated with *rajas* and is the principle of energy and vigour in life; and Durgā, who is the principle of *tamas* in existence and who is associated with darkness and dissolution. Durgā, especially, is associated with *māyā*. So Nature, *prakṛti*, is always essentially unintelligent but is energized by the female aspects of God. And since the energizing of unmanifest *prakṛti* to become manifest, as well as the reverse process, are a result of the power of God, the female forces responsible for this can themselves be identified as the power of God, as part of his being. This does not mean, however, that *prakṛti* is the divine feminine *per se*.

Thus, the female divine force in the form of Śrī, or Lakṣmī, is the force behind the evolutes of *prakṛti* and is the power of God. She is, therefore, like God, all-pervading and eternal, and has never been in the bound state. She, too, can take on many manifestations. But she is limited and dependent on God. Her attributes are limited in comparison to those of God, and her role is one that glorifies him. Since she is the manifestation of the power of God, she is the female creative principle that is subsumed in the male essence. This makes God both male and female, and truly *neti neti*, "not this, not this". But because Śrī is the power of God, one aspect and attribute of his nature, the monotheism that Madhva strives hard to maintain, is not compromised. In any case, as Narain comments: "The position of Lakṣmī in Mādhva philosophy is rather ambiguous and there appears no serious endeavour on the part of its exponents to justify Her existence."[81] The more overt polytheism, and this includes Lakṣmī, is subsumed under the guise of deities that are the dependent instruments of the divine will.

Essentially, then, we are left with a knowable God in Dvaita. Madhva's concept of God is one that permits the intimacy of relationship between divine and human that epitomizes theism as opposed to monism. Narain writes:

> It is in Madhva's philosophy of God that we have a full realization of that spirit of Vaiṣṇavism that rose against the Absolutism of Śaṃkara's creed. The description of Ultimate Reality as an indeterminate, qualityless, immutable and impersonal Infinite as available in Vedānta philosophy is, from the point of view of man, only an example of logical arrogance. Of what use is this Absolute with nothing positive about it to the fallen mortals, to the suffering humanity, to the tragic yearning of man that seeks something immortal in the midst of the fleeting moments of his life? The philosophy of the Absolute may appear as a coherent system and most satisfying to the logical sense of man yet it fails miserably as a doctrine that can impart him strength in the pursuance of a life consistent with human and moral values.[82]

Liberation

According to Madhva: "Release consists in shaking off all extraneous associations and regaining one's own selfhood."[83] There are basic prerequisites that aid the devotee on the path to such release in most areas of Hindu praxis, but particularly so for Vedānta schools where the concepts of God and liberation are highly developed. These include the following:

- *Vairāgya* is freedom from attachment to the things of the world and from the inner drives that promote this. Thus, desires and aversions have to be quelled in order to develop the kind of dispassionate nature that allows the individual to disconnect emotionally from world materiality. Many of the prerequisites of classical Yoga – *yama*, *niyama*, *āsana*, and *prāṇayāma*, and the practices and state of mind these include – are also necessary.
- *Bhakti* is devotion to God and, for Dvaita, the concomitant realization of the self as utterly dependent on, but separate from, the transcendent nature of the divine. *Bhakti*, writes Raghavendrachar, is "one's firm attachment to God accompanied by the correct knowledge of His greatness. It is not only the means for realisation, but

also for liberation (*mokṣa*) and enjoyment (*bhoga*) after liberation. Without *bhakti* discipline loses value".[84]

- *Śravaṇa* is study of the scriptures that will dispel ignorance and lay down the foundation of knowledge that is essential for the spiritual path. A *guru* is important in directing such study.
- *Manana* is reflection or consideration of the knowledge of God found in scripture such as to remove any doubts one may have about God. It is an internalizing of the knowledge acquired through study, a pursuit of the truth until one is absolutely certain about the final knowledge.
- *Dhyāna or nididhyāsana* is the meditation on, or contemplation of, the attributes of God or the truths of scripture. *Dhyāna*, along with *śravaṇa* and *manana*, are collectively known as *jijñāsā*.
- *Darśana*, the final stage, is direct realization of God.

Of these, like Rāmānuja, Madhva believed devotion and knowledge were essential. Continued devotion to God, he believed, would result in God's grace. Concentration on God thus promotes the reciprocal love of God for his devotee and, in this two-way dimension of devotion and grace, the soul evolves, and is drawn to God more and more. The soul comes to know its own dependent nature, and the utter independent nature of the God to whom it is inextricably bound.

Bhakti is important at every stage. It is continuous devotion. It is focus on the greatness and transcendence of God to the exclusion of all else in the world. It is constant communion with God. But because it is underpinned by knowledge, it lacks in Dvaita, that ecstatic and erotic dimension that characterizes the *bhakti* of the earlier southern Tamils, or the Vaiṣṇavism of the north Indian Jayadeva. Sharma depicts the *bhakti* of Madhva as "in essence an ineffable blending of the emotion and the intellect".[85] This to Madhva was the true nature of *bhakti* and, while he did not go as far as rejecting other modes of devotion, he certainly graded them as inferior. Concomitant with his grades of *jīvas* who have different natures – some better than others – is his concept of three different kinds of *bhakti* to suit such different innate natures of individuals. Not all, then, would be capable of the specific blend of knowledge and emotional love that characterized the higher grade of *jīvas*. Only the best of them would be innately capable of this intense devotion to God.

But if a certain type of *bhakti* is a major prerequisite to liberation, it is the realization of the dependent nature of the self that is its counterpart and outcome. Any devotion that does not bring the *jīva* to such a point of knowledge is inferior. The greater the depth and intensity of devotion, the more the *jīva* needs knowledge that recognizes, in the depths of its own self, the reality that is its self. It comes to know the ways in which that self is both a reflection of Brahman on the one hand, and separate from him on the other. In fact, it is this knowledge and realization that, with God's grace, is the very state of *mokṣa*. For the dependence of the self on God is eternally so, and is intrinsic to each self: the true nature of it just has to be realized. *Bhakti* does not cease in the liberated state: the vision of God is clearer, and the devotion to him becomes even more intense once the full state of *mokṣa* is experienced, along with the full intensity of the relationship with the divine. The self and God at *mokṣa* are dualistically related in communal fellowship in which the individual natures of selves and God are thoroughly maintained, with the former always dependent on the latter. The self has moved closer to God, but does not become God.

Madhva identified three stages in devotion to God – the devotion that precedes indirect and mediate knowledge of God, that which comes after it, and that which occurs with the final and direct realization of the true nature of the self and God. Madhva, then, accepts different modes of *bhakti*, as well as different innate capacities for it, in each *jīva*. At each stage, however, it is God who rewards his devotee by granting the kind of knowledge that will lift that devotee to the next stage. Eventually, God lifts the final veil to full knowledge and liberation.

Those eligible for *mokṣa* are divided into three classes – lowest, middling and highest – depending on their innate propensities for devotion. The lowest class consists of those who study the *Vedas*, but those of the middling class also add the practices of tranquillity and meditation. Those in the highest class are able, in addition, to turn away from the materiality of the physical world and quell their attachments to it through complete devotion to God. Innate characteristics of a particular *jīva* will limit or expand the means by which that *jīva* approaches the divine, the quality of devotion, the nature of the released state, and the quality of the final vision of the divine. Similarly, there are three types of beings that are eligible for the highest goal of liberation – the gods, the sages and the best among men. Thus, just as there are distinctions between individuals in the pluralistic perspective of reality of the world, so such distinctiveness and plurality is maintained in the state of release. Innate distinction in this world necessarily involves gradation in liberation. Alongside the three classes of those eligible for *mokṣa* are three types of grace of God. The lowest brings heaven (not *mokṣa*) for those with good *karma*. The middling brings *Janaloka*, the world of great gods for those who have heard of the true nature of God. The highest brings *mokṣa* for those with the kind of knowledge of God that reveals his true nature and the self as dependent on him.

The devotion of the self to God – as, indeed, all its other actions in life – will reap its appropriate reward through the law of *karma*, and that reward must, therefore, be different for each person when liberated. To expect the gods to have the same quality of experience of liberation as human beings, seemed illogical to Madhva. Generally, the harder path of disciplined devotion and knowledge is only for those with the innate potential for it, and the quality of the liberated experience is greater for those equipped to tread this path. A path of surrender, *prapatti*, to God is much easier, and should not, therefore, reap the same high quality of liberated experience. And since notions of inequality and disparity do not obtain among liberated selves, each is fully satisfied with his or her liberated lot, and is perfect in his or her own fulfilled nature. It is just that each nature, each *svarūpa*, is different.

The gods are the most fervent devotees of God. As his overseers of various functions in the universe, they are mediators of the grace of God and facilitators of the right kinds of devotion amongst the human selves. Because they oversee the activities of mind and intellect, as much as physical functioning of the material world, they can assist *jīvas* on their spiritual path to liberation. In the same way, *gurus* are necessary for those on their spiritual journey. *Gurus*, also, can bestow their grace on their devotees, and without them, personal effort is minimalized.

All kinds of qualities are required for the devotee – purity in all aspects of life;

control of the mind, the desires and the emotions; calmness and equanimity. But, above all, love of God and continuous concentration on him, are essential: thought of God should pervade the whole mind. Morality is also essential, and the obligatory regulations of scripture should be upheld disinterestedly. No individual can be a devotee of God without moral perfection, and all actions done are done morally for God. The *Veda* provides the guidance necessary for such moral perfection, and for the *dharma* that should inform all human behaviour and interaction. But Madhva eschewed animal sacrifice – so prolific in the *Vedas*. Instead, he substituted animals made from flour for sacrificial ceremony.

The paths of *karma*, *jñāna* and *bhakti* are pertinent to different kinds of individuals, and are related to the preponderance of physical, intellectual and emotional balances, respectively, in the human make-up. It is *karma* that causes one to be reborn, unless it is performed without egoistic desire for the fruits of its actions. No one is able to abandon action altogether, but if actions can be performed without desire, with complete devotion to God and with developing knowledge of the truths of the *śāstras*, the scriptures, then one is well on the way to liberation. This suggests that the path of egoless action, *karmamarga*, is not in itself a complete path. It is one aspect of the means to *mokṣa*, one dimension of recognition of the dependency of the self on the divine. Knowledge is far more important in Dvaita, but the combination of knowledge, devotion and selfless action is more the ideal. This is true renunciation of the fruits of actions because the *jīva* has abandoned any sense of independence from God. Every action is offered to God as the only independent Reality through such abandonment of independent agency. But, in the spirit of the *Gītā*, renunciation of life as in the fourth stage of life, *saṃnyāsa*, was not essential to Madhva. His was a theism that supported *active* devotion to God without withdrawal from the world.

Knowledge

Knowledge is crucial to both the path of *bhakti* and the state of liberation: "It should not be supposed that Karma alone is a sufficient means of Mokṣa. For the śrutis clearly say that there is no other (final) way to attain Mokṣa than by Jñāna", said Madhva.[86] At its highest, it is full consciousness of the independent nature of God and the dependence of each self on him. As Sharma neatly writes: "It is not extinction of individual consciousness in Mokṣa but its sublimation in tune with the Infinite"[87] that is the basis of the relationship between the self and the divine. This is ultimate knowledge for the self, and intimates just how important knowledge is in informing the devotional path. It is through study of the scripture (*śravana*), reflection (*manana*), and meditation (*nididhyasana*), that ignorance is overcome. Given the dualism of Dvaita, and the nature of liberation as the continued contemplation on the nature of God in order for continued devotion to take place, consciousness/knowledge never leaves the self: knowledge must always have an object. In the liberated state the sole object of knowledge is God. It is the highest point that each individual *jīva* can reach, though is dependent in quality on the innate inner potential of each one. Knowledge, then, is an ingredient of *bhakti*, and *bhakti* is an ingredient of knowledge. The whole purpose of *bhakti* is to reveal the dependent–independent nature of the self–God relationship, and this presupposes correct knowledge. Madhva interpreted the *śruti* statement "he who knows Brahman becomes Brahman" as knowledge of the transcendence and greatness of Brahman that contrasts with the dependent nature of the self. It is knowledge of the difference between the self and God, the difference between self and world, self and self, world and God, and between self and matter.

Inquiry into the nature of God is, then, essential, and reaps the best rewards through the full measure of God's grace. Knowledge of God is obtainable through the scriptures, and it is a process. It is *jijñāsā* "inquiry", "desire for knowledge", and is the combination, as noted above, of *śravaṇa*, *manana* and *nididhyāsana* – study, reflection and contemplation, respectively. And, as each piece of knowledge of God is obtained, the desire for the next piece occurs. And so knowledge grows, and can only grow, if at each stage the knowledge gained is right. Here, the *sākṣin* has the function of being the final arbiter of the knowledge acquired. But such knowledge will only occur when attachment to other desires in the world is lessened, and it will only occur through the grace of God. The combination of *jijñāsā* and the grace of God, brings the self ultimately to a state of harmony with the will of God.

While *dhyāna* brings the self to the highest point of mental reflection and contemplation, and to a state of knowledge in which God is known in the mind, *ultimate* knowledge, and the final vision of God that transcends mental formation, comes only through God's grace. It is this that brings liberation. It is a direct and immediate realization of what God really is. Because this knowledge *is* ultimate, it is the result of the *fullness* of God's grace. Since there is no mediate way in which this kind of knowledge can be gained, only God can grant it, and it has to be immediate, visionary, intuitive and mystical. And yet the knowledge gained is real, for it is knowledge of the true nature of the self as dependent, and a vision of God as the sole independent Reality. The *bimba–pratibimba* reflection of God in the self becomes fully understood.

Meditation

Despite ultimate knowledge being the final intuitive experience, it is dependent on meditation, *dhyāna*, without which it cannot occur. Meditation, *upāsana*, "is a mental process of absorbed thought in unbroken continuity and with deep attachment to the subject".[88] Madhva believed that the best kind of meditation was that on the *Ātman* within that is identified with the pervading will of Brahman. The *Ātman* is the perfection of the infinite qualities of Brahman. This *Ātman* is not so much the real self, as the immanent Brahman on whom the self depends. The self is only a reflection of this. It is through such meditation on one or more of the qualities[89] of God that the self can become intensely absorbed in the Reality of the divine. Unless such intense meditation occurs, there can be no direct vision of God granted through his grace. According to Madhva:

> Release from Samsāra is possible only through God's grace. It is bestowed on those who have had a direct vision of God. Such vision is vouchsafed to those who have constantly meditated on Him in loving devotion, after going through the discipline of sincere study of Śāstras and cogitation, termed "Jijñāsa", which sets one's doubts at rest, and clears the ground for meditation.[90]

The vision of God is beyond the means of *dhyāna*, but is a result of it. *Dhyāna* is essentially *devotional* meditation in which there is an intense mental vision of God as he is worshipped and adored. It is thus a mental representation of God, of Viṣṇu, that is meditated on here – even though God is essentially formless. Yet Madhva also said: "The Supreme Being should always be meditated upon as 'BRAHMAN' i.e. as the Highest being endowed with infinite attributes and which transcends all."[91] It is the higher direct experience of God that will bring knowledge of the true, formless Brahman, but devotional meditation is the precursor of this. Realization is the goal of meditation. What one meditates on, one comes to know in the fullest sense, but what one comes to know is also that on which one meditates further. However, such realization alongside continued *bhakti* is still incomplete for final release for it needs the grace of God for absolute liberation. Self-realization is impossible in Dvaita Vedānta. For liberation of the Self, God has to grant the appropriate knowledge: "God thus implants in the heart of the devotees all knowledge about Himself and makes them qualified to receive His Divine Grace."[92]

In meditation Brahman is *reflected* in the mind. The real vision of God comes only through his grace: "Tho' He remains unmanifest always, by His own grace He reveals Himself to the Upāsaka, by His own inscrutable power. Without His choosing to reveal Himself in this way, who can ever see Him, the limitless one?"[93] Sharma writes of this direct, immediate knowledge (*aparokṣajñāna*): "It is a flash-like revelation of the Supreme at the fruition of a long and arduous process of *śravaṇa*, *manana*, and *nididhyāsana*, in the fulness of absolute self-surrendering devotion to the Lord, as our Bimba. Ultimately it is He that must choose to reveal Himself, pleased by the hungering love of the soul. The Pratibimba (soul) must turn in and *see his Bimba in himself*."[94]

Bhakti, "emotional sublimation in God",[95] is also expressed in meditative practice, as in every aspect of life. It is essential for God's grace, along with knowledge. There is, thus, an interplay between devotion and knowledge, and both bring the individual devotee to the stage of *dhyāna* that prepares that individual for the direct experience of God. *Bhakti*, although pervasive at every point before and after liberation, is not pre-eminent over knowledge. Narain considers that *bhakti* for Madhva "could not acquire that supreme status as was expected from a doyen of the bhakti-movement".[96] He believes it is inferior to knowledge as the ultimate means to evoke the grace of God. It seems this was echoed by Jayatīrtha. But it seems to me that devotion and knowledge were thoroughly concomitant at all stages, each promoting the other. Madhva explained, "wherever Scripture speaks of Jñāna as the means of release, the inclusion of Bhakti within the sense of the word Jñāna is certainly intended and presupposed. For clearness, sometimes, the two are also separately referred to as means of release".[97] To Madhva *bhakti* is an intensive love of God *combined* with knowledge of him: "The firm and unshakable love of God, which rises above all other ties of love and affection, based upon an adequate knowledge and conviction of His great majesty, is called 'Bhakti'. That alone is the means of Mokṣa."[98] At these higher stages on the path to liberation, there is a surrender of the self to God in the sense of a complete trust in God as the Reality that directs each individual life. The self belongs to God like a shadow to a subject and, while individuality is retained in the liberated relationship with God, it is so subsumed in God as to lack the kind of egoistic individuality that sees the self as agent, as possessor, and as independent.

Bhakti will pervade every stage towards *mokṣa*. According to Madhva: "From Bhakti one reaches (mediate) knowledge, thence again ripe Bhakti, thence vision and thence again very ripe devotion to the Lord. Then comes Mukti (release) and thereby Bhakti again, which is of the essence of bliss and an end in itself."[99] But, again, meditation can only be appropriate to the innate dispositions of each individual. Thus Madhva said: "God is to be meditated upon as all-pervasive by some; as in their heart by others; and externally (in Pratīkas, images etc,) by some others."[100] He also said: "Those who worship thro' rituals in fire and images worship God outwardly; the Ṛṣis meditate upon Him as the Antaryāmī in the heart; and the still higher Adhikāris as the all-pervasive One."[101] However important knowledge and devotion are, only God can remove the final veils of ignorance to grant full liberation: "Because bondage is real it cannot be removed through knowledge. Knowledge may destroy a false appearance caused by ignorance but it cannot remove a real fact. Bondage, according to Madhva, has its cause in the *māyā* of *Īśvara* and as such it is He alone who can exonerate the jīva from its clutches."[102]

Predestination and the grace of God

Since Madhva accepted an innate difference in every individual – an innate difference that would determine how good, evil, or devoted to God each person may be – it stands to reason that not every individual would have the necessary character – more specifically, *viśeṣas* – to be liberated. Further, some are so innately evil, that they are destined for eternal hell. Predestination is, thus, a pronounced feature of Dvaita. This is not to say that every action and thought of each individual are predetermined, but that each individual can act and think only within the limits of his or her innate capacities. Nevertheless, the balance between such predestined determinism and freedom of the self varies in the different sects of the Dvaita school. Those destined for eternal hell are many of the bound selves, other bound selves being eligible for liberation. More certainly destined for hell are beings like demons and ghosts.

The grace (*prasāda*) of God, then, does not extend to those whose innate propensities for evil prevent their ever becoming his devotee. It is an elitist view of liberation.[103] But for those individuals who are devoted to God, reward in the form of God's grace assists them on their path to liberation. Because God is the only independent Reality, he is the only one that can grant such release: anything that is dependent cannot be relied on to do so, either for his own self or for others. The fact that God *does* assist his devotees through his grace is, for Dvaita, the greatest expression of the independent Reality that God is. And such assistance takes the form of granting greater and greater knowledge of God, and of the self as dependent on him. It was only by the grace of God that *anything* – the world, selves, eternal Space and Time – existed. Without the grace of God, liberation is impossible. Potter calls this a "leap philosophy",[104] that is to say knowledge and devotion bring one to the point of realization of the true nature of God, but that leap to the fuller vision of God can come about only because God wills it.

Grace is a response to the love of the devotee for the Lord, it is the reward of knowledge of the self and knowledge of God, and it is the *ultimate* key to liberation. But such grace is mediated. Lakṣmī is one important mediator of God's grace, in as far as her grace is a prerequisite to the grace of Viṣṇu. Vāyu is also a mediator of God's grace by propagation of true knowledge. Madhva believed that he himself was Vāyu, and that he had been the monkey general Hanumān in a past existence.[105] As was seen in the context of causality, however, God's grace operates in the context of *karma*, in the context of the just deserts of each individual. So there is considerable responsibility placed on the individual to procure the grace of God. Such grace reflects the idea in the *Gītā* that, in whatever way people approach God, he responds accordingly. Those who pray for heaven will get it, but those who devote themselves to God in total loving surrender of the self, will achieve the higher goal of the true blissful vision of God. The grace of God is proportionate to the faith of the devotee. Madhva was clear about this: "There is a natural gradation among released souls as also disparity in their Sādhanas. The difference in the nature and quality of Sādhanas must necessarily have a relation to the result. The existence of such a gradation in Mokṣa is established by reason and revelation. How can any one oppose it?"[106] And, again, Madhva said: "Variations in results, in accordance with diversity of means, is inevitable in release."[107] The more logical acceptance of the grace of God operating according to the *karmic* law is, as discussed previously, considerably offset by the fact that many are initially doomed to be devoid of that grace by innate and unchangeable characteristics given originally by God himself.

The nature of mokṣa

There are four states of liberated Selves. From lowest to highest they are:

- *Sālokya* souls living in Vaikuṇṭha the abode of God.
- *Sāmīpya* souls existing in a greater proximity with God in Vaikuṇṭha.
- *Sārūpya* souls gaining such closeness to God in Vaikuṇṭha that they acquire physical likeness to God.
- *Sāyujya* souls experiencing the greatest similarity of enjoyment and bliss to that of God, and that become unified with, though not identical to, him.

The soul that is liberated receives everything as if by the hand of God, walks with the feet of God, and sees through his eyes. The state of *mokṣa* or *mukti* is the arrival at the core of one's own self, the deep innate being that one is. It is a blissful and intoxicating devotional surrender to a God that is now more fully known, and a relationship with that God that is fully dependent. It is a highly positive state of bliss that is rid of the negative dust that hid the divine and brought worldly attachment. Since liberation is a sudden, experiential and intuitive vision granted by the grace of God, it might be expected that Dvaita would accept the *jīvanmukta*, one liberated while still possessing an earthly body. But certainly for most in the Dvaita school the state of *jīvanmukti* is that which precedes the final vision granted by God's grace: it is the devotee that is at the point of final liberation. In this state, there is no distraction by the world of matter, there is no sense of agency of the self and there is complete realization of Viṣṇu as the agent of all action, yet it is not ultimate liberation. This, indeed, is the more sensible view of the *jīvanmukta*, as one still waiting for that final moment of complete release beyond the confines of the physical body, though it is a view of the *jīvanmukta* that contrasts with theories elsewhere. Given Madhva's insistence on the continued observance of ritual, it would seem that he must have conceived of final release as beyond death. Certain *karmas* would, in any case, affect the physical body until it was shed. As Sharma points out, since there is still *karma* to be worked out, that may even take another lifetime.[108] This pre-liberated state, too, is characterized by dreams from past subconscious impressions, unlike dreamless sleep that is indicative of complete rest and release. This stage of *jīvanmukti* Madhva preferred to call *aparokṣajñāna*, immediate knowledge.

In the liberation that comes beyond death, the individual *jīva* has reached the fullness of its own potential for love of, and devotion to, God. The liberated Self acquires its true nature of consciousness (*cit*) and bliss (*ānanda*). Its ignorance is overcome when God removes the veil of *māyā* that allows such ignorance to conceal the truth. There is no need for it to be reborn. Negative *karma* that was in the process of being formed is nullified, but any positive *karma* is added to the measure of the quality of the experience in the liberated state. For the purpose of enjoyment of the positive fruits of one's devotion, the liberated soul is able, if it so wishes, to take on an external form, though it exists normally in a subtle form.

The nature of the released *jīva*, then, is one of blissful relationship with God. Of it, Madhva said: "The worship of the Lord there is an unalloyed bliss in itself. It is not a means to any further end. It is an end in itself and a fulfilment of our selfhood."[109] Meditation on, and devotion to, God are still possible, and the wishes of each self are fulfilled. This presupposes ongoing desires, but whereas such desires are normally associated with *karma*, and any *karma* normally results in continued rebirth, desire that is orientated to, and through, God is acceptable. Presupposed, too, is a retention of the egoistic self, but with an ego that is purified of the taints of involvement with matter. Being at one with God, in harmony with God, the liberated soul desires only that which is God-centred. And since God is of the nature of bliss, such harmony with God is an overwhelming experience of harmony with the bliss that is God. There is no pain, no suffering, no evil, only perpetual pleasure of the experience of bliss. It follows, then, that the released soul is still a *being*, though a subtle one, and is a being characterized by continued consciousness, continued knowledge. Without such consciousness there would be no possibility of experiential release. To Madhva, *śruti* texts that taught the necessity of overcoming desire referred only to the quelling of the desires that are focused on the material world. Desires that are focused on God, however, are actively to be encouraged.

The dual nature of the self and God facilitates the retention of individuality that recognizes that duality and that continues to relate to the divine in devotional love. The emancipated souls always remain different from God. Being once bound, they can never be like God who is never so: they remain limited. But, not only are the liberated souls different from God, as in existence in the world, they are different from each other. Individual differences between selves are very real in the state of liberation in the Dvaita schools. And this is so, not only in the retention of the plurality of liberated selves, but also, as we have seen, in the gradation in the quality of experience of *mokṣa* from one individual to the next. It is a gradation that reflects the differences in the quality and degree of spiritual effort of each individual in the pre-liberated existences. Madhva depicted this graphically:

> Just as vessels of different sizes, the rivers and the Ocean are all "full" of water according to their respective capacities, even so, in respect of the Jīvas, from ordinary human beings to Brahmadeva, their fulness of bliss attained thro' Sādhanas is to be understood with reference to their varying (intrinsic) capacities. The Sādhanas practised by them such as Bhakti, Jñāna etc. are nothing more than an expression of their intrinsic potentialities, which are the core of their being – going back to beginningless eternity. Those with limited capacities are satisfied with limited bliss and those with comparatively greater capacities reach fulfilment with still more.[1104]

Thus, the limitations of the innate nature of each individual follow that individual to liberation, and serve to limit or expand the experience of liberation in the same way that it coloured the bound state. And because different kinds of approaches to God are prescribed for different classes and groups of people, this, too, affects the nature of the released soul. So in liberation "one is perfect according to one's capacity".[111]

Individuality, then, is not lost at liberation. To Madhva, liberation would be meaningless without individual consciousness with which to experience it. His view was that: "Mokṣa would not be worth having, if the ātman does not survive as a self-luminous entity there. For, the ātman is the ultimate goal and target of all desires."[112] There is no need in Dvaita to differentiate between some pure, non-egoistic self and the egoistic personality. The "I", or *aham*, is that which is involved with the world of matter, is that which knows that it has slept dreamlessly, and is that which knows it is liberated. This "I" experiences the bliss of liberation, the pleasures of liberation, and its own particular vision of the divine. It is not so much that ego is lost, but that it is redirected. The "I" comes to know the true nature of itself and of God. It sees all in a different light than it did in the bound state, but it is the same "I" that experiences both. To Madhva, there would be no point in the interminably long aeons of reincarnation if the liberated soul had no consciousness of being at the end of its journey. Not to *know* that one is released makes the goal an unworthy one. So individuality is retained at *mokṣa* and makes the experience of it different for each released soul. With individuality comes individual activity. The theism of the Dvaita system is as devotional in release as it is in the pre-released state. The liberated souls are able to sing praises to God, to adore him, and to worship him in whatever mode they wish. Nothing is obligatory; individuals are free to show their devotion to God in a variety of ways.

Thus we have the dualism of Dvaita. It attempts to answer the problem of the relationship between the finite world and the infinity and absolute nature of the divine by that dualism. God is transcendent, and sufficiently removed from the world as to be beyond human comprehension in his ultimate essence. And yet, such transcendence is combined with a thorough realism that allows God to be known through his qualities. Being thoroughly theistic, God is sufficiently knowable to be an object of intense devotion. The outcome of this devotion brings one to the solution – the dualistic and realistic separate natures of the independent Reality that is God, and the dependent reality that is the world and the selves existing in it – the crux of this dualistic philosophy. It is an uncompromising dualism. Narain considers that, "Madhva has tried to strengthen the defence of theistic tradition by adding new bulwarks at places where it has been weakened by Rāmānuja's compromise with the *advaitin*".[113]

The outstanding contribution of Madhva, and the hallmark of the school, is the doctrine of *viśeṣas*, a doctrine important enough to make sense of its many theories, as well as to appeal to common sense. Narain writes: "But for this category many knotty problems which this school could scant avoid would have been left unsolved and this system would, verily, have been a conglomeration of glittering contradictions."[114] Shanbag, too, says of the doctrine of *viśeṣas*: "The beauty and vitality of this concept are such that it is hardly possible to overlook its place and value to logic and metaphysics."[115] Ultimately, the concept of *viśeṣas* brings us to the most logical perspective of reality that we as human beings can have. We can only be realists and pragmatists, given the nature of our ordinary existences, and Dvaita Vedānta gives full rein to a common-sense view of the nature of things as they are, and God as he should be.

Conclusion

Philosophy can be viewed from two major perspectives: that related to the personal, and that which reaches beyond the personal to the world at large, to the cosmic setting of the world in which we live and have our being. Our immediate perspectives of reality are personal. In Susan Greenfield's words: "What counts is what goes on inside our heads and what happens there is completely personal. It's not so much that our visual system rebuilds the outside world but, rather, that we create from scratch our own private universe, our own reality."[1] Our perspectives of reality, then, are governed a great deal by the kinds of individuals we are, by the lives that we live, the people with whom we share our lives, and so on. But there are many times in life when we are almost forced to look beyond the confines of our own rather myopic view of life and extend it to ponder about the deeper meanings of life. And it is often those greater, sadder, joyous moments that pepper our lives, as well as the life-cycles that life includes, that cause us to pause and reflect on the broader issues of our own humanity.

It is these broader issues with which religious philosophy is concerned, and it is philosophical perspectives of this nature that seek to draw us out of our "private universe" to reflect on deeper concerns. This may occur in the context of one's own culture. But leaving our "private universe" is far more meaningful when we are able to reach out beyond our own cultures to see how others have responded to the deeper questions of life. This need never jeopardize what we feel is valuable about our own cultural ethos, but can enrich and widen our own personal views of what life is about. In the geographical vastness of India, and the long span of accommodated traditions, this kind of sharing of philosophical traditions has been endemic. Its numerous strands reflect different pathways to ultimate perspectives of reality and inevitably have influenced each other. Yet, even here, there has been no real influence from outside India until relatively recently, and what we have in the philosophical views of reality are exclusively Indian views. Such views add invaluable pieces of the jigsaw by which humanity assesses its purpose, its goals and its ultimate fate. They are the Indian answers to fundamental questions about life, worked out in the intricacies of teaching, debate and contemplation over many centuries. Although Hindu philosophy, no more than any other, does not have the ultimate answers, it provides perspectives that contribute superbly to our overall inquiries about life, adding to the many brush strokes that help to paint clearer views on the canvas that is life.

From the perspective of ordinary mortals there can never be one *ultimate* Truth. The best we can ever hope for are approximations of reality. The Hindu *darśanas* reflect this very clearly, as do the Hindu scriptures. They provide very different philosophies about what is ultimately real: truth is variously conceived of. One thing, however, is certain. Each school seeks to lift the self from its egoistic and self-centred view of life, suggesting that there is a level to the self that is beyond its "private universe". Each school also tries to reach out to the metaphysical realities that are by nature difficult to confine and convey in ordinary language. Bahadur wrote of this difficulty:

> Philosophical knowledge is beyond name and form (*nama* and *rupa*) which are the basis of the manifest world. It is an excursion into the world of the unknown, and tries to explain the unseen which is beyond the field of ordinary experience. Yet it must use the written word, which indeed is the only medium of communication between the writer and the reader. Herein lies its difficulty. To explain what is abstract and beyond experience by concrete words, is not easy."[2]

Despite the constraints of language, the search for what is real was seen as important because it seemed the only way that the human being could transcend the egoism of the individual world for a more cosmic perspective. Very often, this was a soteriological quest. As Eliade points out: "It is not the possession of truth that is the supreme end of the Indian sage; it is liberation, the conquest of absolute freedom."[3]

Such is the nature and depth of Indian philosophy that it is a privilege to inherit the immense legacy of thought and erudition of its great thinkers past and present. It is fortunate that Hinduism is so accommodating in its accepting of different traditions. For it is in this way that the differing perspectives of reality have been allowed to blossom, rather than having been assimilated by a more ruthless desire for homogeneity of tradition and practice. It comes as something of a surprise to those who encounter Hinduism for the first time that its analysis of the human self, its soteriology, and particularly its concepts of the divine, can reach such depths. A Roman Catholic student recently remarked to me how much her life and perspective of God had been enriched by her study of Rāmānuja. "I love it! I love it! I love it!" were the words that expressed her study of this particular school of Hindu thought. The student's response demonstrates all too well how relevant inquiry into the ideas of these old philosophers can be in the modern context. Indeed, who can but be impressed at the breadth and depth of the concept of divinity as expressed in the Viśiṣṭādvaita school?

The great advantage of the study of these different responses to life and reality lies in its aids to personal evolution. To lose the self, one has to first know the self. And to expand the self, one has to broaden its horizons. In terms of human existence, and in the words of Feuerstein: "We can either become congealed on one particular level, or we can broaden out and learn to master other sectors of this enormous keyboard, to explore the different dimensions of reality, or at least open ourselves to them."[4]

Notes

Introduction

1 S. Chatterjee and D. Datta, *An Introduction to Indian Philosophy* (Calcutta: University of Calcutta, 1984 reprint of 1939 edn), p. 1.

1 B. N. K. Sharma, *Philosophy of Srī Madhvācārya* (Delhi: Motilal Banarsidass, 1991 reprint of 1986 revised edn), p. 3.

3 In order to differentiate between Reality as *sat* and ordinary reality (*asat*), I shall use the upper case for the former – *R*eality – throughout the text.

4 The knowing subject of valid knowledge is termed the *pramātā*, and the object of valid knowledge, the *prameya*.

5 Sharma, *Philosophy of Śrī Madhvācārya*, p. 5.

6 For an excellent overview of ontology in western and eastern contexts, see W. Halbfass, *On Being and What There Is: Classical Vaiśeṣika and the History of Indian Ontology* (Albany, New York: State University of New York Press, 1992), chapters 1–3 and *passim*.

Chapter 1 *Types of belief*

1 P. A. Bertocci, "Theism" in M. Eliade (ed.), *The Encyclopedia of Religion* (hereafter *ER*), vol. 14 (New York: Macmillan, 1987), pp. 421–7.

2 Ontological arguments for proof of the existence of God originate with the great churchman and scholar Saint Anselm (*c.*1033–1109). He claimed that we can conceive of nothing greater than God. Whether we believe this or not, we still *understand*, and have a conception of the nature of God as greater than anything we can think of. But if we cannot think of anything greater than God, then he must exist, otherwise we *would* be able to think of something greater than God – an *existing* God. So God must also have existence as his nature. Further, since we *are* able to conceive of such a being, and cannot have a conception of a non-existent being, then he must exist. Lacking no attributes, then he is bound to have the attribute of existence.

3 Cosmological arguments for the existence of God are concerned with causes and their effects. Because everything we experience has a cause or event that brings it about we can trace things back to their causes. But in this case there must be some *ultimate* cause which caused all other causes and there must also be a *first* cause, because otherwise there can be no succession of causes, no second one, third one, and so on. And when we look at the world we can see results from successive causes. It is this first cause that is said to be God.

4 Teleological proofs for the existence of God are arguments based on the observation of the

ordered patterns of existence that conform to certain natural laws, and that seem to have some sort of pattern of motion and change that leads to a purposeful outcome. Acorns, for example, always grow into oak trees and not any other trees. So everything has a purpose to which it moves, and this is characteristic of all matter. But if all matter is moving towards some purposeful outcome, then there must be a reason why this happens and that reason cannot itself be changing and altering towards its ultimate goal. Aristotle, the Greek philosopher associated with this particular metaphysical argument, posited an Unmoved Mover as the ultimate goal to which all was moving. Although it does not itself change or move, and though it is not involved in the world, the Unmoved Mover is the non-material to which all aspires but can never reach or become. Later developments on the Aristotelian metaphysics accepted the Ummoved Mover as the Creator-Architect of the world. Teleological arguments for the existence of God are closely aligned with arguments to design. The orderliness and interrelatedness of all aspects of the created world are stressed, as well as the similarity of causes and their effects. Since the world displays a degree of design that surpasses anything the human being can equal, even though human wisdom, intellect and ingenuity are considerable, there must be an intelligent God who is the cause of the order and design in the natural world.

5 P. Quinn and C. Taliafero (eds), *A Companion to Philosophy of Religion* (Oxford: Blackwell, 1997), p. 2.

6 W. J. Wainwright, "Christianity" in Quinn and Taliafero, *ibid.*, p. 58.

7 C. Evans, "Moral Arguments", in Quinn and Taliafero, *ibid.*, p. 345.

8 See T. Ludwig, "Monotheism" in *ER*, vol. 10, p. 69.

9 *Ibid.*

10 *Ibid.*, p. 73.

11 The presence of the *ātman*, the divine, in all things is fundamental to much Hindu philosophy and metaphysics and makes the self an integral part of divinity or even makes the self identical to the divine. The world, however, is sometimes considered as a part of divinity, also, but can be designated as illusory. This will become clear in the analysis of the schools of philosophical thought.

12 This is sometimes called *dualistic monotheism.*

13 R. J. Zwi Werblowsky, "Polytheism" in *ER*, vol. 11, p. 436.

14 *Ibid.*

15 *Ibid.*, p. 439.

16 A. Daniélou, *The Myths and Gods of India* (Rochester, Vermont: Inner Traditions International, 1991, first published under the title *Hindu Polytheism* by Bollingen Foundation, New York, 1964), p. 5.

17 *Ibid.*, p. 7.

18 Werblowsky, "Polytheism" in *ER*, vol. 11, p. 438.

19 *Ibid.*

20 The concept of *prakṛti* exists in the *Bhagavadgītā* as the manifest aspect of Brahman. In the theophany of chapter 11, Kṛṣṇa as the manifestation of Brahman on earth gives Arjuna the experience of the divine eye, which reveals how manifest existence is subsumed in Kṛṣṇa: "Behold my forms, Pārtha, by hundreds and by thousands, of various kinds, divine, and of various colours and shapes, says Kṛṣṇa in verse 5. Here, since all phenomena are manifestations of Brahman, there is no end to the diversity contained by the cosmic entity of Brahman. In verse 7 Kṛṣṇa speaks of "this whole universe centred in one, with the moving and unmoving in my body". There is certainly much pantheistic expression here, and the *Gītā* illustrates well how the changeability of the finite world need not compromise the absolute nature of the divine. Although there is much pantheistic thought in the *Gītā*, the overall impression, I feel is,

nevertheless, one of panentheism. In contrast, the philosophical school of Sāṃkhya, which developed the theory of *prakṛti*, had no concept of an Absolute at all.

21 William Wordsworth "The Prelude": Book 2, lines 400–409 *The Works of William Wordsworth* (The Wordsworth Poetry Library, Hertfordshire: Wordsworth Editions Limited, 1994), p. 648.

22 "Lines Composed a Few Miles above Tintern Abbey, on Revisiting the Banks of the Wye during a Tour", *ibid.*, p. 207.

23 "Essence", I suggest, is much stronger than immanence, the latter term being more applicable to theism than pantheism, which sees the divine identified with the world in a much more powerful and dynamic way than the word immanence can suggest.

24 For an excellent discussion of Hartshorne's view, and of pantheism and panentheism in general, see his article "Pantheism and Panentheism" in *ER*, vol. 11, pp. 165–71.

25 See, for example Wayne Grudem, *Systematic Theology: An Introduction to Biblical Doctrine* (Leicester: Inter-Varsity Press, 1994), p. 268. Grudem's view is a very western and confessionalist perspective of pantheism.

26 Hartshorne, "Pantheism and Panentheism" in *ER*, vol. 11, p. 166.

27 Cf., for example, some aspects of Sufism, the mystical element of Islam. As a western type of belief, deism would be dualistic but not theistic.

28 R. Goring (ed.), *Larousse Dictionary of Beliefs and Religions* (Edinburgh: Larousse, 1994, first published 1992), p. 407.

29 R. A. McDermott, "Monism" in *ER*, vol. 10, p. 57.

30 *Ibid.*

31 Such as G. W. F. Hegel in the West and Sarvepalli Radhakrishnan in the East.

32 Goring, *Larousse Dictionary of Beliefs and Religions*, p. 346.

33 So McDermott, "Monism" in *ER*, vol. 10, p. 60.

34 Lao-tzu, *Tao Te Ching*, 2:42. Translated by Gia-fu Feng and Jane English (New York: Vintage Books, 1989, first published 1972).

35 The two refers to *yin* and *yang*; the three refers to the result of the harmony of *yin* and *yang*; the ten thousand things represent all existence.

36 Daniélou, *The Myths and Gods of India*, pp. 6–7.

Chapter 2 *Veda*

1 S. Dasgupta, *A History of Indian Philosophy, Vol. 1* (Delhi: Motilal Banarsidass, 1997, first published 1922), p. 12.

2 See M. Hiriyanna, *The Essentials of Indian Philosophy* (Delhi: Motilal Banarsidass, 1995), p. 9, also K. P. Bahadur, *The Wisdom of Upanishads* (New Delhi: Sterling Publishers Private Limited, 1989), p. 1, who believes that the *Ṛg Veda* dates back to 3000 BCE, making it the oldest literature in the world.

3 M. Hiriyanna, *Outlines of Indian Philosophy* (Delhi: Motilal Banarsidass, 1993), p. 36.

4 Hiriyanna, *Essentials of Indian Philosophy*, p. 17.

5 Dasgupta, *A History of Indian Philosophy, Vol. 1*, p. 22.

6 Strictly speaking, the Sanskrit term for the priestly class is *Brāhmaṇa*. But since this is also the term for a commentary on a *Saṃhitā* or *Veda*, and might be confusing for the reader, I shall retain the anglicized and better-known transliteration, *Brahmin*, for a priest/the priestly class.

7 The *Atharva Veda* and its associated traditions are probably an exception here since it is the latest of the *Vedas*, see P. Olivelle, *Upaniṣads* (Oxford and New York: Oxford University Press, 1996), p. xxx, note 11.

8 See Dasgupta, *A History of Indian Philosophy, Vol. 1*, p. 26.
9 *Ibid.*, p. 17.
10 Hiriyanna, *Outlines of Indian Philosophy*, p. 38.
11 *Ṛg Veda* 1:164:46, translator R. T. H. Griffith, *The Hymns of the Ṛgveda* (Delhi: Motilal Banarsidass, 1991 reprint of 1973 new, revised edn), p. 113.
12 A. L. Basham, *The Wonder that was India* (London: Sidgwick and Jackson, 1982 reprint of 1967 third revised edn), p. 235.
13 *Ṛg Veda* 8:10:2, translator Griffith, *The Hymns of the Ṛgveda*, p. 470.
14 *Śatapatha Brāhmaṇa* V i 2: 10 and 13.
15 *Ṛg Veda* 10: 121: 1–4, translator Griffith, *The Hymns of the Ṛgveda*, p. 628.
16 *Ibid.*, verse 7.
17 *Ṛg Veda* 10:90, 1–4, translator Griffith, *The Hymns of the Ṛgveda*, p. 602.
18 S. Radhakrishnan, *The Principal Upaniṣads* (New Delhi: Indus, 1994, first published in 1953), p. 39.
19 Basham, *The Wonder that was India*, p. 247.
20 *Ibid.*, pp. 247–8.
21 Suggested by Radhakrishnan, *The Principal Upaniṣads*, p. 35.
22 Hiriyanna, *Outlines of Indian Philosophy*, p. 42.
23 C. Sharma, *A Critical Survey of Indian Philosophy* (Delhi: Motilal Banarsidass, 1994 reprint of 1960 edn), p. 16.
24 A rare occasion when pure pantheism might obtain is to be found in *Ṛg Veda* 1:89:10, which features Aditī the mother of the Ādityas. "Aditī is the heaven, Aditī is mid-air, Aditī is the Mother and the Sire and Son. Aditī is all Gods, Aditī five-classed men, Aditī all that hath been born and shall be born." Translator Griffith, *The Hymns of the Ṛgveda*, p. 57.
25 Dasgupta, *A History of Indian Philosophy, Vol. 1*, p. 13.
26 1:3:28, translator Radhakrishnan, *The Principal Upaniṣads*, p. 162.
27 Against this view see Dasgupta, *A History of Indian Philosophy, Vol. 1*, p. 52, where he suggests that the fact that deities such as *Viśvakarman* and *Hiraṇyagarbha* as well as *Puruṣa* were not discussed and developed in the *Upaniṣads* indicates that the monotheistic trends of the *Vedas* were not taken up in them and that the *Upaniṣads* are more distinctively separate from the *Vedas*. This kind of reasoning tends to follow the acceptance of an incomplete monotheism in the *Vedic* period, a flowering of which might be expected in later thought. But we do not get a move to full-blown monotheism in the *Vedānta*; *Vedic* monotheism went as far as it needed to, the monism of the *Upaniṣads* is the logical outcome.
28 Olivelle, *Upaniṣads*, p. xxxvi.
29 *Ibid.*
30 R. N. Dandekar, "Vedānta" in M. Eliade (ed.), *The Encyclopedia of Religion* (hereafter *ER*), vol. 15 (New York: Macmillan, 1987), p. 208.
31 A. Daniélou, *The Myths and Gods of India* (Rochester USA: Inner Traditions International, 1991 reprint of 1985 edn), p. 5. See also A. Shearer and P. Russell, *The Upanishads* (New York: Harper and Row, 1978), p. 11.
32 P. Deussen, *The Philosophy of the Upanishads* (New Delhi: Oriental Books Reprint Corporation, second edn 1979, first published 1906), pp. 10–15.
33 Dasgupta, *A History of Indian Philosophy, Vol. 1*, p. 43.
34 *Ibid.*, p. 7.
35 Olivelle, *Upaniṣads*, p. lvi.
36 E. Gough, *The Philosophy of the Upanishads: Ancient Indian metaphysics* (New Delhi: Cosmo, 1979), p. 38.

37 See J. C. Heesterman, "Brahman" in *ER*, vol. 2, p. 295.
38 Radhakrishnan, *The Principal Upaniṣads*, p. 53.
39 Sharma, *A Critical Survey of Indian Philosophy*, p. 29.
40 Radhakrishnan, *The Principal Upaniṣads*, p. 73.
41 *Ibid.*
42 W. Halbfass, *On Being and What There Is: Classical Vaiśeṣika and the History of Indian Ontology* (Albany, New York: State University of New York Press, 1992), p. 26.
43 *Chāndogya Upaniṣad* 6:1:3, translator Radhakrishnan, *The Principal Upaniṣads*, p. 446.
44 *Ibid.*, 6:12:2,3, translator Radhakrishnan, *ibid.*, p. 462.
45 Radhakrishnan, *ibid.*, p. 90.
46 Sharma, *A Critical Survey of Indian Philosophy*, p.19.
47 *Kaṭha Upaniṣad*, 1:2:23.
48 Radhakrishnan, *The Principal Upaniṣads*, p. 92.
49 See Hiriyanna, *Outlines of Indian Philosophy*, p. 63.
50 *Bhagavadgītā*, 7:12–15.
51 S. Chatterjee and D. Datta, *An Introduction to Indian Philosophy* (Calcutta: University of Calcutta, 1984), pp. 21–22.
52 Radhakrishnan, *Indian Philosophy, Vol. 2* (Delhi: Oxford University Press, 1994 impression, first published 1923), p. 22.
53 *Ibid.*, pp. 22–23.
54 T. Bernard, *Hindu Philosophy* (Delhi: Motilal Banarsidass, 1981 reprint of 1947 edn), p. 4.
55 Dasgupta, *A History of Indian Philosophy, Vol. 1*, p. 8.
56 Chatterjee and Datta, *An Introduction to Indian Philosophy*, p. 4.

Chapter 3 *Pūrva Mīmāṃsā*

1 T. Bernard, *Hindu Philosophy* (Delhi: Motilal Banarsidass, 1981 reprint of 1947 edn), p. 103.
2 A. B. Keith, *The Karma-Mīmāṃsā* (New Delhi: Oriental Books Reprint Corporation, second edn 1978, first published 1921), p. 97.
3 C. Sharma, *A Critical Survey of Indian Philosophy* (Delhi: Motilal Banarsidass, 1994 reprint of 1960 edn), p. 211. Compare the meaning suggested by S. Chatterjee and D. Datta as "solution of some problem by reflection and critical examination", *An Introduction to Indian Philosophy* (Calcutta: University of Calcutta, 1984 reprint of 1939 edn), p. 316.
4 F. X. Clooney, *Thinking Ritually: Rediscovering the Pūrva Mīmāṃsā of Jaimini* (Vienna: Publications of the De Nobili Research Library Vol. XVII general ed. G. Oberhammer, 1990), p. 19.
5 See B. K. Matilal, "Mīmāṃsā" in M. Eliade (ed.), *The Encyclopedia of Religion* (hereafter *ER*, New York: Macmillan, 1987), vol. 9, p. 537.
6 A third school, whose writings have not survived seems to be evident: see S. Radhakrishnan, *Indian Philosophy, Vol. 2* (Delhi: Oxford University Press, 1994 impression, first published 1923), p. 378.
7 See Radhakrishnan, *Indian Philosophy, Vol. 2*, p. 376, S. Dasgupta, *A History of Indian Philosophy Vol. 1* (Delhi, Mumbai, Chennai, Calcutta, Bangalore, Varanasi, Patna, Pune: Motilal Banarsidass, 1997 reprint, first published 1922), p. 370, and M. Gaṇgānātha Jhā, *The Prābhākara School of Pūrva Mīmāṃsā* (Delhi: Motilal Banarsidass, 1978, first published 1911), p. 7.
8 See Bernard, *Hindu Philosophy*, p. 113.
9 See Keith, *The Karma-Mīmāṃsā*, p. 9.
10 See M. Hiriyanna, *Outlines of Indian Philosophy* (Delhi: Motilal Banarsidass, 1993), p. 302.

11 It was, in fact, Prabhākara's major commentator, Śālikanātha, who is credited with rescuing Prabhākara's works from obscurity. See G. P. Bhatt, "Mīmāṃsā as a Philosophical System: A survey" in R. C. Dwivedi (ed.), *Studies in Mīmāṃsā* (Delhi: Motilal Banarsidass, 1994), p. 12.

12 Bhatt, *ibid.*, p. 9.

13 See Radhakrishnan, *Indian Philosophy, Vol. 2*, pp. 377–8.

14 See Bernard, *Hindu Philosophy*, p. 114, and Bhatt, "Mīmāṃsā as a Philosophical System" p. 9.

15 Bhatt, *ibid.*, p. 6.

16 Clooney, *Thinking Ritually*, pp. 152–4.

17 *Ibid.*, p. 155.

18 M. Gaṇgānātha Jhā (translator), *The Sacred Books of the Hindus, Vol. X: The Pūrva Mimāmsā Sūtras of Jaimini (Chapters 1–111)* (Allahabad: Sudhīndranātha Vasu, 1916), *Adhikaraṇa* 11 *Sūtra* 2, p. 4.

19 A word better translated as "classes".

20 W. Halbfass, *Studies in Kumārila and Śaṅkara*. Studien zur Indologie und Iranistik, monograph 9 (Reinbeck: Orientalistiche Fachpublikationen, 1983), pp. 16–17.

21 Kumārila, *Ślokavārtika* 79, translator M. Ganganatha Jha, *Pūrva-Mīmāṃsā in its Sources* (Varanasi: The Banaras Hindu University, second edn 1964, first published 1942), p. 52.

22 Keith, *The Karma-Mīmāṃsā*, p. 44.

23 In any case, Kumārila pointed out, even Buddhist argumentation needs a subject and an object to make sense, and if the object is unreal, then there can be no differentiated subject and, so, no argument.

24 Hiriyanna claims that for Kumārila, such particles are divisible, for Kumārila rejects an atomic theory of basic substances. However, without basic elemental and indivisible particles, it is difficult to see how a theory of identity underlying change and difference can be maintained. See M. Hiriyanna, *The Essentials of Indian Philosophy* (Delhi: Motilal Banarsidass, 1995), p. 132, and the section below on Causality.

25 Dasgupta, *A History of Indian Philosophy, Vol. 1*, p. 12.

26 Sharma, *A Critical Survey of Indian Philosophy*, p. 225.

27 J. A. Taber, "Kumārila's Refutation of the Dreaming Argument: The *Nirālmbanavāda-adhikaraṇa*" in Dwivedi (ed.), *Studies in Mīmāṃsā*, p. 44.

28 Gaṇgānātha Jhā, *The Prābhākara School of Pūrva Mīmāṃsā*, p. 22.

29 This is not far from present neuro-scientific views of the way the brain operates. In a recent BBC television documentary, Professor Susan Greenfield stated: "Once we've named an object we don't normally need to take the recognition task any further and so a more basic part of the brain is used. But even with all these specialized systems working away, the brain would be overloaded if it tried to tackle every detail of every object at once. So we just don't bother: we're all equipped with a means of selecting the key aspects of a scene one at a time. This attention system allows us to concentrate on one thing while the rest of the world falls into the background." *Brain Story* 1 August 2000.

30 Gaṇgānātha Jhā, *The Prābhākara School of Pūrva Mīmāṃsā*, p. 35.

31 Radhakrishnan, *Indian Philosophy, Vol. 2*, p. 387.

32 Sharma, *A Critical Survey of Indian Philosophy*, p. 220.

33 *Pāda* 2, *Adhikaraṇa* 1, *Sūtra* 7. See M. Gaṇgānātha Jhā, *The Sacred Books of the Hindu, Vol. X: The Pūrva Mimāmsā Sūtras of Jaimini.*

34 *Adhikaraṇa* V, *Sūtra* 5, translator Gaṇgānātha Jhā, *ibid.*

35 Clooney, *Thinking Ritually*, pp. 133, 134.

36 In Sanskrit each letter carries with it the vowel sound *a*, which is pronounced as the *u* in *but.* This is why so many Sanskrit words have a number of *a*s, for example, *Mahābhārata.* This means that each letter is also a syllable – *Ma ha bha ra ta.*

37 It is Francis Clooney's thesis, however, that, in so far as Jaimini's *Sūtras* is concerned, there is no profound anthropocentrism. The individual is "simply one element in a much broader network of values and connections". *Thinking Ritually*, p. 163. Clooney's claim is that Jaimini "decentred" the human.

38 Keith, *The Karma-Mīmāṃsā*, p. 65.

39 *Ibid.*, p. 91.

40 *Adhiyāya* VI, *Pāda* I, *Adhikaraṇa* 3, see Gaṇgānātha Jhā (translator), *Shabara-Bhāṣya* Vol. 2 (Baroda: Oriental Institute, 1934, Gaekwad's Oriental Series no. LXX. General editor B. Bhattacharya), p. 977.

41 *Ibid.*, p. 981.

42 *Adhiyāya* VI, *Pāda* I, *Adhikaraṇa* 6, *ibid.*

43 Kumārila, *Ślokavārtika*, *Ātma* 73, translator Jha, *Pūrva-Mīmāṃsā in its Sources*, p. 29.

44 Kumārila, *Nyāyaratnākara*, translator Jha, *ibid.*

45 Chatterjee and Datta, *An Introduction to Indian Philosophy*, p. 338.

46 Clooney, *Thinking Ritually*, p. 145.

47 Hiriyanna, *The Essentials of Indian Philosophy*, p. 147.

48 Chatterjee and Datta, *An Introduction to Indian Philosophy*, p. 334.

49 Prabhākara preferred the term *niyoga*, which means "prompting" – namely, the *Vedic* prompting of an *individual* to correct action. It is this action/cause that brings about the appropriate result. See Gaṇgānātha Jhā, *The Prābhāraka School of Pūrva Mīmāṃsā*, pp. 163–4. There can be no cause– effect without the individual. Gaṇgānātha Jhā likens the relationship between *niyoga* and result as "similar to that between the master and the servant: without the servant the master cannot be a true "master," (*sic*) and yet it is the master that is the more important of the two" (p. 164).

50 S. Radhakrishnan and C. A. Moore (eds), *A Sourcebook in Indian Philosophy* (Princeton, New Jersey: Princeton University Press, 1989, first published 1957), p. 486.

51 *Ibid.*, p. 496. It is likely that for both Jaimini and Prabhākara *apūrva* was not as developed as it became with Śabara and Kumārila. As *apūrva* became increasingly more important, it is Clooney's claim that there is a "devaluation of the action of the sacrifice" (*Thinking Ritually*, p. 223). He points out that, as far as *apūrva* is concerned, "Jaimini nowhere uses the word to refer to the unseen result which bridges the gap between the end of the sacrifice and the still future intended result" (*ibid.*, p. 235). In short, *apūrva* is less of a transcendent reality for Jaimini. This is not so in the case of Śabara and Kumārila where, since the *apūrva* is located in the self, the *ātman* of the individual, there is a more obvious connection with action and its distant fruit(s). Kumārila, indeed, applies equivalent potencies of *apūrva* more widely in the context of secular activity, rather than confine it to *Vedic* ritual.

52 See Dasgupta, *A History of Indian Philosophy, Vol. 1*, p. 72.

53 Radhakrishnan, *Indian Philosophy, Vol. 2*, p. 422.

54 P. T. Raju, "Activism in Indian Thought" in Dwivedi (ed.), *Studies in Mīmāṃsā*, p. 138.

55 *Ibid.*, pp. 138–9.

56 *Ibid.*, p. 145.

57 Halbfass, *Studies in Kumārila and Śaṅkara*, p. 17.

58 For an excellent account of this, see P. S. Sharma's article, "Kumārila Bhaṭṭa's denial of creation and dissolution of the world" in Dwivedi (ed.), *Studies in Mīmāṃsā*, pp. 53–67.

59 Hiriyanna, *Outlines of Indian Philosophy*, p. 324.

60 Radhakrishnan, *Indian Philosophy, Vol. 2*, p. 428.

61 Radhakrishnan and Moore, *A Sourcebook in Indian Philosophy*, p. 486.

62 *Ibid.*, pp. 498–503.

63 See K. S. Murty, *Philosophy in India: Traditions, teachings and research* (New Delhi: Indian Council of Philosophical Research and Delhi: Motilal Banarsidass, 1985), p. 39.
64 Chatterjee and Datta, *An Introduction to Indian Philosophy*, p. 339.
65 *Ibid.*, p 342.
66 See Raju, "Activism in Indian thought", p. 152.
67 *Shabara-Bhāṣya*, *Adhiyāya* VI, *Pāda* I, *Adhikaraṇa* 1, translator Gaṇgānātha Jhā.
68 Kumārila, *Ślokavārtika* (*Sambandhākṣepa-parihāra* 108–10), translator Jha, *Pūrva-Mīmāṃsā in its Sources*, p. 32.
69 See Hiriyanna, *Outlines of Indian Philosophy*, p. 300.
70 Raju, "Activism in Indian thought", pp. 131–2. Compare Clooney's point here: "The science of Mīmāṃsā exegesis developed unhampered, but the philosophy of Mīmāṃsā became more and more like that of the Vedānta, a borrowed metaphysics of self and other permanent realities, uneasily juxtaposed with the older ritual values embodied in the bulk of the Sūtra text and its commentaries" (*Thinking Ritually*, p. 252).
71 Halbfass, *Studies in Kumārila and Śaṅkara*, p. 16.
72 *Ibid.*, p. 18.
73 Dwivedi, *Studies in Mīmāṃsā*, p. xi.

Chapter 4 *Vaiśeṣika*

1 K. H. Potter, *Encyclopedia of Indian Philosophies, Vol. II: The tradition of Nyāya-Vaiśeṣika up to Gaṅgeśa* Delhi: Motilal Banarsidass, 1995 reprint of 1977 edn), p. 1.
2 For a concise critique of this and other suggestions for the meaning of the name of the school, see W. Halbfass, *On Being and What There Is: Classical Vaiśeṣika and the history of Indian ontology* (Albany, New York: State University of New York Press, 1992), Appendix 2 "The Concept of *Viśeṣa* and the Name of the Vaiśeṣika System", pp. 269–73.
3 S. Mookerji, "Nyāya-Vaiśeṣika" in H. Bhattacharyya (ed.), *The Cultural Heritage of India: Vol. 3 The Philosophies* (Calcutta: The Ramakrishna Mission Institute of Culture, 1953 revised and enlarged 2nd edn, first published 1937), p. 91.
4 *Ibid.*, p. 93.
5 For this date of the amalgamation of the two schools see A. Hiltebeitel, "Hinduism" in M. Eliade, *The Encyclopedia of Religion* (hereafter *ER*, London and New York: Macmillan, 1987), vol. 6, p. 346. Others, however, put the formal combining of the two schools much later. See, for example, M. Hiriyanna, *Outlines of Indian Philosophy* (Delhi: Motilal Banarsidass, 1993, first Indian edn), p. 225.
6 Potter, *Encyclopedia of Indian Philosophies, Vol. II*, p. 12.
7 M. Hiriyanna, *The Essentials of Indian Philosophy* (Delhi: Motilal Banarsidass, 1995), p. 84.
8 Vaiśeṣika has certain affinities with the school of Pūrva Mīmāṃsā, in particular its pluralistic and realistic world-view. See S. Dasgupta, *A History of Indian Philosophy, Vol. 1* (Delhi, Mumbai, Chennai, Calcutta, Bangalore, Varanasi, Patna, Pune: Motilal Banarsidass, 1997 reprint of 1922 edn), p. 285.
9 See P. T. Raju, *The Philosophical Traditions of India* (Delhi: Motilal Banarsidass, 1998 reprint of 1992 edn), p. 143, who dates the alleged author of the *Vaiśeṣikasūtras*, Kaṇāda, to this date.
10 See K. K. Chakrabarti, "Vaiśeṣika" in *ER*, vol. 15, p. 167.
11 See H. Zimmer, *Philosophies of India* (Princeton, New Jersey: Princeton University Press, 1989 reprint of 1969 edn), p. 608.
12 See S. Radhakrishnan and C. A. Moore (eds), *A Sourcebook in Indian Philosophy* (Princeton, New

Jersey: Princeton University Press, 1989 reprint of 1957 edn), p. 386, who suggest a date after 300 BCE, A. Hiltebeital, "Hinduism" *ER*, vol. 6, p. 346, who suggests a date for the *Sūtras* as somewhere between 200–100 BCE, and Dasgupta, *A History of Indian Philosophy, Vol. 1*, who suggested a date before 80 CE.

13 Potter, *Encyclopedia of Indian Philosophies, Vol. II*, p. 211.

14 Another legend suggests that as an ascetic, he used to survive on the grains he gathered from the fields – hence an alternative meaning for his name as "grain-eater", "particle eater".

15 Potter, *Encyclopedia of Indian Philosophies, Vol. II*, p. 211.

16 E. Frauwallner, *History of Indian Philosophy, Part 2* (Delhi, Varanasi, Patna: Motilal Banarsidass, 1984 reprint of 1973 edn), p. 3.

17 T. R. V. Murti, *Studies in Indian Thought: Collected Papers of Prof. T. R. V. Murti*, edited by H. G. Coward (Delhi: Motilal Banarsidass, 1996 reprint of 1983 edn), p. 136.

18 Halbfass, *On Being and What There Is*, p. 48.

19 *Ibid.*, p. 57.

20 Frauwallner, *A History of Indian Philosophy, Part 2*, p. 56.

21 S. Radhakrishnan, *Indian Philosophy, Vol. 2* (Delhi, Bombay, Calcutta, Madras: Oxford University Press, 1994 impression, first published 1923), p. 229.

22 *Ibid.*, p. 239.

23 See Dasgupta, *A History of Indian Philosophy, Vol. 1*, p. 350.

24 C. Sharma, *A Critical Survey of Indian Philosophy* (Delhi: Motilal Banarsidass, 1994 reprint of 1960 edn), p. 176.

25 Halbfass, *On Being and What There Is*, p. 93.

26 See Sharma, *A Critical Survey of Indian Philosophy*, p. 177. Ether might normally be expected to be an immaterial, non-physical substance, and is often depicted as such elsewhere. However, as the medium for sound, which is perceptible to the senses, it could be argued that it needs a physical nature for this to occur, corresponding to the other material, elemental substances that are the medium for perceptible knowledge via the sense organs.

27 Radhakrishnan, *Indian Philosophy, Vol. 2*, pp. 197–8.

28 BBC television broadcast, 1998.

29 Interestingly, neuroscientists today have established that people suffering from brain damage to specific parts of the brain can recognize all the *parts*, say, of a human face, but not the *whole* face. As a result, identifying the whole – the face – becomes impossible: only the parts are seen. Also interesting is the discovery that people who cannot decode sense impressions to provide a sensible view of the visual world are helped by the memory of *universals* to function in life. Expansive blueness, for example, will suggest the sky, a lake or the sea. Sky-ness, lake-ness and sea-ness are retained in the memory and recalled even though the brain cannot decode visual perception of such objects. (*Brain Story*, part 1, BBC television series, 1st August 2000).

30 So Theos Bernard, *Hindu Philosophy* (Delhi, Varanasi, Patna: Motilal Banarsidass, 1981 reprint of 1947 edn), p. 48.

31 Radhakrishnan, *Indian Philosophy, Vol. 2*, p. 235.

32 Relevant here might be the nature of qualities as *new* effects, for this suggests that substances can, at some points, be devoid of qualities. "A quality comes to reside only in that substance which has no quality as yet. The atom of earth, when being cooked, loses its qualities and remains without any quality. Therefore, a new quality produced by cooking comes to reside in it. Qualities and motions have no qualities." Summary of *Vaiśeṣikasūtras* VII:i:12–14, translator Masaaki Hattori, in Potter, *Encyclopedia of Indian Philosophies, Vol. II*, p. 218.

33 Halbfass, *On Being and what There Is*, p. 55.

34 The Self here, the *ātman,* should not be viewed in the same way as the *Upaniṣadic* unifying

essence that makes all ultimately one. Neither should it be viewed as any kind of ultimate Absolute that indwells the subjective personality.

35 Kaṇāda, *Vaiśeṣikasūtras,* 1. i. 7, translators Radhakrishnan and Moore (eds), *A Sourcebook in Indian Philosophy*, p. 398.

36 Frauwallner, *History of Indian Philosophy, Part 2*, p. 101.

37 S. H. Phillips, *Classical Indian Metaphysics* (Delhi: Motilal Banarsidass, 1997, first published 1996), p. 59.

38 See S. Chatterjee and D. Datta, *An Introduction to Indian Philosophy* (Calcutta: University of Calcutta, 1984), p. 237, and Raju, *The Philosophical Traditions of India*, p. 151. Kaṇāda's *Vaiśeṣikasūtras* does not make the distinction into three kinds of universals, see Radhakrishnan and Moore (eds), *A Sourcebook in Indian Philosophy*, pp. 398–9, and pp. 420–1.

39 Halbfass, *On Being and What There Is*, p. 143.

40 B. K. Matilal, *Perception: An essay on classical Indian theories of knowledge* (Oxford: Clarendon, 1991, first published 1986), p. 383.

41 Murti, in H. G. Coward (ed.), *Studies in Indian Thought*, p. 146.

42 Chakrabarti, "Vaiśeṣika", in *ER*, vol. 15, p. 167.

43 It is for this reason that particularity is not necessarily synonymous with individuality in Vaiśeṣika physics. Raju summarizes this neatly: "The individual (*vyakti*) is the origin, the manifester of qualities and actions, whereas the particular (*viśeṣa*) is that which differentiates the ultimate infinitesimals and infinites from one another. It is not the ultimate difference, but that which is the basis of that ultimate difference." *The Philosophical Traditions of India*, p. 152.

44 *Padārthadharmasaṃgraha* 156, summarized by Karl Potter in *Encyclopedia of Indian Philosophies, Vol. II*, p. 302.

45 Halbfass, *On Being and What There Is*, p. 74.

46 Hiriyanna, *Outlines of Indian Philosophy*, p. 235.

47 Halbfass, *On Being and what There Is*, p. 149.

48 Sharma, *A Critical Survey of Indian Philosophy*, p. 187.

49 Radhakrishnan and Moore (eds), *A Sourcebook in Indian Philosophy*, p. 399, original translator Gaṇgānātha Jhā (Allahabad: E. J. Lazarus & Co., 1916).

50 Potter, *Encyclopedia of Indian Philosophies, Vol. II*, p. 144.

51 However, there is some discussion of non-existence in Kaṇāda's *Vaiśeṣikasūtras*, see, in particular, IX:i:1–10. This might suggest that Kaṇāda's acceptance of it as a separate category of knowledge is not so wide of the mark as some scholars suggest. See Chatterjee and Datta, *An Introduction to Indian Philosophy*, p. 240. On the other hand, it does not seem to be fully worked out into a separate category by Kaṇāda.

52 *The Vaiśeṣika Sūtras of Kaṇāda with the Commentary of Śaṅkara Miśra and Extracts from the Gloss of Jayanārāyaṇa* translated by Nandalal Sinha, The Sacred Books of the Hindus, Vol. 7 (Allababad: Sudhīdranātha Vasu, 1911).

53 *Vaiśeṣikasūtras* VII:i:22, translator Sinha, *ibid.*

54 *Ibid.*, III:ii:3.

55 *Ibid.*, VIII:i:2 and commentary.

56 *Ibid.*, III:ii:1.

57 Sharma, *A Critical Survey of Indian Philosophy*, p. 189.

58 J. Pereira (ed. and translator), *Hindu Theology: Themes, Texts and Structures* (Delhi: Motilal Banarsidass, 1991, first published 1976), pp. 106–7. Translated form Praśastapāda's *Bhāṣya* on Kaṇāda's *Vaiśeṣikasūtrāṇi*, ed. Dhundiraj Sastri with Hindi commentary, in Kashi Sanskrit Series, no. 173 (Benares: Chowkhamba Sanskrit Series Office, 1966), pp. 29–34.

59 See Radhakrishnan, *Indian Philosophy*, *Vol. 2*, p. 201 note 1.

60 *Ibid.*, p. 208.
61 Potter, *Encyclopedia of Indian Philosophies, Vol. II*, p. 130.
62 *Vaiśeṣikasūtras* V. i. 15, translator Sinha, *The Vaiśeṣika Sūtras of Kaṇāda.* (My brackets).
63 *Ibid.*, V. 2. 19–20.
64 Although there are two of his aphorisms, 1. i. 3 and 10. ii. 9, that are sometimes cited as evidence of acceptance of a God, the Sanskrit of both is unclear. Radhakrishnan and Moore, for example translate 1. i. 3 as "The authoritativeness of the Veda (arises from its) being the Word of God [or being an exposition of *dharma*]", a translation close to that of Sinha's. But in a footnote to the verse, they note that the text does not use the word "God", but *tat*, "that". The problem lies with the term *tadvachana*, which could refer to God, the seers, or even *Tat*, "that". See Radhakrishnan and Moore (eds), *A Sourcebook in Indian Philosophy*, p. 387 and p. 387 note 1. The translation of the verse to refer to God, might suggest the acceptance of *śabda* as an additional *pramāṇa*, and this Vaiśeṣika does not do. Either way, reference to God is not explicit and is only shakily inferred here, and in X:ii:9. Cf. also Sinha's translation at X:ii:8 and VII:ii:20.
65 Potter, *Encyclopedia of Indian Philosophies, Vol. II*, p. 34.
66 Sharma, *A Critical Survey of Indian Philosophy*, p. 190.
67 *Vaiśeṣikasūtras* I:i:2, translator Sinha, *The Vaiśeṣika Sūtras of Kaṇāda.*
68 Vaiśeṣika accepted that those with *yogic* powers could perceive both *dharma* and *adharma.*
69 *Padārthadharmasaṃgraha*, 6. ii. 2, 5, 8, 9, translators Radhakrishnan and Moore (eds), *A Sourcebook in Indian Philosophy*, p. 416.
70 Yet the system accepts a condition of enlightenment before death, when the self operates in the world with right knowledge, right actions and so on. Clearly, qualities must still obtain in the self for this to occur, and the *manas* must remain the mediator of sense perceptions and inner qualities until final death, when the body is shed for good.
71 Hiriyanna, *The Essentials of Indian Philosophy*, p. 103.
72 Radhakrishnan, *Indian Philosophy, Vol. 2*, p. 244.
73 Sharma, *A Critical Survey of Indian Philosophy*, p. 186.

Chapter 5 *Nyāya*

1 T. Bernard, *Hindu Philosophy* (Delhi: Motilal Banarsidass, 1981 reprint of 1947 edn), p. 20.
2 S. Radhakrishnan, *Indian Philosophy, Vol. 2* (Delhi: Oxford University Press, 1994 impression, first published 1923), p. 43.
3 The term, according to Potter and Bhattacharyya, is used in two ways, "On the one hand, it is frequently employed to identify Nyāya-Vaiśeṣika literature that appeared from Gaṅgeśa's time onwards, but a more precise sense of the term applies to that literature which, as Gaṅgeśa's does, utilizes a certain technical vocabulary to explicate Nyāya concepts." K. H. Potter and S. Bhattacharyya, *Encyclopedia of Indian Philosophies, Vol. VI: Indian Philosophical Analysis Nyāya-Vaiśeṣika from Gaṅgeṣa to Raghunātha Śiromaṇi* (Delhi: Motilal Banarsidass, 1993), p. 3.
4 S. Chatterjee, *The Nyāya Theory of Knowledge: A critical study of some problems of logic and metaphysics* (Calcutta: University of Calcutta, 1965 reprint of 1939 edn), p. 5.
5 See B. K. Matilal, *A History of Indian Literature: Nyāya-Vaiśeṣika* (Wiesbaden: Otto Harrassowitz, 1977), p. 76.
6 Bernard, *Hindu Philosophy*, p. 23.
7 Radhakrishnan, *Indian Philosophy, Vol. 2*, p. 34.
8 See Radhakrishnan, *ibid.*, p. 36.
9 It may be that the alternative name of Akṣapāda refers to a different person, Gautama being

the earlier of the two, and Akṣapāda he who developed the earlier material of Gautama into a recognizable system. See Matilal, *A History of Indian Literature*, p. 78. If this is so, then the dating of the *Nyāyasūtras* in this final redacted form would be in the first few centuries CE.

10 K. H. Potter, *Encyclopedia of Indian Philosophies, Vol. II: The tradition of Nyāya-Vaiśeṣika up to Gaṅgeśa* (Delhi: Motilal Banarsidass, 1995 reprint of 1977 edn), pp. 220–21.

11 N. L. Sinha (ed.) and S. C. Vidyâbhûṣaṇa (translator), *The Nyâya Sûtras of Gotama* (Delhi: Motilal Banarsidass, 1990 reprint of 1930 edn), p. i.

12 Potter, *Encyclopedia of Indian Philosophies, Vol. II*, pp. 4, 239.

13 Potter and Bhattacharyya, *Encyclopedia of Indian Philosophies, Vol. VI*, p. 6.

14 Chatterjee, *The Nyāya Theory of Knowledge*, p. 108.

15 S, Chatterjee and D. Datta, *An Introduction to Indian Philosophy* (Calcutta: University of Calcutta, 1984) p. 166.

16 K. K. Chakrabarti, *The Logic of Gotama*. Monographs of the Society for Asian and Comparative Philosophy no. 5 (Hawaii: University Press of Hawaii, 1977), p. 116.

17 N. S. Junankar, *Gautama: The Nyāya Philosophy* (Delhi, Varanasi, Patna: Motilal Banarsidass, 1978), p. 486.

18 S, Chatterjee and D. Datta, *An Introduction to Indian Philosophy* (Calcutta: University of Calcutta, 1984), p. 165.

19 Junankar, *Gautama*, p. 486.

20 *Nyāyasūtras* 1:1:4 translator K. P. Bahadur, *The Wisdom of Nyaaya* (New Delhi: Sterling Publishers Private Limited, 1978), p. 42.

21 B. K. Matilal, *Logic, Language and Reality: Indian Philosophy and Contemporary Issues* (Delhi: Motilal Banarsidass, 1997 reprint of 1985 edn), p. 210.

22 C. Sharma, *A Critical Survey of Indian Philosophy* (Delhi: Motilal Banarsidass, 1994 reprint of 1960 edn), p. 195.

23 Chatterjee, *The Nyāya Theory of Knowledge*, p. 197.

24 *Ibid.*, p. 198.

25 It is Vātṣāyana who first seems to have included the mind as a sense.

26 Radhakrishnan, *Indian Philosophy, Vol. 2*, p. 68.

27 Chatterjee, *The Nyāya Theory of Knowledge*, p. 85.

28 Potter, *Encyclopedia of Indian Philosophies, Vol. II*, p. 179.

29 Chatterjee, *The Nyāya Theory of Knowledge*, p. 233.

30 Gautama did not provide any examples of his five-membered syllogism, so it is later Naiyāyikas that furnish us with such examples.

31 Chakrabarti, *The Logic of Gotama*, p. 136.

32 A few of the earlier Naiyāyikas suggested as many as ten. See Chatterjee, *The Nyāya Theory of Knowledge*, p. 273.

33 *Nyāyasūtras* 1:1:32–39.

34 A distinct difference from the Aristotelian syllogism. On this point, see Chakrabarti, *The Logic of Gotama*, p. 64.

35 Sharma, *A Critical Survey of Indian Philosophy*, p. 199.

36 For an excellent outline of this, see Potter, *Encyclopedia of Indian Philosophies, Vol. 2*, pp. 179–208.

37 Chakrabarti, *The Logic of Gotama*, p. 103. *Pentapod* is another word for a five-membered syllogism.

38 *Nyāyasūtras* 1:1:6 translator Bahadur, *The Wisdom of Nyaaya*.

39 *Ibid.*, 1:1:7.

40 *Ibid.*, 1:1:8.

41 See Potter, *Encyclopedia of Indian Philosophies, Vol. II*, p. 153.

42 *Nyāyasūtras* 1:1:57 translator Bahadur, *The Wisdom of Nyaaya.*

43 Intelligence and intellect are distinguished here. The former, *buddhi*, is seen as the ability of the mind to understand, to discriminate between things, to apprehend objects of knowledge and to make judgements about them. The latter, *manas*, is the process of the mind that enables reflection and cognition through inference. It includes such aspects as wit, doubt, memory, desires and aversions and the ability to experience pleasure and pain. It is the intellect that binds the self to the world whereas intelligence, *buddhi*, in its pure state, is the medium for liberation.

44 Vātsyāyana's *Bhāṣya* on *Nyāyasūtra* 1:1:9, translator M. Gaṅgānāṭha Jhā, *The Nyāya-Sūṭras of Gauṭama, Vol. 1* (4 vols. Delhi: Motilal Banarsidass, 1984 reprint of 1912–19 edn), p. 211.

45 *Nyāyasūtras* 1:1:10 translator Bahadur, *The Wisdom of Nyaaya.*

46 Junankar, *Gautama*, p. 550.

47 *Ibid.*, p. 478.

48 Vātsyāyana's *Bhāṣya* on *Nyāyasūtras* 3:2:45 translator Gaṅānāṭha Jhā, *The Nyāya-Sūṭras of Gauṭama, Vol. 3*, p. 1382.

49 Radhakrishnan, *Indian Philosophy, Vol. 2*, pp. 152–62.

50 *Nyāyasūtras* 4:1:6 translator Bahadur, *The Wisdom of Nyaaya.*

51 Jununkar, *Gautama*, p. 478.

52 Vātsyāyana's *Bhāṣya* on *Nyāyasūtras* 3:2:16, translator Gaṅgānāṭha Jhā, *The Nyāya-Sūṭras of Gauṭama, Vol. 3*, p. 1325.

53 *Ibid.*, 4:1:18, *Vol. 4*, p. 1455.

54 Radhakrishnan, *Indian Philosophy, Vol. 2*, p. 101.

55 Junankar, *Gautama*, p. 479.

56 Vātsyāyana's *Bhāṣya* on *Nyāyasūtras* 4:1:65 translator Gaṅgānāṭha Jhā, *The Nyāya-Sūṭras of Gauṭama, Vol. 4*, p. 1571.

57 Sinha, *The Nyâya Sûtras of Gotama*, p. xiv.

58 *Ibid.*, p. xvi.

59 Potter, *Encyclopedia of Indian Philosophies, Vol. II*, p. 100.

60 J. Vattanky, *Gaṅgeśa's Philosophy of God* (Madras: The Adyar Library and Research Centre, 1984), p. 4.

61 *Īśvaraḥ kāraṇam purṣakarmāphalyadarśanāt.*

62 *na puruṣakarmābhāve phalānispatteḥ.*

63 *tatkāritatvādahetuḥ.*

64 Bahadur, *The Wisdom of Nyaaya*, *sūtras* 4:1:19–21.

65 *Ibid.*, p. 194.

66 However, Vācaspati and Udayana consider 19 to establish God as the material cause of the universe, 20 to be the objection, and 21 to be Gautama's view.

67 Vattanky, *Gaṅgeśa's Philosophy of God*, p. 6.

68 See Chatterjee and Datta, *An Introduction to Indian Philosophy*, p. 208.

69 Vātsyāyana's *Bhāṣya* on *Nyāyasūtras* 4:1:21 translator Gaṅgānāṭha Jhā, *The Nyāya-Sūṭras of Gauṭama, Vol. 4*, pp. 1460–1.

70 C. Bulcke, *The Theism of Nyaya-Vaisesika: Its origin and early development* (Delhi: Motilal Banarsidass, 1968 reprint of 1947 edn), p. 54.

71 Junankar, *Gautama*, p. 571.

72 Bulcke, *The Theism of Nyaya-Vaisesika*, p. 27.

73 *Nyāyasūtras* 1:1:22 translator Bahadur, *The Wisdom of Nyaaya.*

74 Vātsyāyana's *Bhāṣya* on *Nyāyasūtras* 4:2:38 translator Gaṅgānāṭha Jhā, *The Nyāya-Sūṭras of Gauṭama, Vol. 4*, p. 1648.

75 *Nyāyasūtras* 1:1:2 translator Bahadur, *The Wisdom of Nyaaya.*

76 Potter, *Encyclopedia of Indian Philosophies, Vol. II*, p. 44.
77 *Nyāyasūtras* 4:2:47–50 translator Bahadur, *The Wisdom of Nyaaya.*
78 "One is enjoined to practice meditation in a forest, in a cave or by the side of a river." *Nyāyasūtras* 4:2:42 translator Bahadur, *The Wisdom of Nyaaya.*
79 *Nyāyasūtras* 4:2:46.
80 *Ibid.*, translator Bahadur, *The Wisdom of Nyaaya.*
81 Junankar, *Gautama*, p. 572.
82 Sharma, *A Critical Survey of Indian Philosophy*, p. 210.
83 Radhakrishnan, *Indian Philosophy, Vol. 2*, p. 152.
84 Junankar, *Gautama*, p. 553.

Chapter 6 *Sāṃkhya*

1 The modern scholar and ascetic Swami Hariharānanda Āraṇya who died in 1947 founded a monastery in Madhupur, and was a follower of Sāṃkhya-Yoga.
2 G. J. Larson, *Classical Sāṃkhya: An Interpretation of its History and Meaning* (Delhi: Motilal Banarsidass, second, revised edn 1979, first published 1969), p. 154.
3 E. Frauwallner, for example, believes that it dates back to the oral tradition, *History of Indian Philosophy, Vol. 1: The philosophy of the Veda and of the epic, the Buddha and the Jina, the Sāṃkhya and the Classical Yoga System*, translated from the original German by V. M. Bedekar (Delhi: Motilal Banarsidass, 1993 reprint of 1973 edn), p. 221.
4 E. Harzer, "Sāṃkhya" in M. Eliade, *The Encyclopedia of Religion* (hereafter *ER*, New York: Macmillan, 1987), vol. 13, p. 49.
5 Larson, *Classical Sāṃkhya*, p. 71.
6 *Ibid.*, p. 99.
7 *Māhabhārata* 12: 187–240; *Bhagavadgītā* chapters 2 and 6: 23–40.
8 Harzer, "Sāṃkhya" in *ER*, vol. 13, p. 49.
9 *Buddhacarita* 12: 15–44 and 45–67, see E. B. Cowell, *The Buddha-Karita or Life of the Buddha* (New Delhi: Cosmo Publications, 1977, first published 1894), pp. 124–30.
10 Larson, *Classical Sāṃkhya*, p. 95.
11 *Ibid.* I am indebted to this particularly clear analysis given in *Classical Sāṃkhya* for the present chapter.
12 Larson, *Classical Sāṃkhya*, p. 133.
13 *Ibid.*, p. 122.
14 S. Dasgupta, *A History of Indian Philosophy, Vol. 1* (Delhi, Mumbai, Chennai, Calcutta, Bangalore, Varanasi, Patna, Pune: Motilal Banarsidass, 1997, first published 1922), p. 229.
15 *Ibid.*, p. 238.
16 Neverthless, a late collection of *sūtras* dated to the fifteenth or sixteenth century does exist. See G. Larson, "Introduction to the philosophy of Sāṃkhya" in G. Larson and R. S. Bhattacharya, *Encyclopedia of Indian Philosophies, Vol. IV Sāṃkhya: A dualist tradition in Indian philosophy* (Delhi, Varanasi, Patna, Madras: Motilal Banarsidass, 1987), p. 84.
17 *Ibid.*, pp. 85, 93–4, 127–8.
18 This is perhaps the most important and thorough commentator. Dasgupta, in his analysis of Sāṃkhya in *A History of Indian Philosophy, Vol. 1*, relies heavily on Vijñanabhikṣu's works which are dated to about the sixteenth century.
19 See Harzer, "Sāṃkhya" in *ER*, vol. 13, p. 50.
20 See Larson, "Introduction to the philosophy of Sāṃkhya", p. 19.

21 Frauwallner, *History of Indian Philosophy, Vol. 1*, p. 222.
22 Pañcaśikha, indeed, is likely to have pre-empted much of Īśvarakṛṣṇa's analysis of reality, and it was he who used the terms *puruṣa* and *prakṛti* to depict the dual aspects of the Sāṃkhya system. On this point, see Frauwallner, *ibid.*, pp. 248–9. Pañcaśikha's assigning of *puruṣa* to the male, knowing principle, and of *prakṛti* to the female, creative principle, through the metaphor of man and wife, was to have its effect on Hindu and Indian thought to the present day.
23 See Larson, "Introduction to the philosophy of Sāṃkhya", p. 9.
24 Dasgupta, *A History of Indian Philosophy, Vol. 1*, p. 212.
25 Larson, *Classical Sāṃkhya*, p. 252.
26 Larson, "Introduction to the philosophy of Sāṃkhya", p. 19.
27 K. H. Potter and G. J. Larson in *Encyclopedia of Indian Philosophies, Vol. IV*, p. 150.
28 Dasgupta, *A History of Indian Philosophy, Vol. 1*, p. 216.
29 Larson, *Classical Sāṃkhya*, p. 171.
30 It is possible that these fifty categories represent an earlier doctrine than the eight dispositions of the intellect (to be analysed below), but were included in the *Sāṃkhyakārikā* alongside the eight. See Frauwallner, *History of Indian Philosophy, Vol. 1*, pp. 269–70.
31 For a very full analysis and discussion of the term, see K. A. Jacobsen, *Prakṛti in Sāṃkhya-Yoga: Material principle, religious experience, ethical implications*, Asian Thought and Culture, vol. 30 (New York, Washington D.C., Baltimore, Boston, Bern, Frankfurt am Main, Berlin, Vienna, Paris: Peter Lang, 1999), pp. 25–121.
32 Jacobsen, *Prakṛti in Sāṃkhya-Yoga*, p. 52.
33 S. Chatterjee and D. Datta, *An Introduction to Indian Philosophy* (Calcutta: University of Calcutta, 1984), p. 259.
34 Dasgupta, *A History of Indian Philosophy, Vol. 1*, p. 245.
35 Jacobsen, *Prakṛti in Sāṃkhya-Yoga*, p. 54.
36 See Larson, *Classical Sāṃkhya*, p. 236.
37 *Sāṃkhyakārikā* 10, translator Larson, *Classical Sāṃkhya*, p. 259.
38 Weerasinghe terms *mahat* "the great germ of the universe" and sees the *Vedic* Hiraṇyagarbha, the "golden germ" from which all things spring (*Ṛg Veda* 10:21) as its older prototype. S. G. M. Weerasinghe, *The Sāṅkhya Philosophy: A critical evaluation of its origins and development*, Sri Garib Das Series, no. 167 (Delhi: Sri Satguru, 1993), pp. 155–9. A full discussion of the origins of the term *mahat* and its links to the Sāṃkhya concept can be found on pp. 159–68 of Weerasinghe's work.
39 In the *Sāṃkhyakārikā* 46–51 fifty *bhāvas* are indicated, contrasting with the eight identified in 42–45 and 52.
40 Frauwallner, *History of Indian Philosophy, Vol. 1*, p. 268. Frauwallner sees the influence of the Vaiśeṣika system here (*ibid.*, pp. 270–1).
41 M. Hiriyanna, *Outlines of Indian Philosophy* (Delhi: Motilal Banarsidass, 1993), p. 292.
42 Weerasinghe, *The Sāṅkhya Philosophy*, p. 169.
43 Larson, *Classical Sāṃkhya*, p. 186.
44 Translator Larson, *Classical Sāṃkhya*, p. 264.
45 See Larson, *ibid.*, p. 187.
46 *Ibid.*
47 *Ibid.*, p. 268.
48 Translator Larson, *ibid.*
49 Weerasinghe, *The Sāṅkhya Philosophy*, p. 203.
50 Dasgupta, *History of Indian Philosophy, Vol. 1*, p. 251.
51 *Ibid.*

52 Larson, "Introduction to the philosophy of Sāṃkhya", p. 50.
53 An excellent account of Śāṃkara's critique of Sāṃkhya, along with possible responses that Sāṃkhya might have given, is to be found in Larson, *Classical Sāṃkhya*, "Epilogue", pp. 209–35.
54 S. Radhakrishnan, *Indian Philosophy, Vol. 2* (Delhi: Oxford University Press, 1994 impression, first published 1923), p. 262.
55 Larson provides a detailed account of these in "Introduction to the philosophy of Sāṃkhya", pp. 65–7.
56 M. Hiriyanna, *The Essentials of Indian Philosophy* (Delhi: Motilal Banarsidass, 1995), p. 109.
57 *Sāṃkhyakārikā* 12, translator Larson, *Classical Sāṃkhya*, p. 259.
58 Chatterjee and Datta, *An Introduction to Indian Philosophy*, p. 261.
59 Dasgupta, *A History of Indian Philosophy, Vol. 1*, p. 264.
60 Chatterjee and Datta, *An Introduction to Indian Philosophy*, p. 261.
61 *Sāṃkhyakārikā* 54, translator Larson, *Classical Sāṃkhya*, p. 272.
62 C. Sharma, *A Critical Survey of Indian Philosophy* (Delhi: Motilal Banarsidass, 1994 reprint of 1960 edn), p. 163.
63 *Sāṃkhyakārikā* 13, translator Larson, *Classical Sāṃkhya*, p. 260.
64 Radhakrishnan, *Indian Philosophy, Vol. 2*, p. 311.
65 See Chatterjee and Datta, *An Introduction to Indian Philosophy*, p. 263.
66 Hiriyanna, *Outlines of Indian Philosophy*, p. 272.
67 This is not unlike the view of error in the Nyāya-Vaiśeṣika schools.
68 Radhakrishnan, *Indian Philosophy, Vol. 2*, p. 302.
69 Weerasinghe, *The Sāṅkhya Philosophy*, p. 227.
70 *Ṛg Veda* 10:129.
71 Radhakrishnan, *Indian Philosophy, Vol. 2*, p. 286.
72 Larson, *Classical Sāṃkhya*, p. 171.
73 *Sāṃkhyakārikā* 19.
74 *Ibid.*, 62, translator Larson, *Classical Sāṃkhya*, p. 274.
75 So, Hiriyanna, *Outlines of Indian Philosophy*, p. 293.
76 Larson, "Introduction to the philosophy of Sāṃkhya", p. 54.
77 *Ibid.*, 41–2.
78 *Sāṃkhyakārikā* 17.
79 J. Davies, *Hindu Philosophy: An exposition of the system of Kapila* (New Delhi: Cosmo Publications, 1981), p. 47.
80 Translator Larson, *Classical Sāṃkhya*, p. 262.
81 Sharma, *A Critical Survey of Indian Philosophy*, p. 168.
82 *Ibid.*
83 Chatterjee and Datta, *An Introduction to Indian Philosophy*, p. 273.
84 Hiriyanna, *Outlines of Indian Philosophy*, p. 273.
85 *Sāṃkhyakārikā* 21.
86 *Ibid.* 20, translator Larson, *Classical Sāṃkhya*, p. 62.
87 Radhakrishnan, *Indian Philosophy, Vol. 2*, p. 329.
88 Sharma, *A Critical Survey of Indian Philosophy*, p. 166.
89 See Dasgupta, *A History of Indian Philosophy, Vol. 1*, pp. 247–8.
90 Frauwallner, *History of Indian Philosophy, Vol. 1*, p. 297.
91 *Sāmkhyakārikā* 60, translator Larson, *Classical Sāṃkhya*, p. 273.
92 *Ibid.*, 61, p. 274.
93 *Sāmkhyakārikā* 66.
94 Radhakrishnan, *Indian Philosophy, Vol. 2*, p. 303.

95 Sharma. *A Critical History of Indian Philosophy*, p. 165.
96 Hiriyanna, *Outlines of Indian Philosophy*, p. 287.
97 Dasgupta, *A History of Indian Philosophy, Vol. 1*, p. 257.
98 Translator Larson, *Classical Sāṃkhya*, p. 260.
99 Dasgupta, *A History of Indian Philosophy, Vol. 1*, p. 245.
100 *Ibid.*, p. 247.
101 Radhakrishnan, *Indian Philosophy Vol. 2*, p. 279.
102 *Ibid.*, p. 308.
103 *Ibid.*, p. 257.
104 See Larson, *Classical Sāṃkhya*, p. 104 and Dasgupta, *A History of Indian Philosophy, Vol. 1*, pp. 216–17.
105 Translator Larson, *Classical Sāṃkhya*, p. 271.
106 *Ibid.*, p. 256.
107 *Sāṃkhyakārikā*, 37.
108 Larson, *Classical Sāṃkhya*, p. 205.
109 *Sāṃkhyakārikā* 62, translator Larson, *ibid.*, p. 274.
110 So, Sharma, *A Critical Survey of Indian Philosophy*, p. 168.
111 Hiriyanna, *Essentials of Indian Philosophy*, p. 115.
112 Davies, *Hindu Philosophy*, p. 112.

Chapter 7 *Classical Yoga*

1 *The Yoga-system of Patañjali*, translator J. H. Woods (Delhi: Motilal Banarsidass, 1992 reprint of 1914 edn), 1:2.
2 In other schools, where union of the self with the Supreme Self as Brahman is accepted, the word is often translated as "to unite" or "to connect". This is less applicable to a dualist school that separates, not unifies, spirit and matter.
3 K. Werner, *Yoga and Indian Philosophy* (Delhi: Motilal Banarsidass, 1989 reprint of 1977 edn), pp. 93–4.
4 R. Ravindra, "Yoga: The royal path to freedom" in K. Sivaraman, *Hindu Spirituality, Vol. 1: Vedas through Vedanta* (London: SCM, 1989), p. 177.
5 I. Whicher, *The Integrity of the Yoga Darśana: A reconsideration of Classical Yoga* (New Delhi: D. K. Printworld (P) Ltd., 2000, first published 1998), p. 28.
6 Werner, *Yoga and Indian Philosophy*, p. 102.
7 Such figures feature on three well-known seals and are often depicted as representing a single deity who was the precursor of the Hindu deity Śiva, the great ascetic God of Hinduism. However, the figures on the seals may not be identical and there are many reasons why the identity with Śiva is suspect. See J. Fowler, *Hinduism: Beliefs and practices* (Brighton, Sussex and Portland, Oregon: Sussex Academic Press, 1997), pp. 86–8.
8 *Ṛg Veda* 10:31, translator R. T. H. Griffith, *The Hymns of the Ṛgveda* (Delhi: Motilal Banarsidass, 1991 reprint of 1973 new revised edn), pp. 552–3.
9 See the *Chāndogya Upaniṣad* 7:6:1.
10 A good critique of those scholars who minimalize the nature of Yoga in comparison to Sāṃkhya can be found in G. Feuerstein, *The Philosophy of Classical Yoga* (Rochester, Vermont: Inner Traditions International, 1996, first published 1980), pp. 109–20.
11 Yoga uses some different terminology from Sāṃkhya. The unmanifest *prakṛti* is generally termed *aliṅga*. The three *guṇas* in their unmanifest state and in their multifarious collocations of

manifest existence are called *dṛśya* "the seeable" – in other words, all that *puruṣas* are capable of seeing. *Puruṣa*, then, is often known as the "seer", *draṣṭṛ*. The Sāṃkhya *mahatbuddhi* is generally termed the Designator, the *liṅgamātra*. The Sāṃkhya *ahaṃkāra*, pure I-ness, is termed *asmitāmātra*, but when this is transferred to I-ness in the sense of "I am", "me", it is sometimes simply termed *asmitā*, self-identity. Yoga groups the *asmitāmātra* (Sāṃkhya *ahaṃkāra*) and the five subtle elements (*tanmātras*) together as the six *aviśeṣas* or "non-particularized", "undifferentiated". *Manas*, the ten *indriyas* and the five gross elements are grouped together as the *viśeṣas*, the "particularized", "differentiated".

12 M. Eliade, "Yoga" in *The Encyclopedia of Religion* (hereafter *ER*, New York: Macmillan, 1987), vol. 15, p. 519.

13 Werner, *Yoga and Indian Philosophy*, p. 94.

14 E. Wood, *Seven Schools of Yoga* (Wheaton, Illinois, Madras, London: The Theosophical Publishing House, 1988, first published 1976), p. 19.

15 S. Chatterjee and D. Datta, *An Introduction to Indian Philosophy* (Calcutta: University of Calcutta, 1984), p. 301.

16 S. N. Dasgupta, *Yoga Philosophy: In relation to other systems of Indian thought* (Delhi: Motilal Banarsidass, 1996, first published 1930), p. 51.

17 Werner, *Yoga and Indian Philosophy*, p. 131.

18 See Woods, "Introduction" in *The Yoga-system of Patañjali*, pp. xiii–xxiii for a detailed analysis of the authorship and dating of the *Yogasūtras*.

19 *Ibid.*, pp. xv–xvii.

20 Whicher, *The Integrity of the Yoga Darśana*, p. 1.

21 F. Tola and C. Dragonetti, *The Yogasūtras of Patañjali on Concentration of Mind*, translated from Spanish by K. D. Prithipaul (Delhi: Motilal Banarsidass, 1991 reprint of 1987 edn), p. x.

22 *Yogasūtras* 1:14, translator Woods, *The Yoga-system of Patañjali.*

23 *Ibid.*, 1:39.

24 I. K. Taimni, *The Science of Yoga: The Yoga-Sūtras of Patañjali in Sanskrit with Transliteration in Roman, Translation and Commentary in English* (Madras: The Theosophical Publishing House, 1986 reprint of 1961 edn), p. 29.

25 *Yogasūtras* 1:33, translator Woods, *The Yoga-system of Patañjali.*

26 *Ibid.*, 4:14.

27 Dasgupta, *Yoga Philosophy*, p. 209.

28 See note 11 above.

29 Feuerstein, *The Philosophy of Classical Yoga*, p. 29.

30 Feuerstein, *The Yoga-Sūtra of Patañjali*, p. 14.

31 K. A. Jacobsen, *Prakṛti in Sāṃkhya-Yoga: Material principle, religious experience, ethical implications.* Asian Thought and Culture Series, vol. 30 (New York, Washington D.C./Baltimore, Boston, Bern, Frankfurt am Main, Berlin, Vienna, Paris: Peter Lang, 1999), p. 242.

32 A. Daniélou, *Yoga: Mastering secrets of matter and the universe* (Rochester, Vermont: Inner Traditions International, 1991), p. 2.

33 G. Feuerstein, "The Meaning of Suffering in Yoga" in G. Feuerstein and J. Miller, *The Essence of Yoga: Essays on the development of yogic philosophy from the Vedas to modern times* (Rochester, Vermont: Inner Traditions International 1998. First published in 1971 under the title *A Reappraisal of Yoga* and in 1972 under the title *Yoga and Beyond*), p. 88.

34 T. Berry, *Religions of India: Hinduism, Yoga, Buddhism* (New York: Columbia University Press, 1996, first published 1992), p. 90.

35 Jacobsen, *Prakṛti in Sāṃkhya-Yoga*, p. 3.

36 *Yogasūtras*, 1:7, translator Woods, *The Yoga-system of Patañjali.*

37 Whicher, *The Integrity of the Yoga Darśana*, p. 145.
38 Commentary on *Yogasūtras* 1:43, translator Woods, *The Yoga-system of Patañjali.*
39 Translator, Woods, *ibid.*
40 "Mind-stuff" is a translation rejected by Feuerstein because it lacks the awareness supplied by the *puruṣa* in order to function (*Philosophy of Classical Yoga*, p. 59). Elsewhere he calls the translation a *horrific* word (*The Yoga-Sūtra of Patañjali: A new translation and commentary* [Rochester, Vermont: Inner Traditions International, 1989, first published 1979], p. 26). But his translation of *citta* as "consciousness" is misleading, as would be Larson's as "awareness" (G. Larson and R. S. Bhattacharya eds, *Encyclopedia of Indian Philosophies, Vol. IV: Sāṃkhya a dualist tradition in Indian philosophy* [Delhi, Varanasi, Patna, Madras: Motilal Banarsidass, 1987], p. 26), for this is the nature of *puruṣa* only.
41 The word actually has a wide number of meanings, see Whicher, *The Integrity of the Yoga Darśana*, p. 91.
42 G. M. Koelman, *Pātañjala Yoga: From Related Ego to Absolute Self* (Poona: Papal Athenaeum, 1970), p. 101.
43 Larson, "Introduction to the philosophy of Sāṃkhya" in Larson and Bhattacharya, *Encyclopedia of Indian Philosophies, Vol. 4*, p. 26.
44 S. Radhakrishnan, *Indian Philosophy, Vol. 2* (Delhi, Bombay, Calcutta, Madras: Oxford University Press, 1994 impression, first published 1923), p. 345.
45 Dasgupta, for example, believed it is important to differentiate between the *citta* as the mind, and the intellect and ego. Each he believed, has a separate role in the process of knowledge. (*Yoga Philosophy*, p. 265). This is true, but the total mind functioning must incorporate all three, not only in ordinary exixtence but in all the stages of *yogic* training.
46 Radhakrishnan, *Indian Philosophy, Vol. 2*, p. 349.
47 Wood, *Seven Schools of Yoga*, p. 16.
48 Feuerstein, "The Essence of Yoga" in Feuerstein and Miller, *The Essence of Yoga*, p. 30.
49 Mental abstraction, *vikalpa*, can also mean conceptualization, that is to say the bringing into the mind of ideas and verbal thought that is not connected with objects. This the *yogin* would do in stages of concentration and meditation. Mental abstraction here, however, is referring to the more ordinary thought processes.
50 A. Bailey, *The Light of the Soul Its Science and Effect: The Yoga Sutras of Patanjali* (London and New York: Lucis, 1983 reprint of 1927 edn), pp. 19–20.
51 R. Mehta, *The Secret of Self-Transformation: A synthesis of Tantra and Yoga* (Delhi: Motilal Banarsidass, 1995 reprint of 1987 edn), p. 54.
52 Commentary on 1:12, translator Woods, *The Yoga-system of Patañjali.*
53 Chatterjee and Datta, *An Introduction to Indian Philosophy*, pp. 299–300.
54 Commentary on 1:4, translator Woods, *The Yoga-system of Patañjali.*
55 Commentary on 2:27, translator Woods, *ibid.*
56 Feuerstein, *The Philosophy of Classical Yoga*, p. 60.
57 J. Varenne, *Yoga and the Hindu Tradition* (Chicago and London: University of Chicago Press, 1976, first published in French in 1973), p. 101.
58 Feuerstein, "The Meaning of Suffering in Yoga" in Feuerstein and Miller, *The Essence of Yoga*, p. 87.
59 Feuerstein, "The Essence of Yoga" in *ibid.*, p. 14.
60 While progressive, this does not mean that each stage is abandoned as a higher one is achieved. When in the final three stages, the *yogin* glides backwards and forwards from one to another depending on skill. When not in meditative practice, the *yogin* still observes the earlier *aṅgas.*
61 Some readers may be surprised to find an absence of references to the *cakras* and to the power

of *kuṇḍalini* – both commonly associated with Yoga in the western mind. However, while Patañjali certainly had knowledge of the *cakras*, no mention of *kuṇḍalini* occurs in the *Yogasūtras*. It was a development of Tantric Yoga.

62 Clearly, even *Kṣatriyas*, the warrior class would offend this principle of Yoga, despite the necessity of war presented by the *Bhagavadgītā*.

63 Jacobsen, *Prakṛti in Sāṃkhya-Yoga*, p. 6.

64 *Ibid.*, p. 246.

65 *Ibid.*, p. 342.

66 Werner, *Yoga and Indian Philosophy*, p. 135.

67 Feuerstein, "The Essence of Yoga" in Feuerstein and Miller, *The Essence of Yoga*, p. 18.

68 *Ibid.*, p. 19.

69 M. Eliade, *Yoga: Immortality and Freedom.* Translated from the French by W. R. Trask. Bollingen Series 56 (Princeton, New Jersey: Princeton University Press, 1990 reprint of second, revised edn 1969, first published 1958), p. 55.

70 Eliade, "Yoga" in *ER*, vol. 15, p. 521.

71 Feuerstein, "The Essence of Yoga" in Feuerstein and Miller, *The Essence of Yoga*, p. 26.

72 Eliade, *Yoga*, p. 58.

73 Commentary on 2:54, translator Woods, *The Yoga-system of Patañjali.*

74 Varenne, *Yoga and the Hindu Tradition*, p. 120.

75 Whicher, *The Integrity of the Yoga Darśana*, p. 29.

76 H. Āraṇya, *Yoga Philosophy of Patañjali*, translated by P. N. Mukerji (Albany: State University of New York Press, 1983, first published 1963), p. xvii.

77 Commentary on *Yogasūtras* 3:3, translator Āraṇya, *Yoga Philosophy of Patañjali.*

78 Dasgupta, *Yoga Philosophy*, p. 345.

79 Radhakrishnan, *Indian Philosophy, Vol. 2*, p. 360.

80 Āraṇya, *Yoga Philosophy of Patañjali*, p. 100.

81 Eliade, *Yoga*, p. 340.

82 Whicher, *The Integrity of the Yoga Darśana*, p. 212.

83 Commentary on 1:51, translator Woods, *The Yoga-system of Patañjali.* This is termed *dharma-megha-samādhi* (*dharma* "rightness", *megha* "cloud") and is translated rather well by Ravindra as "silence in the cloud of right order" (Ravindra, "Yoga: The royal path to freedom" in Sivaraman, *Hindu Spirituality, Vol. 1*, p. 186).

84 Commentary on 2:55, translator Woods, *The Yoga-system of Patañjali.*

85 M. Hiriyanna, *Outlines of Indian Philosophy* (Delhi: Motilal Banarsidass, 1993), p. 297.

86 Radhakrishnan. *Indian Philosophy, Vol. 2*, p. 366.

87 Feuerstein, *The Philosophy of Classical Yoga*, p. 108.

88 Radhakrishnan. *Indian Philosophy, Vol. 2*, p. 367.

89 Feuerstein, "The Essence of Yoga" in Feuerstein and Miller, *The Essence of Yoga*, p. 34.

90 *Ibid.*

91 Whicher, *The Integrity of the Yoga Darśana*, p. 259.

92 *Ibid.*, p. 153.

93 *Yogasūtras* 2:5, translator Woods, *The Yoga-system of Patañjali.*

94 Vyāsa's commentary on *Yogasūtras* 2:8, translator Āraṇya, *Yoga Philosophy of Patañjali.*

95 Vācaspati Miśra's explanation and Vyāsa's comments on Patañjali's *Yogasūtras* 2:9, translator Woods.

96 Commentary on 2:15, translator Woods, *The Yoga-system of Patañjali.*

97 Feuerstein believes that *nirodha*, "cessation" of the mind fluctuations (*vṛttis*) refers *only* to those involved with the *kleśas*. He bases his evidence for this on *Yogasūtras* 2:11, which tells us that

mind fluctuations are overcome by meditative absorption. But Feuerstein has to insert the *kleśas* in parentheses, for they are not actually referred to in the text. His suggestion that, "whatever cognitive elements are to be met with in the enstatic frame of mind, they are definitely not of the nature of the *vṛttis*" (*Yoga-Sūtras of Patañjali*, p. 66), is a difficult one, for any cognitions *must* take place in the mind-complex. In Feuerstein's view, concentration in *samādhi* on any object, whether gross or subtle, cannot produce a *vṛtti* of the mind. But it must be remembered that it is *vṛttis* that engender bondage, and to be devoid of them is to be free. Yet concentration is not liberation. *Ekāgra*, single-pointedness, must involve mind function – a single, still arresting of the mind, but a *vṛtti*, nevertheless.

98 On this point, see Āraṇya, *Yoga Philosophy of Patañjali*, p. 426.
99 Jacobsen, *Prakṛti in Sāṃkhya-Yoga*, p. 64.
100 Eliade, *Yoga*, p. 42.
101 Dasgupta, *Yoga Philosophy*, p. 286.
102 For example in *The Philosophy of Classical Yoga*, p. 60 *et al.*
103 *Ibid.*, p. 67.
104 F. W. J. Humphries, "Yoga Philosophy and Jung" in K. Werner (ed.), *The Yogi and the Mystic: Studies in Indian and comparative mysticism* (Richmond, Surrey: Curzon Press: 1994, first published 1989), p. 142.
105 The term *saṃskāra* carries the nuance of purification in its meanings. Thus it is applicable to birth, marriage and death rites.
106 Dasgupta certainly equates the two (see *Yoga Philosophy*, pp. 324 and 325), but I think there is some measure in recognizing a difference in the nuances of meaning of the two terms, though perhaps not as definitive as others suggest, see G. Feuerstein, *The Philosophy of Classical Yoga* (Rochester, Vermont: Inner Traditions International, 1996), p. 67.
107 Dasgupta, *Yoga Philosophy*, p. 324.
108 For example in *The Philosophy of Classical Yoga*, p. 21.
109 Eliade, *Yoga*, p. 42.
110 Whicher, *The Integrity of the Yoga Darśana*, p. 102.
111 This suggests that a *liṅgaśarīra* as in Sāṃkhya is unnecessary.
112 Āraṇya, *Yoga Philosophy of Patañjali*, p. 428.
113 *Ibid.*
114 Translator Āraṇya, *ibid.* p. 358.
115 Feuerstein, *The Philosophy of Classical Yoga*, p. 66.
116 Feuerstein, *The Yoga-Sūtras of Patañjali*, p. 58.
117 Āraṇya, *Yoga Philosophy of Patañjali*, p. 440.
118 Whicher, *The Integrity of the Yoga Darśana*, p. 149.
119 Āraṇya, *Yoga Philosophy of Patañjali*, p. 442.
120 Dasgupta, *Yoga Philosophy*, pp. 196–7.
121 Jacobsen, *Prakṛti in Sāṃkhya-Yoga*, p. 227.
122 Vyāsa's commentary on *Yogasūtras* 4:12, translator Āraṇya, *Yoga Philosophy of Patañjali*, p. 367.
123 Whicher, *The Integrity of the Yoga Darśana*, p. 18.
124 Radhakrishnan, *Indian Philosophy, Vol. 2*, p. 371.
125 Koelman, *Pātañjala Yoga*, p. 57.
126 *Ibid.*, p. 58.
127 See Chatterjee and Datta, *An Introduction to Indian Philosophy*, p. 309 and *Yogasūtras* 1:23, translator Woods, *The Yoga-system of Patañjali.*
128 Āraṇya, *Yoga Philosophy of Patañjali*, p. 215.
129 Feuerstein, *The Philosophy of Classical Yoga*, p. 5.

130 Eliade, *Yoga*, p. 75.
131 This is somewhat problematic in that it serves to diminish the nature of the liberated *puruṣa* as totally separate from *prakṛti*. It is projecting something beyond *puruṣa* that *puruṣa* can never be, and to which it will always be inferior.
132 Commentary on 1:24 of Patañjali's *Yogasūtras* translator Woods, *The Yoga-system of Patañjali*.
133 Koelman, *Pātañjala Yoga*, pp. 61–3.
134 So, Whicher, *The Integrity of the Yoga Darśana*, p. 85.
135 Eliade, *Yoga*, p. 75.
136 Feuerstein, *The Philosophy of Classical Yoga*, p. 13.
137 Eliade, *Yoga*, p. 74.
138 Whicher, *The Integrity of the Yoga Darśana*, p. 151.
139 Jacobsen, *Prakṛti in Sāṃkhya-Yoga*, p. 299.
140 Eliade, *Yoga*, p. 39.
141 The five *tanmātras*, I-ness, *buddhi* and unmanifest *prakṛti* are known as the eight *prakṛtis*.
142 Feuerstein, *The Yoga-Sūtra of Patañjali*, p. 14.
143 *Yogasūtras* 3:55, translator Āraṇya, *Yoga Philosophy of Patañjali*, p. 344.
144 Vyāsa's commentary on *Yogasūtras* 3:5, translator Āraṇya, *ibid*.
145 *Ibid*. This is usually understood to be the cessation of all mind activity, the *nirodha* of the *cittavṛtti*. I shall have occasion below to examine the different view of Whicher on the nature of liberation. It is his view that an "expansion of perception" takes place, not a cessation (*nirodha*) of the *prakṛtic* mind.
146 Feuerstein, *The Yoga-Sūtra of Patañjali*, p. 144.
147 *Ibid*., p. 145.
148 Feuerstein, "The Essence of Yoga" in Feuerstein and Miller, *The Essence of Yoga*, p. 47.
149 Whicher, *The Integrity of the Yoga Darśana*, p. 2.
150 Cf. *Yogasūtras* 3:55.
151 Whicher, *The Integrity of the Yoga Darśana*, p. 157.
152 *Ibid*., p. 158.
153 *Ibid*., p. 157.
154 *Ibid*., p. 161.
155 *Ibid*., p. 167.
156 *Ibid*.
157 Radhakrishnan, *Indian Philosophy, Vol. 2*, p. 364.
158 Whicher, *The Integrity of the Yoga Darśana*, p. 172.
159 *Ibid*., p. 281.
160 *Ibid*., p. 293.
161 Eliade, *Yoga*, p. 95.
162 *Ibid*., p. 96.
163 Feuerstein, *The Yoga-Sūtra of Patañjali*, p. 142.
164 See also G. J. Larson, "*On* The integrity of the Yoga Darśana: *A review* in *International Journal of Hindu Studies*, 3 (1999), 183–6, and Whicher's response to this "*On* The integrity of the Yoga Darśana: *A response to Larson's review*" in the same volume, pp. 187–97.
165 Jacobsen, *Prakṛti in Sāṃkhya-Yoga*, p. 287. This concept of *prakṛtilaya* possibly illustrates the likelihood of different sects accepting a merging of the Self with *prakṛti* as the ultimate goal. This must necessitate an acceptance of twenty-four evolutes of *prakṛti*, rather than accepting the separate twenty-fifth as *puruṣa*.

See Jacobsen, *ibid*., p. 300, and *Yogasūtras* 1:19. As Jacobsen points out: "The *kevalin* has realized the subjective principle, his own *puruṣa*, and has become free from materiality. The *prakṛtilīna* has realized the objective principle and he has merged with the transcendent material principle." *Ibid.*, p. 302.

166 Feuerstein, "The Essence of Yoga" in Feuerstein and Miller, *The Essence of Yoga*, p. 21.

167 See Whicher, *The Integrity of the Yoga Darśana*, p. 80 and G. Feuerstein, *The Philosophy of Classical Yoga*, p. 23.

168 For example, Tola and Dragonetti, *The Yogasūtras of Patañjali*, p. x.

169 Berry, *Religions of India*, pp. 88–9.

170 *Ibid.*, p. 89.

171 Eliade, *Yoga*, p. 7.

172 V. Worthington, *A History of Yoga* (London: Arkana, 1989, first published 1982), p. 88.

173 Radhakrishnan, *Indian Philosophy, Vol. 2*, p. 337.

Chapter 8 *Advaita Vedānta*

1 The interpretations of *pūrva* and *uttara* may vary, some suggesting "former" and "later", that is to say, in time. The interpretation I have here seems the most sensible, but for a closer analysis, see H. Nakamura, *A History of Early Vedānta Philosophy*, translated by T. Leggett, S. Mayeda, T. Unno *et al.* (Delhi: Motilal Banarsidass, 1990 reprint of 1983 edn), pp. 411–12.

2 Also called the *Vedāntasūtras*, *Śārirakasūtras*, *Śārīramīmāṃsā* and *Uttaramīmāṃsā*.

3 According to Mayeda, Bādarāyaṇa is unlikely to have been the composer of the *Brahmasūtras*. He considers the text to have been a composite work. Even if this were so, as Mayeda points out, the *Brahmasūtras* was invaluable in the unifying and systematizing of *Upaniṣadic* thought. As such, it was a highly important work. S. Mayeda, *A Thousand Teachings: The Upadeśasāhasrī of Śaṅkara* (Albany, New York: State University of New York Press, 1992), p. 12.

4 See S. Dasgupta, *A History of Indian Philosophy, Vol. 1* (Delhi: Motilal Banarsidass, 1998 reprint of 1922 Cambridge edn), p. 418.

5 *Ibid.*, p. 422.

6 A thorough account of this is to be found in Dasgupta, *A History of Indian Philosophy, Vol. 1*. pp. 418–20.

7 See K. H. Potter (ed.), *Encyclopedia of Indian Philosophies, Vol. III: Advaita Vedānta up to Śaṃkara and his Pupils* (Delhi, Varanasi, Patna: Motilal Banarsidass, first Indian edn 1981), p. 6.

8 *Ibid.*, p. 9.

9 *Ibid.*, p. 10.

10 For these, see Mayeda, *A Thousand Teachings*, p. 3, A. J. Alston, *Śaṃkara on the Absolute: A Śaṃkara Source-Book, Vol. 1* (London: Shanti Sadan, 1981 reprint of 1980 edn), p. 43, Potter, *Encyclopedia of Indian Philosophies, Vol. III*, p. 14, and B. Malkovsky, "The Personhood of Śaṃkara's *Para Brahman*", *The Journal of Religion* 77 (1997), 541.

11 A much earlier date of the fifth or sixth century is also courted for Gauḍapāda, see N. Isayeva, *Shankara and Indian Philosophy* (Albany, New York: State University of New York Press, 1993), p. 49.

12 For a more detailed analysis of the traditions about his life and works, see Isayeva, *ibid.*, pp. 69–104.

13 For his Vaiṣṇava background, see H. V. S. Murthy, *Vaiṣṇavism of Śaṃkaradeva and Rāmānuja: A Comparative Study* (Delhi, Varanasi, Patna: Motilal Banarsidass, 1973).

14 Alston, *Śaṃkara on the Absolute*, p. 47. See also the *Śivāndalaharī*, a long hymn in praise of Śiva that tradition ascribes to Śaṃkara, in T. M. P. Mahadevan, *The Hymns of Śaṅkara* (Delhi: Motilal Banarsidass, 1995 reprint of 1980 edn), pp. 84–171.

15 Atheism, indeed, is world affirming, accepting the plurality and independence of world forms one from another. Such concepts would be alien to the philosophy of Śaṃkara who sought to prove the unreality of all except Brahman. While a theistic deity as Īśvara is accepted as a means to elevate consciousness to its pure state, as we shall see, this more theistic conception of a divine being is as unreal as the rest of existence.

16 Potter, *Encyclopedia of Indian Philosophies*, *Vol. III*, p. 119.

17 M. Hiriyanna, *Outlines of Indian Philosophy* (Delhi: Motilal Banarsidass, 1993), p. 339.

18 Mayeda, *A Thousand Teachings*, p. 6.

19 R. Das, *Introduction to Shankara* (Calcutta: Firma KLM Private Limited, 1983), p. xviii.

20 For Śaṃkara's views on rival schools, see A. J. Alston, *Śaṃkara on Rival Views: A Śaṃkara Source-Book, Vol. 5* (London: Shanti Sadan, 1989).

21 C. Sharma, *The Advaita Tradition in Indian Philosophy: A Study of Advaita in Buddhism, Vedānta and Kāshmīra Shaivism* (Delhi: Motilal Banarsidass, 1996), p. 273. Sharma notes that the terms *māyā*, *avidyā*, *ajñāna*, *adhyāsa*, *adhyāropa*, *anirvachanīya*, *vivarta*, *bhrānti*, *bhrama*, *nāma-rūpa*, *avyakta*, *akṣara*, *bījashakti*, *mula-prakṛti*, etc., are used synonymously. *Ibid.*

22 Sāṃkhya gives the analogy here of the unconscious flow of milk from a cow to her calf as an example of an unconscious act that serves a purpose. But, as the Vedāntins point out, the cow gives her milk out of affection for the calf; the act, therefore, is more purposeful than unconscious.

23 With some justification, Loy comments, "perhaps the term Ātman should be rejected as superfluous, because it suggests another entity apart from Brahman". But, as he notes, "the two terms do serve a function, since they emphasize different aspects of the Absolute: Brahman, that is the ultimate reality which is the ground of all the universe; Ātman, that is my true nature". D. Loy, *Non-Duality: A study in comparative philosophy* (New Haven and London: Yale University Press, 1988), p. 198. However, since we cannot assign "different aspects" to the non-dual Brahman, the difficulty of the two terms for the same essence is not removed.

24 S. Chatterjee and D. Datta, *An Introduction to Indian Philosophy* (Calcutta: University of Calcutta, 1984), p. 379.

25 Śaṃkara, *Upadeśasāhasrī* 1:13:18, translator Mayeda, *A Thousand Teachings*, p. 133.

26 *Ibid.*, 1:13:2, p. 132.

27 D. Sinha, *Metaphysic of Experience in Advaita Vedānta: A phenomenological approach* (Delhi: Motilal Banarsidass, 1995 reprint of 1983 edn), p. 45.

28 R. N. Dandekar, "Vedānta" in M. Eliade, *The Encyclopedia of Religion* (hereafter *ER*, New York: Macmillan, 1987), vol. 15, p. 210.

29 Śaṃkara, *Upadeśasāhasrī* 1:10:1–3, translator Mayeda, *A Thousand Teachings*, p. 123.

30 W. M. Indich, *Consciousness in Advaita Vedānta* (Delhi: Motilal Banarsidass, 1995 reprint of 1980 edn), *passim.*

31 Raphael, *The Pathway of Non-Duality: Advaitavāda*, translated from the Italian by Kay McCarthy (Delhi: Motilal Banarsidass, 1992), p. 11.

32 Sharma, *The Advaita Tradition in Indian Philosophy*, p. 182.

33 Potter, *Encyclopedia of Indian Philosophies, Vol. III*, p. 20.

34 Trevor Leggett's translation of Śaṃkara's commentary on the *Yogasūtras* prompts him to write: "If he has chosen to write a commentary on Yoga meditation, it must have been a central part of his own standpoint, although he was opposed to some of the philosophical doctrines of the official Yoga school." T. Leggett, *Śaṅkara on the Yoga Sūtras: A full translation of the newly discovered text* (Delhi: Motilal Banarsidass, 1992 first Indian edn), p. 1. There seems good evidence to suggest Leggett is right when he says that for Śaṃkara, "the Yoga system is accepted as an authority on meditation practice and some other things like ethics and renunciation" (*ibid.*, p.

8) though, naturally, there are profound differences in thought. The need to discipline the mind was certainly accepted by Śaṃkara.

35 Śaṃkara, *Brahmasūtrabhāṣya* 1:1:1, translator Alston, *Śaṃkara on the Absolute*, p. 94.

36 Potter, *Encyclopedia of Indian Philosophies, Vol. III*, p. 89.

37 Indich, *Consciousness in Advaita Vedānta*, p. 46.

38 Malkovsky, "The Personhood of Śaṃkara's *Para Brahman*", p. 545.

39 Śaṃkara, *Upadeśasāhasrī* 1:8:1,3,4, translator Mayeda, *A Thousand Teachings*, p. 116.

40 Das, *Introduction to Shankara*, p. v.

41 Alston, *Śaṃkara on the Absolute*, pp. 170, 221, 224–31.

42 R. Puligandla, *Fundamentals of Indian Philosophy* (London, Lanham, New York: University Press of America, 1985 second edn), p. 217.

43 For example Sarvajnātmamuni in his *Saṃkṣepaśārīraka*.

44 Das, *Introduction to Shankara*, p. xxii.

45 Alston, *Śaṃkara on the Absolute*, pp. 37–8.

46 Śaṃkara, *Brahmasūtrabhāṣya* 2:1:9, translator A. J. Alston, *Śaṃkara on Creation: A Śaṃkara Source-Book, Vol. 2* (London: Shanti Sadan, 1980), p. 78.

47 C. Sharma, *A Critical Survey of Indian Philosophy* (Delhi: Motilal Banarsidass, 1994 reprint of 1960 edn), p. 253.

48 Das, *Introduction to Shankara*, p. xxvi.

49 Vivekananda, *Jnana-Yoga* (New York: Ramakrishna-Vivekananda Center, 1982, first published 1955), p. 35.

50 Potter, *Encyclopedia of Indian Philosophies, Vol. III*, p. 70.

51 See Alston, *Śaṃkara on the Absolute*, p. 42.

52 A. J. Alston, *Śaṃkara on the Soul: A Śaṃkara Source-Book, Vol. 3* (London: Shanti Sadan, 1985 reprint of 1981 edn), p. 112.

53 Sharma, *The Advaita Tradition in Indian Philosophy*, p. 175.

54 *Ibid.*, p. 274.

55 S. Rao, 'Two "Myths" in Advaita', *Journal of Indian Philosophy* 24 (1996), 267.

56 *Ibid.*, p. 268.

57 *Ibid.*, p. 271.

58 K. N. Tiwari, *Dimensions of Renunciation in Advaita Vedānta* (Delhi, Varanasi, Patna: Motilal Banarsidass, 1977), pp. 73–4.

59 *Ibid.*, p. 74.

60 Śaṃkara, *Upadeśasāhasrī* 1:17:20, translator Mayeda, *A Thousand Teachings*, p. 162.

61 Das, *Introduction to Shankara*, p. viii.

62 Alston, *Śaṃkara on Creation*, p. 120.

63 S. Radhakrishnan, *Indian Philosophy, Vol. 2* (Delhi: Oxford University Press, 1994 impression, first published 1923), p. 575. Radhakrishnan believed that for Śaṃkara *avidyā* had an "objective reality", a positive character, and existed in gross and subtle form (*ibid.*, p. 582). But if this were so, it could only be from the perspective of ignorance. For Śaṃkara, *avidyā/māyā* cannot obtain at all once liberation reveals the *Ātman*.

64 Dasgupta, *A History of Indian Philosophy, Vol. 1*, p. 440.

65 Vivekananda, *Jnana-Yoga*, p. 18.

66 Śaṃkara, *Upadeśasāhasrī* 1:6:3, translator Mayeda, *A Thousand Teachings*, p. 116.

67 E. Lott, *Vedantic Approaches to God.* Library of Philosophy and Religion, general ed. J. Hick (London and Basingstoke: Macmillan, 1980), p. 43.

68 Radhakrishnan, *Indian Philosophy, Vol. 2*, p. 583.

69 *Ibid.*, p. 584.

70 Alston, *Śaṃkara on the Absolute*, p. 67.
71 *Ibid.*, p. 68.
72 Mayeda, *A Thousand Teachings*, p. 82.
73 Indich, *Consciousness in Advaita Vedānta*, p. 6.
74 Radhakrishnan, *Indian Philosophy, Vol. 2*, p. 519.
75 Potter, *Encyclopedia of Indian Philosophies, Vol. III*, p. 39.
76 Śaṃkara, *Upadeśasāhasrī* 1:13:25, translator Mayeda, *A Thousand Teachings*, p. 134.
77 Indich, *Consciousness in Advaita Vedānta*, p. 9.
78 *Ibid.*, p. 55.
79 Sharma, *The Advaita Tradition in Indian Philosophy*, p. 178.
80 Śaṃkara, *Upadeśasāhasrī* 1:15:27–9, translator Mayeda, *A Thousand Teachings*, pp. 144–5.
81 Sharma, *A Critical Survey of Indian Philosophy*, pp. 283–4.
82 Śaṃkara, *Upadeśasāhasrī* 1:13:25, translator Mayeda, *A Thousand Teachings*, p. 134.
83 *Ibid.*, 1:16:6, p. 149.
84 *Ibid.*, 1:17:54, p. 165.
85 *Ibid.*, 1:17:73, p. 167.
86 *Ibid.*, 1:16:61, p. 155.
87 Śaṃkara, *Upadeśasāhasrī* 18:57–8, translator A. J. Alston, *Śaṃkara on Enlightenment: A Śaṃkara Source-Book, Vol. 6* (London: Shanti Sadan, 1989), p. 119.
88 Radhakrishnan, *Indian Philosophy, Vol. 2*, p. 507.
89 *Ibid.*, p. 509.
90 Śaṃkara, *Chāndogya Upaniṣad Bhaṣya* 6:3:2, translator A. J. Alston, *Śaṃkara on the Soul*, p. 14.
91 Śaṃkara, *Upadeśasāhasrī* 1:5:4, translator Mayeda, *A Thousand Teachings*, p. 114.
92 *Ibid.*, 2:2:79, p. 241.
93 *Ibid.*, 1:17:4, p. 160.
94 *Ibid.*, 1:17:21, p. 162.
95 *Ibid.*, 2:1:42, p. 226.
96 Swami Atmananda, *Sankara's Teachings in His Own Words* (Bombay: Bharatiya Vidya Bhawan, 1989), p. xxv.
97 Lott, *Vedantic Approaches to God*, p. 72.
98 Isayeva, *Shankara and Indian Philosophy*, pp. 120–1.
99 For this method of explanation followed by negation of supportive material in using the *Veda*, see Sri Swami Satchidānandendra, *The Method of the Vedanta: A critical account of the Advaita tradition*, translated by A. J. Alston (Delhi: Motilal Banarsidass, first Indian edn 1997, first published 1989), pp. 41–7.
100 Only "twice-born" Hindus were permitted access to the *Veda*. *Śūdras* and women were amongst those excluded.
101 Śaṃkara, *Bṛhadāraṇyaka Upaniṣad Bhāṣya* 2:3:6, translator Alston, *Śaṃkara on the Absolute*, p. 141.
102 W. Halbfass, *Studies in Kumārila and Śaṅkara* Studien zür Indologie und Iranistik Monograph 9 (Reinbeck: Orientalistische Fachpublikationen, 1983), p. 31.
103 A point examined in detail by Halbfass, *ibid.*, pp. 27–70.
104 Hiriyanna, *Outlines of Indian Philosophy*, p. 351.
105 Śaṃkara, *Brahmasūtrabhāṣya* 1:1:1, translator Alston, *Śaṃkara on the Absolute*, p. 94.
106 Alston, *Śaṃkara on the Absolute*, p. 63.
107 Śaṃkara, *Upadeśasāhasrī* 1:14:19, translator Mayeda, *A Thousand Teachings*, p. 138.
108 It might have been more logical to have dispensed with the term *Ātman* and retained only Brahman, for the use of *Ātman* implies Brahman individuated. Sinari maintains that the subsequent relation between *Ātman* and *jīva* is "not logically warranted" (R. A. Sinari, *The Structure of*

Indian Thought [Delhi, Bombay, Calcutta, Madras: Oxford University Press, 1984, first published 1970], p. 114), and the metaphysics would have been significantly clearer without the two terms. See also Loy's point above, note 23.

109 Sinha, *Metaphysic of Experience*, p. 54.

110 P. Deussen, *The System of the Vedanta* (Delhi: Low Price Publications, 1995 reprint of 1912 edn), p. 324.

111 Śaṃkara, *Kaṭha Upaniṣad Bhāṣya*, translator A. J. Alston, *Śaṃkara on Discipleship: A Śaṃkara Source-Book, Vol. 5* (London: Shanti Sadan, 1989), p. 18.

112 Mayeda, *A Thousand Teachings*, p. 31.

113 Chatterjee and Datta, *An Introduction to Indian Philosophy*, p. 404.

114 Potter, *Encyclopedia of Indian Philosophies, Vol. III*, p. 84.

115 Deussen, *The System of the Vedanta*, p. 172.

116 Mayeda, *A Thousand Teachings*, p. 45.

117 Śaṃkara, *Bṛhadāraṇyaka Upaniṣad Bhāṣya* 4:3:21, translator Alston, *Śaṃkara on the Soul*, p. 128.

118 Indich, *Consciousness in Advaita Vedānta*, p. 62.

119 Indich argues for a "radical discontinuity" between these stages of waking, dreaming, deep sleep and enlightenment, corresponding to the same "radical discontinuity" between the ultimate Reality that is the true Self and the reality of the phenomenal world (*ibid.*, p. 18). However, the same Consciousness that is *Ātman* is *reflected* in all states, and it is this that lends continuity. Nevertheless, it is difficult to posit Pure Consciousness from three illusory states of consciousness and, as Indich later states: "Having established a radical distinction between reality and appearance, the one and the many, eternal rest and temporal change, the Advaitin's attempts to argue from the latter back to the former may be systematically instructive and spiritually edifying, but they cannot be logically conclusive" (*ibid.*, p. 122).

120 Śaṃkara, *Upadeśasāhasrī* 2:17:26–7, translator Potter, *Encyclopedia of Indian Philosophies, Vol. III*, pp. 240–1.

121 *Ibid.*, 1:14:9, p. 137.

122 *Ibid.*, 1:19:8, p. 204.

123 Puligandla, *Fundamentals of Indian Philosophy*, p. 215.

124 Vivekananda, *Jnana-Yoga*, p. 16.

125 Raphael, *The Pathway of Non-Duality*, p. 60.

126 Alston, *Śaṃkara on the Absolute*, p. 139.

127 Raphael, *The Pathway of Non-Duality*, p. 54.

128 Śaṃkara, *Aitareya Upaniṣad Bhāṣya* 2:1:1, translator Alston, *Śaṃkara on the Absolute*, pp. 142–3.

129 Deussen, *The System of the Vedanta*, p. 135.

130 M. Hiriyanna, *Essentials of Indian Philosophy* (Delhi: Motilal Banarsidass, 1995), p. 157.

131 Satchidānandendra, *The Method of the Vedanta*, p. 111.

132 Deussen, *The System of the Vedanta*, p. 286.

133 *Ibid.*

134 Vivekananda, *Jnana-Yoga*, p. 59.

135 Deussen, *The System of the Vedanta*, p. 278.

136 Śaṃkara, *Bhagavadgītābhāṣya* 2:16, translator Alston, *Śaṃkara on the Absolute*, p. 189.

137 Śaṃkara, *Muṇḍaka Upaniṣad* and *Gauḍapādakārikābhāṣya* 3:19, translator Alston, *Śaṃkara on Creation*, p. 202.

138 Alston, *Śaṃkara on Creation*, p. 95.

139 *Ibid.*, p. 3

140 *Ibid.*, p. 6.

141 Śaṃkara, *Brahmasūtrabhāṣya* 2:1:14, translator Alston, *Śaṃkara on Creation*, p. 6.

142 Satchidānandendra, *The Method of the Vedanta*, p. 75.
143 Śaṃkara, *Brahmasūtrabhāṣya* 2:1:27, translator Alston, *Śaṃkara on Creation*, p. 26.
144 Śaṃkara, *Bṛhadāraṇyaka Upaniṣad Bhāṣya* 1:4:7, translator Alston, *ibid.*, p. 141.
145 Mayeda, *A Thousand Teachings*, p. 22.
146 Hence, a theory of *bhedābheda*, identity-in-difference, would be rejected by Śaṃkara.
147 Lott, *Vedantic Approaches to God*, p. 101.
148 For a full analysis of these processes see Potter, *Encyclopedia of Indian Philosophies, Vol. III*, pp. 23–7.
149 Śaṃkara, *Brahmasūtrabhāṣya* 2:1:14, translator Alston, *Śaṃkara on Creation*, p. 41.
150 Primarily, Śaṃkara depicted the Absolute as Pure Consciousness, *cit*, secondarily as Truth, *sat*, and rarely as Bliss, *ānanda*.
151 Lott, *Vedantic Approaches to God*, p. 75.
152 A. Sharma, *The Philosophy of Religion and Advaita Vedānta: A comparative study in religion and reason* (Pennsylvania: The Pennsylvania State University Press, 1995), p. 2.
153 Sharma, *A Critical Survey of Indian Philosophy*, p. 280.
154 Radhakrishnan, *Indian Philosophy, Vol. 2*, p. 519.
155 Śaṃkara, *Bhagavadgītābhāṣya* 3:4:8, translator Alston, *Śaṃkara on Creation*, p. 14.
156 Radhakrishnan, *Indian Philosophy, Vol. 2*, p. 540.
157 Śaṃkara, *Bhagavadgītābhāṣya* 13:12, translator Alston, *Śaṃkara on Discipleship*, p. 304. The quotation actually makes full sense without the intrusion of Alston's words in parentheses.
158 Dasgupta, *A History of Indian Philosophy, Vol. 1*, p. 477.
159 Hiriyanna, *Outlines of Indian Philosophy*, p. 369.
160 Radhakrishnan, *Indian Philosophy, Vol. 2*, p. 545.
161 Vivekananda, *Jnana-Yoga*, p. 73.
162 Alston, *Śaṃkara on the Soul*, p. 146.
163 Dandekar, "Vedānta" in *ER*, vol. 15, p. 210.
164 Hiriyanna, *Outlines of Indian Philosophy*, p. 365.
165 Potter, *Encyclopedia of Indian Philosophies, Vol. III*, p. 77.
166 *Ibid.*, p. 78.
167 Radhakrishnan, *Indian Philosophy, Vol. 2*, pp. 555–6.
168 Radhakrisnan wrote: "There is a gap between the intuited Brahman which is devoid of logical determinations and the conceived Brahman which is the productive principle, which explains difference and at the same time overcomes it. The indeterminate Brahman in itself will seem to the logical intellect, as the dark in which all colours become grey. If it should serve as an explanation of the finite at all, it can only be through the introduction of the very form of the finite into the heart of the absolute" *ibid.*, p. 561.
169 Sharma, *A Critical Survey of Indian Philosophy*, p. 281.
170 Potter, *Encyclopedia of Indian Philosophies, Vol. III*, p. 32.
171 Śaṃkara, *Bṛhadāraṇyaka Upaniṣad Bhāṣya* 4:4:6, translator Alston, *Śaṃkara on Enlightenment*, p. 211.
172 Śaṃkara, *Upadeśasāhasrī* 1:16:63, translator Mayeda, *A Thousand Teachings*, p. 155.
173 Śaṃkara, *Chāndogya Upaniṣad Bhāṣya* 8:1:1, translator Alston, *Śaṃkara on Enlightenment*, p. 22.
174 *Gauḍapādakārikābhāṣya* 4:93, translator Alston, *Śaṃkara on Enlightenment*, p. 288.
175 Alston, *Śaṃkara on Enlightenment*, p. 1.
176 Śaṃkara, *Chāndogya Upaniṣad Bhāṣya*, Introduction 1:1:1, translator Alston, *Śaṃkara on Enlightenment*, p. 8.
177 Śaṃkara, *Bṛhadāraṇyaka Upaniṣad Bhāṣya* 1:4:10, translator Alston, *Śaṃkara on Discipleship*, p. 18.
178 Alston, *Śaṃkara on Enlightenment*, p. 20.

179 Satchidānandendra, *The Method of the Vedanta*, p. 147.
180 *Ibid.*, p. 146.
181 Comans, for example, concurs that the knowledge that brings about liberation can occur directly from hearing *śruti*. M. Comans, "Śaṅkara and the Prasaṅkhyānavāda", *Journal of Indian Philosophy*, 24 (1996), 24.
182 Śaṃkara, *Upadeśasāhasrī* (verse) chapter 13, translator Alston, *Śaṃkara on Enlightenment*, p. 152.
183 Alston, *Śaṃkara on Enlightenment*, p. 82.
184 See Śaṃkara, *Kaṭha Upaniṣad Bhāṣya* 2:2:13, translator Alston, *Śaṃkara on Enlightenment*, p. 85.
185 *Kaṭha Upaniṣad* 1:3:13, translator Alston, *Śaṃkara on Enlightenment*, p. 85.
186 Śaṃkara, *Muṇḍaka Upaniṣad Bhāṣya* 3:1:9, translator Alston, *ibid.*, p. 88.
187 Śaṃkara, *Gauḍapādakārikābhāṣya* 3:41, translator Alston, *ibid.*, p. 91.
188 Śaṃkara, *Māṇḍūkya Upaniṣad* and *Gauḍapādakārikābhāṣya* 3:37, translator Alston, *Śaṃkara on the Absolute*, p. 164.
189 Potter, *Encyclopedia of Indian Philosophies, Vol. III*, p. 45.
190 Sharma, *A Critical Survey of Indian Philosophy*, p. 287.
191 Śaṃkara, *Praśna Upaniṣad Bhāṣya* 5:3, translator Alston, *Śaṃkara on Enlightenment*, p. 170.
192 Śaṃkara, *Upadeśasāhasrī* 2:1:, translator Mayeda, *A Thousand Teachings*, p. 211.
193 Mayeda, *A Thousand Teachings*, p. 88.
194 Śaṃkara, *Upadeśasāhasrī* 2:1:30, translator Mayeda, *ibid.*, p. 220.
195 *Ibid.*, 2:1:44, pp. 226–7.
196 *Ibid.*, 1:17:22, p. 162.
197 *Ibid.*, 1:17:49, p. 165.
198 Potter, *Encyclopedia of Indian Philosophies, Vol. III*, p. 41.
199 Śaṃkara, *Upadeśasāhasrī* 1:1:6, translator Mayeda, *A Thousand Teachings*, p. 103.
200 *Ibid.*, 1:14:22, 23, p. 138.
201 Deussen, *The System of the Vedanta*, p. 409.
202 Indich, *Consciousness in Advaita Vedānta*, p. 16.
203 Though Radhakrishnan, for one, does not accept that Śaṃkara saw *saṃnyāsins* as *jīvanmuktas*. He believed they were simply better placed for intuitive realization of Brahman as *Ātman*. *Indian Philosophy, Vol. 2*, p. 617.
204 Śaṃkara, *Gauḍapādakārikābhāṣya* 4:94, translator Alston, *Śaṃkara on Enlightenment*, p. 290.
205 Loy, *Non-Duality*, p. 242.
206 Translator Alston, *Śaṃkara on Enlightenment*, p. 285.
207 *Ibid.* This suggests a view of the mind as atomic rather than as a mere sense.
208 4:4:23, translator Alston, *Śaṃkara on Enlightenment*, p. 294.
209 Dasgupta, *A History of Indian Philosophy, Vol. 1*, p. 440.
210 Śaṃkara, *Gauḍapādakārikābhāṣya* 90, translator Alston, *Śaṃkara on the Soul*, p. 171.
211 Mayeda, *A Thousand Teachings*, p. 12.
212 N. Smart, *Doctrine and Argument in Indian Philosophy* (Leiden, New York, Köln: E. J. Brill, 1992), p. 87.
213 Radhakrishnan, *Indian Philosophy, Vol. 2*, p. 649.
214 *Ibid.*, p. 652.
215 Smart, *Doctrine and Argument in Indian Philosophy*, p. 91.
216 Loy, *Non-Duality*, p. 297.
217 R. Sinari, *The Structure of Indian Thought* (Delhi, Bombay, Calcutta, Madras: Oxford University Press, first Indian edn 1984, first published 1970), p. 107.
218 Mayeda, *A Thousand Teachings*, p. 94.
219 Deussen, *The System of the Vedanta*, p. 404.

220 Potter, *Encyclopedia of Indian Philosophies, Vol. III*, p. 100.
221 G. Larson, in G. Larson and R. S. Bhattacharya, *Encyclopedia of Indian Philosophies, Vol. IV: Sāṃkhya* (Delhi, Varanasi, Patna, Madras: Motilal Banarsidass, 1987), p. 84.
222 Isayeva, *Shankara and Indian Philosophy*, p. 11.
223 Sinari, *The Structure of Indian Thought*, p. 112.
224 Vivekananda, *Jnana-Yoga*, p. 99.

Chapter 9 *Viśiṣṭādvaita Vedānta*

1 S. Radhakrishnan, *Indian Philosophy, Vol. 2* (Delhi: Oxford University Press, 1994 impression, first published 1923), p. 720.
2 See, for example, A. L. Basham, *The Wonder that was India* (London: Sidgwick & Jackson, 1982, first published 1954), p. 332, and I. Kesarcodi-Watson, "Śaṅkara, Rāmānuja and Bhakti" in G. M. Bailey and I. Kesarcodi-Watson (eds), *Bhakti Studies* (New Delhi: Sterling Publishers Private Ltd., 1992), p. 112.
3 See K. K. Klostermaier, *A Survey of Hinduism* (Albany: State University of New York, second edn 1994), p. 419.
4 See the discussion on monism in chapter 1.
5 See E. Lott, *Vedantic Approaches to God* (London and Basingstoke: Macmillan, 1980), p. 46.
6 See S. M. Srinivasa Chari, *Fundamentals of Viśiṣṭādvaita Vedānta: A study based on Vedānta Deśika's Tattva-muktā-kalāpa* (Delhi: Motilal Banarsidass, 1988), p. 18.
7 Rāmānuja, *Vedārthasaṃgraha* 4, translator J. A. B. van Buitenen, *Rāmānuja's Vedārthasaṃgraha: Introduction, critical edition and annotated translation* (Poona: Deccan College Postgraduate and Research Institute, 1956), pp. 184–5.
8 Radhakrishnan, *Indian Philosophy, Vol. 2*, p. 659.
9 K. H. Potter, *Presuppositions of India's Philosophies* (Delhi: Motilal Banarsidass, 1999 reprint of 1991 first Indian edn), p. 153.
10 This is a dating put forward by S. M. S. Chari, *Philosophy and Theistic Mysticism of the Āḻvārs* (Delhi: Motilal Banarsidass 1997, pp. 1–2). Others accept a later dating of seventh to ninth centuries CE, see C. Sharma, *A Critical Survey of Indian Philosophy* (Delhi: Motilal Banarsidass, 1994 reprint of 1960 edn), p. 337. Unanimity of dating is, as Chari points out (p. 11), not to be found.
11 Kesarcodi-Watson, "Śaṅkara, Rāmānuja, and Bhakti" in Bailey and Kesarcodi-Watson (eds), *Bhakti Studies*, p. 113. Given this kind of respect for devotional practice – despite the ecstatic fanaticism of it – Kesarcodi-Watson is somewhat misleading in referring to the devotion of the Āḻvārs as "the crazed lusting of an unbridled appetite for Divine Vision". There is no evidence to suggest that Rāmānuja set out to "bridle this lunacy and lust, by systematizing its impetus into a socially constructive phenomenon, purged of this anti-social menace" (p. 118).
12 Bhatt, however, considers that Rāmānuja was not a Śrī Vaiṣṇavite, and that it was his followers who associated him thus. If this is the case, then it might explain the absence of any reference to the Āḻvars, though not the synonymy of ideas, nor the many references to Nārāṇaya in Rāmānuja's works. See S. R. Bhatt, *Studies in Rāmānuja Vedānta* (New Delhi: Heritage Publishers, 1975, pp. 181 and 187–8.
13 See Chari, *Philosophy and Theistic Mysticism of the Āḻvārs*, pp. 2–3 and *passim*.
14 In fact, tradition considers the Āḻvārs themselves to be incarnations of Viṣṇu.
15 Justification for the acceptance of the *Pāñcarātra* corpus was supplied by Yāmuna for the following reason: "The Lord, to Whose unerring and innate vision the entire corpus of Vedic Revelation is directly displayed, saw that His devotees' minds were too infirm to study and

retain the many branches of the Vedic schools embodying scattered and multifarious injunctions, preceptive explications and incantations. Moved to compassion for the devotees, He condensed the meaning of the Vedas in a manner easy to comprehend, and then promulgated it [the Pañcarātra corpus]". Translator J. Pereira, *Hindu Theology: Themes, Texts and Structures* (Delhi: Motilal Banarsidass 1991, first published 1976), p. 285.

16 See V. Rangacharya, "Historical Evolution of Śrī-Vaiṣṇavism in South India", in H. Bhattacharya (ed.), *The Cultural Heritage of India, Vol. 4: The Religions* (Calcutta: The Ramakrishna Mission Institute of Culture, 1956 revised edn, first published 1937), p. 178. However, the more recent view of Chari is that there are few major differences that divide the two schools so radically as to separate them entirely: the fact that both accept the foundational work of the *Śrībhāṣya* of Rāmānuja, he suggests, is sufficient evidence to favour a less overt split. See Chari, *Philosophy and Theistic Mysticism of the Āḷvārs*, pp. 240–4.

17 Van Buitenen, *Rāmānuja's Vedārthasaṃgraha*, p. 3.

18 Tradition has it that, when Rāmānuja went to see Yāmuna, the teacher had died, but with three fingers closed on the right hand. Rāmānuja interpreted this as evidence that he should fulfil three vows – to honour the memories of Vyāsa, said to have written the *Vedas*, and Parāśara, said to have written the *Viṣṇu Purāṇa*, to write what became the *Tiruvāimoli*, a *bhāṣya* on the hymns of the Āḷvār Nammāḷvār, and to write a *bhāṣya* on Bādarāyana's *Brahmasūtras* (*Vedāntasūtras*). All three vows were fulfilled during his lifetime.

19 Kesarcodi-Watson, "Śaṅkara, Rāmānuja, and Bhakti" in Bailey and Kesarcodi-Watson (eds), *Bhakti Studies*, p. 110.

20 *Ibid.*, pp. 134–5.

21 Van Buitenen, *Rāmānuja's Vedārthasaṃgraha*, p. 30.

22 M. Hiriyanna, *The Essentials of Indian Philosophy* (Delhi: Motilal Banarsidass, 1995), p. 176.

23 S. M. S Chari, *Advaita and Viśiṣṭādvaita: A study based on Vedānta Deṣikā's Śatadūṣaṇ"* (Delhi, Varanasi, Patna: Motilal Banarsidass, 1976 reprint of 1961 edn), p. 2.

24 For a highly detailed account of this, the reader is directed to S. Dasgupta, *A History of Indian Philosophy, Vol. 3* (Delhi, Varanasi, Patna, Bangalore and Madras: Motilal Banarsidass, 1991, first published 1922), pp. 114–33.

25 Such a separation of one *guṇa* from another two would have been impossible in the *prakṛtic* reality of Sāṃkhya.

26 Presumably always in combination, since pure *sattva* is isolated as the transcendental substance *śuddhasattva.*

27 Rejected in Viśiṣṭādvaita are the categories of *karma*, *sāmānya*, *samavāya*, *viśeṣa*, and *abhāva.*

28 *Śvetāśvatara Upaniṣad* 1:12, translator R. E. Hume, *The Thirteen Principal Upanishads* (Delhi, Bombay, Calcutta, Madras: Oxford University Press, 1989 Indian impression, first published 1921), p. 396). Cf also 1:9.

29 Radhakrishnan, *Indian Philosophy, Vol. 2*, p. 717.

30 Rāmānuja, *Gītābhāṣya* 9:4, translator J. A. B. van Buitenen, *Rāmānuja on the Bhagavadgītā: A condensed rendering of his Gītābhāṣya with copious notes and an introduction* (Delhi, Varanasi, Patna: Motilal Banarsidass, 1974 reprint of 1968, second edn), pp. 113–14.

31 See Chari, *Philosophy and Theistic Mysticism of the Āḷvārs*, pp. 116–17.

32 *Ibid.*, p. 237.

33 *The Vedānta Sūtras with the Commentary of Rāmānuga*, translated by George Thibaut, *Sacred Books of the East, Vol. 48* (Oxford: Clarendon Press, 1904), cited in S. Radhakrishnan and C. A. Moore, *A Sourcebook in Indian Philosophy* (Princeton, New Jersey: Princeton University Press, 1989 reprint of 1957 edn), p. 552.

34 Translator Hume, *The Thirteen Principal Upanishads*, p. 116.

35 Sharma, *A Critical Survey of Indian Philosophy*, p. 369.
36 Rāmānuja, *Vedārthasaṃgraha*, translator van Buitenen, *Rāmānuja's Vedārthasaṃgraha*, p. 231.
37 The issue is an interesting one in that it seems to suggest a pantheistic conception of absolute divinity – God is the sum total of the parts that compose the whole. Despite its monistic emphasis, however, there is much to be said for viewing Viśiṣṭādvaita as panentheistic, maintaining the perspective that there is an essence of Brahman that is over and above the manifestation (the body) of Brahman as the universe. Yet it is difficult to see how God as a substance can transcend his own attributes. Without his attributes he cannot exist, since a substance is only such by virtue of its attributes.
38 Van Buitenen, *Rāmānuja on the Bhagavadgītā*, p. 2.
39 Dasgupta, *A History of Indian philosophy, Vol. 3*, p. 193.
40 S. M. S. Chari, *Fundamentals of Viśiṣṭādvaita Vedānta: A study based on Vedānta Deśika's Tattva-muktā-kalāpa* (Delhi, Varanasi, Patna, Bangalore, Madras: Motilal Banarsidass, 1988), p. 272.
41 J. B. Carman, *The Theology of Rāmānuja: An essay in interreligious understanding* (New Haven and London: Yale University Press, 1974), p. 116.
42 Translator Hume, *The Thirteen Principal Upanishads*, p. 241.
43 For example, *Bṛhadāraṇyaka Upaniṣad* 4:4:19; 4:5:15.
44 Radhakrishnan, *Indian Philosophy, Vol. 2*, p. 682.
45 Bhatt, *Studies in Rāmānuja Vedānta*, p. 91.
46 *Ibid.* p. 53.
47 Radhakrishnan, *Indian Philosophy, Vol. 2*, p. 685.
48 Sharma, *A Critical Survey of Indian Philosophy*, p. 341.
49 Bhatt, *Studies in Rāmānuja Vedānta*, p. 28.
50 Nevertheless, since Rāmānuja accepts a beginningless *saṃsāra*, this must surely suggest that ignorance that produces *karma* is also beginningless. This is a point he does not seem to solve. It is difficult to see how a pure Self – one characterized by knowledge and bliss – can become deluded by the world in the first place, without positing *avidyā* as some kind of eternal "real".
51 Rāmānuja, *Vedārthasaṃgraha* 82, translator van Buitenen, *Rāmānuja's Vedārthasaṃgraha*, p. 240.
52 J. B. Chethimattam, *Consciousness and Reality: An Indian approach to metaphysics* (London: Chapman, 1971), p. 62.
53 Chari, *Fundamentals of Viśiṣṭādvaita Vedānta*, p. 148.
54 Some Viśiṣṭādvaitins, however, reject knowledge as a *dravya* because of its dependency on the self: see Chari, *ibid.*, p. 152. Such rejection reflects the basic weakness of the principle.
55 J. J. Lipner, *The Face of Truth* (London: Macmillan, 1986), pp. 49–50.
56 See Chari, *Advaita and Viśiṣṭadvaita*, p. 37.
57 Rāmānuja rejected class or universality as a separate category. What we mean by class is that something, a cow, perhaps, is *like* other cows. But there is insufficient identity of qualities in all cows to suggest a separate category of class/universality.
58 Lott, *Vedantic Approaches to God*, p. 76.
59 Radhakrishnan, *Indian Philosophy, Vol. 2*, p. 675.
60 Rāmānuja, *Vedārthasaṃgraha* 4, translator Carman, *The Theology of Rāmānuja*, p. 108.
61 Lipner, *The Face of Truth*, p. 9.
62 Rāmānuja, *Vedārthasaṃgraha* 139, translator van Buitenen, *Rāmānuja's Vedārthasaṃgraha*, p. 294.
63 *Ibid.*, 21, p. 197.
64 S. Chatterjee and D. Datta, *An Introduction to Indian Philosophy* (Calcutta: University of Calcutta, 1984 reprint of 1939 edn), p. 422.
65 Radhakrishnan, *Indian Philosophy, Vol. 2*, p. 719.
66 Sharma, *A Critical Survey of Indian Philosophy*, p. 368.

67 Rāmānuja, *Vedārthasaṃgraha* 78, translator van Buitenen, *Rāmānuja's Vedārthasaṃgraha*, p. 238.
68 Rāmānuja, *Gītābhāṣya* 2:30, translator van Buitenen, *Rāmānuja on the Bhagavadgītā*, p. 56.
69 *Ibid.*, 5:18–19, cf. 6:29, translator van Buitenen, p. 89.
70 Van Buitenen, *Rāmānuja's Vedārthasaṃgraha*, pp. 186–7, note 37.
71 Rāmānuja, *Gītābhāṣya* 13:16, translator van Buitenen, *Rāmānuja on the Bhagavadgītā*, p. 143.
72 Rāmānuja, *Vedārthasaṃgraha* 42, translator van Buitenen, *Rāmānuja's Vedārthasaṃgraha*, p. 213.
73 *Vedārthasaṃgraha* 43, see van Buitenen, *ibid.*, p. 215.
74 According to the *Śvetāśvatara Upaniṣad* 5:9, the atomic Self is smaller than a hundredth part of the point of a hair that has been divided a hundred times.
75 Cf. *cit* and *cetana* referring to the consciousness of the self, *ahaṃpadārtha* the "I" of the self, and *kṣetrajña* or "knower of the field of knowledge".
76 See Chari, *Philosophy and Theistic Mysticism of the Āḷvārs*, p. 111.
77 The *sattva* in this state is different from *prakṛtic sattva* since the latter always exists with the other two *guṇas* of *rajas* and *tamas*. *Śuddhasattva* is pure *sattva*, transparent and subtle, not like the *prakṛtic* qualities, or Sāṃkhya substances.
78 Radhakrishnan, *Indian Philosophy, Vol. 2*, p. 677.
79 Rāmānuja, *Vedārthasaṃgraha* 20, translator van Buitenen, *Rāmānuja's Vedārthasaṃgraha*, p. 196.
80 See, for example, the *Chāndogya Upaniṣad* 8:12 and 4:5.
81 Rāmānuja, *Vedārthasaṃgraha* 5, translator van Buitenen, *Rāmānuja's Vedārthasaṃgraha*, p. 186.
82 Van Buitenen, *ibid.*, p. 186, note 36.
83 Rāmānuja, *Vedārthasaṃgraha* 24, translator van Buitenen, *ibid.*, p. 199.
84 Van Buitenen, *ibid.*, p. 212, note 183.
85 This is not an issue that lends itself well to any solution, and the reader is advised to be aware of the difficulties that obtain by a substance that is at once both substance and attribute in this instance.
86 See Chari, *Advaita and Viśiṣṭādvaita*, pp. 57–60.
87 Radhakrishnan, *Indian Philosophy, Vol. 2*, p. 703.
88 H. V. S. Murthy, *Vaiṣṇavism of Śaṃkaradeva and Rāmānuja* (Delhi, Varanasi, Patna: Motilal Banarsidass, 1973), p. 180.
89 Rāmānuja, *Śrībhāṣya* 1:1:1, translator G. Thibaut, *The Vedānta-Sūtras with the Commentary of Rāmānuja*, Part 3, Sacred Books of the East, vol. 48, general ed. M. Müller (Oxford: Clarendon Press, 1904), p. 4.
90 Dasgupta, *A History of Indian Philosophy, Vol. 3*, p. 195.
91 S. S. Raghavachar, *Śrī Rāmānuja on The Gītā* (Mangalore: Sri Ramakrishna Ashrama, 1969), p. xii.
92 Rāmānuja, *Vedārthasaṃgraha* 18, translator van Buitenen, *Rāmānuja's Vedārthasaṃgraha*, p. 194.
93 Rāmānuja, *Gītābhāṣya* 10:39, translator van Buitenen, *Rāmānuja on the Bhagavadgītā*, p. 126.
94 3:7:3, translator Hume, *The Thirteen Principal Upanishads*, p. 115.
95 Rāmānuja, *Gītābhāṣya* 7:7, translator Carman, *The Theology of Rāmānuja*, p. 83.
96 From the introduction to the *Vedārthasaṃgraha*, translator Murthy, *Vaiṣṇavism of Śaṃkaradeva and Rāmānuja*, p. 85.
97 Bhatt, *Studies in Rāmānuja Vedānta*, p. 25.
98 Rāmānuja, *Vedārthasaṃgraha* 134, trans. van Buitenen, *Rāmānuja's Vedārthasaṃgraha*, pp. 289–90.
99 Bhatt, *Studies in Rāmānuja Vedānta*, p. 54.
100 Though this is no less a problem for the nature of God than it was for that of the self.
101 Chari, *Philosophy and Theistic Mysticism of the Āḷvārs*, p. 53.
102 See Kesarcodi-Watson, "Śaṅkara, Rāmānuja, and Bhakti" in Bailey and Kesarcodi-Watson (eds), *Bhakti Studies*, p. 137.

103 See Chari, *Fundamentals of Viśiṣṭādvaita Vedānta*, p. 228.
104 Dasgupta, *A History of Indian Philosophy, Vol. 3*, p. 159.
105 Radhakrishnan, *Indian Philosophy, Vol. 2*, p. 698.
106 Rāmānuja, *Vedārthasaṃgraha* 90, translator van Buitenen, *Rāmānuja's Vedārthasaṃgraha*, p. 247.
107 Rāmānuja, *Śrībhāṣya* 1:2:1, translator Carman, *The Theology of Rāmānuja*, p. 132.
108 *Bhagavadgītā* 18: 64–66.
109 Bhatt, *Studies in Rāmānuja Vedānta*, p. 41.
110 See Dasgupta, *A History of Indian Philosophy, Vol. 3*, p. 158.
111 *Ibid.*, p. 304.
112 Rāmānuja, *Vedārthasaṃgraha* 90, translator van Buitenen, *Rāmānuja's Vedārthasaṃgraha*, p. 247.
113 K. Ward, *Images of Eternity* (Oxford: Oneworld, 1993, first published 1987), p. 39.
114 *Vedārthasaṃgraha* 127.
115 See Chari, *Philosophy and Theistic Mysticism of the Āḷvārs*, p. 63.
116 See for example Bhatt, *Studies in Rāmānuja Vedānta*, p. 59.
117 *Ibid.*, p. 94.
118 From the *Glory Commentary on the "Aphorisms of the Brahman"*, Rāmānuja's *Śrībhāṣya*, translator J. Pereira, *Hindu Theology: Themes, Texts and Structures* (Delhi: Motilal Banarsidass, 1991, first published 1976), p. 287.
119 Rāmānuja, *Gītābhāṣya* 13:2, translator van Buitenen, *Rāmānuja on the Bhagavadgītā*, p. 140.
120 Carman, *The Theology of Rāmānuja*, p. 115.
121 Rāmānuja, *Vedārthasaṃgraha* 74, translator van Buitenen, *Rāmānuja's Vedārthasaṃgraha*, p. 234.
122 Bhatt, *Studies in Rāmānuja Vedānta*, p. 92.
123 Rāmānuja, *Śrībhāṣya* 1:4:26, translator G. Thibaut, *Vedānta-Sūtras*, p. 402.
124 Bhatt, *Studies in Rāmānuja Vedānta*, p. 26.
125 Advaita proponents were quick to criticize Rāmānuja for having the point both ways. God is either removed from the world, or he is not. To say that he is only half removed is, said his critics, like having half a chicken for cooking and the other half for laying eggs!
126 J. B. Chethimattam, *Consciousness and Reality: An Indian approach to metaphysics* (London: Chapman, 1971), p. 73.
127 Rāmānuja, *Śrībhāṣya* 1:4:27, translator G. Thibaut, *Vedānta-Sūtras*, p. 405.
128 *Ibid.*, p. 406.
129 Rāmānuja, *Gītābhāṣya* 4:14, translator van Buitenen, *Rāmānuja on the Bhagavadgītā*, p. 79.
130 Carman, *The Theology of Rāmānuja*, p. 119.
131 Rāmānuja, *Vedārthasaṃgraha* 42, translator Carman, *ibid.*, p. 70.
132 Bhatt, *Studies in Rāmānuja Vedānta*, p. 25.
133 For example, the *Muṇḍaka Upaniṣad* 3:1:3.
134 See Dasgupta, *A History of Indian Philosophy, Vol. 3*, p. 104.
135 See Murthy, *Vaiṣṇavism of Śaṃkaradeva and Rāmānuja*, p. 151.
136 See also Bhatt, *Studies in Rāmānuja Vedānta*, p. 158.
137 Rāmānuja, *Gītābhāṣya* 9:29, translator van Buitenen, *Rāmānuja on the Bhagavadgītā*, p. 120.
138 Murthy, *Vaiṣṇavism of Śaṃkaradeva and Rāmānuja*, p. 216.
139 *Ibid.*, p. 201.
140 See Rangacharya, "Historical Evolution of Śrī-Vaiṣṇavism in South India", in Bhattacharya (ed.), *The Cultural Heritage of India, Vol. 4: The Religions*, p. 176.
141 Lipner, *The Face of Truth*, p. 104.
142 Bhatt, *Studies in Rāmānuja Vedānta*, p. 151.
143 Radhakrishnan, *Indian Philosophy, Vol. 2*, p. 704.
144 Bhatt, *Studies in Rāmānuja Vedānta*, p. 150.

145 Rāmānuja, *Vedārthasaṃgraha* 92, translator van Buitenen, *Rāmānuja's Vedārthasaṃgraha*, p. 250.
146 See, for example, 7:17 and 10:10.
147 Rāmānuja, *Gītābhāṣya* 15:5, translator van Buitenen, *Rāmānuja on the Bhagavadgītā*, p. 152.
148 Carman, *The Theology of Rāmānuja*, p. 85.
149 Rāmānuja, *Śrībhāṣya* 3:2:37, translator Carman, *ibid.*, p. 86.
150 Van Buitenen, *Rāmānuja on the Bhagavadgītā*, p. 28.
151 See Chari, *Philosophy and Theistic Mysticism of the Āḻvārs*, p. 239.
152 Bhatt, *Studies in Rāmānuja Vedānta*, pp. 151–6.
153 *Ibid.*, p. 156.
154 Van Buitenen, *Rāmānuja on the Bhagavadgītā*, p. 24.
155 *Vedārthasaṃgraha* 91.
156 Murthy, *Vaiṣṇavism of Śaṃkaradeva and Rāmānuja*, p. 154.
157 See Chari, *Philosophy and Theistic Mysticism of the Āḻvārs*, pp. 122–6.
158 Bhatt, *Studies in Rāmānuja Vedānta*, p. 124.
159 Puligandla, *Fundamentals of Indian Philosophy*, p. 237.
160 Murthy, *Vaiṣṇavism of Śaṃkaradeva and Rāmānuja*, p. 125.
161 Bhatt, *Studies in Rāmānuja Vedānta*, p. 53.
162 On this point, cf. the words of Chethimattam: "Rāmānuja's theory of *tâdâtmya*, or 'ensoulment', of things by Brahman is dangerously close to a pantheistic formal or material causality", and "the accusation of pantheism or panentheism seems rather difficult to avoid". *Consciousness and Reality*, p. 77.
163 Sharma, *A Critical Survey of Indian Philosophy*, pp. 366–7.
164 Chethimattam, *Consciousness and Reality*, p. 78.

Chapter 10 *Dvaita Vedānta*

1 For example, Chandradhar Sharma, *A Critical Survey of Indian Philosophy* (Delhi: Motilal Banarsidass, 1994 reprint of 1960 edn), p. 372, and S. Dasgupta, *A History of Indian Philosophy, Vol. 4: Indian Pluralism* (Delhi, Varanasi, Patna, Bangalore, Madras: Motilal Banarsidass, 1988 reprint of 1975 Indian edn, first published 1922), pp. 51–2, 54.
2 B. N. K. Sharma, *Madhva's Teachings in His Own Words* (Bombay: Bharatiya Vidya Bhavan, 1979), p. 4. See also K. K. Klostermaier, *A Survey of Hinduism* (New York: State University of New York Press, second edn 1994), p. 422.
3 Sharma, *Madhva's Teachings in His Own Words*, p. 17.
4 *Ibid.*, p. 19.
5 *Ibid.*, p. 101.
6 Madhva, *Viṣṇutattvanirṇaya*, translator Sharma, *ibid.*, p. 36.
7 Madhva, *Tattvaviveka*, translator Sharma, *ibid.*, p. 37.
8 Madhva, *Viṣṇutattvanirṇaya*, translator Sharma, *ibid.*, p. 84.
9 K. Narain, *An Outline of Madhva Philosophy* (Allahabad: Udayana Publications, 1962), p. 61.
10 *Ibid.*, p. 97.
11 Madhva, *Viṣṇutattvanirṇaya*, translator Sharma, *Madhva's Teachings in His Own Words*, p. 85.
12 The concept differs from that in Nyāya and Vaiśeṣika by virtue of the fact that it refers to attributes not just eternal substances.
13 B. N. K. Sharma, *The Philosophy of Śrī Madhvācārya* (Delhi, India: Motilal Banarsidass, 1986), p. 79.
14 *Ibid.*, p. 86.

15 H. N. Raghavendrachar, *The Dvaita Philosophy and its Place in the Vedānta* (Mysore: University of Mysore, 1941), p. 185.
16 D. N. Shanbag, *Some Problems of Dvaita Philosophy in their Dialectical Setting* (Dharwad: Shri Rama Prakashana, 1982), p. 127.
17 Narain, *An Outline of Madhva Philosophy*, p. 120.
18 *Ibid.*
19 Madhva, *Viṣṇutattvanirṇaya*, translator Sharma, *Madhva's Teachings in His Own Words*, p. 80.
20 Narain, *An Outline of Madhva Philosophy*, p. 155.
21 Sharma, *Madhva's Teachings in His Own Words*, p. 98.
22 Madhva, *Dvādaśastotra* 3:6, translator Sharma, *Madhva's Teachings in His Own Words*, p. 100.
23 Here, eternal Space, like eternal Time, is infinite, and should not be confused with the limited space in which finite existents have their transient manifestation. Ordinary physical space, or ether, is a product of *prakṛti*, unlike eternal Space. It is the latter that provides space for existence, and for movement within it. *Prakṛti* itself is in infinite Space. Both Space and Time are divisible into parts of Space and parts of Time in Madhva's school, otherwise, there could be no created and dissolved universe. But both are, themselves, uncreated.
24 Here, *sattva*, *rajas*, and *tamas* are classed as substances, though they are also the characteristic properties of *prakṛti*. The principle of *saviśeṣābheda*, the identity between the substance (*prakṛti*) and its characteristics (*guṇas*) supports their being substances in some senses and independent attributes in others.
25 Time can only be perceived supersensually and intuitively by the inner self, the *sākṣin*. It is this, for example, that enables the self to know that it has slept a long time.
26 A reflection is an entity that is inseparable from the object that it reflects. *Jīvas* are reflections of God and, as such, are eternal.
27 Madhva, *Anuvyākhyāna*, translator Sharma, *Madhva's Teachings in His Own Words*, p. 50.
28 Sharma, *Philosophy of Śrī Madhvācārya*, p. 163.
29 Narain, *An Outline of Madhva Philosophy*, p. 19.
30 Madhva, *Pramāṇalakṣaṇa*, translator Sharma, *Madhva's Teachings in His Own Words*, p. 42.
31 Translator Shanbag, *Some Problems of Dvaita in their Dialectical Setting*, p. 36.
32 Other *pramāṇas* accepted by other schools are rejected as cases of inference.
33 Madhva, *Pramāṇalakṣaṇa*, translator Sharma, *Madhva's Teachings in His Own Words*, p. 46.
34 Madhva, *Tattvodyota*, translator Sharma, *ibid.*, pp. 66–7.
35 Narain, *An Outline of Madhva Philosophy*, p. 46.
36 H. N. Raghavendrachar, "Madhva's Brahma-Mīmāṃsā" in H. Bhattacharya (ed.), *The Cultural Heritage of India, Vol. 3: The Philosophies* (Calcutta: The Ramakrishna Mission Institute of Culture, revised edn 1953, first published 1937), p. 314.
37 Shanbag, *Some Problems of Dvaita Philosophy in their Dialectical Setting*, p. 48.
38 E. Lott, *Vedantic Approaches to God* (London: Macmillan, 1980), p. 142.
39 Narain, *An Outline of Madhva Philosophy*, p. 149.
40 Madhva, *Anuvyākhyāna*, translator Sharma, *Madhva's Teachings in His Own Words*, p. 74.
41 Raghavendrachar, *The Dvaita Philosophy and its Place in the Vedānta*, p. 176.
42 *Ibid.*, p. 189.
43 Madhva, *Upādhikhaṇḍana* 11, translator Sharma, *Madhva's Teachings in His Own Words*, p. 89.
44 For Rāmānuja there was certainly an essential essence of nature that was the same in all, even if variety overlaid that essence to account for differences in the liberated state. There is no such same essential essence for Madhva.
45 Sharma, *Madhva's Teachings in His Own Words*, p. 89.
46 Madhva, *Brahmasūtrabhāṣya* 2:3:33, translator Sharma, *ibid.*, p. 133.

47 Sharma, *Philosophy of Śrī Madhvācārya*, p. 362.
48 *Ibid.*, p. 365.
49 Raghavendrachar, *The Dvaita Philosophy and its Place in the Vedānta*, p. 191.
50 Madhva, *Viṣṇutattvanirṇaya*, translator Sharma, *Madhva's Teachings in His Own Words*, p. 87.
51 Sharma, *ibid.*, pp. 47 and 51.
52 *Ibid.*, p. 51.
53 See, for example, the *Bhagavadgītā* 16: 5, 6.
54 Sharma, *Philosophy of Śrī Madhvācārya*, p. 269.
55 Madhva, *Dvādaśastotra* 6:3, translator Sharma, *Madhva's Teachings in His Own Words*, p. 33.
56 Lott, *Vedantic Approaches to God*, p. 35.
57 *Ibid.*, p. 117.
58 Jayatīrtha came to accept *prakṛti* in its primordial state as the body of God, though he still did not concede that it was God himself who was the material cause of the universe: this could only be primordial matter. God is but the *deus ex machina.*
59 Madhva, *Brahmasūtrabhāṣya* 2:3:11, translator Sharma, *Madhva's Teachings in His Own Words*, p. 126.
60 Madhva, *Tattvodyota*, translator Sharma, *ibid.*, p. 110.
61 M. Hiriyanna, *The Essentials of Indian Philosophy* (Delhi: Motilal Banarsidass, 1995), p. 191.
62 Sharma, *Madhva's Teachings in His Own Words*, p. 39.
63 Madhva, *Brahmasūtrabhāṣya* 1, translator Narain, *An Outline of Madhva Philosophy*, p. 121.
64 Madhva, *Karmaniṇaya*, translator Sharma, *Madhva's Teachings in His Own Words*, p. 119.
65 Hiriyanna, *The Essentials of Indian Philosophy*, p. 191.
66 Madhva, *Viṣṇutattvanirṇaya*, translator Sharma, *ibid.*, p. 120.
67 Raghavendrachar, "Madhva's Brahma-Mīmāṃsā" in Bhattacharya (ed.), *The Cultural Heritage of India, Vol. 3*, p. 314.
68 Narain, *An Outline of Madhva Philosophy*, p. 203.
69 Hiriyanna, *The Essentials of Indian Philosophy*, p. 192.
70 Radhakrishnan, *Indian Philosophy Vol. 2*, p. 751.
71 Sharma, *Philosophy of Śrī Madhvācārya*, p. 298.
72 *Ibid.*, p. 351.
73 *Ibid.*, p. 370.
74 There can be no "partial" *avatāras* such as Rāma is sometimes thought to be. All *avatāras* – and Madhva accepts more than the usual ten – are accepted as full manifestations of God.
75 Unlike Rāmānuja, however, Madhva did not accept that God was manifested in temple images.
76 Madhva, *Brahmasūtrabhāṣya* 3:2:14, translator Sharma, *Madhva's Teachings in His Own Words*, p. 121.
77 *Ibid.* 1:4:27, translator Sharma, *ibid.*, p. 125.
78 Lott, *Vedantic Approaches to God*, p. 184.
79 Sharma, *Madhva's Teachings in His Own Words*, p. 28.
80 *The Vedānta-sūtras with the Commentary of Sri Madhwacharya*, translated by S. Subba Rao (Tirupati: Sri Vyasa Press, second revised edn 1936), cited in S. Radhakrishnan and C. A. Moore (eds), *A Sourcebook in Indian Philosophy* (Princeton, New Jersey: Princeton University Press, 1989 reprint of 1957 edn), p. 569.
81 Narain, *An Outline of Madhva Philosophy*, p. 78.
82 *Ibid.*, p. 107.
83 Madhva, *Brahmasūtrabhāṣya* 1:1:17, translator Sharma, *Madhva's Teachings in His Own Words*, p. 163.
84 Raghavendrachar, *The Dvaita Philosophy and its Place in the Vedānta*, p. 209.

85 Sharma, *Philosophy of Śrī Madhvācārya*, p. 393.
86 Madhva, *Nyāyavivaraṇa* 3:1: adh. 7, translator Sharma, *Madhva's Teachings in His Own Words*, p. 139.
87 Sharma, *Philosophy of Śrī Madhvācārya*, p. 45.
88 Sharma, *Madhva's Teachings in His Own Words*, p. 141.
89 The number of qualities on which one is able to meditate is infinite but, since the *jīva* is limited in its ability to concentrate on many of God's attributes, it usually confines meditation to one or two. Gods, however, particularly the highest god, Brahmā, are able to meditate on many more.
90 Madhva, *Anuvyākhyāna*, translator Sharma, *Madhva's Teachings in His Own Words*, pp. 102–3.
91 Madhva, *Brahmasūtrabhāṣya* 4:1:5, translator Sharma, *ibid.*, p. 152.
92 Narain, *An Outline of Madhva Philosophy*, p. 114.
93 Madhva, *Brahmasūtrabhāṣya* 3:2:27, translator Sharma, *Madhva's Teachings in His Own Words*, p. 159.
94 Sharma, *ibid.*, p. 159.
95 *Ibid.*, p. 161.
96 Narain, *An Outline of Madhva Philosophy*, p. 174.
97 Madhva, *Anuvyākhyāna* 3:4, translator Sharma, *Madhva's Teachings in His Own Words*, p. 104.
98 Madhva, *Mahābhārata Tātparyanirṇaya* 1:86, translator Sharma, *ibid.*, p. 105.
99 Madhva, *Anuvyākhyāna* 3:4, translator Sharma, *ibid.*, p. 106.
100 Madhva, *Brahmasūtrabhāṣya* 1:1:31, translator Sharma, *ibid.*, p. 144.
101 *Ibid.*
102 Narain, *An Outline of Madhva Philosophy*, p. 171.
103 Evidence is slim to suggest the influence of Christianity here, though the possibility remains, given the unusual nature of the tenet in Indian ideas.
104 K. H. Potter, *Presuppositions of India's Philosophies* (Delhi: Motilal Banarsidass, 1999 reprint of 1991 edn), p. 250.
105 He also believed himself to be the son of God – perhaps another influence from the Christian religion.
106 Madhva, *Anuvyākhyāna* p. 48, translator Sharma, *Madhva's Teachings in His Own Words*, p. 169. *Sādhanas* are the means to liberation through self-effort and self-discipline.
107 *Ibid.*, p. 45, translator Sharma, *ibid.*, p. 90.
108 *Ibid.*, pp. 159–60.
109 Madhva, *Brahmasūtrabhāṣya* 4:4:21, translator Sharma, *ibid.*, p. 107.
110 Madhva, *Bṛhadāraṇyaka Upaniṣad Bhāṣya*, translator Sharma, *ibid.*, p. 170.
111 Raghavendrachar, *The Dvaita Philosophy and its Place in the Vedānta*, p. 211.
112 Madhva, *Anuvyākhyāna* 57b, translator Sharma, *Madhva's Teachings in His Own Words*, p. 163.
113 Narain, *An Outline of Madhva Philosophy*, p. 178.
114 *Ibid.*, p. 97.
115 Shanbag, *Some Problems of Dvaita Philosophy in their Dialectical Setting*, p. 35.

Conclusion

1 Greenfield, *Brain Story* (BBC, 1st August 2000).
2 K. P. Bahadur, *The Wisdom of Nyaaya* (New Delhi: Sterling Publishers Private Ltd., 1978), p. 1.
3 M. Eliade, *Yoga: Immortality and Freedom* (Princeton, New Jersey: Princeton University Press, 1990 reprint, first published in French, 1954), p. 4.
4 G. Feuerstein, *The Yoga-Sūtra of Patañjali: A new translation and commentary* (Rochester, Vermont: Inner Traditions International, 1989, first published 1979), p. 12.

Glossary

A guide to pronunciation of Sanskrit words

Sanskrit consonants carry the vowel '*a*' with them, which is why transliterated Sanskrit words have so many '*a*'s in them, like *Mahabharata.* This '*a*' is normally more like the '*u*' in the "English word *but.* Where this is not so, diacritical marks can be added in transliteration to indicate a change of sound. Such diacritical marks are also helpful on vowels to indicate where the stress occurs in pronouncing a word. Sanskrit has a number of letters representing English '*s*'. Where it occurs without any diacritical marks its pronunciation is as the '*s*' in *is*. Sanskrit *ś* and *ṣ* are pronounced as the *sh* in English *ship.* Sanskrit also has a number of aspirated letters indicated with an '*h*' following the consonant. When these combinations of letters occur, the reader is advised to separate the two consonants in pronunciation to gain a more accurate sound. Thus *artha* "wealth" is *art* (as in English *art*) plus *ha* as in English *have*, though since there are no diacritical marks on the vowels, the '*a*'s are better pronounced as '*u*'s – *urt-hu.*

abhāva	non-existence, non-being, non-apprehension.
abheda	non-difference; identity.
abhiniveśa	fear of death and annihilation; attachment to life; the will to live.
abhyasa	continuous practice and effort; repetition.
Ācāryas	great theologians, teachers and spiritual guides, also a title attached to their names.
acit	non-sentient matter.
ādhāra-ādheya	controller of the controlled, supporter and supported.
adharma	what is not right; demerit.
adhikaraṇa	arrangement of *sūtras* under a topic consisting of five parts.
adhyāsa	superimposition.
adhyātmayoga	meditation on the Supreme Self.
adhyāya	arrangement of material into a chapter.
adravya	that which is not a substance.
adṛṣṭa	the unseen potency that links appropriate effects to their causes. *See also apūrva.*
adṛṣṭaphalakarma	*karma* accumulated by unconscious, innate actions that becomes manifest at a later time.
advaita	"non-dualism".
Advaita Vedānta	the school of non-dualism, one of the six orthodox schools of Indian/Hindu philosophy.

āgama	testimony; scriptural tradition.
Āgamas	scriptures bearing testimony to a personal deity.
āgāmikarma	*karma* that is being formed now in the present existence and that still has to mature.
Agni	*Vedic* god identified as fire.
ahaṃkāra	egoity; the individuating principle; the ego of the self; individuality; the "I".
ahiṃsā	abstention from injury and violence to any form of life.
aiśvarya	power; lordship.
ajñāna	ignorance
ākāśa	ether.
akhyāti	non-apprehension.
akliṣta	unafflicted (mind content).
alaukika	extraordinary, extra-sensory, *yogic* intuition.
aliṅga	the term for unmanifest *prakṛti* in classical Yoga, synonymous with Sāṃkhya *avyakta*; lacking in any characteristics.
Āḷvār	devotional mystic who "dives" into the divine.
aṃśi	the whole.
anādiviśeṣa	the intrinsic peculiarity of an entity; eternal differentiators.
ānanda	bliss.
ānanda samādhi	experience of bliss in *samādhi.*
andhakāra	darkness.
aṇga	part, limb, individual.
anonyābhāva	mutual negation; mutual non-existence.
antaḥkaraṇa	"internal organ" consisting of the intellect, ego and mind.
antaryāmin	the divine as inner controller and ruler of the world and selves.
anthropomorphism	the giving of human form, attributes and character to the divine; the giving of human personality to what is impersonal and irrational, for example, animals.
aṇu	atomic, minute.
anubhava	intuitive knowledge; direct perception; experience.
anubhūti	direct apprehensions of knowledge.
anumāna	inference; syllogism.
anupramāṇa	secondary means of knowledge through *pramāṇas.*
Anuvyākhyāna	a major work of the Dvaitist Madhva.
aparāvidyā	lower knowledge.
aparigraha	non-acceptance of gifts; non-grasping; non-possession.
aparokṣajñāna	sudden, intuitive knowledge of God; immediate, direct knowledge.
apauruṣeya	superhuman; extraordinary.
apavarga	release; realization of the Self; deliverance from pain.
apṛthaksiddhi	inseparability between a substance and its attributes, a whole and its parts.
āpta	a trustworthy person.
aptavacana	the testimony of reliable persons. *See also śabda.*
apūrva	the unseen potency that links appropriate effects to their causes. *See also adṛṣṭa.*
Āraṇyakas	forest writings; part of the *śruti* sacred literature.
artha	wealth.
arthāpaṭṭi	presumption, implication, postulation.
Aryans	the invaders of India who brought with them the foundations of *Brahminical* Hinduism.

asādhāraṇakāraṇa	non-common, specific and special causes of effects.
asaṃprajñāta samādhi	the highest stage of *samādhi* when there is total cessation of mind fluctuations, and there is no consciousness of objects, either gross or subtle.
āsana	bodily posture.
asatkāryavāda	the theory of causality which accepts that effects do not exist until they are manifest, that effects are new, and that effects are different from their causes.
asmitā	egoism; false notions of a self; "I-am-ness".
asmitāmātra	pure "I-ness", egoity, the term used in classical Yoga instead of Sāṃkhya *ahaṃkāra*.
asmitā samādhi	experience of the *mahātbuddhi*, the first evolute of *prakṛti* in the process of *samādhi*.
āśramas	four stages of Hindu life.
asteya	abstinence from theft.
āstika	literally "it is", the orthodox systems of belief.
asvatantra	dependent.
Atharva Veda	one of the four *Vedas* containing knowledge of incantations, magical formulas and spells.
atheism	absence of any belief in the divine.
ātman	the self; the eternal soul.
atyantābhāva	absolute negation and non-existence.
Aum	the sacred symbol that is Brahman.
autpattika	the relation between a word and its meaning.
avatāras	"descents" of the Hindu deity Viṣṇu to the human realm.
avayava	parts of a syllogism; member, premise.
avayavin	whole.
avidyā	ignorance, nescience.
aviśeṣas	the six unparticularized and indeterminate evolutes of Sāṃkhya and classical Yoga comprised of egoity and the five *tanmātras*.
aviveka	failure to discriminate, non-discrimination.
avyākṛta	unmanifest; the subtle potential material of the universe.
avyākṛtākāśa	unmanifest Space.
avyakta	unmanifest, potential effects of all existence.
Bādarāyaṇa	founder of Vedānta philosophy and composer of the *Brahmasūtras* that condensed the major teachings of the *Upaniṣads*.
baddhas	those bound to reincarnation.
Bhagavadgītā	sacred Hindu devotional epic poem.
Bhagavad Purāṇa	devotional, theistic legends.
bhakta	devotee; one who loves God.
bhakti	loving devotion to the divine, and from the divine to the devotee.
bhaktimārga	the path of loving-devotion.
bhaktiyoga	the *yoga* of loving-devotion to the divine.
bhāṣya	a commentary on a text.
Bhaṭṭa, Kumārila	major proponent of the school of Pūrva Mīmāṃsā.
bhāva	being-ness, being-hood; predisposition of the intellect.
bheda	difference.

bhedābheda	literally "different yet not different", the theory of identity-in-difference.
bhoga	experience, enjoyment.
bhūtas	gross elements.
bīja samādhi	*samādhi* "with seed", *samādhi* with the aid of an object for one-pointed focus.
Bimba	the principle or prototype of reality.
Brahmā	Hindu God responsible for the creation process.
brahmacarya	chastity; celibate student, the first of the four stages of life.
Brahman	the divine Absolute of Hinduism.
Brāhmaṇas	commentaries on the *Vedas*; part of the *śruti* sacred literature.
Brahmapariṇāmavāda	real transformations of Brahman from cause to effect.
Brahmasūtras	the condensed major teachings of the *Upaniṣads*, compiled by Bādarāyaṇa.
Brahmin	member of the priestly class of Hinduism.
buddhi	knowledge; intellect; consciousness; the discerning faculty.
buddhīndriyas	five capacities for sense in the Sāṃkhya theory of evolution.
buddhisattva	the *sattvic* nature, or experience, of the pure *sattva* of the *buddhi*, the intellect.
chela	disciple.
cit	consciousness; intelligence; sentient beings; spirit.
citta	mind; mind complex including intellect and ego; awareness; consciousness; memory.
cittavṛttinirodha	cessation of the fluctuations of the mind.
cittavṛttis	mind-fluctuations.
darśana	"view", "to have sight of" a holy person or divine image; a philosophical "view" or school of philosophy.
deism	belief in a Creator who has no further involvement with what he has created.
dhāraṇā	focused concentration and attention; single-mindedness.
dharma	what is right for individuals, society, class and the universe; right and morally good behaviour.
dharmabhūtajñāna	knowledge that is both the substance for modifying change in subjective knowledge, and an attribute of the self; qualitative, attributive consciousness.
dharmijñāna	knowledge that is the unchanging nature of the self.
dharmisvarūpa	the essential nature of an entity.
dhvaṃsābhāva	the non-existence of something after it has been destroyed.
dhyāna	meditation.
dik	space.
doṣa	defect, fault.
draṣṭr	the seer, perceiver, *puruṣa*.
dravya	substance.
dṛṣṭa	perception.
dṛśya	the seeable, what is perceived, the world of matter.
dualism	"of two parts", belief in two independent and juxtaposed principles.
duḥkha	suffering, pain, disharmony, dissatisfaction.
Dūrga	one of the great female Goddesses of Hinduism.
Dvaita	"duality", "dualism"; a school of Vedānta philosophy.
dvandva	pairs of opposites.
dveṣa	aversion to what is painful in life; hatred, dislike.

dvyaṇuka	dyad, or binary molecule consisting of two atoms.
ekāgra/ekāgratā	one-pointedness of the mind.
emanationism	theory that the universe emanates from one primary source.
empiricism	theory that knowledge can be acquired only through the senses.
epistemology	theory of knowledge.
gandha	smell.
Gauḍapāda	early proponent of non-dualism.
Gauḍapādakārikā	text written by Gauḍapāda containing the earliest known exposition of *advaita* or non-dualism.
Gautama	the traditional founder of the school of Nyāya and composer of the *Nyāyasūtras.*
gṛhastha	householder, one at the second of the four stages of life.
guṇa	generally a quality, attribute; also a substance.
guru	a spiritual teacher.
Hari	"Lord", another name for Viṣṇu.
henotheism	belief in one deity as supreme, while recognizing the existence of other deities.
hetu	the reason or cause by which something is inferred; the second part and middle term of a five-membered syllogism.
Hiraṇyagarbha	one of the *Vedic* deities posited as the source of creation.
Indra	*Vedic* god identified as lightning, rain and storm.
indriyas	external sense organs.
Īśvara	"Lord", a term to depict Brahman with qualities and manifest form; God; supreme deity.
Īśvarakṛṣṇa	writer of the Sāṃkhya text, the *Sāṃkhyakārikā.*
Īśvarapraṇidhāna	devotion to Īśvara, God.
Itihāsas	literally, "so it was", mythological stories and historical sagas about human heroes.
Jaimini	the traditional founder of the school of Pūrva Mīmāṃsā, author of the *Mīmāṃsāsūtras.*
Jainism	an atheistic religious tradition in India.
Jayatīrtha	commentator on the works of Madhva.
jijñāsā	philosophical inquiry into the nature of God through study, reflection and meditation.
jīvanmukta	one who is liberated, enlightened, while still alive.
jīvanmukti	liberation while still living.
jīvātman/jīva	the individual, personality self; the bound self; the soul.
jñā	knower.
jñāna	knowledge.
jñānakāṇḍa	"knowledge portion"; the more mystical texts of the *Veda* related to knowledge of Brahman.
jñānakaraṇa	resultant object of knowledge.
jñānalakṣaṇa	extraordinary perception that permits knowledge of something additional to that perceived, for example the *softness* of grass.

jñānamārga	the path to liberation that involves knowledge.
jñānayoga	the *yoga* of knowledge.
jñānin	one possessing knowledge; one on the path of knowledge.
jñātā	knower.
jñātatā	cognition; state of being known.
jñeya	the object to be known.
kaivalya	isolation, aloneness, the Sāṃkhya and Yoga state of liberation.
kāla	time.
kalpa	one cycle of creation and dissolution of the universe, consisting of four ages.
kāma	pleasure, love, desire; one of the four goals of human life.
kāmyakarmas	*Vedic* injunctions that are optional.
Kaṇāda	legendary founder of the school of Vaiśeṣika, and compiler of the *Vaiśeṣikasūtras*.
Kapila	legendary founder of the school of Sāṃkhya.
kāraṇa	instrumental, efficient cause.
kāraṇāvasthā	Brahman in the causal state.
karma	"activity", "action", "motion"; the law of cause and effect by which each individual reaps according to that which he or she sows.
karmakāṇḍa	"ritual portion" of the *Veda*.
karmamārga	the path to liberation that involves egoless action.
karmāśaya	the balance between good and bad *karmic* causes that produce a particular life form in the present. It is formed from the subconscious impressions left after all past actions, thought, speech and memory activity.
karmayoga	the *yoga* of egoless action.
karmendriyas	five capacities for actions in the Sāṃkhya theory of evolution.
kārya	effect.
kāryāvastha	Brahman in the effect state.
keśin	one with uncut hair.
kevala advaita	absolute non-dualism.
kevalapramāṇa	true knowledge of an object as it is.
kleśas	afflictions or hindrances of the mind.
kliṣṭa	afflicted (mind content).
Kṣatriya	member of the warrior/administrator class of Hinduism.
Lakṣmī	the consort of the deity Viṣṇu, also called Śrī, the Goddess of fortune and beauty.
laukika	ordinary, worldly, secular.
līlā	sport, play.
līlāvibhūti	"cosmic sport" or "play", the divine means of interaction with the world.
liṅga	mark, sign, characteristic that is universally related to something else that can be inferred from it, for example *smoke* is the mark of/infers fire.
liṅgamātra	the Designator, the term in classical Yoga for Sāṃkhya *mahatbuddhi*, the first evolute of *prakṛti*.
liṅgaśarīra	the subtle body that is the means of reincarnation; the hidden container of the soul.
lotus of the heart	an inner light visualized as an inverted lotus, and used as a focus of one-pointed concentration.

Madhva	twelfth-century philosopher, founder of the Vedānta school of Dvaita.
Mahābhārata	great epic poem of the *smṛti* tradition.
mahābhūtas	the five great elemental substances of ether, fire, air, water and earth that form the material world.
mahāpralaya	a great dissolution of the universe.
mahat/mahatbuddhi	cosmic intellect the first evolute of *prakṛti* in the Sāṃkhya system.
manana	reflection on the meaning of the scriptures; discriminative understanding.
manas	the mind; mental powers; thinking faculty.
mānasakarma	*karma* acquired through thought.
maṇḍalas	the sections into which the books of the *Vedas* are divided.
mantras	hymns of the *Vedas*.
Manusmṛti	an ancient law book said to have been composed by Manu.
mārga	path, way.
Materialists	those belonging to the Indian Materialist school, known as Cārvāka or Lokāyata.
māyā	"illusion", "appearance", obscuring veil of Nature; "marvellous creation"; God's creative energy.
Mīmāṃsā	one of the six orthodox schools of Indian/Hindu philosophy.
Mīmāṃsāsūtras	the foundational text of the Pūrva Mīmāṃsā school, ascribed to Jaimini.
mokṣa	(also termed *mukti*) liberation, the end of the cycle of reincarnation; spiritual enlightenment.
monism	the belief that reality is one single principle, which is to say that all things are ultimately one with, and identical to, another. In terms of the divine, the same unity and identity of all things with it obtains.
monotheism	belief in one divine being (male, female or other) with whom the individual has a dualistic and personal relationship.
mukta	one who is enlightened, liberated, and no longer subject to reincarnation.
mukti	see *mokṣa*.
muktiyoga	discipline that leads to liberation.
mūlaprakṛti	unformed, unmanifest *prakṛti*; primordial matter.
muni	a sage, seer, great devotee.
naimittikarmas	actions that, according to the *Veda*, must be performed at auspicious times.
Nāḷāyira-divya-prabandham	hymns of the devotional poets, the Āḻvārs.
Nārāyana	another name for the deity Viṣṇu.
nāstika	literally, "it is not", the heterodox systems of Indian belief; atheist.
Nāthamuni	devotional mystic, one of the most prominent of the Āḻvārs.
Navya-Nyāya	"new", later or modern Nyāya.
nescience	ignorance.
neti neti	"not this, not this" referring to the nature of Brahman as beyond dualities.
nididhyāsana	deep, sustained meditation; contemplation.
nidrā	sleep.
nigamana	the concluding part of a five-membered syllogism; the summing up of an argument.
nirākāra	"without form", referring to the nature of Brahman as unmanifest.
nirguṇa	"without qualities" referring to the nature of Brahman as unmanifest.
nirodha	cessation (of mind fluctuations).

niruddha	restrained, restricted.
nirvicāra samādhi	the fourth stage of *samādhi* when language, thought and memory are abandoned in one-pointed concentration on a subtle object.
nirvikalpaka	indeterminate (perception).
nirviśeṣa	without qualities; undifferentiated.
nirvitarka samādhi	the second stage of *samādhi* when language and memory are abandoned in one-pointed concentration on a gross object.
niṣedha	*Vedic* prohibitions.
nityakarmas	obligatory actions that, according to the *Veda* have to be performed daily.
nityamuktas	those beings eternally free from reincarnation.
niyama	discipline; observance; regulation.
niyantā-niyāmya	controller of the controlled; sustainer of the sustained.
Nyāya	"logic"; one of the six orthodox schools of Indian/Hindu philosophy.
Nyāyasūtras	foundational aphorisms of the Nyāya school, said to have been composed by Gautama.
ontology	philosophy that is concerned with the nature of Being.
pāda	part; chapter; arrangement of *sūtras* into a section.
Padārthadharmasaṃgraha	Praśastapāda's commentary on Jaimini's *Vaiśeṣikasūtras.*
padārthas	categories of reality; real entities.
Padmapāda	a notable Advaitin.
pakṣa	the minor term in a syllogism and the subject in which the major term is inferred.
pañcabheda	doctrine of five differences of reality in the Dvaita school.
Pañcarātra Āgamas	sectarian literature devoted to Viṣṇu as a personal God.
pañcāvayavanyāya	"reasoning with five members", the five parts of a Nyāya syllogism.
panentheism	belief that God is in all things, and all things are in God, but that God is greater than all things.
pantheism	belief that the divine is the totality of all things, though each is dualistically related to the divine.
parābhakti	supreme, highest devotion to God.
Parabrahman	Supreme, Highest Brahman.
paramāṇu	a primary, indivisible atom, the smallest division of matter.
pāramārthika	reality that is absolute.
Paramātman	Supreme Self; God; Brahman.
paratantra	dependent.
paratantratā	inherence.
paravairāgya	supreme detachment, the highest state of *yogic samādhi.*
parāvidyā	"higher knowledge"; wisdom.
pariṇāma	transformation; modification; change.
pariṇāmavāda	the belief that effects are real transformations of their causes, but in a way that makes cause and effects the same.
Patañjali	founder of the school of Yoga, composer of the *Yogasūtras.*
phala	the fruit of action; result.
pitṛ	ancestor, "father".

pluralism	belief in the lack of total unity between the human and the divine and between the world and the divine; the assigning of an independent reality to all things in the perceived world, and the absence of any unifying force to connect them.
polytheism	belief in more than one deity, or a plurality of deities, with whom there is a dualistic (and sometimes personal) relationship.
pradhāna	the primordial material principle; *prakṛti*; the source of the universe.
prāgabhāva	the non-existence of something before it comes into being.
Prajāpati	"Lord of Creatures", one of the *Vedic* deities posited as the source of creation.
prajñā	wisdom; the subtlest self.
prakāra	dependent mode, attribute, quality, adjunct.
Prakārin	possessor of modes or attributes.
prakṛti	unmanifest potential existence and manifest existence; the uncaused cause of material existence in the Sāṃkhya system; cosmic substance.
prakṛtilaya	lower form of highest *samādhi* when the liberated Self is at one with all matter, *prakṛti*.
prakṛtilīna	one who experiences and remains in a state of unity with matter until rebirth.
pralaya	cyclical dissolved state of the universe.
pramā	real, valid knowledge.
pramāṇa	right knowledge; a means of valid knowledge.
pramātā	the person knowing; the cognizer.
prameya	the object of valid knowledge.
prāṇa	vital breath, life breath.
prāṇāyāmā	rhythmic control of respiration.
prapatti	total surrender to God.
prārabdhakarma	*karma* that is about to, or has already begun, to take effect and must be experienced by the individual.
Praśastapāda	author of the earliest commentary on Jaimini's *Vaiśeṣikasūtras*.
prātibhāsika	impossibilities in reality like the horns of a hare; apparent reality, like a mirage.
pratibimba	reflection.
pratijnā	the proposition to be proved in a syllogism, the first part of a five-membered syllogism.
pratiṣiddhakarmas	actions that are prohibited by the *Veda*.
pratyāhāra	withdrawal of the senses from the external world of stimuli.
pratyakṣa	perception.
pratyaya	modification, condition of the mind.
pravṛtti	activity, effort.
pretyabhāva	the state after death, afterlife.
Purāṇas	"ancient narratives", sacred legends.
puruṣa	the individual soul; the cosmic soul that is Brahman; the self; pure spirit.
puruṣakārakarma	*karma* accumulated through individual free will and effort.
puruṣārtha	what exists for the end achievement of something; the four goals of life.
Puruṣasūkta	a *Vedic* creation hymn.
Puruṣottama	the Highest Self, Brahman, and his *avatāra* Kṛṣṇa.
Pūrva Mīmāṃsā	"inquiry", "investigation"; one of the six orthodox schools of Indian/Hindu philosophy.

pūrvavat	inference from lesser to greater, cause to effect, or *a priori*.
rāga	attachment, desire.
rājamārga	"Royal Path", the path of Yoga as a means to liberation.
Rājamārtaṇḍa	commentary by King Bhoja on Patañjali's *Yogasūtras*.
rajas	one of the three *guṇas*, of the nature of energy, activity, passion.
Rāmānuja	eleventh-century philosopher and theologian, founder of the Vedānta school of Viśiṣṭādvaita.
rasa	taste.
realism	belief that the world is real and that everything in it has an independent reality.
Ṛg Veda	"Royal knowledge", one of the four *Vedas*.
ṛṣis	seers, great sages, poets.
ṛta	the cosmic norm of the *Vedas*; Truth; Order.
rūpa	form; colour.
śabda	verbal testimony; sound; word.
śabdabodha	verbal understanding.
sadasatkāryavāda	the belief that effects partly exist in their causes and yet do not exist in them.
sādhāraṇakāraṇa	common causes of effects.
sādhya	the major term in a syllogism, and the subject to be proved.
sādṛśya	similarity.
saguṇa	"with qualities" referring to the qualities of Brahman.
Śaivism	one of the three great sects of Hinduism whose followers are devoted to the God Śiva.
sākāra	"with form" referring to the manifest aspects of Brahman.
sākṣin	the inner, witnessing, neutral self (Advaita); the inner self as consciousness that perceives absolute knowledge (Dvaita).
śakti	potency, power, energy.
samādhi	concentration; absorption of consciousness into the object of contemplation; the state of stilled consciousness; the highest state in *yoga*.
sāmānya	generality, genus, class.
sāmānyaguṇa	universal qualities.
sāmānyalakṣaṇa	extraordinary perception that permits knowledge of the universal through the perceived particular.
sāmānyatodṛṣṭa	inference without causal relationship.
samavāya	inherence, inseparable connection, concomitance.
Sāma Veda	"Knowledge of chants", one of the four *Vedas*.
Saṃhitās	another name for the four *Vedas*.
Śaṃkara	eighth-century philosopher and founder of the school of Advaita Vedānta.
saṃkhyā	number.
Sāṃkhya	"enumeration" (of objects of knowledge); one of the six orthodox schools of Indian/Hindu philosophy.
saṃnyāsa	renunciation; the final, fourth stage of life as a wandering mendicant.
saṃnyāsin	mendicant in the fourth stage of life.
Sāṃkhyakārikā	(or *Kārikā*) foundational, extant text of the Sāṃkhya school, composed by Īśvarakṛṣṇa.
sāṃkhyayoga	non-differentiated, combined ideas of Sāṃkhya and Yoga.

Sāṃkhya-Yoga	combined schools of Sāṃkhya and Yoga.
saṃprajñāta samādhi	cognitive stage of *samādhi* with the support of an object of concentration.
saṃsāra	reincarnation; empirical existence.
saṃśaya	doubt, uncertainty.
saṃskāras	impressions, tendencies, predispositions formed in the subconscious from actions of thought, body and memory; purificatory ritual.
saṃyama	combined practice; *dhārana*, *dhyāna* and *samādhi* combined in *yogic* concentration; restraint, self-control.
saṃyoga	conjunction, contact; union.
sañcitakarma	*karma* from past and present lives that is in the process of maturing.
santoṣa	serenity and contentment of mind.
Santoṣī Mā	a modern Hindu goddess.
śarīra	body.
śarīrin	soul; Brahman in Viśiṣṭādvaita.
ṣaṣṭitantra	"system of sixty topics", a non-extant Sāṃkhya source.
śāstras	scriptures, sacred teachings.
sat/satya	"truth", "reality", "existence", "being".
satkāraṇavāda	the theory of causality which accepts that only causes exist; there are no real effects.
satkāryavāda	the theory of causality which accepts that effects are latent in their causes and therefore exist prior to their manifestation.
satta	being-hood; existence.
sattva	one of the three *guṇas* of the nature of goodness, evolution, pureness, blissfulness, illumination.
śauca	purity.
savicāra samādhi	the third stage of *samādhi* when a gross aid is abandoned for a subtle one in one-pointed concentration.
savikalpaka	determinate (perception).
saviśeṣa	with qualities.
saviśeṣābheda	the theory of identity between a substance and its attributes that is characterized and conditioned by essential differences.
savitarka samādhi	the lowest stage of *samādhi* with concentration on a gross object involving language, memory and cognition.
śeṣavat	inferring from effect to cause or *a posteriori*.
śeṣi-śeṣa	master of the enslaved; owner of the owned.
siddhis	extraordinary, supernormal powers of advanced *yogins*.
Śiva	a major deity of Hinduism.
Ślokavārtika	Pūrva Mīmāṃsā text written by Kumārila Bhaṭṭa.
smṛti	memory; recollection.
smṛtis	"recollections", "traditions", Hindu literature that is not revealed, but recollected.
sparśa	touch.
śraddhā	faith.
śramaṇas	non-*Vedic* wandering holy men in search of Truth.
śravaṇa	hearing and study of the scriptures.
Śrī	consort of the deity Viṣṇu, also called Lakṣmī.
Śrībhāṣya	Rāmānuja's commentary on the *Vedāntasūtras* or *Brahmasūtras*.
śruti	"that which is heard", the revealed scriptures of the *Veda*.

śuddhasattva	"pure *sattva*", an unconscious, immaterial, transcendental substance.
Śūdra	member of the servant class of Hinduism, the lowest of the four classes.
śūnyata	Buddhist theory of emptiness or "voidness".
Sureśvara	a notable Advaitin.
Sūrya	*Vedic* god identified as the sun.
sūtras	"threads" or aphoristic statements that became the foundational texts of each philosophical school.
svabhāva	the inherent nature of something.
svabhāvabheda	real difference in being.
svādhyāya	regular, religious study.
svarga	heaven.
svarūpa	"own form", the essential essence or nature of an entity.
svarūpabheda	difference in the essential natures of entities.
svarūpajñāna	knowledge that is the unchanging nature of the self.
svarūpanirūpaka-dharmas	five basic attributes of the essence of Brahman.
svataḥprāmāṇya	self-validity of knowledge.
svatantra	independent.
svatantratattva	independent reality.
syllogism	reasoning by inference set out in three or more established parts.
taijasa	the self in the dreaming state.
tamas	one of the three *guṇas* of the nature of inertia, indifference, darkness.
tanmātras	five subtle essences in the Sāṃkhya theory of evolution, from which evolve the five gross elements.
Tantravārtika	Pūrva Mīmāṃsā text written by Kumārila Bhaṭṭa.
tapas	"heat"; austerities.
tarka	a hypothetical contradiction raised against a proposed conclusion to demonstrate that that conclusion must be true; confutation; argument.
Tat/Tat Ekam	"That"/"That One" referring to the indescribable divinity beyond all the deities.
Tattvacintāmaṇi	Navya-Nyāya work composed by Gaṅgeśa.
Tat tvam asi	"That you are" the association of the self with Brahman.
tattvas	literally "reals", "truths", essences of things; the evolutes of evolution.
Tengalais school	branch of Viśiṣṭādvaita advocating total surrender to God as a means to liberation.
theism	belief in a deity or deities (God, Goddess, Gods and/or Goddesses) with whom human beings have a dual and personal relationship.
theodicy	the problem of the existence of evil in the world in the light of a good and all-powerful God, and hypotheses for its solution.
tryaṇuka	triad of three binary molecules.
Ṭupṭika	Pūrva Mīmāṃsā text written by Kumārila Bhaṭṭa.
turya/turīya	"fourth", the fourth and enlightened state of the self in Advaita.
udāharaṇa	the third part of a syllogism that gives an example in order to corroborate the reason.
Udayana	proponent of Navya-Nyāya.
Uddyotakara	author of the Nyāyavārtika.

Upadeśasāhasrī	*Thousand Teachings*, an authentic work by the Advaita Vedāntin, Śaṃkara.
upādhi	limiting adjunct.
upamāna	analogy, comparison.
upanaya	the fourth part of a syllogism that applies the reason to the minor term.
Upaniṣads	the final part of the Veda, generally more philosophical and metaphysical.
upāsana	meditation.
Uṣas	*Vedic* goddess identified as the dawn.
Uttara Mīmāṃsā	term given to the later Mīmāṃsā tradition that bases its views on the "latter" part of the *Veda*, the *Vedānta*.
Vācaspati Miśra	author of the *Nyāyavārtika* and commentator on Patañjali's *Yogasūtras*.
Vaḍagalais school	branch of Viśiṣṭādvaita that advocates surrender to God alongside personal effort as a means to liberation.
vāhyakarma	*karma* acquired through physical action.
Vaikuṇṭha	the heaven of the deity Viṣṇu.
vairāgya	detachment, dispassion, renunciation.
Vaiśeṣika	"distinction", "excellence"; one of the six orthodox schools of Indian/Hindu philosophy.
Vaiśeṣikasūtras	foundational aphorisms of the *Vaiśeṣika* school, said to have been composed by Kaṇāda.
Vaiṣṇavism	one of the three great sects of Hinduism whose followers are devoted to the God Viśṇu.
Vaiśya	member of the merchant and farmer class of Hinduism.
varṇa	sounds of speech; religious class.
vānaprasthas	those at the third of four stages of life who retire for a spiritual existence in the forest.
vārrtika	commentaries on what has been said, what has not been said, and not said clearly.
Varuṇa	*Vedic* god of cosmic order.
vāsaṇās	deep-rooted habits, traits, tendencies accumulated in the subconscious.
Vāsudeva	another name for the deity Viṣṇu.
Vātsyāyana	earliest and outstanding commentator on the *Nyāyasūtras*.
Vāyu	*Vedic* god of the wind.
Veda	"knowledge", "wisdom"; the sacred scriptures of the four *Vedas*, the *Brāhmaṇas*, *Āraṇyakas* and *Upaniṣads*, collectively referred to as *śruti*.
Vedānta	name given to a number of different philosophical schools founded on *Vedānta*, the major ones being Advaita, Viśiṣṭādvaita and Dvaita.
Vedānta	"end of the Veda", the texts and teachings of the Upaniṣads.
Vedānta Deśika	famous proponent of the Viśiṣṭādvaita school.
Vedārthasaṃgraha	earliest work of the philosopher Rāmānuja.
Vedas	the four scriptures of the *Ṛg Veda*, the *Sāma Veda*, the *Yajur Veda* and the *Atharva Veda*.
vibhāga	disjunction, separation.
vibhūti	divine manifestations; manifest divine power.
vidhi	*Vedic* injunctions.
vidyā	knowledge, wisdom.
vijñāna	pure Knowledge; pure Consciousness; discriminative knowledge.
Vijñānabhikṣu	commentator on the *Yogasūtras* of Patañjali.

vikalpa	conceptualization, mental abstraction, fancy, imagination.
viparyaya	incorrect knowledge.
virāga	non-attachment.
virāj	(also *vaiśvānara*), the self in the waking state; the manifest universe.
viśeṣa	"particularity", the distinctive nature of primary atoms in the Vaiśeṣika system; the sixteen particularized of classical Yoga – ten *indriyas*, mind, and the five gross elements; the essential characteristics that differentiate one entity from another in Dvaita Vedānta.
viśeṣaguṇa	"particular quality".
viśeṣaṇa	subordinate particular or attribute of a substance; predication.
viśesya	substantive element to which particulars and attributes are subordinate.
viśiṣṭa	a unitary whole of substance and attributes.
Viśiṣṭādvaita	qualified non-dualism; a school of Vedānta philosophy.
Viṣṇu	a major deity of Hinduism who was incarnate in the forms of Kṛṣṇa and Rāma amongst others.
Viśvadevas	"All gods", the *Vedic* source of all the deities.
Viśvakarman	"Maker of Everything", one of the *Vedic* deities posited as the source of creation.
vivarta	appearance; apparent and not real change.
vivartavāda	the belief that the world we see is but a false appearance and illusory.
viveka	discriminative discernment.
vivekajñāna	discriminative knowledge.
vrātyas	wandering ascetics.
vṛttis	modes, modifications, or fluctuations, of the mind; mental state.
vyakta	the manifest, material world.
vyāvahārika	apparent reality that is capable of being contradicted; empirical perspectives of life.
vyāpti	the universal and major premise asserted in inferential knowledge; universal pervasion; universal concomitance.
Vyāsa	major commentator on Patañjali's *Yogasūtras*.
Vyāsatīrtha	commentator and writer on Dvaita philosophy.

yajña	sacrificial ritual.
Yajur Veda	"Knowledge of sacrificial ritual", one of the four *Vedas*.
yama	restraint, self-control.
Yāmuna	teacher of qualified monism who preceded and influenced Rāmānuja.
yoga	discipline; union.
Yoga	"union", "discipline"; one of the six orthodox schools of Indian/Hindu philosophy.
Yogabhāsya	Vyāsa's commentary on the *Yogasūtras* of Patañjali.
yogaja	extraordinary perception of *yogins*.
Yogasūtras	the foundational aphorisms composed by Patañjali of the school of classical Yoga.
Yogavārttika	commentary on Patañjali's *Yogasūtras* and its earlier commentators by Vijñānabhikṣu.
yogin	one disciplined in the practice and beliefs of Yoga.

Bibliography

Two books that will be helpful for the reader in explaining **Sanskrit terms** are the following. For straightforward definitions of general Hindu terms, *The Rider Encyclopedia of Eastern Philosophy and Religion* (London, Melbourne, Auckland, Johannesburg: Rider, 1986) gives comprehensive definitions and clear background information. Slightly more specialist, and covering all the necessary terms to be found in the philosophical schools, is John Grimes' *A Concise Dictionary of Indian Philosophy: Sanskrit terms defined in English* (New York: State University of New York Press, 1989) – an excellent book, of great benefit to students. Also very good indeed is N. N. Bhattacharyya's *A Glossary of Indian Religious Terms and Concepts* (New Delhi: Manohar, 1990).

Chapter 1 *Types of Belief*

A very useful source is *The Encyclopedia of Religion* (hereafter *ER*) edited by M. Eliade (New York: Macmillan, 1987). This is a sixteen-volume work, but for those students who have access to it, there are a range of entries on each of the types of belief dealt with in chapter 1, as well as many other areas relevant to Hindu philosophy as a whole. A good bibliography is given for each entry. In particular, the following would be relevant for chapter 1:

P. A. Bertocci, "Theism". In *ER*, vol. 14, pp. 421–7.
C. Hartshorne, "Pantheism and Panentheism". In *ER*, vol. 11, pp. 165–71.
T. Ludwig, "Monotheism". In *ER*, vol. 10, pp. 68–76.
R. A. McDermott, "Monism". In *ER*, vol. 10, pp. 57–65.
R. J. Zwi Werblowsky, "Polytheism". In *ER*, vol. 11, pp. 435–9.

Hindu polytheism, in particular, is dealt with comprehensively by Alain Daniélou in *The Myths and Gods of India* (Rochester, Vermont: Inner Traditions International, 1991, first published under the title *Hindu Polytheism* by Bollingen Foundation, New York, 1964). Those new to the study of the philosophy of religion would find *A Companion to Philosophy of Religion* helpful. It is edited by P. Quinn and C. Taliafero (Oxford: Blackwell, 1997).

Chapter 2 *Veda*

There are numerous works on the *Vedas* and *Upaniṣads*. As far as **primary sources** are concerned, the standard text on the *Ṛg Veda* is the translation by R. T. H. Griffith, *The Hymns of the Ṛgveda* (Delhi: Motilal Banarsidass, 1991 reprint of 1973 new, revised edn). David Frawley's work, *Wisdom of the Ancient Seers* (Salt Lake City: Passage Press, 1992) contains translations of many hymns from the *Ṛg Veda*, with comments. One of the most recent and readily available translations of the *Upaniṣads* is the work by P. Olivelle, *Upaniṣads* (Oxford and New York: Oxford University Press, 1996). *The Early Upaniṣads: Annotated text and translation*, also by Olivelle (New York and Oxford:

Oxford University Press, 1998), is also an excellent source. Another good anthology of teachings from the *Vedas*, *Brāhmaṇas*, and *Upaniṣads* is R. Panikkar's *The Vedic Experience: Mantramañjari – An anthology of the Vedas for modern man and contemporary celebration* (Los Angeles: University of California Press, 1977). Translations of selections from *Vedic* texts can also be found in R. C. Zaehner's *Hindu Scriptures* (London, Melbourne and Toronto: Dent, 1982 reprint of 1966 edn, first published 1966). Other such primary source texts are the following:

Aurobindo, Sri 1986 impression, first published 1971: *The Upanishads: Texts, translations and commentaries.* Pondicherry: Sri Aurobindo Ashram.

Bahadur, K. P. 1989: *The Wisdom of Upanishads.* New Delhi: Sterling Publishers Private Limited.

Deussen, P. 1995 reprint of first Indian edn, 1980; first published 1897: *Sixty Upaniṣads of the Veda* 2 vols. Translated from the German by V. M. Bedekar and G. B. Palsule. Delhi: Motilal Banarsidass.

Embree, A. T. (ed.) 1972, first published 1966: *The Hindu Tradition: Readings in oriental thought.* New York: Vintage Books.

Frawley, D. 1986: *Hymns from the Golden Age: Selected hymns from the Rig Veda with yogic interpretation.* Delhi, Varanasi, Patna, Madras: Motilal Banarsidass.

Goodall, D. (ed.) 1996: *Hindu Scriptures.* London: Phoenix.

Hume, R. E. 1989 impression, first published 1921: *The Thirteen Principal Upanishads.* Delhi: Oxford University Press.

O' Flaherty, W. 1975: *Hindu Myths.* Harmondsworth: Penguin.

—— 1983 reprint of 1981 edn: *The Rig Veda: An Anthology.* Harmondsworth: Penguin.

Olivelle, P. 1998: *The Early Upanisads: Annotated text and translation.* New York and Oxford: Oxford University Press.

Parrinder, G. 1975: *The Wisdom of the Forest: Sages of the Indian Upanishads.* London: Sheldon Press.

Radhakrishnan, S. 1994, first published 1953: *The Principal Upaniṣads.* New Delhi: Harper Collins.

Shearer, A. and Russell, P. 1978: *The Upanishads.* New York: Harper and Row.

Swami, Shree, P. and W. B. Yeats, 1985 reprint of 1970 edn, first published 1937: *The Ten Principal Upanishads.* London and Boston: Faber and Faber.

Selected general secondary sources on the *Vedas* and *Upaniṣads*

Aurobindo, Sri 1987 impression, first published 1956: *The Secret of the Veda.* Pondicherry: Sri Aurobindo Ashram.

Dayananda, S. 1989: *Introduction to Vedanta.* Vision Books.

Deussen, P. second edn 1979, first published 1906: *The Philosophy of the Upanishads.* New Delhi: Oriental Books Reprint Corporation.

Gough, E. 1979, first published 1882: *Philosophy of the Upanishads: Ancient Indian metaphysics.* New Delhi: Cosmo.

Keith, A. B. 1998 reprint of 1925 edn: *The Religion and Philosophy of the Veda and Upanishads.* 2 vols. Delhi: Motilal Banarsidass.

Mehta, R. 1990 reprint of 1970 edn: *The Call of the Upanishads.* Delhi: Motilal Banarsidass.

Müller, M. 1985, first published 1904: *Vedanta Philosophy.* New Delhi: Cosmo.

Radhakrishnan, S. 1994 impression, first published 1923: *Indian Philosophy, Vol. 1.* Delhi: Oxford University Press.

Sources specific to Hindu philosophy

The following list contains themes and issues related to Hindu philosophy, such as epistemology, theories of reality, and concepts of the self, consciousness and the mind. These, and other topics that inform Hindu philosophy, are areas taken up for discussion by the different philosophical schools of Hinduism.

Adams, G. C. Jr. 1993: *The Structure and Meaning of Bādarāyana's Brahma Sūtras.* Delhi: Motilal Banarsidass.

Chakraborty, A. 1997: *Mind-Body Dualism.* New Delhi: D. K. Printworld (P) Ltd.

Chatterjee, M. (ed.) 1974: *Contemporary Indian Philosophy.* Muirhead Library of Philosophy, Series 2. London: George Allen & Unwin, and New York: Humanities Press Inc.

Chaube, D. B. 1991: *Mind-Body Relation in Indian Philosophy.* Varanasi: Tara Book Agency.

Chennakesavan, S. 1991 reprint of second, revised edn, first published 1960: *Concept of Mind in Indian Philosophy.* Delhi: Motilal Banarsidass.

Chethimattam, J. B. 1971: *Consciousness and Reality: An Indian approach to metaphysics.* London: Chapman.

Coward, H. G. (ed.) 1996 reprint of 1983 edn: *Studies in Indian Thought: Collected papers of Prof. T. R. V. Murti.* Delhi: Motilal Banarsidass.

Dasgupta, S. N. 1976, first published 1927: *Hindu Mysticism.* Delhi, Varanasi, Patna: Motilal Banarsidass.

Halbfass, W. 1991: *Tradition and Reflection: Explorations in Indian Thought.* Albany: State University of New York Press.

King, R. 1999: *Indian Philosophy: An introduction to Hindu and Buddhist thought.* Edinburgh: Edinburgh University Press.

Klostermeier, K. 1984: *Mythologies and Philosophies of Salvation in the Theisitic Traditions of India.* Waterloo, Ontario: Wilfred Laurier University Press.

Krishna, D. 1997 impression, first published 1991: *Indian Philosophy: A counter perspective.* Delhi, Calcutta, Chennai, Mumbai: Oxford University Press.

Masih, Y. 1983: *The Hindu Religious Thought (3000 B.C.–200 A.D.).* Delhi, Varanasi, Patna: Motilal Banarsidass.

Matilal, B. K. 1971: *Epistemology, Logic and Grammar in Indian Philosophical Analysis.* The Hague: Morton.

—— 1990: *Logic, Language and Reality.* Delhi: Motilal Banarsidass.

—— 1986: *Perception: An essay on classical Indian theories of knowledge.* Oxford: Clarendon Press.

Mohanty, J. N. 1992: *Reason and Tradition in Indian Thought: An essay on the nature of Indian philosophical thinking.* Oxford: Clarendon Press.

Murty, K. S. 1985: *Philosophy in India: Traditions, teaching and research.* Delhi: Motilal Banarsidass and New Delhi: Indian Council of Philosophical Research.

Oberhammer, G. 1989: *Philosophy of Religion in Hindu Thought.* Translated from German and edited by Anand Amaladass. Sri Garib Dass Oriental Series 93. Delhi: Sri Satguru Publications.

Panda, N. C. 1995: *The Vibrating Universe.* Delhi: Motilal Banarsidass.

Phillips, S. H. 1997, first published, 1996: *Classical Indian Metaphysics.* Delhi: Motilal Banarsidass.

Potter, K. H. 1988: *Guide to Indian Philosophy.* Boston, MA: G. K. Hall.

—— 1999 reprint of first Indian edn, 1991: *Presuppositions of India's Philosophies.* Delhi: Motilal Banarsidass.

Radhakrishnan, S. 1971 reprint of 1960 edn: *The Brahma Sūtra: The philosophy of spiritual life.* London: George Allen & Unwin.

Sinari, R. A. 1984, first published 1970: *The Structure of Indian Thought.* Delhi: Oxford University Press.

Sinha, J. 1996 reprint of 1958 second edn: *Indian Psychology, Vol. 1: Cognition.* 1996 reprint of 1961 first edn: *Vol. 2: Emotion and Will.* 1996 reprint of 1969 first edn: *Vol. 3: Epistemology and Perception.* Delhi: Motilal Banarsidass.

Sivaraman, K. (ed.) 1989: *Hindu Spirituality: Vedas through Vedanta.* London: SCM Press Ltd.

Smart, N. 1992: *Doctrine & Argument in Indian Philosophy.* Leiden, New York, Köln: E. J. Brill.

Ward, K. 1993: *Images of Eternity.* Oxford: Oneworld.

Warder, A. K. 1998 second edn: *A Course in Indian Philosophy.* Delhi: Motilal Banarsidass.

Zimmer, H. 1989 reprint of 1951 edn: *Philosophies of India.* Princeton, New Jersey: Princeton University Press.

The schools of Hindu philosophy

There are a large number of sources pertinent to Indian philosophy in general, and to the Hindu orthodox philosophical schools: most of these are published in India. Sources that provide **selected primary source extracts** of the writings of all the various schools of philosophy are:

Pereira, J. 1991, first published 1976: *Hindu Theology: Themes, Texts and Structures.* Delhi: Motilal Banarsidass.

Radhakrishnan, S. and Moore, C. A. (eds) 1989 reprint of 1957 edn: *A Sourcebook in Indian Philosophy.* Princeton, New Jersey: Princeton University Press.

The following **secondary sources** provide a background to the philosophical schools, as well as dealing with them individually. In this field of the philosophy of Hinduism the reader is advised that older texts should not, by any means, be shunned. They are still outstanding standard works – mostly by Indian scholars – and have never been replaced in intensity and depth of study or outstanding erudition.

Bernard, T. 1981 reprint of 1947 edn: *Hindu Philosophy.* Delhi: Motilal Banarsidass.

Dasgupta, S. 1997 reprint of 1975 Indian edn, first published, 1922: *A History of Indian Philosophy, Vol. 1.* Delhi, Mumbai, Chennai, Calcutta, Bangalore, Varanasi, Patna, Pune: Motilal Banarsidass. *Vols. 2–5* 1991 reprint of 1975 Indian edn, first published 1922. Delhi, Varanasi, Patna, Bangalore, Madras).

Frauwallner, E. 1993 reprint of 1973 edn: *History of Indian Philosophy, Vol. 1.* Delhi: Motilal Banarsidass.

Hiriyanna, M. 1993: *Outlines of Indian Philosophy.* Delhi: Motilal Banarsidass.

—— 1995: *The Essentials of Indian Philosophy.* Delhi: Motilal Banarsidass.

Koller, J. M. and Koller, P. J. 1998: *Asian Philosophies.* New Jersey: Prentice-Hall.

Lott, E. 1980: *Vedantic Approaches to God.* London: Macmillan.

Puligandla, R. second edn 1985: *Fundamentals of Indian Philosophy.* London, Lanham and New York: University Press of America.

Radhakrishnan, S. 1994 impression, first published 1923: *Indian Philosophy, Vol. 2.* Delhi: Oxford University Press.

Raju, R. T. 1998 reprint of 1992 edn: *The Philosophical Traditions of India.* Delhi: Motilal Banarsidass.

Sharma, C. 1994 reprint of 1960 edn: *A Critical Survey of Indian Philosophy.* Delhi: Motilal Banarsidass.

Tigunait, R. 1983: *Seven Systems of Indian Philosophy.* Honesdale, PA: Himalayan International Institute of Yoga.

Chapter 3 *Pūrva Mīmāṃsā*

Bhatt, G. P. 1994: "Mīmāṃsā as a philosophical system: A survey". In R. C. Dwivedi (ed.) *Studies in Mīmāṃsā*. Delhi: Motilal Banarsidass.

Clooney, F. X. 1990: *Thinking Ritually: Rediscovering the Pūrva Mīmāṃsā of Jaimini*. Publications of the De Nobili Research Library, edited by G. Oberhammer, Vol. 17. Vienna: Gerold & Co. and Delhi: Motilal Banarsidass.

Dwivedi, R. C. (ed.) 1994: *Studies in Mīmāṃsā*. Delhi: Motilal Banarsidass.

Halbfass, W. 1983: *Studies in Kumārila and Śankara*. Studien zur Indologie und Iranistik. Monograph 9. Reinbeck: Orientalistiche Fachpublikationen.

Jha, G. M. second edn 1964, first published 1942: *Pūrva Mīmāṃsā in its Sources*. Varanasi: The Banaras Hindu University.

—— 1978, first published, 1911: *The Prābhākara School of Pūrva Mīmāṃsā*. Delhi: Motilal Banarsidass.

—— (translator) 1916: *The Sacred Books of the Hindus Vol. X: The Pūrva Mīmāṃsā Sūtras of Jaimini (Chapters I–III)*. Allahabad: Sudhīndranātha Vasu.

Keith, A. B. 1978 second edn, first published 1921: *The Karma-Mīmāṃsā*. New Delhi: Oriental Books Reprint Corporation.

Matilal, B. K. 1987: "Mīmāṃsā". In *ER*, vol. 9, pp. 536–7.

Raju, P. T. 1994: "Activism in Indian thought". In R. C. Dwivedi (ed.) 1994: *Studies in Mīmāṃsā*. Delhi: Motilal Banarsidass.

Rao, B. S. 1996, first published 1984: *Jaiminisutras*. Delhi: Motilal Banarsidass.

Śābara 1933–6: *The Śābara Bhāṣya* translated into English by Ganganatha Jha. 3 vols. Baroda: Gaekwad's Oriental Series 66, 70, 73.

Sharma, P. S. 1994: "Kumārila Bhaṭṭa's denial of creation and dissolution of the world". In R. C. Dwivedi (ed.) 1994: *Studies in Mīmāṃsā*. Delhi: Motilal Banarsidass.

Chapter 4 *Vaiśeṣika*

The following titles include some sources that deal with the united schools of Nyāyā and Vaiśeṣika and are pertinent to the following chapter on Nyāya also.

Chakrabarti, K. K. 1987: "Vaiśeṣika". In *ER*, vol. 15, pp. 167–8.

Halbfass, W. 1992: *On Being and What There Is: Classical Vaiśeṣika and the history of Indian Ontology*. Albany: State University of New York Press.

Matilal, B. K. 1977: *Nyāya-Vaiśeṣika*. A History of Indian Literature, vol. 6, edited by Jan Gonda. Wiesbaden: Otto Harrassowitz.

Mookerji, S. 1953 revised and enlarged second edn, first published 1937: "Nyāya-Vaiśeṣika". In H. Bhattacharya (ed.), *The Cultural Heritage of India, Vol. 3: The Philosophies*. Calcutta: The Ramakrishna Mission Institute of Culture, pp. 91–124.

Potter, K. H. 1995 reprint of 1977 edn: *Encyclopedia of Indian Philosophies, Vol. II: The tradition of Nyāya-Vaiśeṣika up to Gaṅgeśa*. Delhi: Motilal Banarsidass.

Potter, K. H. and S. Bhattacharya (eds) 1993: *Encyclopedia of Indian Philosophies, Vol. VI: Indian philosophical analysis. Nyāya-Vaiśeṣika from Gaṅgeśa to Raghunātha Śiromaṇi*. Delhi: Motilal Banarsidass.

Sinha, N. (translator) 1923: *The Vaiśeṣika Sūtras of Kanāda with the Commentary of Śaṅkara Miśra and extracts from the Gloss of Jayanārāyaṇa*. The Sacred Books of the Hindus no. 6. Allahabad: Sudhindranātha Vasu.

Chapter 5 *Nyāya*

Bahadur, K. P. 1978: *The Wisdom of Nyaaya*. The Wisdom of India Series. New Delhi: Sterling Publishers.

Bulcke, C. 1968 reprint of 1947 edn: *The Theism of Nyaya-Vaisesika: Its origin and early development*. Delhi: Motilal Banarsidass.

Chakrabarti, K. K. 1977: *The Logic of Gotama*. Monograph no. 5 of the Society for Asian and Comparative Philosophy. Honolulu: University of Hawaii Press.

Chatterjee, S. C. 1965 third edn, first published 1950: *The Nyāya Theory of Knowledge: A critical study of some problems of logic and metaphysics*. Calcutta: University of Calcutta.

Jhā, M. G. 1984 reprint of 1912–19 edns: *The Nyāya-Sūtras of Gauṭama*, 4 vols. Delhi, Varanasi, Patna, Madras: Motilal Banarsidass.

Junankar, N. S. 1978: *Gautama: The Nyāya Philosophy*. Delhi, Varanasi, Patna: Motilal Banarsidass.

Sinha, N. L. (ed.) and M. M. S. Vidyābhūṣaṇa (translator) 1990 reprint of 1930 edn: *The Nyāya Sūtras of Gotama*. Delhi: Motilal Banarsidass.

Vattanky, J. 1984: *Gaṅgeśa's Philosophy of God*. The Adyar Library Series No. 115, general ed. K. K. Raja. Madras: The Adyar Library and Research Centre.

Chapter 6 *Sāṃkhya*

Bahadur, K. P. 1988 reprint: *The Wisdom of Sankhya*. The Wisdom of India Series. New Delhi: Sterling Publishers.

Davies, J. 1981: *Hindu Philosophy: An Exposition of the System of Kapila*. New Delhi: Cosmo.

Harzer, E. 1987: "Sāṃkhya". In *ER*, vol. 13, pp. 47–51.

Jacobsen, K. A. 1999: *Prakrti in Sāṃkhya-Yoga: Material principle, religious experience, ethical implications*. Asian Thought and Culture no. 30. New York etc.: Peter Lang.

Larson, G. L. 1979 revised edn, first published 1969: *Classical Sāṃkhya: An interpretation of its history and meaning*. Delhi, Varanasi, Patna: Motilal Banarsidass.

Larson, G. J. and R. S. Bhattacharya (eds) 1987: *Encyclopedia of Indian Philosophies, Vol. IV, Sāṃkhya: A dualist tradition in Indian philosophy*. Princeton: Princeton University Press, also Delhi, Varanasi, Patna, Madras: Motilal Banarsidass.

Weerasinghe, S. G. M. 1993: *The Sāṅkhya Philosophy: A critical evaluation of its origins and development*. Sri Garib Das Oriental Series, 167. Delhi: Sri Satguru.

Wilson, H. H. 1978: *Sāṃkhya Kārikā*. Delhi: Indological Book House.

Chapter 7 *Yoga*

Abhedananda, Swami 1967: *The Yoga Psychology*. Calcutta: Ramakrishna Vedanta Math.

Āraṇya, Swami H. 1983 reprint of 1981 revised edn: *Yoga Philosophy of Patañjali*, translated by P. N. Mukerji. Albany: University of New York Press.

Bahm, A. J. 1993, first published 1961: *Yoga Sutras of Patañjali*. Berkeley, California: Asian Humanities Press.

Bailey, A. 1983 reprint of 1927 edn: *The Light of the Soul: The Yoga Sutras of Patanjali*. Albany, New York: Lucis Press Ltd.

Bernard, T. 1974 impression of 1950 edn: *Hatha Yoga*. London: Rider & Company.

Daniélou, A. 1991, first published 1949: *Yoga: Mastering the secrets of matter and the universe*. Rochester, Vermont: Inner Traditions International.

Dasgupta, S. N. 1996 reprint of 1930 Calcutta edn: *Yoga Philosophy in Relation to Other Systems of Indian Thought*. Delhi: Motilal Banarsidass.

Deshpanda, P. Y. 1978: *The Authentic Yoga: A fresh look at Patañjali's Yoga Sutras with a new translation, notes and comments.* London: Rider.

Eliade, M. 1990, first published 1958: *Yoga: Immortality and freedom.* Translated from the French by W. R. Trask. Bollingen Series, 56. Princeton, New Jersey: Princeton University Press.

—— 1975: *Patanjali and Yoga.* Translated from the French by C. L. Markmann. New York: Schocken Books.

—— 1987: "Yoga" in *ER*, vol. 15, pp. 519–23.

Feuerstein, G. (translator) 1979: *The Yoga-Sutra of Patanjali: A new translation and commentary.* Folkestone: Dawson and Sons. Also 1989 edn, Rochester: Inner Traditions International.

—— 1996, first published 1980: *The Philosophy of Classical Yoga.* Rochester, Vermont: Inner Traditions International.

—— 1990: *Encyclopedic Dictionary of Yoga.* London, Sydney, Wellington: Unwin Paperbacks.

—— 1975: *Textbook of Yoga.* London: Rider & Company.

—— 1974: *The Essence of Yoga: A contribution to the psychohistory of Indian civilisation.* London: Rider and Company.

—— and J. Miller 1998: *The Essence of Yoga: Essays on the development of yogic philosophy from the Vedas to modern times.* Rochester, Vermont: Inner Traditions International. Published in 1971 under the title *A Reappraisal of Yoga: Essays in Indian Philosophy*, London: Rider and Company and in 1972 under the title *Yoga and Beyond: Essays in Indian philosophy*, New York: Schocken Books.

——1989: *Yoga: The technology of ecstasy.* Los Angeles: J. P. Tarcher.

Filliozat, J. 1991: *Religion, Philosophy, Yoga.* Delhi: Motilal Banarsidass.

Fuller, J. F. C. 1988: *Yoga: A study of the mystical philosophy of the Brahmins and Buddhists.* Sri Garib Dass Oriental Series, 63. Delhi: Sri Satguru.

Koelman, S. J. 1970: *Pātañjala Yoga: From related ego to absolute self.* Poona: Papal Athenaeum.

Leggett, T. 1978: *The Chapter of the Self.* London and Henley: Routledge and Kegan Paul.

Mehta, R. 1995 reprint of 1987 edn: *The Secret of Self-transformation: A synthesis of tantra and yoga.* Delhi: Motilal Banarsidass.

Mishra, R. S. 1972: *The Textbook of Yoga Psychology: A new translation and interpretation of Patañjali's Yoga Sutras for meaningful application in all modern psychologic disciplines.* London: The Lyrebird Press Ltd.

Taimni, I. K. 1986 reprint of 1961 edn: *The Science of Yoga.* London, Wheaton, Illinois and Madras: The Theosophical Publishing House.

Tola, F. and C. Dragonetti 1991 reprint of 1987 edn: *The Yogasūtras of Patañjali.* Delhi: Motilal Banarsidass.

Varenne, J. 1976, first published 1973: *Yoga and the Hindu Tradition*, translated from the French by Derek Coltman. Chicago and London: University of Chicago Press.

Werner, K. (ed.) 1994, first published 1989: *The Yogi and the Mystic: Studies in Indian and comparative mysticism.* Richmond, Surrey: Curzon Press.

——- 1989 reprint of 1977 edn: *Yoga and Indian Philosophy.* Delhi, Varanasi, Patna, Bangalore, Madras: Motilal Banarsidass.

Whicher, I. 1992: *A Study of Patañjali's Definition of Yoga: Uniting theory and practice in the Yoga-Sūtras.* Cambridge University Ph.D. thesis.

—— 1997: *The Integrity of the Yoga Darśana. A reconsideration of Classical Yoga.* Albany: State University of New York Press.

Whiteman, J. H. M. 1993: *Aphorisms on Spiritual method: The "Yoga Sutras of Patanjali" in the light of mystical experience.* Sanskrit text, interlinear & idiomatic English translations, commentary & supplementary aids. Gerrards Cross: Colin Smythe.

Wood, E. 1967: *Yoga.* Baltimore: Penguin Books.

—— 1988: *Seven Schools of Yoga.* Wheaton, Madras, London: Theosophical Publishing House.

Woods, J. H. 1992 reprint of 1914 edn: *The Yoga-System of Patanjali*. The Harvard Oriental Series vol. 17. Delhi: Motilal Banarsidass.

Worthington, V. 1989, first published 1982: *A History of Yoga*. London: Arkana.

Chapter 8 *Advaita Vedānta*

Alston, A. J. 1981 reprint of 1980 edn: *A Śaṃkara Source-Book, Vol. 1: Śaṃkara on the Absolute*. London: Shanti Sadan.

—— 1980: *A Śaṃkara Source-Book, Vol. 2: Śaṃkara on the creation*. London: Shanti Sadan.

—— 1981: *A Śaṃkara Source-Book, Vol. 3: Śaṃkara on the soul*. London: Shanti Sadan.

—— 1989: *A Śaṃkara Source-Book, Vol. 4: Śaṃkara on rival views*. London: Shanti Sadan.

—— 1989: *A Śaṃkara Source-Book, Vol. 5: Śaṃkara on discipleship*. London: Shanti Sadan.

—— 1989: *A Śaṃkara Source-Book, Vol. 6: Śaṃkara on enlightenment*. London: Shanti Sadan.

—— 1990: *The Thousand Teachings of Śaṃkara*. London: Shanti Sadan.

Atmananda, Swami 1989: *Sankara's Teachings in His Own Words*. Bombay: Bharatiya Vidya Bhavan.

Bahadur, K. P. 1983: *The Wisdom of Vedaanta*. The Wisdom of India Series, no. 5. New Delhi: Sterling Publishers Private Ltd.

Carr, B. 2000: "Śaṅkara on memory and the continuity of the self". In *Religious Studies* 36, pp. 419–34.

Chinmayananda, Swami 1982: *Atma Bodha of Bhagawan Sri Sankaracharya*. Bombay: Central Chinmaya Mission Trust.

Comans, M. 1996: "Śaṅkara and the Prasaṅkhyānavāda". In *The Journal of Indian Philosophy* vol. 24, pp. 49–71.

Das, R. 1983 reprint of 1968 edn: *Introduction to Shankara*. Calcutta: Firma KLM Private Limited.

Deussen, P. 1995 reprint of 1912 edn: *The System of the Vedanta*. Delhi: Low Price Publications.

Deutsch, E. 1973 reprint: *Advaita Vedanta: A philosophical reconstruction*. Honolulu: University of Hawaii.

—— and J. A. B. van Buitenen 1971: *A Source Book of Advaita Vedānta*. Honolulu: University of Hawaii.

Gambhirananda, Swami (translator) 1977: *The Brahma Sūtra Bhāṣya of Śrī Śaṅkarācārya*. English translation. Calcutta: Advaita Ashrama.

Gangolli, D. B. 1991: *The Essential Ādi Shankara*. Bangalore: Adhyatma Prakasha Karyalaya.

Gupta, B. 1991: *Perceiving in Advaita Vedānta: Epistemological analysis and interpretation*. Lewisburg: Bucknell University Press, London and Toronto: Associated University Presses.

Halbfass, W. 1983: *Studies in Kumārila and Śankara*. Studien zur Indologie und Iranistik, monograph 9. Reinbeck: Orientalistiche Fachpublikation.

Indich, W. M. 1995 reprint of 1980 edn: *Consciousness in Advaita Vedānta*. Delhi: Motilal Banarsidass.

Isayeva, N. 1993: *Shankara and Indian Philosophy*. Albany: State University of New York Press.

Isayeva, N. 1992: *Shankara and Indian Philosophy*. Albany, New York: State University of New York Press.

Leggett, T. 1992: *Śaṅkara on the Yoga Sūtras: A full translation of the newly discovered text*. Delhi: Motilal Banarsidass. Also 1990: London and New York: Kegan Paul.

Loy, D. 1988: *Nonduality: A Study in Comparative Philosophy*. New Haven and London: Yale University Press.

Mahadevan, T. M. P. 1995 reprint of 1980 edn: *The Hymns of Śaṇkara*. Delhi: Motilal Banarsidass.

Malkovsky, B. 1997: "The Personhood of Śaṃkara's *Para Brahman*". In *The Journal of Religion* 77, pp. 541–62.

Mayeda, S. (translator and ed.) 1992, first published 1979: *A Thousand Teachings: The Upadeśasāhasrī of Śaṇkara*. Albany: State University of New York Press.

Nakamura, H. 1990 reprint of 1983 edn: *A History of Early Vedānta Philosophy*, translated by T. Leggett, S. Mayeda, T. Unno *et al.* Religions of Asia Series. Delhi: Motilal Banarsidass.

Nikhilānanda, Swāmi (n.d.): *Self-knowledge of Śrī Śaṅkarācārya*. Madras: Sri Ramakrishna Math.

Potter, K. H. (ed.) 1981: *Encyclopedia of Indian Philosophies, Vol. III: Advaita Vedānta up to Śaṃkara and his pupils*. Princeton, New Jersey: Princeton University Press.

Rao, S. 1996: 'Two "Myths" in Advaita'. In *The Journal of Indian Philosophy* 24, pp. 265–79.

Raphael 1992: *The Pathway of Non-Duality: Advaitavāda*. Delhi: Motilal Banarsidass.

Saraswati, Swami S. 1990 second edn, first published 1957: *Salient Features of Śaṅkara's Vedānta*. Bangalore: Adhyatma Prakasha Karyalaya.

Sastri, A. M. 1986 reprint of 1899 edn: *The Vedānta Doctrine of Śrī Sankarāchārya*. Sri Garib Dass Oriental Series no. 38. Delhi: Sri Satguru Publications.

Satchidānandendra, Sri Swami 1997, first published 1989: *The Method of the Vedanta: A critical account of the Advaita tradition*, translated by A. J. Alston. Delhi: Motilal Banarsidass.

Shankara 1962: *Brahma-Sutra, Shankara Bhashya*, translator Swami Nikhilananda. Madras: Sri Ramakrishna Math.

Sharma, A. 1995: *The Philosophy of Religion and Advaita Vedānta: A comparative study in religion and reason*. Pennsylvania: The Pennsylvania State University Press.

Sharma, C. 1996: *The Advaita Tradition in Indian Philosophy: A study of Advaita in Buddhism, Vedānta and Kāshmīra Shaivism*. Delhi: Motilal Banarsidass.

Sinha, D. 1995 reprint of 1983 edn: *Metaphysic of Experience in Advaita Vedānta: A phenomenological approach*. Delhi: Motilal Banarsidass.

Tiwari, K. N. 1977: *Dimensions of Renunciation in Advaita Vedānta*. Delhi, Varanasi, Patna: Motilal Banarsidass.

Torwesten, H. 1985: *Vedanta: Heart of Hinduism*. New York: Grove Weidenfeld.

Venkatesananda (translator) 1984: *The Supreme Yoga*. Freemantle, Australia: Chiltern Yoga Trust.

Vivekananda, Swami, 1982, first published 1955: *Jnana-Yoga*. New York: Ramakrishna-Vivekananda Center.

Chapter 9 *Viśiṣṭadvaita Vedānta*

Abhyankar, V. S. (ed.) 1914: *Śrī-Bhāṣya of Rāmānujāchārya*. Bombay: Government Central Press.

Bailey, G. M. and I. Kesarcodi-Watson (eds) *Bhakti Studies*. New Delhi: Sterling Publishers Private Limited.

Bhatt, S. R. 1975: *Studies in Rāmānuja Vedānta*. New Delhi: Heritage Publishers.

Carman, J. B. 1974: *The Theology of Rāmānuja: An essay in interreligious understanding*. New Haven and London: Yale University Press.

Chari, S. M. S. 1976, first published 1961: *Advaita and Viśiṣṭādvaita: A study based on Vedānta Deśikā's Śatadūṣaṇ"*. Delhi: Motilal Banarsidass.

——— 1988: *Fundamentals of Viśiṣṭadvaita Vedānta: A study based on Vedānta Deśika's Tattva-muktā-kalāpa*. Delhi: Motilal Banarsidass.

——— 1997: *Philosophy and Theistic Mysticism of the Āḷvārs*. Delhi: Motilal Banarsidass.

Grimes, J. 1990: *The Seven Great Untenables: (sapta-vidhā Anupatti)*. Delhi: Motilal Banarsidass.

Lipner, J. L. 1986: *The Face of Truth: A study of meaning and metaphysics in the Vedāntic theology of Rāmānuja*. London: Macmillan.

Lott, E. J. 1976: *God and the Universe in the Vedāntic Theology of Rāmānuja: A study in his use of the self-body analogy*. Madras: Ramanuja Society.

Murthy, H. V. S. 1973: *Vaiṣṇavism of Śaṃkaradeva and Rāmānuja*. Delhi, Varanasi, Patna: Motilal Banarsidass.

Raghavachar, S. S. (ed. and translator) 1956: *Rāmānuja's Vedārthasangraha*. Mysore: Ramakrishna Ashrama.
—— 1957: *Introduction to the Vedāntha Saṃgraha*. Mangalore: Mangalore Trading Association.
—— 1969: *Śrī Rāmānuja on the Gītā*. Mangalore: Sri Ramakrishna Ashrama.
—— 1972: *Śrī Rāmānuja on the Upaniṣads*. Madras.
Sharma, A. 1978: *Viśiṣṭādvaita Vedānta: A study*. New Delhi: Heritage Press.
Sheridan, D. P. 1986: *The Advaitic Theism of the Bhāgavata Purāṇa*. Delhi: Motilal Banarsidass.
Thibaut, G. (translator) 1904: *The Vedānta Sūtras with the Commentary of Rāmānuga* Part 3. Sacred Books of the East, vol. 48, general ed. M. Müller. Oxford: Clarendon Press.
van Buitenen, J. A. B. 1956: *Rāmānuja's Vedārtasaṃgraha: Introduction, critical edition and annotated translation*. Poona: Deccan College Postgraduate and Research Institute.
—— 1974 reprint of 1968 edn: *Rāmānuja on the Bhagavadgītā: A condensed rendering of his Gītābhāṣya with copious notes and an introduction*. Delhi, Varanasi, Patna: Motilal Banarsidass.

Chapter 10 *Dvaita Vedānta*

Narain, K. 1962: *An Outline of Madhva Philosophy*. Allahabad: Udayana Publications.
Raghavendrachar, H. N. 1953 revised edn, first published 1937: "Madhva's Brahma-Mīmāṃsā" in H. Bhattacharya (ed.), *The Cultural Heritage of India Vol. 3: The Philosophies*. Calcutta: The Ramakrishna Mission Institute of Culture.
—— 1941: *The Dvaita Philosophy and its Place in the Vedānta*. Mysore: The University of Mysore.
Rao, S. S. 1936: *Vedāntasūtras with the Commentary of Madhva*. Tirupati: Śrī Vyasa Press.
Shanbag, D. N. 1982: *Some Problems of Dvaita Philosophy in their Dialectical Setting*. Dharwad: Sri Rama Prakashan.
Sharma, B. N. K. third edn 1979, first published 1961: *Madhva's Teachings in His Own Words*. Bombay: Bharatiya Vidya Bhavan.
—— 1960–1: *A History of Dvaita School of Vedanta and its Literature*, 2 vols. Bombay: Bharatiya Vidya Bhavan.
—— 1986: *The Philosophy of Śrī Madhvācarya*. Delhi: Motilal Banarsidass.

Index

एकम् सत् विप्रा बहुधा वदन्ति।

Ekam sat vipraa bahuda vadanti

Truth is one, wise men call it by different names